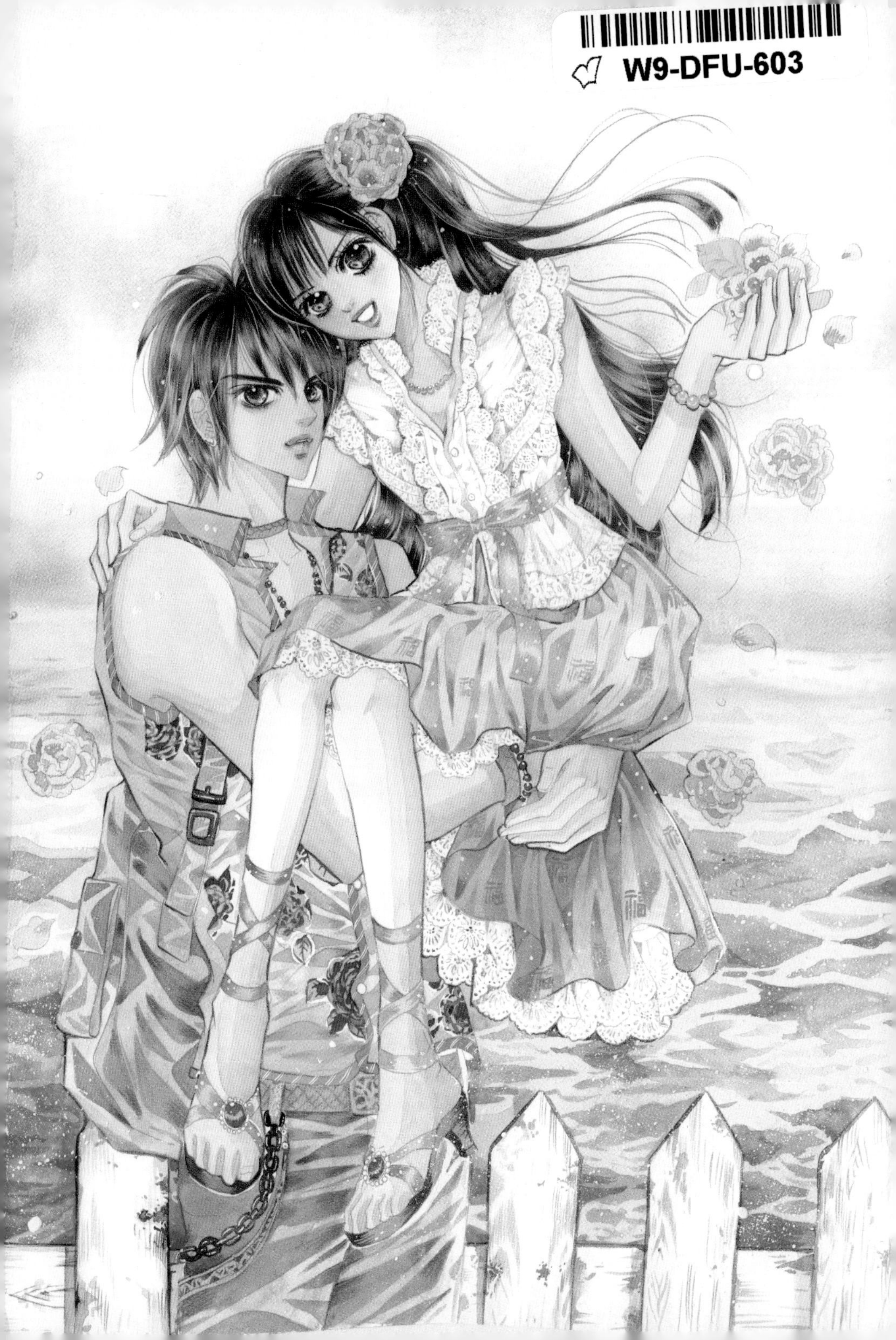

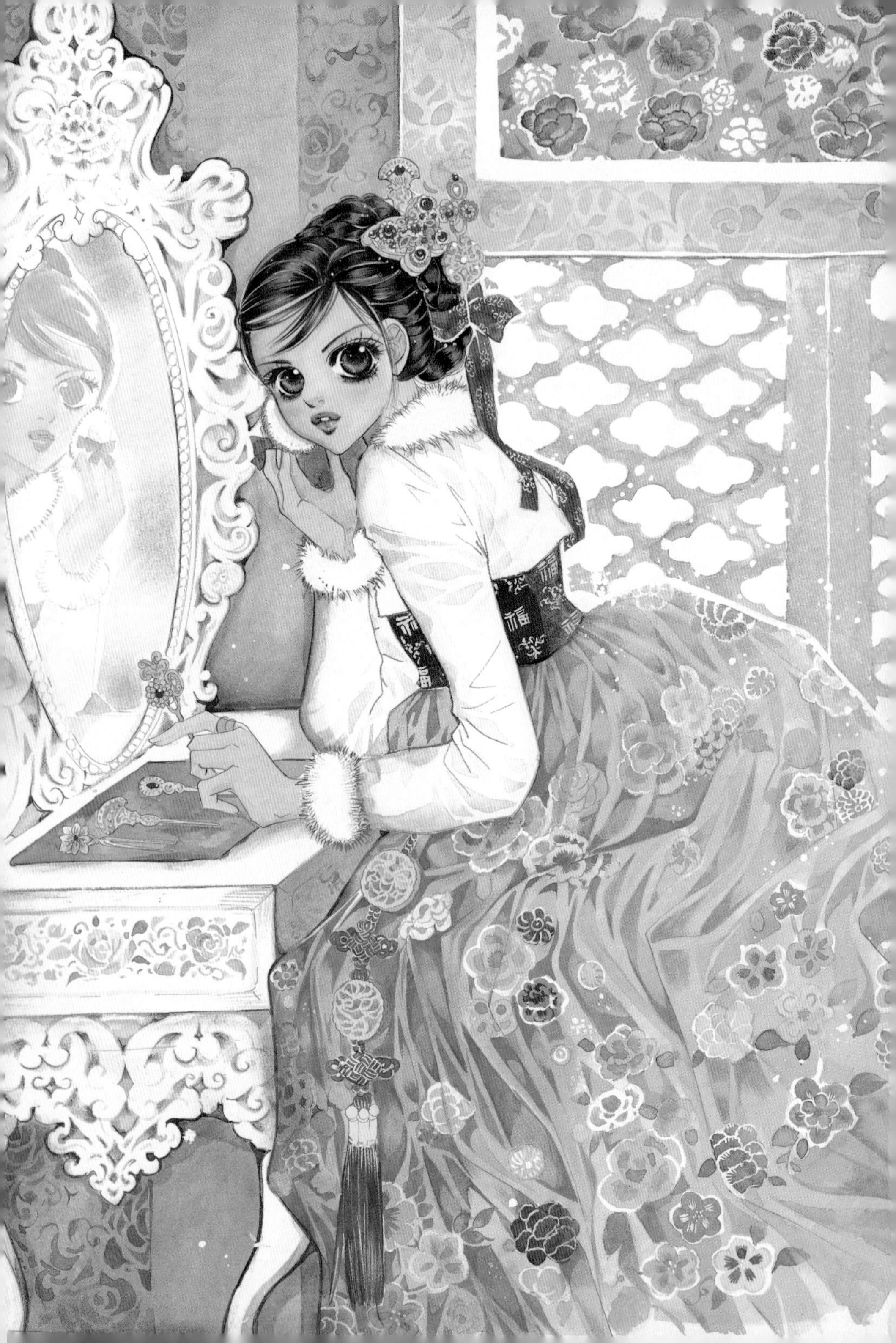

vol. 11

Park SoHee

Yen Press

Words from the Creator

I would like to apologize to you for Volume 13 taking so long to come out. It's a pretty action-packed volume, and I feel like maybe the series is nearing its conclusion. The characters have gone through a lot and have grown up so much. Shin isn't the same as he was back in Volume 1, and neither is Chae-Kyung. But I sometimes want to take them back to the beginning.

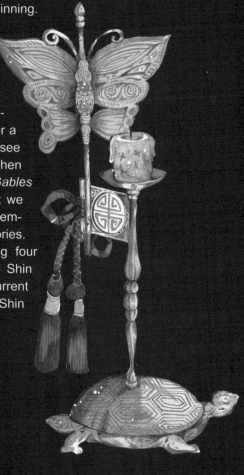

I wish Chae-Kyung had stayed the bright, outgoing, slightly knuckleheaded girl, Shin the mean and selfish boy, and Yul the boy who kept his cold, manipulative side well hidden under a blanket of warmth. When I see them now, I feel sad, like when I watched *Anne of Green Gables* while I was growing up. But we can't turn back time, and memories are just that—memories. I planned on **Goong** lasting four years, and Chae-Kyung and Shin have only grown two. The current versions of Chae-Kyung and Shin are still more precious to me.

SoHee Park

Words from

Volume 14

No matter which characters I like and don't like, Chae-Kyung is the one I put the most of my own emotions into. While I was working on Volume 14, I was worried about her feelings, the changes she was going through, and what the future holds. Since I'm the one creating it, I know where the series is headed and what will happen, but I'm still a slave to my emotions. My mood swings confuse me. I know Chae-Kyung isn't very smart, rational, or wise, but I hope she'll be happy in the end. (And I say this while knowing that I'm the one who causes her suffering...but even so...)

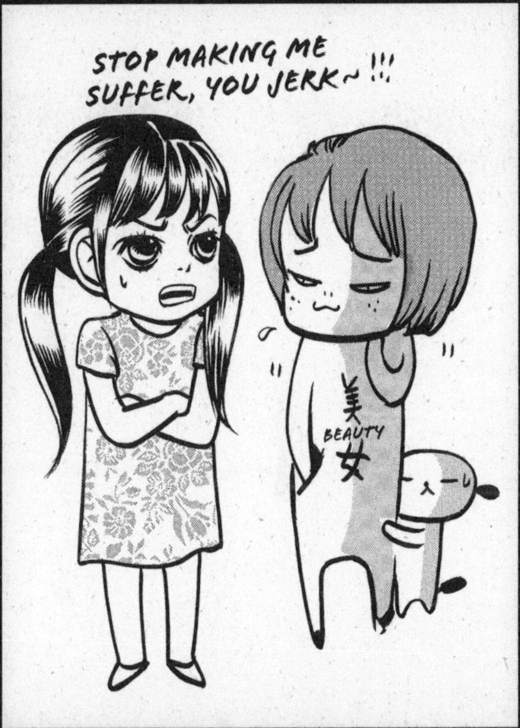
STOP MAKING ME SUFFER, YOU JERK~!!!
美
BEAUTY
女

SoHee Park

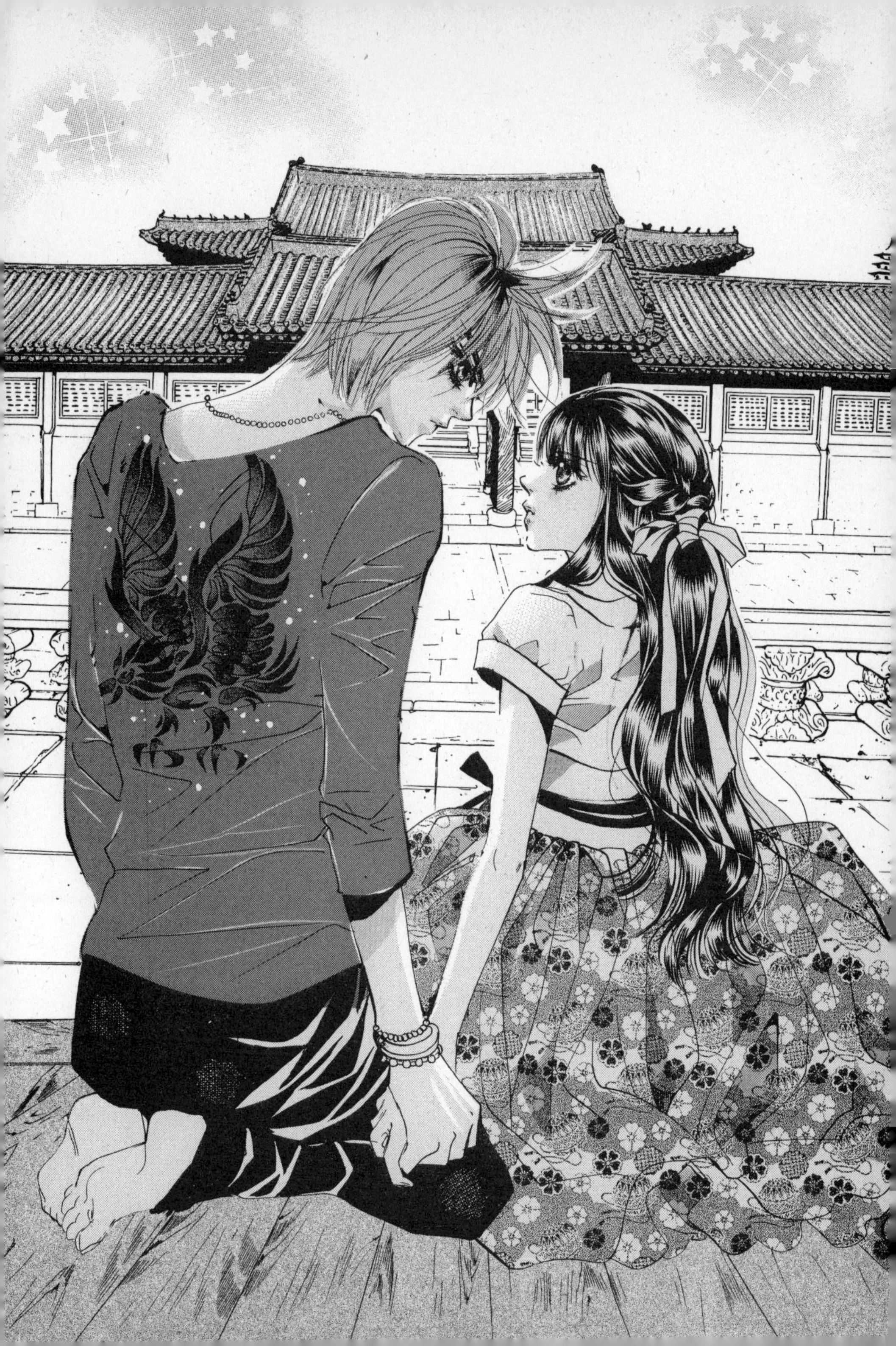

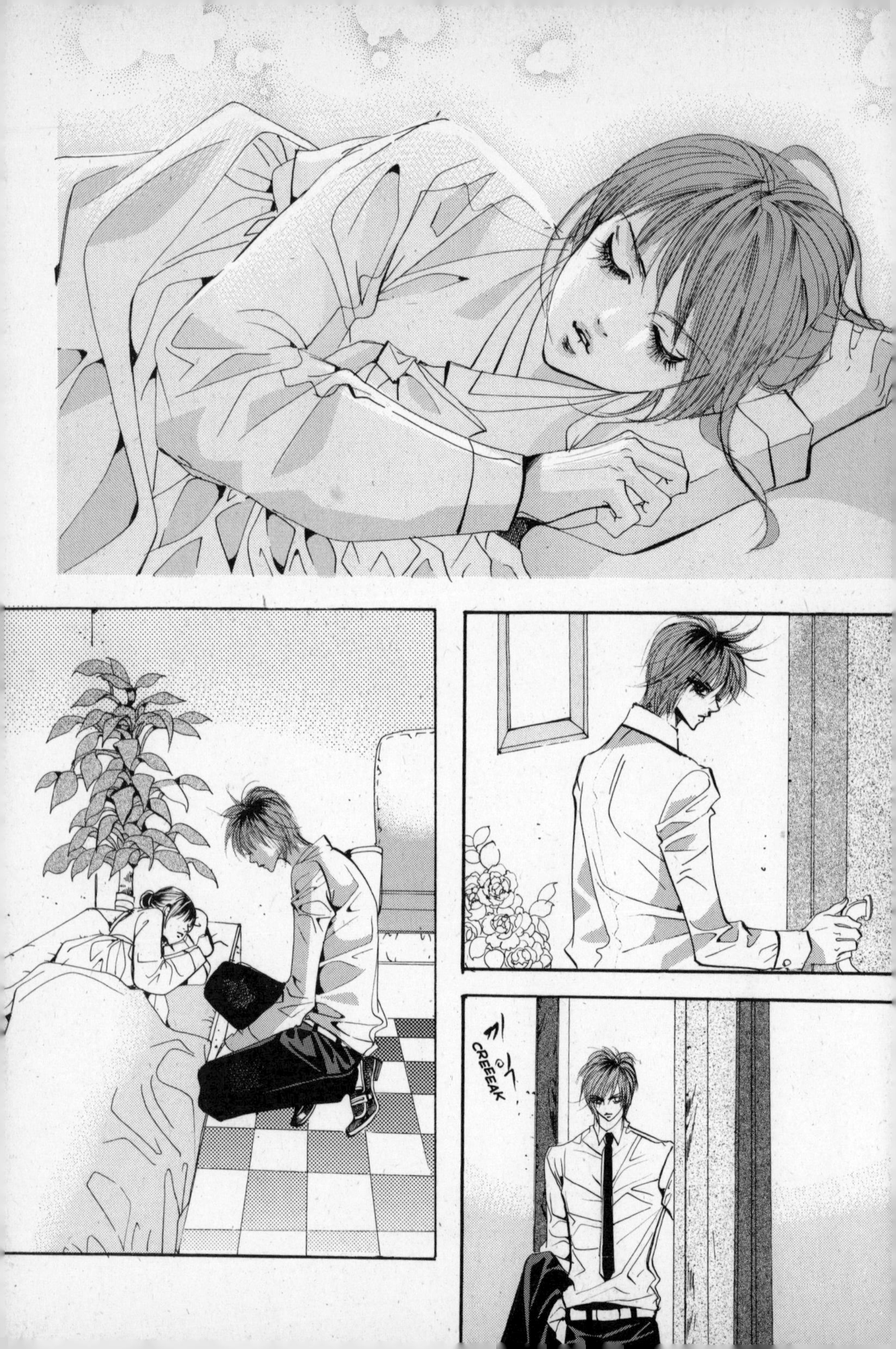
CREEEAK

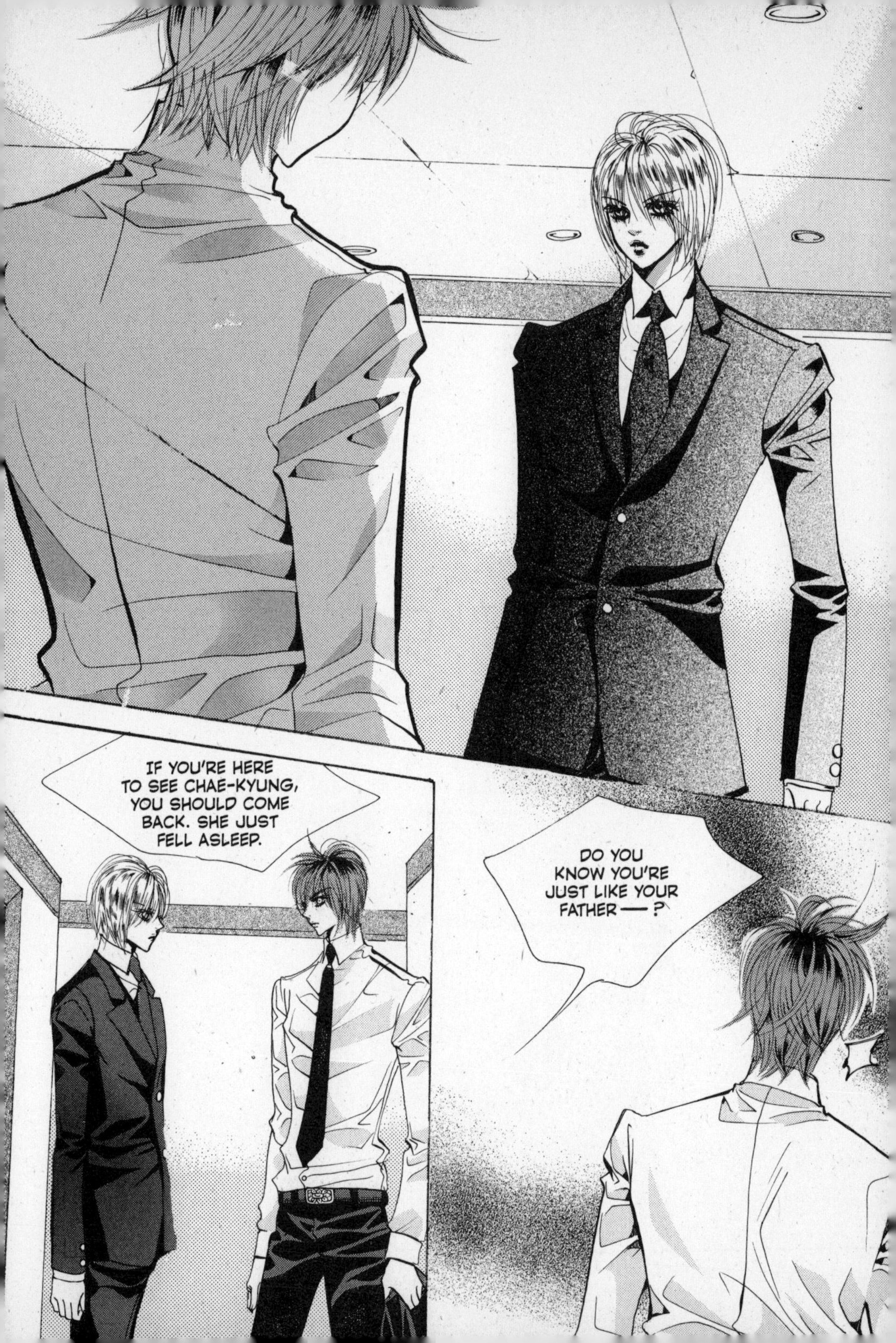
IF YOU'RE HERE TO SEE CHAE-KYUNG, YOU SHOULD COME BACK. SHE JUST FELL ASLEEP.
DO YOU KNOW YOU'RE JUST LIKE YOUR FATHER— ?

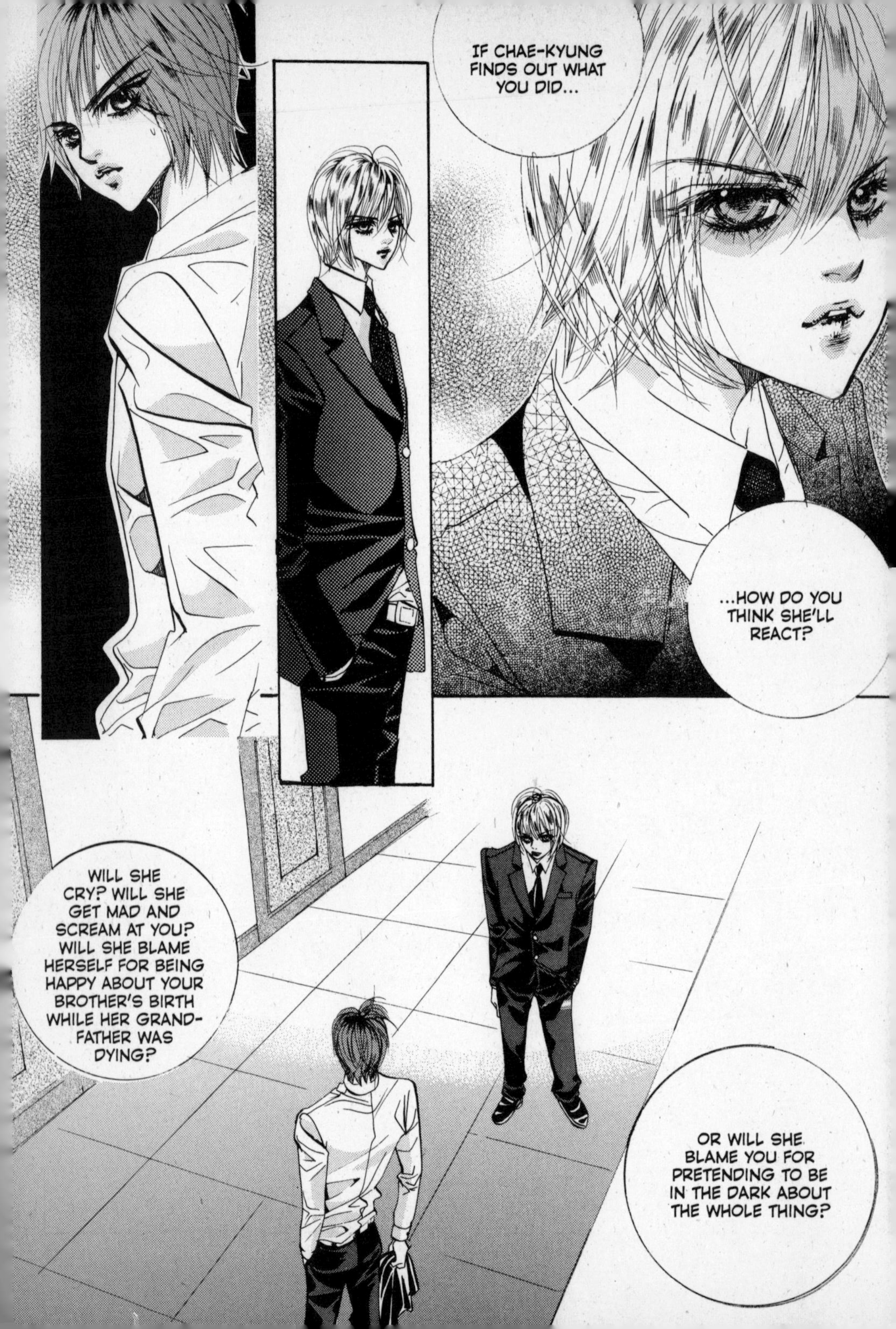
IF CHAE-KYUNG FINDS OUT WHAT YOU DID...
...HOW DO YOU THINK SHE'LL REACT?
WILL SHE CRY? WILL SHE GET MAD AND SCREAM AT YOU? WILL SHE BLAME HERSELF FOR BEING HAPPY ABOUT YOUR BROTHER'S BIRTH WHILE HER GRAND-FATHER WAS DYING?
OR WILL SHE BLAME YOU FOR PRETENDING TO BE IN THE DARK ABOUT THE WHOLE THING?

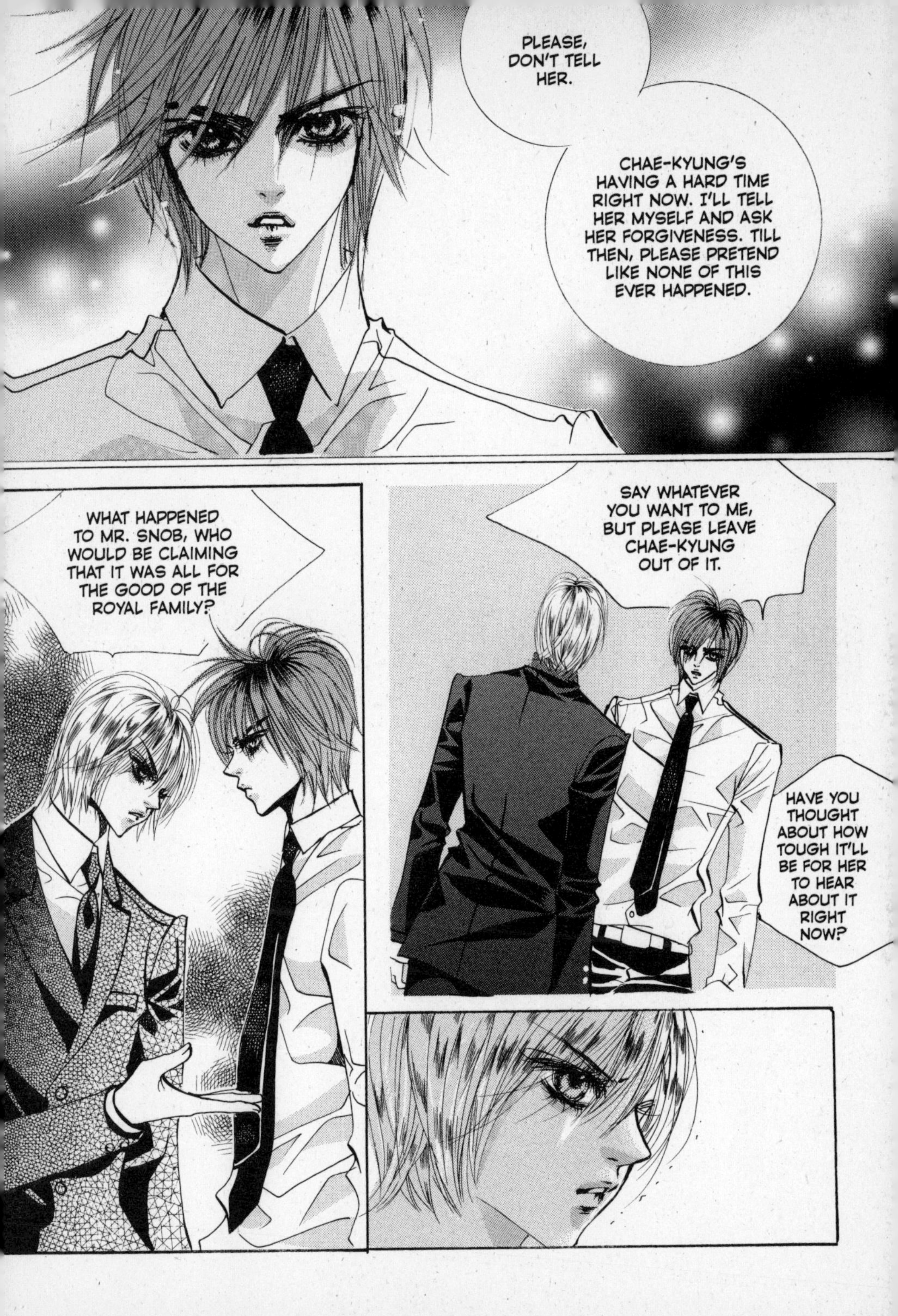
PLEASE, DON'T TELL HER.
CHAE-KYUNG'S HAVING A HARD TIME RIGHT NOW. I'LL TELL HER MYSELF AND ASK HER FORGIVENESS. TILL THEN, PLEASE PRETEND LIKE NONE OF THIS EVER HAPPENED.
WHAT HAPPENED TO MR. SNOB, WHO WOULD BE CLAIMING THAT IT WAS ALL FOR THE GOOD OF THE ROYAL FAMILY?
SAY WHATEVER YOU WANT TO ME, BUT PLEASE LEAVE CHAE-KYUNG OUT OF IT.
HAVE YOU THOUGHT ABOUT HOW TOUGH IT'LL BE FOR HER TO HEAR ABOUT IT RIGHT NOW?

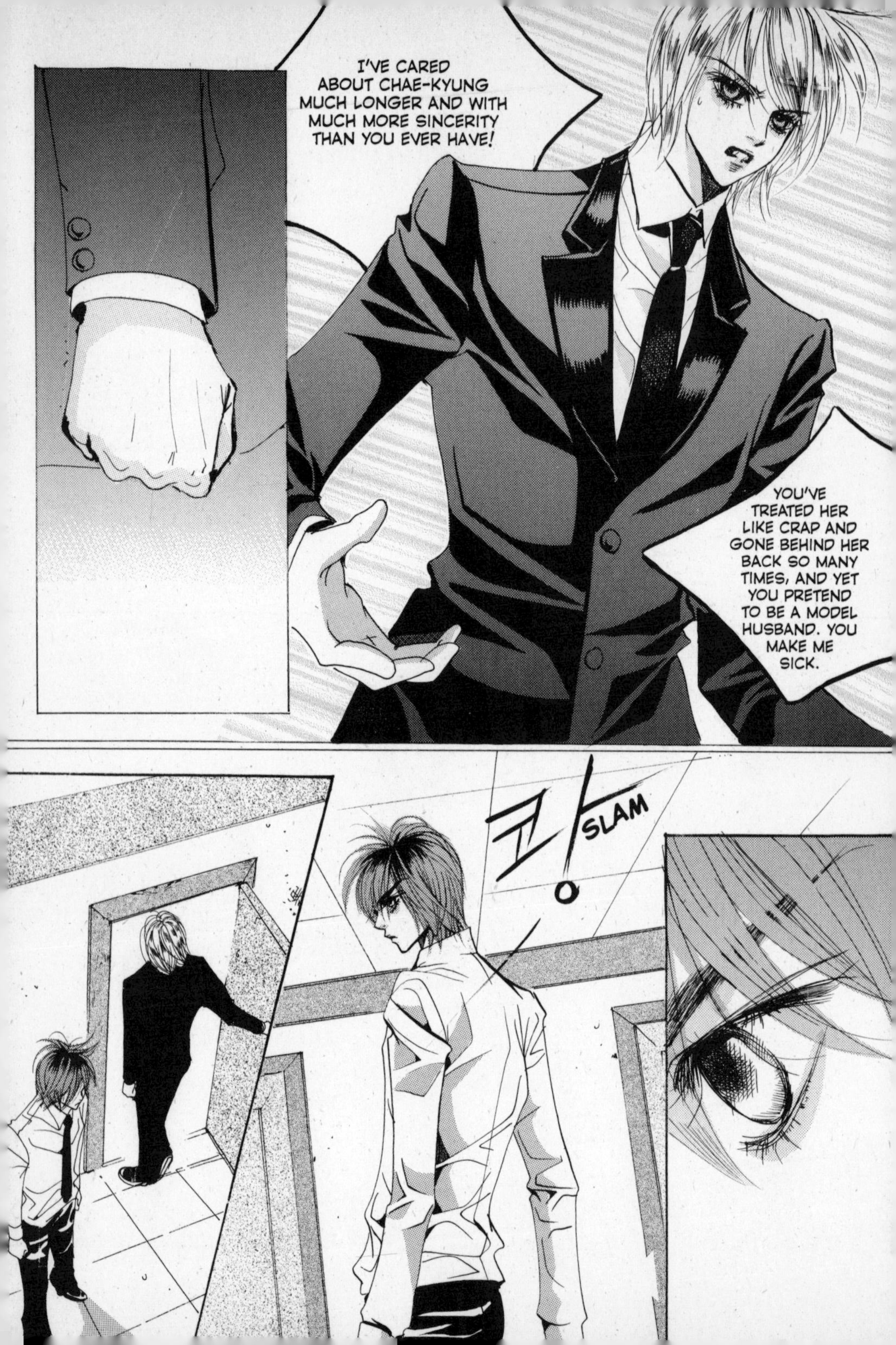
I'VE CARED ABOUT CHAE-KYUNG MUCH LONGER AND WITH MUCH MORE SINCERITY THAN YOU EVER HAVE!
YOU'VE TREATED HER LIKE CRAP AND GONE BEHIND HER BACK SO MANY TIMES, AND YET YOU PRETEND TO BE A MODEL HUSBAND. YOU MAKE ME SICK.
쾅!
SLAM

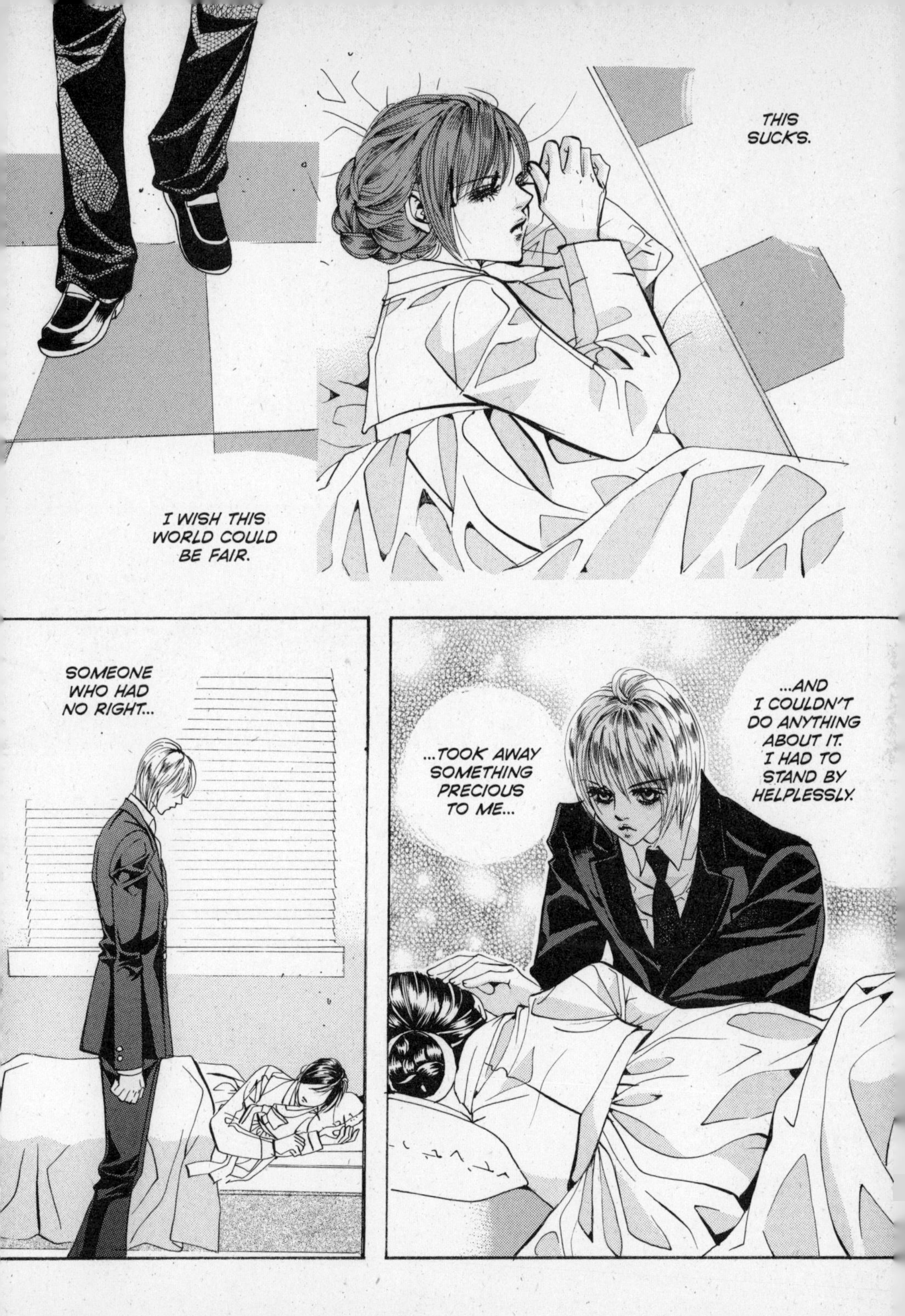
THIS SUCKS.
I WISH THIS WORLD COULD BE FAIR.
SOMEONE WHO HAD NO RIGHT...
...TOOK AWAY SOMETHING PRECIOUS TO ME...
...AND I COULDN'T DO ANYTHING ABOUT IT. I HAD TO STAND BY HELPLESSLY.

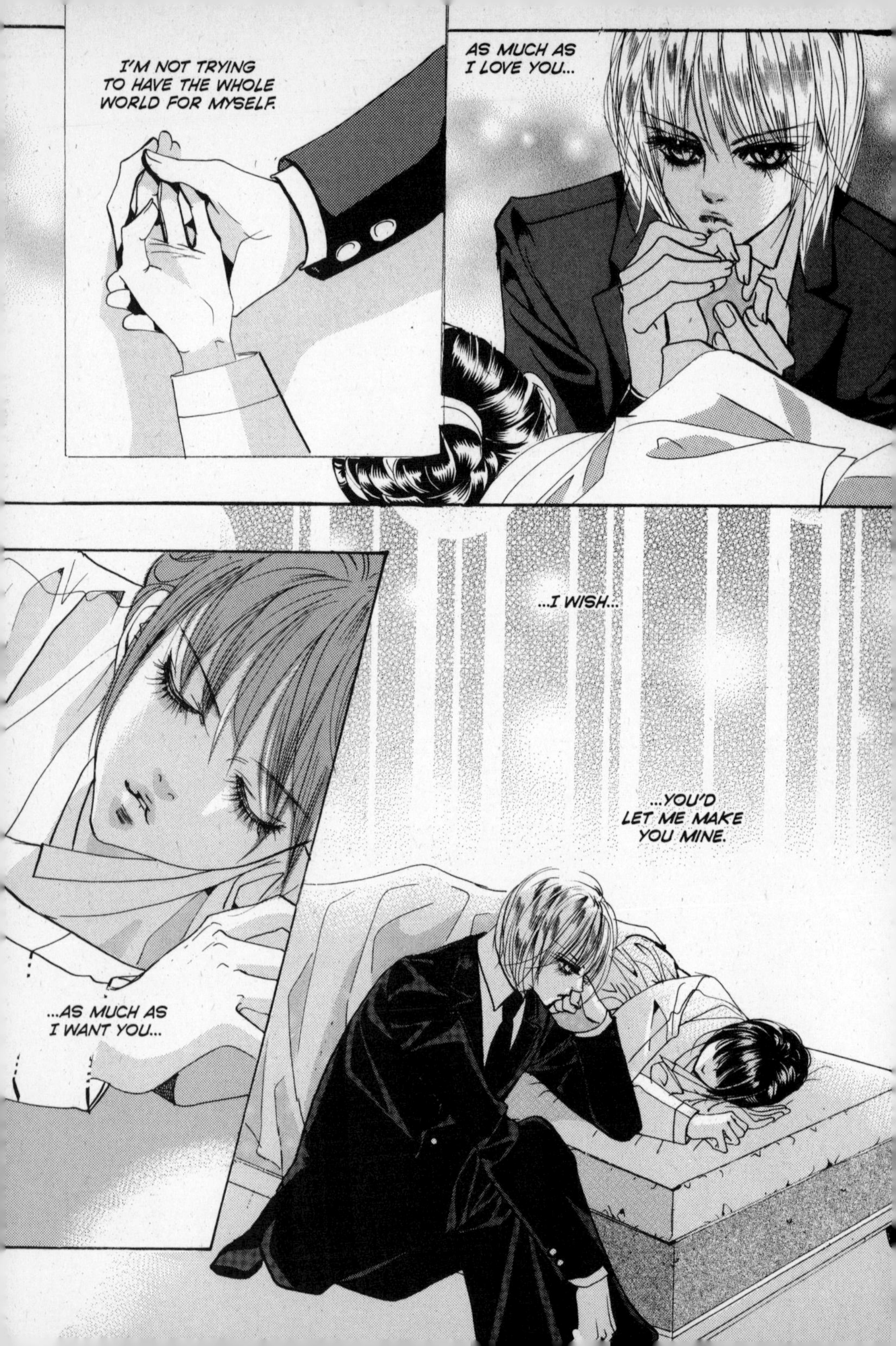
I'M NOT TRYING TO HAVE THE WHOLE WORLD FOR MYSELF.
AS MUCH AS I LOVE YOU...
...AS MUCH AS I WANT YOU...
...I WISH...
...YOU'D LET ME MAKE YOU MINE.

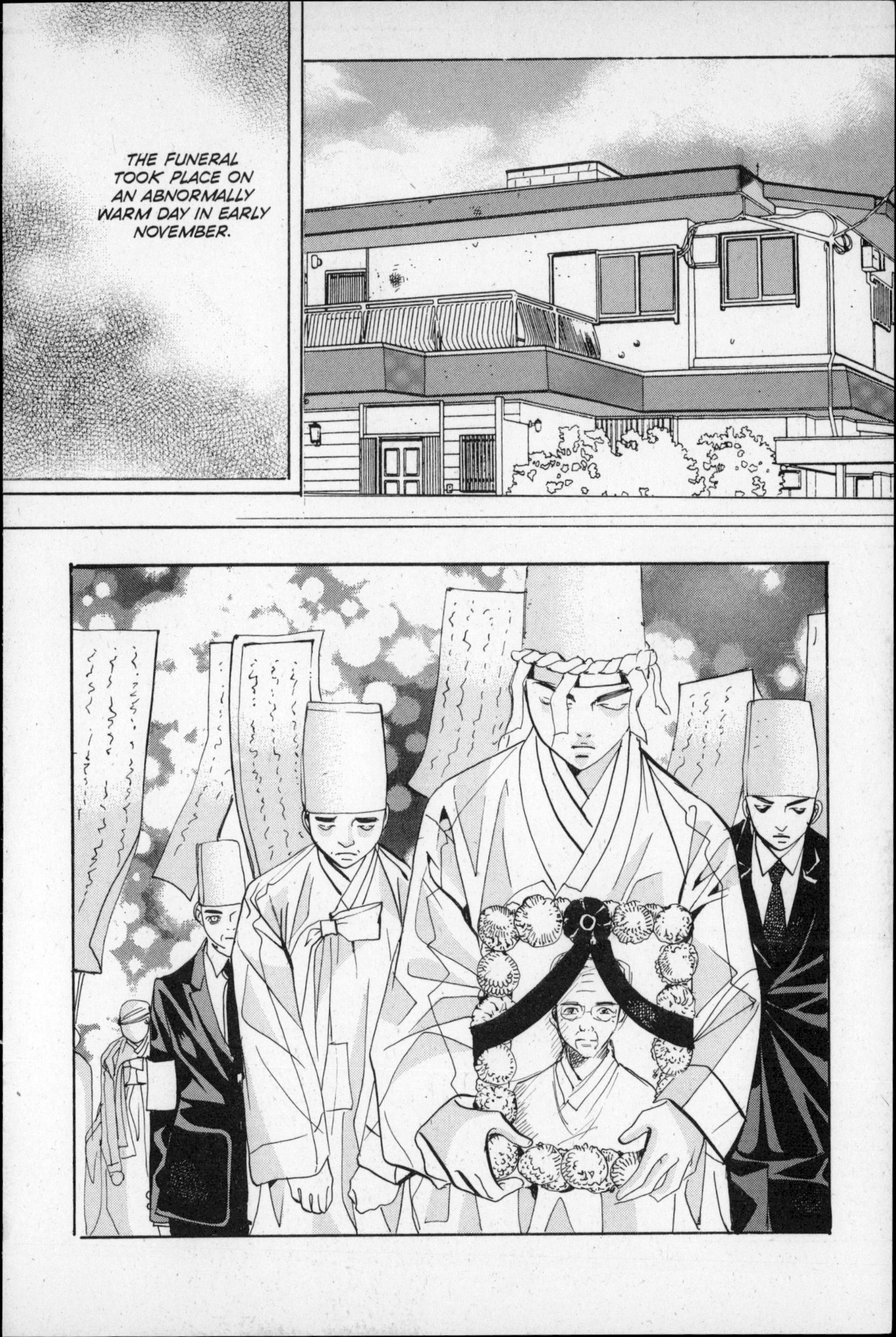
THE FUNERAL TOOK PLACE ON AN ABNORMALLY WARM DAY IN EARLY NOVEMBER.

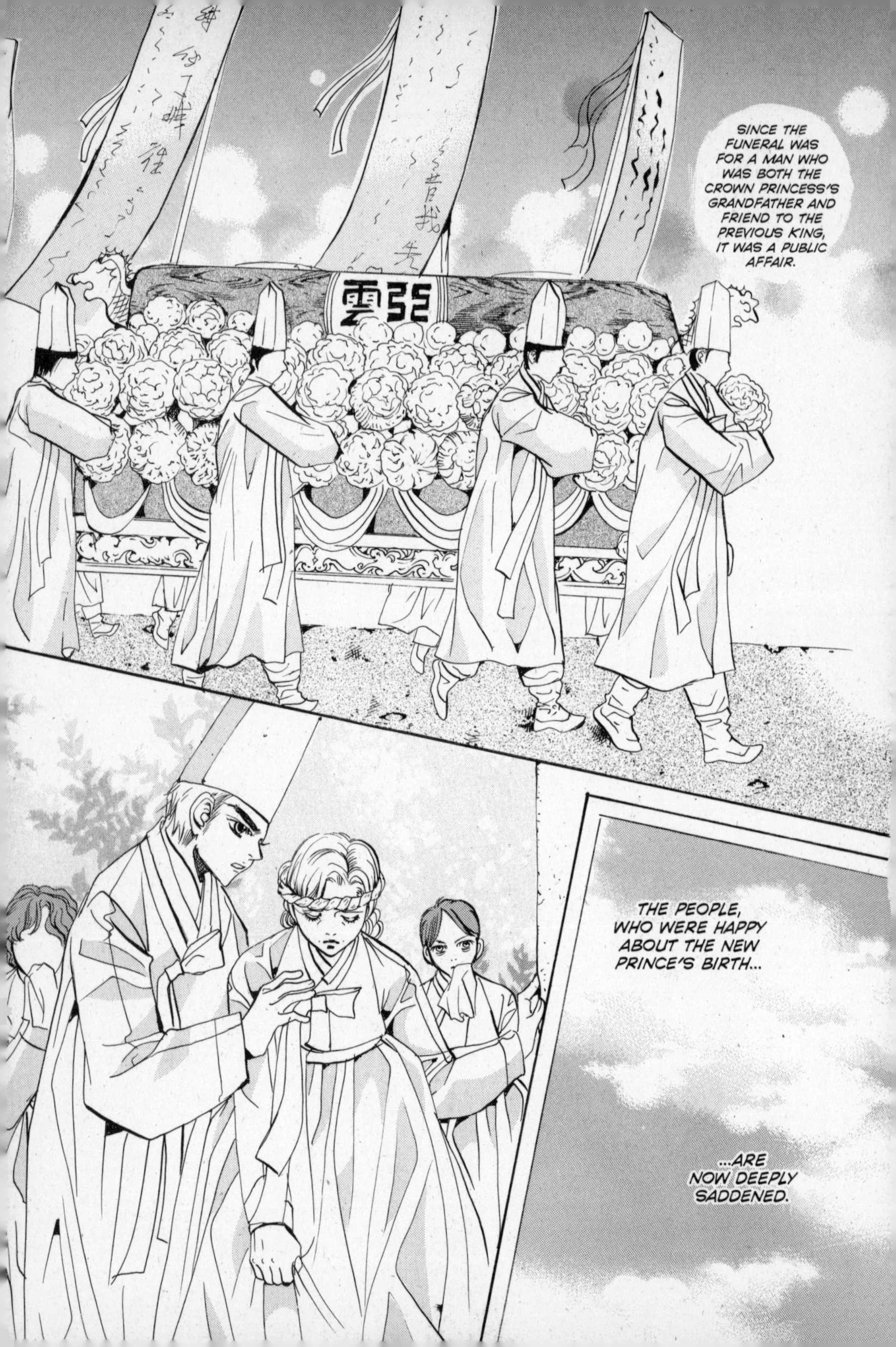
SINCE THE FUNERAL WAS FOR A MAN WHO WAS BOTH THE CROWN PRINCESS'S GRANDFATHER AND FRIEND TO THE PREVIOUS KING, IT WAS A PUBLIC AFFAIR.
THE PEOPLE, WHO WERE HAPPY ABOUT THE NEW PRINCE'S BIRTH...
...ARE NOW DEEPLY SADDENED.

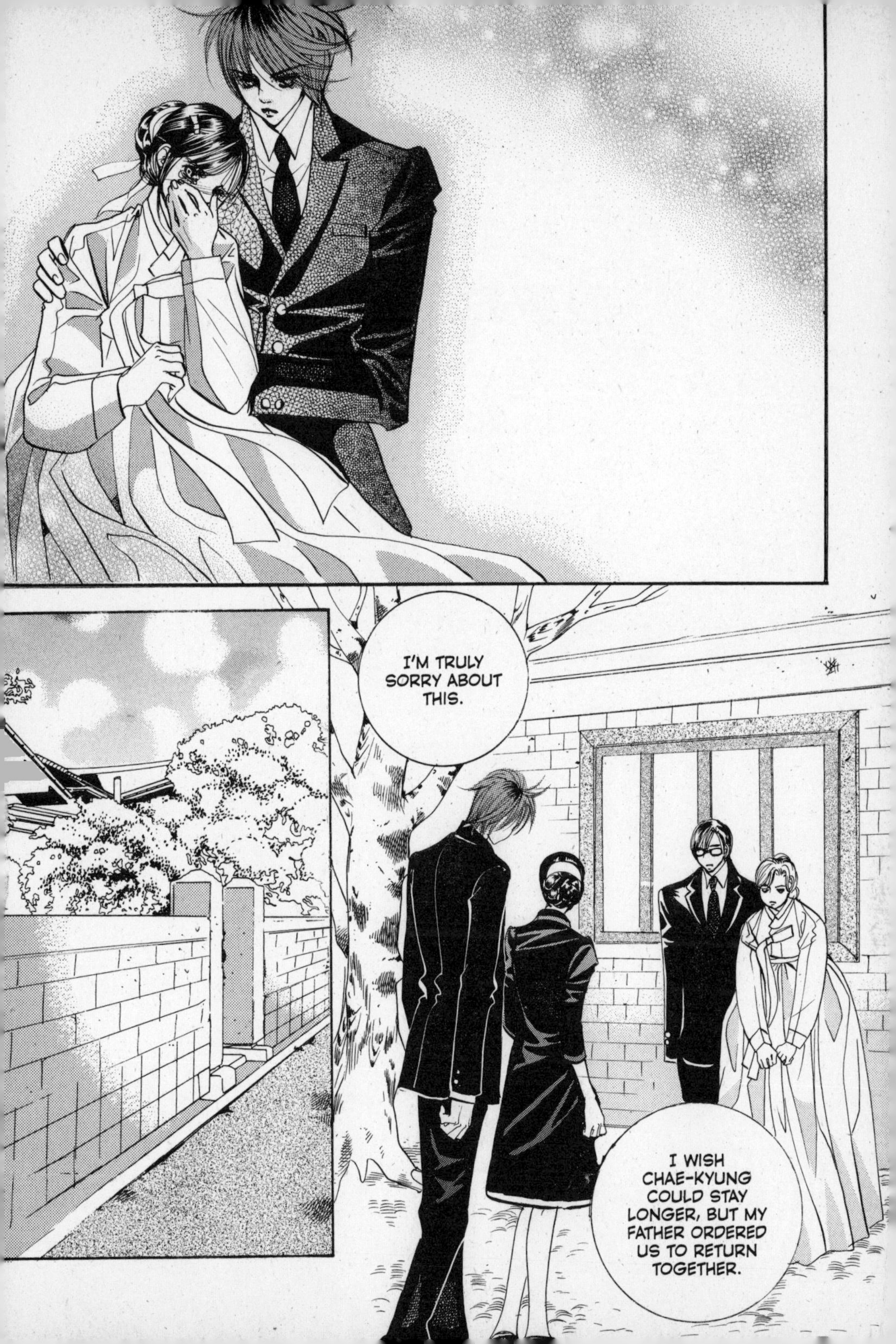
I'M TRULY SORRY ABOUT THIS.
I WISH CHAE-KYUNG COULD STAY LONGER, BUT MY FATHER ORDERED US TO RETURN TOGETHER.

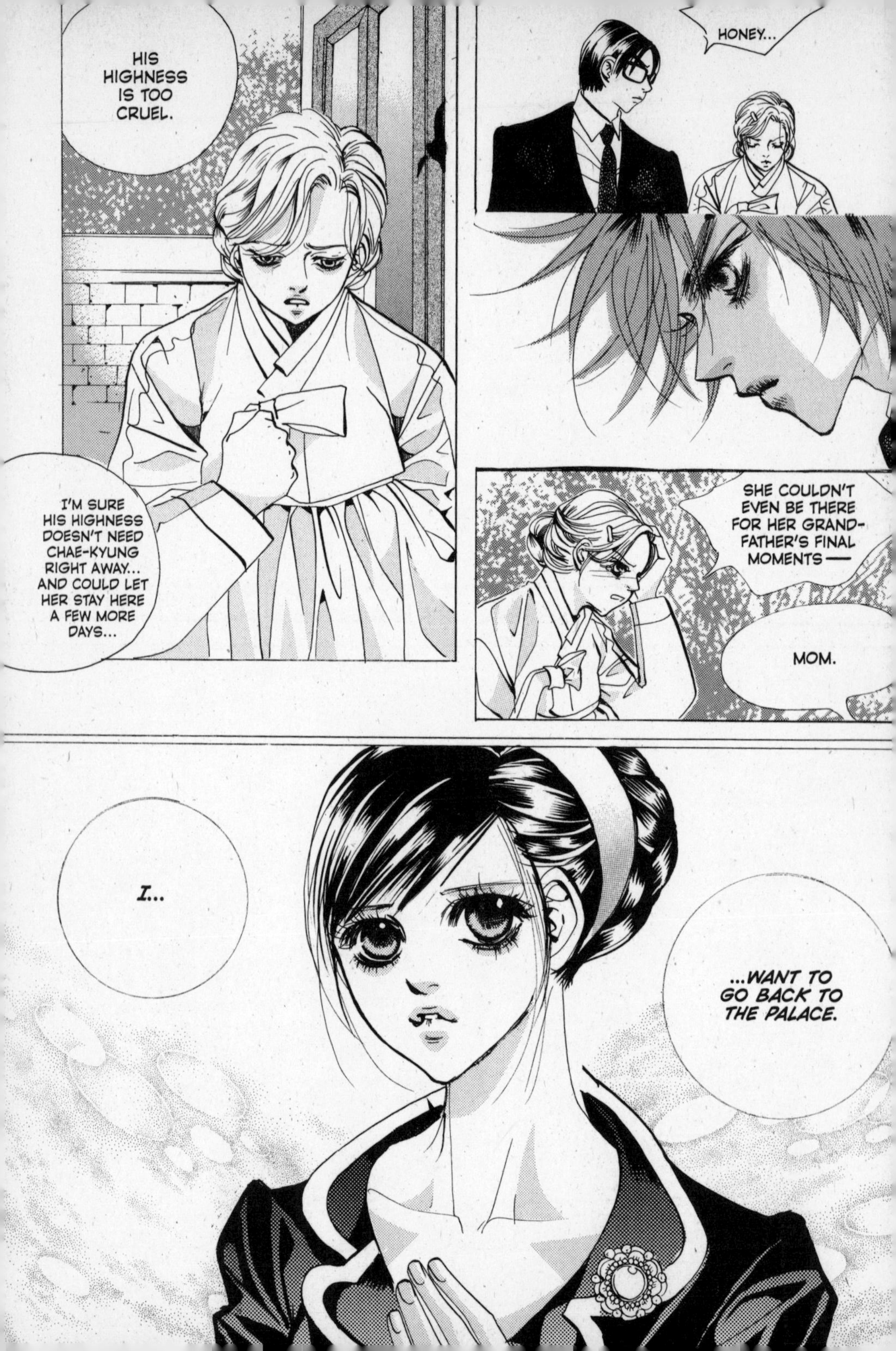
HIS HIGHNESS IS TOO CRUEL.
I'M SURE HIS HIGHNESS DOESN'T NEED CHAE-KYUNG RIGHT AWAY... AND COULD LET HER STAY HERE A FEW MORE DAYS...
HONEY...
SHE COULDN'T EVEN BE THERE FOR HER GRAND-FATHER'S FINAL MOMENTS—
MOM.
I...
...WANT TO GO BACK TO THE PALACE.

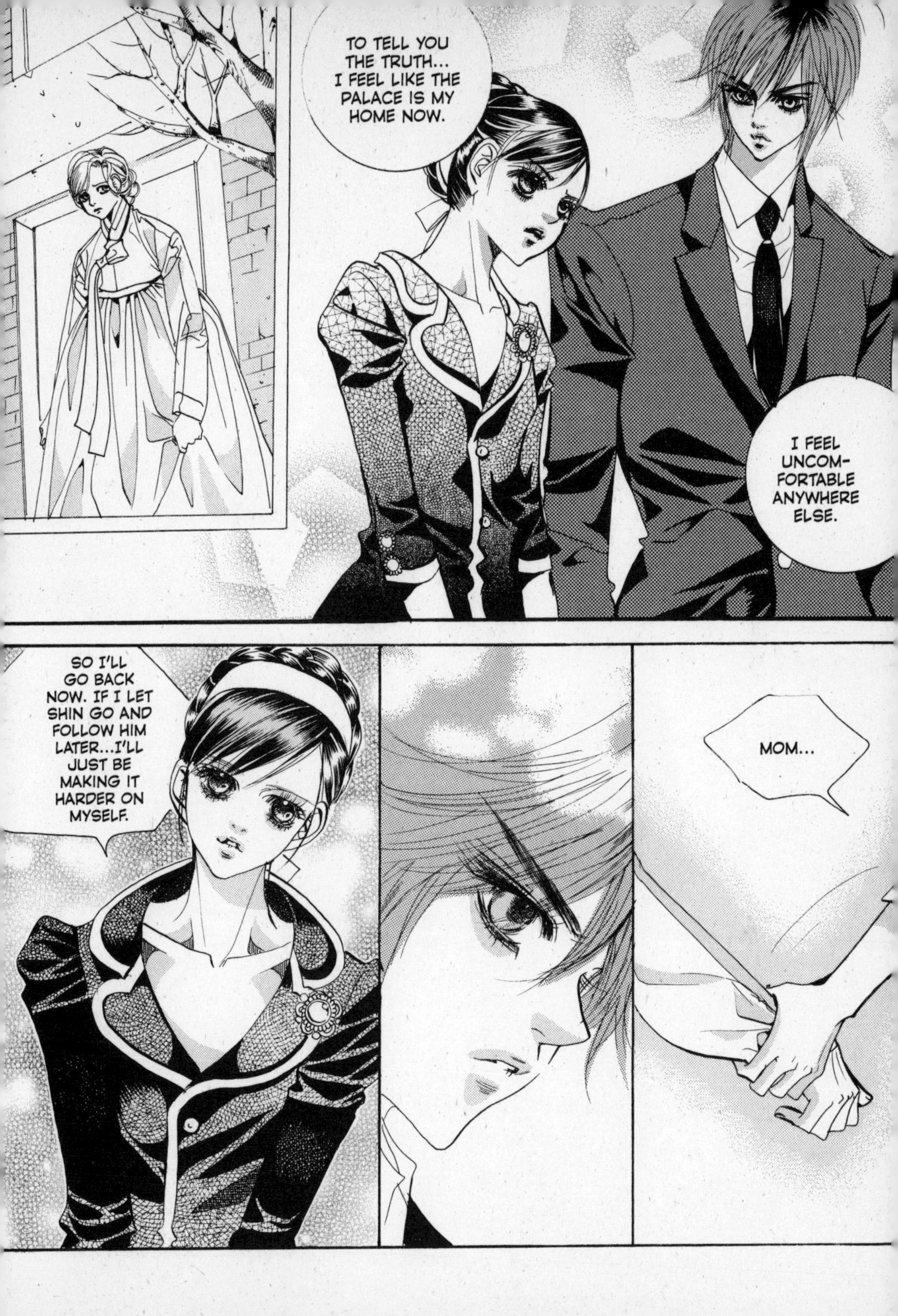
TO TELL YOU THE TRUTH... I FEEL LIKE THE PALACE IS MY HOME NOW.
I FEEL UNCOM-FORTABLE ANYWHERE ELSE.
SO I'LL GO BACK NOW. IF I LET SHIN GO AND FOLLOW HIM LATER...I'LL JUST BE MAKING IT HARDER ON MYSELF.
MOM...

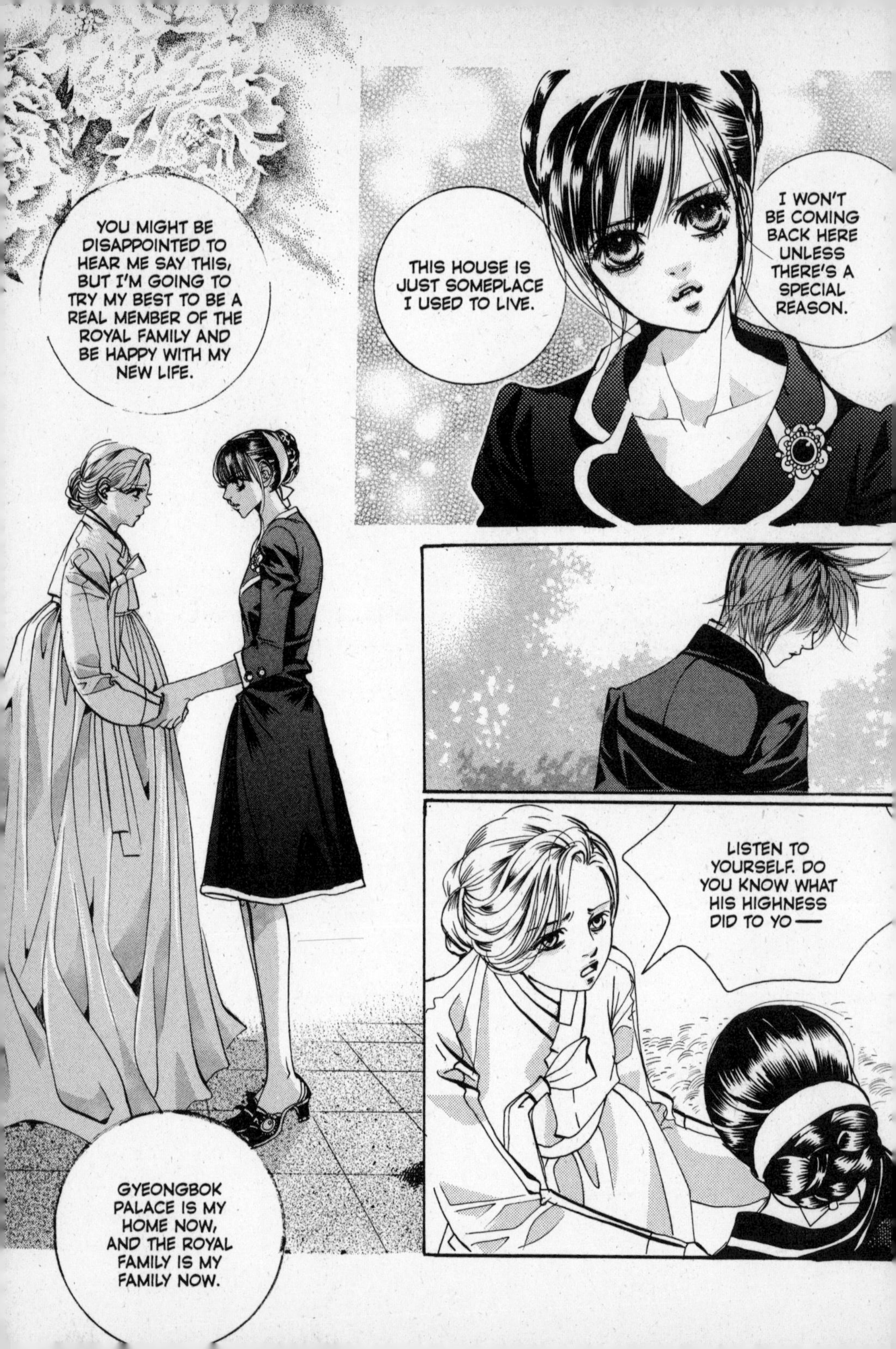
YOU MIGHT BE DISAPPOINTED TO HEAR ME SAY THIS, BUT I'M GOING TO TRY MY BEST TO BE A REAL MEMBER OF THE ROYAL FAMILY AND BE HAPPY WITH MY NEW LIFE.
GYEONGBOK PALACE IS MY HOME NOW, AND THE ROYAL FAMILY IS MY FAMILY NOW.
THIS HOUSE IS JUST SOMEPLACE I USED TO LIVE.
I WON'T BE COMING BACK HERE UNLESS THERE'S A SPECIAL REASON.
LISTEN TO YOURSELF. DO YOU KNOW WHAT HIS HIGHNESS DID TO YO—

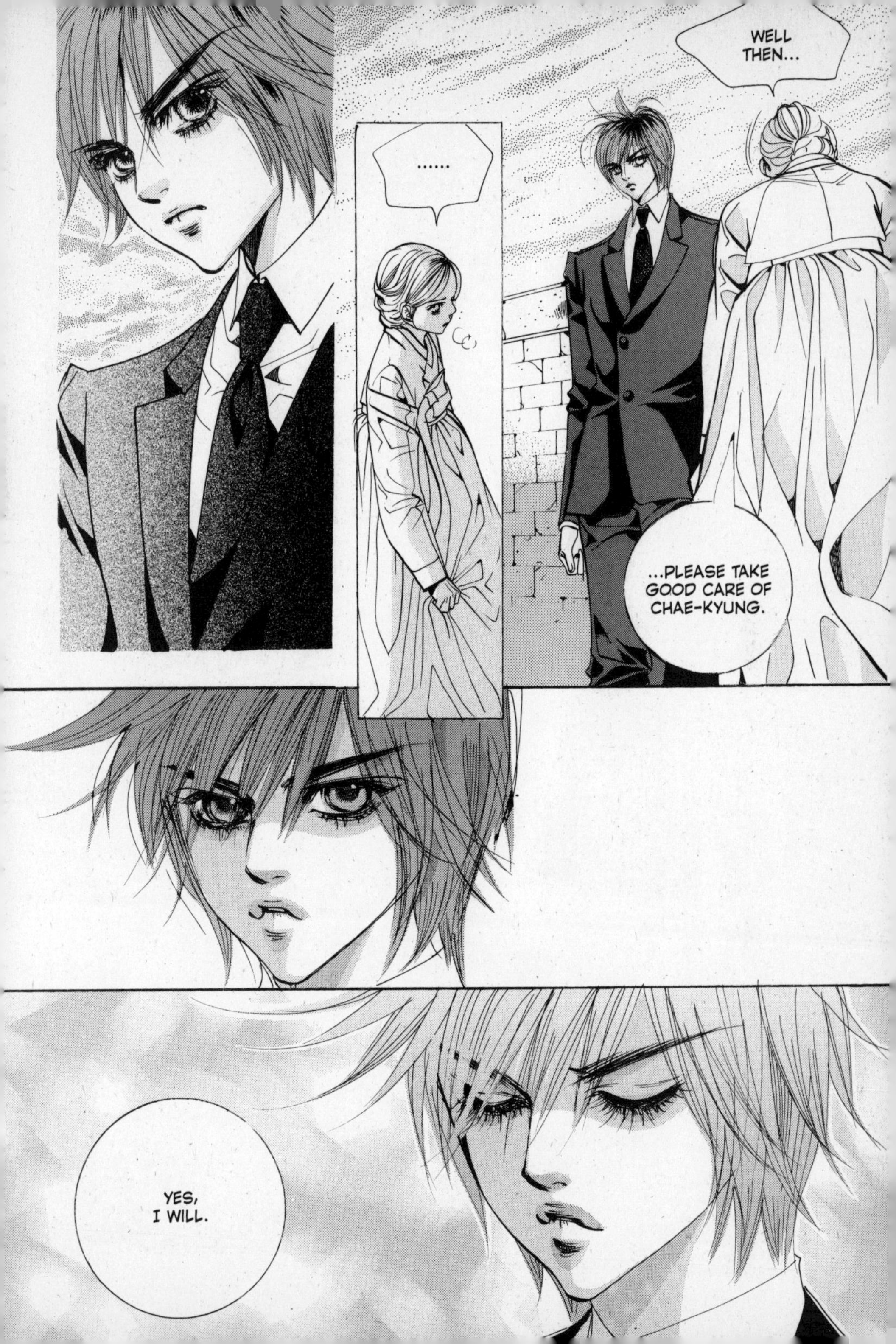

......
WELL THEN...
...PLEASE TAKE GOOD CARE OF CHAE-KYUNG.
YES, I WILL.

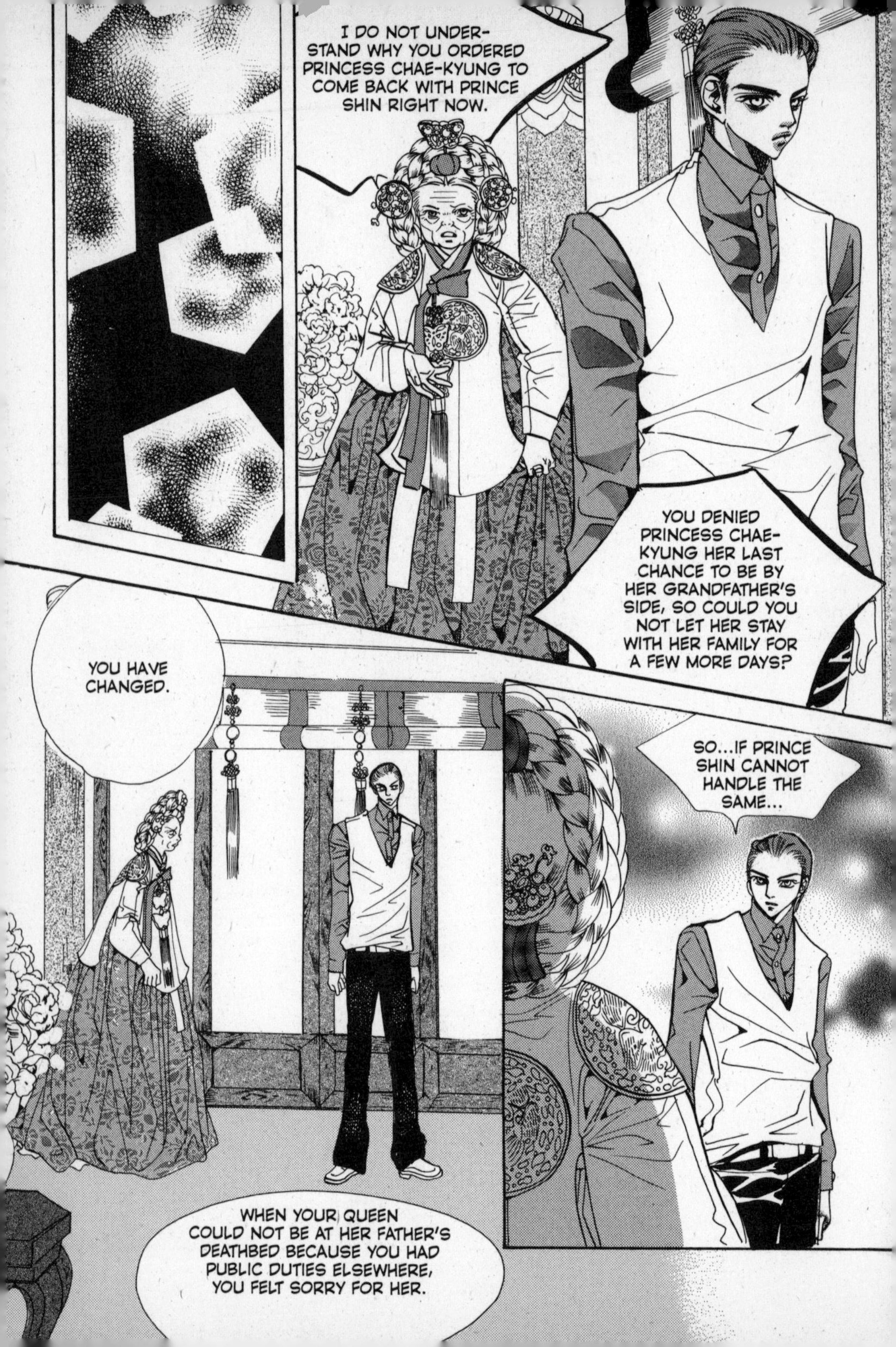
I DO NOT UNDER-STAND WHY YOU ORDERED PRINCESS CHAE-KYUNG TO COME BACK WITH PRINCE SHIN RIGHT NOW.
YOU DENIED PRINCESS CHAE-KYUNG HER LAST CHANCE TO BE BY HER GRANDFATHER'S SIDE, SO COULD YOU NOT LET HER STAY WITH HER FAMILY FOR A FEW MORE DAYS?
YOU HAVE CHANGED.
WHEN YOUR QUEEN COULD NOT BE AT HER FATHER'S DEATHBED BECAUSE YOU HAD PUBLIC DUTIES ELSEWHERE, YOU FELT SORRY FOR HER.
SO...IF PRINCE SHIN CANNOT HANDLE THE SAME...

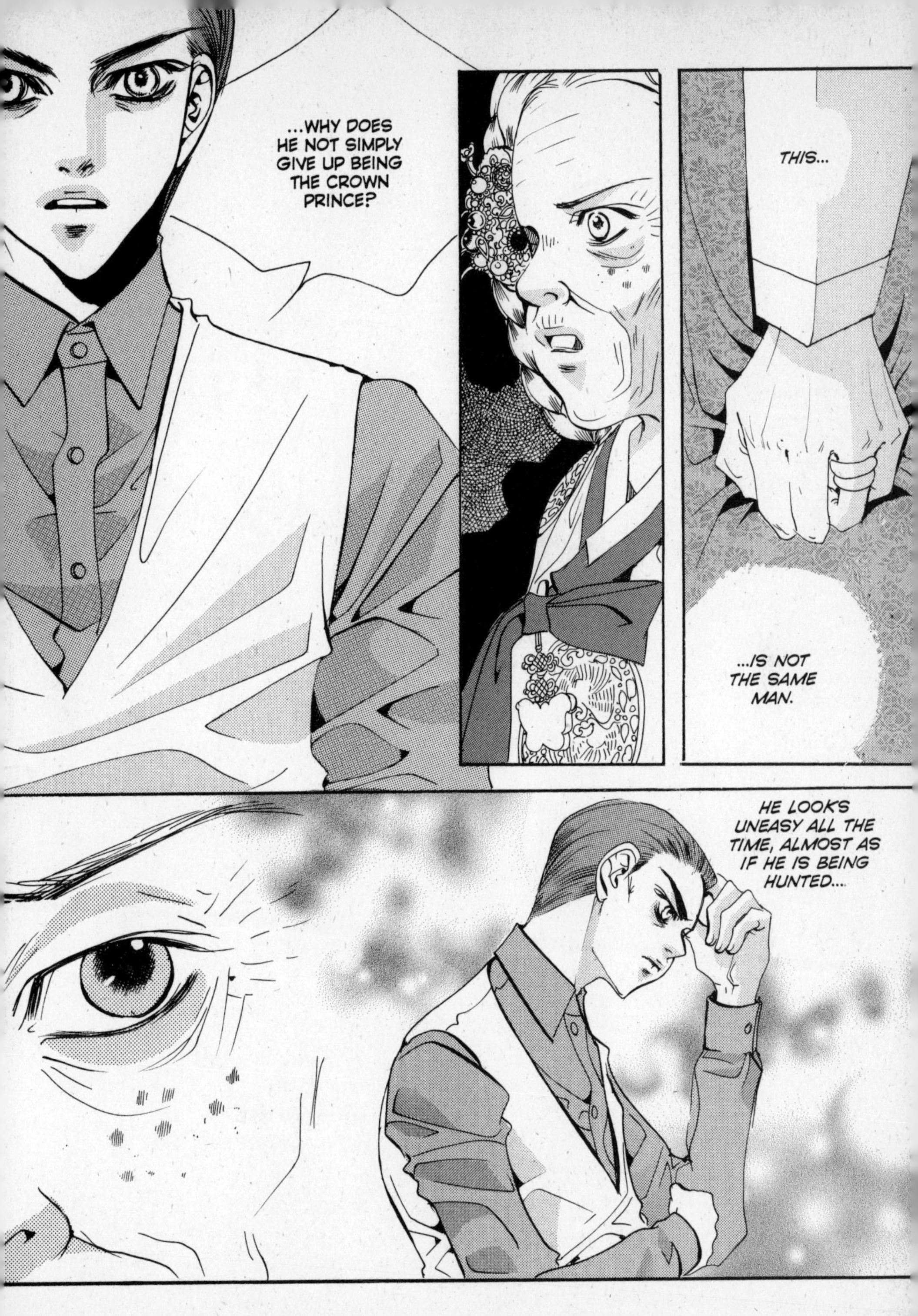
...WHY DOES HE NOT SIMPLY GIVE UP BEING THE CROWN PRINCE?
THIS...
...IS NOT THE SAME MAN.
HE LOOKS UNEASY ALL THE TIME, ALMOST AS IF HE IS BEING HUNTED...

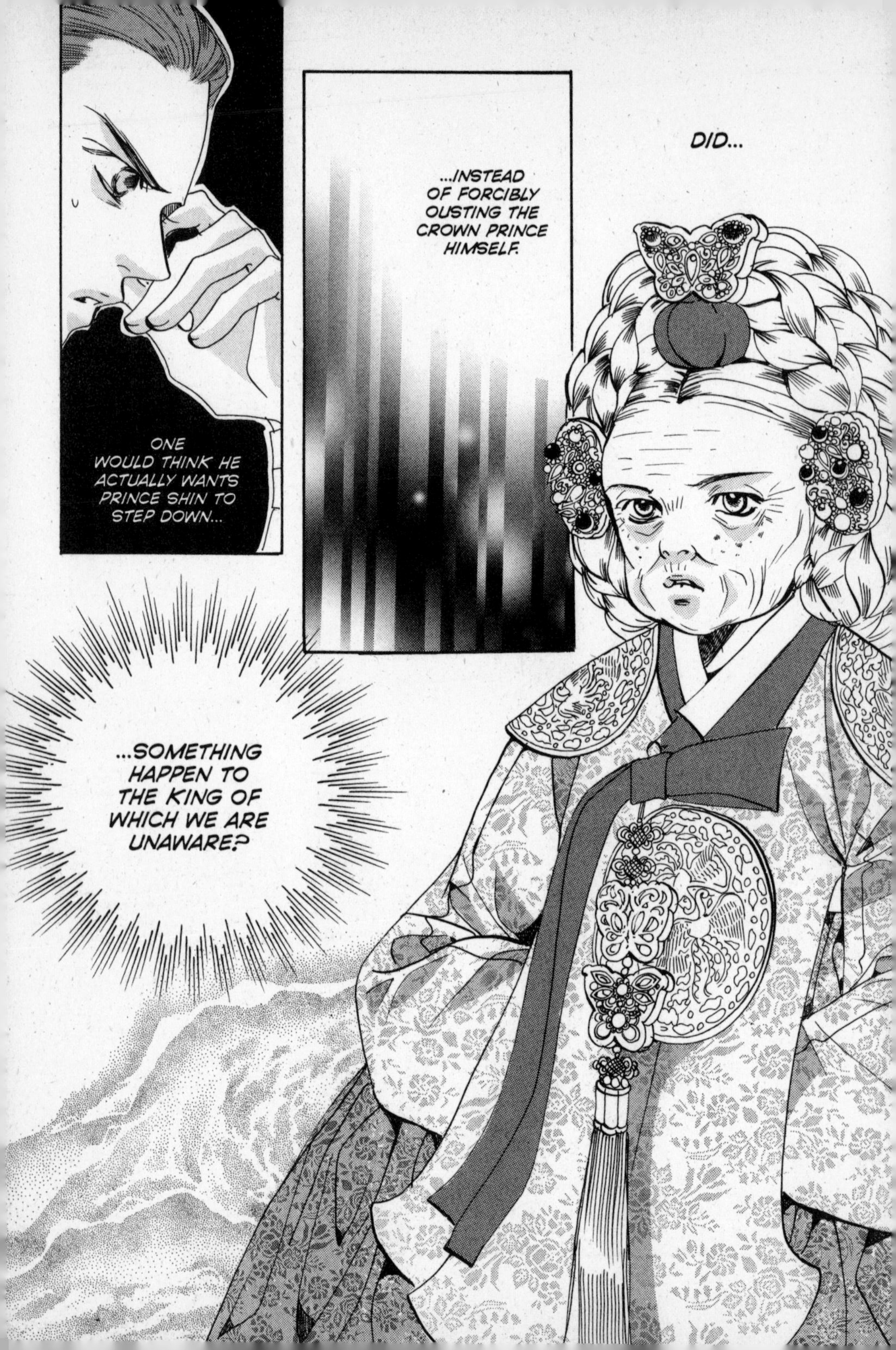
ONE WOULD THINK HE ACTUALLY WANTS PRINCE SHIN TO STEP DOWN...
...INSTEAD OF FORCIBLY OUSTING THE CROWN PRINCE HIMSELF.
DID...
...SOMETHING HAPPEN TO THE KING OF WHICH WE ARE UNAWARE?

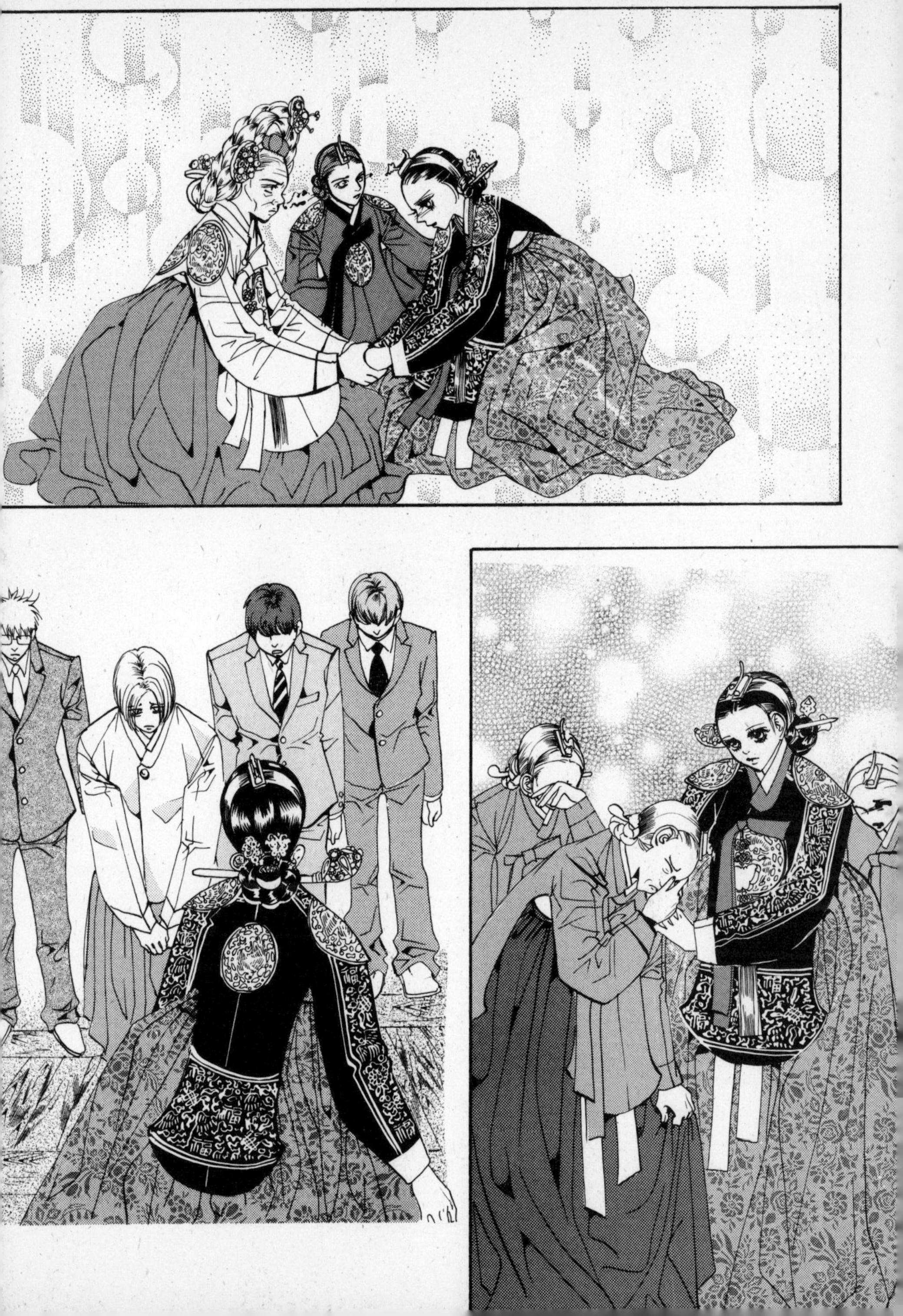

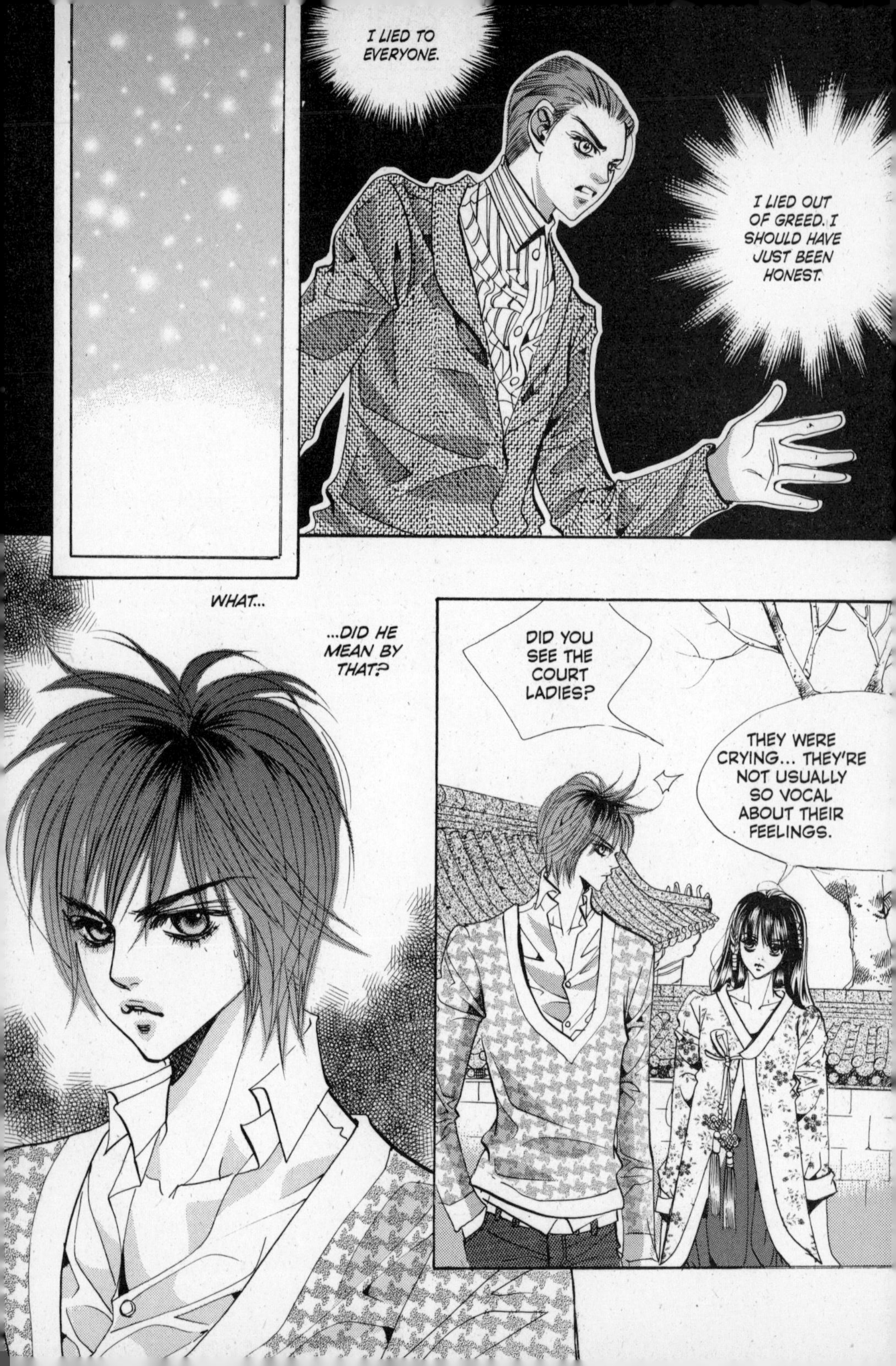
I LIED TO EVERYONE.
I LIED OUT OF GREED. I SHOULD HAVE JUST BEEN HONEST.
WHAT...
...DID HE MEAN BY THAT?
DID YOU SEE THE COURT LADIES?
THEY WERE CRYING... THEY'RE NOT USUALLY SO VOCAL ABOUT THEIR FEELINGS.

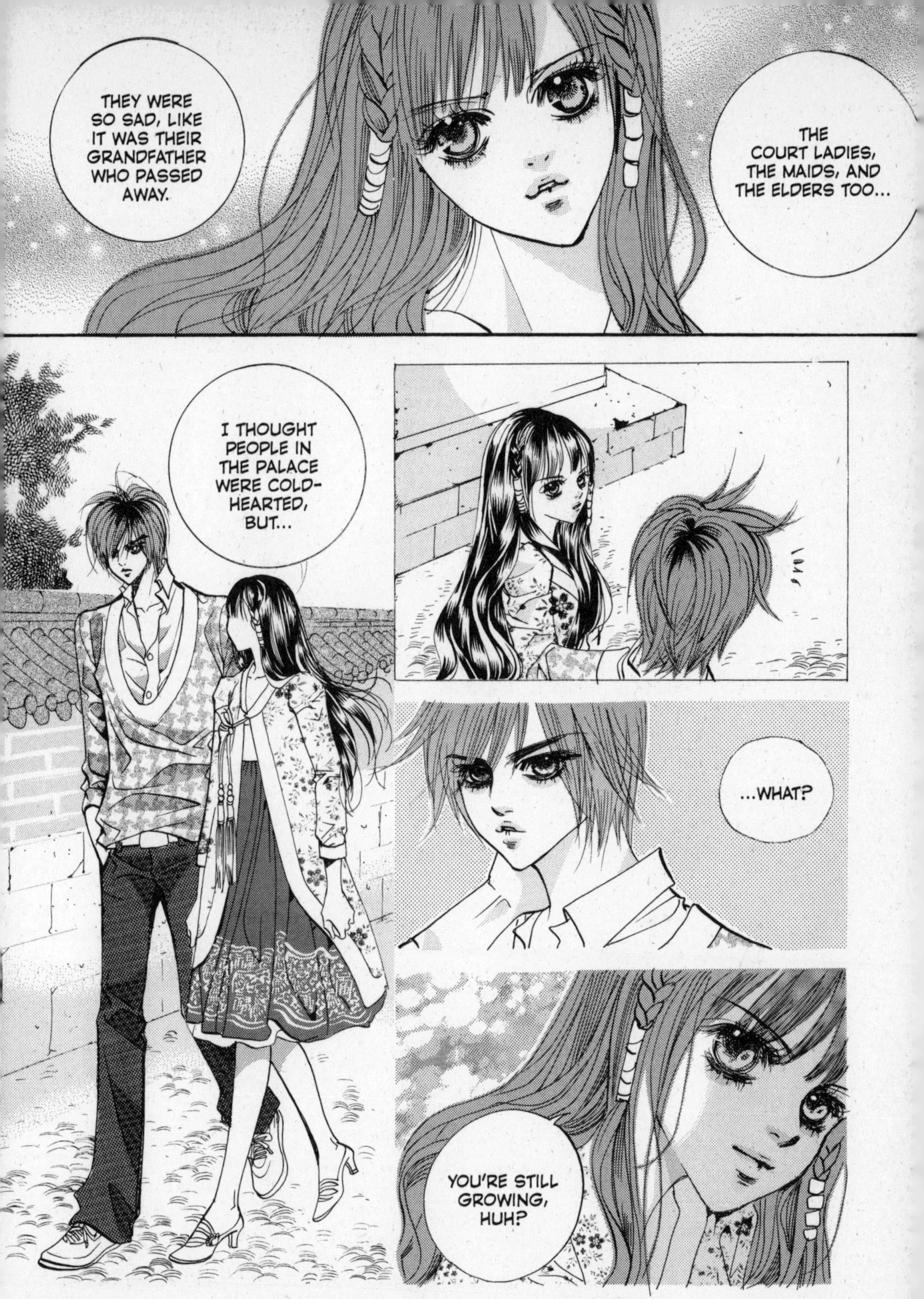
THEY WERE SO SAD, LIKE IT WAS THEIR GRANDFATHER WHO PASSED AWAY.
THE COURT LADIES, THE MAIDS, AND THE ELDERS TOO...
I THOUGHT PEOPLE IN THE PALACE WERE COLD-HEARTED, BUT...
...WHAT?
YOU'RE STILL GROWING, HUH?

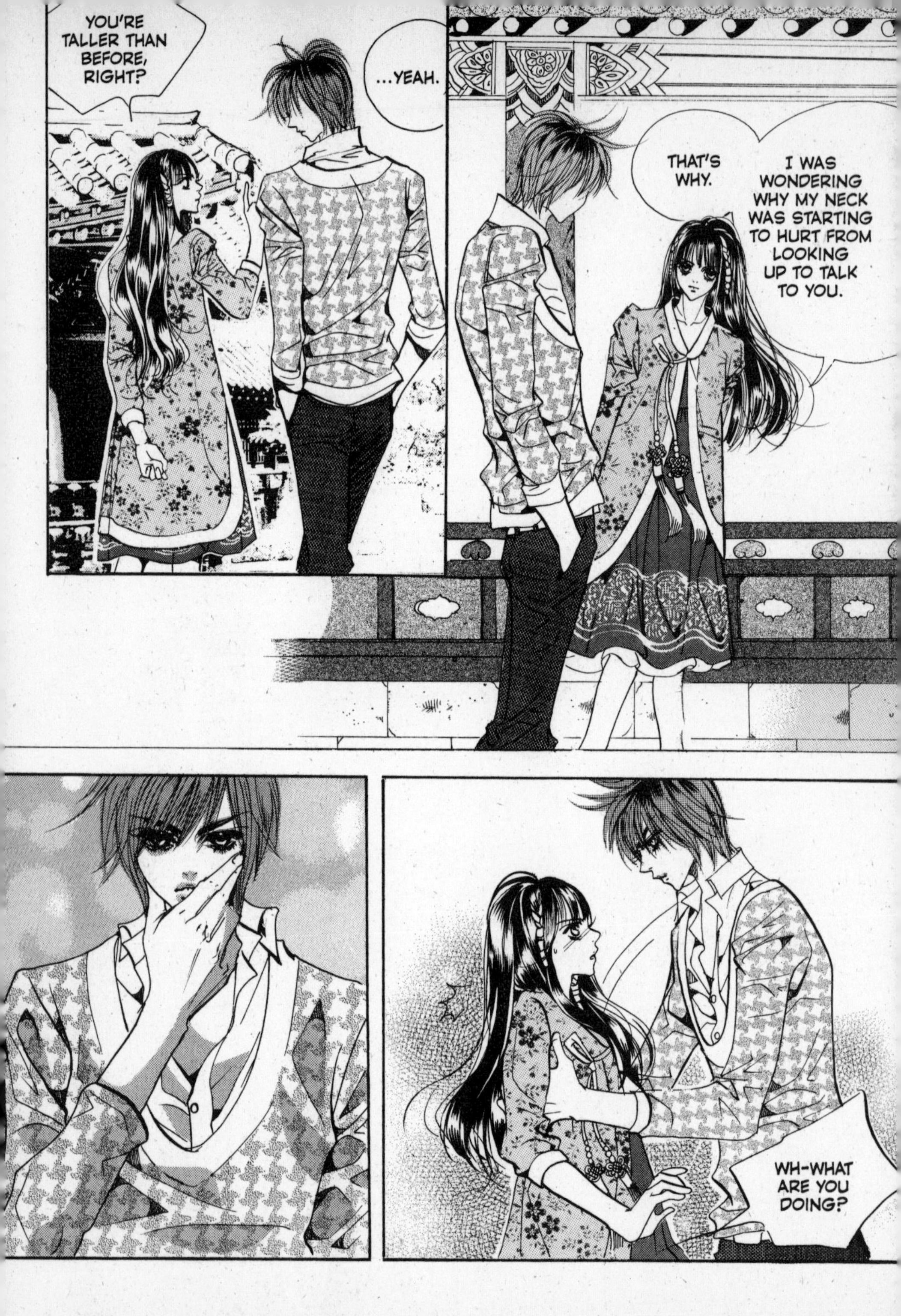
YOU'RE TALLER THAN BEFORE, RIGHT?
...YEAH.
THAT'S WHY.
I WAS WONDERING WHY MY NECK WAS STARTING TO HURT FROM LOOKING UP TO TALK TO YOU.
WH-WHAT ARE YOU DOING?

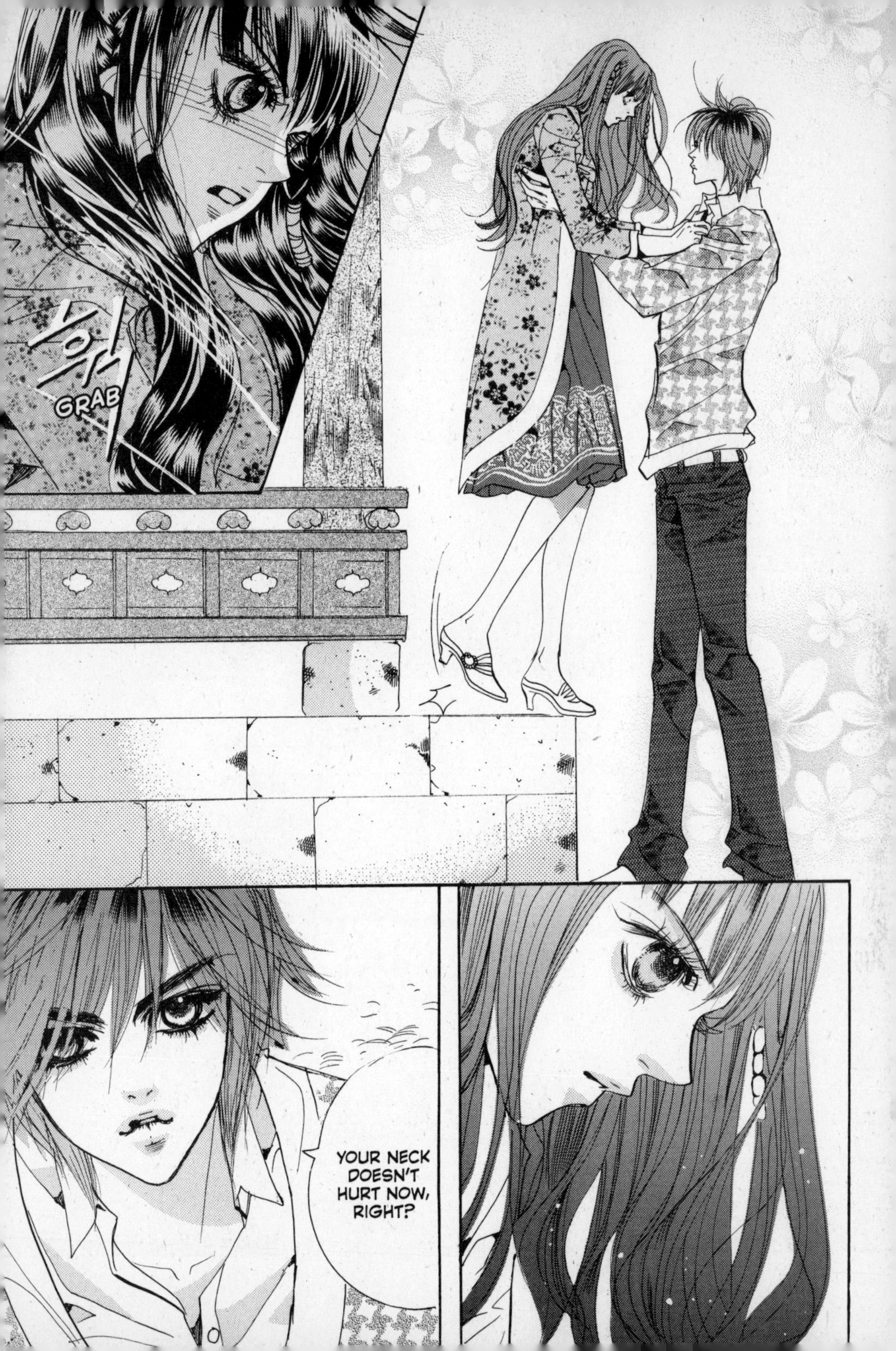
GRAB
YOUR NECK DOESN'T HURT NOW, RIGHT?

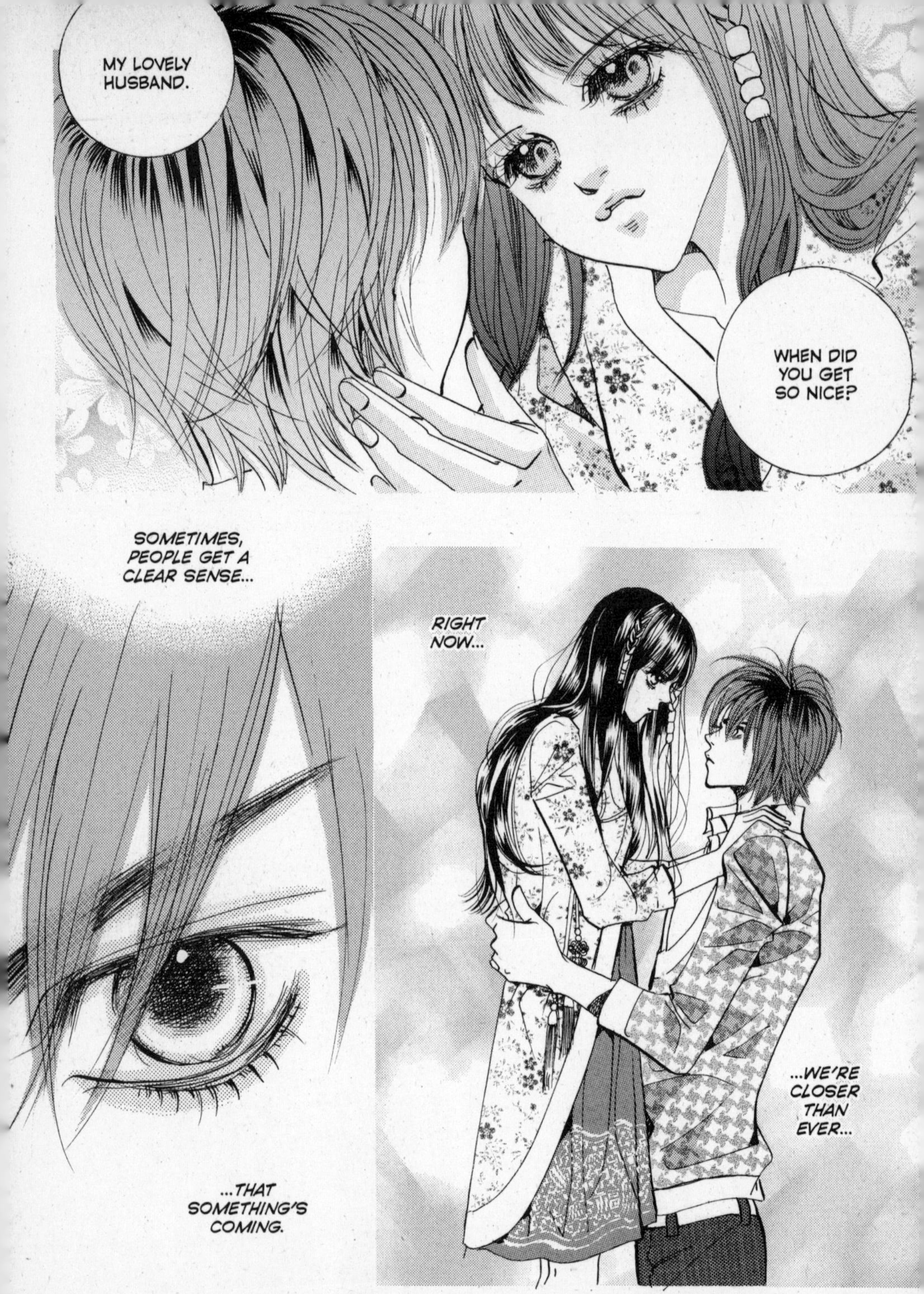
MY LOVELY HUSBAND.
WHEN DID YOU GET SO NICE?
SOMETIMES, PEOPLE GET A CLEAR SENSE...
...THAT SOMETHING'S COMING.
RIGHT NOW...
...WE'RE CLOSER THAN EVER...

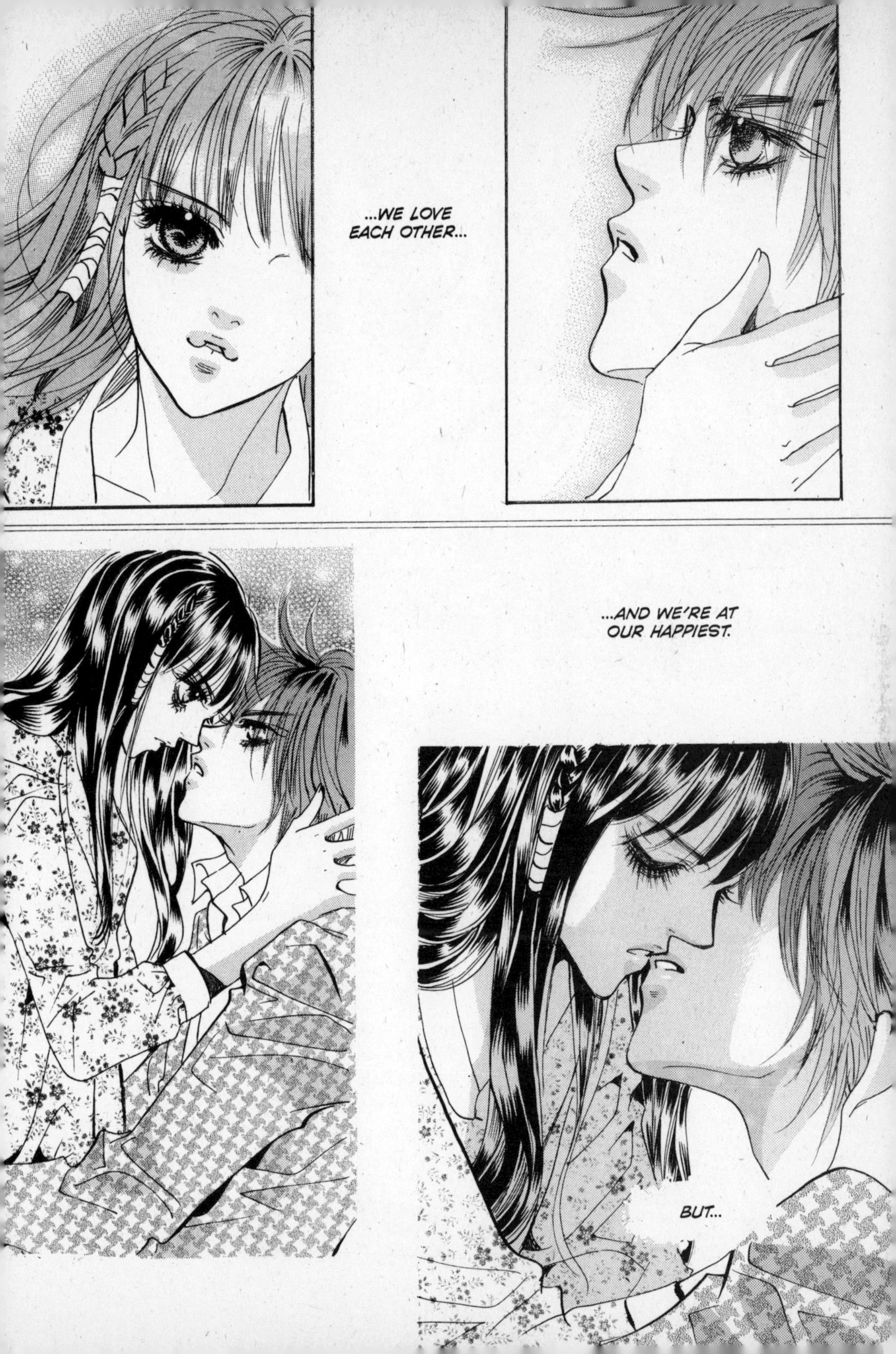
...WE LOVE EACH OTHER...
...AND WE'RE AT OUR HAPPIEST.
BUT...

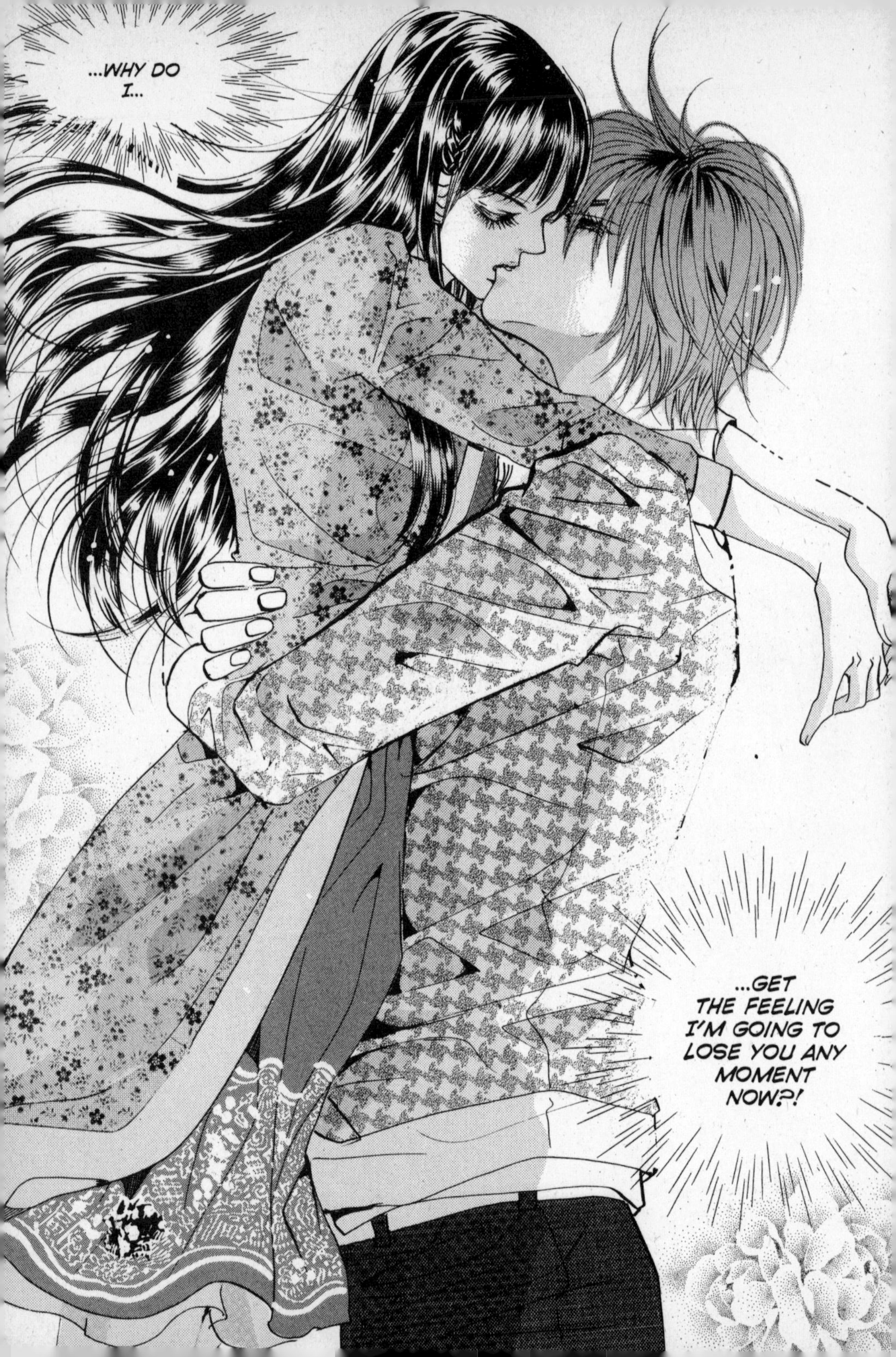
...WHY DO I...
...GET THE FEELING I'M GOING TO LOSE YOU ANY MOMENT NOW?!

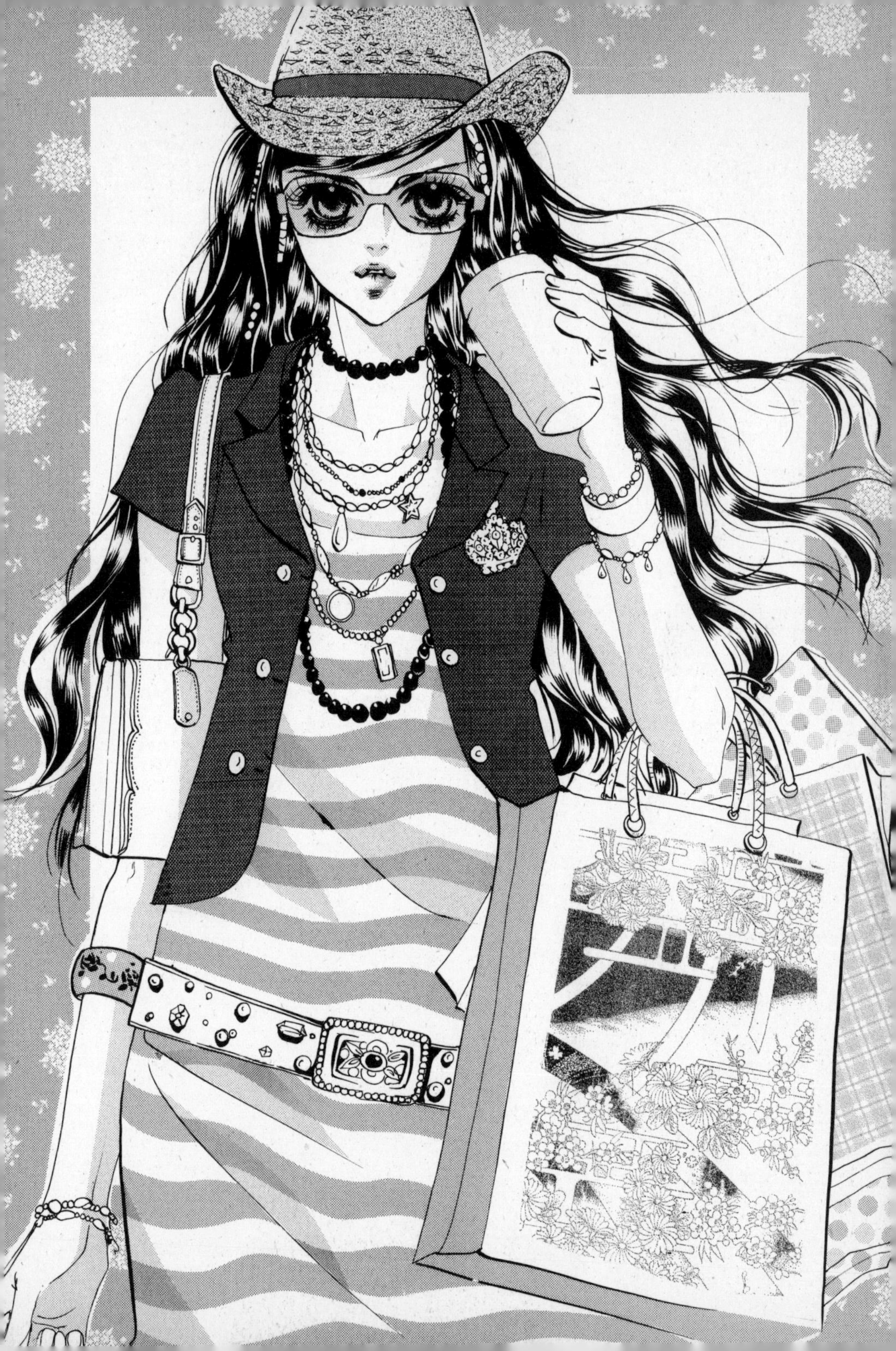

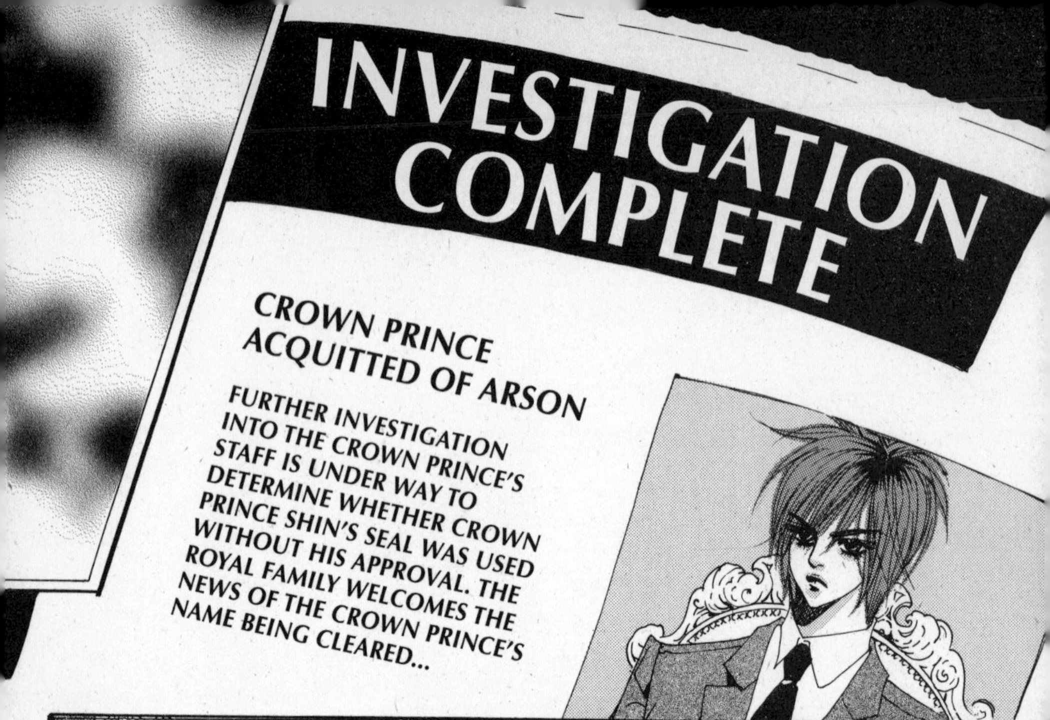
INVESTIGATION COMPLETE
CROWN PRINCE ACQUITTED OF ARSON
FURTHER INVESTIGATION INTO THE CROWN PRINCE'S STAFF IS UNDER WAY TO DETERMINE WHETHER CROWN PRINCE SHIN'S SEAL WAS USED WITHOUT HIS APPROVAL. THE ROYAL FAMILY WELCOMES THE NEWS OF THE CROWN PRINCE'S NAME BEING CLEARED...

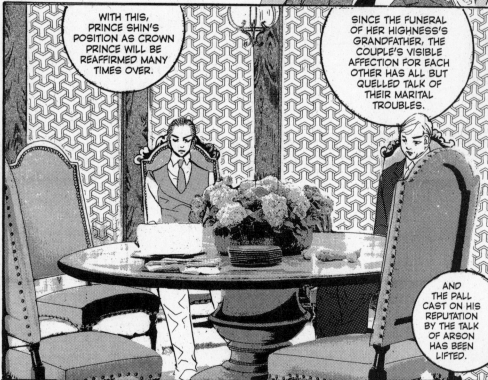

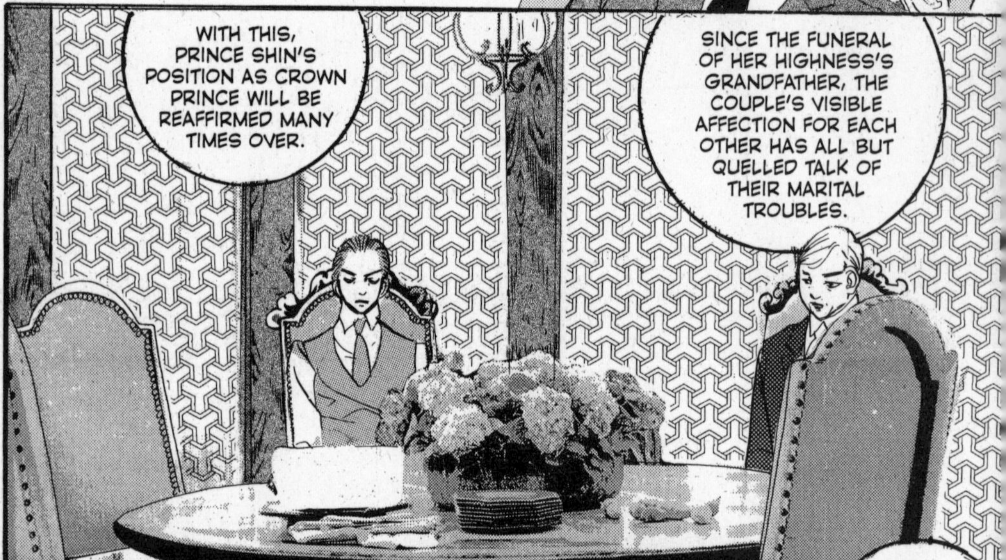
WITH THIS, PRINCE SHIN'S POSITION AS CROWN PRINCE WILL BE REAFFIRMED MANY TIMES OVER.
SINCE THE FUNERAL OF HER HIGHNESS'S GRANDFATHER, THE COUPLE'S VISIBLE AFFECTION FOR EACH OTHER HAS ALL BUT QUELLED TALK OF THEIR MARITAL TROUBLES.
AND THE PALL CAST ON HIS REPUTATION BY THE TALK OF ARSON HAS BEEN LIFTED.

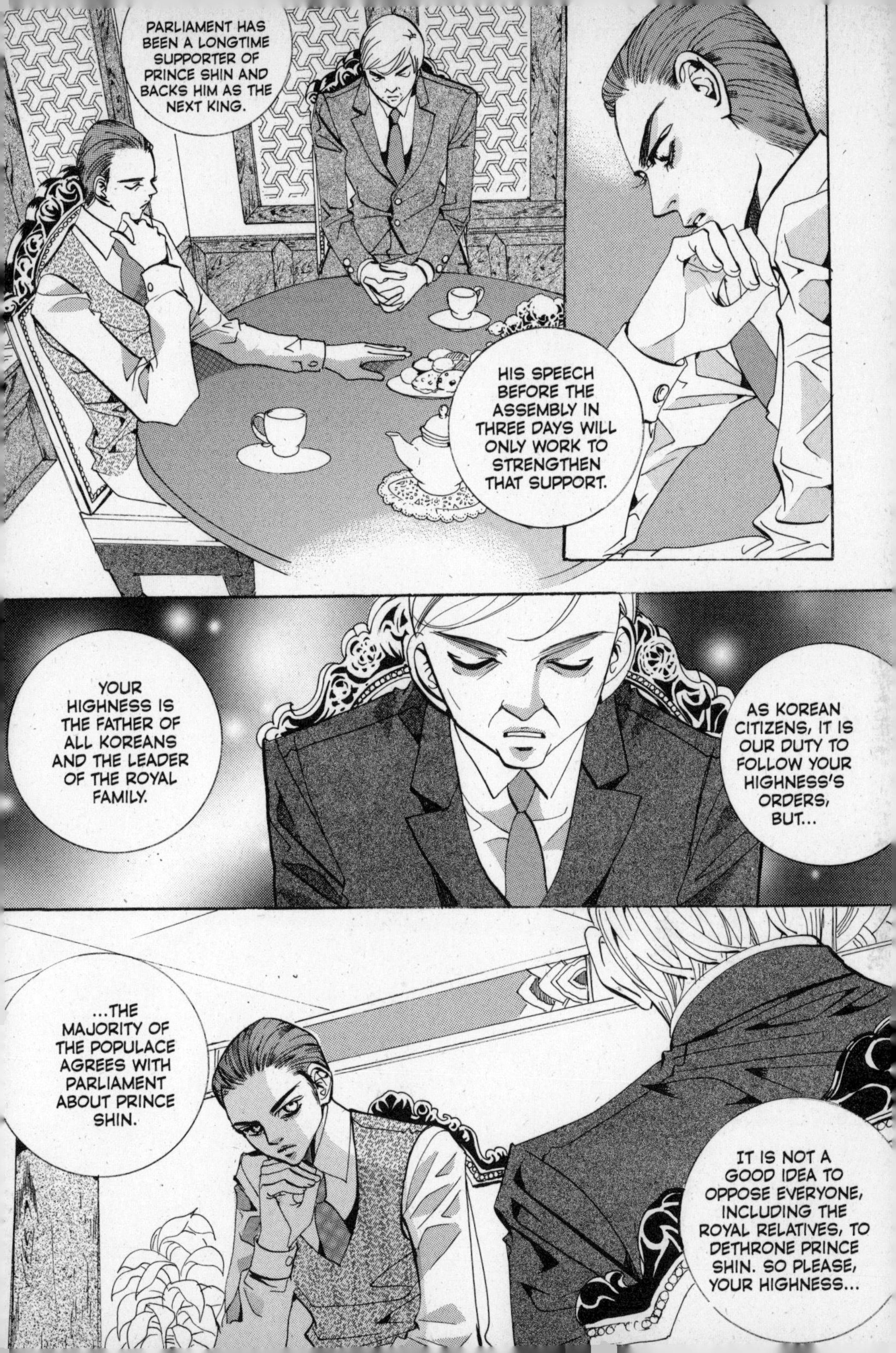
PARLIAMENT HAS BEEN A LONGTIME SUPPORTER OF PRINCE SHIN AND BACKS HIM AS THE NEXT KING.
HIS SPEECH BEFORE THE ASSEMBLY IN THREE DAYS WILL ONLY WORK TO STRENGTHEN THAT SUPPORT.
YOUR HIGHNESS IS THE FATHER OF ALL KOREANS AND THE LEADER OF THE ROYAL FAMILY.
AS KOREAN CITIZENS, IT IS OUR DUTY TO FOLLOW YOUR HIGHNESS'S ORDERS, BUT...
...THE MAJORITY OF THE POPULACE AGREES WITH PARLIAMENT ABOUT PRINCE SHIN.
IT IS NOT A GOOD IDEA TO OPPOSE EVERYONE, INCLUDING THE ROYAL RELATIVES, TO DETHRONE PRINCE SHIN. SO PLEASE, YOUR HIGHNESS...

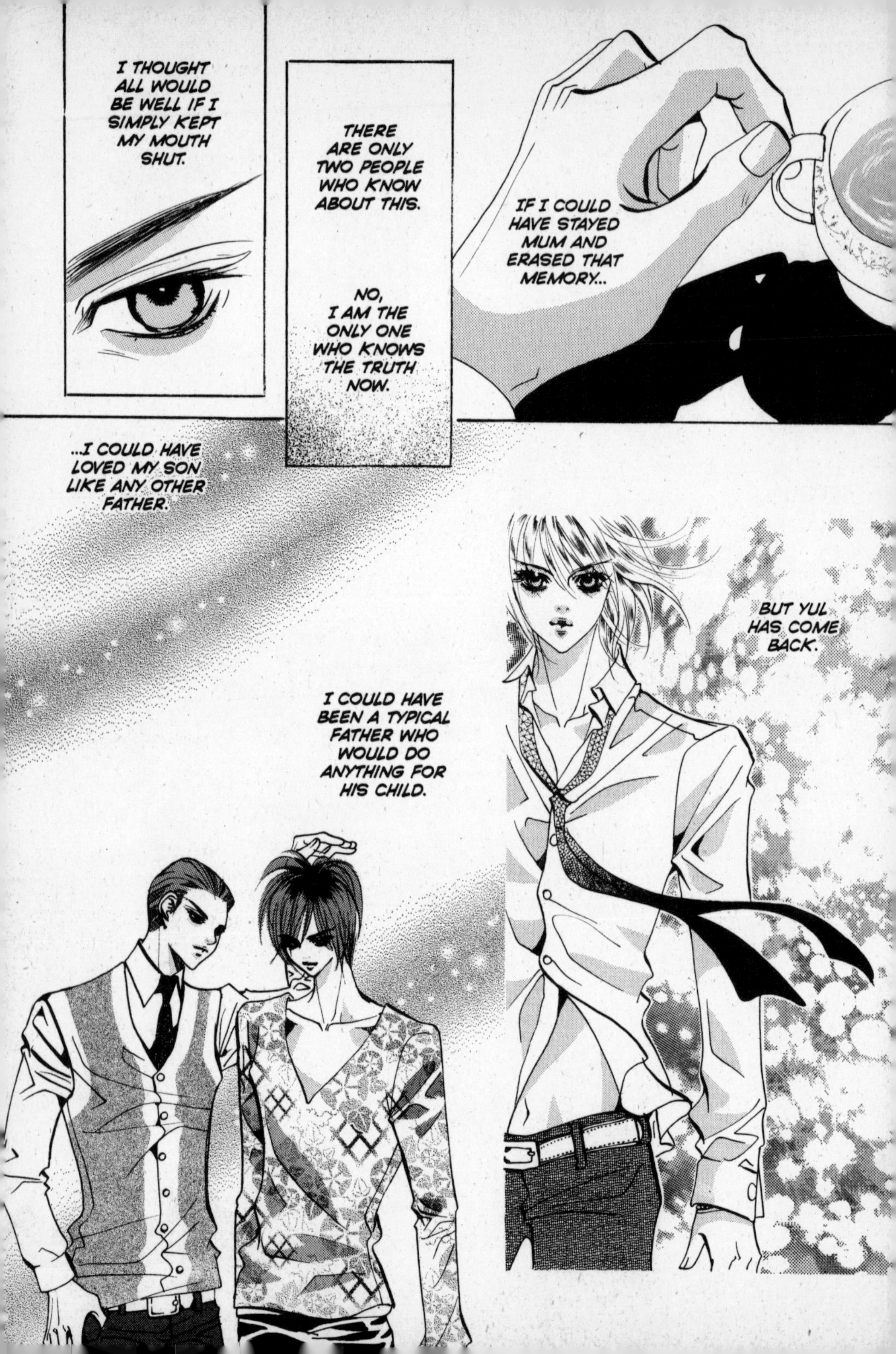
I THOUGHT ALL WOULD BE WELL IF I SIMPLY KEPT MY MOUTH SHUT.
THERE ARE ONLY TWO PEOPLE WHO KNOW ABOUT THIS.
NO, I AM THE ONLY ONE WHO KNOWS THE TRUTH NOW.
IF I COULD HAVE STAYED MUM AND ERASED THAT MEMORY...
...I COULD HAVE LOVED MY SON LIKE ANY OTHER FATHER.
I COULD HAVE BEEN A TYPICAL FATHER WHO WOULD DO ANYTHING FOR HIS CHILD.
BUT YUL HAS COME BACK.

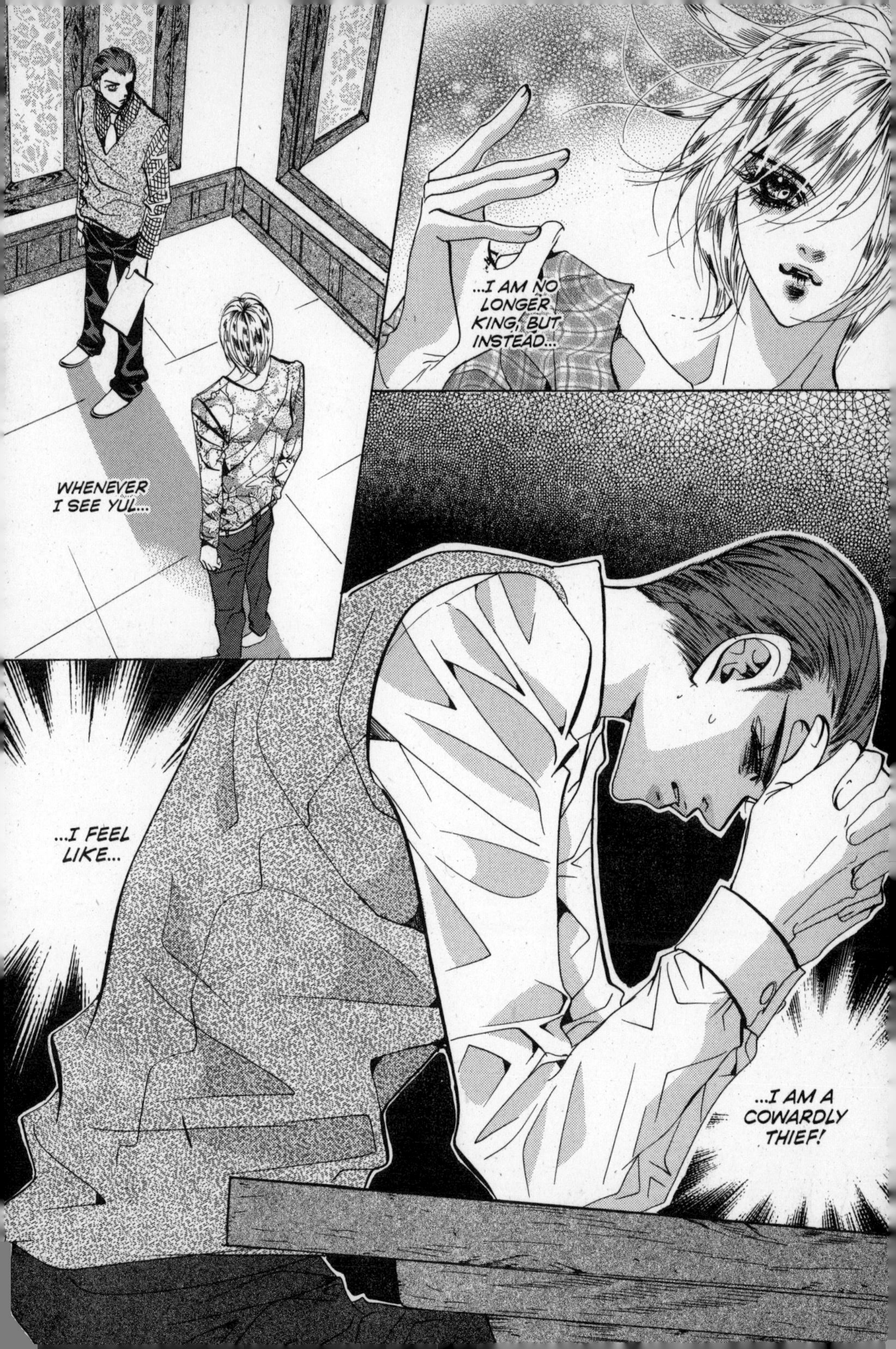
WHENEVER I SEE YUL...
...I AM NO LONGER KING, BUT INSTEAD...
...I FEEL LIKE...
...I AM A COWARDLY THIEF!

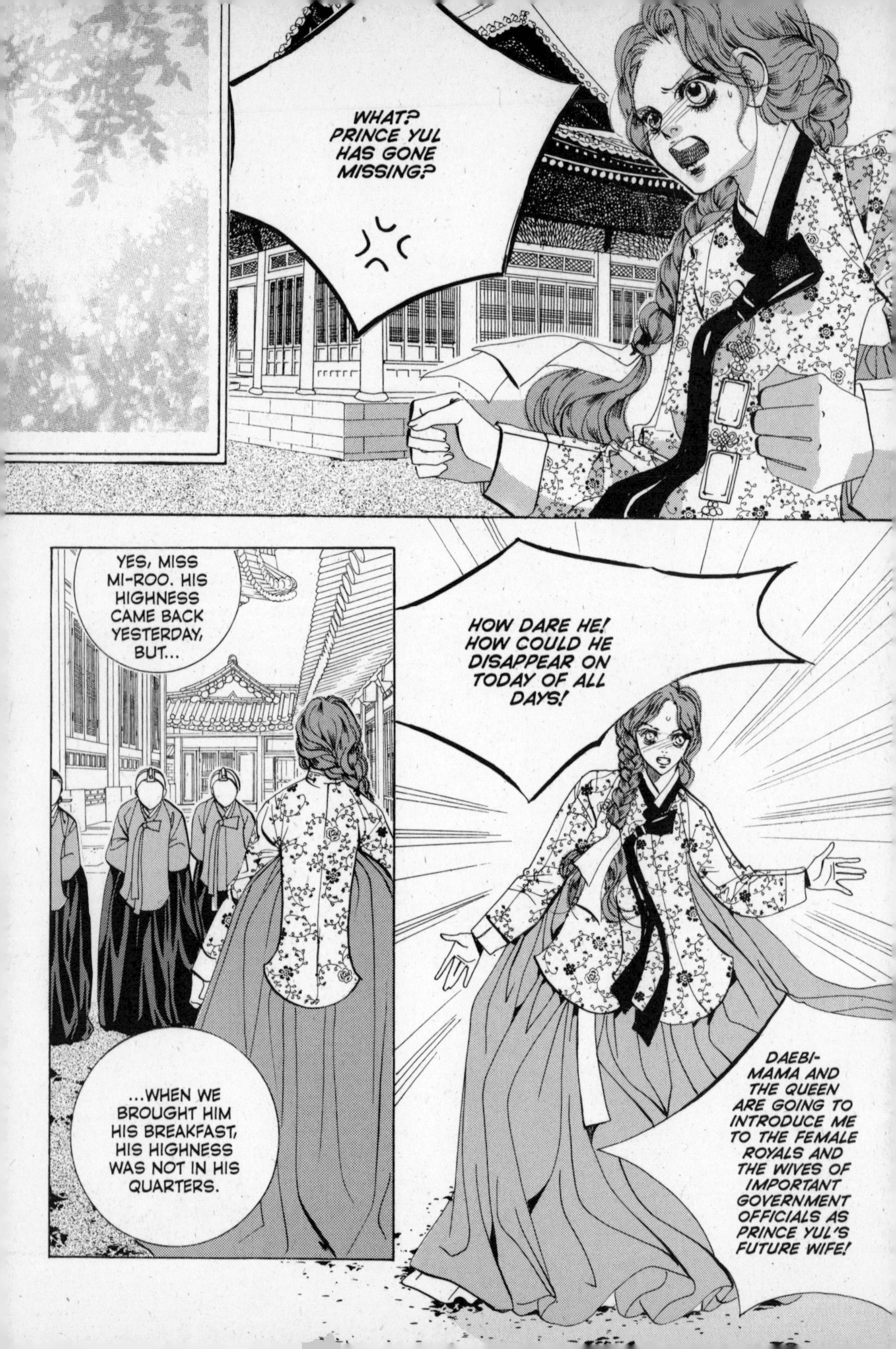
WHAT? PRINCE YUL HAS GONE MISSING?
YES, MISS MI-ROO. HIS HIGHNESS CAME BACK YESTERDAY, BUT...
...WHEN WE BROUGHT HIM HIS BREAKFAST, HIS HIGHNESS WAS NOT IN HIS QUARTERS.
HOW DARE HE! HOW COULD HE DISAPPEAR ON TODAY OF ALL DAYS!
DAEBI-MAMA AND THE QUEEN ARE GOING TO INTRODUCE ME TO THE FEMALE ROYALS AND THE WIVES OF IMPORTANT GOVERNMENT OFFICIALS AS PRINCE YUL'S FUTURE WIFE!

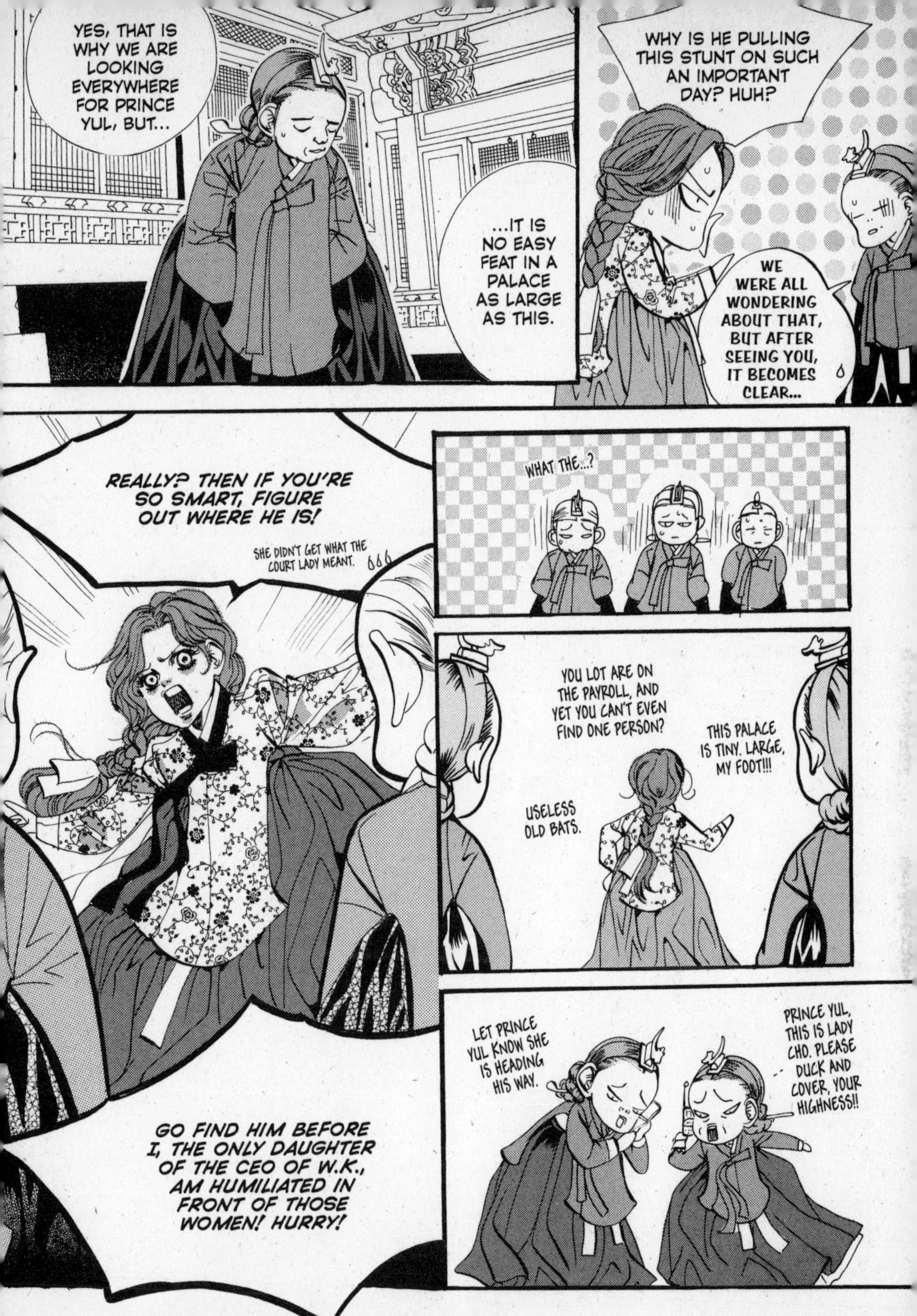

YES, THAT IS WHY WE ARE LOOKING EVERYWHERE FOR PRINCE YUL, BUT...
...IT IS NO EASY FEAT IN A PALACE AS LARGE AS THIS.
WHY IS HE PULLING THIS STUNT ON SUCH AN IMPORTANT DAY? HUH?
WE WERE ALL WONDERING ABOUT THAT, BUT AFTER SEEING YOU, IT BECOMES CLEAR...
REALLY? THEN IF YOU'RE SO SMART, FIGURE OUT WHERE HE IS!
SHE DIDN'T GET WHAT THE COURT LADY MEANT.
GO FIND HIM BEFORE I, THE ONLY DAUGHTER OF THE CEO OF W.K., AM HUMILIATED IN FRONT OF THOSE WOMEN! HURRY!
WHAT THE...?
YOU LOT ARE ON THE PAYROLL, AND YET YOU CAN'T EVEN FIND ONE PERSON?
THIS PALACE IS TINY. LARGE, MY FOOT!!!
USELESS OLD BATS.
LET PRINCE YUL KNOW SHE IS HEADING HIS WAY.
PRINCE YUL, THIS IS LADY CHO. PLEASE DUCK AND COVER, YOUR HIGHNESS!!

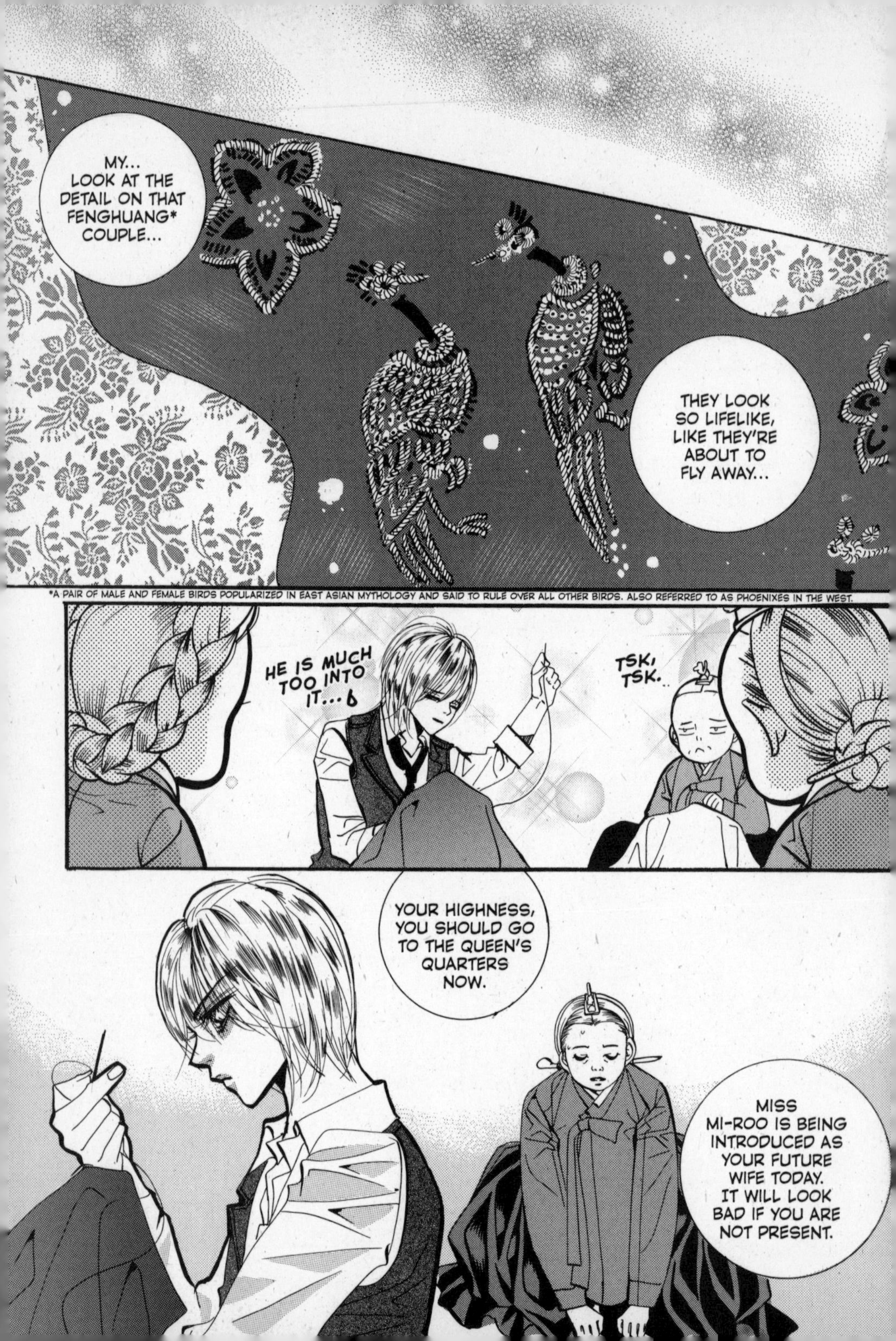
MY... LOOK AT THE DETAIL ON THAT FENGHUANG* COUPLE...
THEY LOOK SO LIFELIKE, LIKE THEY'RE ABOUT TO FLY AWAY...
*A PAIR OF MALE AND FEMALE BIRDS POPULARIZED IN EAST ASIAN MYTHOLOGY AND SAID TO RULE OVER ALL OTHER BIRDS. ALSO REFERRED TO AS PHOENIXES IN THE WEST.
HE IS MUCH TOO INTO IT...
TSK, TSK..
YOUR HIGHNESS, YOU SHOULD GO TO THE QUEEN'S QUARTERS NOW.
MISS MI-ROO IS BEING INTRODUCED AS YOUR FUTURE WIFE TODAY. IT WILL LOOK BAD IF YOU ARE NOT PRESENT.

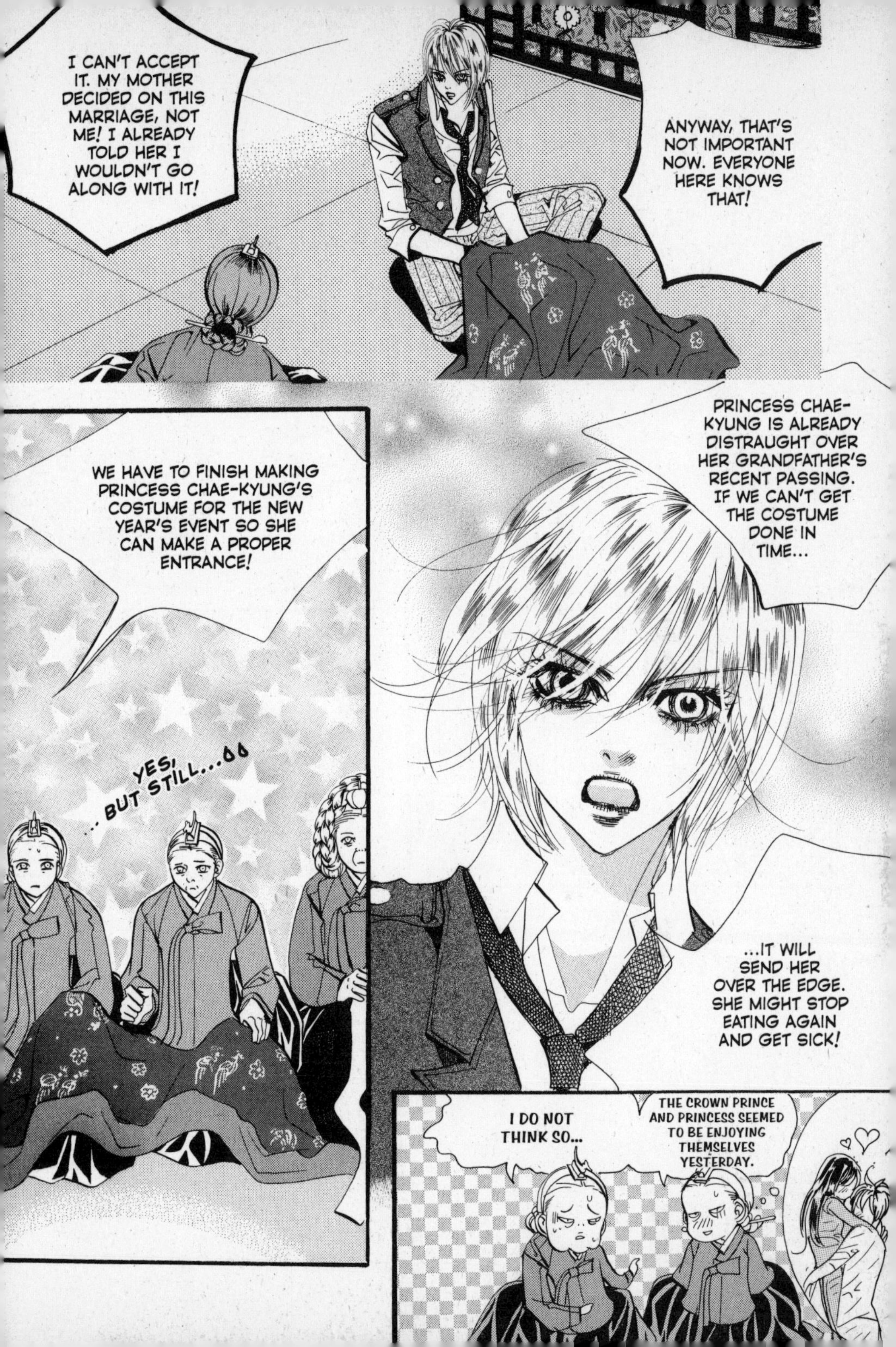
I CAN'T ACCEPT IT. MY MOTHER DECIDED ON THIS MARRIAGE, NOT ME! I ALREADY TOLD HER I WOULDN'T GO ALONG WITH IT!
ANYWAY, THAT'S NOT IMPORTANT NOW. EVERYONE HERE KNOWS THAT!
WE HAVE TO FINISH MAKING PRINCESS CHAE-KYUNG'S COSTUME FOR THE NEW YEAR'S EVENT SO SHE CAN MAKE A PROPER ENTRANCE!
YES, ...BUT STILL...
PRINCESS CHAE-KYUNG IS ALREADY DISTRAUGHT OVER HER GRANDFATHER'S RECENT PASSING. IF WE CAN'T GET THE COSTUME DONE IN TIME...
...IT WILL SEND HER OVER THE EDGE. SHE MIGHT STOP EATING AGAIN AND GET SICK!
I DO NOT THINK SO...
THE CROWN PRINCE AND PRINCESS SEEMED TO BE ENJOYING THEMSELVES YESTERDAY.

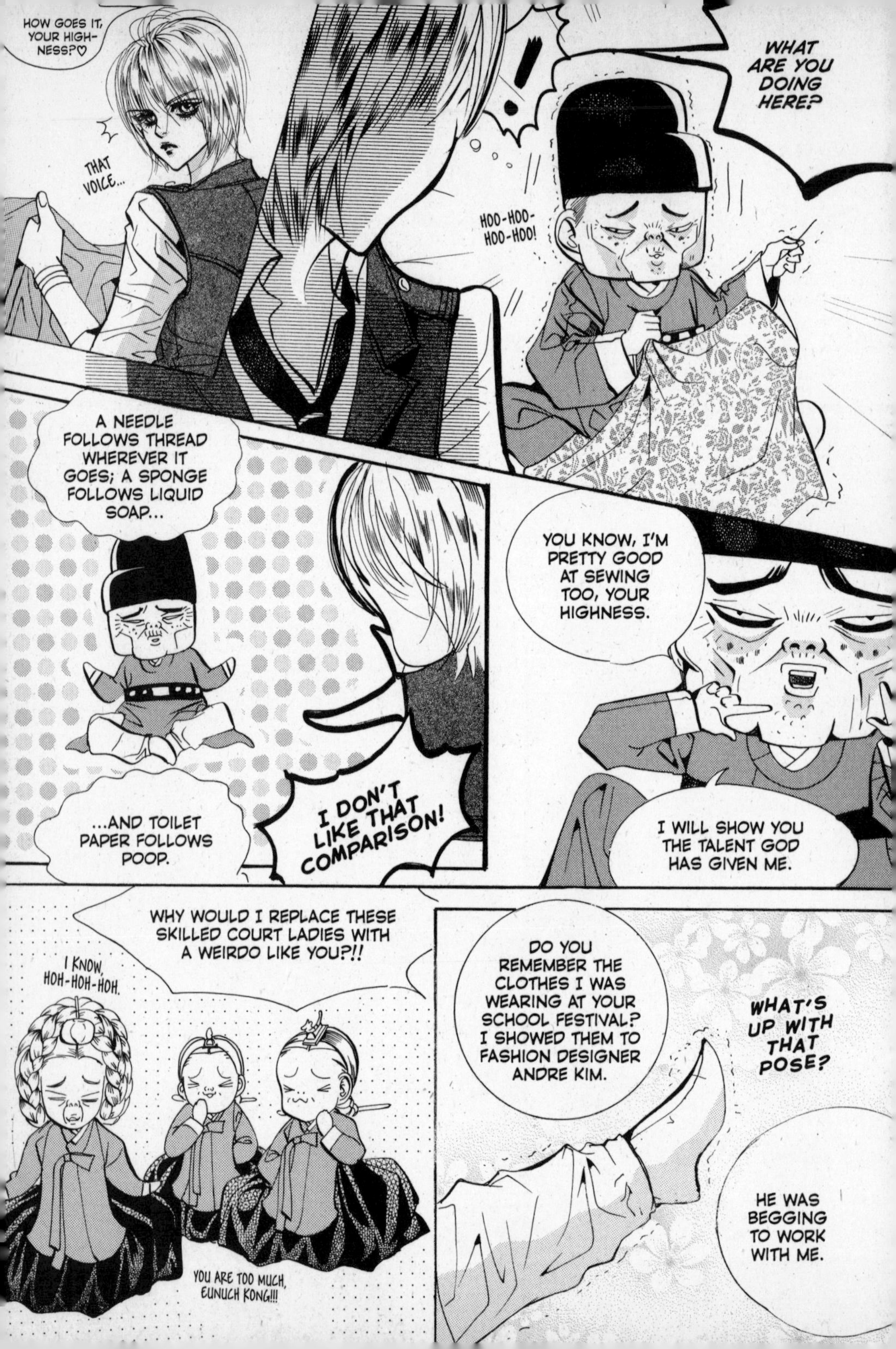
HOW GOES IT, YOUR HIGH-NESS?♡
THAT VOICE...
!
HOO-HOO-HOO-HOO!
WHAT ARE YOU DOING HERE?
A NEEDLE FOLLOWS THREAD WHEREVER IT GOES; A SPONGE FOLLOWS LIQUID SOAP...
...AND TOILET PAPER FOLLOWS POOP.
I DON'T LIKE THAT COMPARISON!
YOU KNOW, I'M PRETTY GOOD AT SEWING TOO, YOUR HIGHNESS.
I WILL SHOW YOU THE TALENT GOD HAS GIVEN ME.
WHY WOULD I REPLACE THESE SKILLED COURT LADIES WITH A WEIRDO LIKE YOU?!!
I KNOW, HOH-HOH-HOH.
YOU ARE TOO MUCH, EUNUCH KONG!!!
DO YOU REMEMBER THE CLOTHES I WAS WEARING AT YOUR SCHOOL FESTIVAL? I SHOWED THEM TO FASHION DESIGNER ANDRE KIM.
WHAT'S UP WITH THAT POSE?
HE WAS BEGGING TO WORK WITH ME.

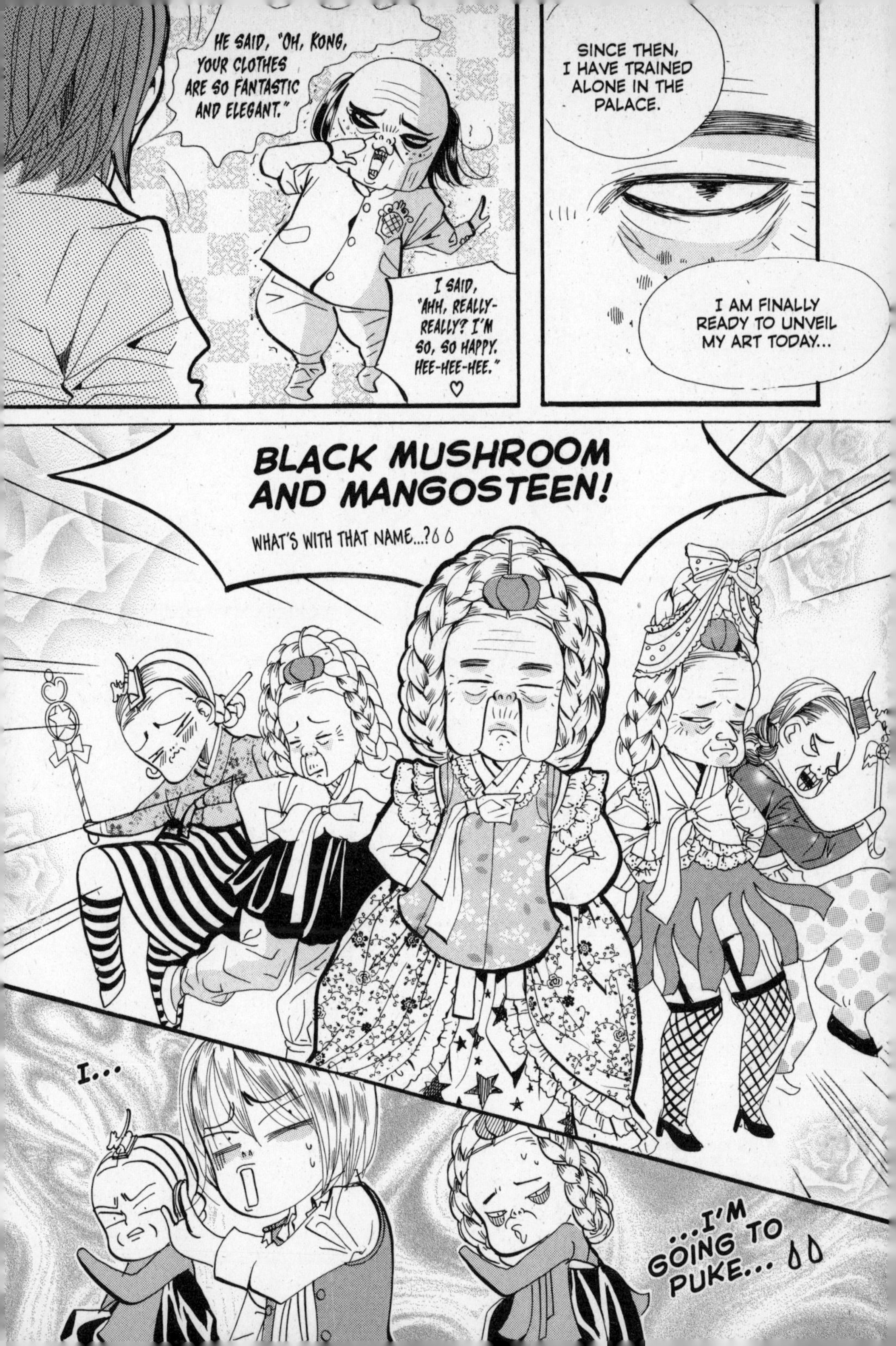
HE SAID, "OH, KONG, YOUR CLOTHES ARE SO FANTASTIC AND ELEGANT."
I SAID, "AHH, REALLY-REALLY? I'M SO, SO HAPPY. HEE-HEE-HEE." ♡
SINCE THEN, I HAVE TRAINED ALONE IN THE PALACE.
I AM FINALLY READY TO UNVEIL MY ART TODAY...
BLACK MUSHROOM AND MANGOSTEEN!
WHAT'S WITH THAT NAME...?
I...
...I'M GOING TO PUKE...

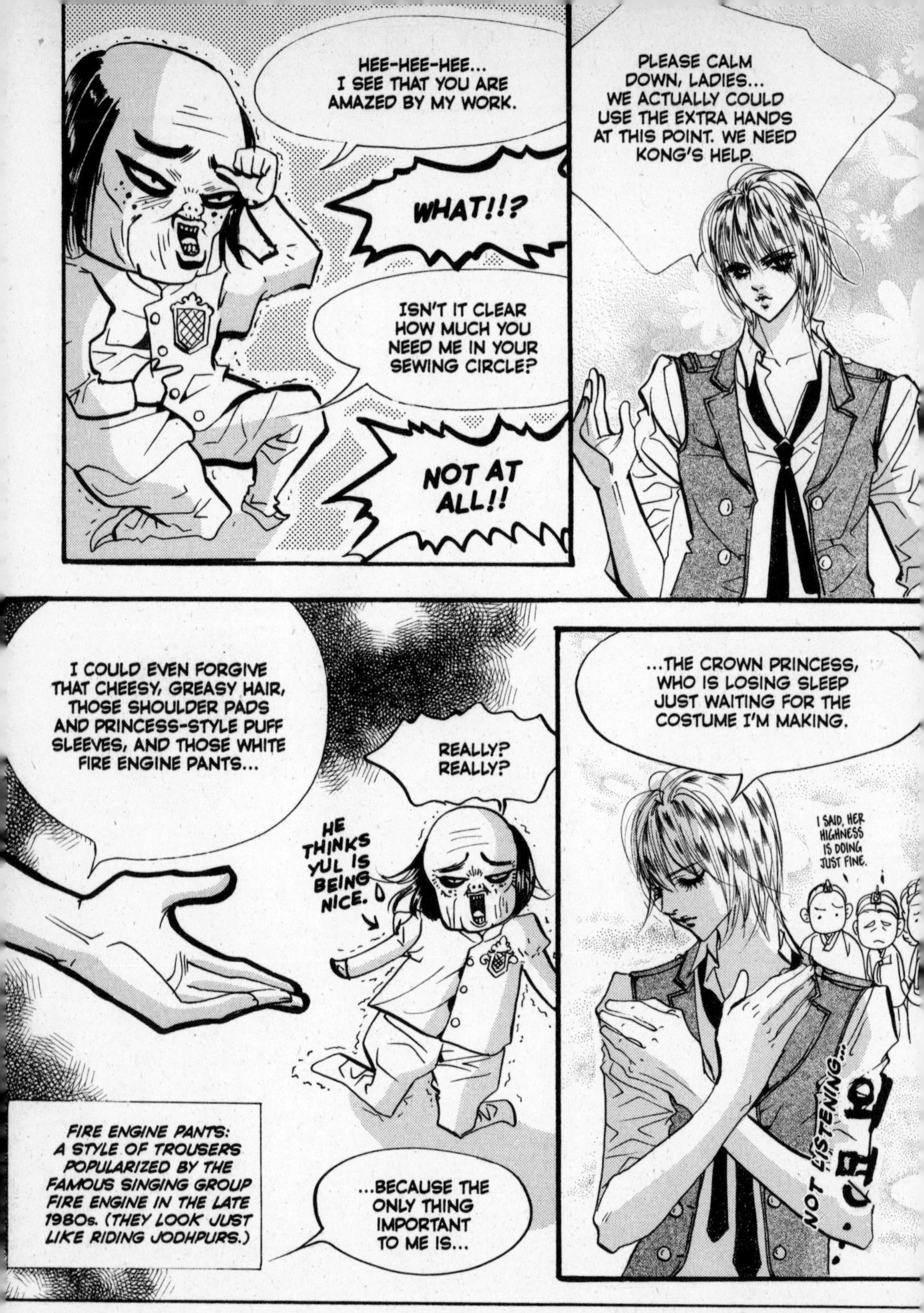
HEE-HEE-HEE... I SEE THAT YOU ARE AMAZED BY MY WORK.
WHAT!!?
ISN'T IT CLEAR HOW MUCH YOU NEED ME IN YOUR SEWING CIRCLE?
NOT AT ALL!!
PLEASE CALM DOWN, LADIES... WE ACTUALLY COULD USE THE EXTRA HANDS AT THIS POINT. WE NEED KONG'S HELP.
I COULD EVEN FORGIVE THAT CHEESY, GREASY HAIR, THOSE SHOULDER PADS AND PRINCESS-STYLE PUFF SLEEVES, AND THOSE WHITE FIRE ENGINE PANTS...
REALLY? REALLY?
HE THINKS YUL IS BEING NICE.
FIRE ENGINE PANTS: A STYLE OF TROUSERS POPULARIZED BY THE FAMOUS SINGING GROUP FIRE ENGINE IN THE LATE 1980s. (THEY LOOK JUST LIKE RIDING JODHPURS.)
...BECAUSE THE ONLY THING IMPORTANT TO ME IS...
...THE CROWN PRINCESS, WHO IS LOSING SLEEP JUST WAITING FOR THE COSTUME I'M MAKING.
I SAID, HER HIGHNESS IS DOING JUST FINE.
NOT LISTENING...

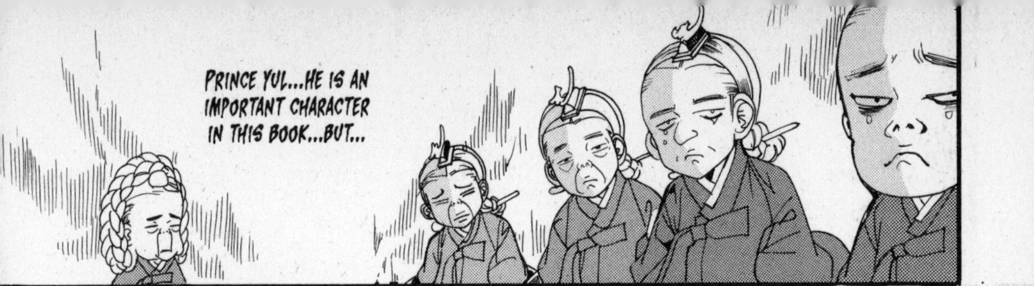
PRINCE YUL...HE IS AN IMPORTANT CHARACTER IN THIS BOOK...BUT...

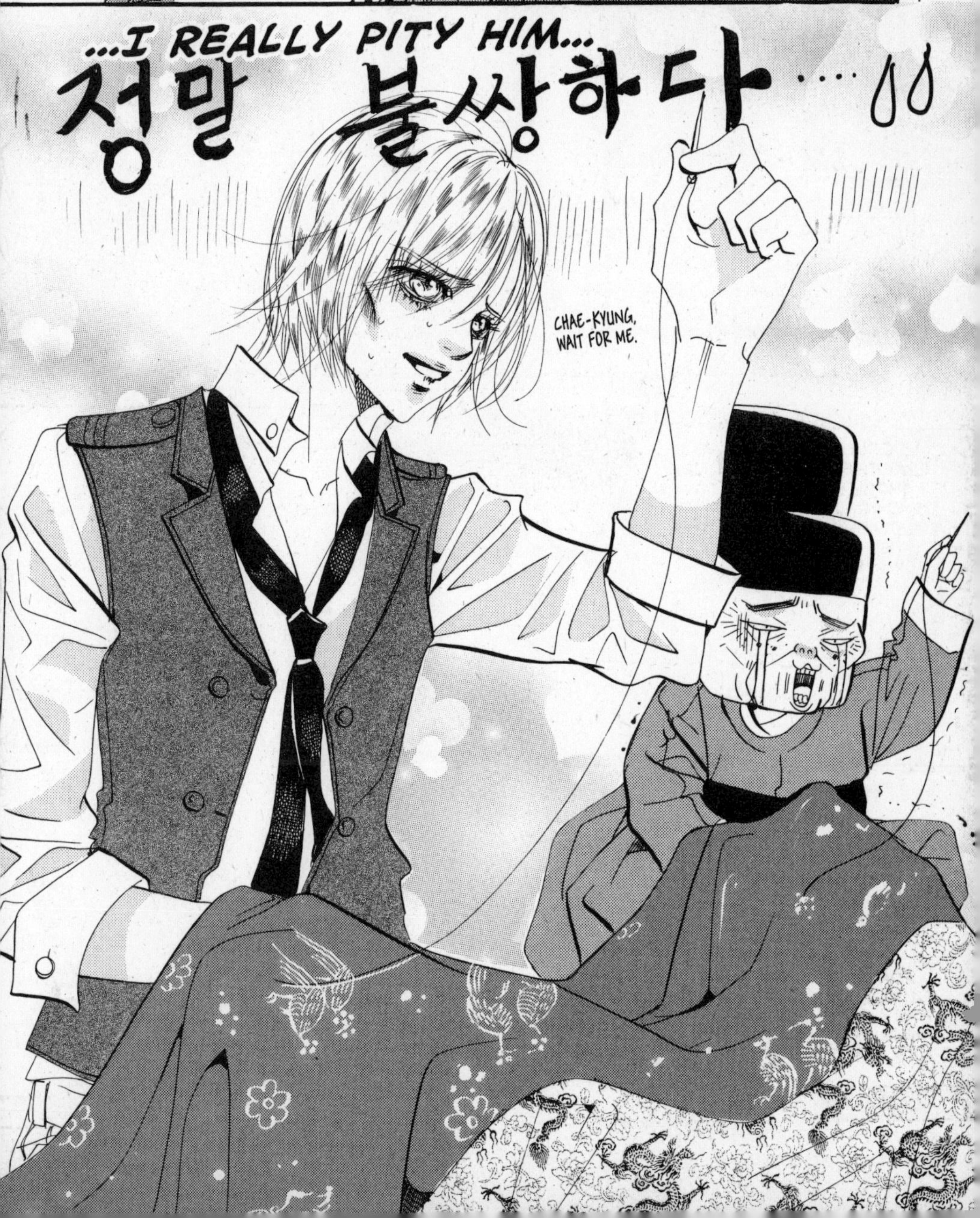
...I REALLY PITY HIM...
정말 불쌍하다....
CHAE-KYUNG, WAIT FOR ME.

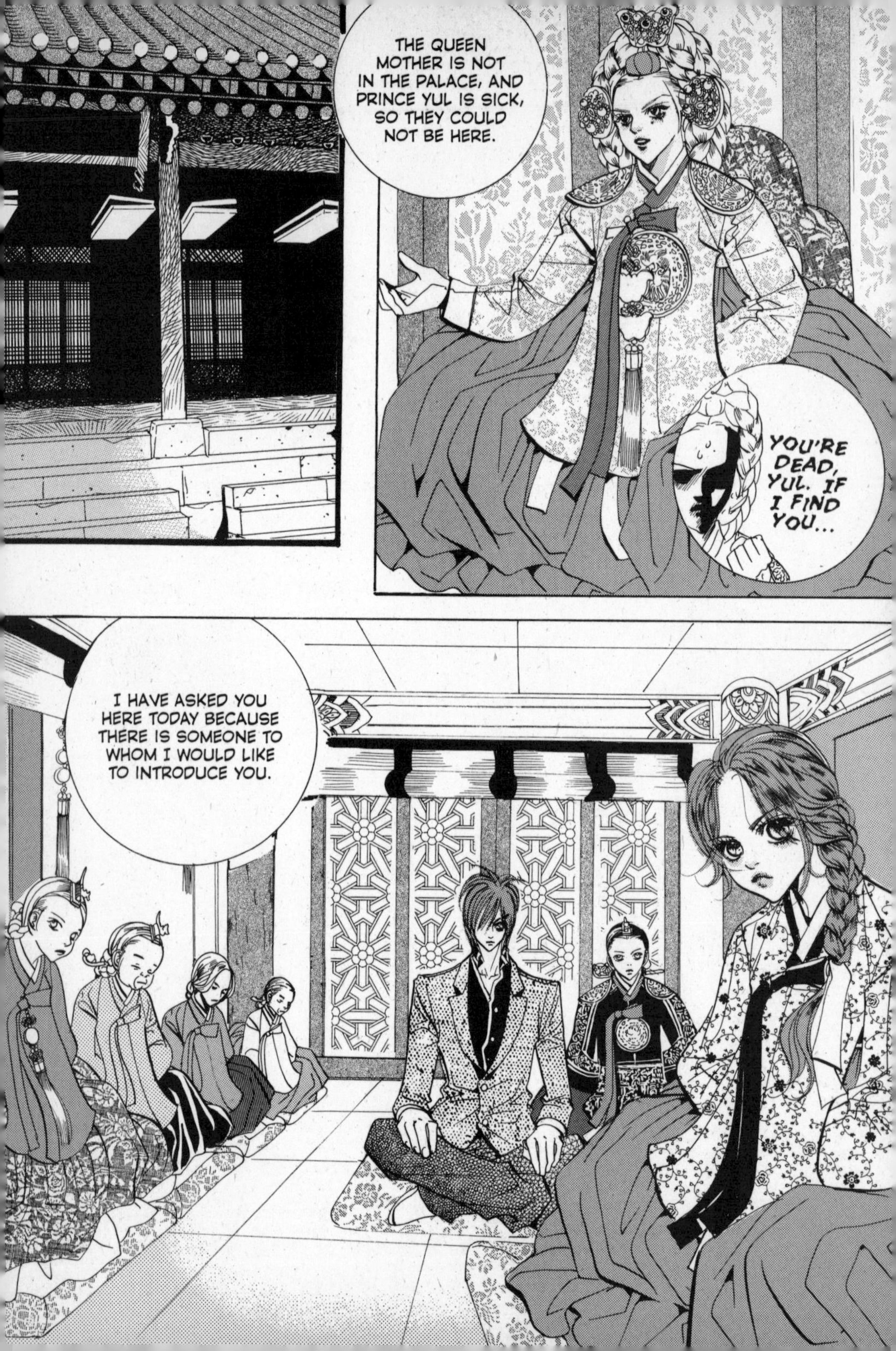
THE QUEEN MOTHER IS NOT IN THE PALACE, AND PRINCE YUL IS SICK, SO THEY COULD NOT BE HERE.
YOU'RE DEAD, YUL. IF I FIND YOU...
I HAVE ASKED YOU HERE TODAY BECAUSE THERE IS SOMEONE TO WHOM I WOULD LIKE TO INTRODUCE YOU.

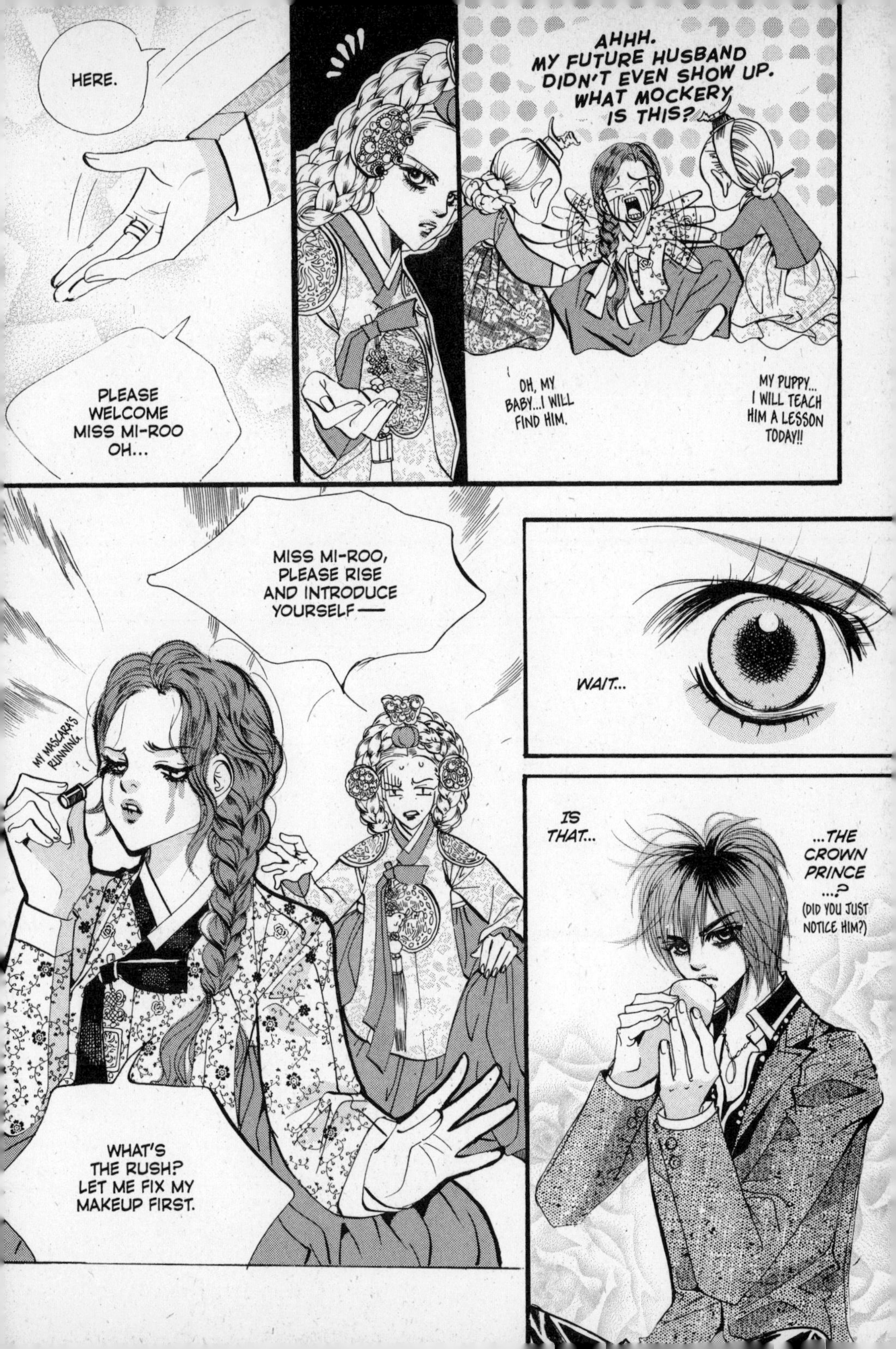
HERE.
PLEASE WELCOME MISS MI-ROO OH...
AHHH. MY FUTURE HUSBAND DIDN'T EVEN SHOW UP. WHAT MOCKERY IS THIS?
OH, MY BABY...I WILL FIND HIM.
MY PUPPY... I WILL TEACH HIM A LESSON TODAY!!
MISS MI-ROO, PLEASE RISE AND INTRODUCE YOURSELF—
MY MASCARA'S RUNNING.
WHAT'S THE RUSH? LET ME FIX MY MAKEUP FIRST.
WAIT...
IS THAT...
...THE CROWN PRINCE ...?
(DID YOU JUST NOTICE HIM?)

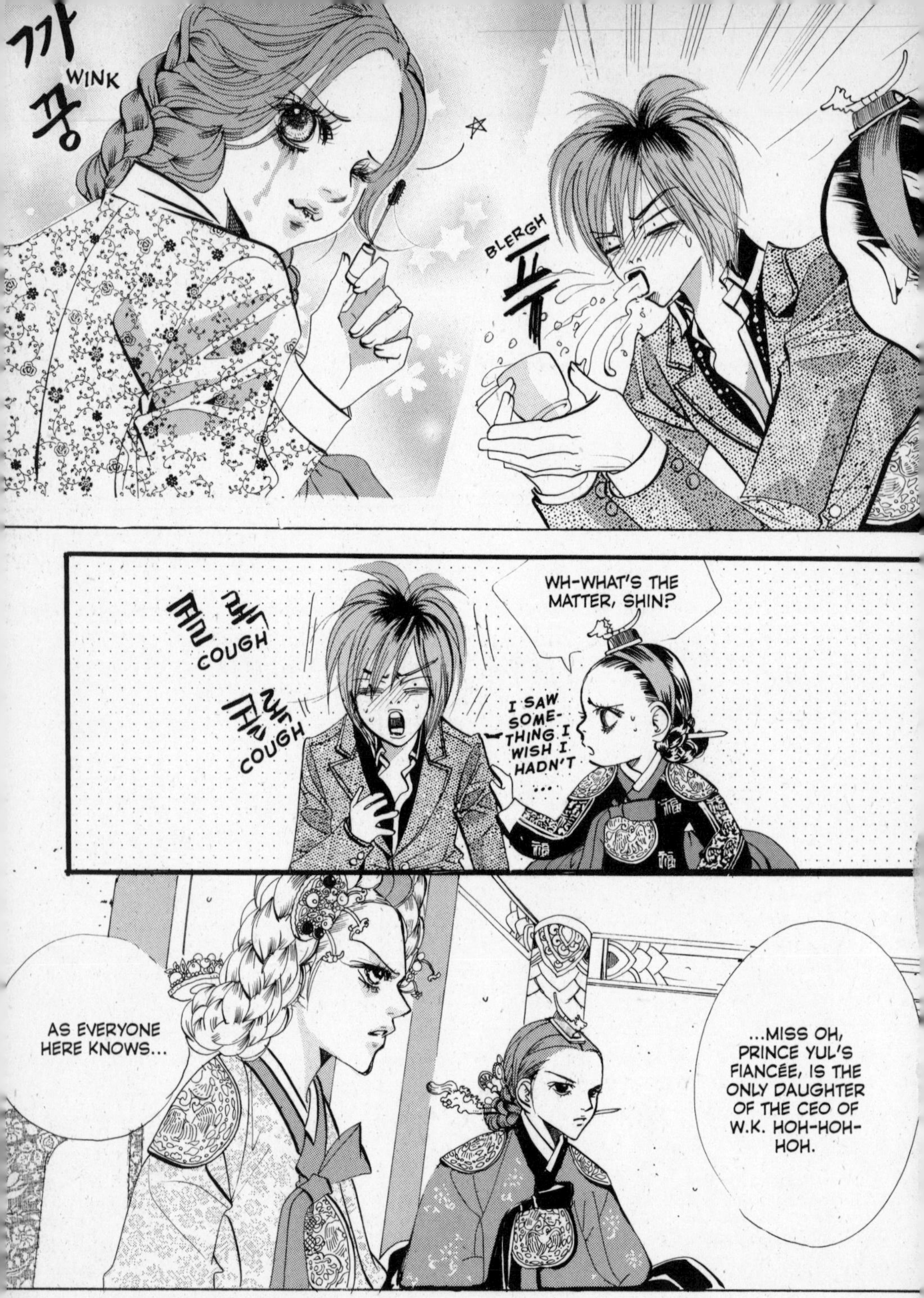

까꿍
WINK
BLERGH
푸
콜록
COUGH
콜록
COUGH
WH-WHAT'S THE MATTER, SHIN?
I SAW SOMETHING I WISH I HADN'T ...
AS EVERYONE HERE KNOWS...
...MISS OH, PRINCE YUL'S FIANCÉE, IS THE ONLY DAUGHTER OF THE CEO OF W.K. HOH-HOH-HOH.

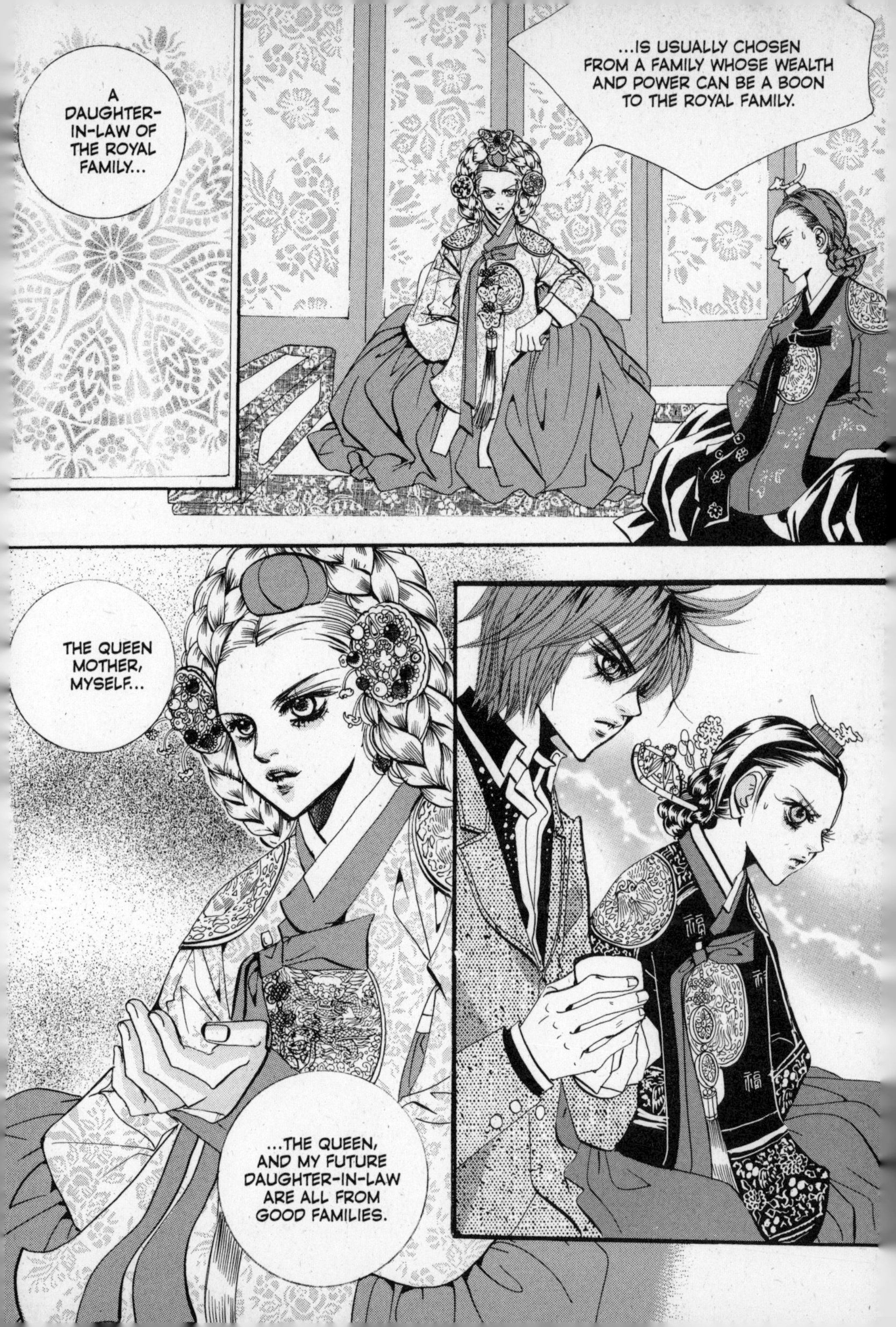

A DAUGHTER-IN-LAW OF THE ROYAL FAMILY...
...IS USUALLY CHOSEN FROM A FAMILY WHOSE WEALTH AND POWER CAN BE A BOON TO THE ROYAL FAMILY.
THE QUEEN MOTHER, MYSELF...
...THE QUEEN, AND MY FUTURE DAUGHTER-IN-LAW ARE ALL FROM GOOD FAMILIES.

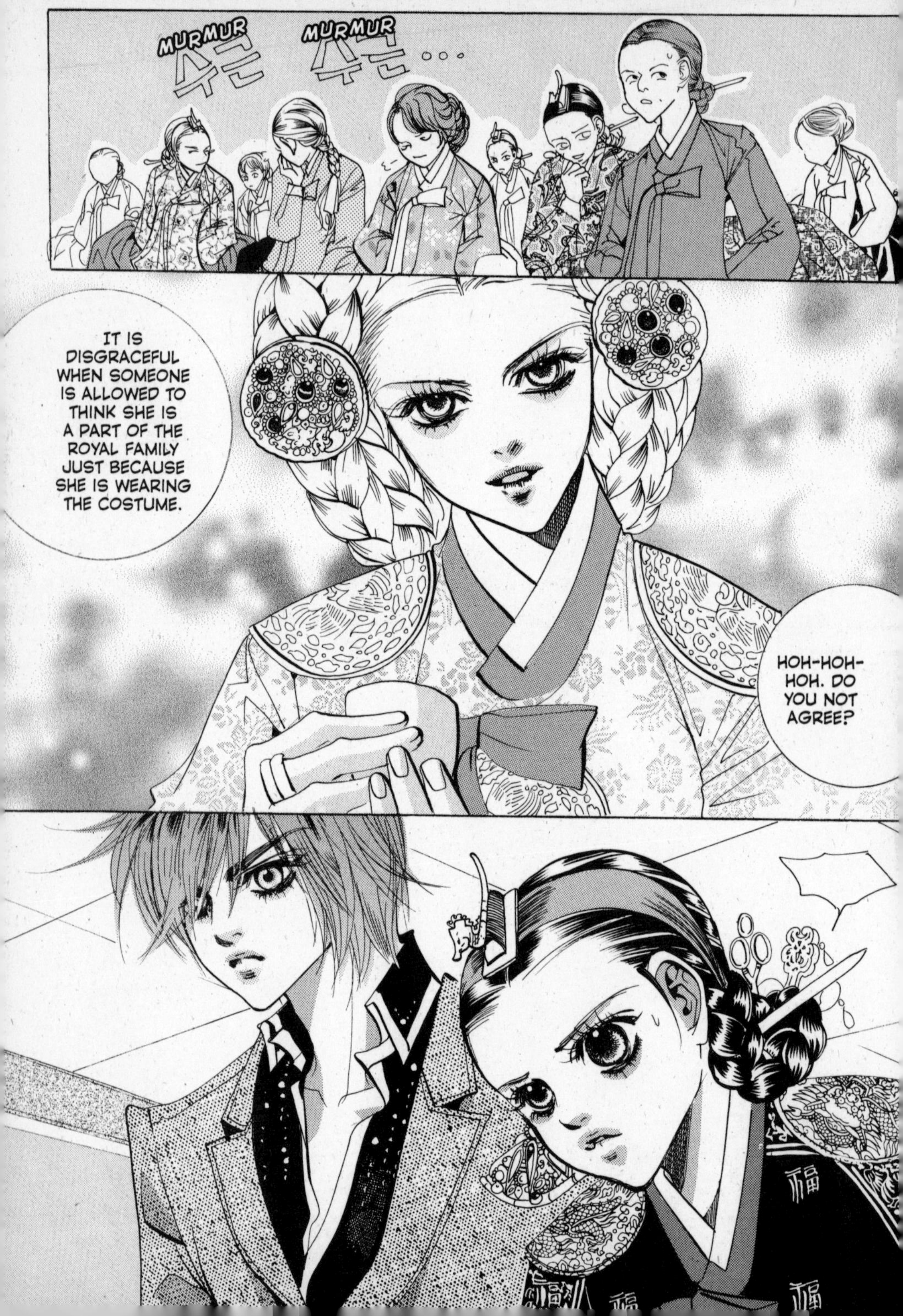

MURMUR
수근
MURMUR
수근...
IT IS DISGRACEFUL WHEN SOMEONE IS ALLOWED TO THINK SHE IS A PART OF THE ROYAL FAMILY JUST BECAUSE SHE IS WEARING THE COSTUME.
HOH-HOH-HOH. DO YOU NOT AGREE?

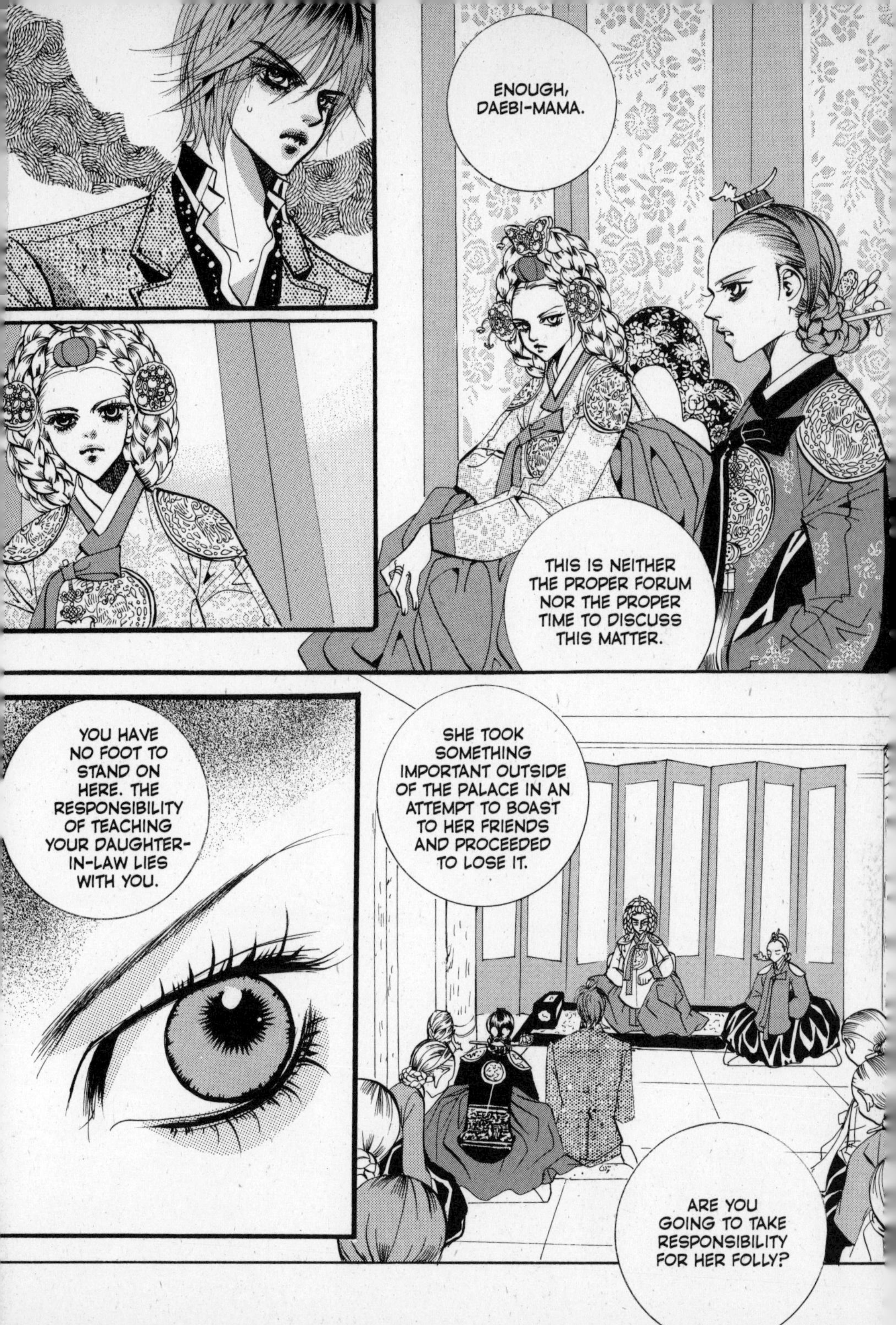
ENOUGH, DAEBI-MAMA.
THIS IS NEITHER THE PROPER FORUM NOR THE PROPER TIME TO DISCUSS THIS MATTER.
YOU HAVE NO FOOT TO STAND ON HERE. THE RESPONSIBILITY OF TEACHING YOUR DAUGHTER-IN-LAW LIES WITH YOU.
SHE TOOK SOMETHING IMPORTANT OUTSIDE OF THE PALACE IN AN ATTEMPT TO BOAST TO HER FRIENDS AND PROCEEDED TO LOSE IT.
ARE YOU GOING TO TAKE RESPONSIBILITY FOR HER FOLLY?

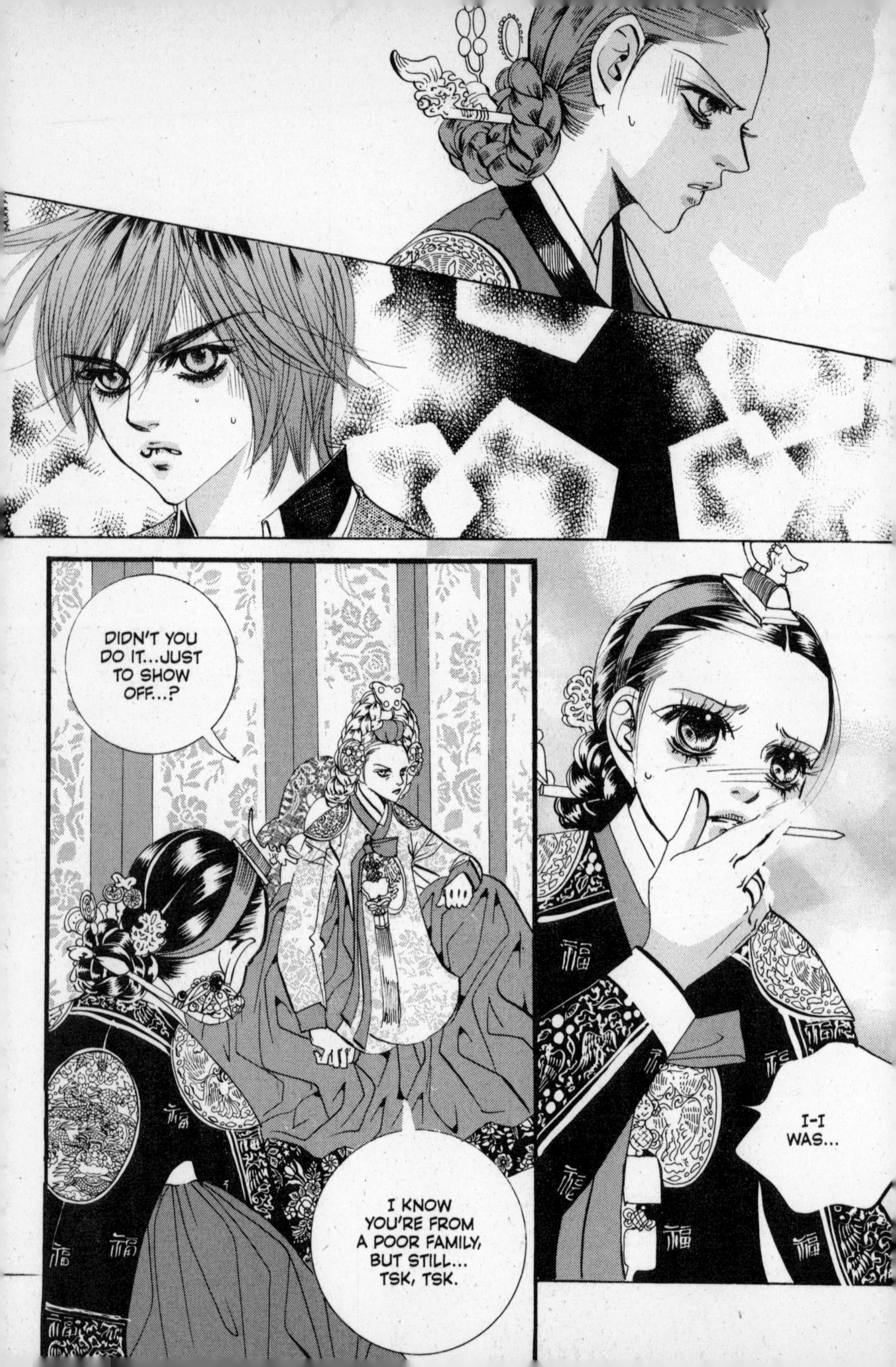
DIDN'T YOU DO IT...JUST TO SHOW OFF...?
I KNOW YOU'RE FROM A POOR FAMILY, BUT STILL... TSK, TSK.
I-I WAS...

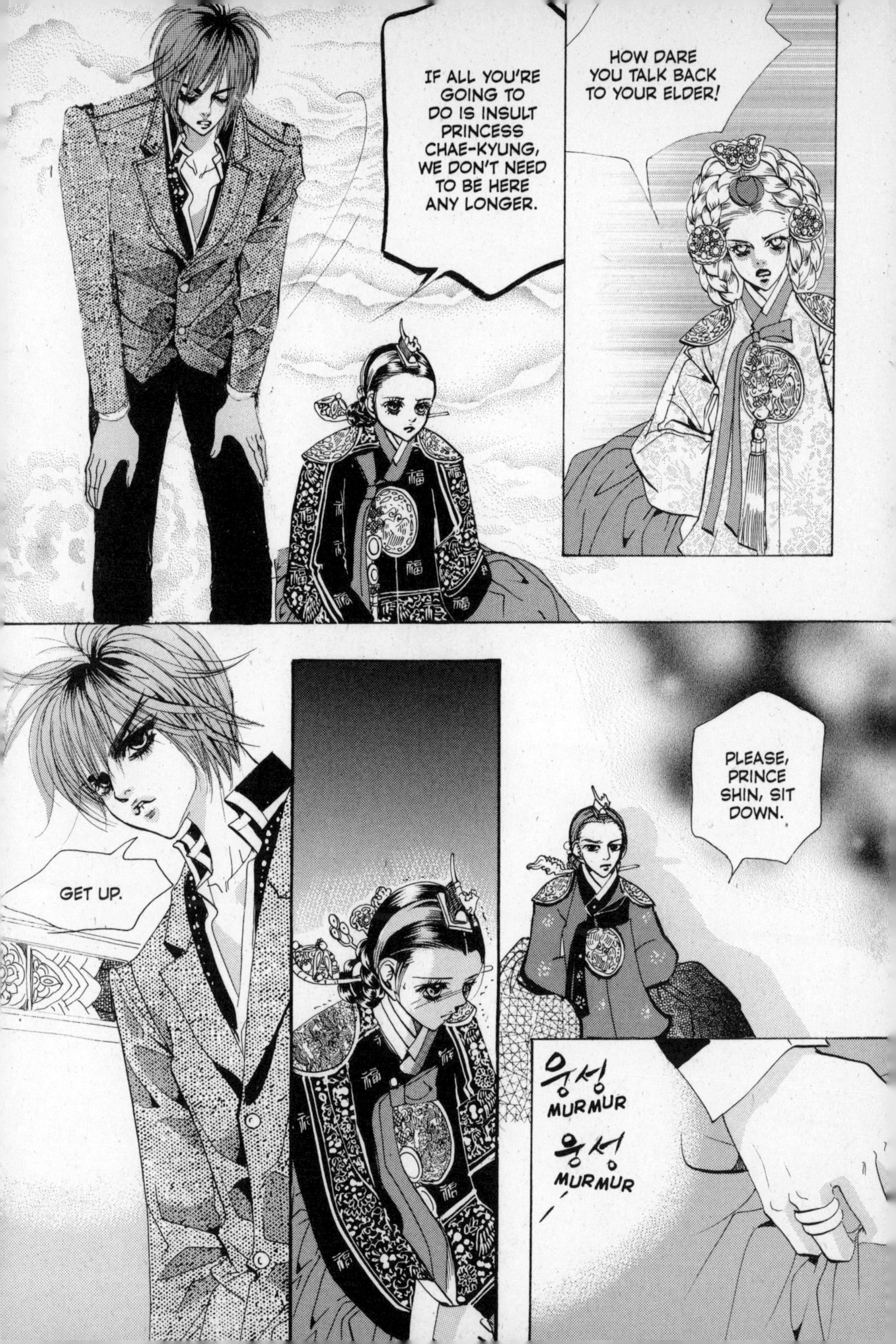
IF ALL YOU'RE GOING TO DO IS INSULT PRINCESS CHAE-KYUNG, WE DON'T NEED TO BE HERE ANY LONGER.
HOW DARE YOU TALK BACK TO YOUR ELDER!
GET UP.
PLEASE, PRINCE SHIN, SIT DOWN.
웅성
MURMUR
웅성
MURMUR

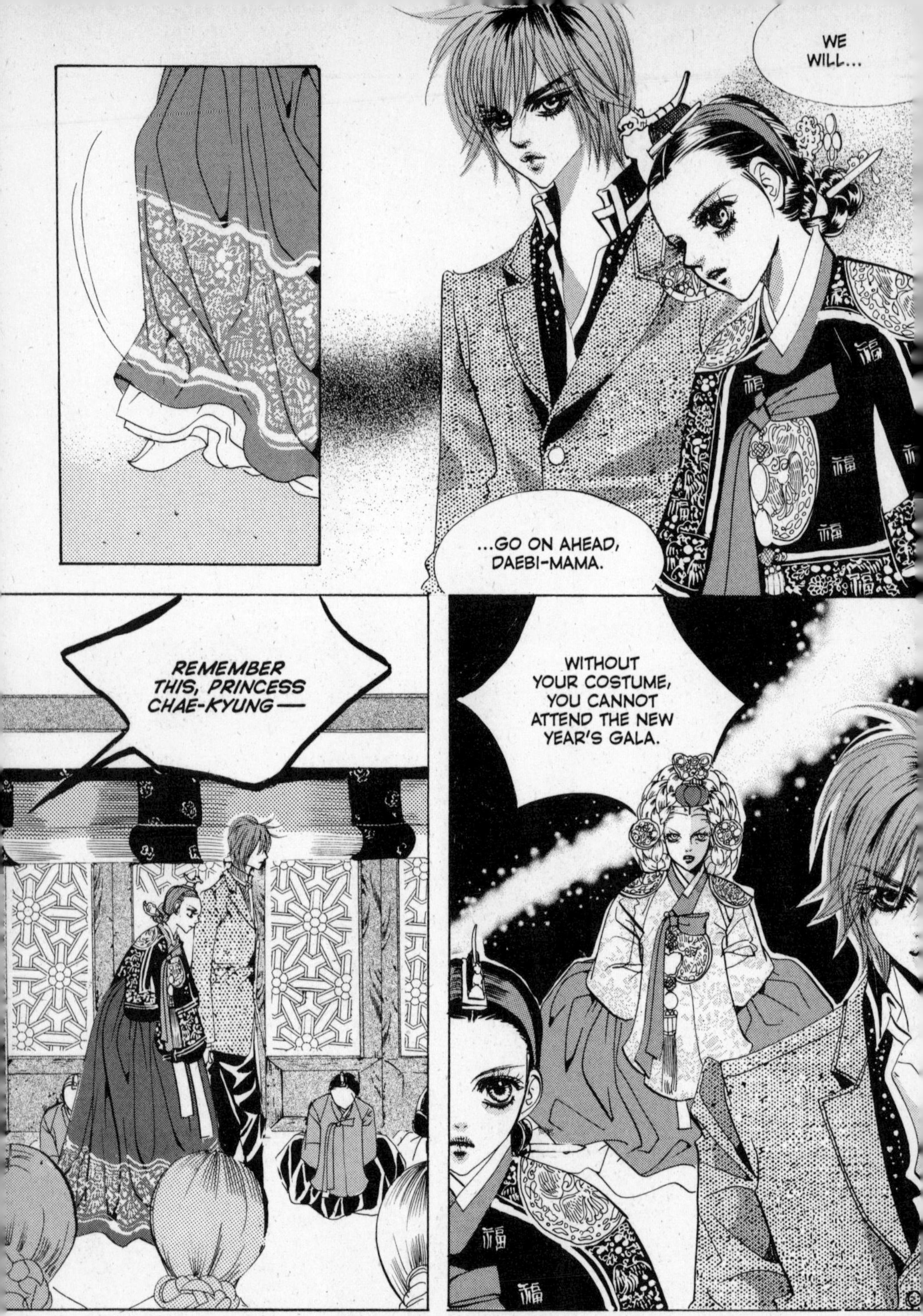
WE WILL...
...GO ON AHEAD, DAEBI-MAMA.
REMEMBER THIS, PRINCESS CHAE-KYUNG—
WITHOUT YOUR COSTUME, YOU CANNOT ATTEND THE NEW YEAR'S GALA.

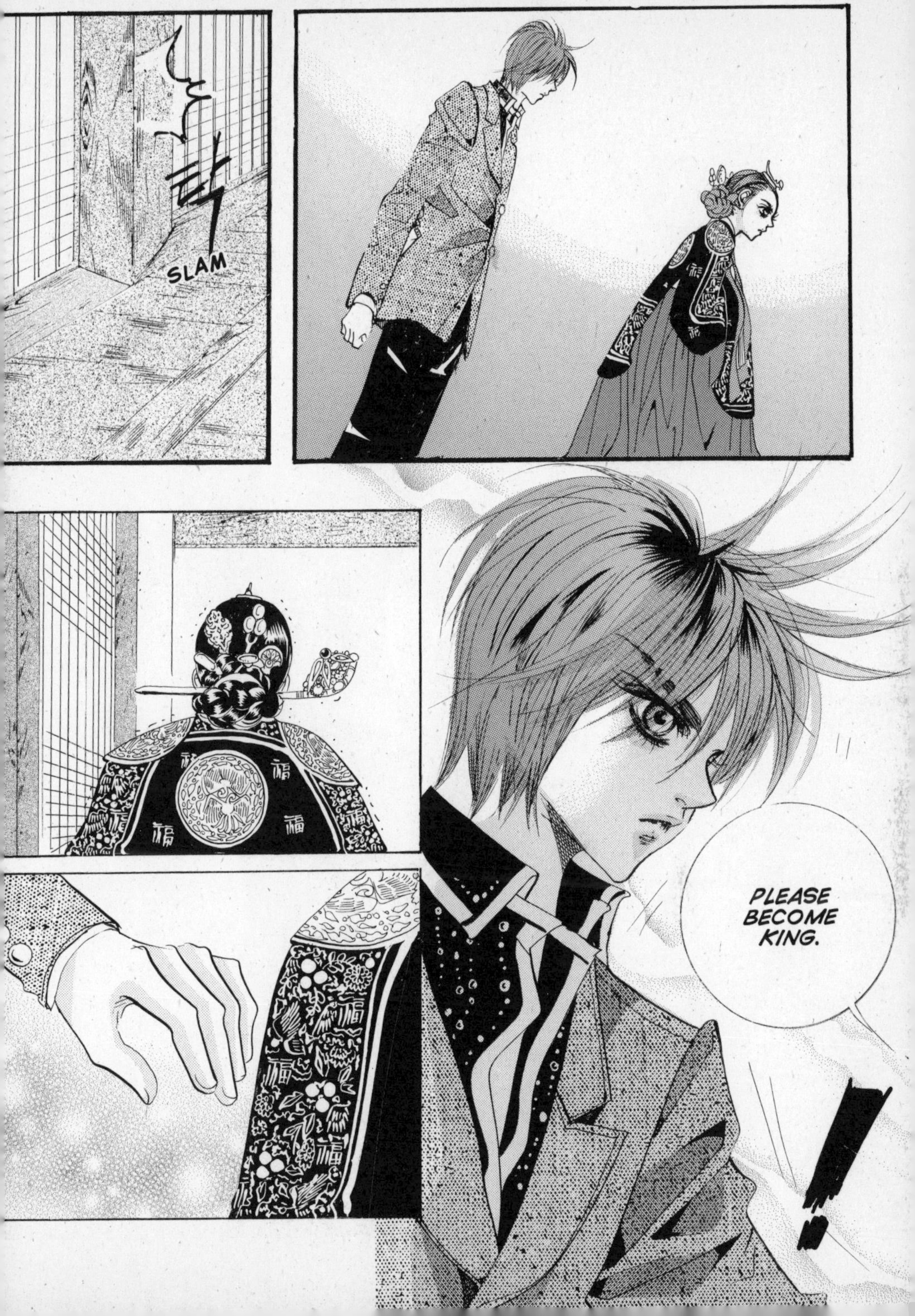
SLAM
PLEASE BECOME KING.

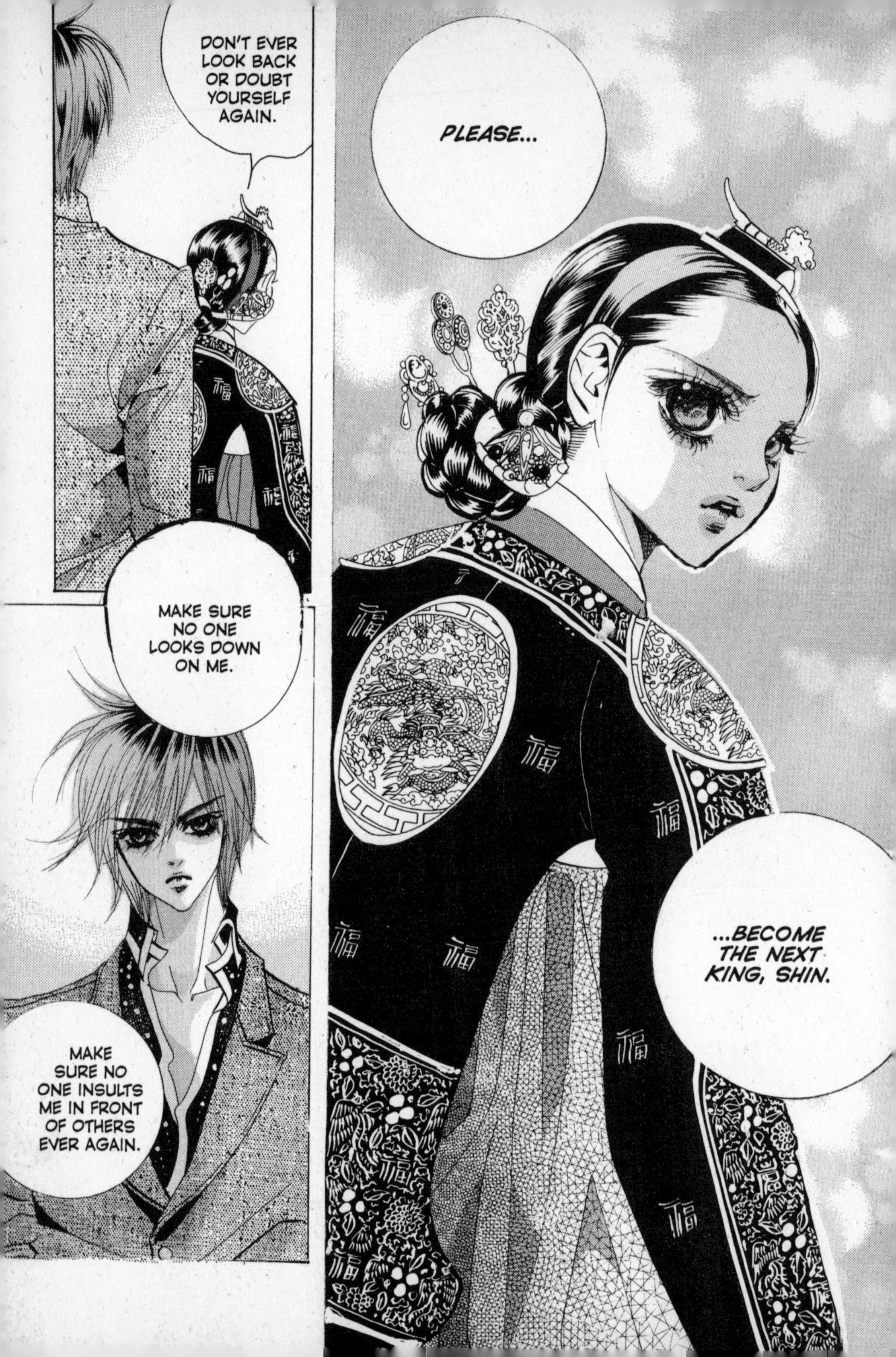
DON'T EVER LOOK BACK OR DOUBT YOURSELF AGAIN.
MAKE SURE NO ONE LOOKS DOWN ON ME.
MAKE SURE NO ONE INSULTS ME IN FRONT OF OTHERS EVER AGAIN.
PLEASE...
...BECOME THE NEXT KING, SHIN.

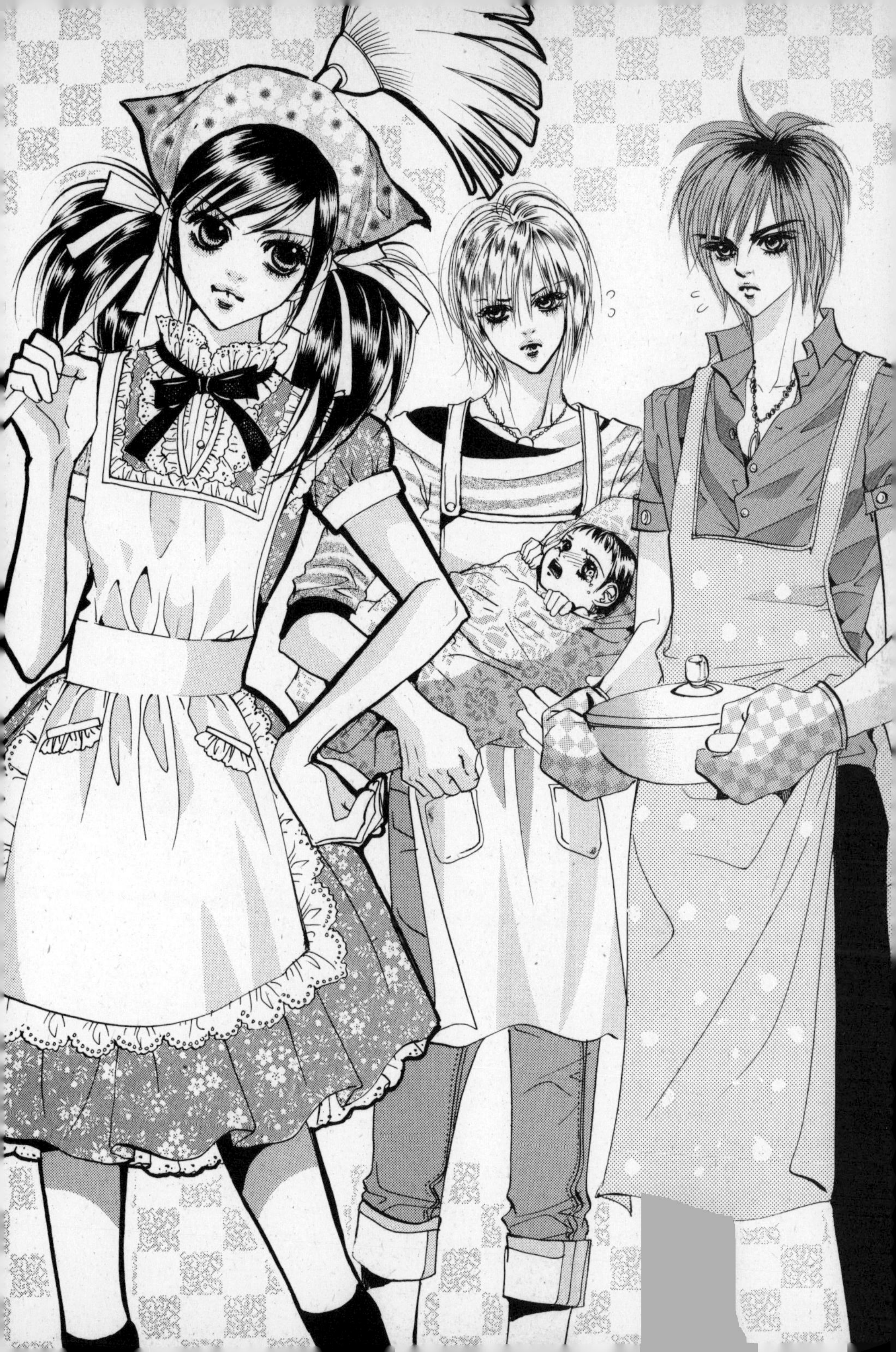

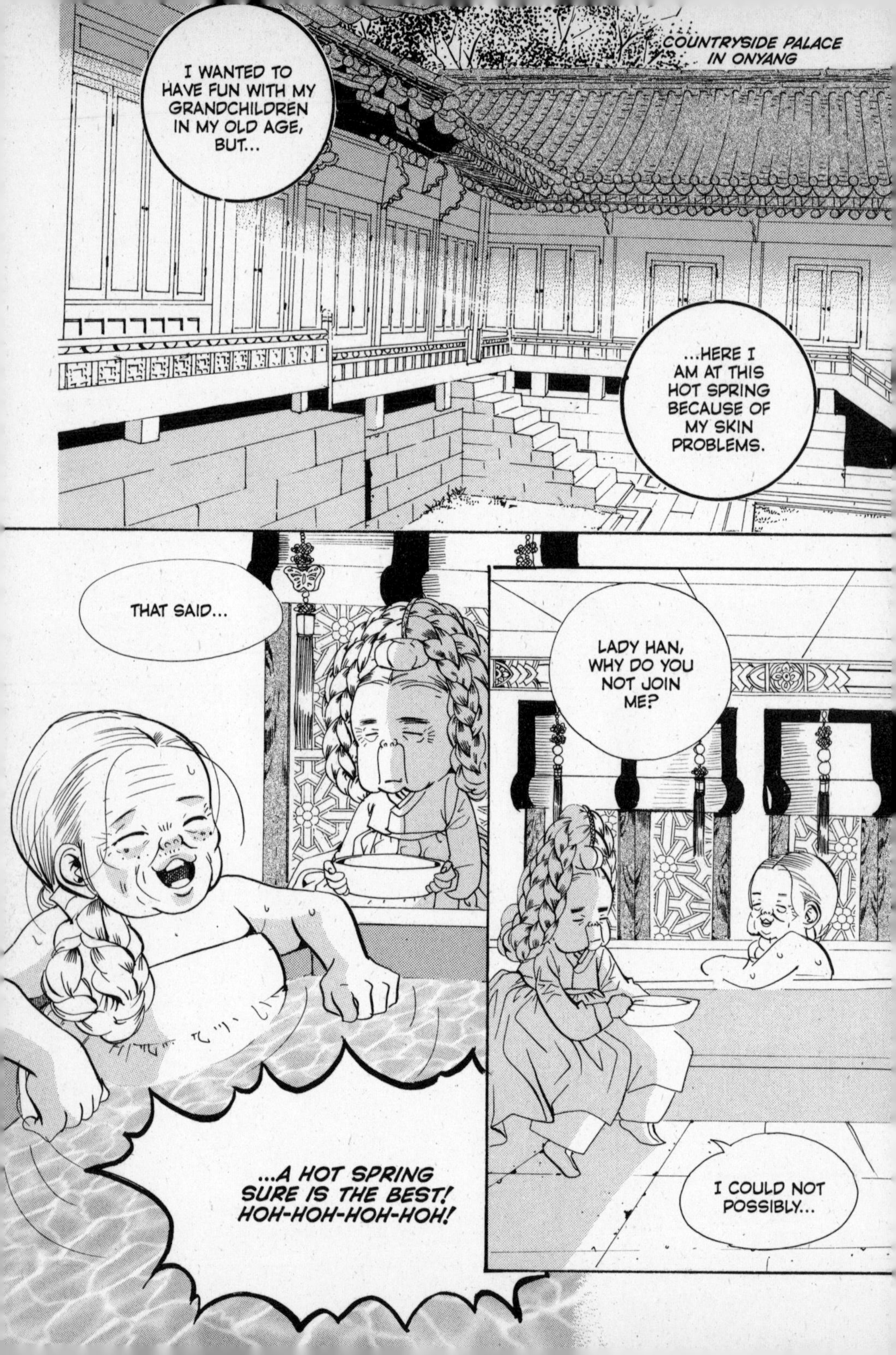
COUNTRYSIDE PALACE IN ONYANG
I WANTED TO HAVE FUN WITH MY GRANDCHILDREN IN MY OLD AGE, BUT...
...HERE I AM AT THIS HOT SPRING BECAUSE OF MY SKIN PROBLEMS.
THAT SAID...
...A HOT SPRING SURE IS THE BEST! HOH-HOH-HOH-HOH!
LADY HAN, WHY DO YOU NOT JOIN ME?
I COULD NOT POSSIBLY...

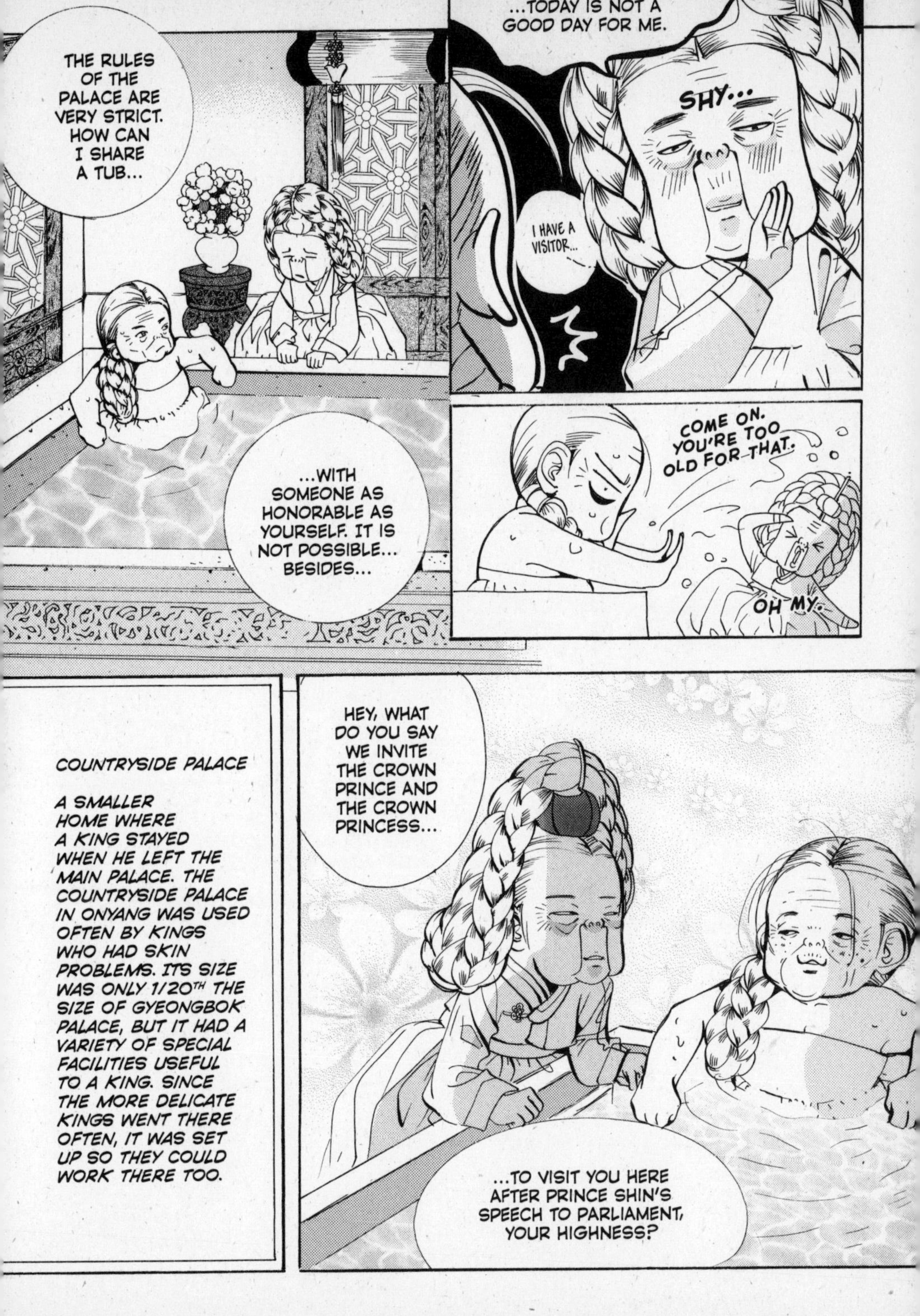
THE RULES OF THE PALACE ARE VERY STRICT. HOW CAN I SHARE A TUB...
...WITH SOMEONE AS HONORABLE AS YOURSELF. IT IS NOT POSSIBLE... BESIDES...
...TODAY IS NOT A GOOD DAY FOR ME.
SHY...
I HAVE A VISITOR...
COME ON. YOU'RE TOO OLD FOR THAT.
OH MY.
COUNTRYSIDE PALACE
A SMALLER HOME WHERE A KING STAYED WHEN HE LEFT THE MAIN PALACE. THE COUNTRYSIDE PALACE IN ONYANG WAS USED OFTEN BY KINGS WHO HAD SKIN PROBLEMS. ITS SIZE WAS ONLY 1/20TH THE SIZE OF GYEONGBOK PALACE, BUT IT HAD A VARIETY OF SPECIAL FACILITIES USEFUL TO A KING. SINCE THE MORE DELICATE KINGS WENT THERE OFTEN, IT WAS SET UP SO THEY COULD WORK THERE TOO.
HEY, WHAT DO YOU SAY WE INVITE THE CROWN PRINCE AND THE CROWN PRINCESS...
...TO VISIT YOU HERE AFTER PRINCE SHIN'S SPEECH TO PARLIAMENT, YOUR HIGHNESS?

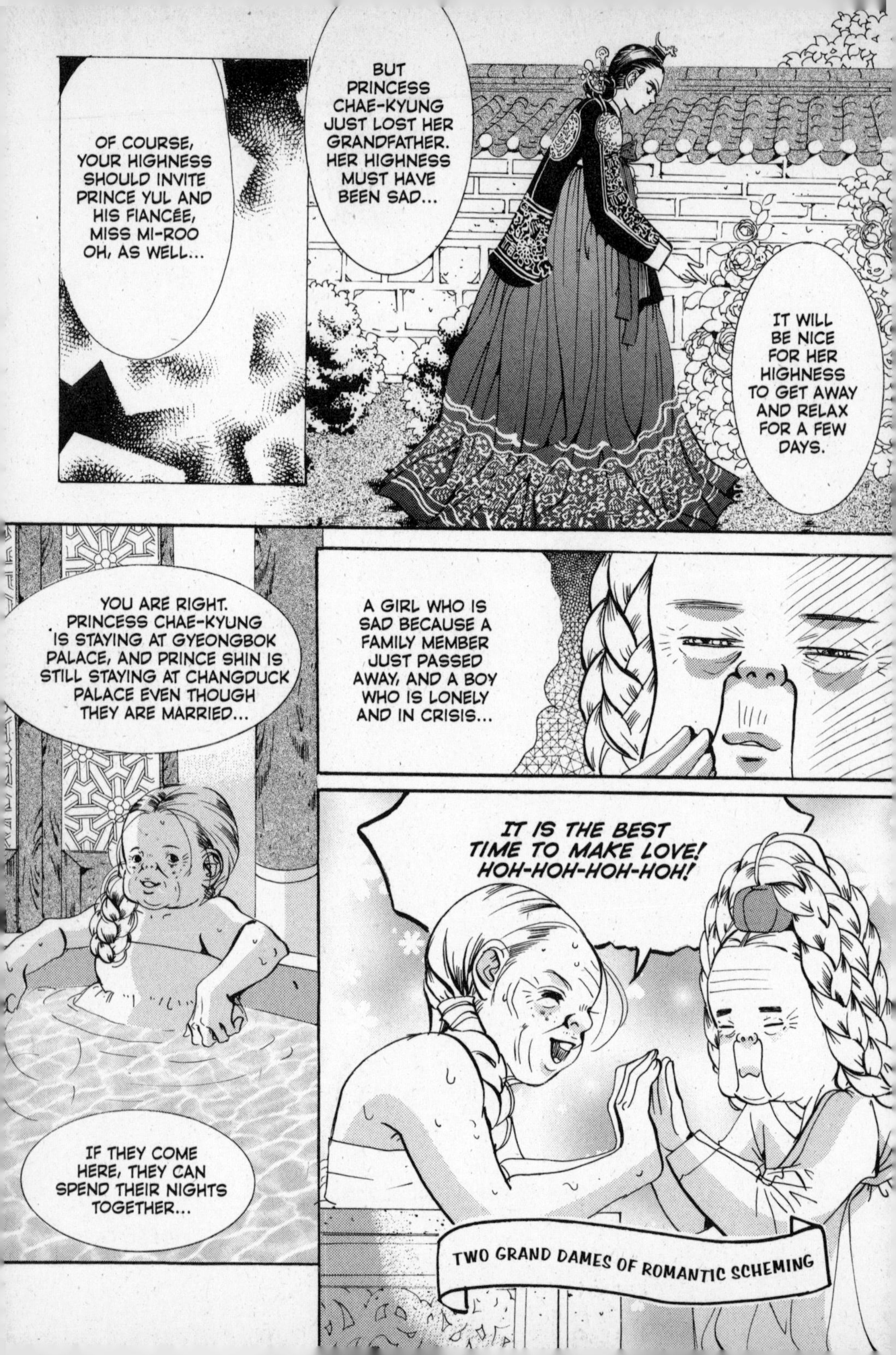
OF COURSE, YOUR HIGHNESS SHOULD INVITE PRINCE YUL AND HIS FIANCÉE, MISS MI-ROO OH, AS WELL...
BUT PRINCESS CHAE-KYUNG JUST LOST HER GRANDFATHER. HER HIGHNESS MUST HAVE BEEN SAD...
IT WILL BE NICE FOR HER HIGHNESS TO GET AWAY AND RELAX FOR A FEW DAYS.
YOU ARE RIGHT. PRINCESS CHAE-KYUNG IS STAYING AT GYEONGBOK PALACE, AND PRINCE SHIN IS STILL STAYING AT CHANGDUCK PALACE EVEN THOUGH THEY ARE MARRIED...
IF THEY COME HERE, THEY CAN SPEND THEIR NIGHTS TOGETHER...
A GIRL WHO IS SAD BECAUSE A FAMILY MEMBER JUST PASSED AWAY, AND A BOY WHO IS LONELY AND IN CRISIS...
IT IS THE BEST TIME TO MAKE LOVE! HOH-HOH-HOH-HOH!
TWO GRAND DAMES OF ROMANTIC SCHEMING

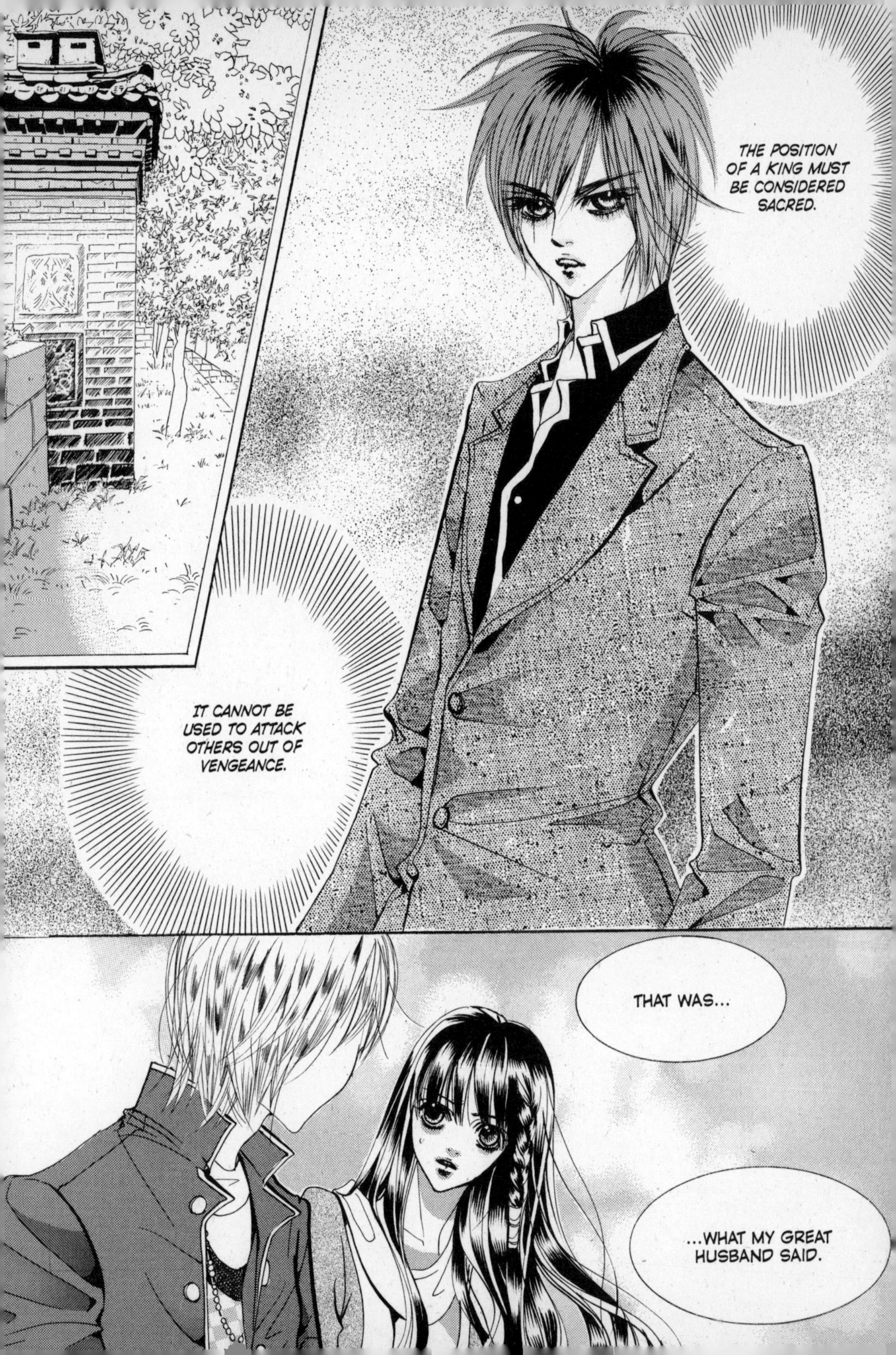
THE POSITION OF A KING MUST BE CONSIDERED SACRED.
IT CANNOT BE USED TO ATTACK OTHERS OUT OF VENGEANCE.
THAT WAS...
...WHAT MY GREAT HUSBAND SAID.

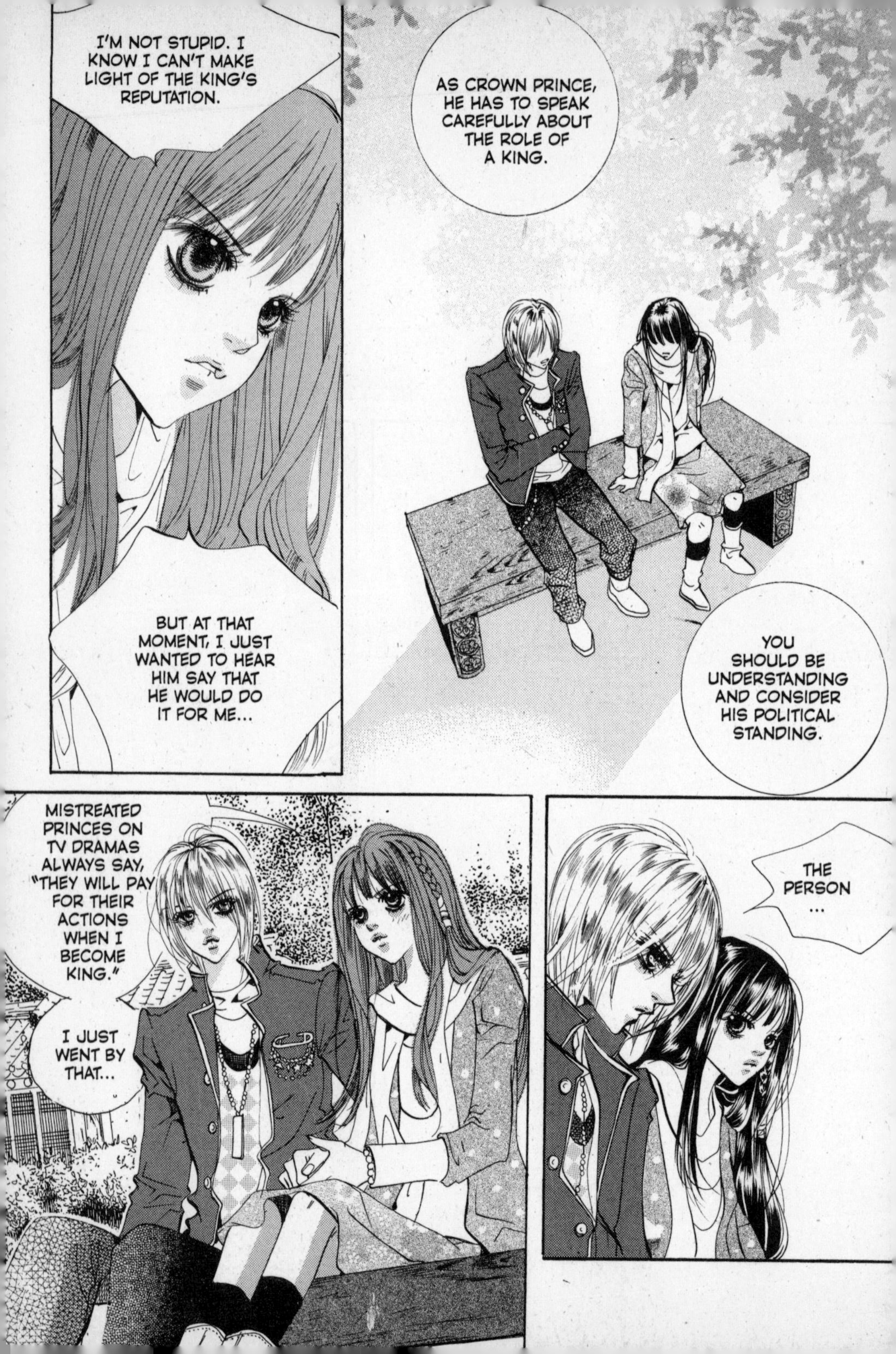
I'M NOT STUPID. I KNOW I CAN'T MAKE LIGHT OF THE KING'S REPUTATION.
BUT AT THAT MOMENT, I JUST WANTED TO HEAR HIM SAY THAT HE WOULD DO IT FOR ME...
AS CROWN PRINCE, HE HAS TO SPEAK CAREFULLY ABOUT THE ROLE OF A KING.
YOU SHOULD BE UNDERSTANDING AND CONSIDER HIS POLITICAL STANDING.
MISTREATED PRINCES ON TV DRAMAS ALWAYS SAY, "THEY WILL PAY FOR THEIR ACTIONS WHEN I BECOME KING."
I JUST WENT BY THAT...
THE PERSON ...

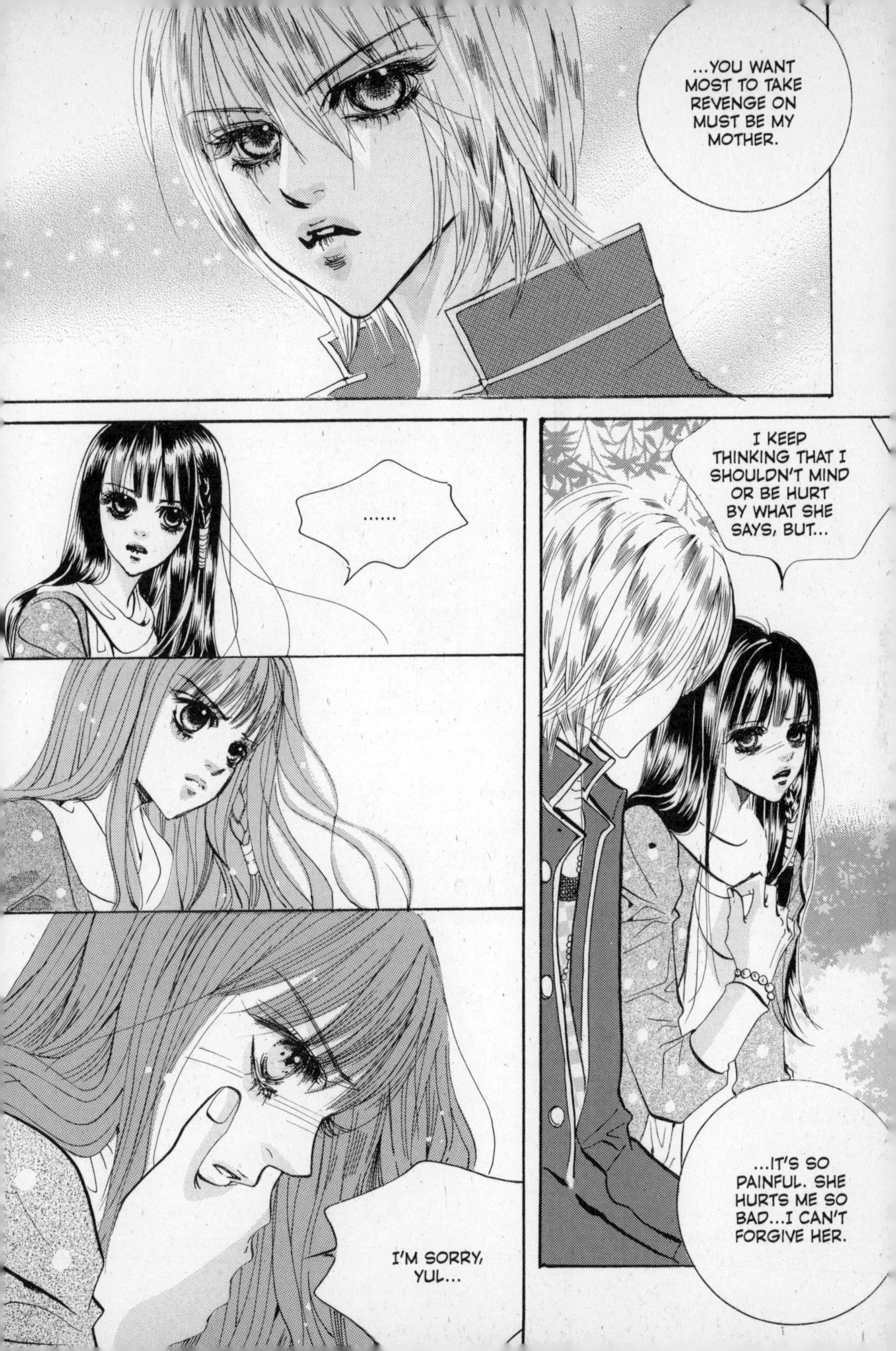
...YOU WANT MOST TO TAKE REVENGE ON MUST BE MY MOTHER.
......
I'M SORRY, YUL...
I KEEP THINKING THAT I SHOULDN'T MIND OR BE HURT BY WHAT SHE SAYS, BUT...
...IT'S SO PAINFUL. SHE HURTS ME SO BAD...I CAN'T FORGIVE HER.

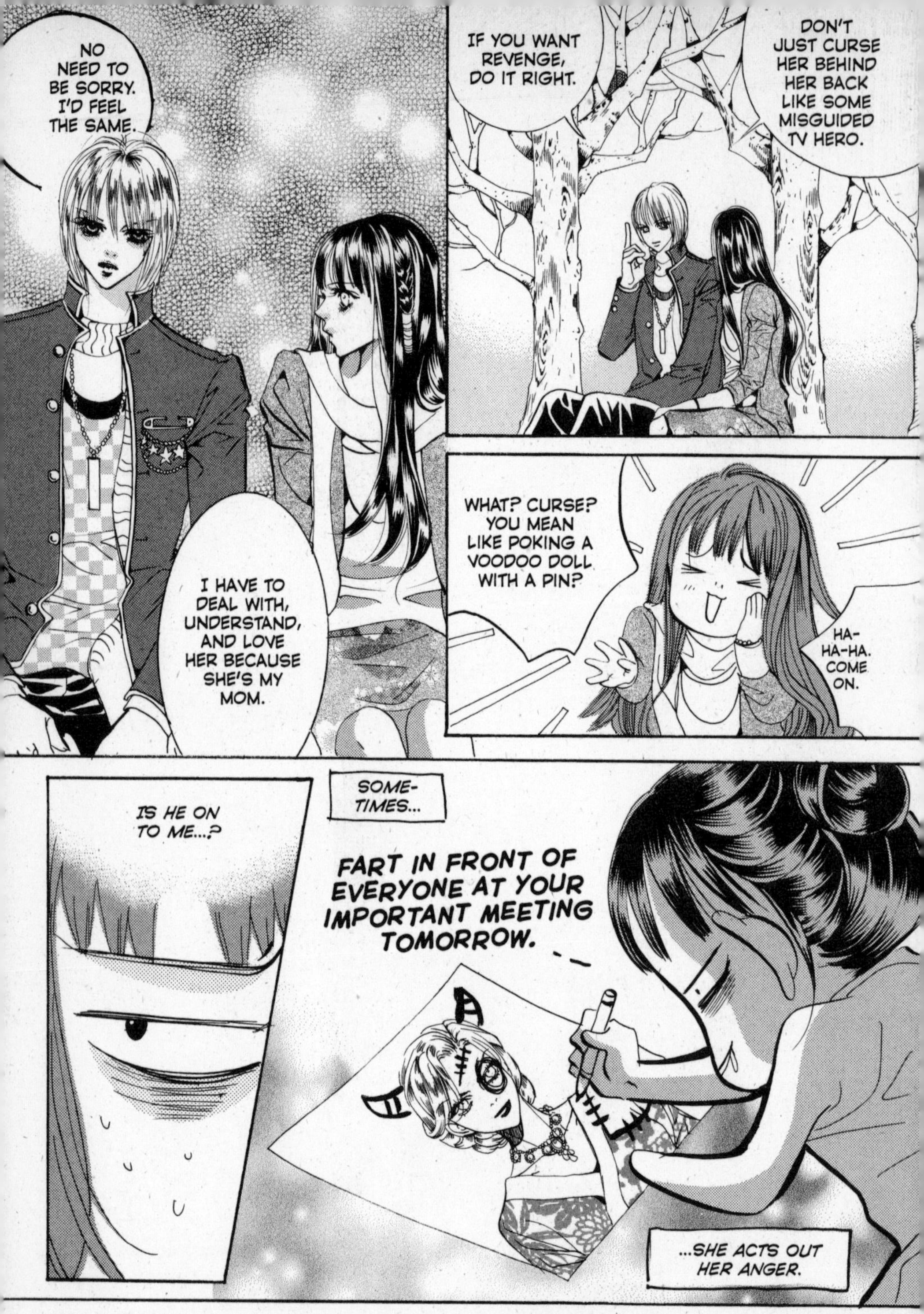
NO NEED TO BE SORRY. I'D FEEL THE SAME.
I HAVE TO DEAL WITH, UNDERSTAND, AND LOVE HER BECAUSE SHE'S MY MOM.
IF YOU WANT REVENGE, DO IT RIGHT.
DON'T JUST CURSE HER BEHIND HER BACK LIKE SOME MISGUIDED TV HERO.
WHAT? CURSE? YOU MEAN LIKE POKING A VOODOO DOLL WITH A PIN?
HA-HA-HA. COME ON.
IS HE ON TO ME...?
SOME-TIMES...
FART IN FRONT OF EVERYONE AT YOUR IMPORTANT MEETING TOMORROW.
...SHE ACTS OUT HER ANGER.

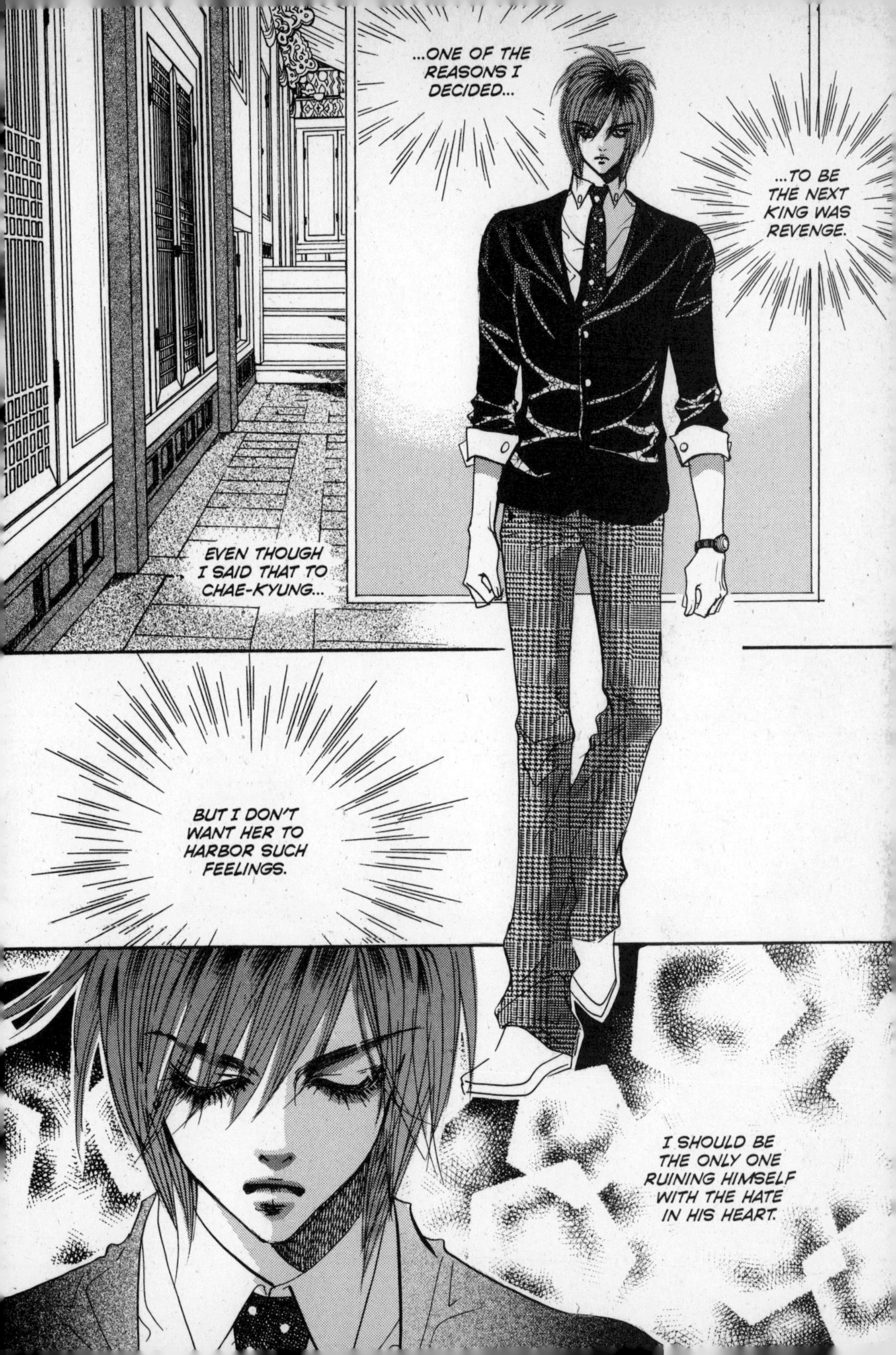
EVEN THOUGH I SAID THAT TO CHAE-KYUNG...
...ONE OF THE REASONS I DECIDED...
...TO BE THE NEXT KING WAS REVENGE.
BUT I DON'T WANT HER TO HARBOR SUCH FEELINGS.
I SHOULD BE THE ONLY ONE RUINING HIMSELF WITH THE HATE IN HIS HEART.

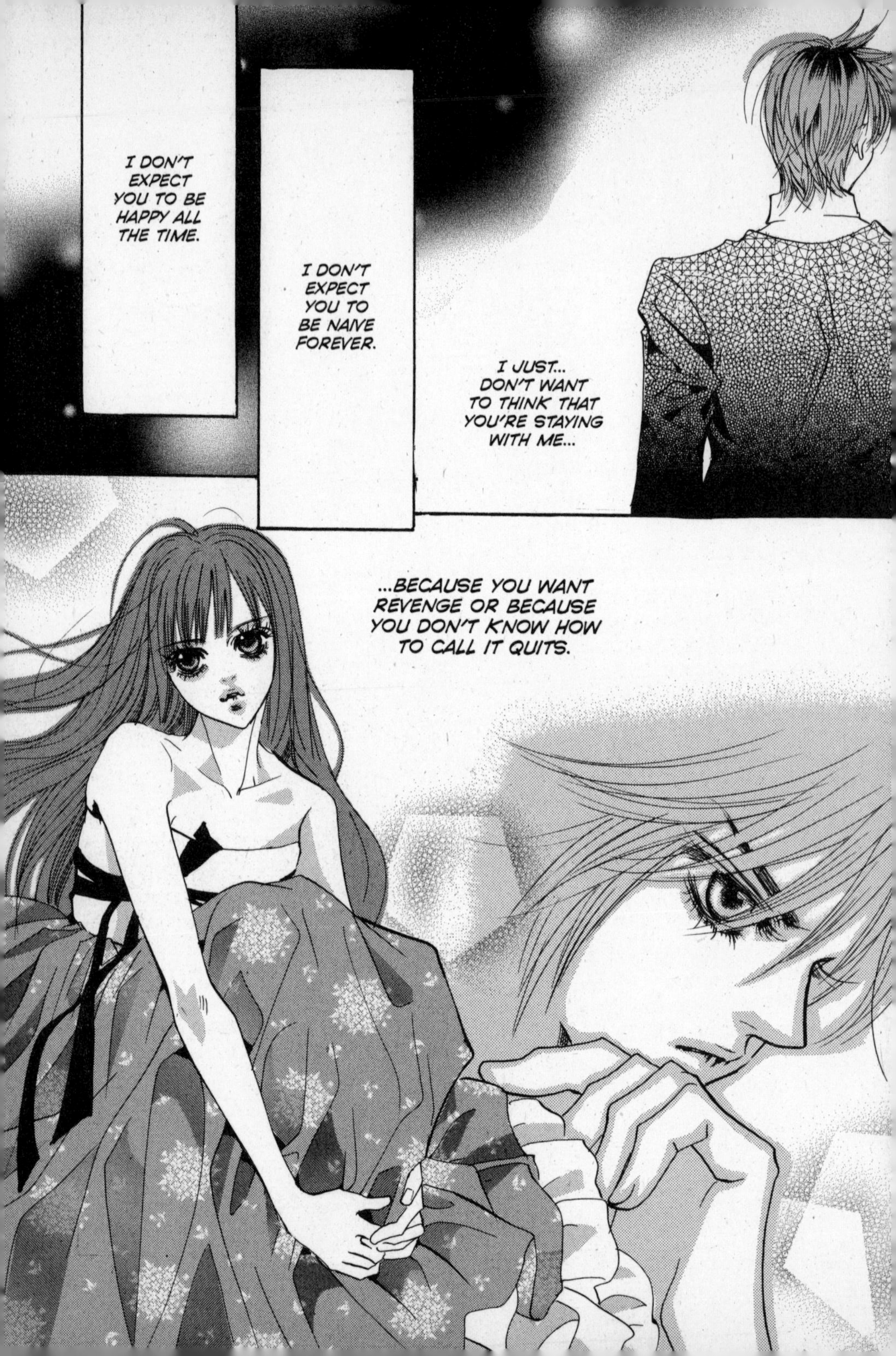
I DON'T EXPECT YOU TO BE HAPPY ALL THE TIME.
I DON'T EXPECT YOU TO BE NAIVE FOREVER.
I JUST... DON'T WANT TO THINK THAT YOU'RE STAYING WITH ME...
...BECAUSE YOU WANT REVENGE OR BECAUSE YOU DON'T KNOW HOW TO CALL IT QUITS.

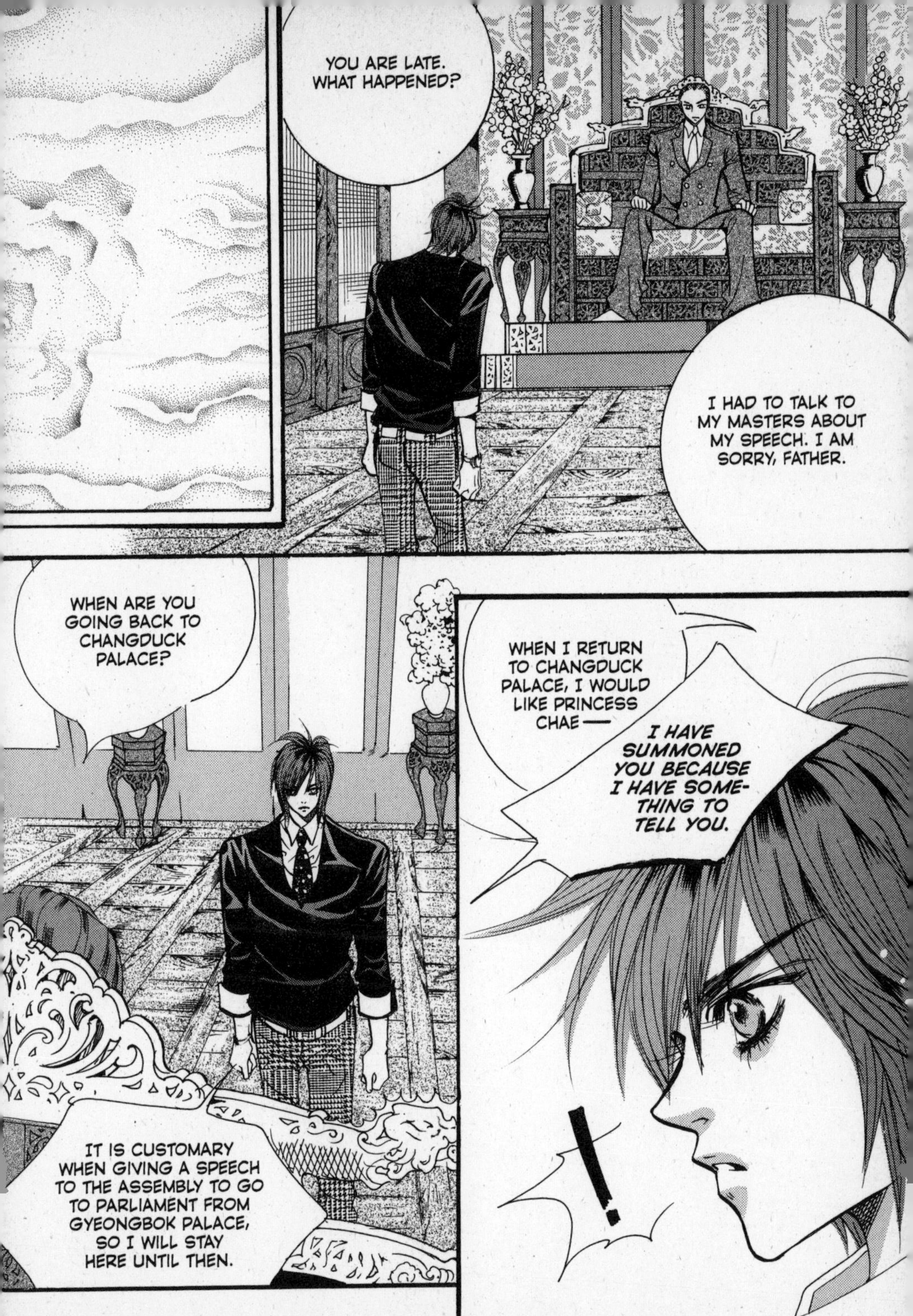
YOU ARE LATE. WHAT HAPPENED?
I HAD TO TALK TO MY MASTERS ABOUT MY SPEECH. I AM SORRY, FATHER.
WHEN ARE YOU GOING BACK TO CHANGDUCK PALACE?
IT IS CUSTOMARY WHEN GIVING A SPEECH TO THE ASSEMBLY TO GO TO PARLIAMENT FROM GYEONGBOK PALACE, SO I WILL STAY HERE UNTIL THEN.
WHEN I RETURN TO CHANGDUCK PALACE, I WOULD LIKE PRINCESS CHAE—
I HAVE SUMMONED YOU BECAUSE I HAVE SOMETHING TO TELL YOU.
!

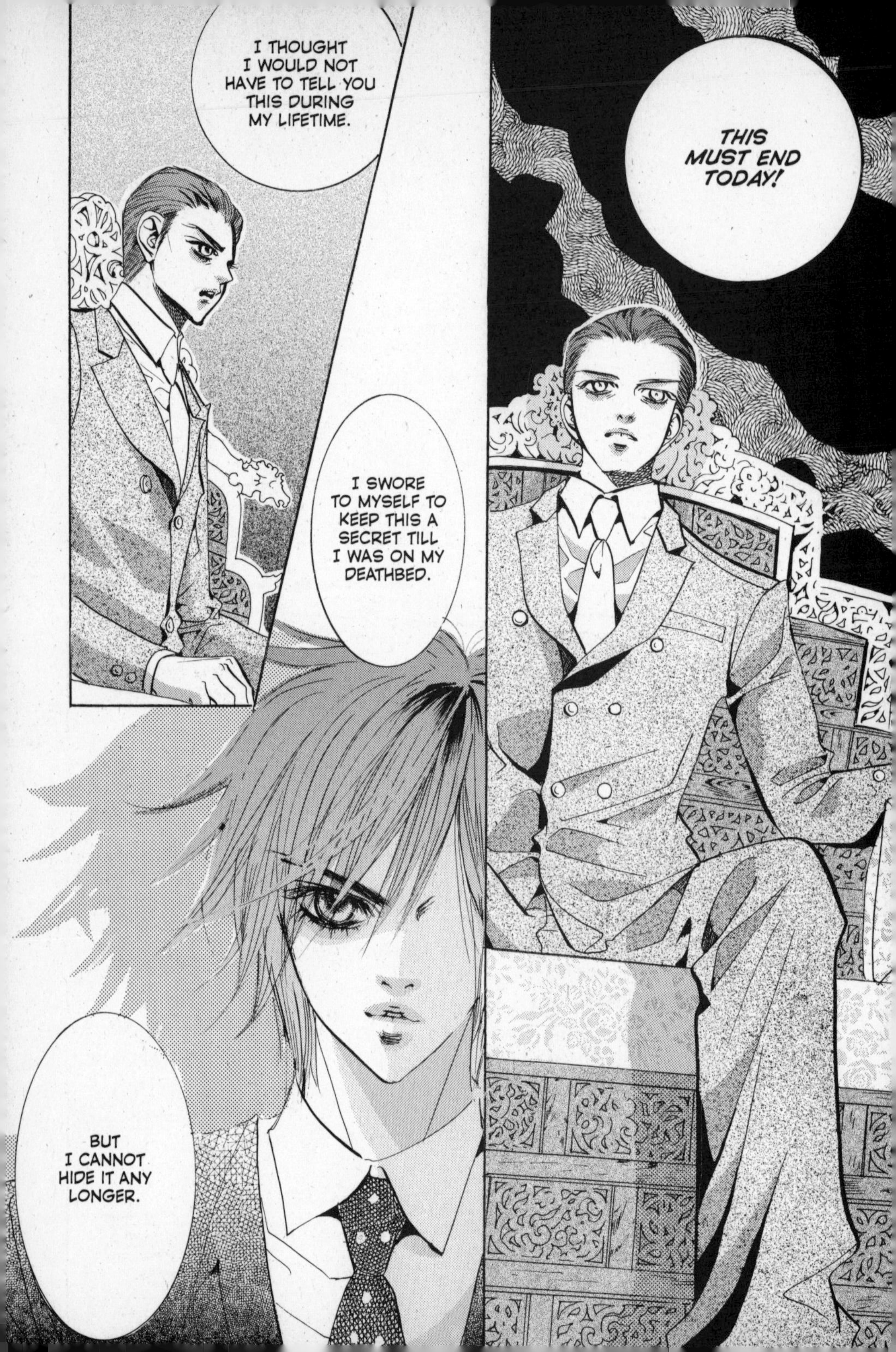
I THOUGHT I WOULD NOT HAVE TO TELL YOU THIS DURING MY LIFETIME.
I SWORE TO MYSELF TO KEEP THIS A SECRET TILL I WAS ON MY DEATHBED.
BUT I CANNOT HIDE IT ANY LONGER.
THIS MUST END TODAY!

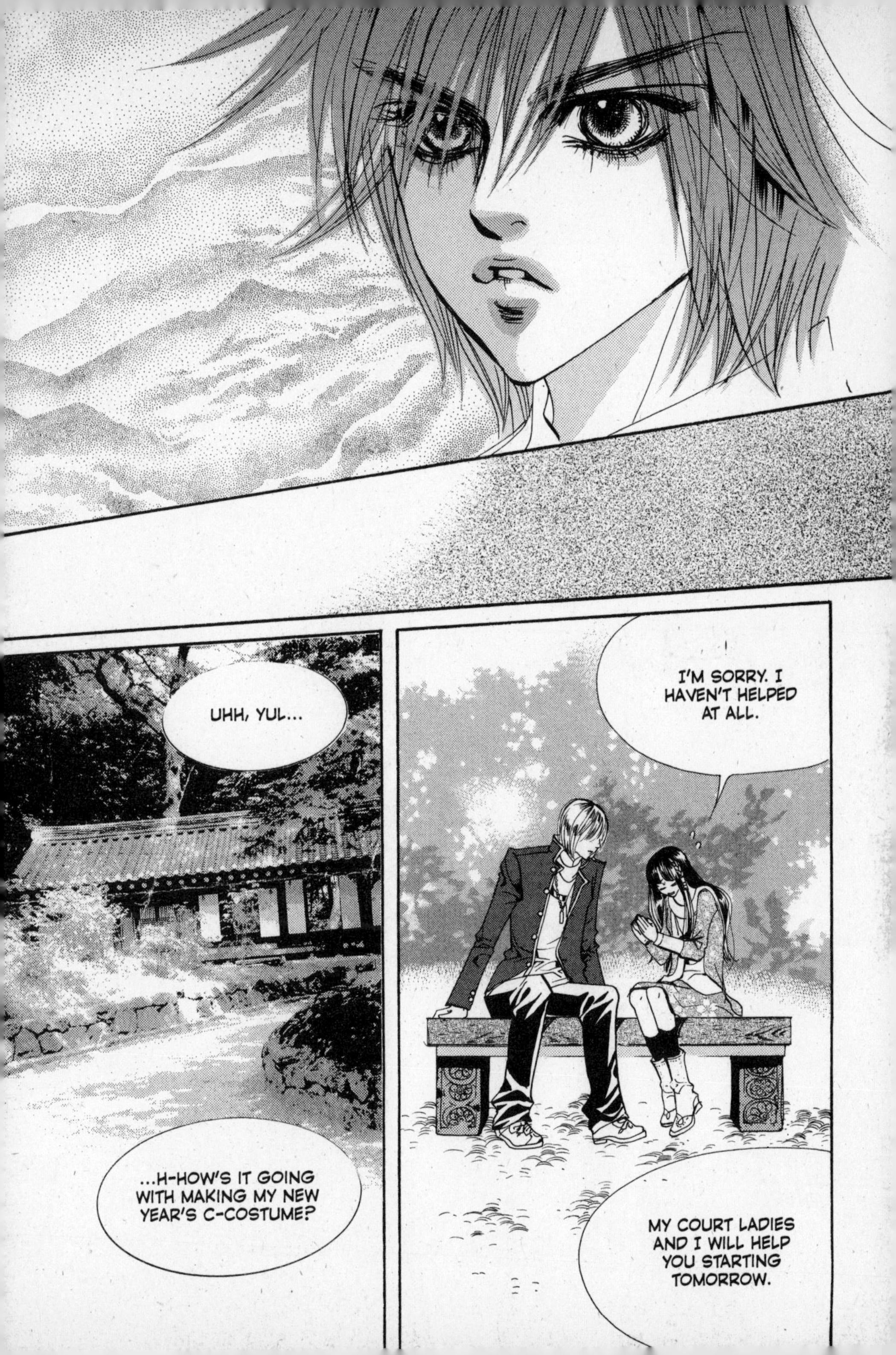
UHH, YUL...
...H-HOW'S IT GOING WITH MAKING MY NEW YEAR'S C-COSTUME?
I'M SORRY. I HAVEN'T HELPED AT ALL.
MY COURT LADIES AND I WILL HELP YOU STARTING TOMORROW.

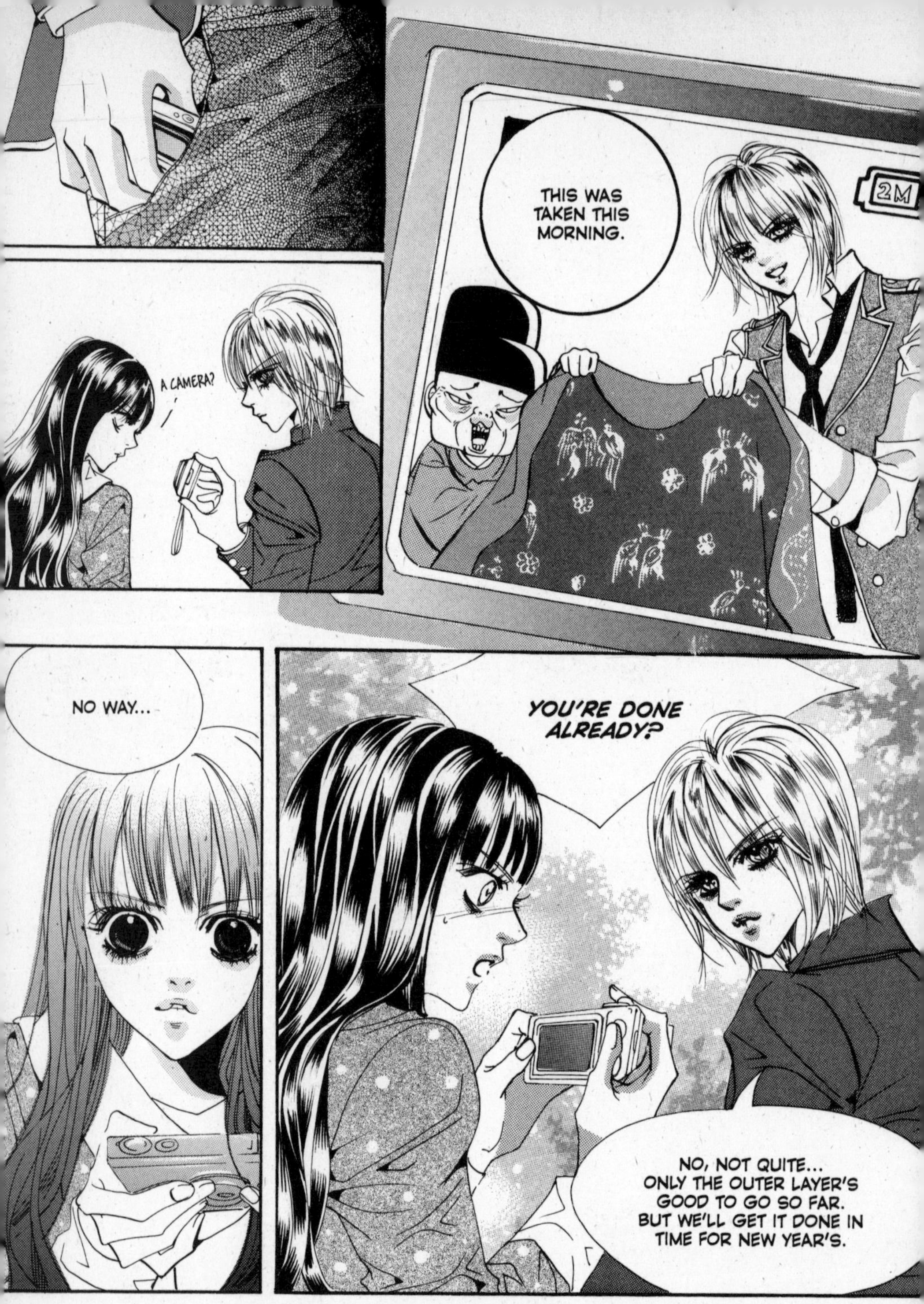
A CAMERA?
THIS WAS TAKEN THIS MORNING.
2M
NO WAY...
YOU'RE DONE ALREADY?
NO, NOT QUITE... ONLY THE OUTER LAYER'S GOOD TO GO SO FAR. BUT WE'LL GET IT DONE IN TIME FOR NEW YEAR'S.

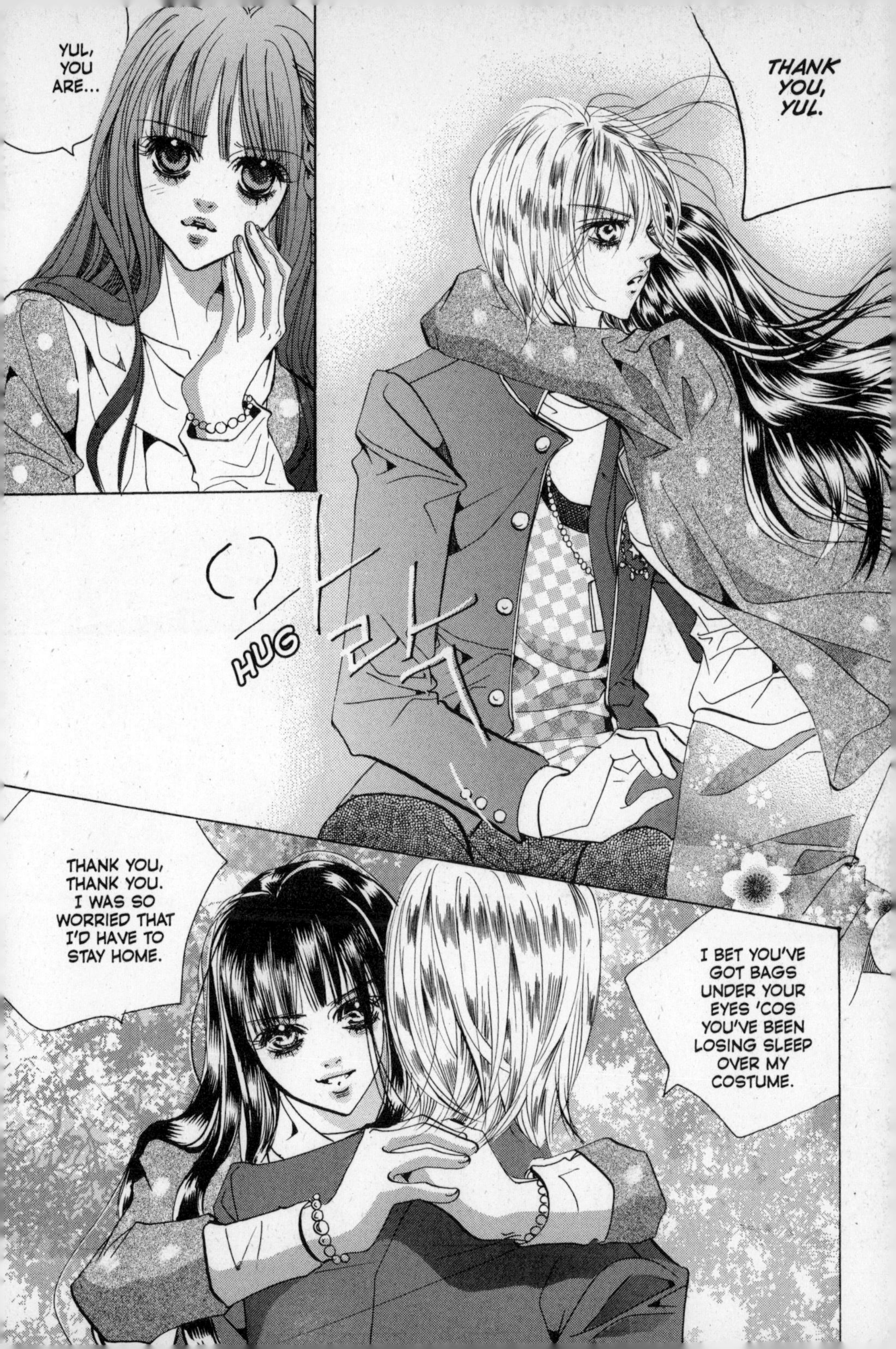
YUL, YOU ARE...
THANK YOU, YUL.
HUG
THANK YOU, THANK YOU. I WAS SO WORRIED THAT I'D HAVE TO STAY HOME.
I BET YOU'VE GOT BAGS UNDER YOUR EYES 'COS YOU'VE BEEN LOSING SLEEP OVER MY COSTUME.

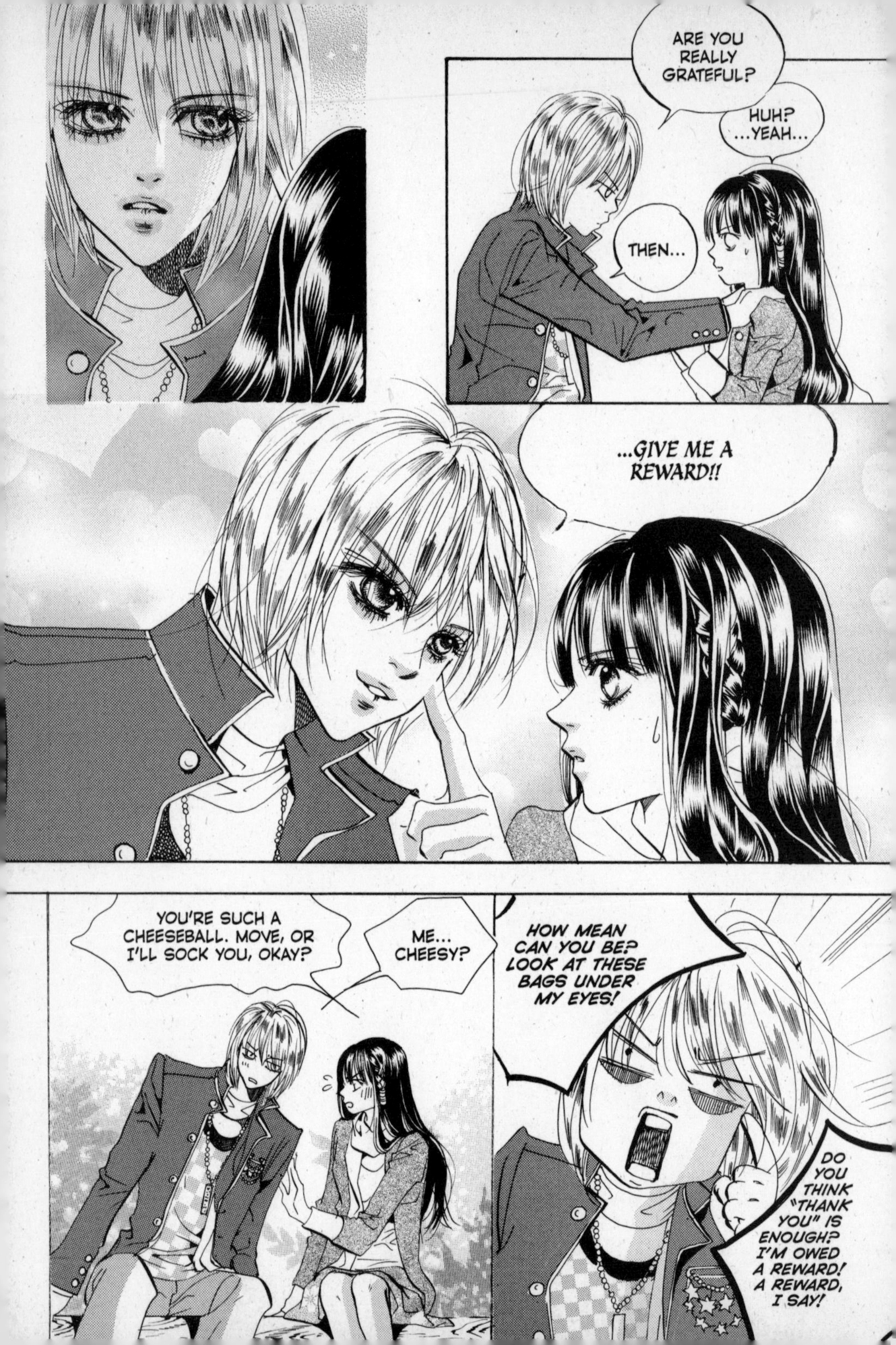
ARE YOU REALLY GRATEFUL?
HUH? ...YEAH...
THEN...
...GIVE ME A REWARD!!
YOU'RE SUCH A CHEESEBALL. MOVE, OR I'LL SOCK YOU, OKAY?
ME... CHEESY?
HOW MEAN CAN YOU BE? LOOK AT THESE BAGS UNDER MY EYES!
DO YOU THINK "THANK YOU" IS ENOUGH? I'M OWED A REWARD! A REWARD, I SAY!

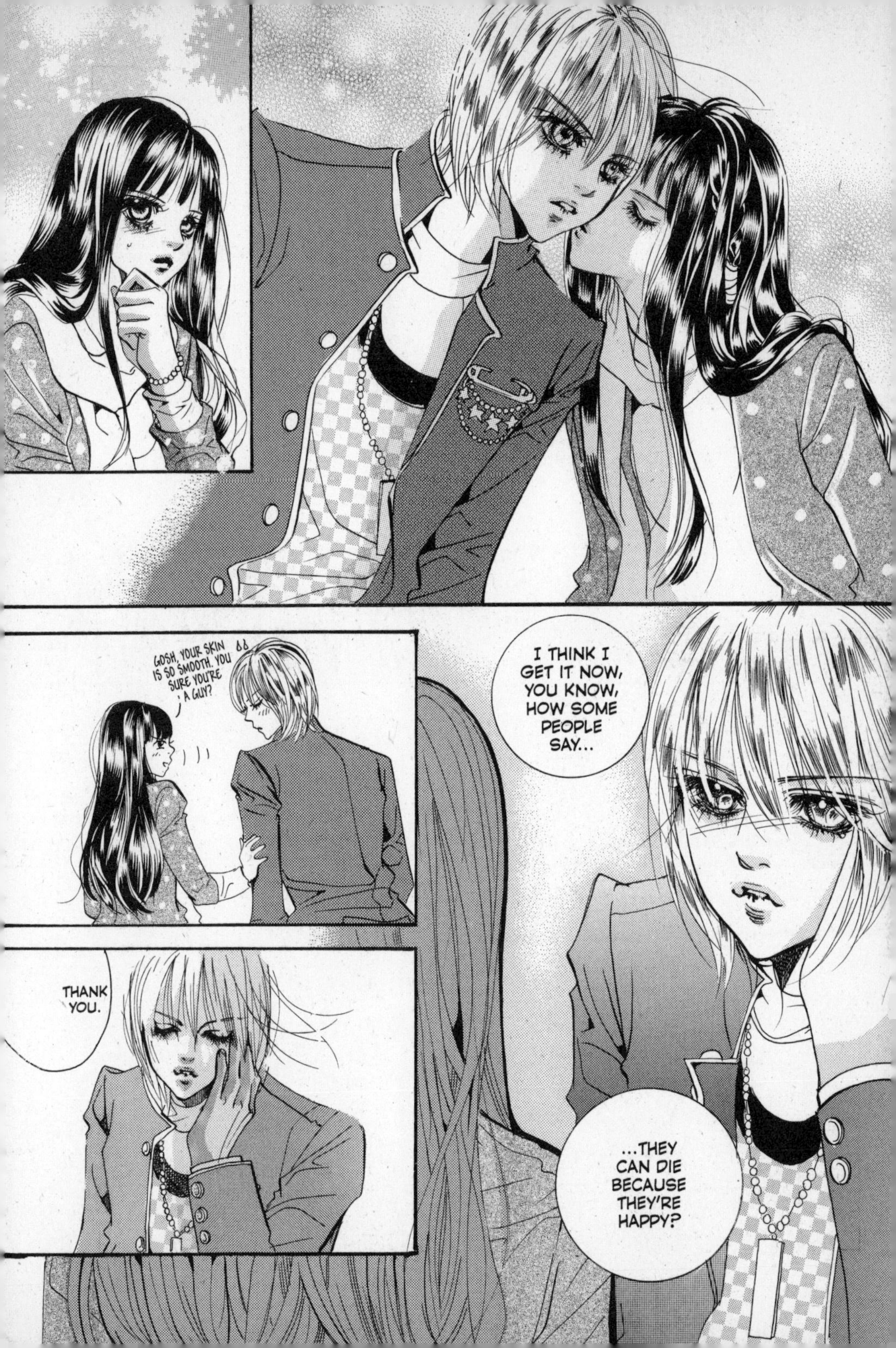
GOSH, YOUR SKIN IS SO SMOOTH. YOU SURE YOU'RE A GUY?
THANK YOU.
I THINK I GET IT NOW, YOU KNOW, HOW SOME PEOPLE SAY...
...THEY CAN DIE BECAUSE THEY'RE HAPPY?

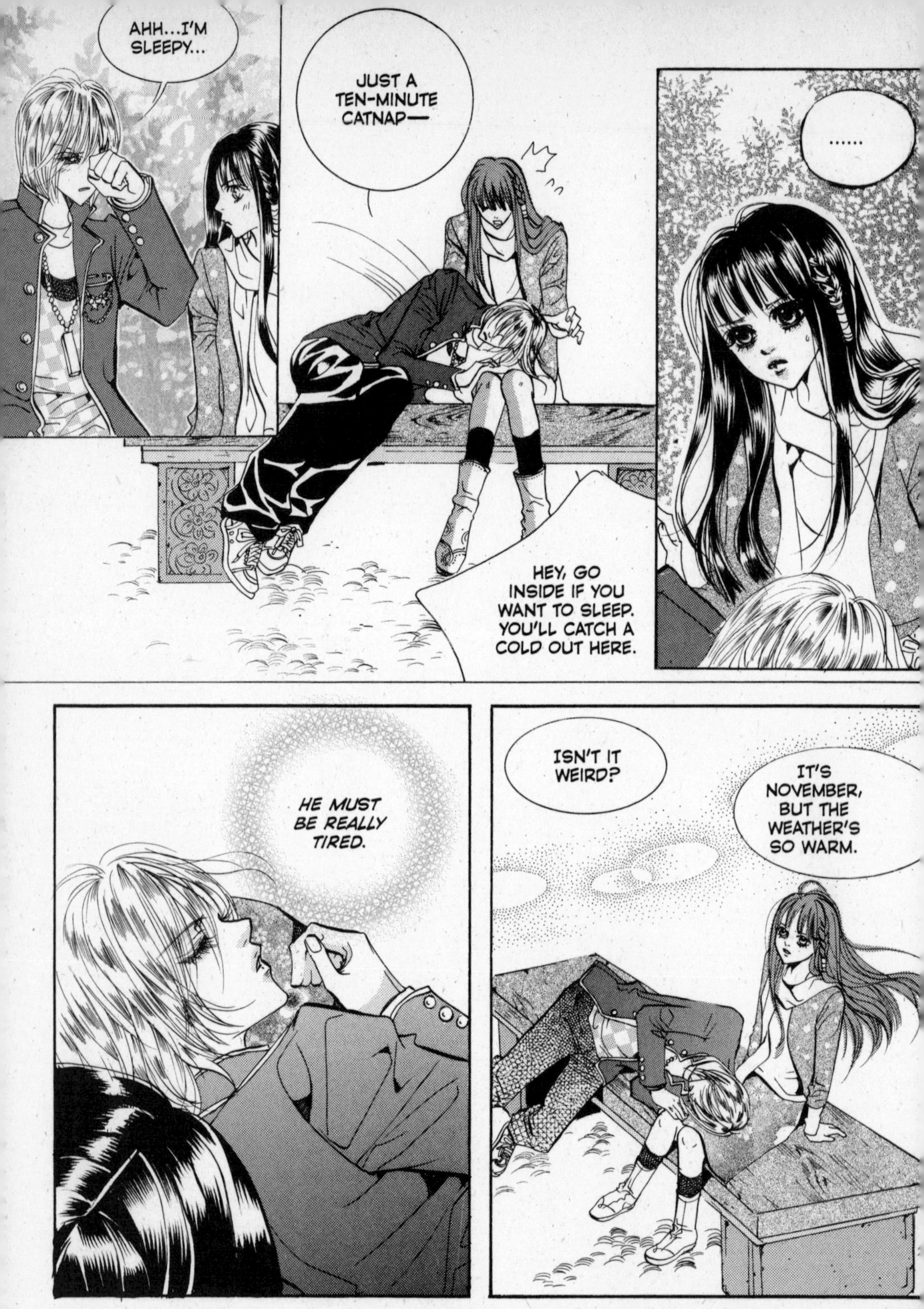
AHH...I'M SLEEPY...
JUST A TEN-MINUTE CATNAP—
......
HEY, GO INSIDE IF YOU WANT TO SLEEP. YOU'LL CATCH A COLD OUT HERE.
HE MUST BE REALLY TIRED.
ISN'T IT WEIRD?
IT'S NOVEMBER, BUT THE WEATHER'S SO WARM.

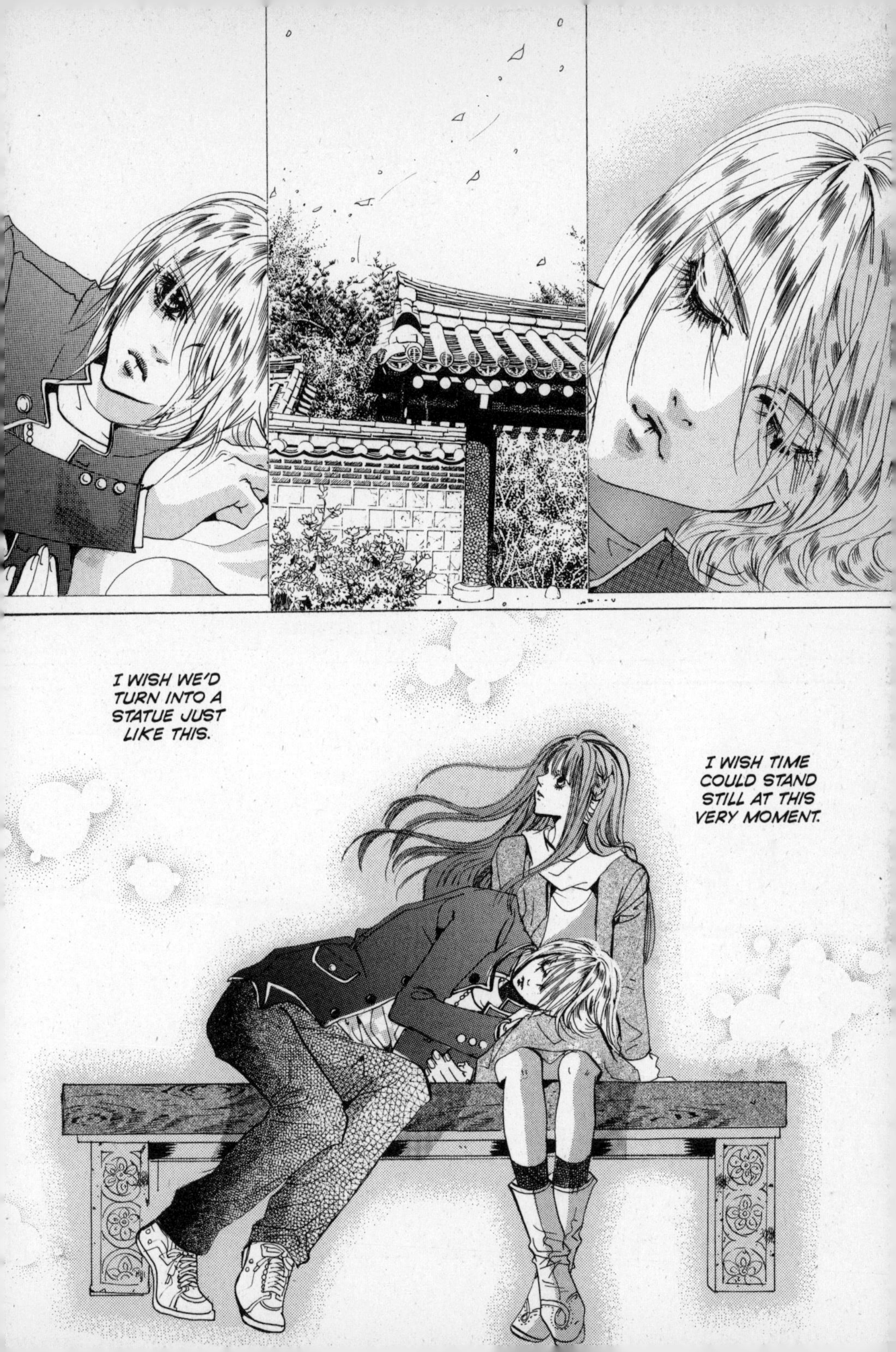
I WISH WE'D TURN INTO A STATUE JUST LIKE THIS.
I WISH TIME COULD STAND STILL AT THIS VERY MOMENT.

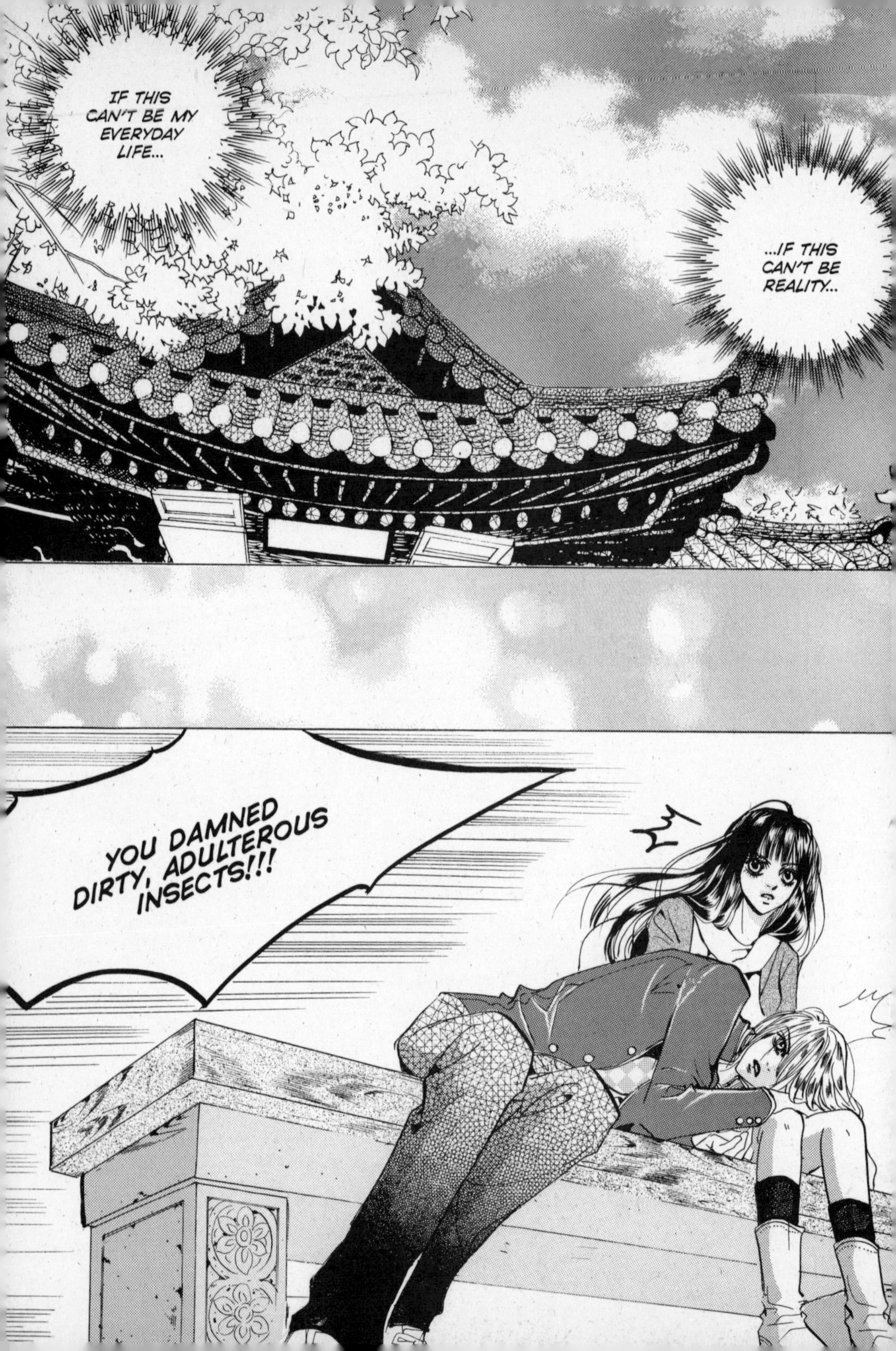
IF THIS CAN'T BE MY EVERYDAY LIFE...
...IF THIS CAN'T BE REALITY...
YOU DAMNED DIRTY, ADULTEROUS INSECTS!!!

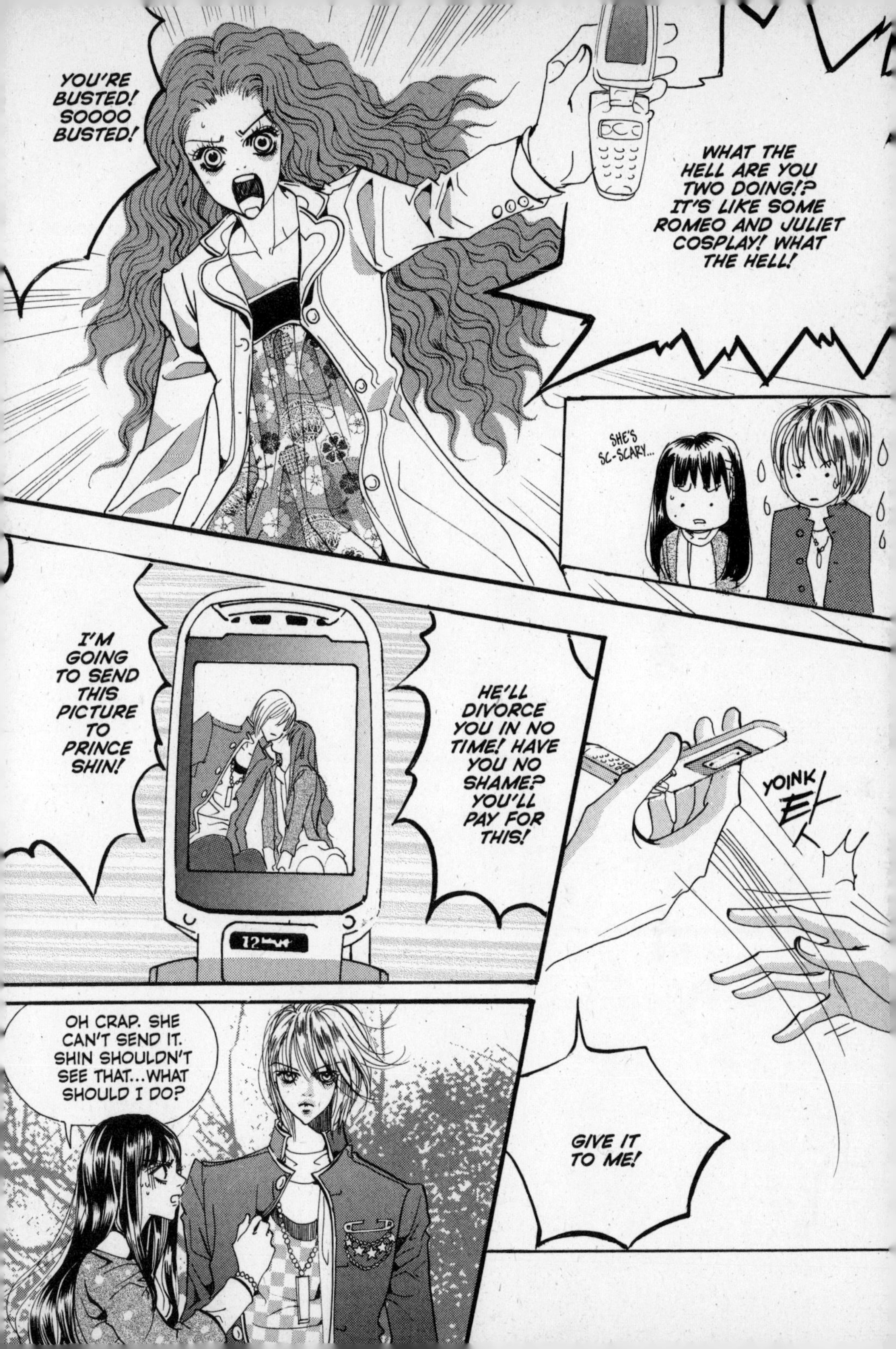
YOU'RE BUSTED! SOOOO BUSTED!
WHAT THE HELL ARE YOU TWO DOING!? IT'S LIKE SOME ROMEO AND JULIET COSPLAY! WHAT THE HELL!
SHE'S SC-SCARY...
I'M GOING TO SEND THIS PICTURE TO PRINCE SHIN!
HE'LL DIVORCE YOU IN NO TIME! HAVE YOU NO SHAME? YOU'LL PAY FOR THIS!
OH CRAP. SHE CAN'T SEND IT. SHIN SHOULDN'T SEE THAT...WHAT SHOULD I DO?
YOINK
GIVE IT TO ME!

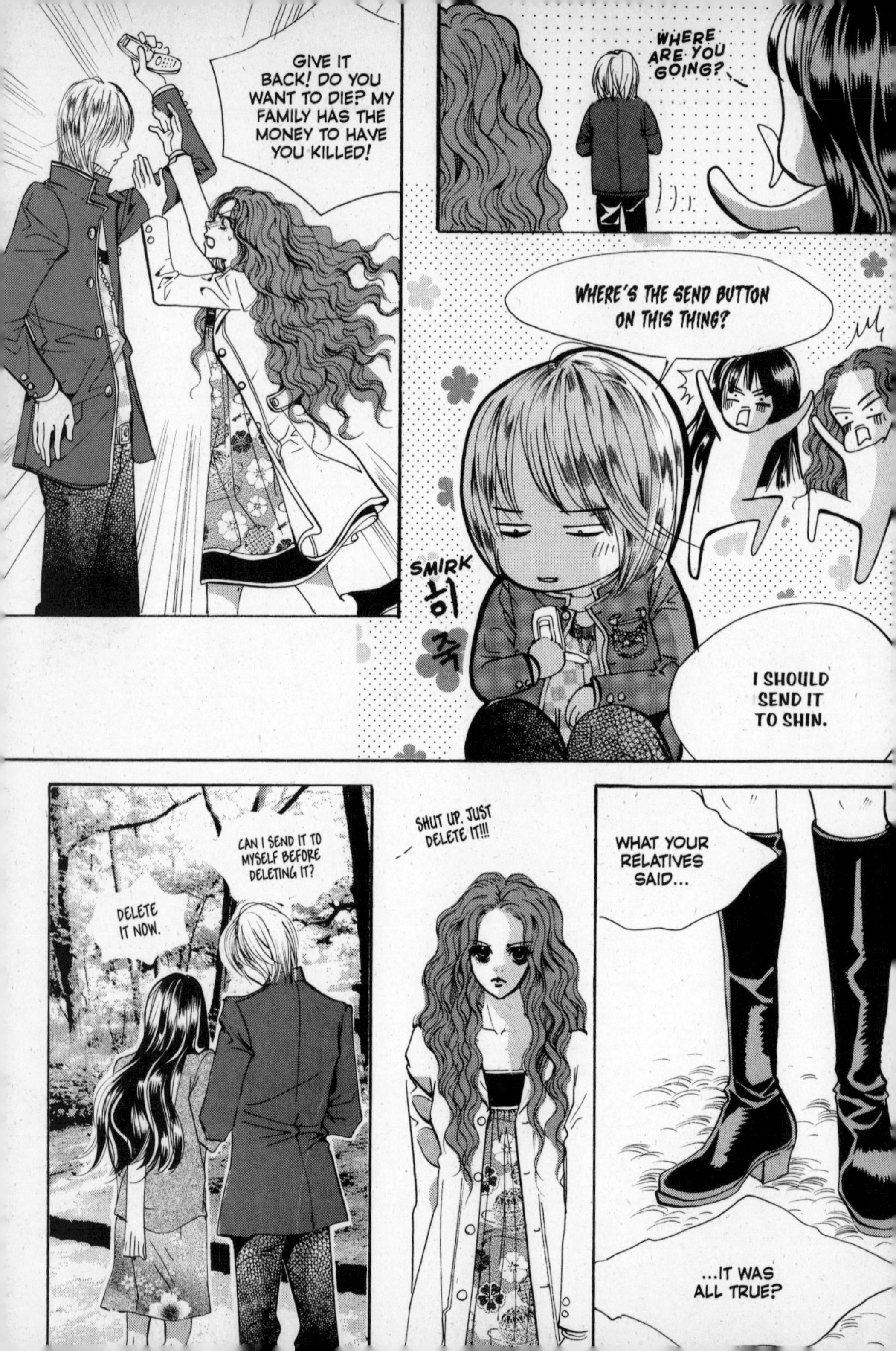
GIVE IT BACK! DO YOU WANT TO DIE? MY FAMILY HAS THE MONEY TO HAVE YOU KILLED!
WHERE ARE YOU GOING?
WHERE'S THE SEND BUTTON ON THIS THING?
SMIRK
히죽
I SHOULD SEND IT TO SHIN.
CAN I SEND IT TO MYSELF BEFORE DELETING IT?
DELETE IT NOW.
SHUT UP. JUST DELETE IT!!!
WHAT YOUR RELATIVES SAID...
...IT WAS ALL TRUE?

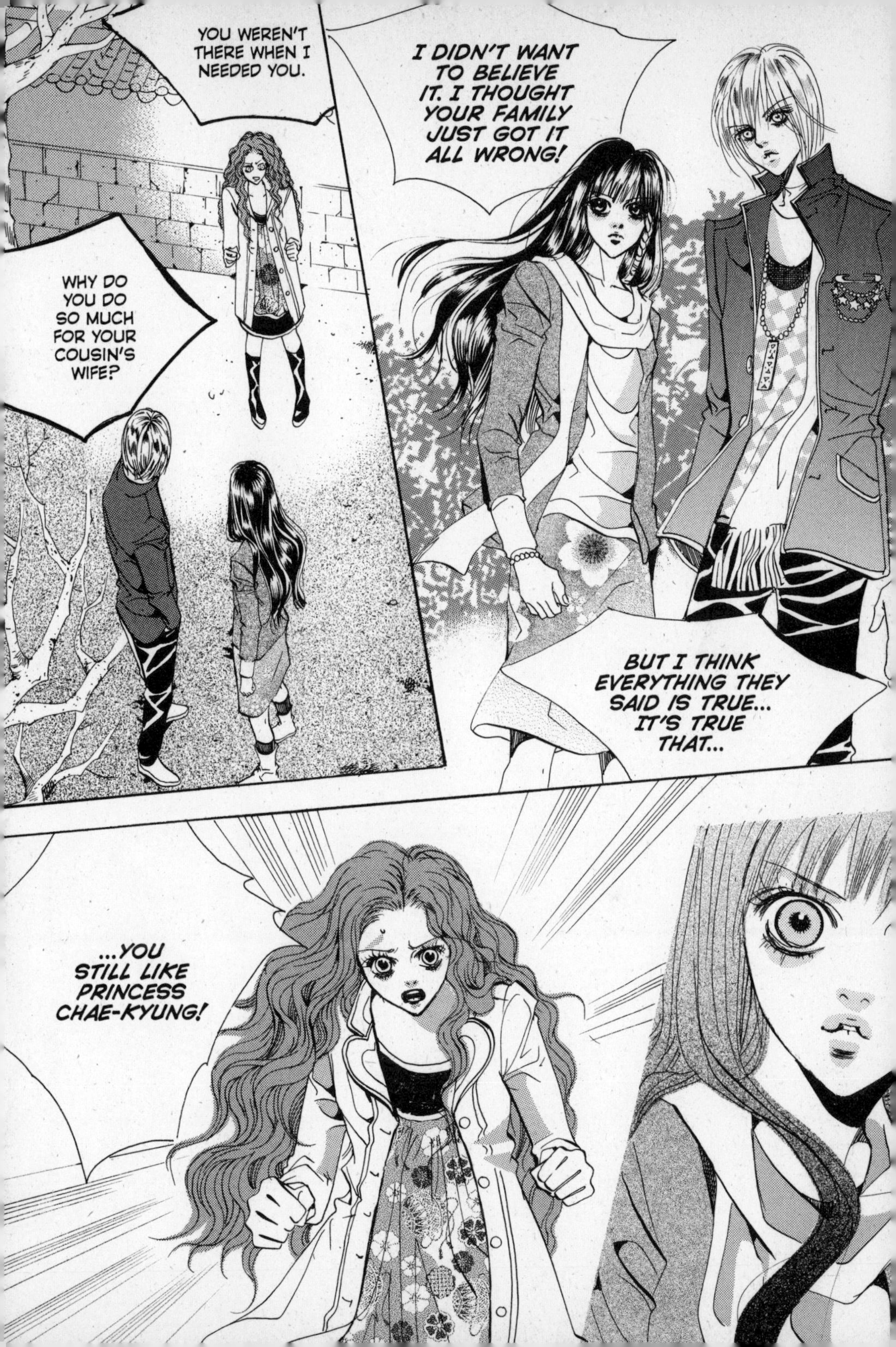
YOU WEREN'T THERE WHEN I NEEDED YOU.
WHY DO YOU DO SO MUCH FOR YOUR COUSIN'S WIFE?
I DIDN'T WANT TO BELIEVE IT. I THOUGHT YOUR FAMILY JUST GOT IT ALL WRONG!
BUT I THINK EVERYTHING THEY SAID IS TRUE... IT'S TRUE THAT...
...YOU STILL LIKE PRINCESS CHAE-KYUNG!

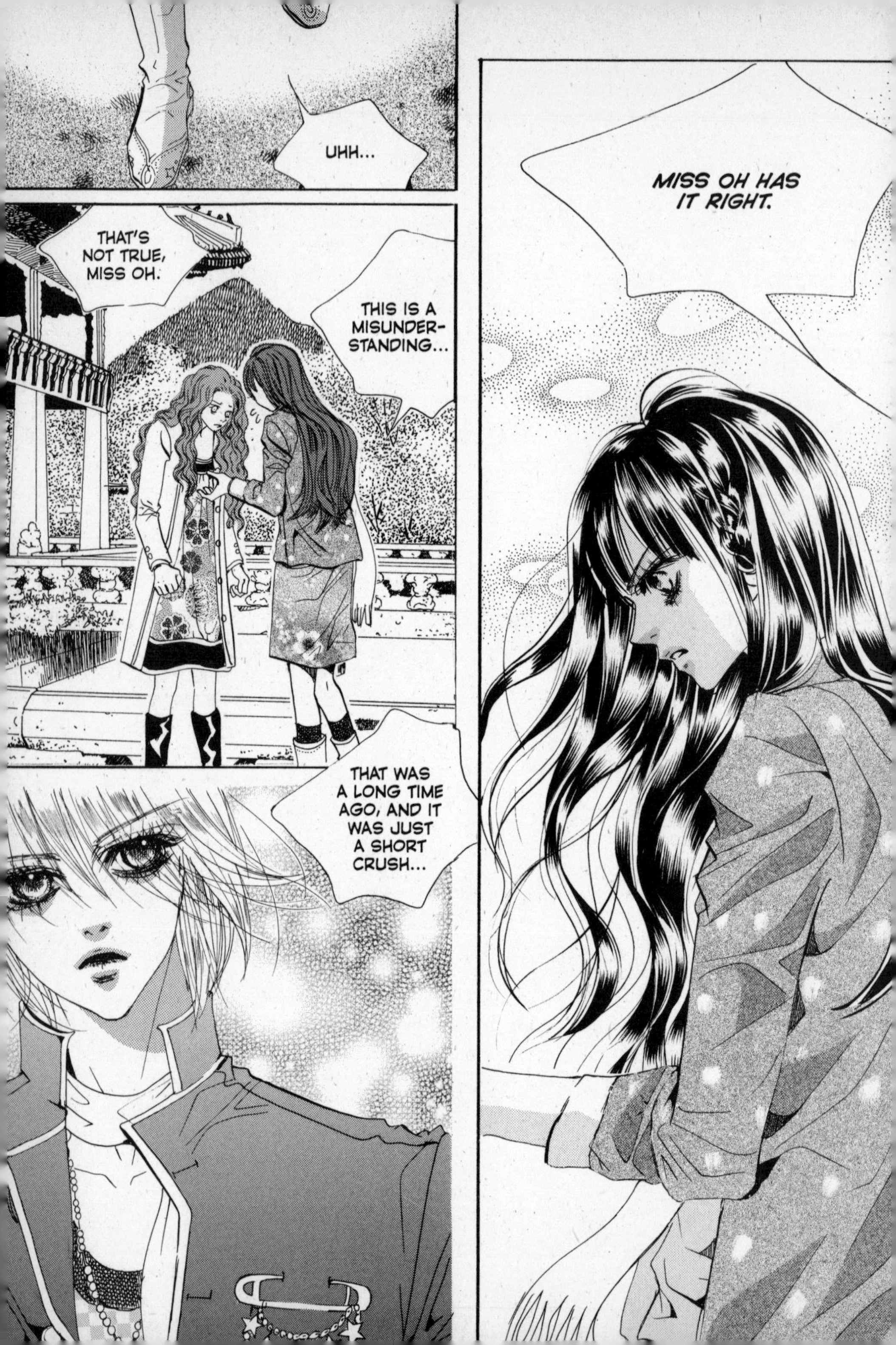
UHH...
THAT'S NOT TRUE, MISS OH.
THIS IS A MISUNDER-STANDING...
THAT WAS A LONG TIME AGO, AND IT WAS JUST A SHORT CRUSH...
MISS OH HAS IT RIGHT.

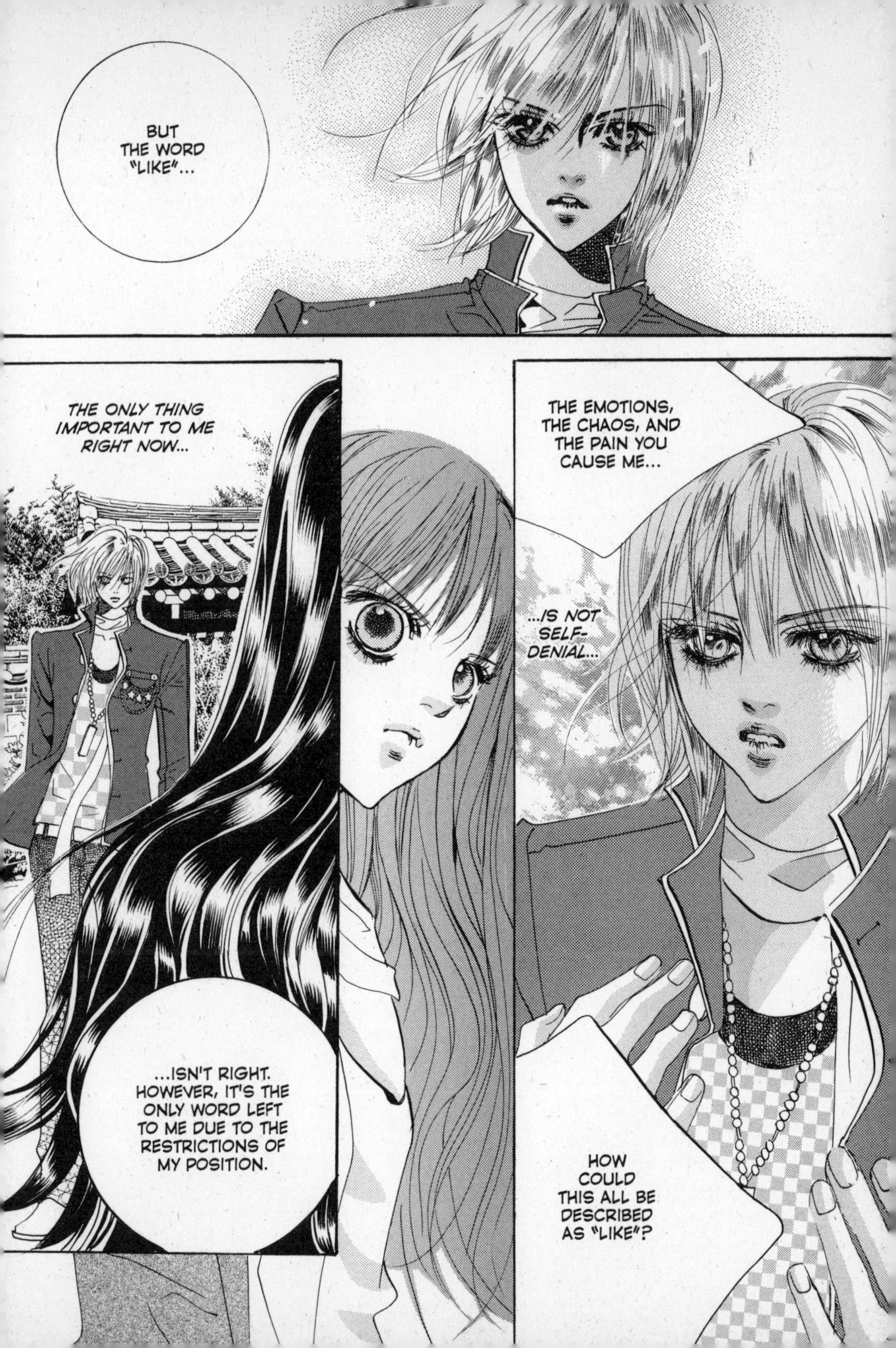
BUT THE WORD "LIKE"...
THE ONLY THING IMPORTANT TO ME RIGHT NOW...
...ISN'T RIGHT. HOWEVER, IT'S THE ONLY WORD LEFT TO ME DUE TO THE RESTRICTIONS OF MY POSITION.
THE EMOTIONS, THE CHAOS, AND THE PAIN YOU CAUSE ME...
...IS NOT SELF-DENIAL...
HOW COULD THIS ALL BE DESCRIBED AS "LIKE"?

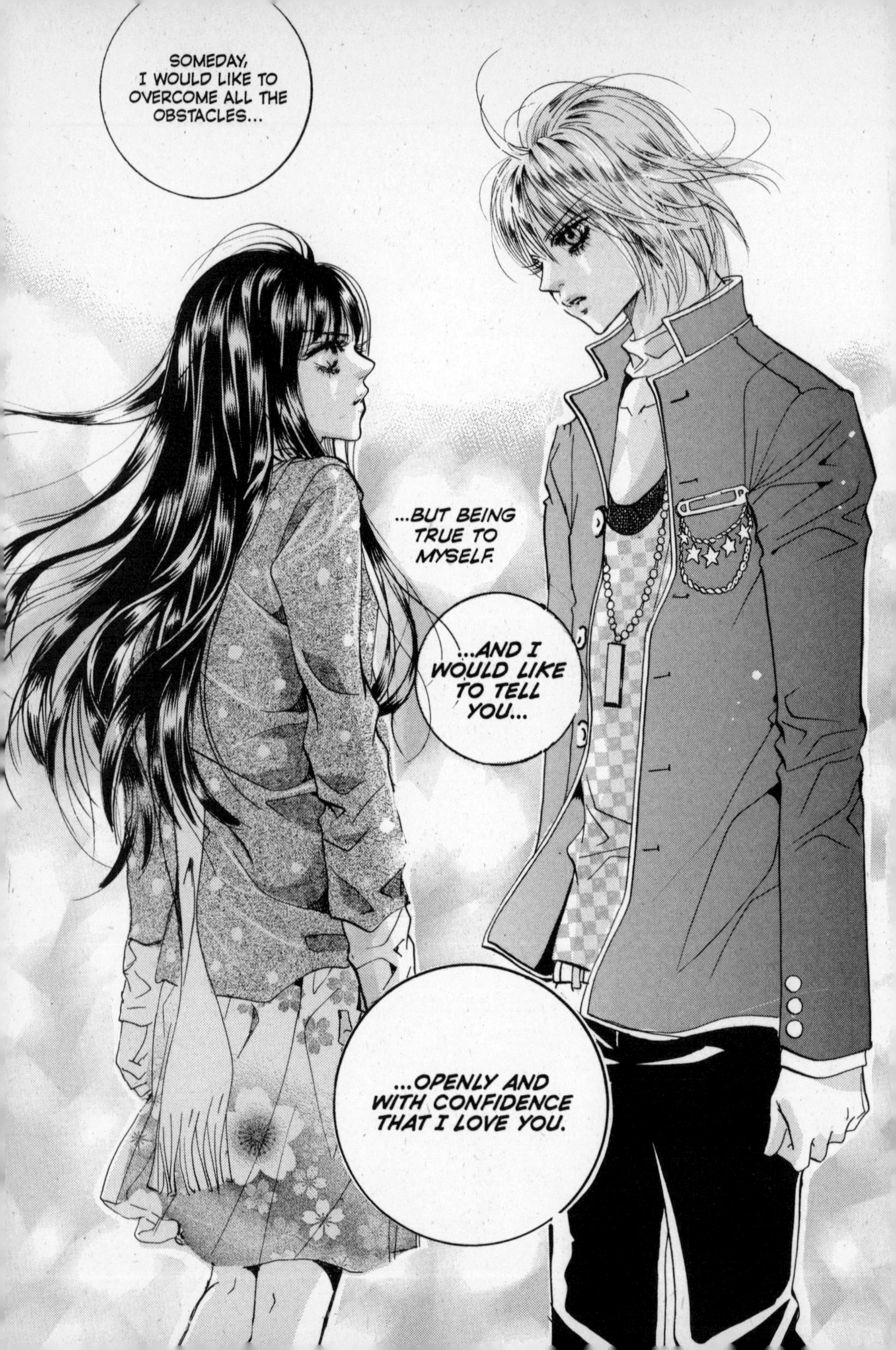
SOMEDAY, I WOULD LIKE TO OVERCOME ALL THE OBSTACLES...
...BUT BEING TRUE TO MYSELF.
...AND I WOULD LIKE TO TELL YOU...
...OPENLY AND WITH CONFIDENCE THAT I LOVE YOU.

THE ROYAL PALACE

Goong

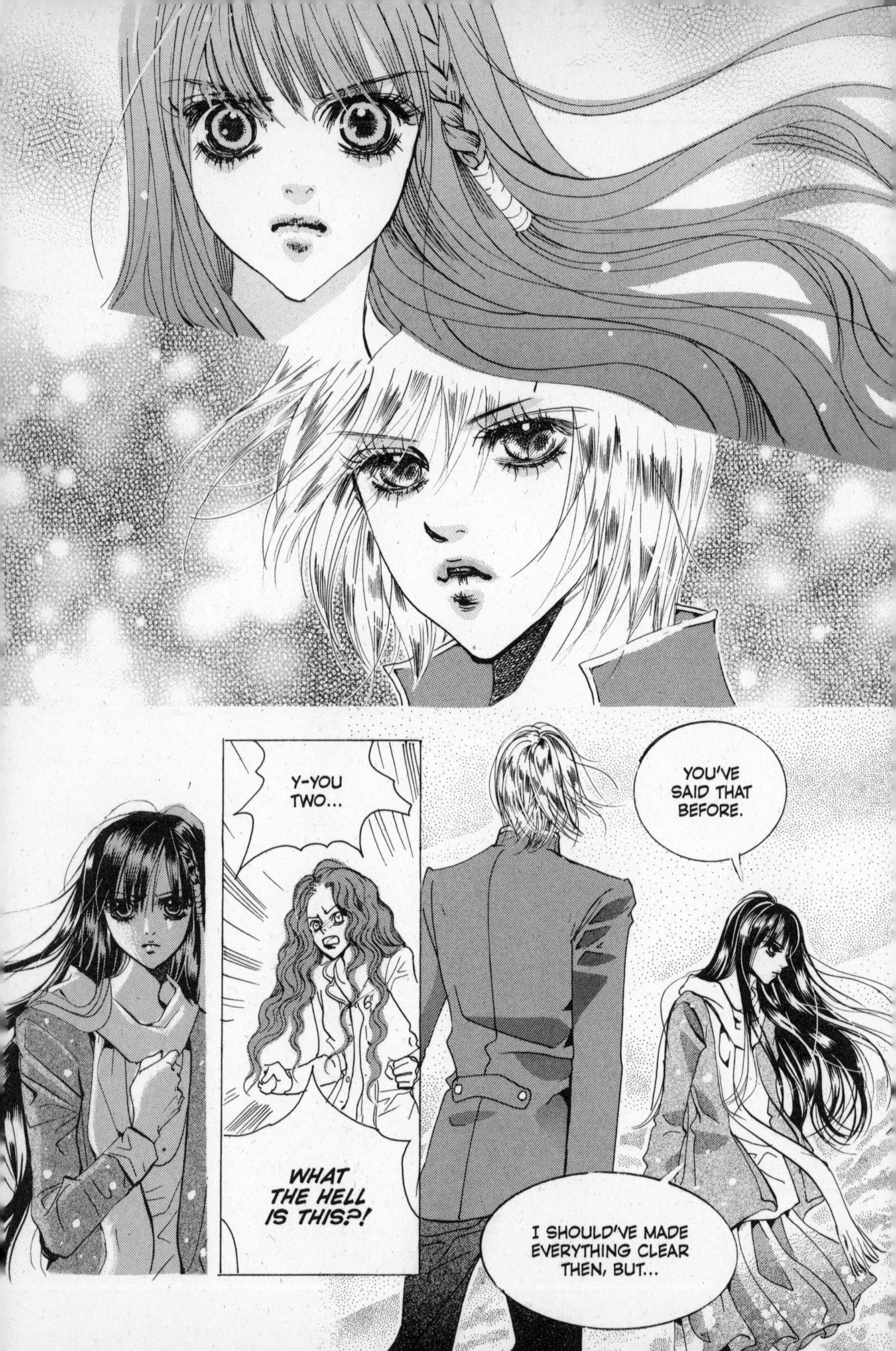
Y-YOU TWO...
WHAT THE HELL IS THIS?!
YOU'VE SAID THAT BEFORE.
I SHOULD'VE MADE EVERYTHING CLEAR THEN, BUT...

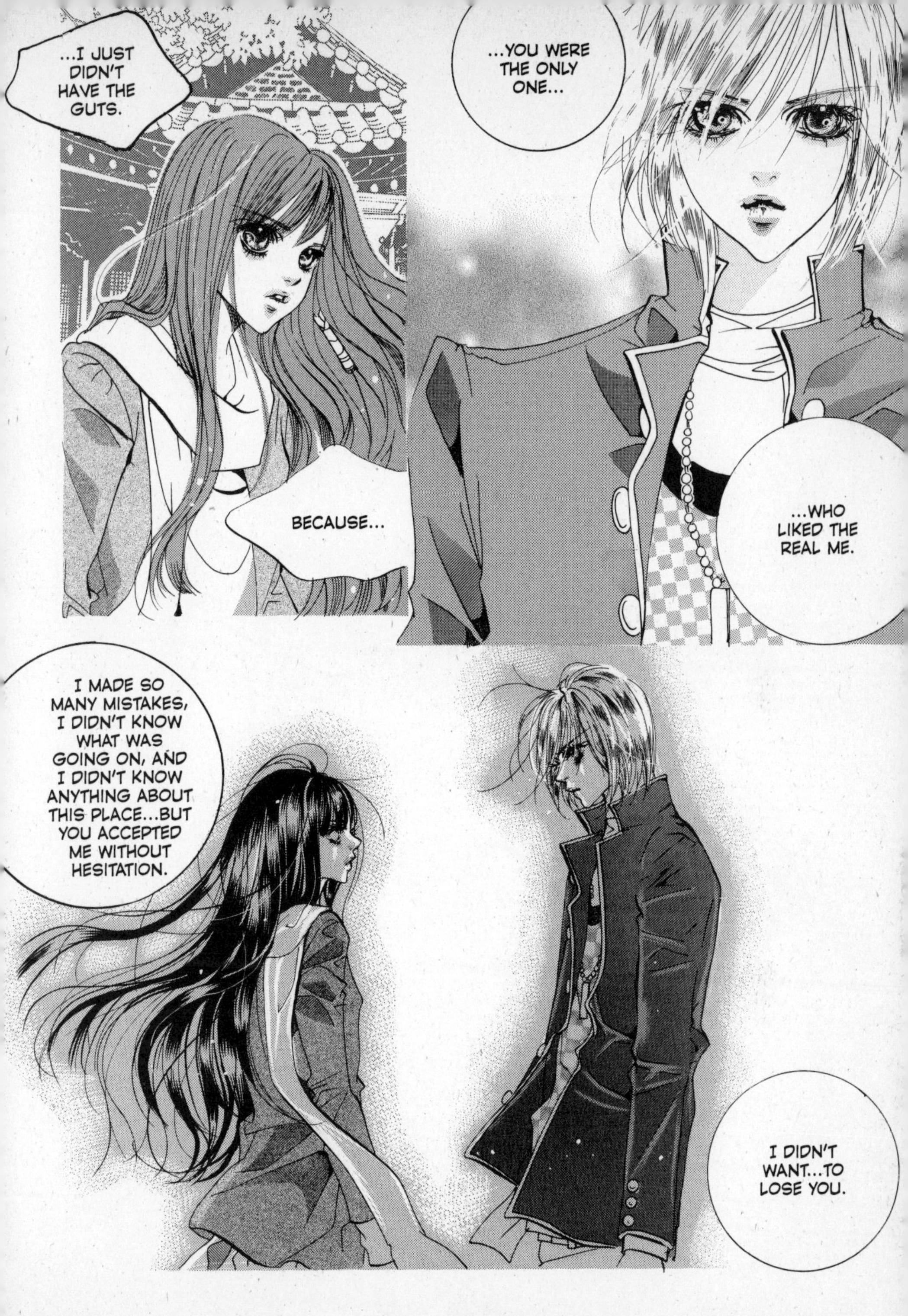
...I JUST DIDN'T HAVE THE GUTS.
BECAUSE...
...YOU WERE THE ONLY ONE...
...WHO LIKED THE REAL ME.
I MADE SO MANY MISTAKES, I DIDN'T KNOW WHAT WAS GOING ON, AND I DIDN'T KNOW ANYTHING ABOUT THIS PLACE...BUT YOU ACCEPTED ME WITHOUT HESITATION.
I DIDN'T WANT...TO LOSE YOU.

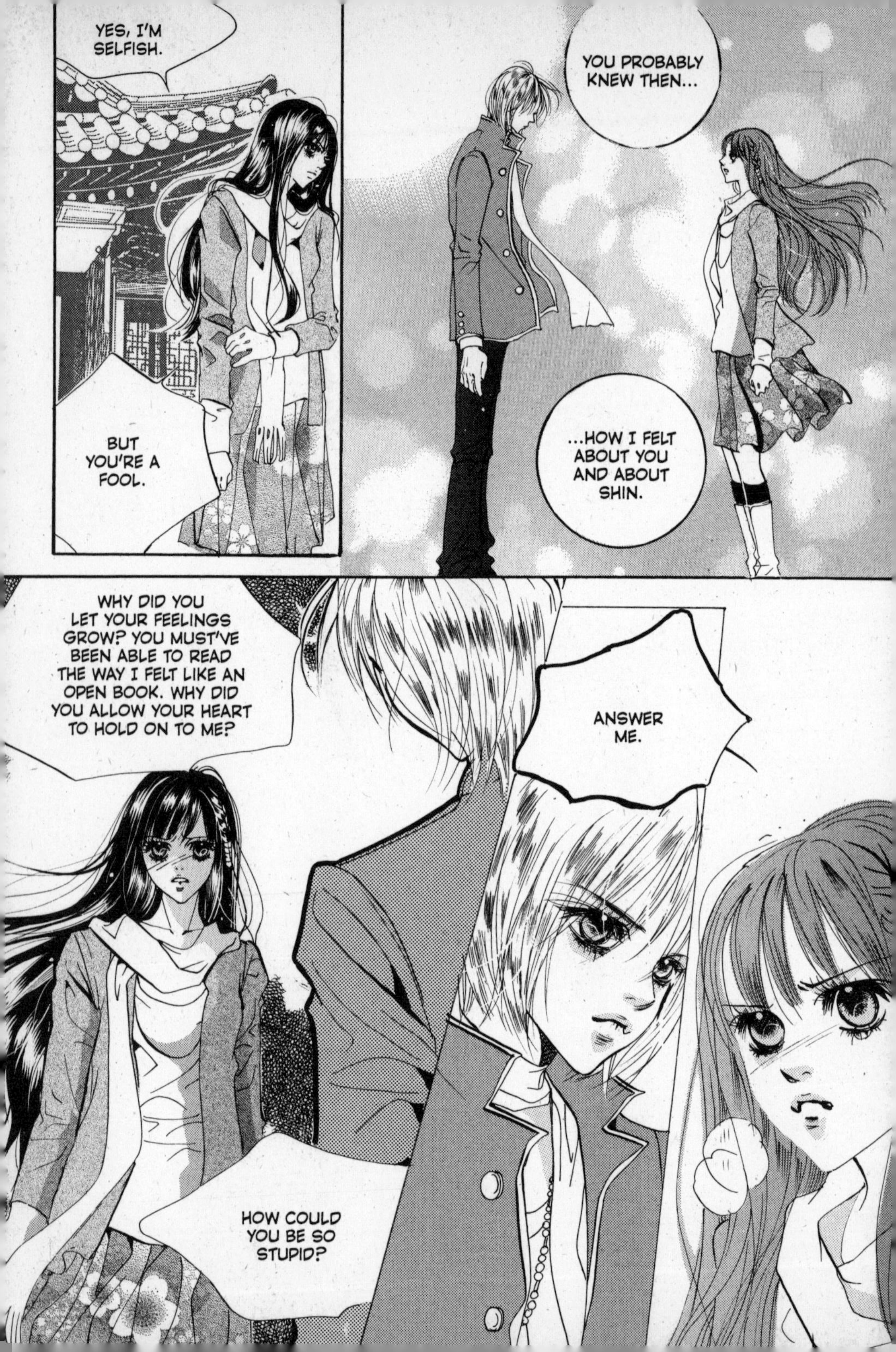
YES, I'M SELFISH.
BUT YOU'RE A FOOL.
YOU PROBABLY KNEW THEN...
...HOW I FELT ABOUT YOU AND ABOUT SHIN.
WHY DID YOU LET YOUR FEELINGS GROW? YOU MUST'VE BEEN ABLE TO READ THE WAY I FELT LIKE AN OPEN BOOK. WHY DID YOU ALLOW YOUR HEART TO HOLD ON TO ME?
ANSWER ME.
HOW COULD YOU BE SO STUPID?

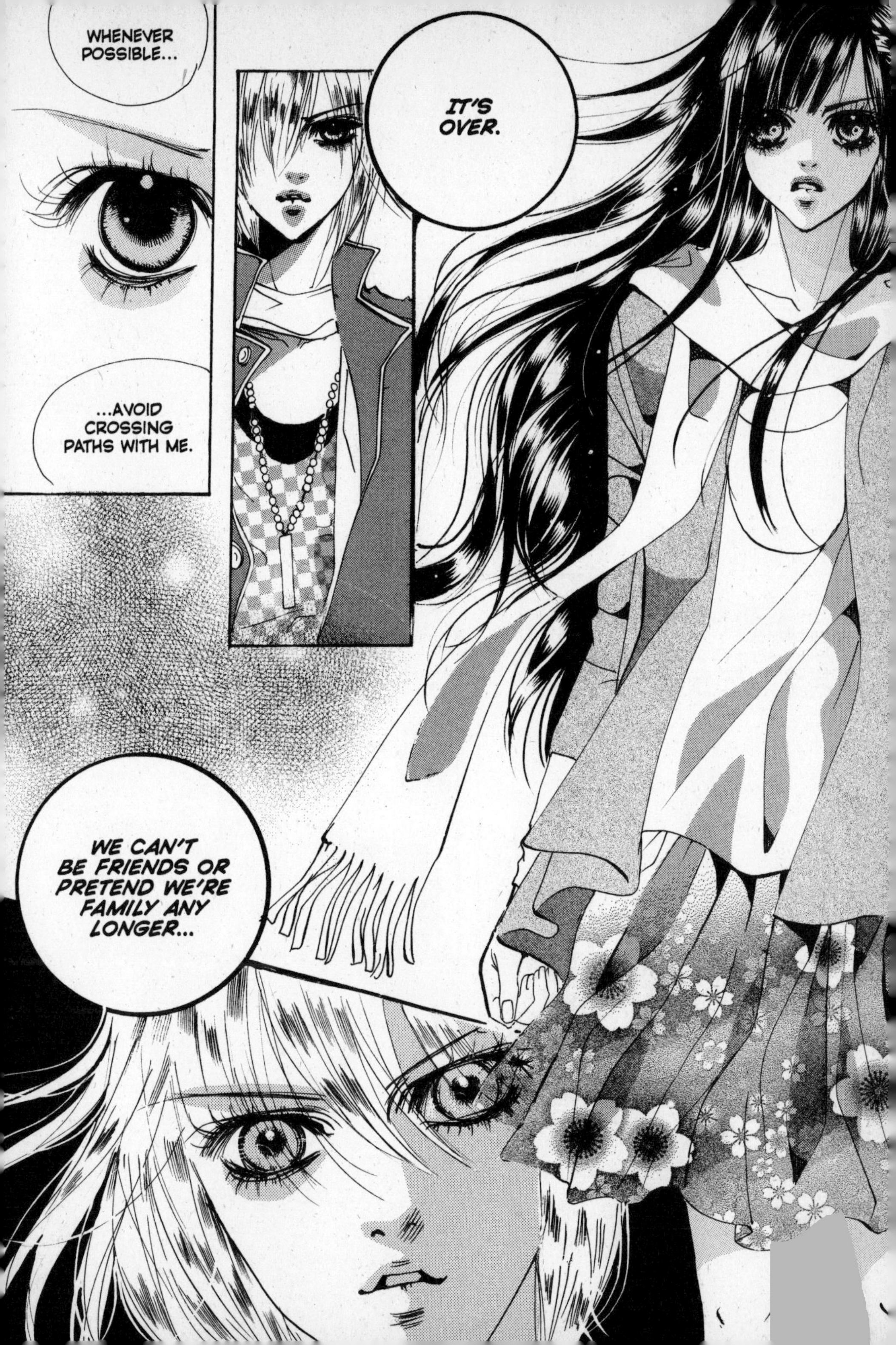
WHENEVER POSSIBLE...
...AVOID CROSSING PATHS WITH ME.
IT'S OVER.
WE CAN'T BE FRIENDS OR PRETEND WE'RE FAMILY ANY LONGER...

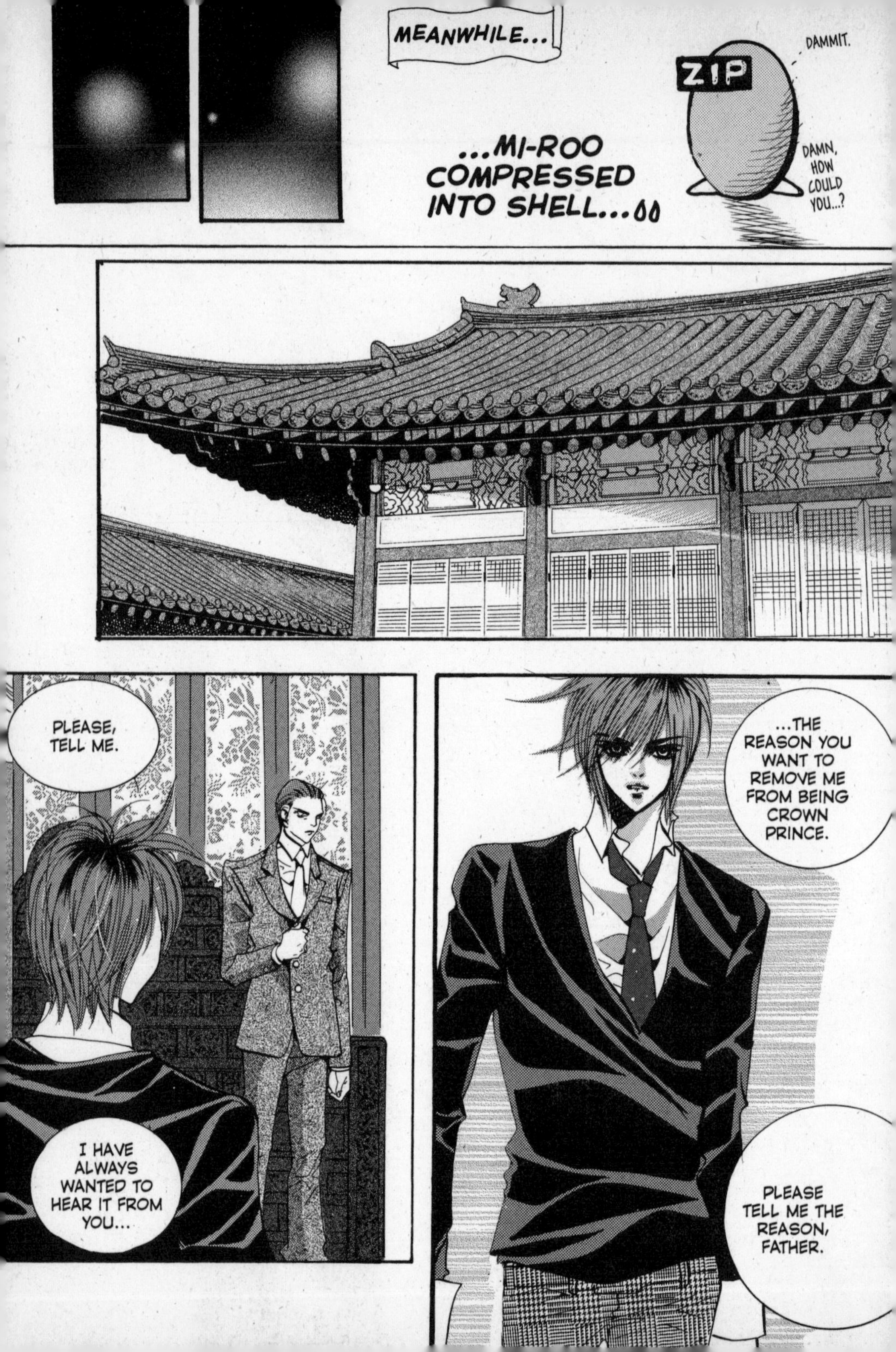
MEANWHILE...
...MI-ROO COMPRESSED INTO SHELL...
ZIP
DAMMIT.
DAMN, HOW COULD YOU...?
PLEASE, TELL ME.
I HAVE ALWAYS WANTED TO HEAR IT FROM YOU...
...THE REASON YOU WANT TO REMOVE ME FROM BEING CROWN PRINCE.
PLEASE TELL ME THE REASON, FATHER.

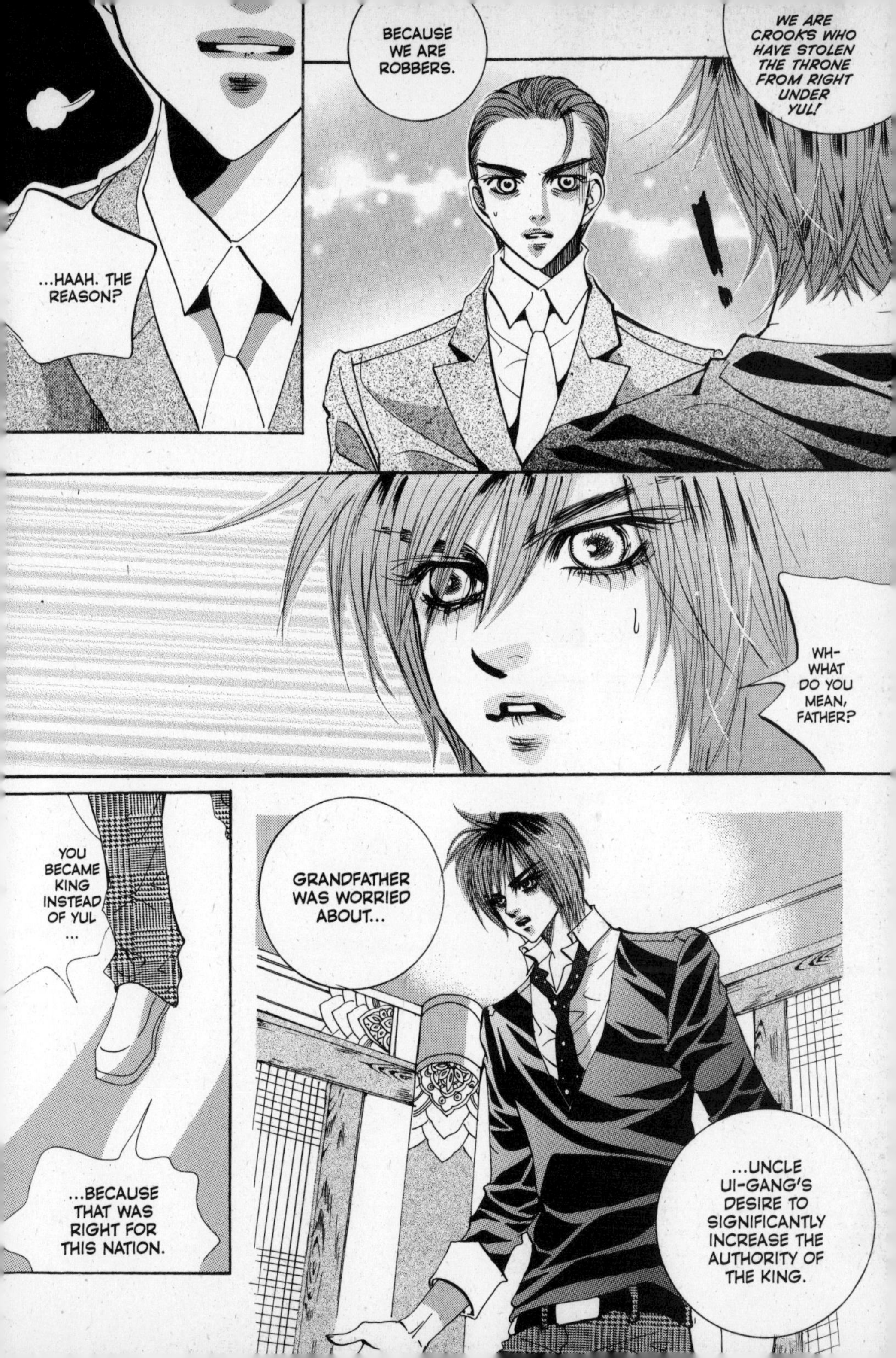
...HAAH. THE REASON?
BECAUSE WE ARE ROBBERS.
WE ARE CROOKS WHO HAVE STOLEN THE THRONE FROM RIGHT UNDER YUL!
WH- WHAT DO YOU MEAN, FATHER?
YOU BECAME KING INSTEAD OF YUL ...
...BECAUSE THAT WAS RIGHT FOR THIS NATION.
GRANDFATHER WAS WORRIED ABOUT...
...UNCLE UI-GANG'S DESIRE TO SIGNIFICANTLY INCREASE THE AUTHORITY OF THE KING.

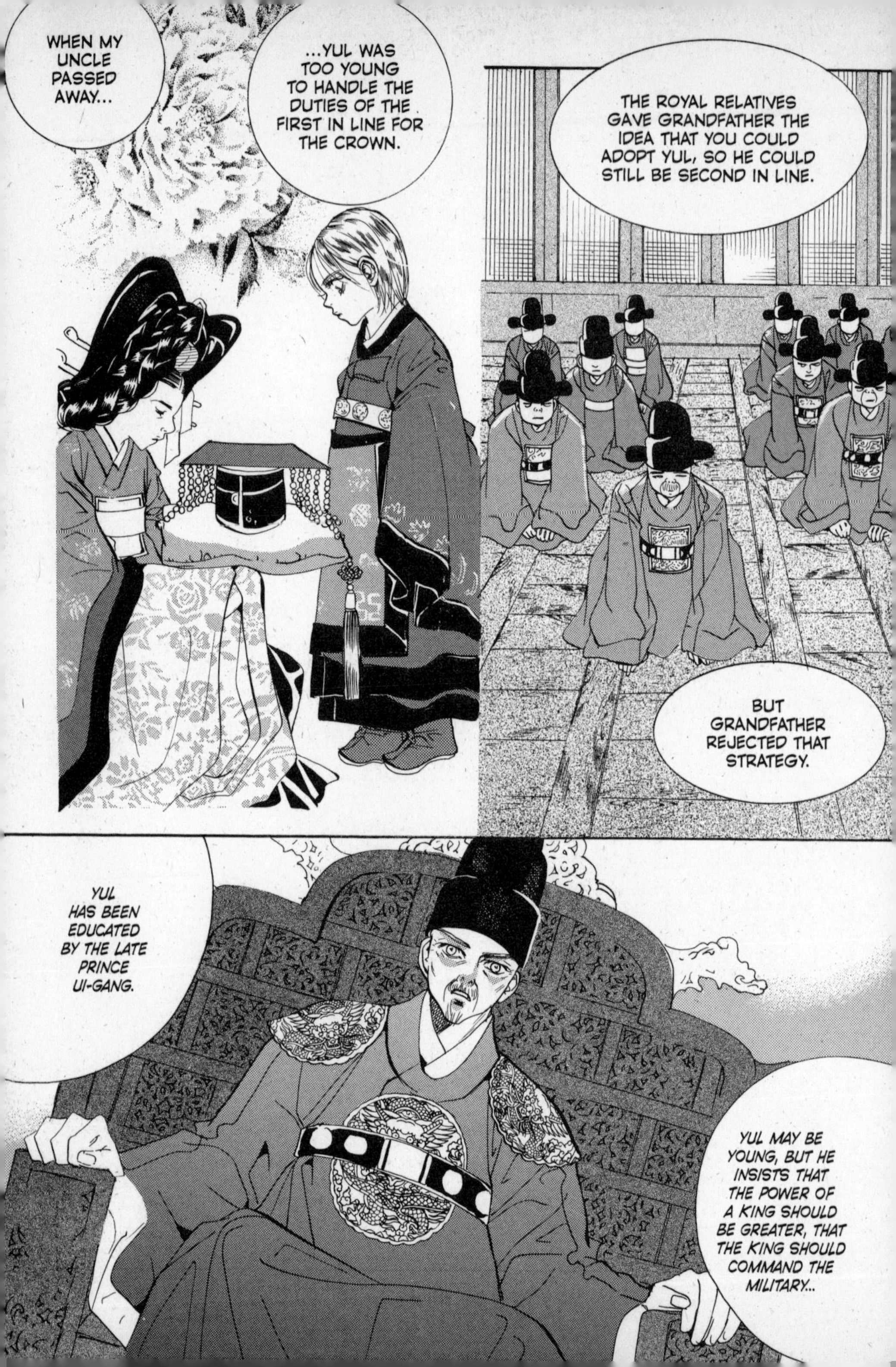
WHEN MY UNCLE PASSED AWAY...
...YUL WAS TOO YOUNG TO HANDLE THE DUTIES OF THE FIRST IN LINE FOR THE CROWN.
THE ROYAL RELATIVES GAVE GRANDFATHER THE IDEA THAT YOU COULD ADOPT YUL, SO HE COULD STILL BE SECOND IN LINE.
BUT GRANDFATHER REJECTED THAT STRATEGY.
YUL HAS BEEN EDUCATED BY THE LATE PRINCE UI-GANG.
YUL MAY BE YOUNG, BUT HE INSISTS THAT THE POWER OF A KING SHOULD BE GREATER, THAT THE KING SHOULD COMMAND THE MILITARY...

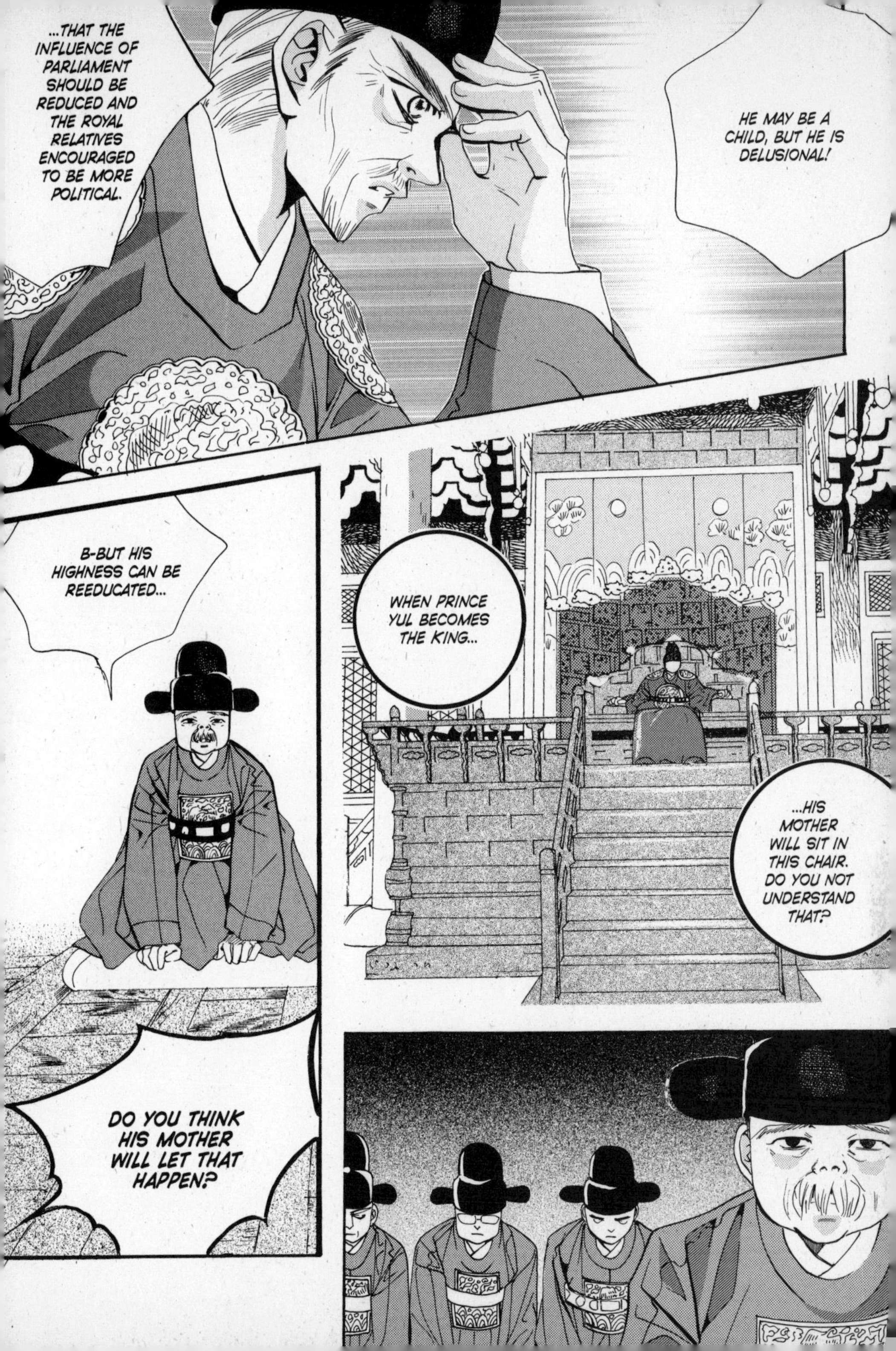
...THAT THE INFLUENCE OF PARLIAMENT SHOULD BE REDUCED AND THE ROYAL RELATIVES ENCOURAGED TO BE MORE POLITICAL.
HE MAY BE A CHILD, BUT HE IS DELUSIONAL!
B-BUT HIS HIGHNESS CAN BE REEDUCATED...
DO YOU THINK HIS MOTHER WILL LET THAT HAPPEN?
WHEN PRINCE YUL BECOMES THE KING...
...HIS MOTHER WILL SIT IN THIS CHAIR. DO YOU NOT UNDERSTAND THAT?

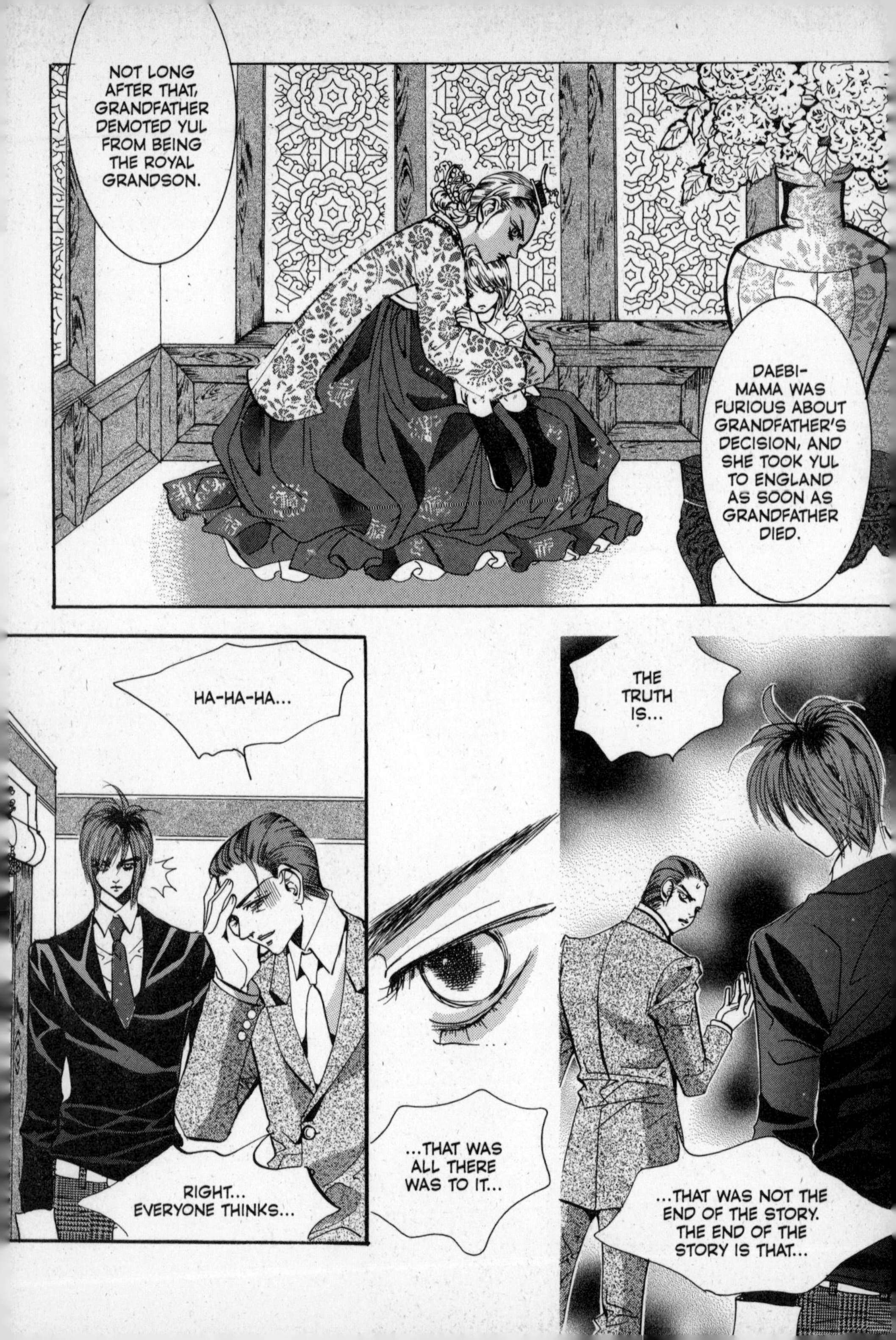
NOT LONG AFTER THAT, GRANDFATHER DEMOTED YUL FROM BEING THE ROYAL GRANDSON.
DAEBI-MAMA WAS FURIOUS ABOUT GRANDFATHER'S DECISION, AND SHE TOOK YUL TO ENGLAND AS SOON AS GRANDFATHER DIED.
HA-HA-HA...
RIGHT... EVERYONE THINKS...
...THAT WAS ALL THERE WAS TO IT...
THE TRUTH IS...
...THAT WAS NOT THE END OF THE STORY. THE END OF THE STORY IS THAT...

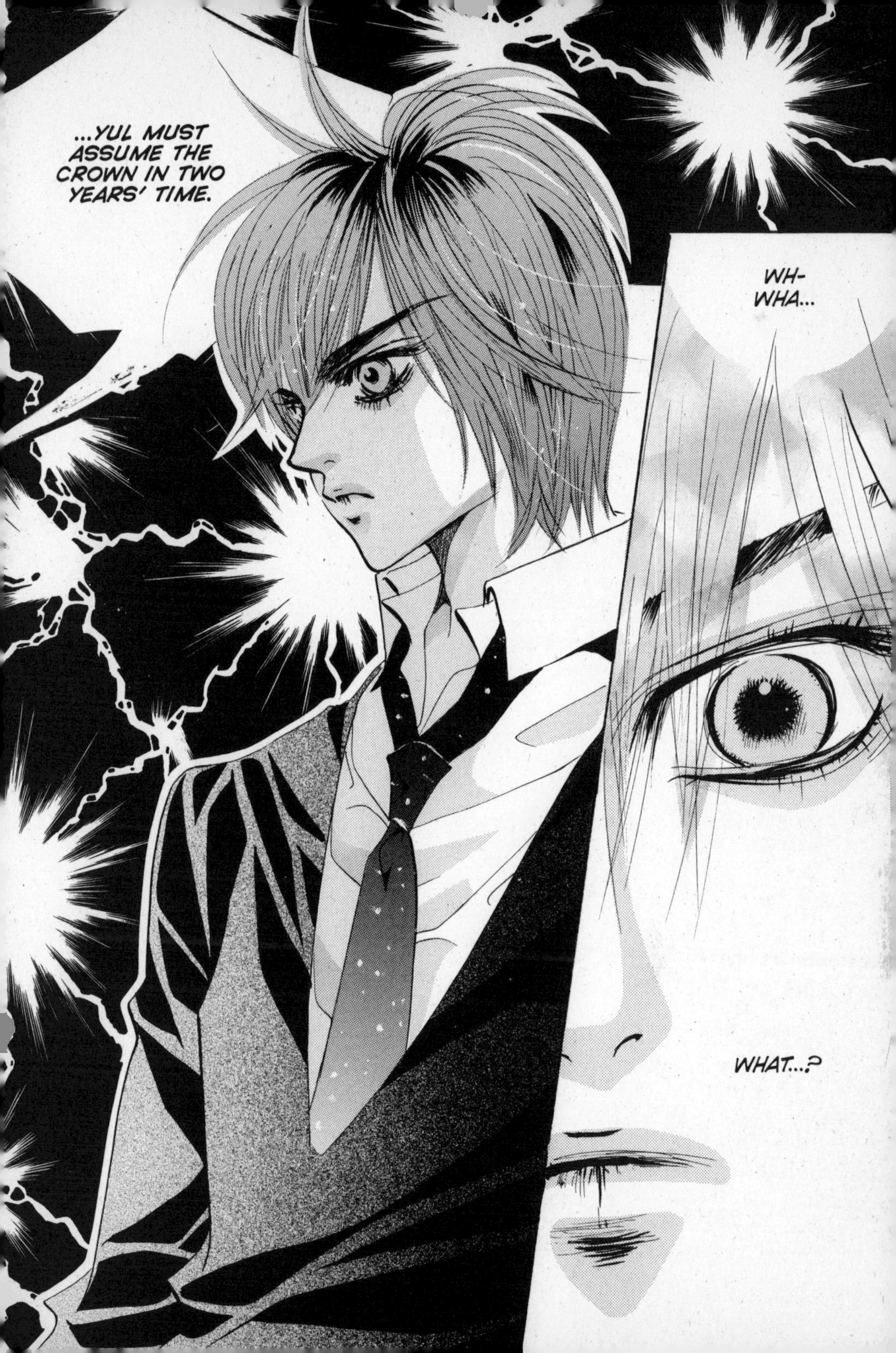
...YUL MUST ASSUME THE CROWN IN TWO YEARS' TIME.
WH- WHA...
WHAT...?

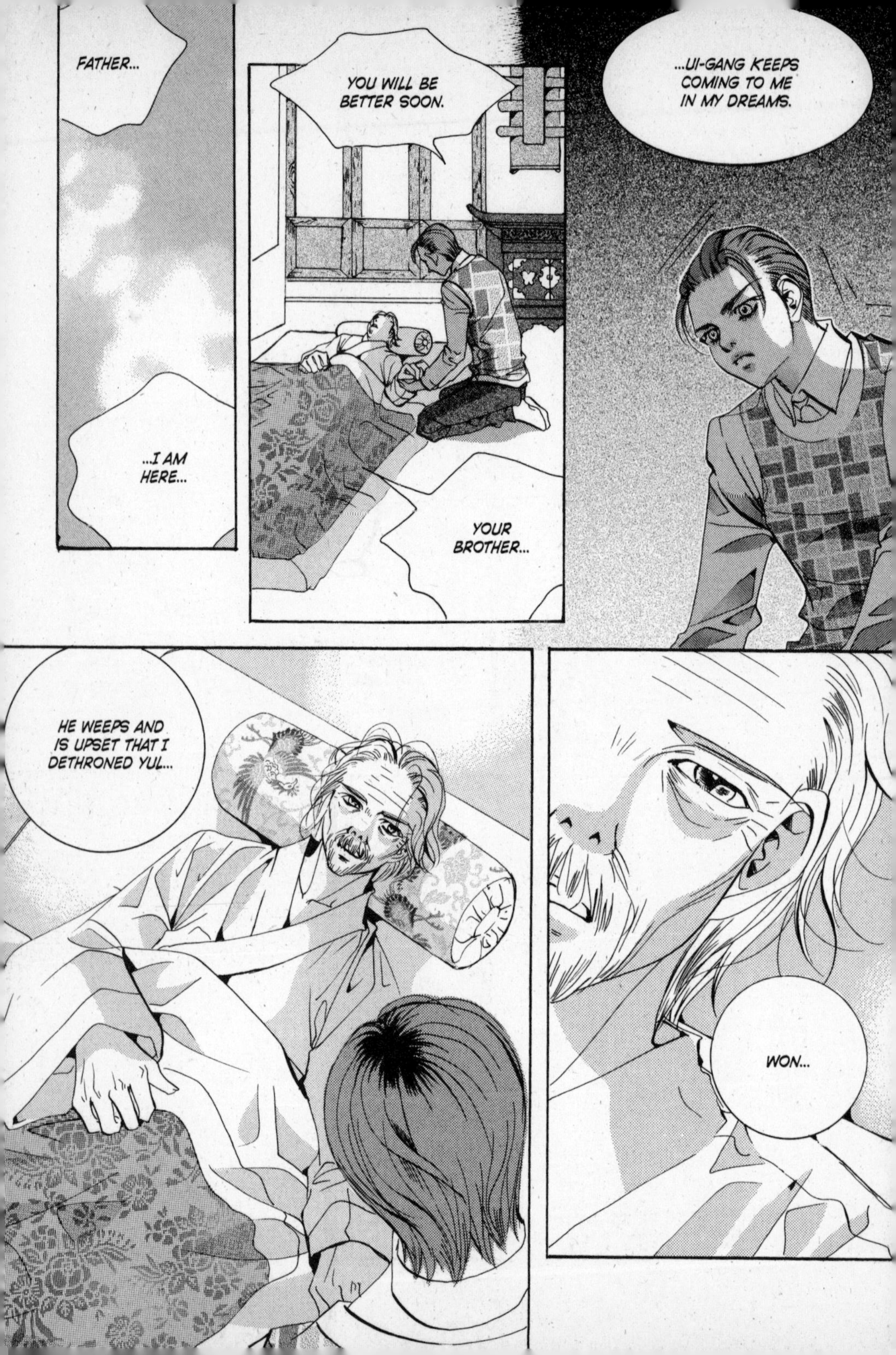
FATHER...
...I AM HERE...
YOU WILL BE BETTER SOON.
YOUR BROTHER...
...UI-GANG KEEPS COMING TO ME IN MY DREAMS.
HE WEEPS AND IS UPSET THAT I DETHRONED YUL...
WON...

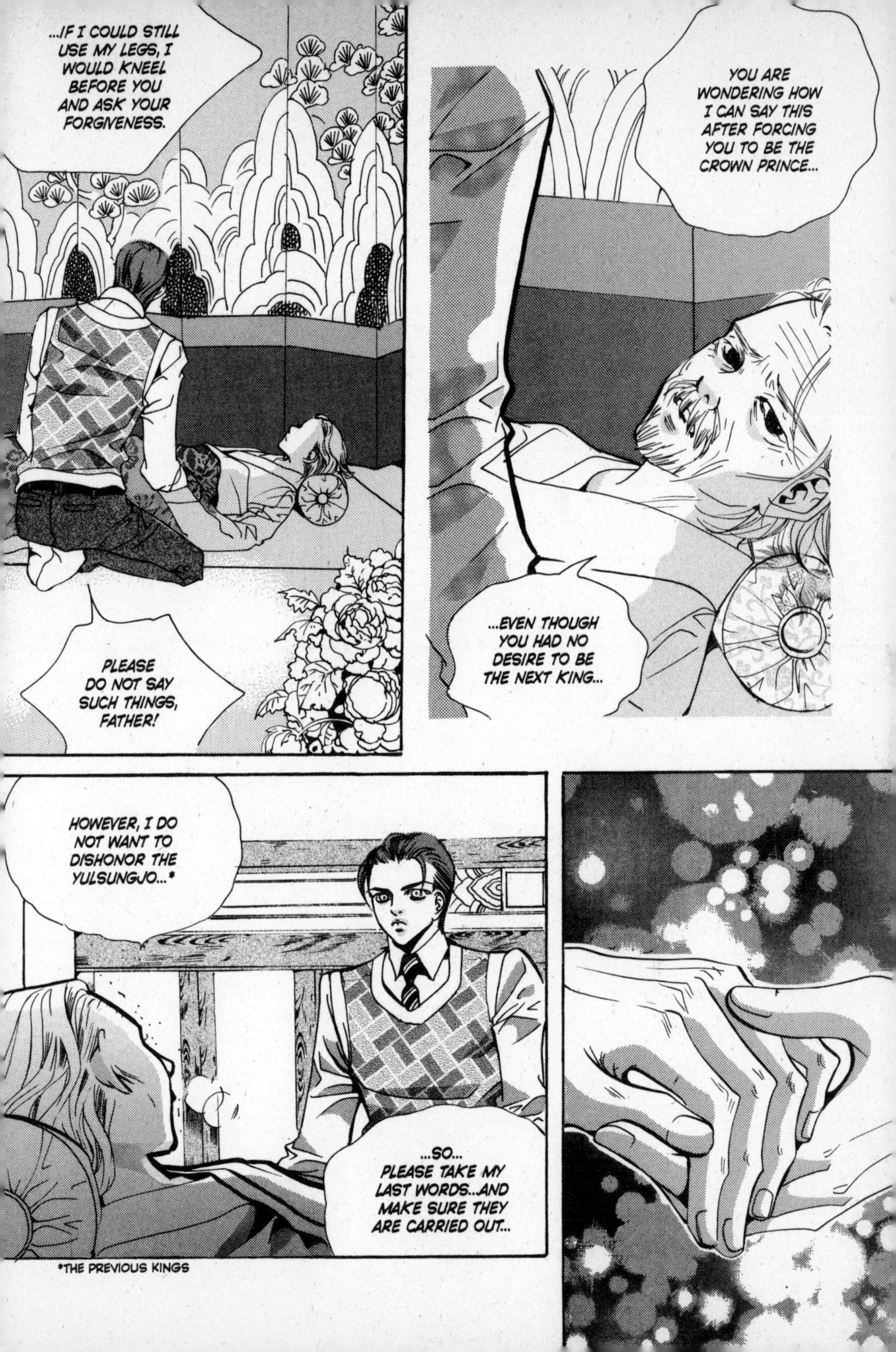
...IF I COULD STILL USE MY LEGS, I WOULD KNEEL BEFORE YOU AND ASK YOUR FORGIVENESS.
PLEASE DO NOT SAY SUCH THINGS, FATHER!
YOU ARE WONDERING HOW I CAN SAY THIS AFTER FORCING YOU TO BE THE CROWN PRINCE...
...EVEN THOUGH YOU HAD NO DESIRE TO BE THE NEXT KING...
HOWEVER, I DO NOT WANT TO DISHONOR THE YULSUNGJO...*
...SO... PLEASE TAKE MY LAST WORDS...AND MAKE SURE THEY ARE CARRIED OUT...

*THE PREVIOUS KINGS

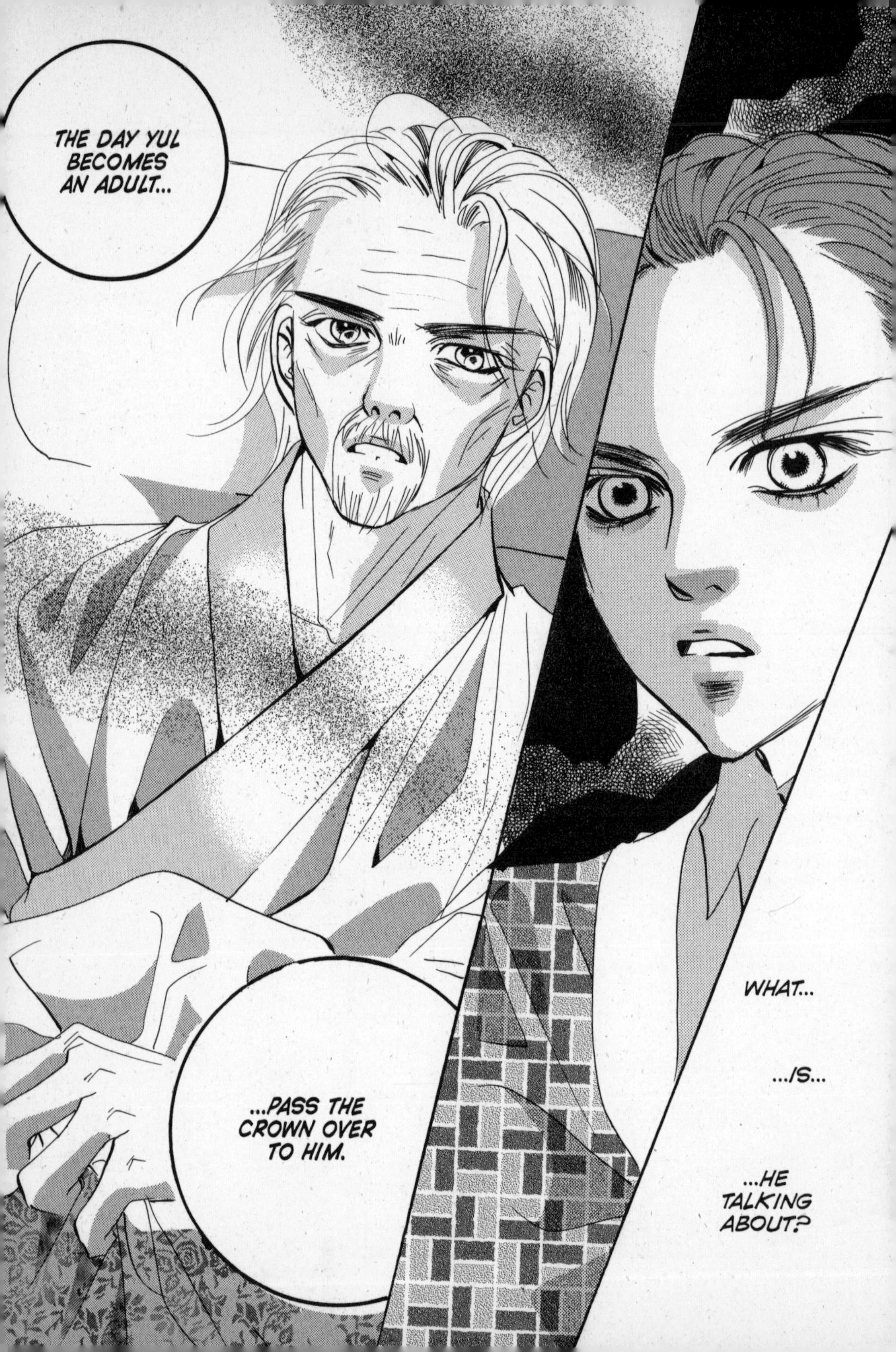
THE DAY YUL BECOMES AN ADULT...
...PASS THE CROWN OVER TO HIM.
WHAT...
...IS...
...HE TALKING ABOUT?

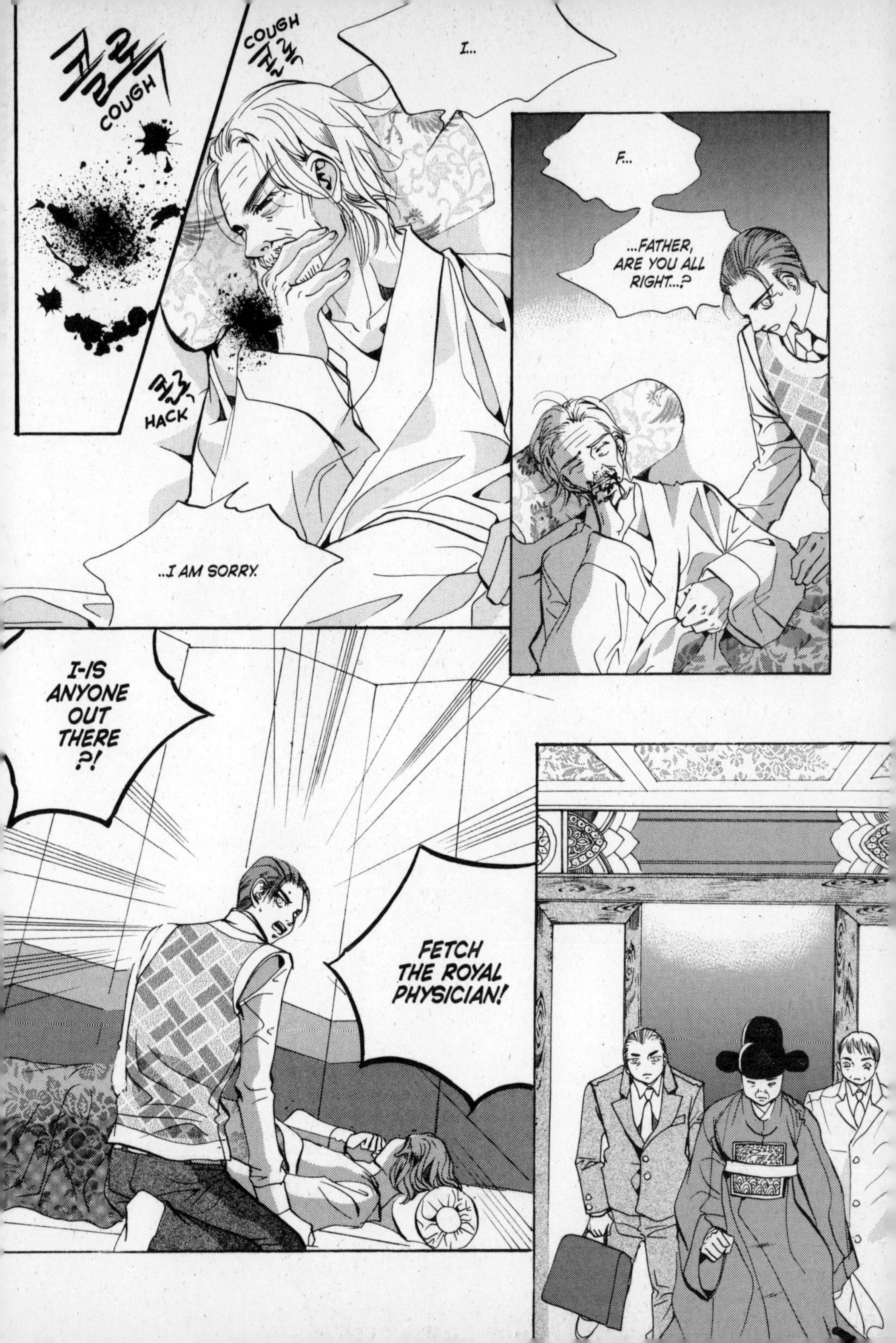
COUGH
COUGH
I...
HACK
...I AM SORRY.
F...
...FATHER, ARE YOU ALL RIGHT...?
I-IS ANYONE OUT THERE ?!
FETCH THE ROYAL PHYSICIAN!

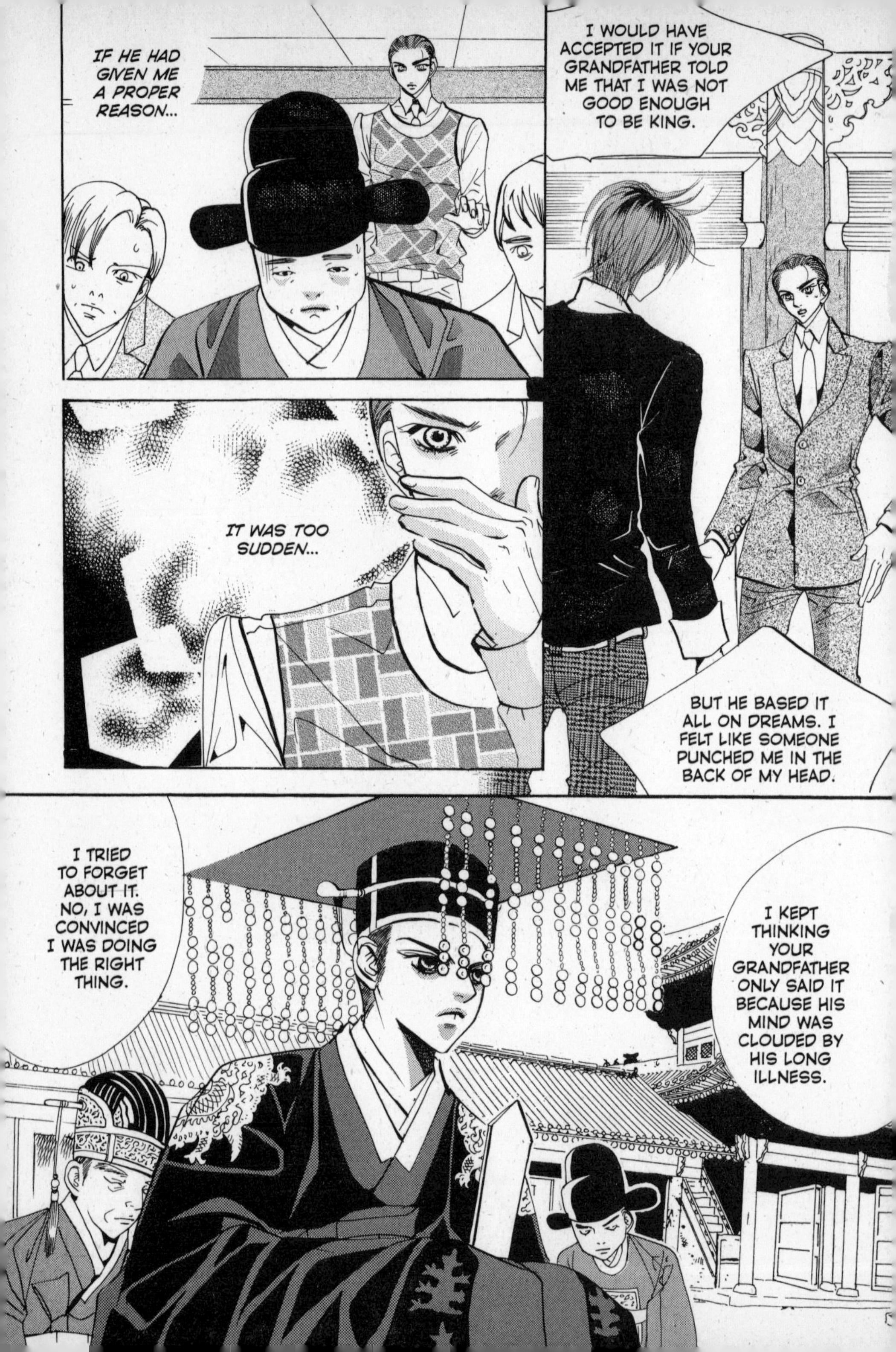
IF HE HAD GIVEN ME A PROPER REASON...
IT WAS TOO SUDDEN...
I WOULD HAVE ACCEPTED IT IF YOUR GRANDFATHER TOLD ME THAT I WAS NOT GOOD ENOUGH TO BE KING.
BUT HE BASED IT ALL ON DREAMS. I FELT LIKE SOMEONE PUNCHED ME IN THE BACK OF MY HEAD.
I TRIED TO FORGET ABOUT IT. NO, I WAS CONVINCED I WAS DOING THE RIGHT THING.
I KEPT THINKING YOUR GRANDFATHER ONLY SAID IT BECAUSE HIS MIND WAS CLOUDED BY HIS LONG ILLNESS.

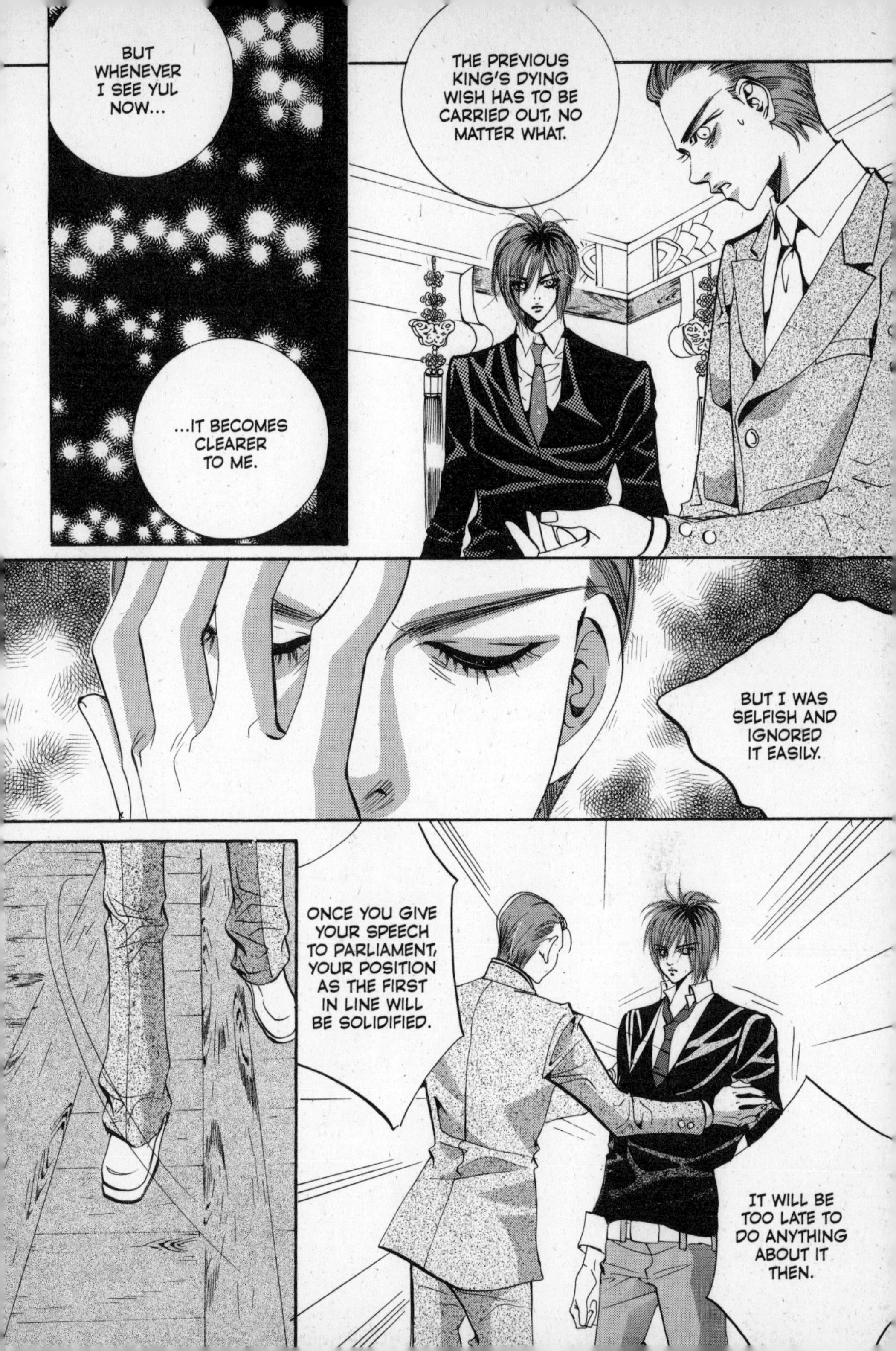
BUT WHENEVER I SEE YUL NOW...
...IT BECOMES CLEARER TO ME.
THE PREVIOUS KING'S DYING WISH HAS TO BE CARRIED OUT, NO MATTER WHAT.
BUT I WAS SELFISH AND IGNORED IT EASILY.
ONCE YOU GIVE YOUR SPEECH TO PARLIAMENT, YOUR POSITION AS THE FIRST IN LINE WILL BE SOLIDIFIED.
IT WILL BE TOO LATE TO DO ANYTHING ABOUT IT THEN.

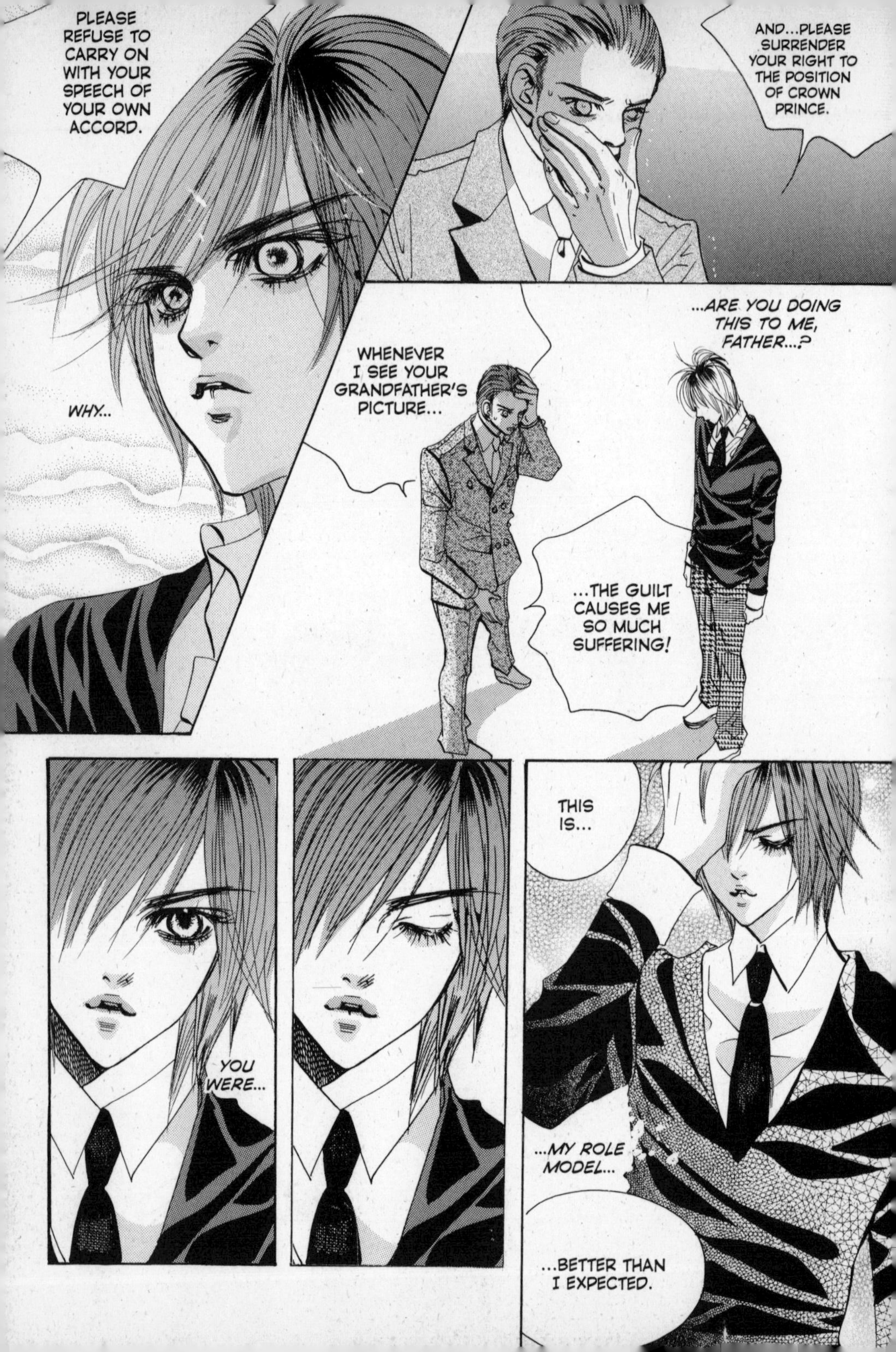
PLEASE REFUSE TO CARRY ON WITH YOUR SPEECH OF YOUR OWN ACCORD.
WHY...
AND...PLEASE SURRENDER YOUR RIGHT TO THE POSITION OF CROWN PRINCE.
WHENEVER I SEE YOUR GRANDFATHER'S PICTURE...
...ARE YOU DOING THIS TO ME, FATHER...?
...THE GUILT CAUSES ME SO MUCH SUFFERING!
YOU WERE...
THIS IS...
...MY ROLE MODEL...
...BETTER THAN I EXPECTED.

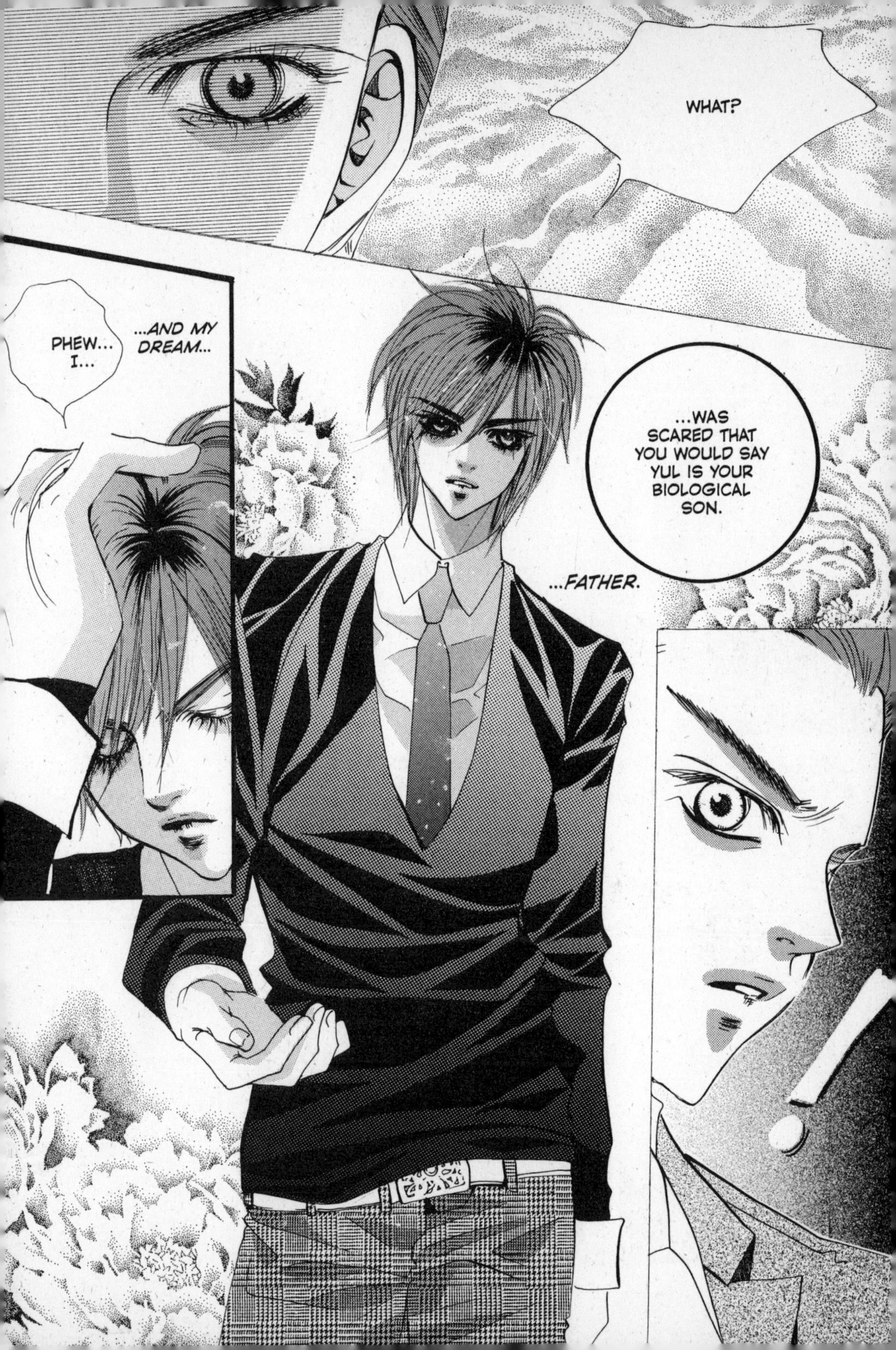
WHAT?
PHEW... I...
...AND MY DREAM...
...WAS SCARED THAT YOU WOULD SAY YUL IS YOUR BIOLOGICAL SON.
...FATHER.

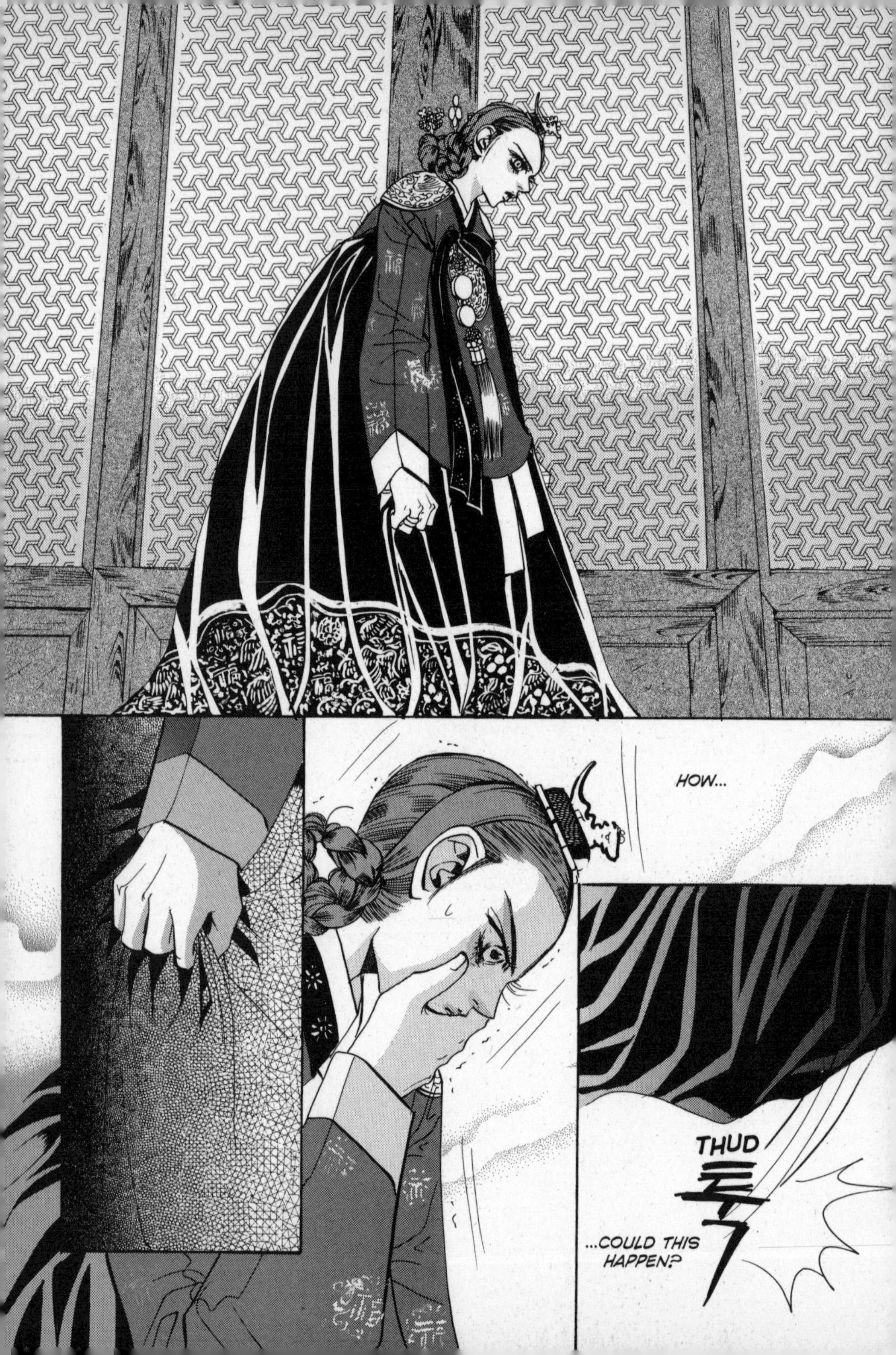
HOW...
...COULD THIS HAPPEN?
THUD
툭

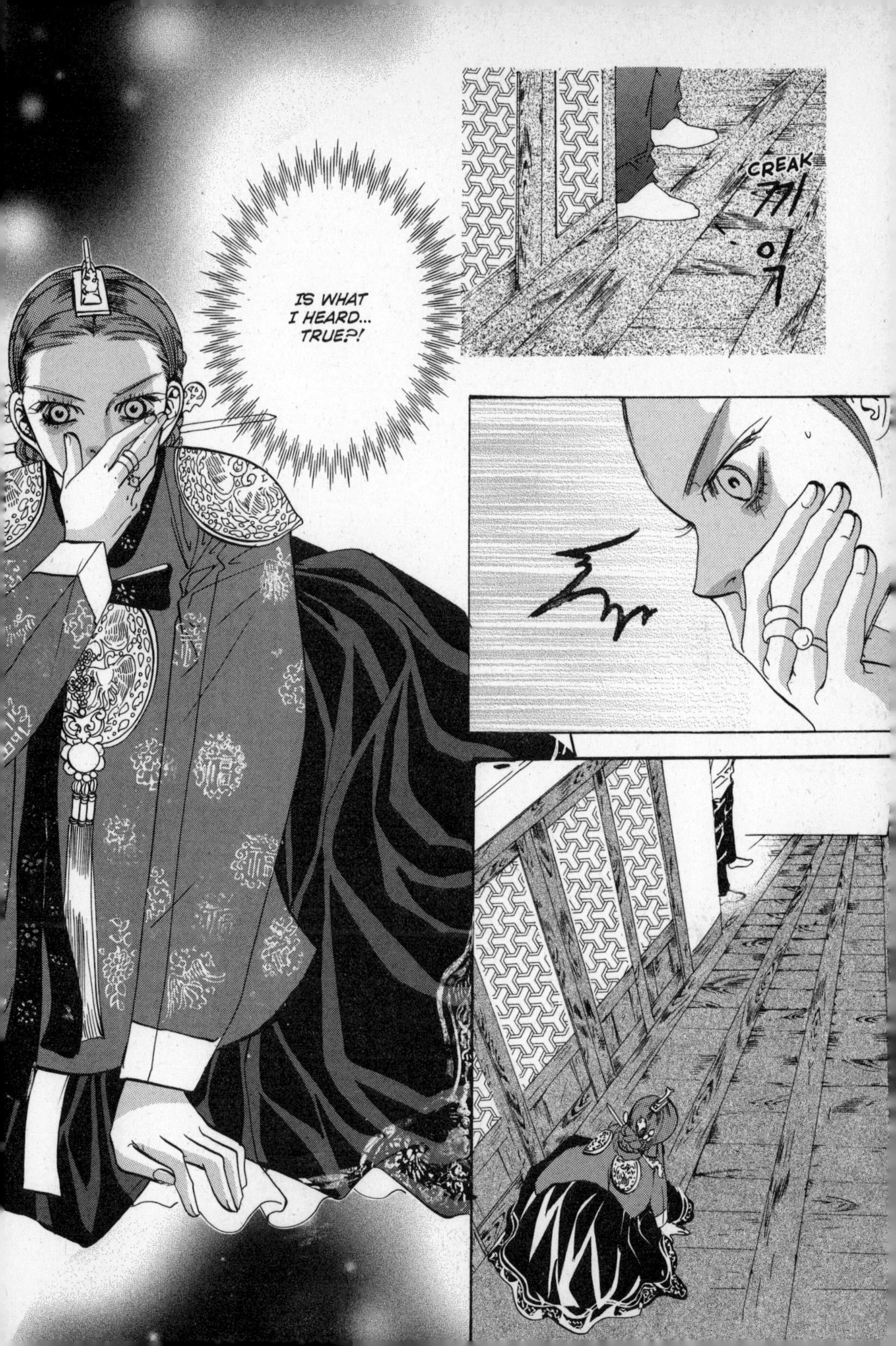
IS WHAT I HEARD... TRUE?!
CREAK

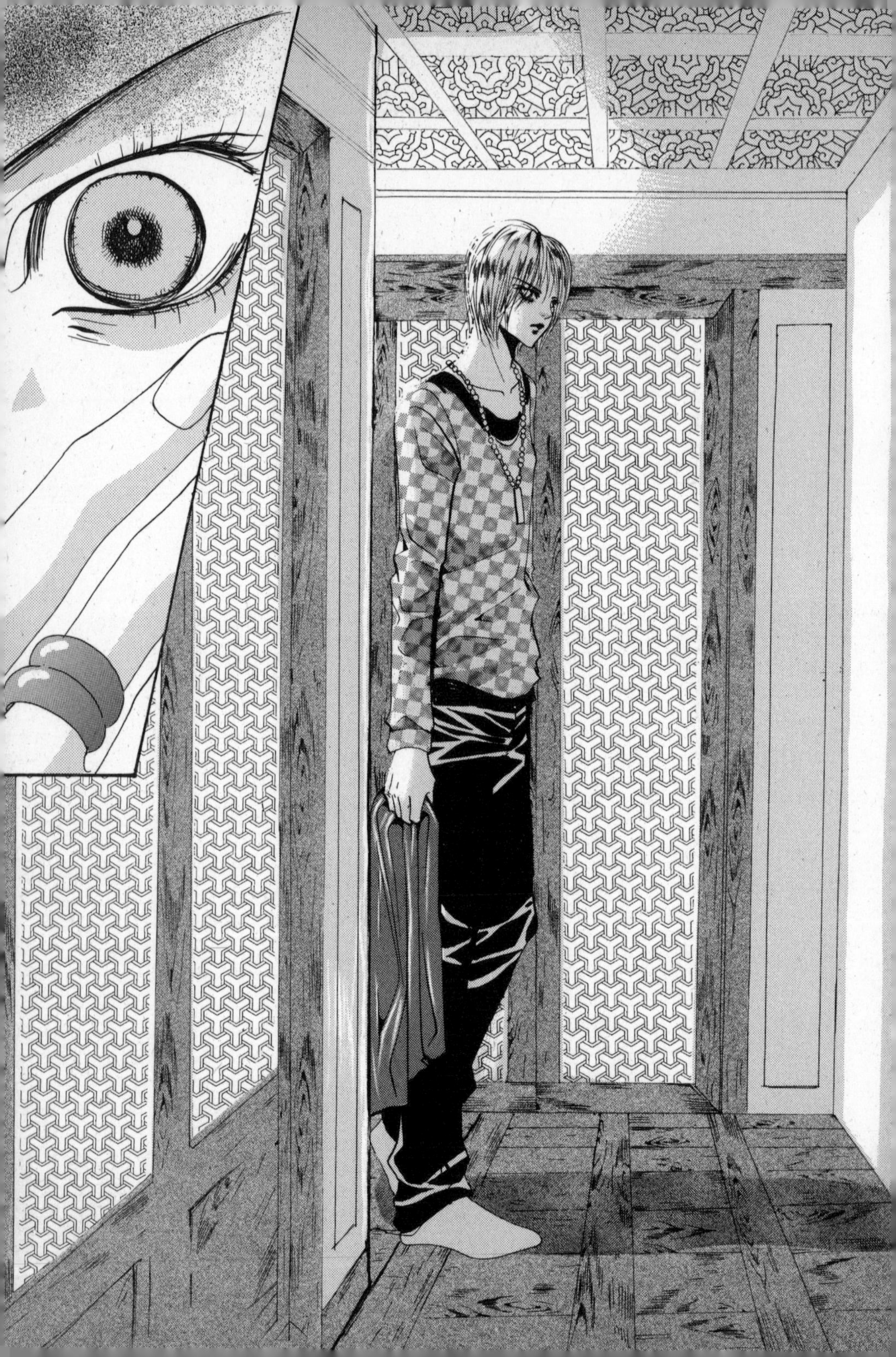

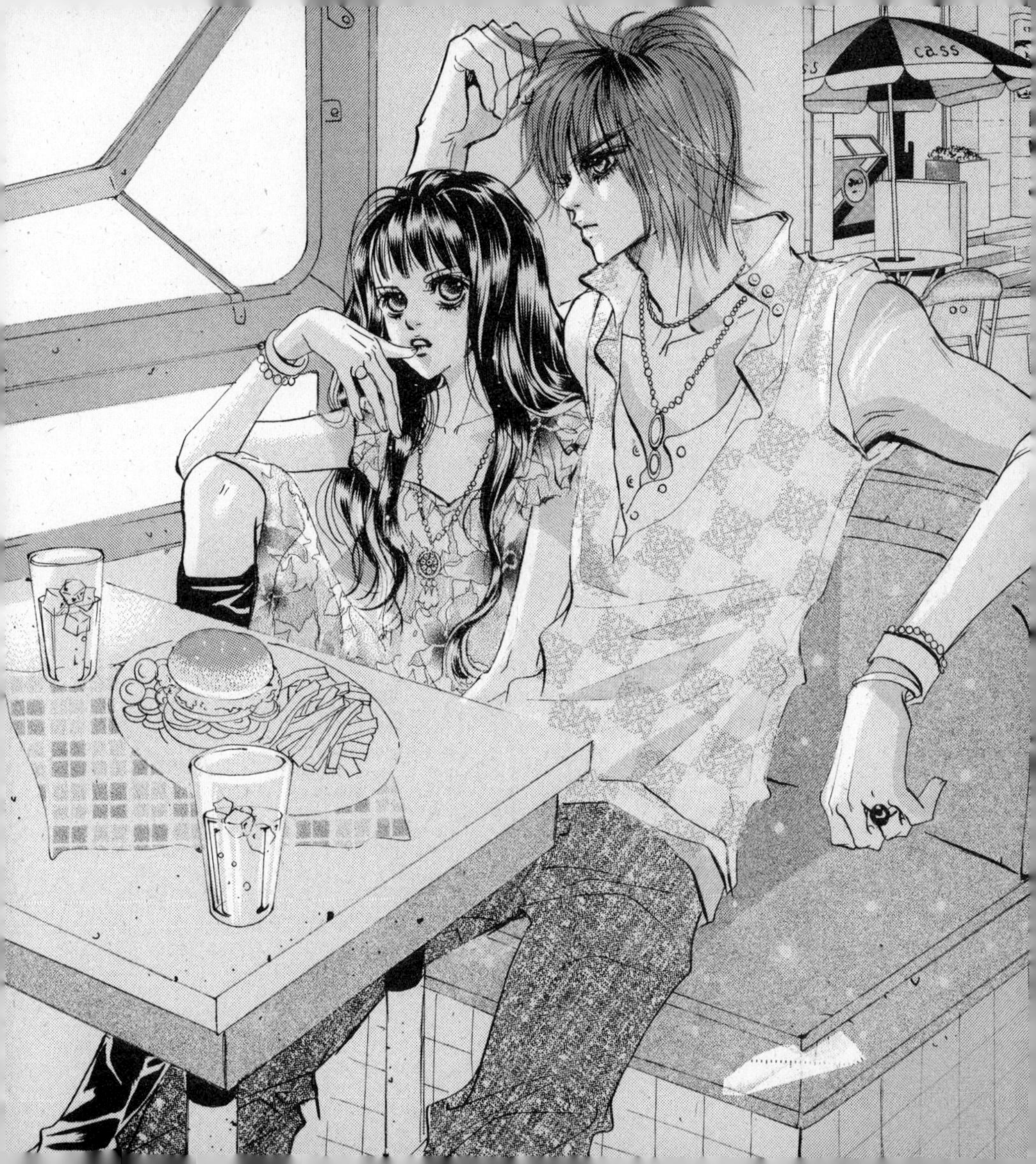
cass

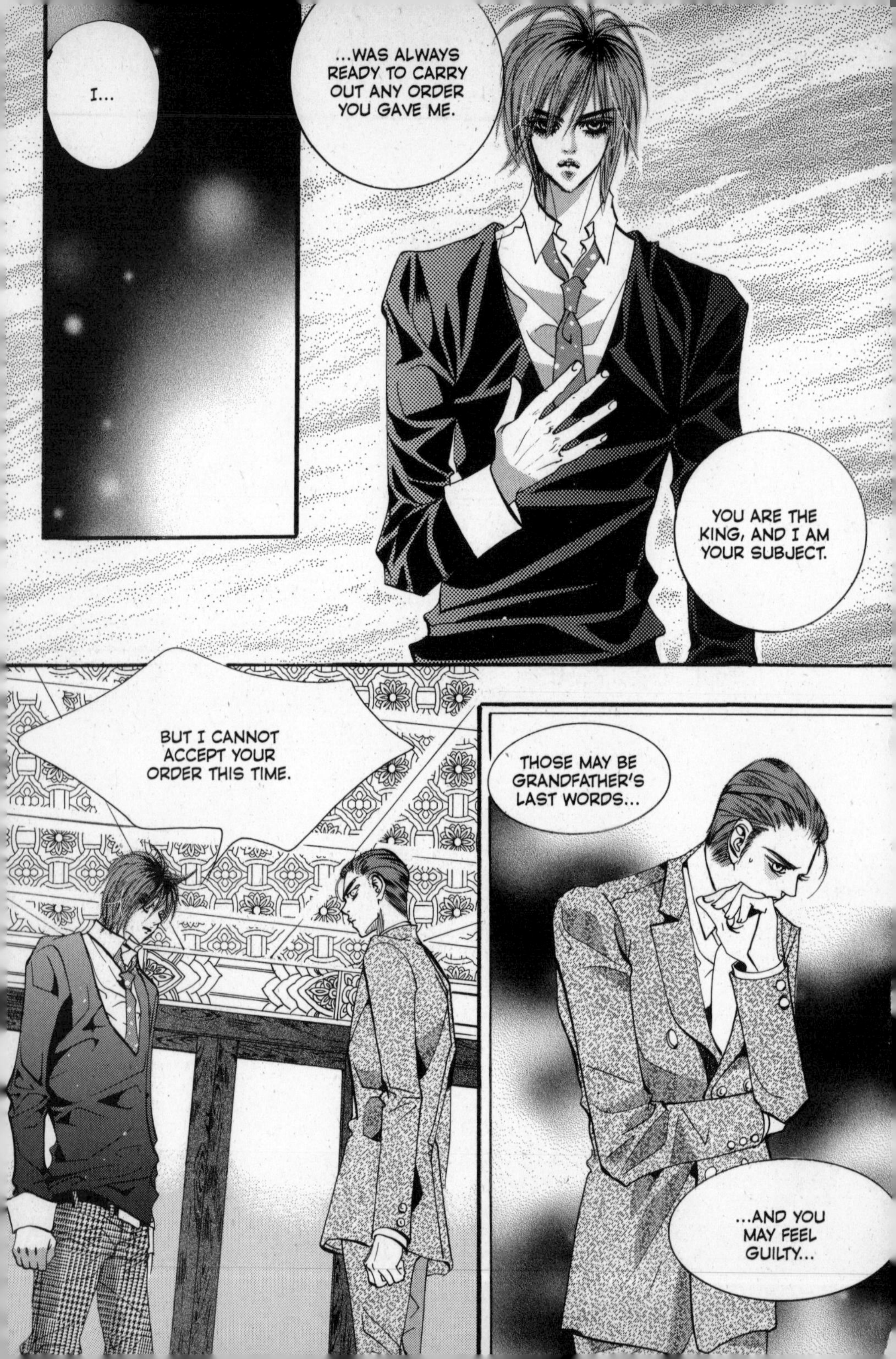
I...
...WAS ALWAYS READY TO CARRY OUT ANY ORDER YOU GAVE ME.
YOU ARE THE KING, AND I AM YOUR SUBJECT.
BUT I CANNOT ACCEPT YOUR ORDER THIS TIME.
THOSE MAY BE GRANDFATHER'S LAST WORDS...
...AND YOU MAY FEEL GUILTY...

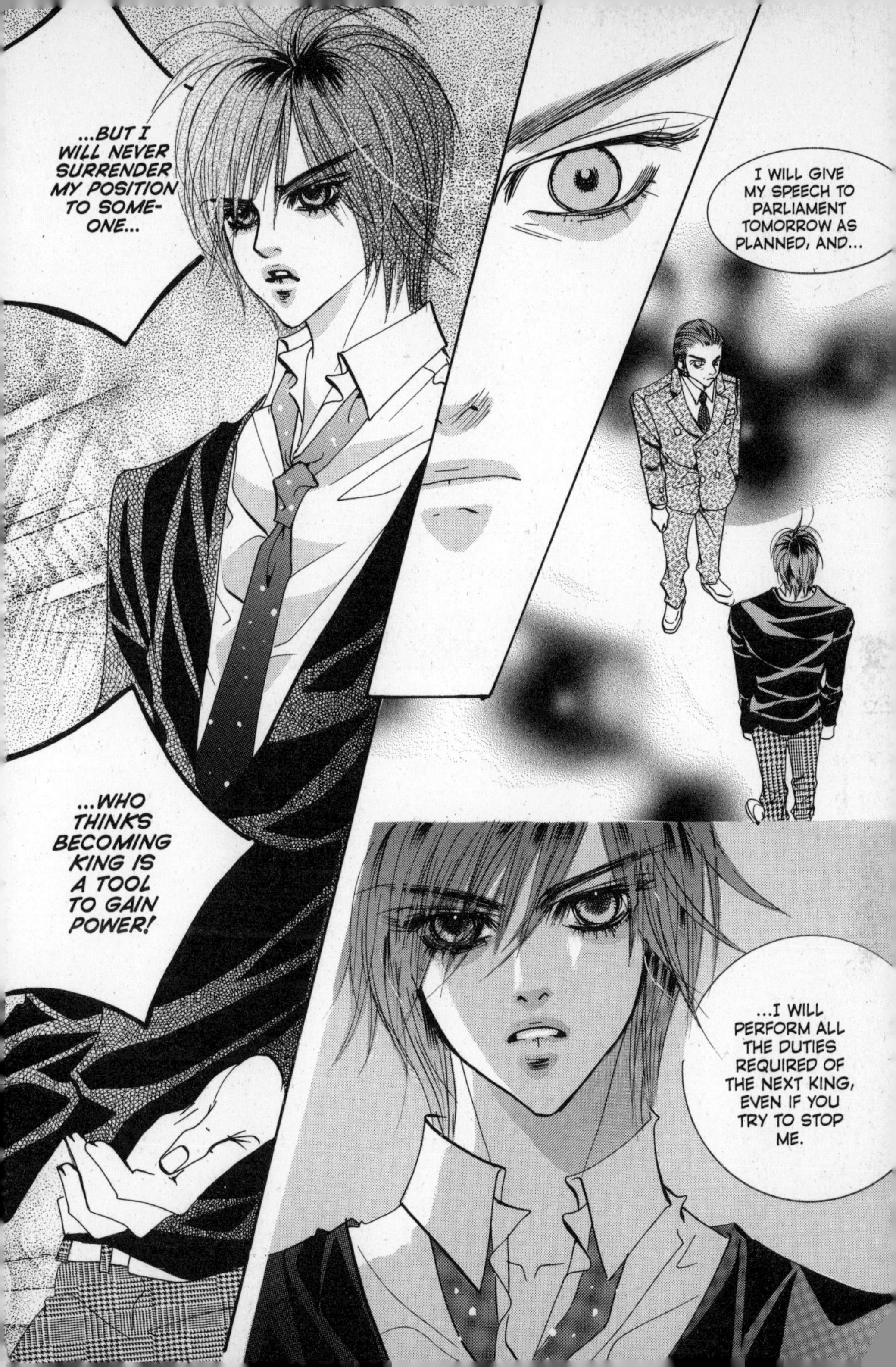
...BUT I WILL NEVER SURRENDER MY POSITION TO SOME-ONE...
...WHO THINKS BECOMING KING IS A TOOL TO GAIN POWER!
I WILL GIVE MY SPEECH TO PARLIAMENT TOMORROW AS PLANNED, AND...
...I WILL PERFORM ALL THE DUTIES REQUIRED OF THE NEXT KING, EVEN IF YOU TRY TO STOP ME.

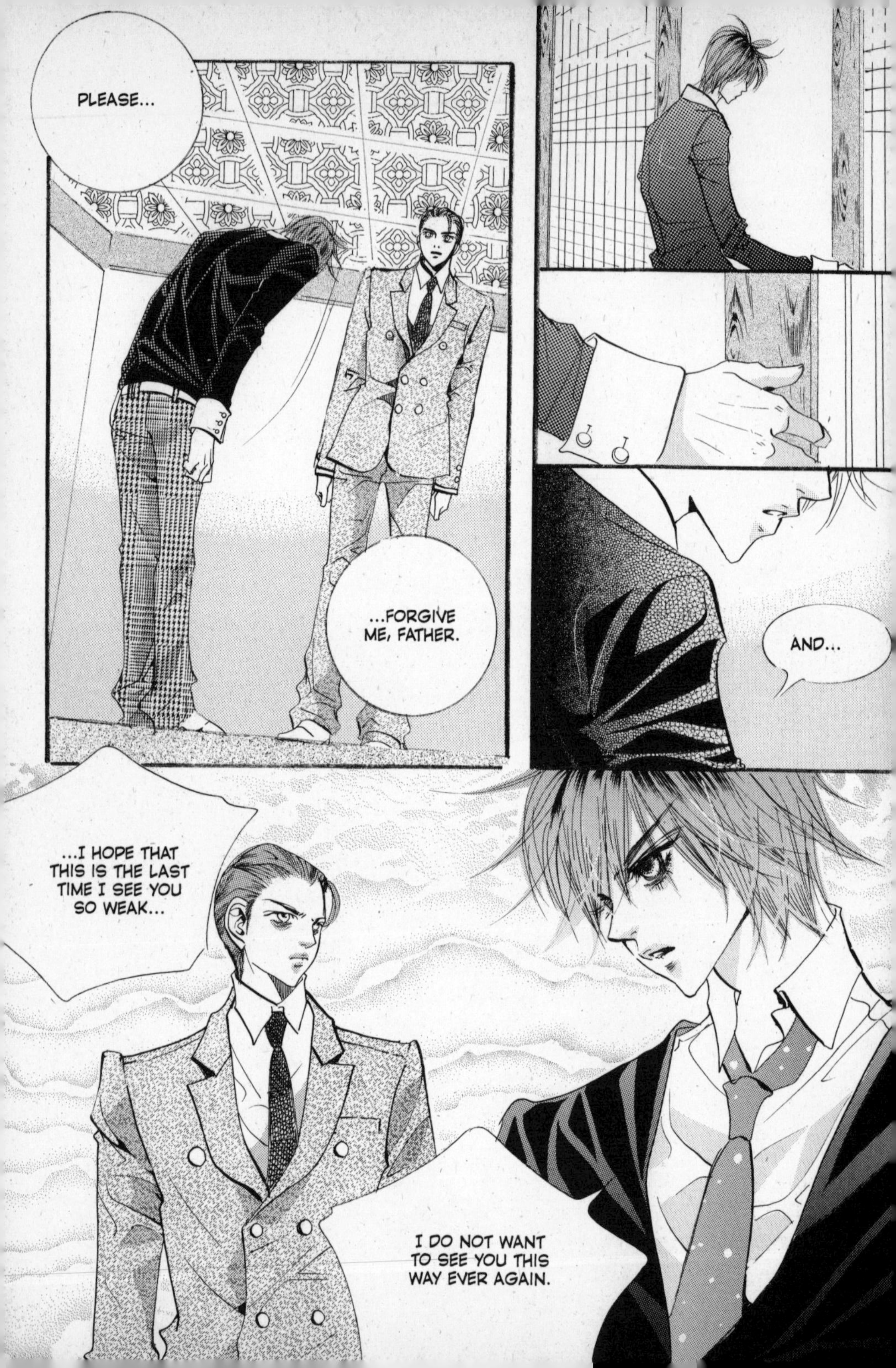
PLEASE...
...FORGIVE ME, FATHER.
AND...
...I HOPE THAT THIS IS THE LAST TIME I SEE YOU SO WEAK...
I DO NOT WANT TO SEE YOU THIS WAY EVER AGAIN.

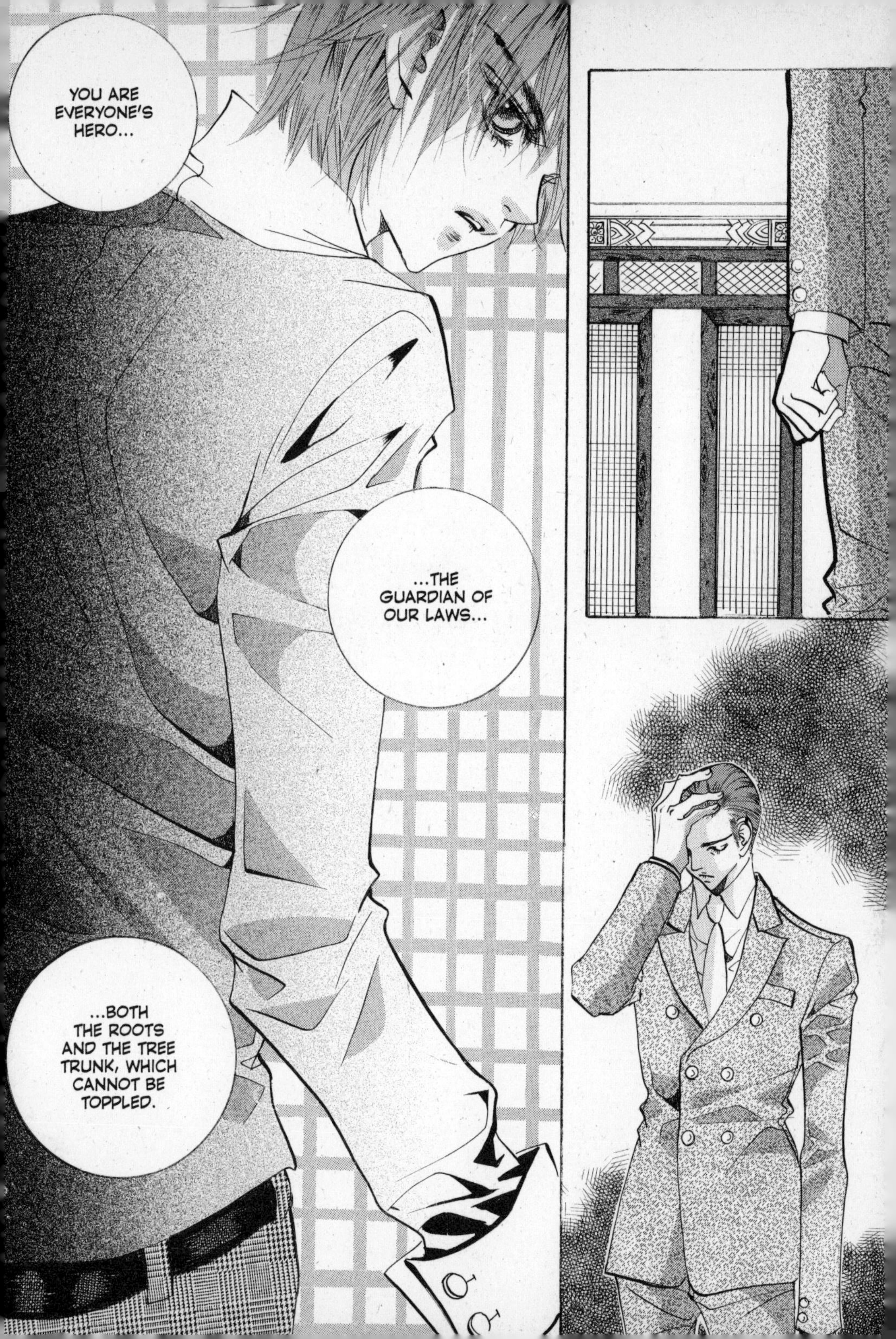
YOU ARE EVERYONE'S HERO...
...THE GUARDIAN OF OUR LAWS...
...BOTH THE ROOTS AND THE TREE TRUNK, WHICH CANNOT BE TOPPLED.

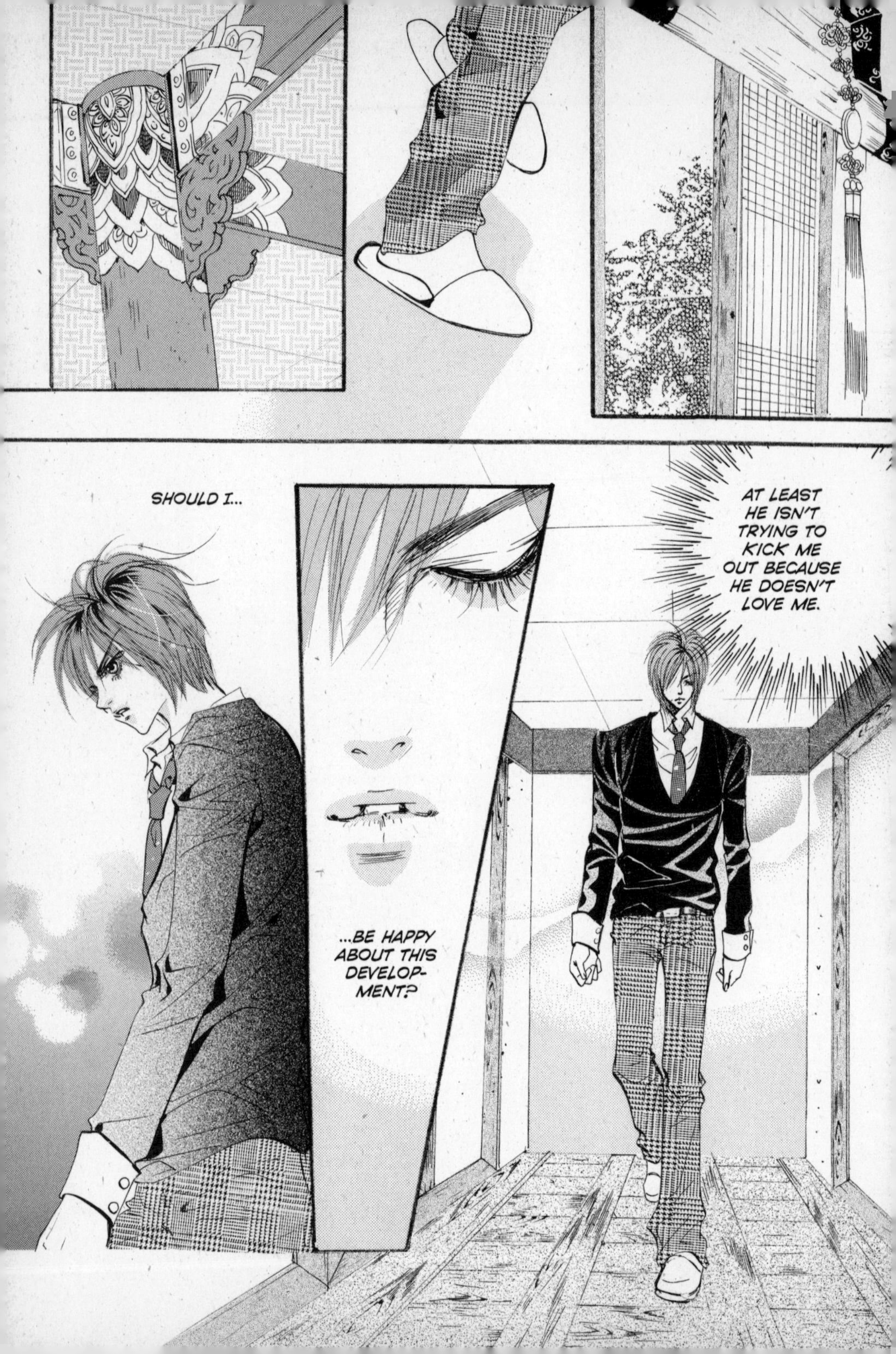
SHOULD I...
...BE HAPPY ABOUT THIS DEVELOP-MENT?
AT LEAST HE ISN'T TRYING TO KICK ME OUT BECAUSE HE DOESN'T LOVE ME.

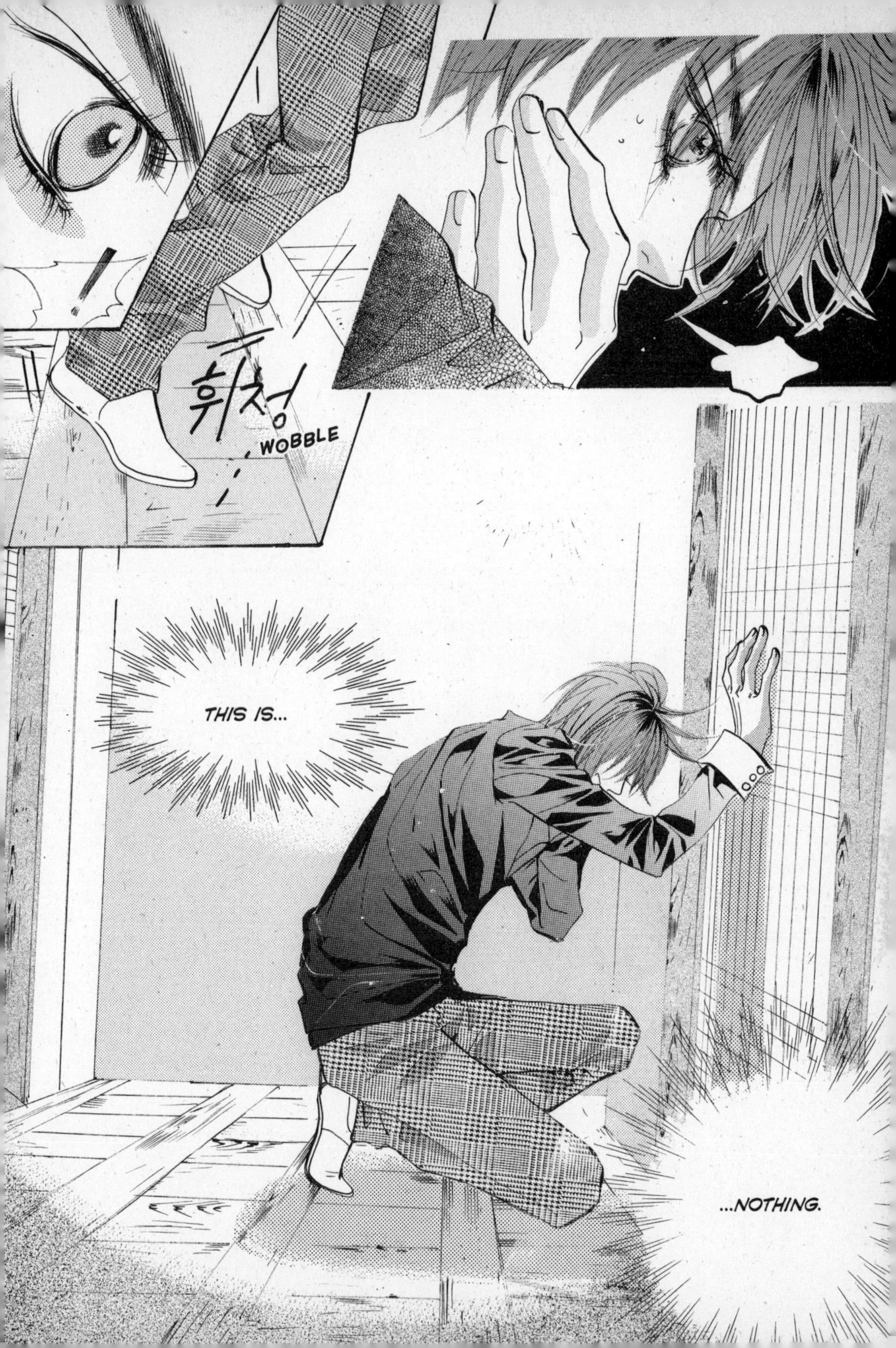

!
휘청
WOBBLE
THIS IS...
...NOTHING.

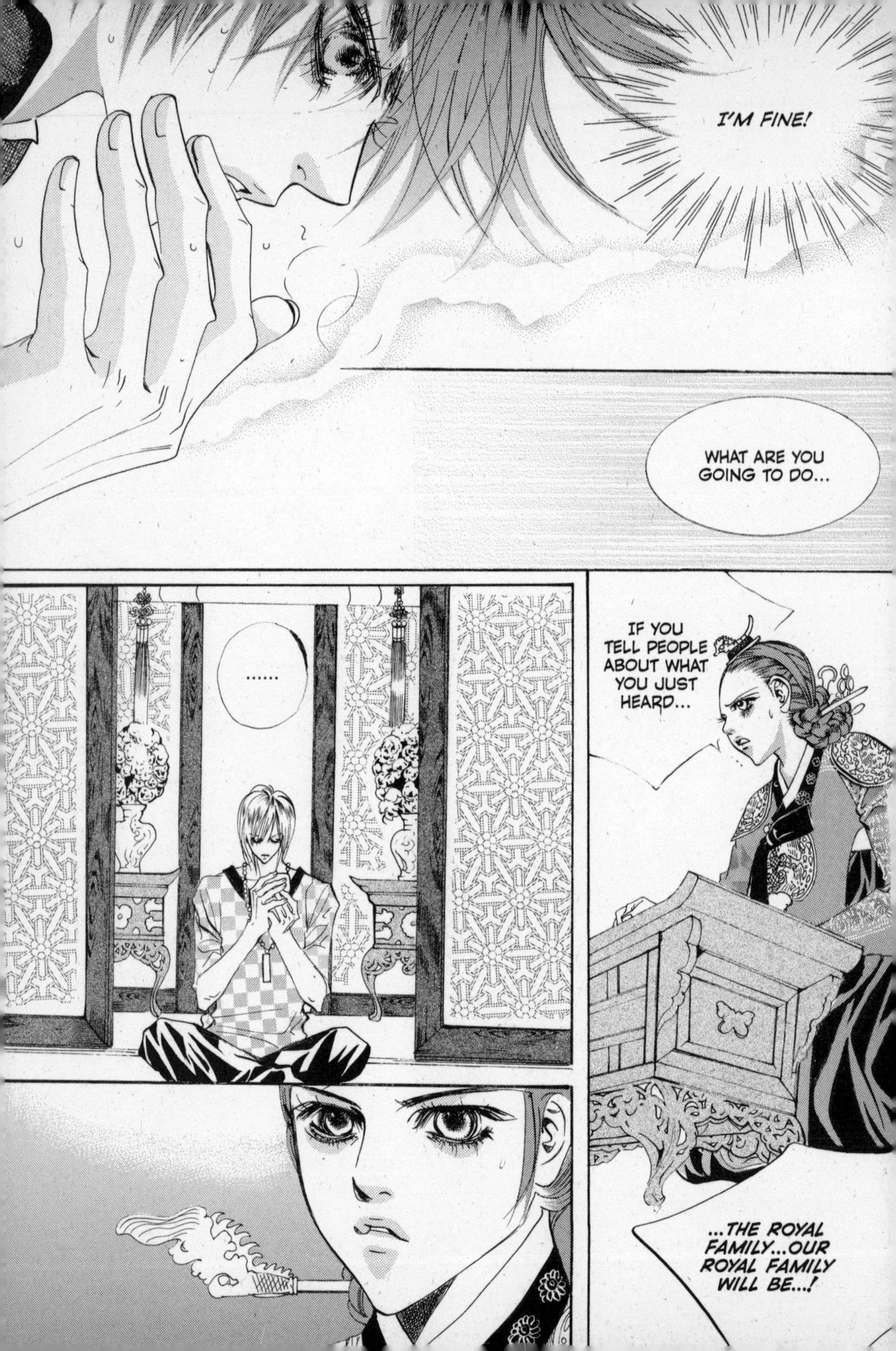
I'M FINE!
WHAT ARE YOU GOING TO DO...
......
IF YOU TELL PEOPLE ABOUT WHAT YOU JUST HEARD...
...THE ROYAL FAMILY...OUR ROYAL FAMILY WILL BE...!

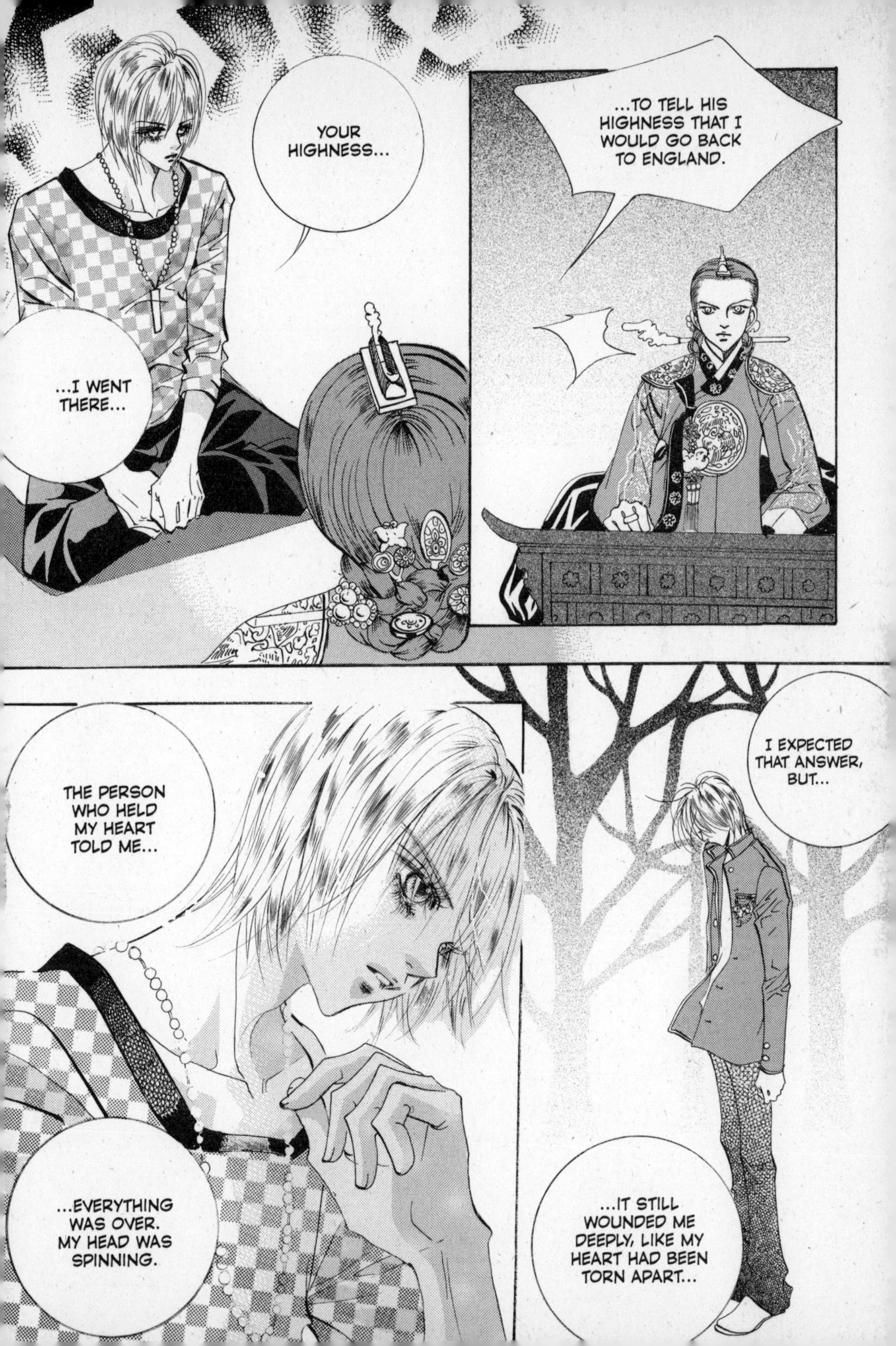
YOUR HIGHNESS...
...I WENT THERE...
...TO TELL HIS HIGHNESS THAT I WOULD GO BACK TO ENGLAND.
THE PERSON WHO HELD MY HEART TOLD ME...
...EVERYTHING WAS OVER. MY HEAD WAS SPINNING.
I EXPECTED THAT ANSWER, BUT...
...IT STILL WOUNDED ME DEEPLY, LIKE MY HEART HAD BEEN TORN APART...

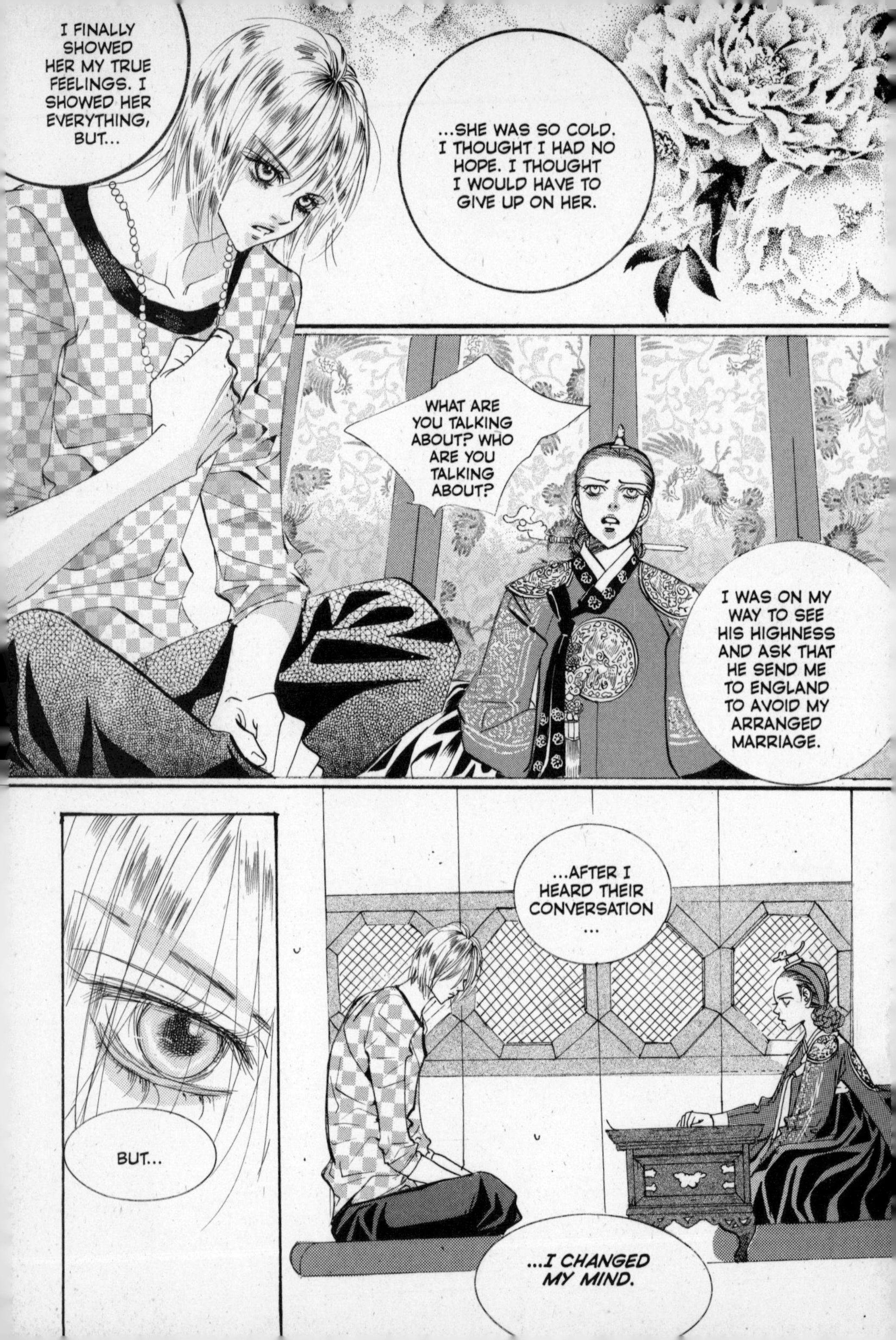
I FINALLY SHOWED HER MY TRUE FEELINGS. I SHOWED HER EVERYTHING, BUT...
...SHE WAS SO COLD. I THOUGHT I HAD NO HOPE. I THOUGHT I WOULD HAVE TO GIVE UP ON HER.
WHAT ARE YOU TALKING ABOUT? WHO ARE YOU TALKING ABOUT?
I WAS ON MY WAY TO SEE HIS HIGHNESS AND ASK THAT HE SEND ME TO ENGLAND TO AVOID MY ARRANGED MARRIAGE.
BUT...
...AFTER I HEARD THEIR CONVERSATION ...
...I CHANGED MY MIND.

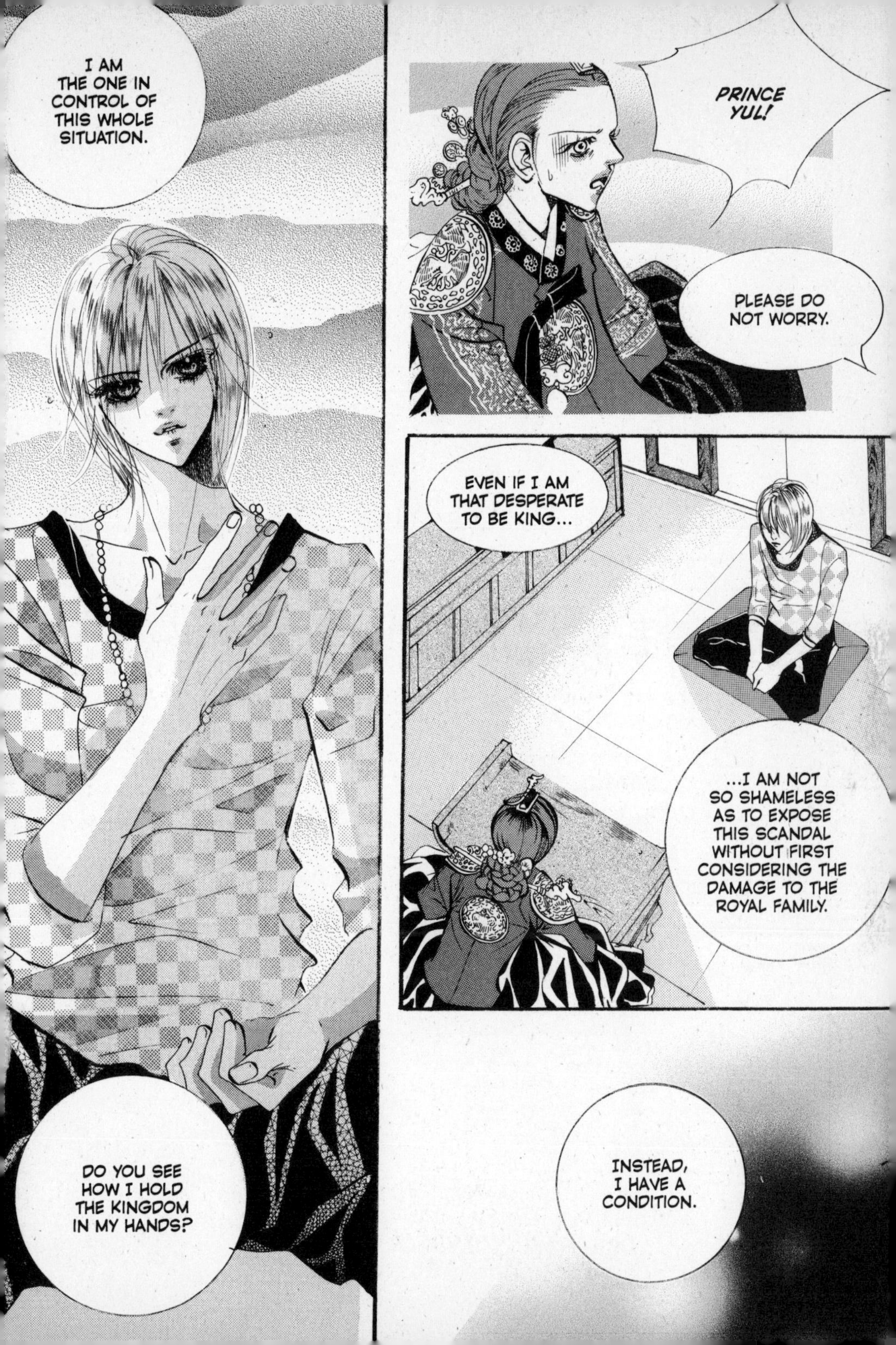
I AM THE ONE IN CONTROL OF THIS WHOLE SITUATION.
DO YOU SEE HOW I HOLD THE KINGDOM IN MY HANDS?
PRINCE YUL!
PLEASE DO NOT WORRY.
EVEN IF I AM THAT DESPERATE TO BE KING...
...I AM NOT SO SHAMELESS AS TO EXPOSE THIS SCANDAL WITHOUT FIRST CONSIDERING THE DAMAGE TO THE ROYAL FAMILY.
INSTEAD, I HAVE A CONDITION.

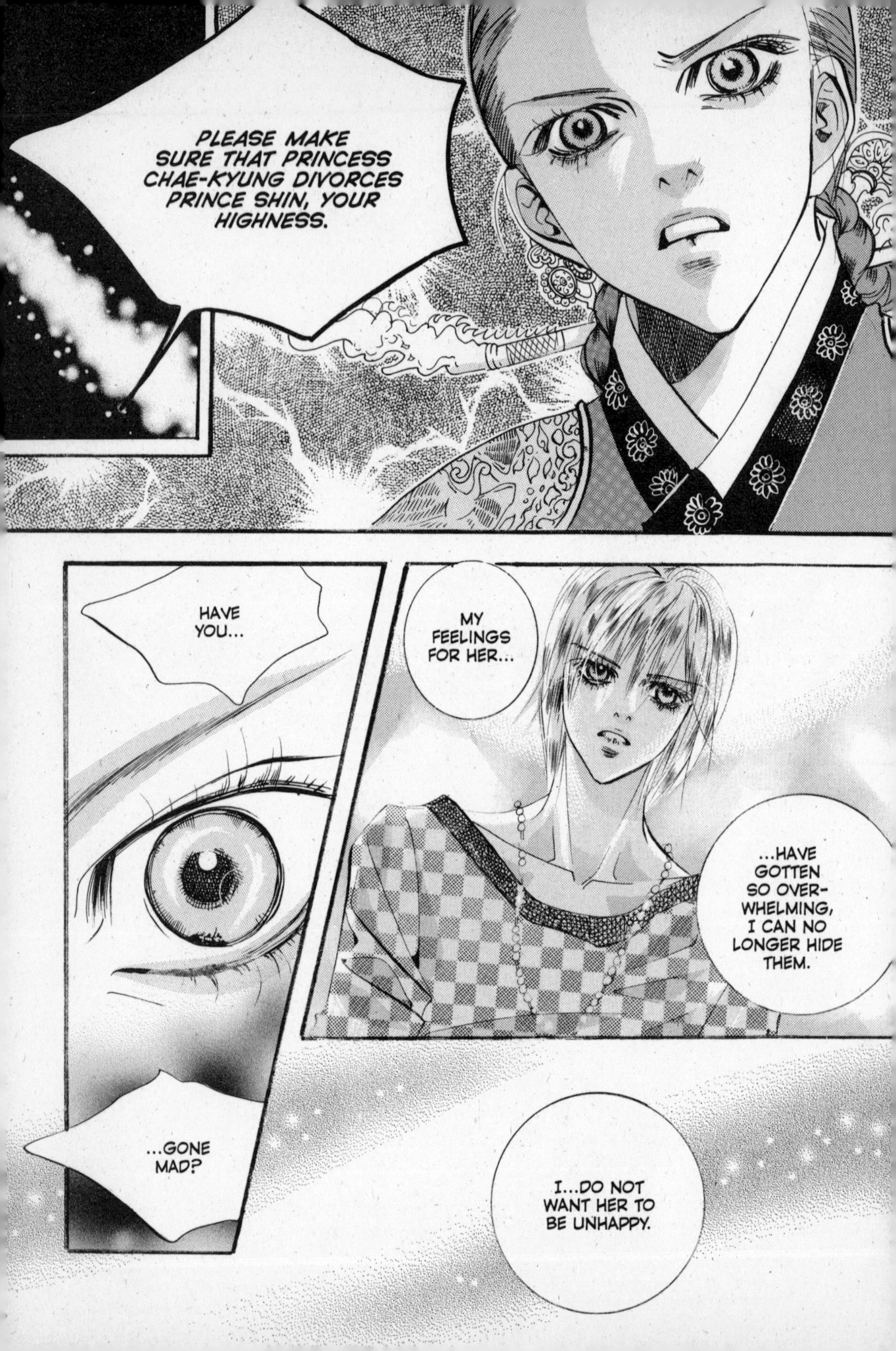
PLEASE MAKE SURE THAT PRINCESS CHAE-KYUNG DIVORCES PRINCE SHIN, YOUR HIGHNESS.
HAVE YOU...
...GONE MAD?
MY FEELINGS FOR HER...
...HAVE GOTTEN SO OVER-WHELMING, I CAN NO LONGER HIDE THEM.
I...DO NOT WANT HER TO BE UNHAPPY.

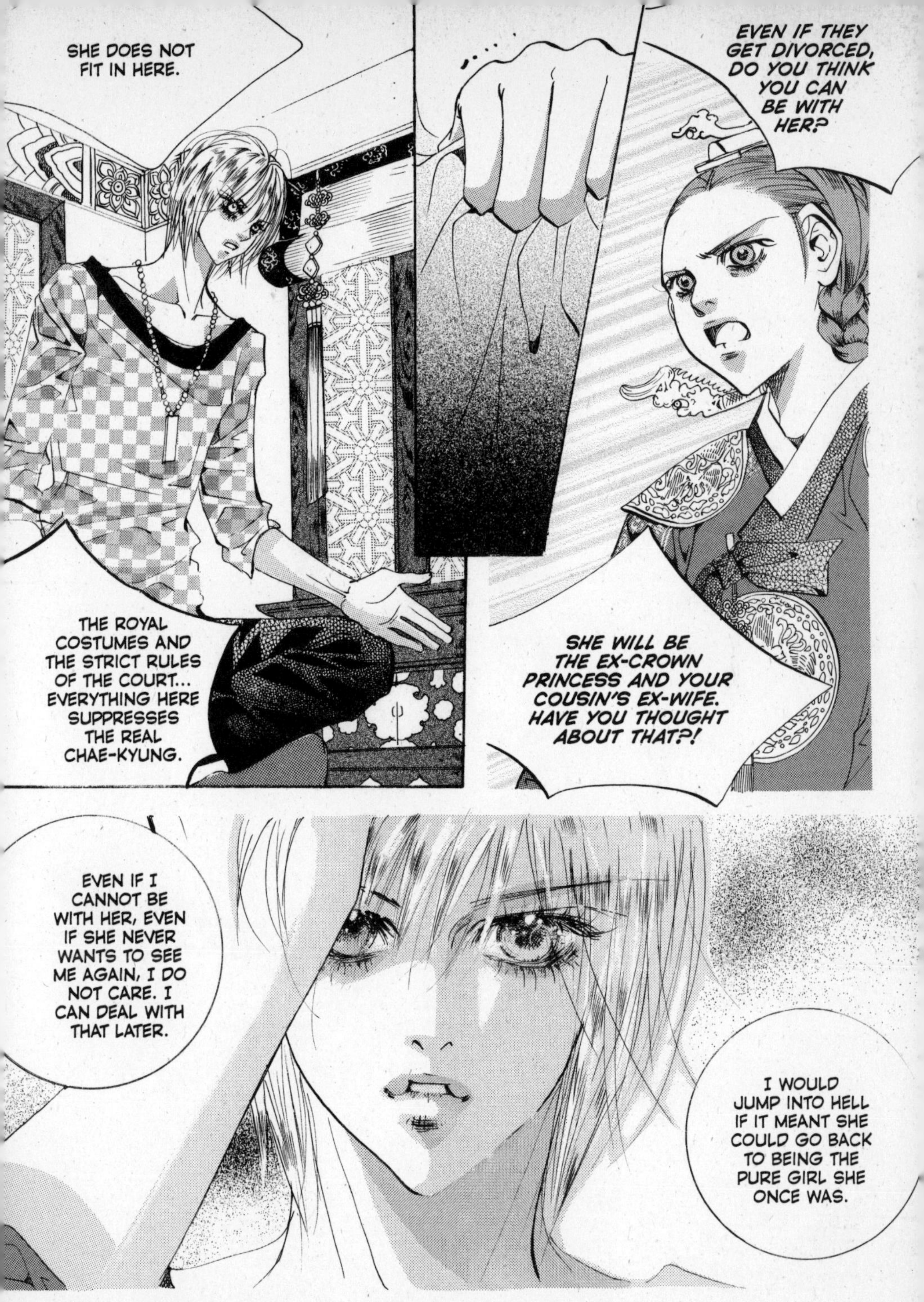
SHE DOES NOT FIT IN HERE.
THE ROYAL COSTUMES AND THE STRICT RULES OF THE COURT... EVERYTHING HERE SUPPRESSES THE REAL CHAE-KYUNG.
...
EVEN IF THEY GET DIVORCED, DO YOU THINK YOU CAN BE WITH HER?
SHE WILL BE THE EX-CROWN PRINCESS AND YOUR COUSIN'S EX-WIFE. HAVE YOU THOUGHT ABOUT THAT?!
EVEN IF I CANNOT BE WITH HER, EVEN IF SHE NEVER WANTS TO SEE ME AGAIN, I DO NOT CARE. I CAN DEAL WITH THAT LATER.
I WOULD JUMP INTO HELL IF IT MEANT SHE COULD GO BACK TO BEING THE PURE GIRL SHE ONCE WAS.

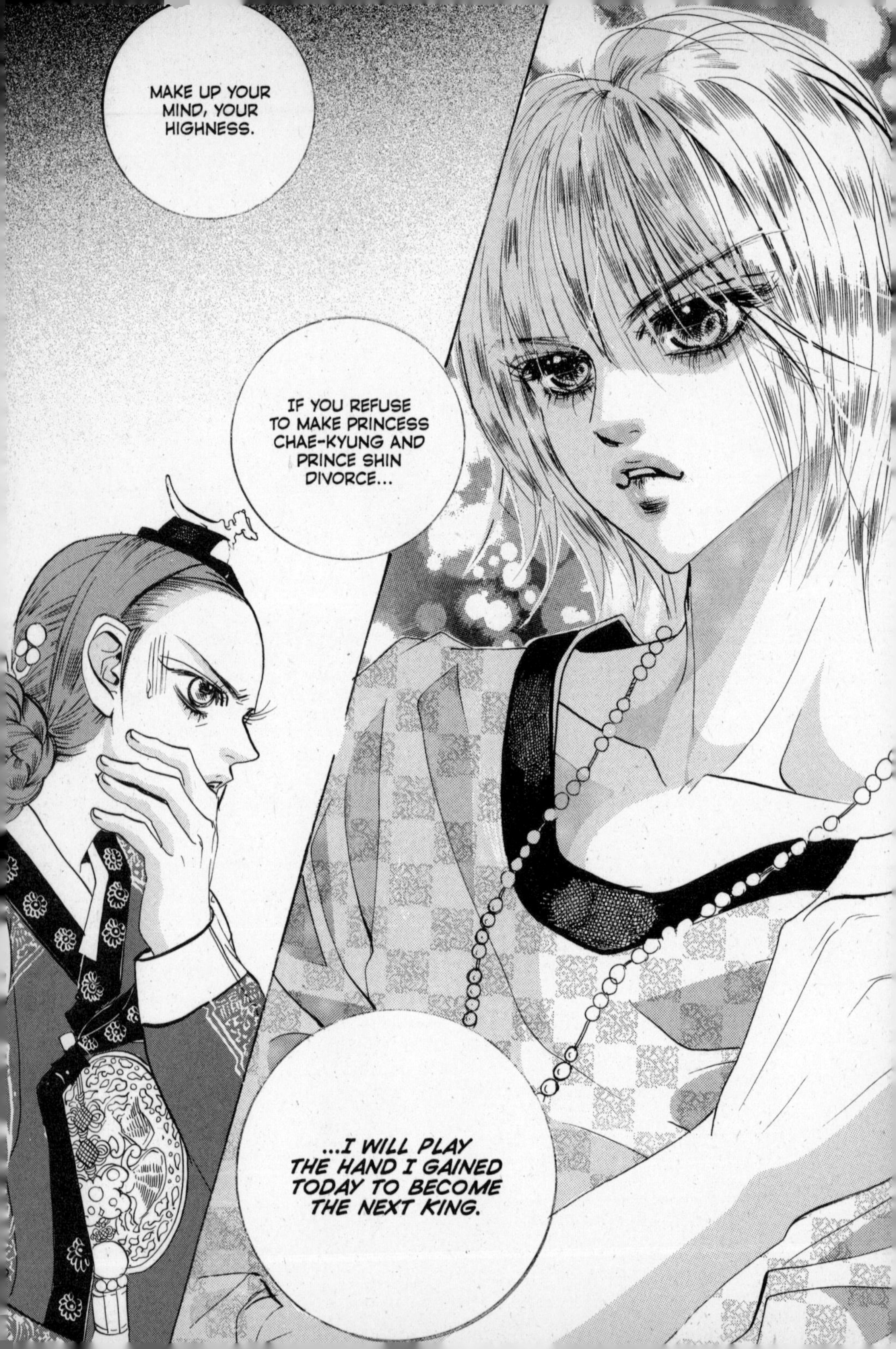
MAKE UP YOUR MIND, YOUR HIGHNESS.
IF YOU REFUSE TO MAKE PRINCESS CHAE-KYUNG AND PRINCE SHIN DIVORCE...
...I WILL PLAY THE HAND I GAINED TODAY TO BECOME THE NEXT KING.

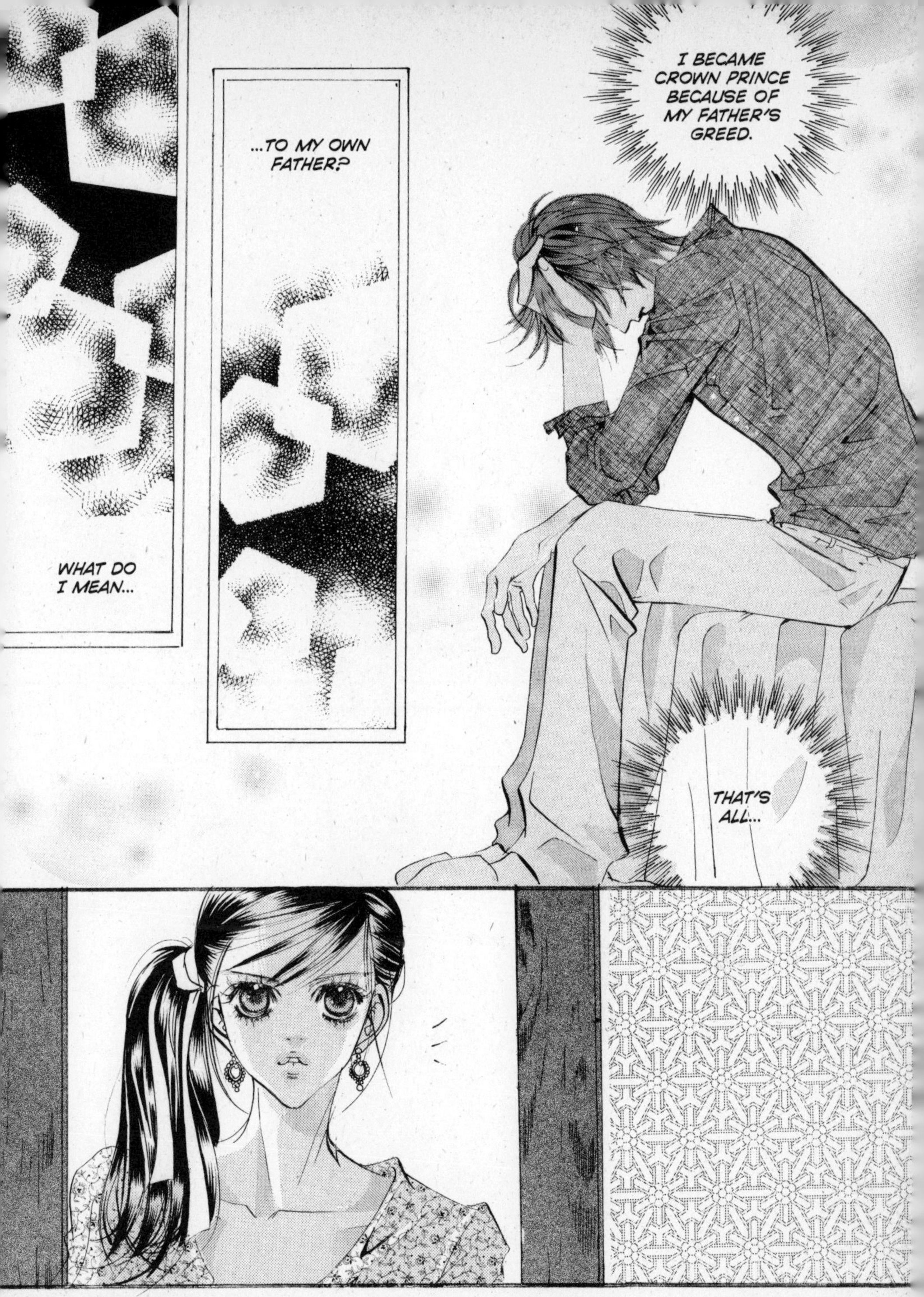
WHAT DO I MEAN...
...TO MY OWN FATHER?
I BECAME CROWN PRINCE BECAUSE OF MY FATHER'S GREED.
THAT'S ALL...

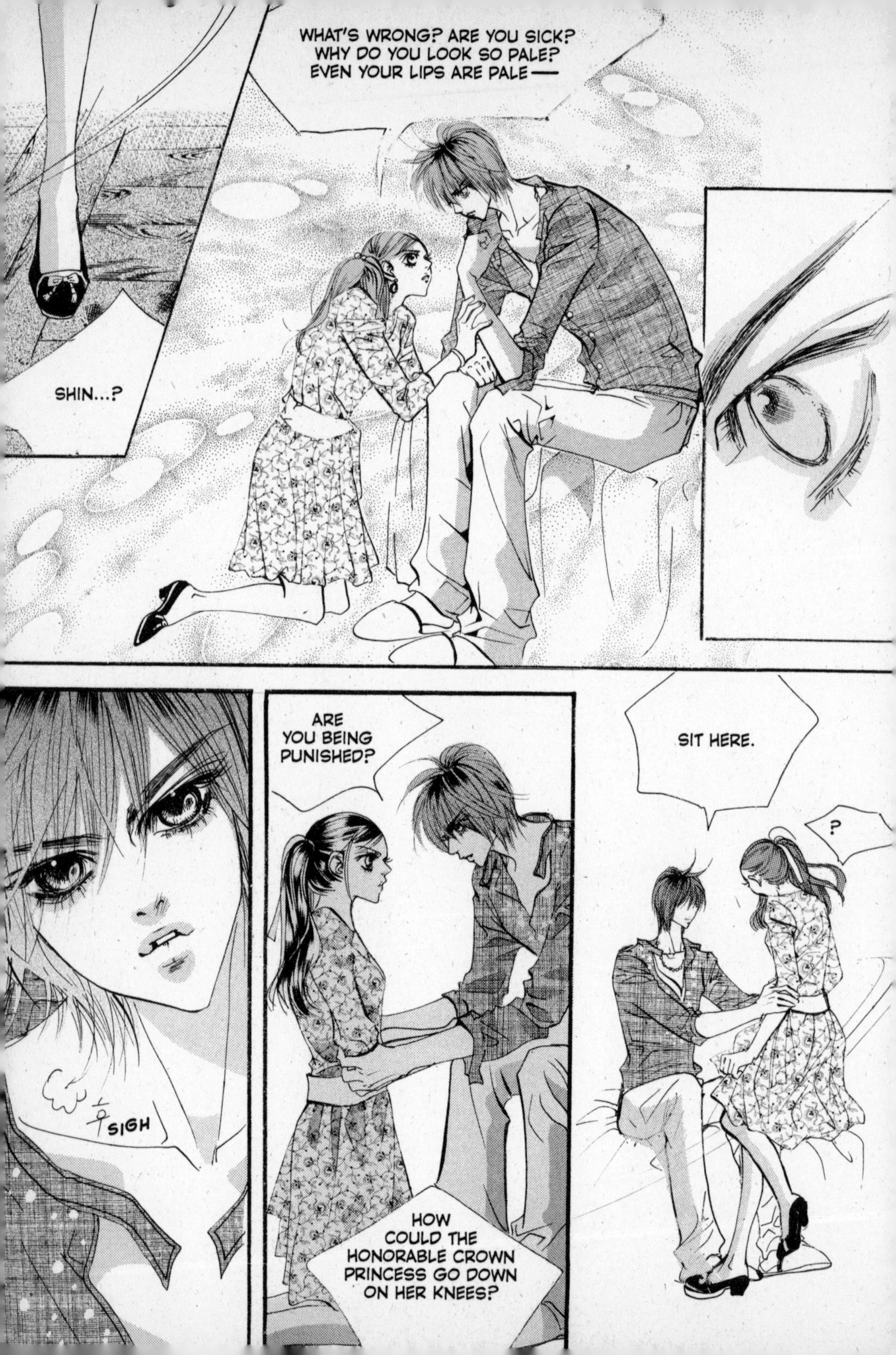
WHAT'S WRONG? ARE YOU SICK? WHY DO YOU LOOK SO PALE? EVEN YOUR LIPS ARE PALE—
SHIN...?
SIGH
ARE YOU BEING PUNISHED?
HOW COULD THE HONORABLE CROWN PRINCESS GO DOWN ON HER KNEES?
SIT HERE.
?

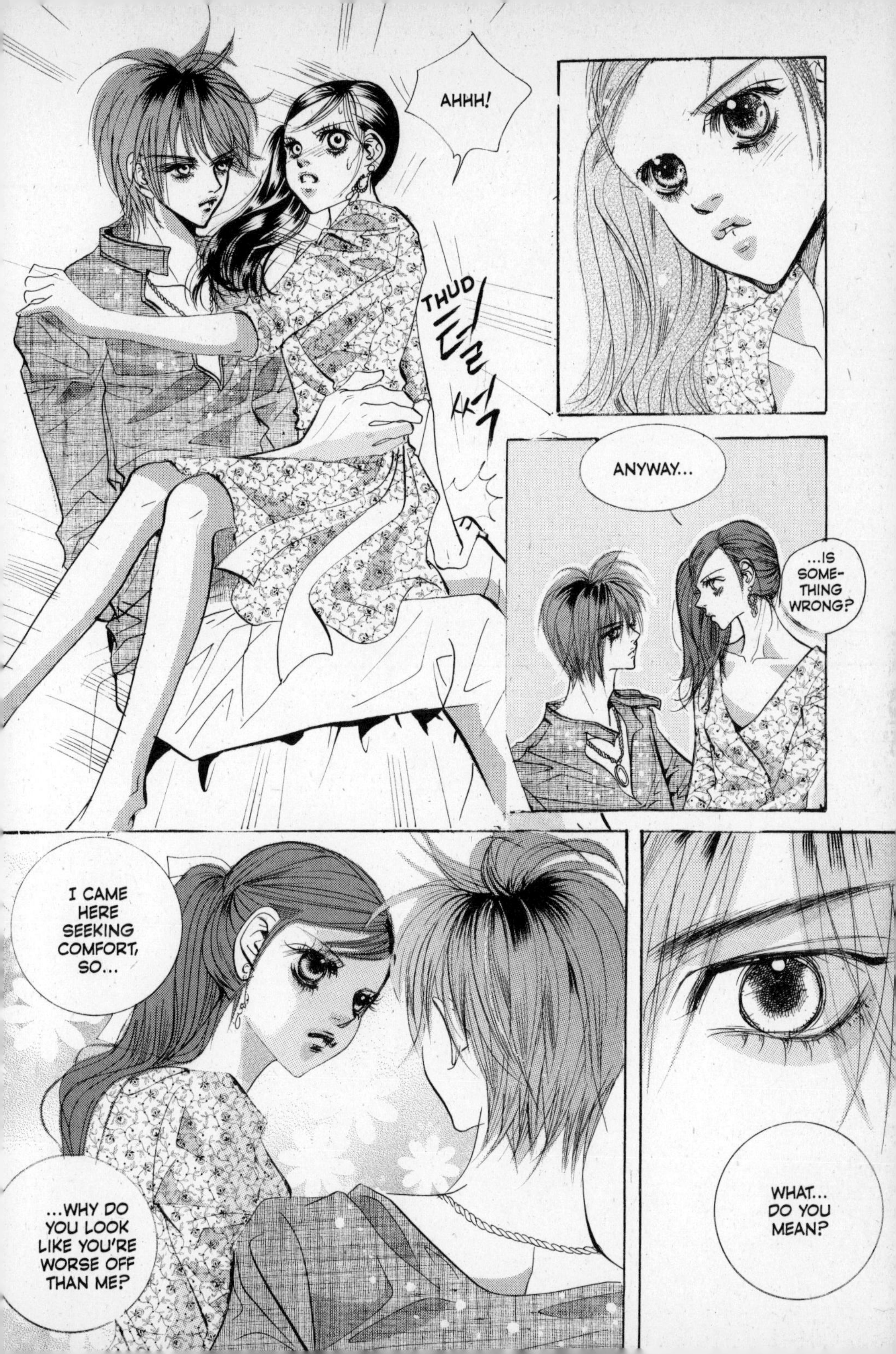
AHHH!
THUD
털썩
ANYWAY...
...IS SOMETHING WRONG?
I CAME HERE SEEKING COMFORT, SO...
...WHY DO YOU LOOK LIKE YOU'RE WORSE OFF THAN ME?
WHAT... DO YOU MEAN?

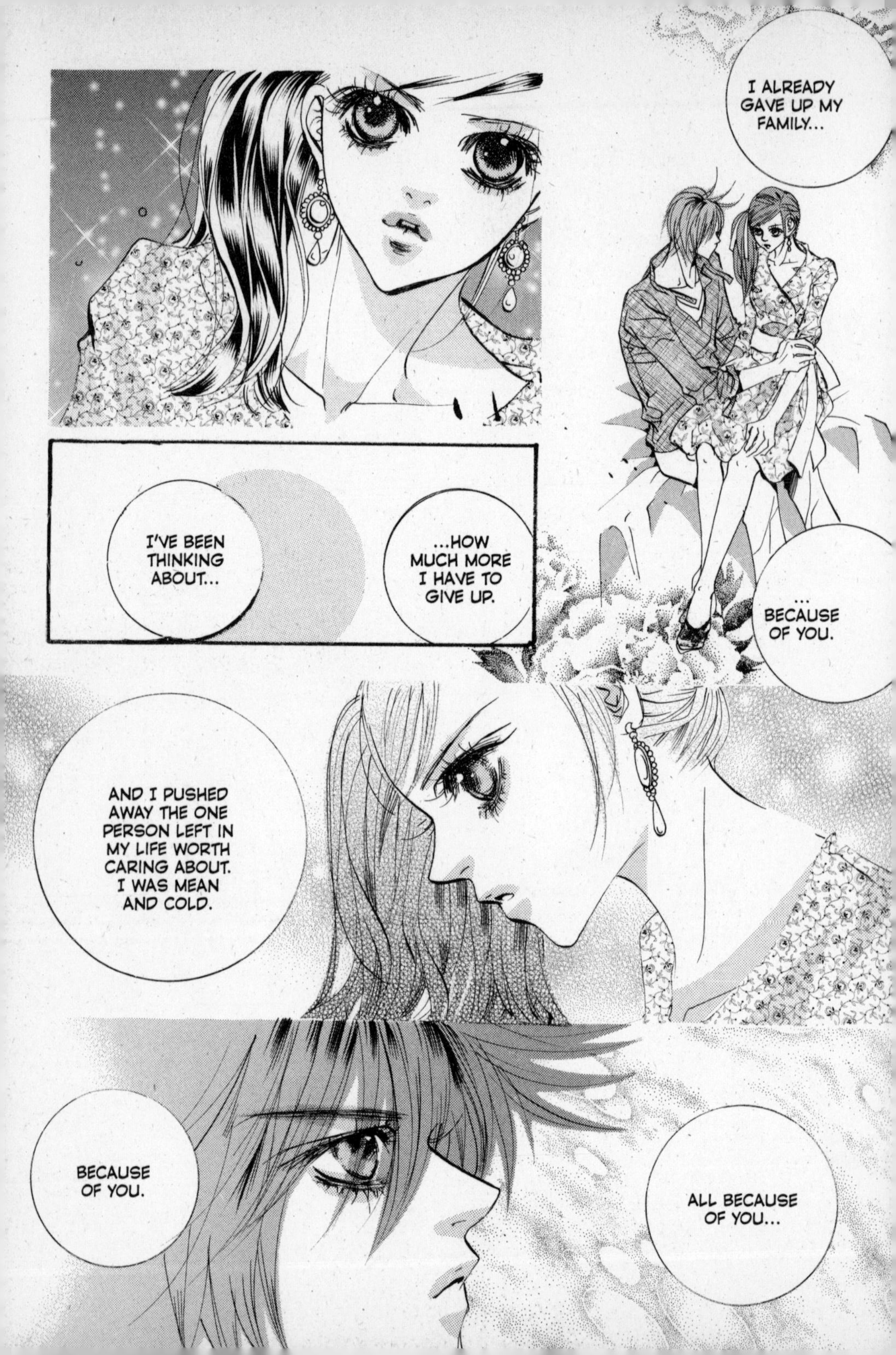
I'VE BEEN THINKING ABOUT...
...HOW MUCH MORE I HAVE TO GIVE UP.
I ALREADY GAVE UP MY FAMILY...
...BECAUSE OF YOU.
AND I PUSHED AWAY THE ONE PERSON LEFT IN MY LIFE WORTH CARING ABOUT. I WAS MEAN AND COLD.
BECAUSE OF YOU.
ALL BECAUSE OF YOU...

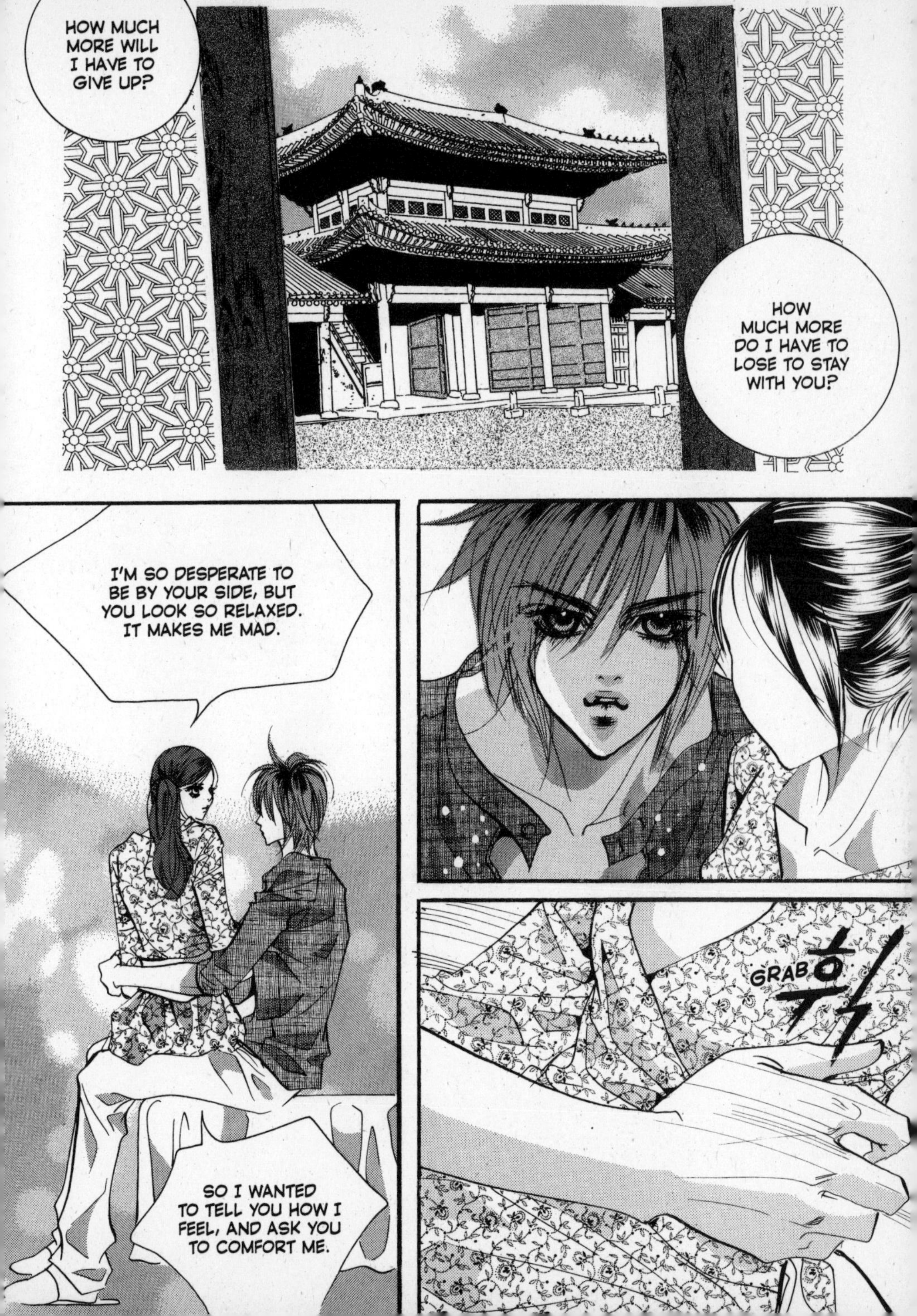
HOW MUCH MORE WILL I HAVE TO GIVE UP?
HOW MUCH MORE DO I HAVE TO LOSE TO STAY WITH YOU?
I'M SO DESPERATE TO BE BY YOUR SIDE, BUT YOU LOOK SO RELAXED. IT MAKES ME MAD.
SO I WANTED TO TELL YOU HOW I FEEL, AND ASK YOU TO COMFORT ME.
GRAB

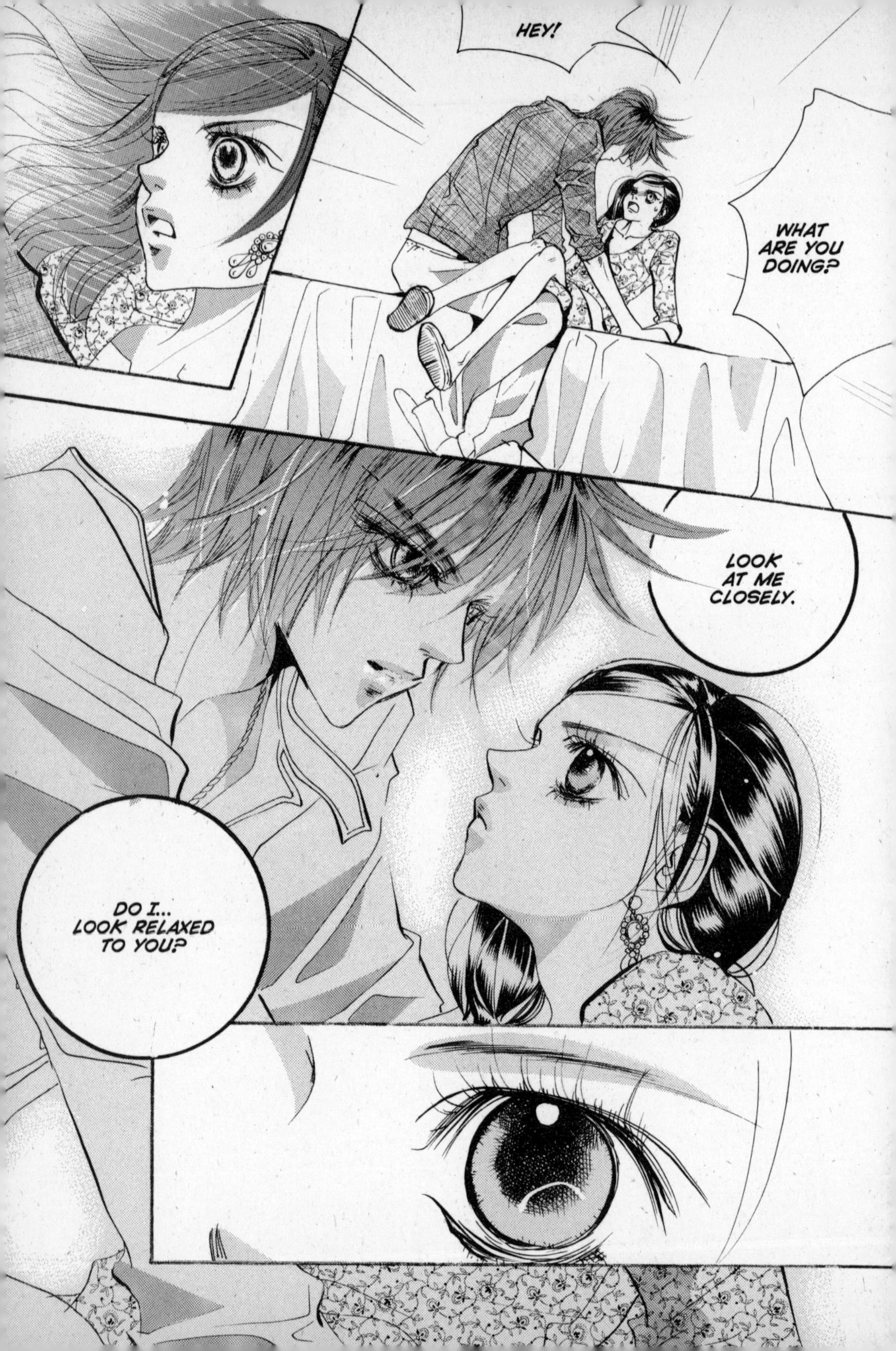
HEY!
WHAT ARE YOU DOING?
LOOK AT ME CLOSELY.
DO I... LOOK RELAXED TO YOU?

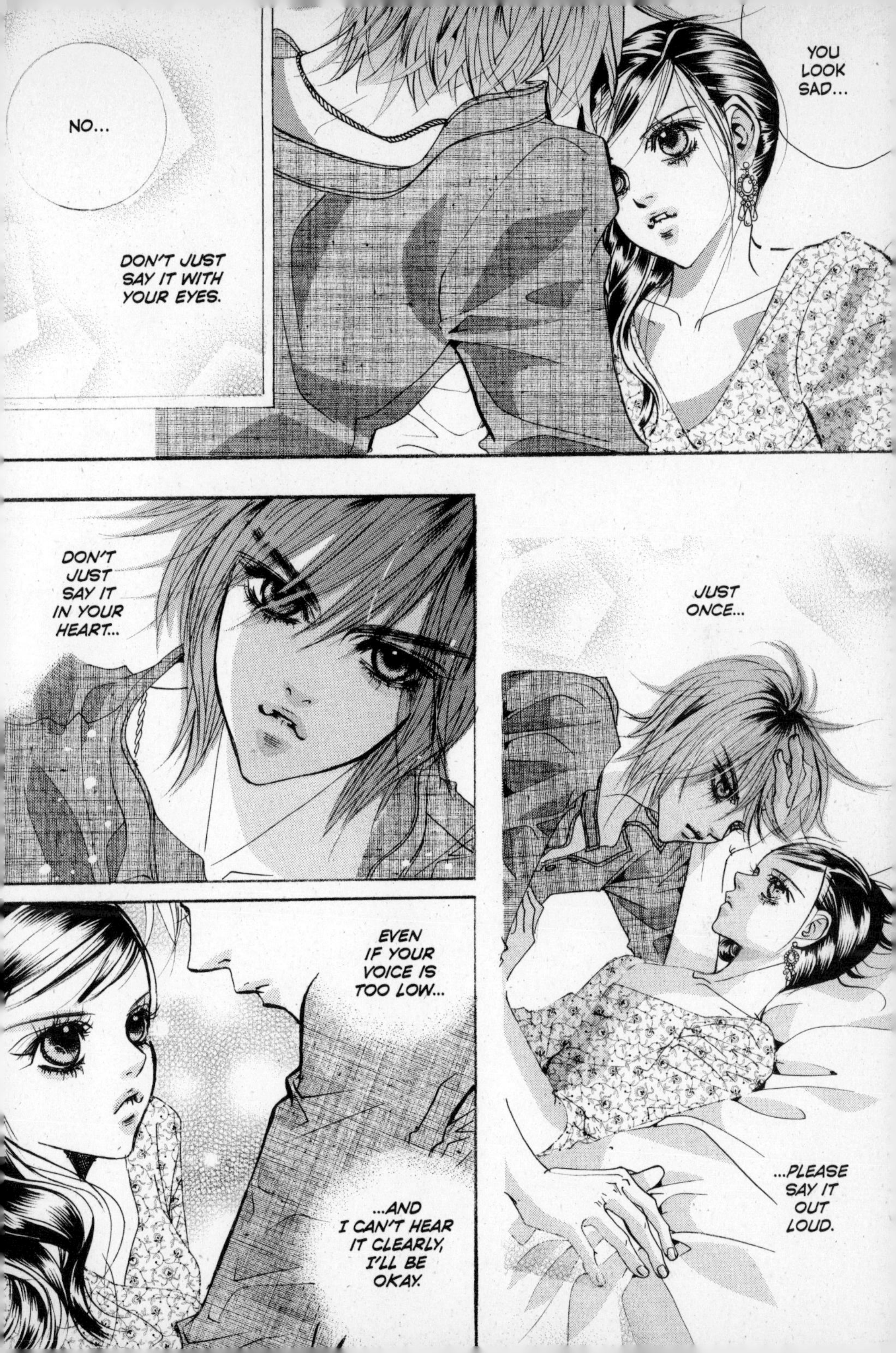
NO...
DON'T JUST SAY IT WITH YOUR EYES.
YOU LOOK SAD...
DON'T JUST SAY IT IN YOUR HEART...
EVEN IF YOUR VOICE IS TOO LOW...
...AND I CAN'T HEAR IT CLEARLY, I'LL BE OKAY.
JUST ONCE...
...PLEASE SAY IT OUT LOUD.

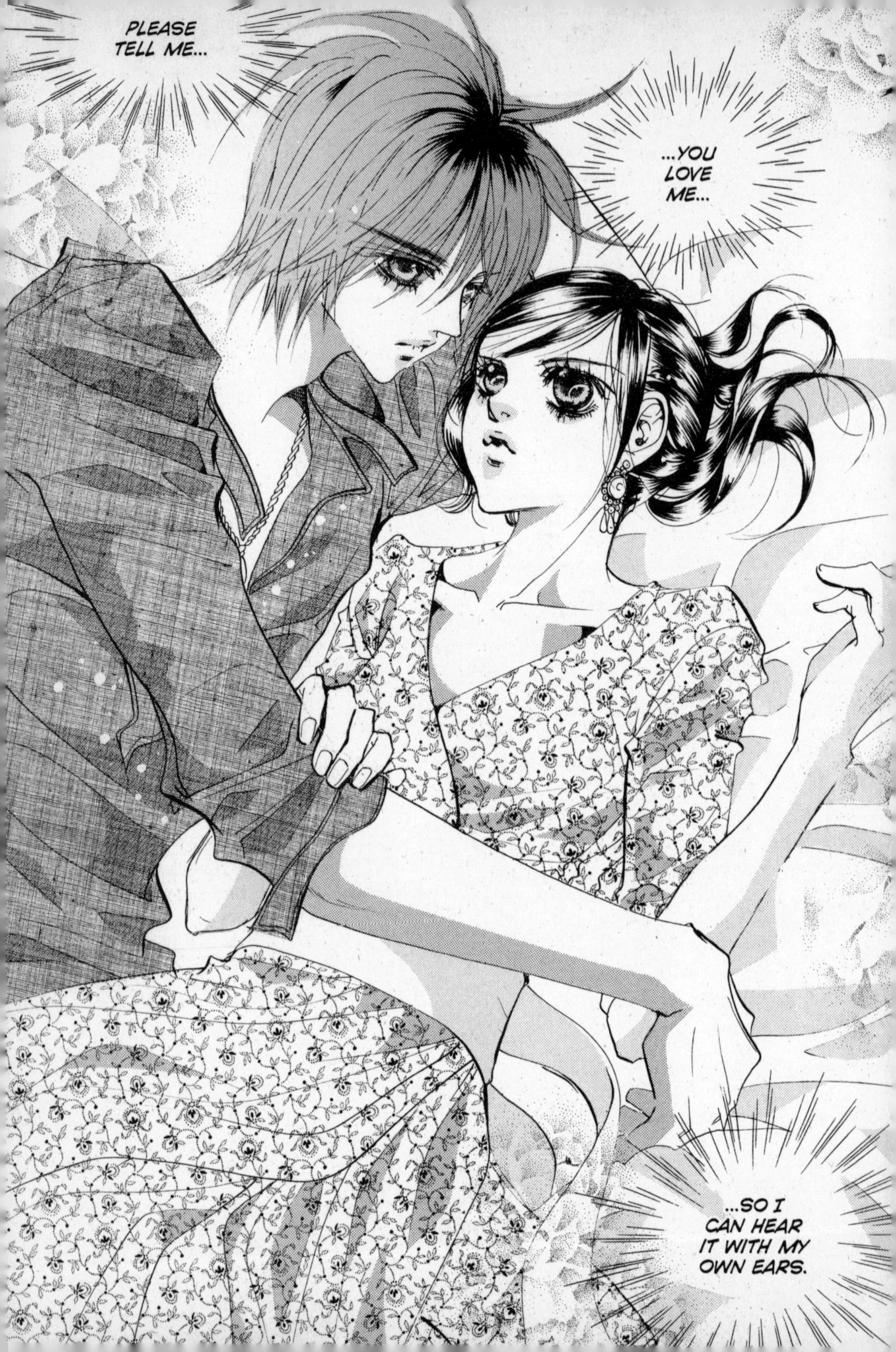
PLEASE TELL ME...
...YOU LOVE ME...
...SO I CAN HEAR IT WITH MY OWN EARS.

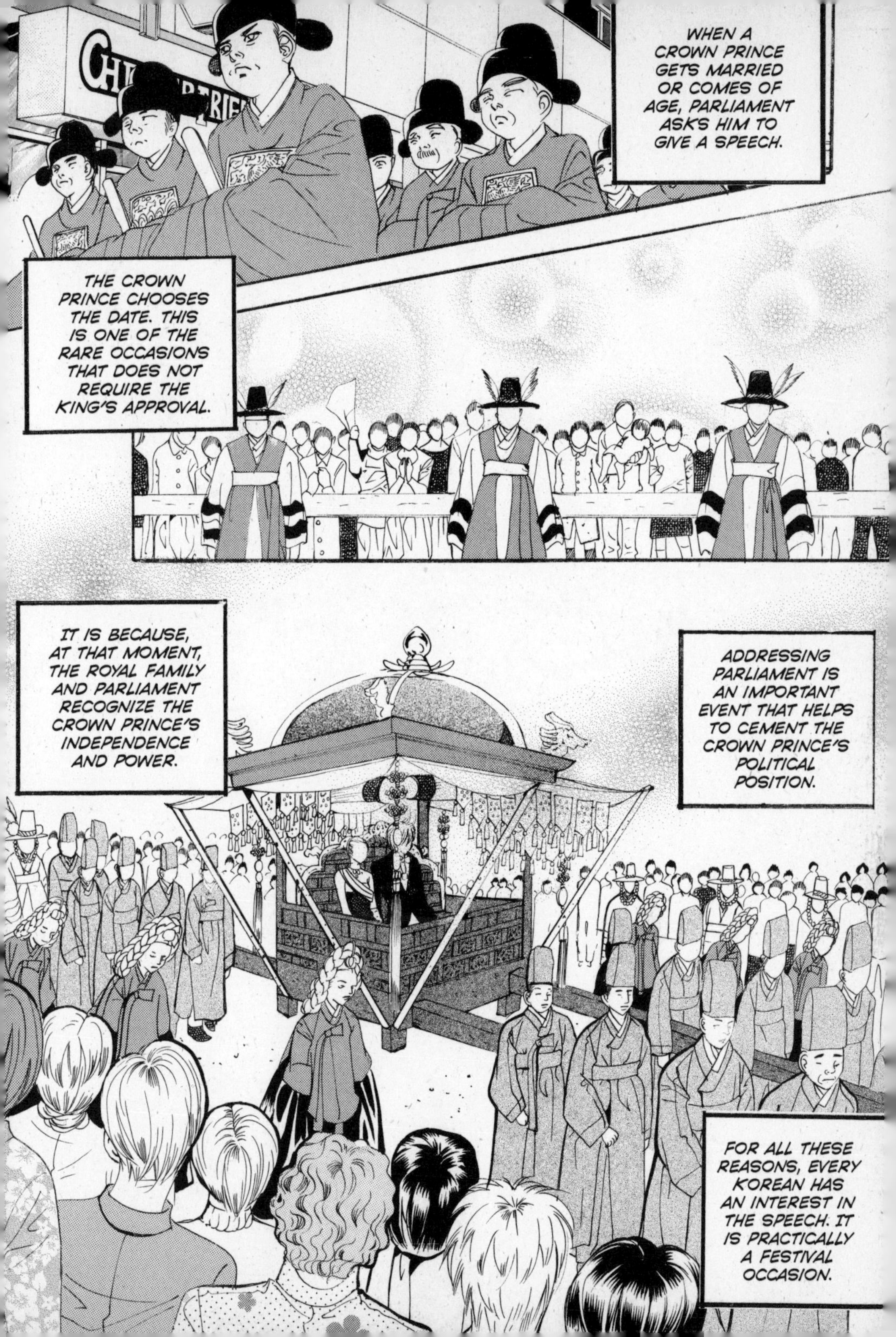
WHEN A CROWN PRINCE GETS MARRIED OR COMES OF AGE, PARLIAMENT ASKS HIM TO GIVE A SPEECH.
THE CROWN PRINCE CHOOSES THE DATE. THIS IS ONE OF THE RARE OCCASIONS THAT DOES NOT REQUIRE THE KING'S APPROVAL.
IT IS BECAUSE, AT THAT MOMENT, THE ROYAL FAMILY AND PARLIAMENT RECOGNIZE THE CROWN PRINCE'S INDEPENDENCE AND POWER.
ADDRESSING PARLIAMENT IS AN IMPORTANT EVENT THAT HELPS TO CEMENT THE CROWN PRINCE'S POLITICAL POSITION.
FOR ALL THESE REASONS, EVERY KOREAN HAS AN INTEREST IN THE SPEECH. IT IS PRACTICALLY A FESTIVAL OCCASION.

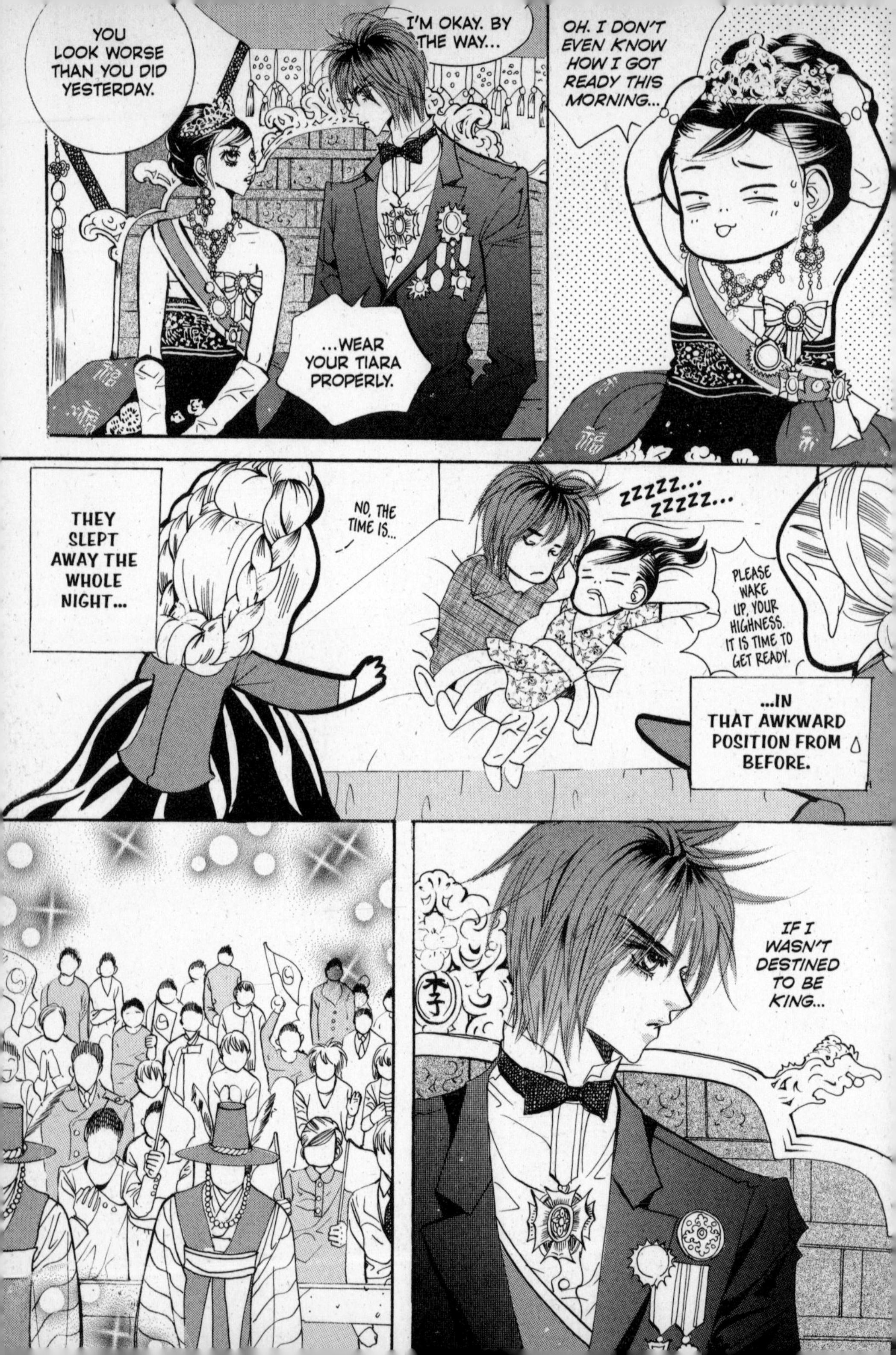

YOU LOOK WORSE THAN YOU DID YESTERDAY.
I'M OKAY. BY THE WAY...
...WEAR YOUR TIARA PROPERLY.
OH. I DON'T EVEN KNOW HOW I GOT READY THIS MORNING...
THEY SLEPT AWAY THE WHOLE NIGHT...
NO, THE TIME IS...
ZZZZZ... ZZZZZ...
PLEASE WAKE UP, YOUR HIGHNESS. IT IS TIME TO GET READY.
...IN THAT AWKWARD POSITION FROM BEFORE.
IF I WASN'T DESTINED TO BE KING...

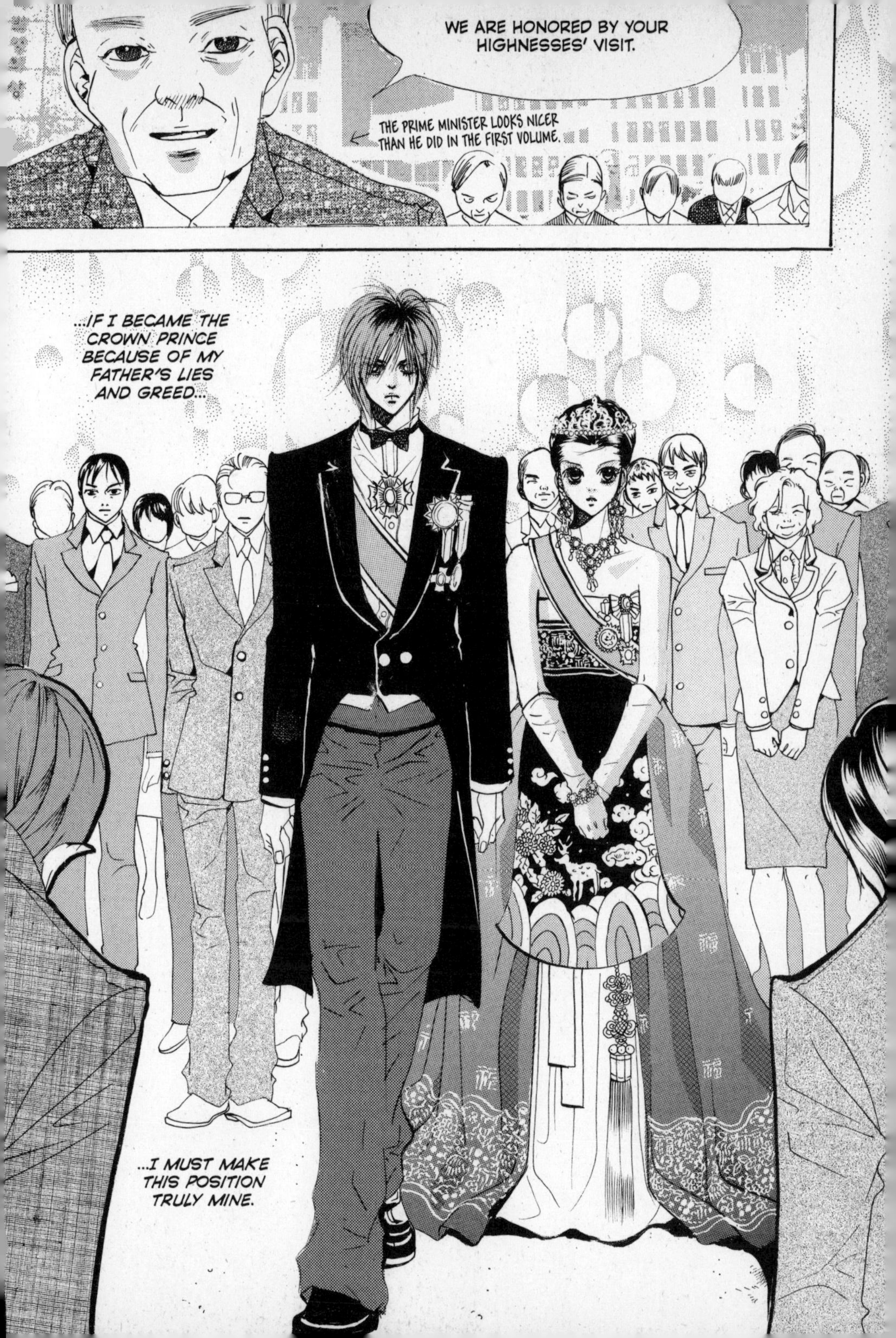
WE ARE HONORED BY YOUR HIGHNESSES' VISIT.
THE PRIME MINISTER LOOKS NICER THAN HE DID IN THE FIRST VOLUME.
...IF I BECAME THE CROWN PRINCE BECAUSE OF MY FATHER'S LIES AND GREED...
...I MUST MAKE THIS POSITION TRULY MINE.

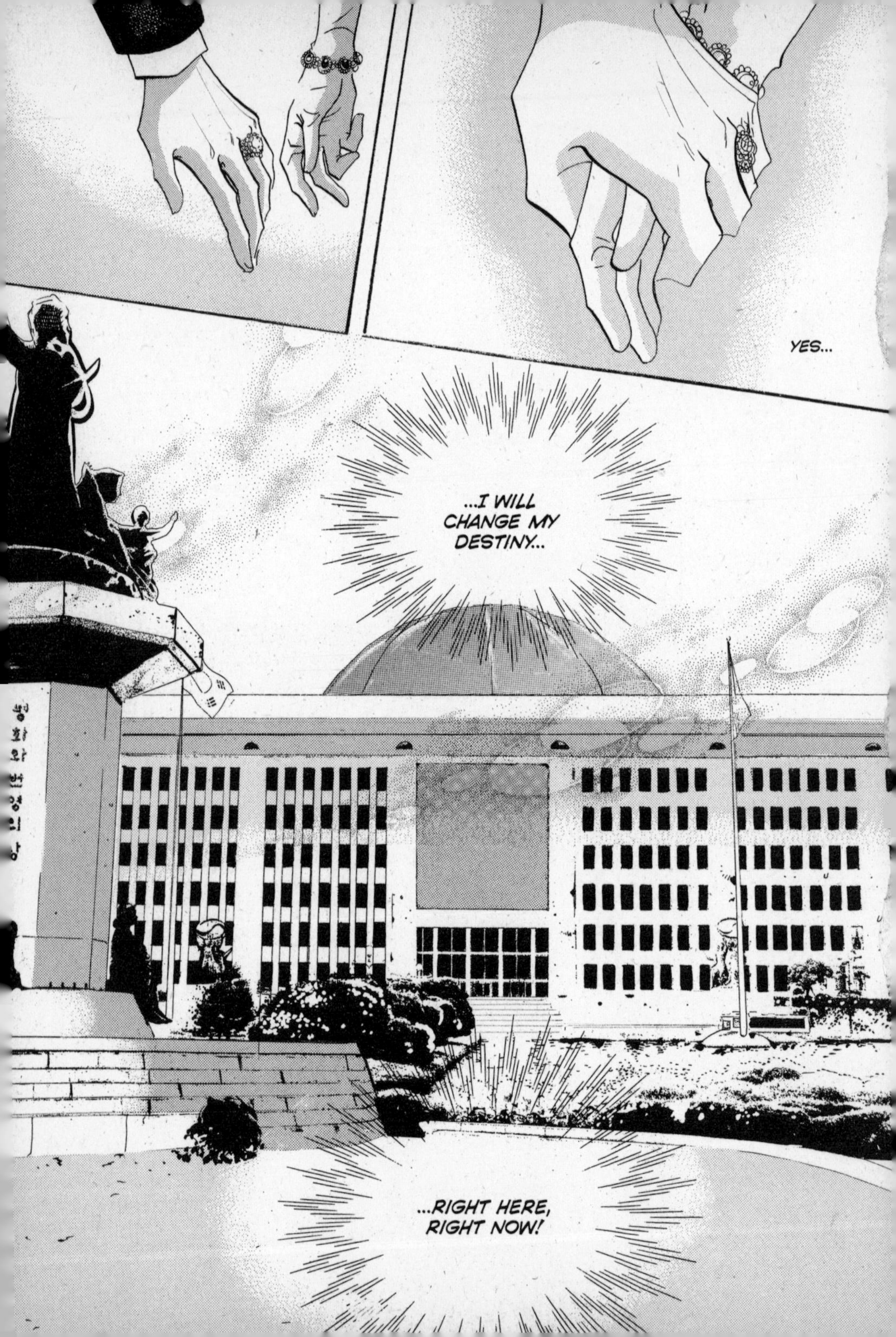
YES...
...I WILL CHANGE MY DESTINY...
평화와 번영의 상
...RIGHT HERE, RIGHT NOW!

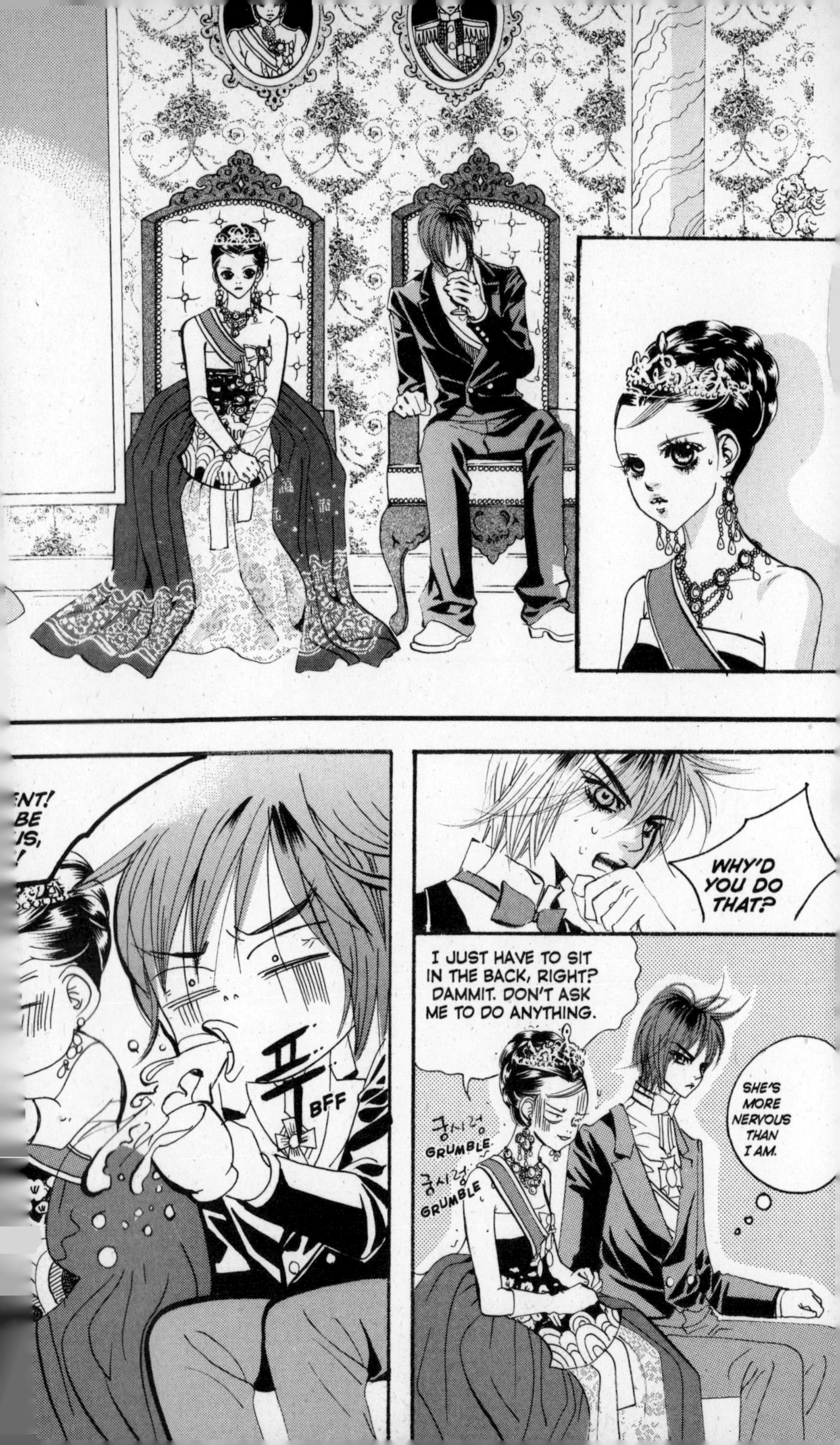
ENT!
BE
US,
프
BFF
WHY'D YOU DO THAT?
I JUST HAVE TO SIT IN THE BACK, RIGHT? DAMMIT. DON'T ASK ME TO DO ANYTHING.
궁시렁
GRUMBLE
궁시렁
GRUMBLE
SHE'S MORE NERVOUS THAN I AM.

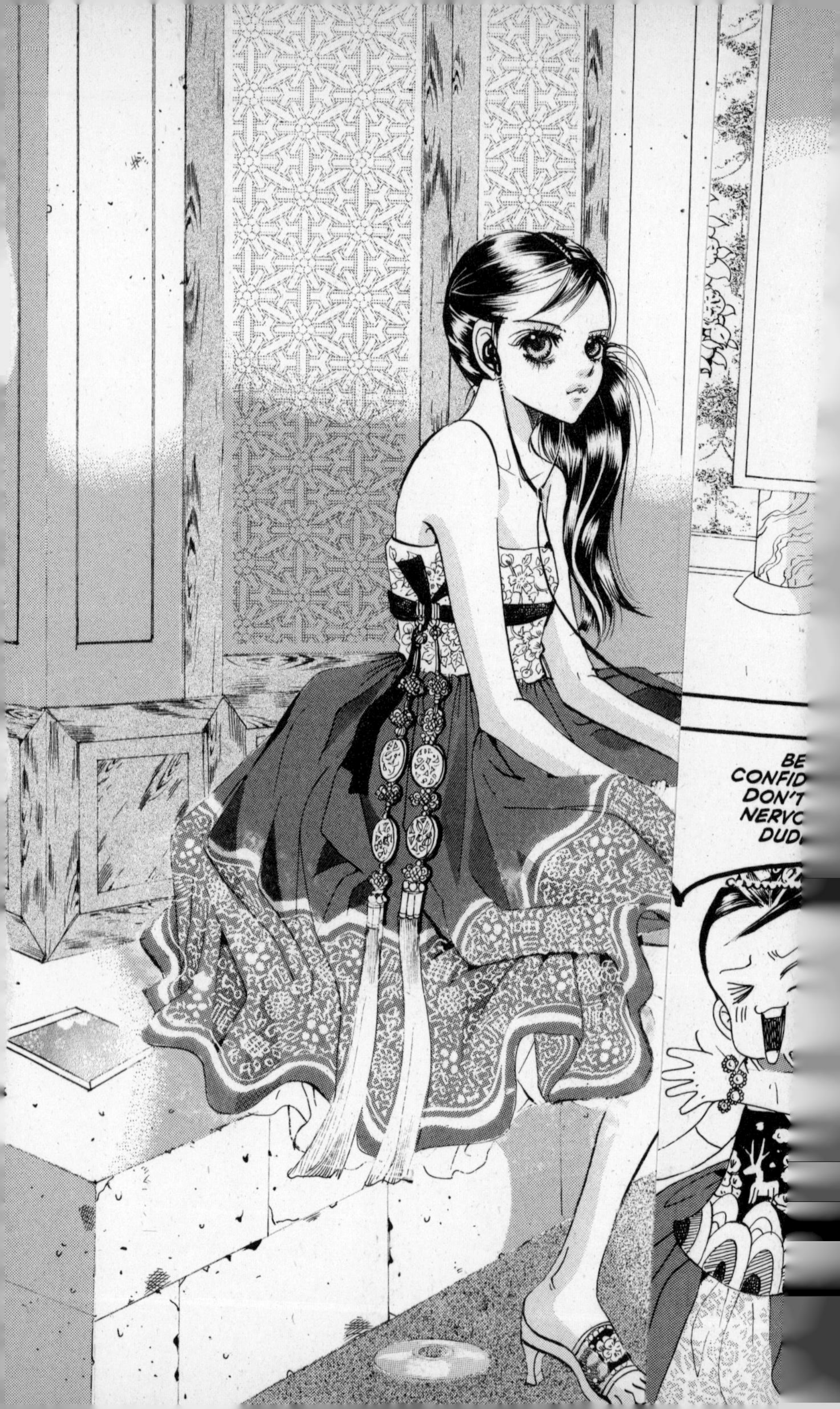
BE CONFID DON'T NERVO DUD

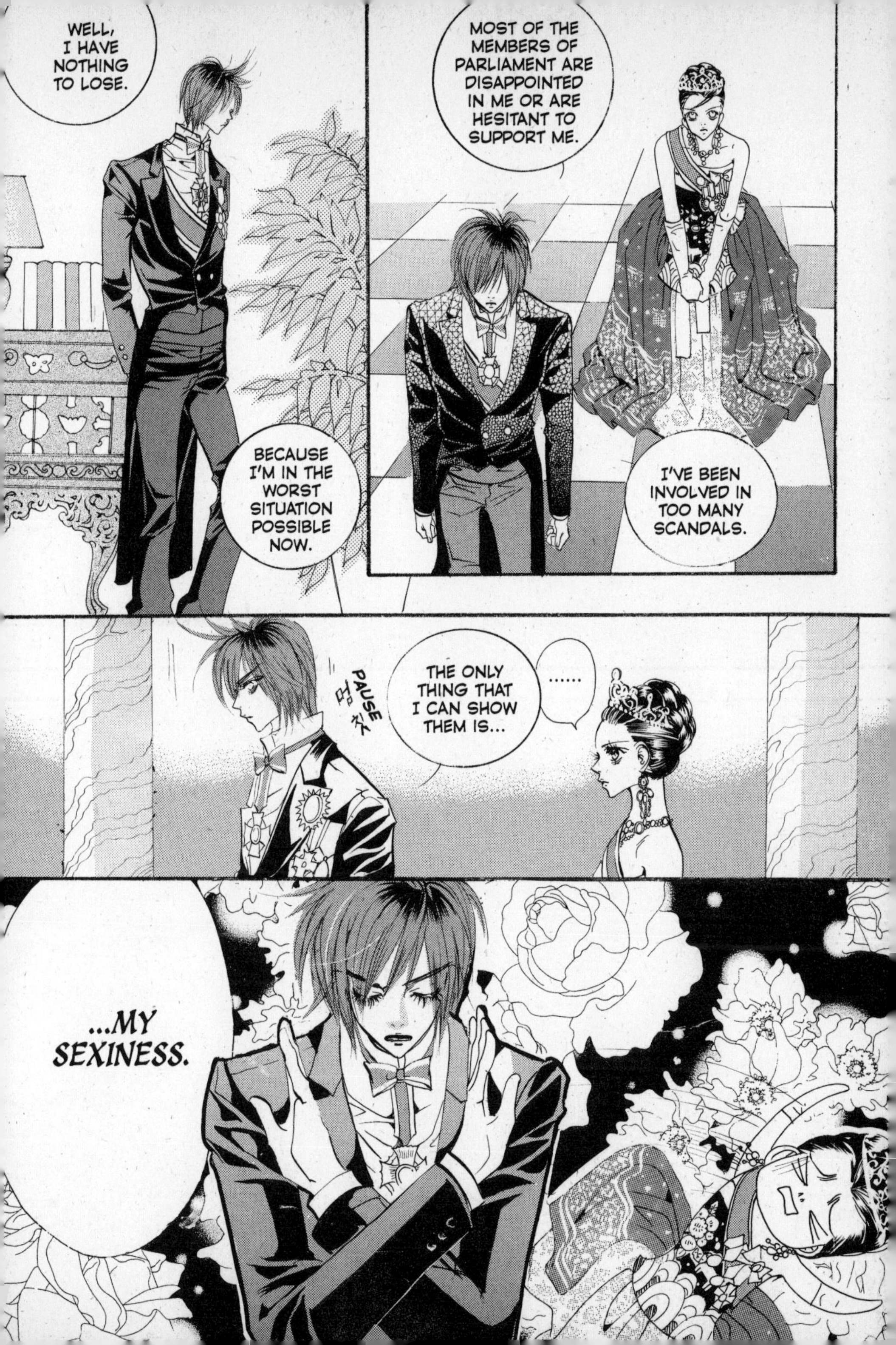
WELL, I HAVE NOTHING TO LOSE.
BECAUSE I'M IN THE WORST SITUATION POSSIBLE NOW.
MOST OF THE MEMBERS OF PARLIAMENT ARE DISAPPOINTED IN ME OR ARE HESITANT TO SUPPORT ME.
I'VE BEEN INVOLVED IN TOO MANY SCANDALS.
PAUSE
멈칫
THE ONLY THING THAT I CAN SHOW THEM IS...
......
...MY SEXINESS.

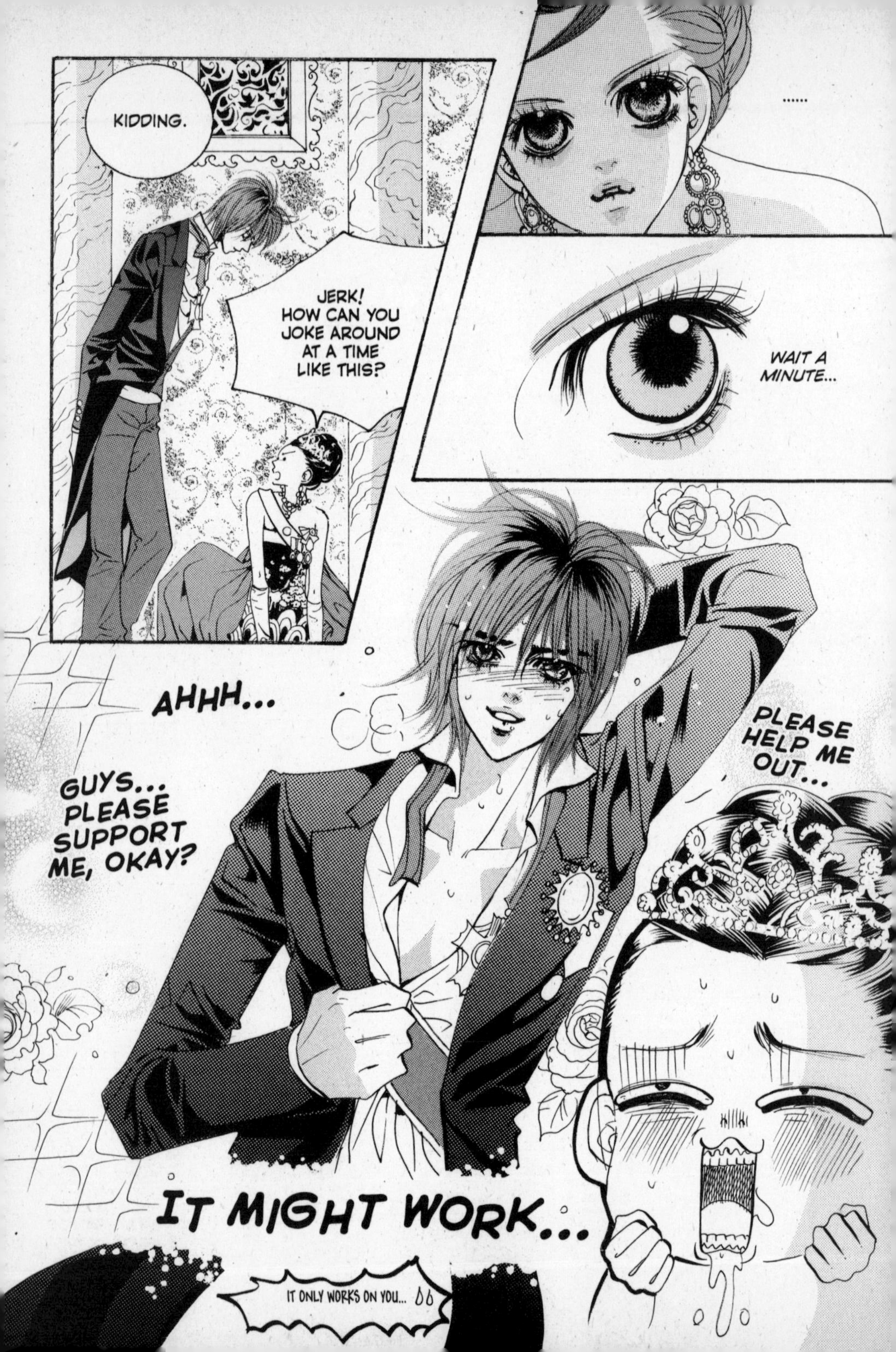
KIDDING.
JERK! HOW CAN YOU JOKE AROUND AT A TIME LIKE THIS?
......
WAIT A MINUTE...
AHHH...
GUYS... PLEASE SUPPORT ME, OKAY?
PLEASE HELP ME OUT...
IT MIGHT WORK...
IT ONLY WORKS ON YOU...

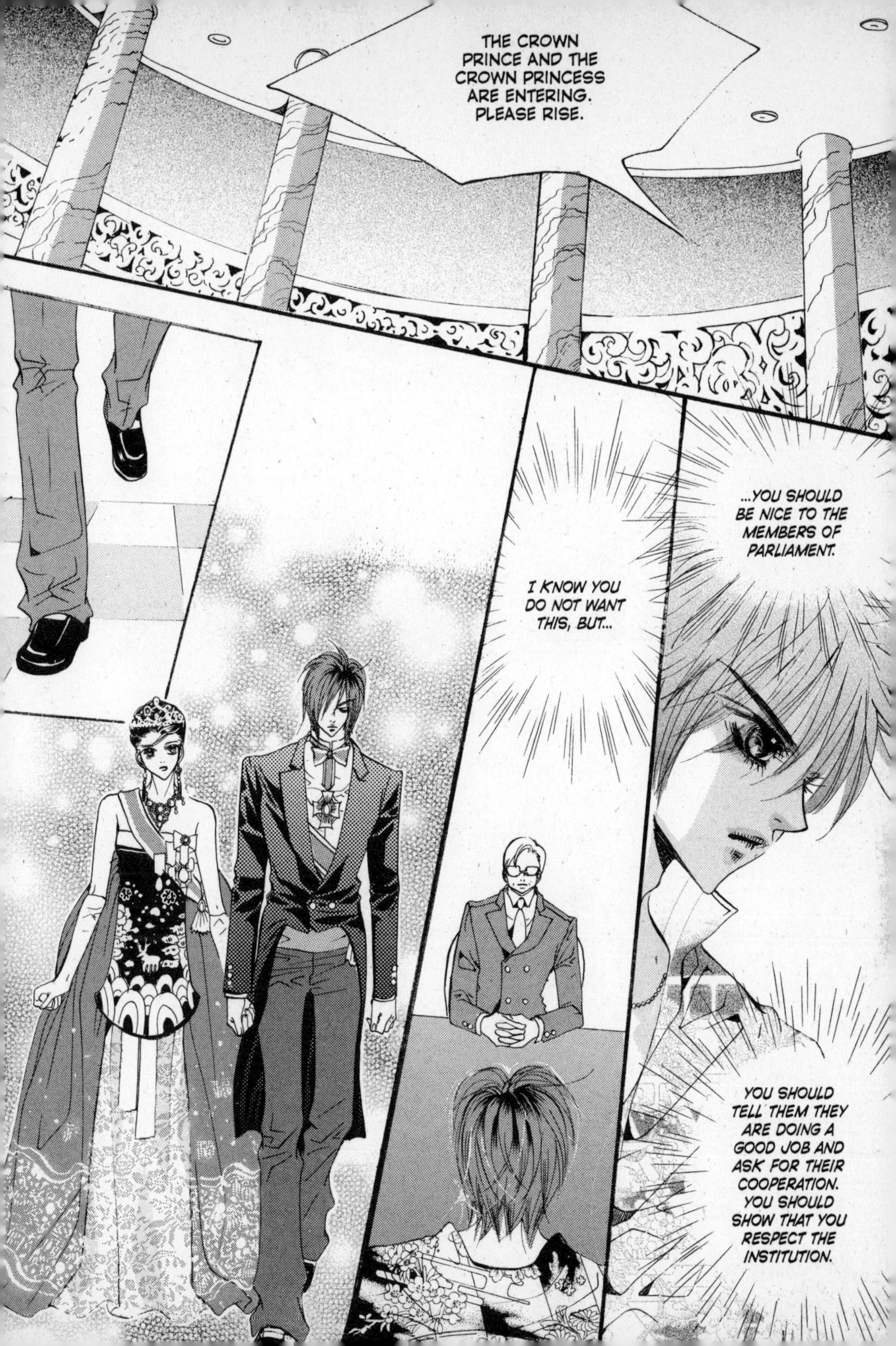
THE CROWN PRINCE AND THE CROWN PRINCESS ARE ENTERING. PLEASE RISE.
I KNOW YOU DO NOT WANT THIS, BUT...
...YOU SHOULD BE NICE TO THE MEMBERS OF PARLIAMENT.
YOU SHOULD TELL THEM THEY ARE DOING A GOOD JOB AND ASK FOR THEIR COOPERATION. YOU SHOULD SHOW THAT YOU RESPECT THE INSTITUTION.

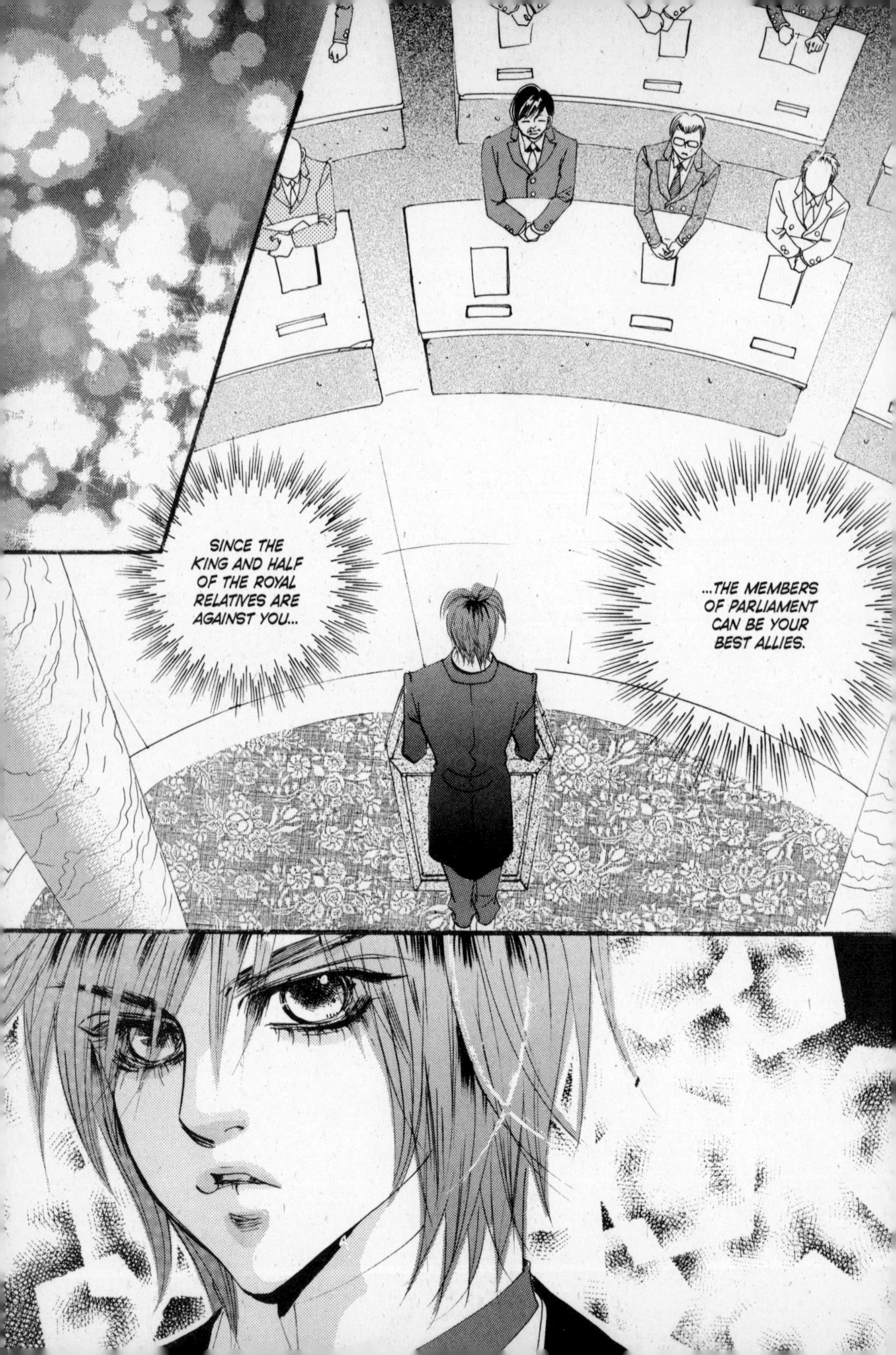
SINCE THE KING AND HALF OF THE ROYAL RELATIVES ARE AGAINST YOU...
...THE MEMBERS OF PARLIAMENT CAN BE YOUR BEST ALLIES.

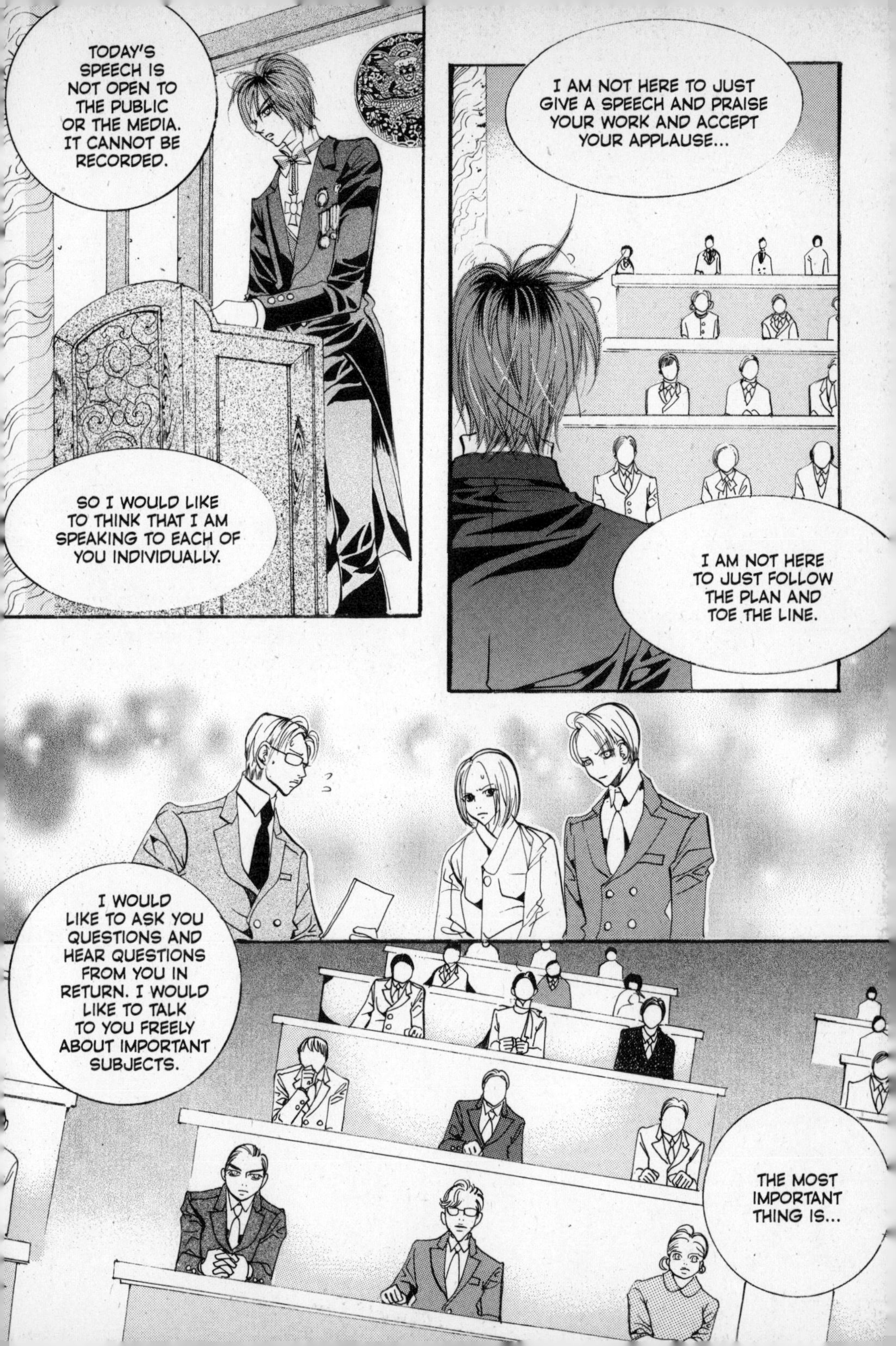
TODAY'S SPEECH IS NOT OPEN TO THE PUBLIC OR THE MEDIA. IT CANNOT BE RECORDED.
SO I WOULD LIKE TO THINK THAT I AM SPEAKING TO EACH OF YOU INDIVIDUALLY.
I AM NOT HERE TO JUST GIVE A SPEECH AND PRAISE YOUR WORK AND ACCEPT YOUR APPLAUSE...
I AM NOT HERE TO JUST FOLLOW THE PLAN AND TOE THE LINE.
I WOULD LIKE TO ASK YOU QUESTIONS AND HEAR QUESTIONS FROM YOU IN RETURN. I WOULD LIKE TO TALK TO YOU FREELY ABOUT IMPORTANT SUBJECTS.
THE MOST IMPORTANT THING IS...

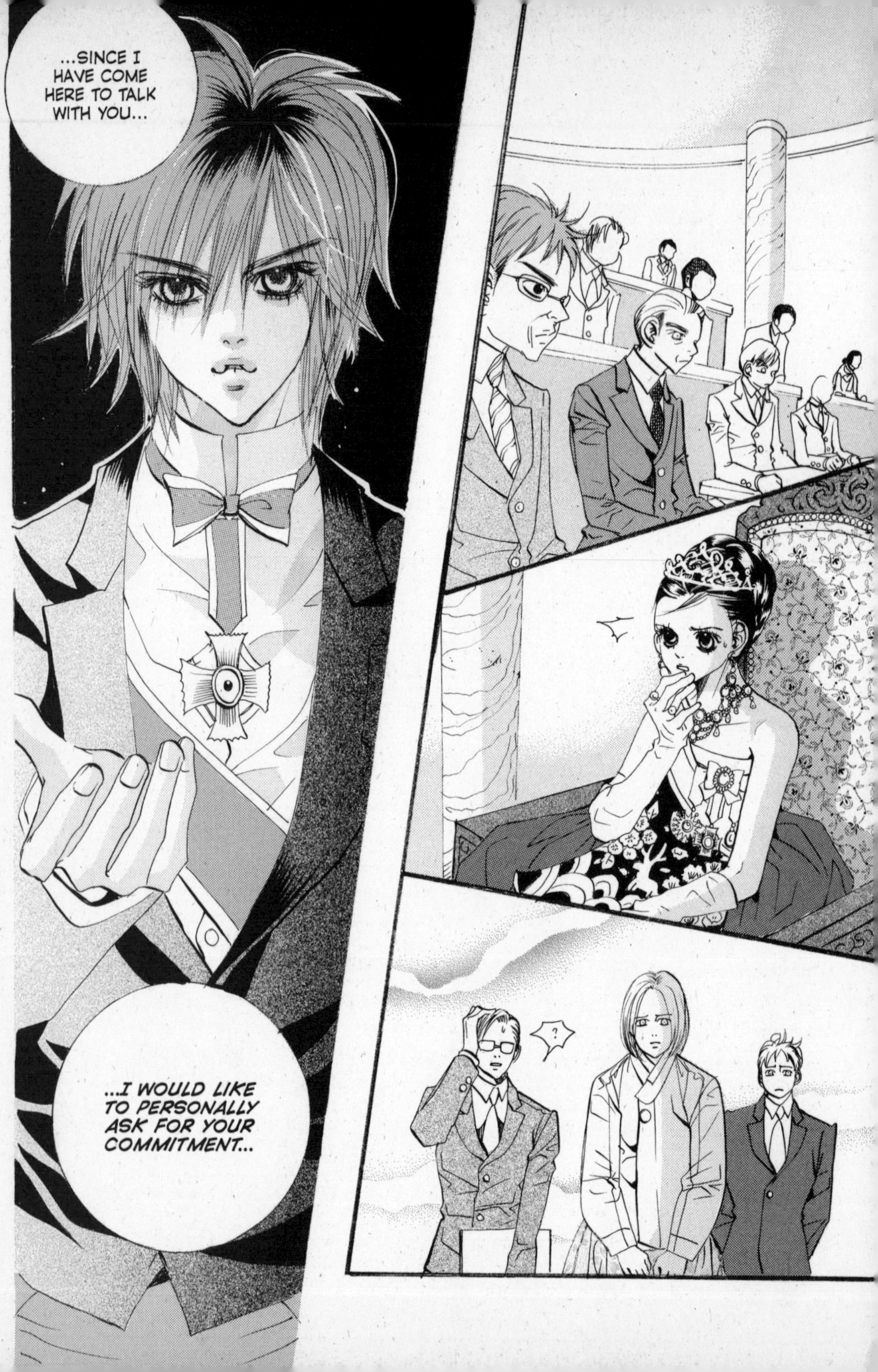
...SINCE I HAVE COME HERE TO TALK WITH YOU...
...I WOULD LIKE TO PERSONALLY ASK FOR YOUR COMMITMENT...
?

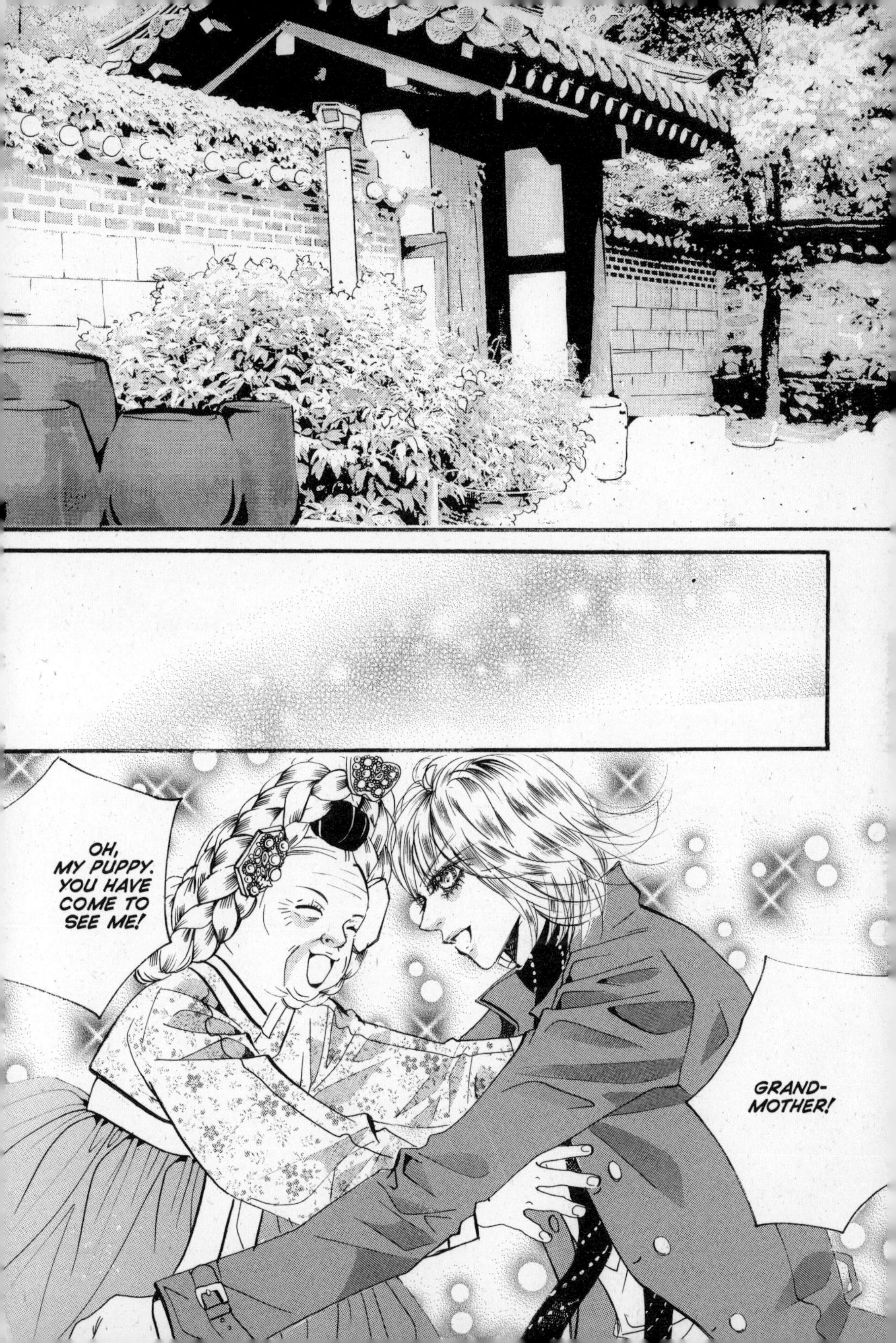
OH, MY PUPPY. YOU HAVE COME TO SEE ME!
GRAND-MOTHER!

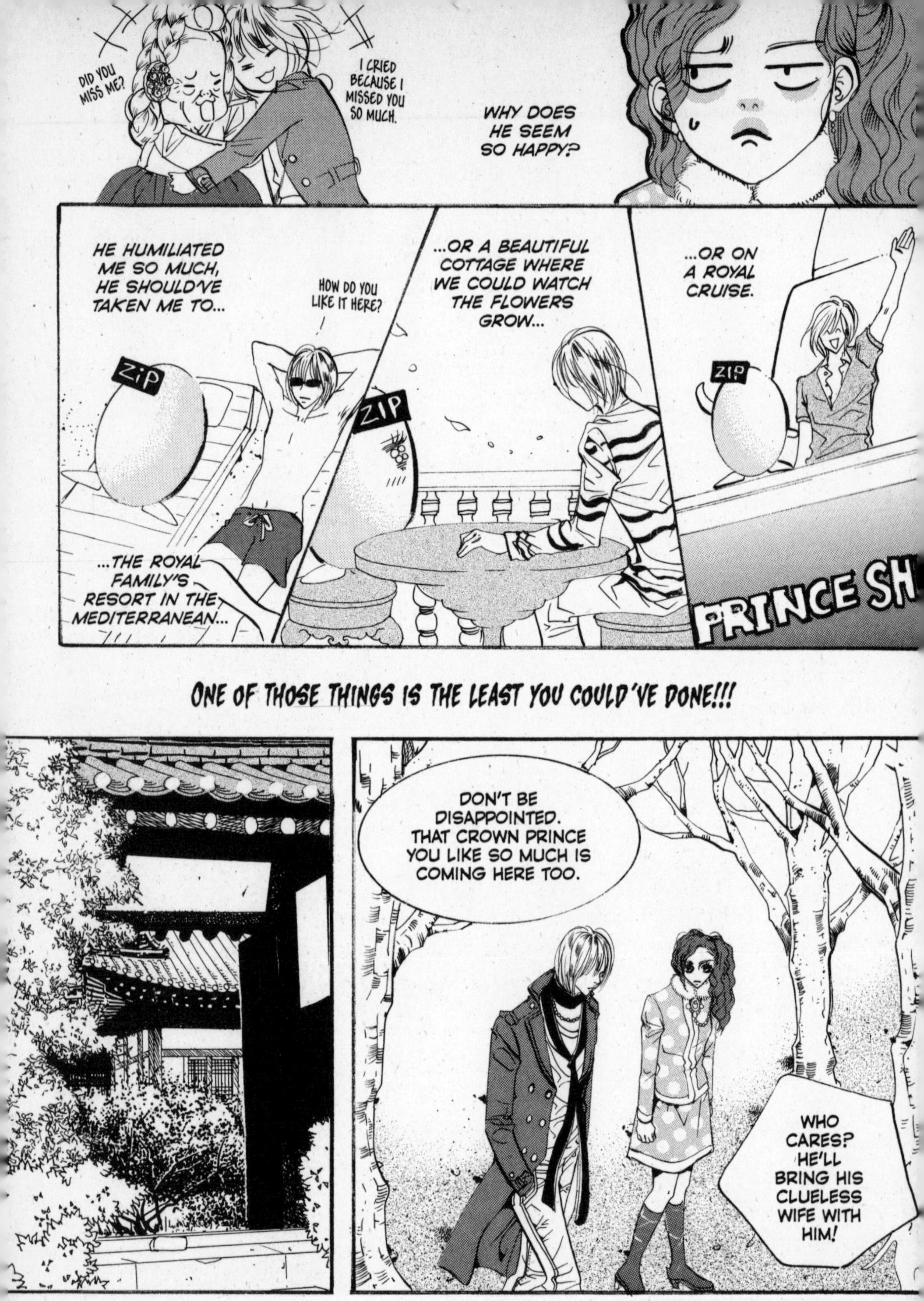
DID YOU MISS ME?
I CRIED BECAUSE I MISSED YOU SO MUCH.
WHY DOES HE SEEM SO HAPPY?
HE HUMILIATED ME SO MUCH, HE SHOULD'VE TAKEN ME TO...
HOW DO YOU LIKE IT HERE?
ZIP
...THE ROYAL FAMILY'S RESORT IN THE MEDITERRANEAN...
ZIP
...OR A BEAUTIFUL COTTAGE WHERE WE COULD WATCH THE FLOWERS GROW...
...OR ON A ROYAL CRUISE.
ZIP
PRINCE SH
ONE OF THOSE THINGS IS THE LEAST YOU COULD'VE DONE!!!
DON'T BE DISAPPOINTED. THAT CROWN PRINCE YOU LIKE SO MUCH IS COMING HERE TOO.
WHO CARES? HE'LL BRING HIS CLUELESS WIFE WITH HIM!

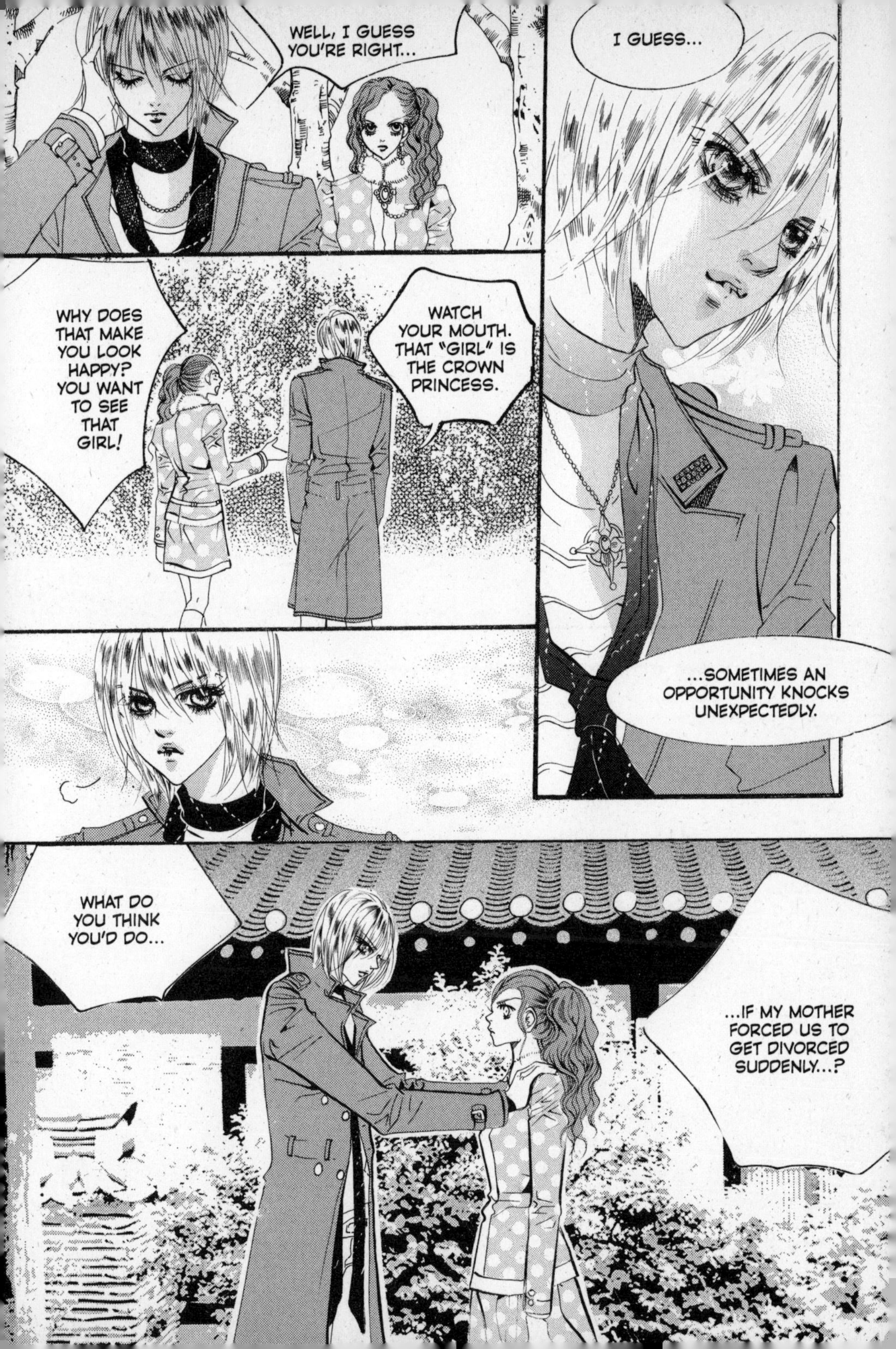
WELL, I GUESS YOU'RE RIGHT...
I GUESS...
WHY DOES THAT MAKE YOU LOOK HAPPY? YOU WANT TO SEE THAT GIRL!
WATCH YOUR MOUTH. THAT "GIRL" IS THE CROWN PRINCESS.
...SOMETIMES AN OPPORTUNITY KNOCKS UNEXPECTEDLY.
WHAT DO YOU THINK YOU'D DO...
...IF MY MOTHER FORCED US TO GET DIVORCED SUDDENLY...?

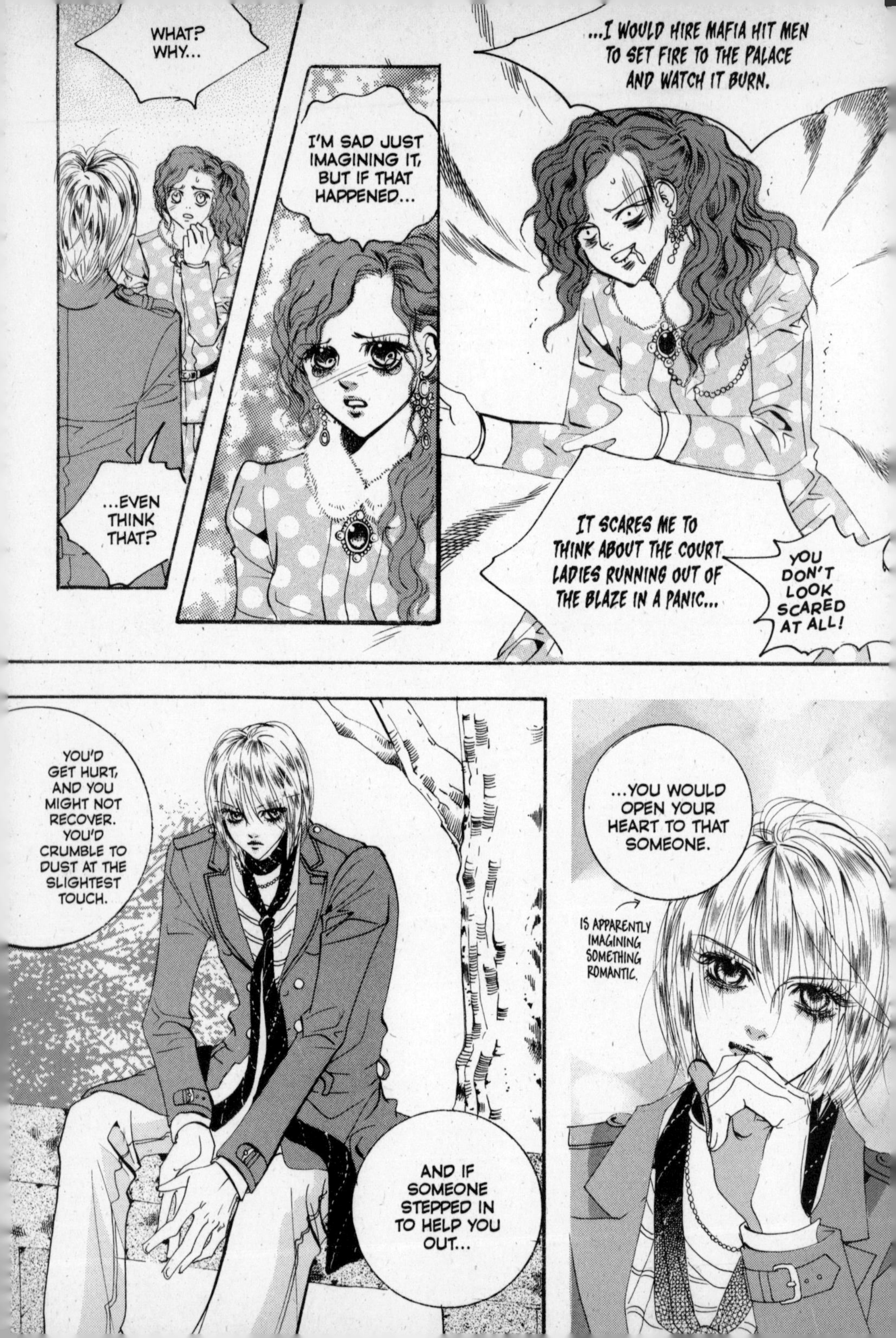
WHAT? WHY...
...EVEN THINK THAT?
I'M SAD JUST IMAGINING IT, BUT IF THAT HAPPENED...
...I WOULD HIRE MAFIA HIT MEN TO SET FIRE TO THE PALACE AND WATCH IT BURN.
IT SCARES ME TO THINK ABOUT THE COURT LADIES RUNNING OUT OF THE BLAZE IN A PANIC...
YOU DON'T LOOK SCARED AT ALL!
YOU'D GET HURT, AND YOU MIGHT NOT RECOVER. YOU'D CRUMBLE TO DUST AT THE SLIGHTEST TOUCH.
AND IF SOMEONE STEPPED IN TO HELP YOU OUT...
...YOU WOULD OPEN YOUR HEART TO THAT SOMEONE.
IS APPARENTLY IMAGINING SOMETHING ROMANTIC.

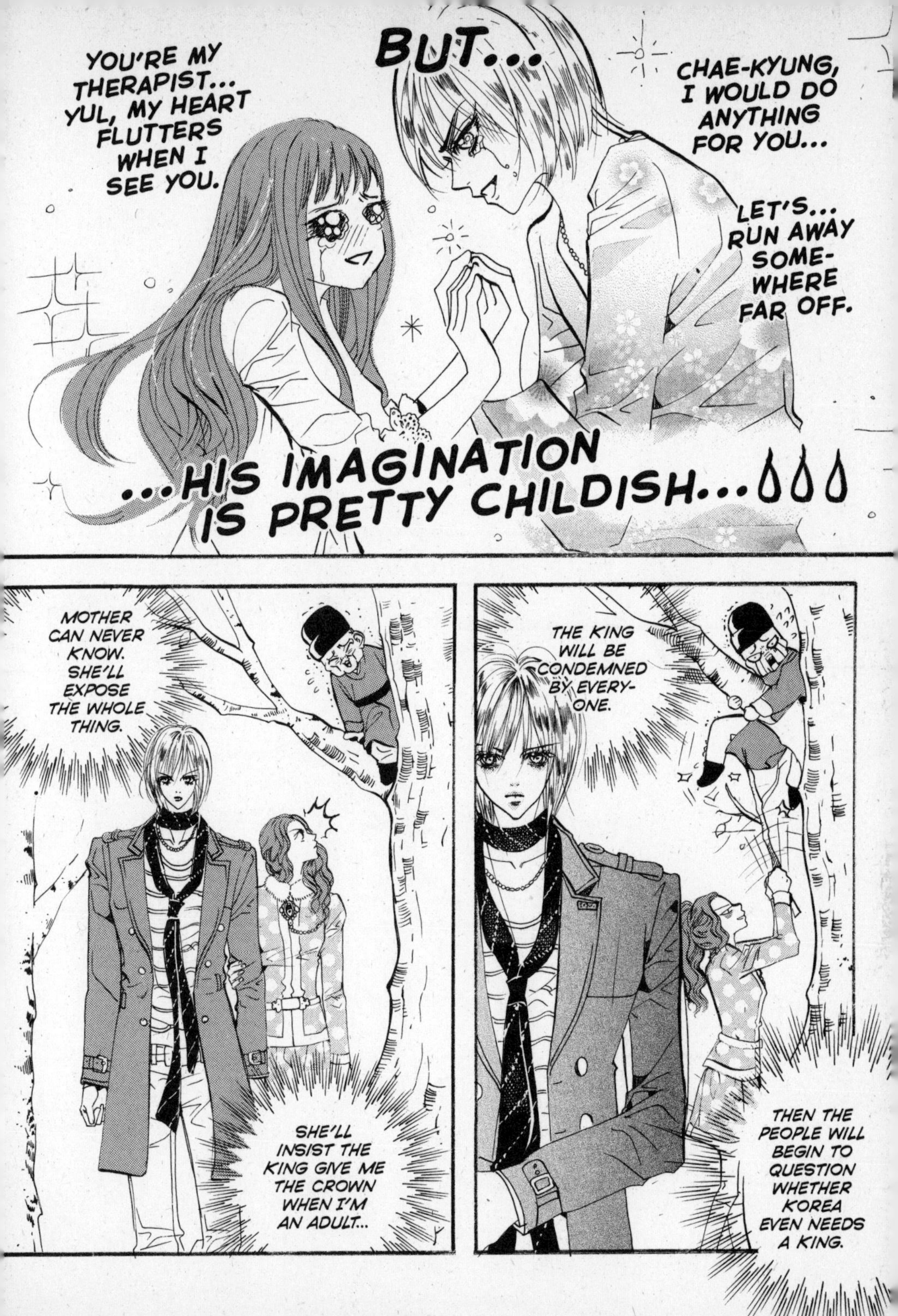
YOU'RE MY THERAPIST... YUL, MY HEART FLUTTERS WHEN I SEE YOU.
BUT...
CHAE-KYUNG, I WOULD DO ANYTHING FOR YOU...
LET'S... RUN AWAY SOME-WHERE FAR OFF.
...HIS IMAGINATION IS PRETTY CHILDISH...
MOTHER CAN NEVER KNOW. SHE'LL EXPOSE THE WHOLE THING.
SHE'LL INSIST THE KING GIVE ME THE CROWN WHEN I'M AN ADULT...
THE KING WILL BE CONDEMNED BY EVERY-ONE.
THEN THE PEOPLE WILL BEGIN TO QUESTION WHETHER KOREA EVEN NEEDS A KING.

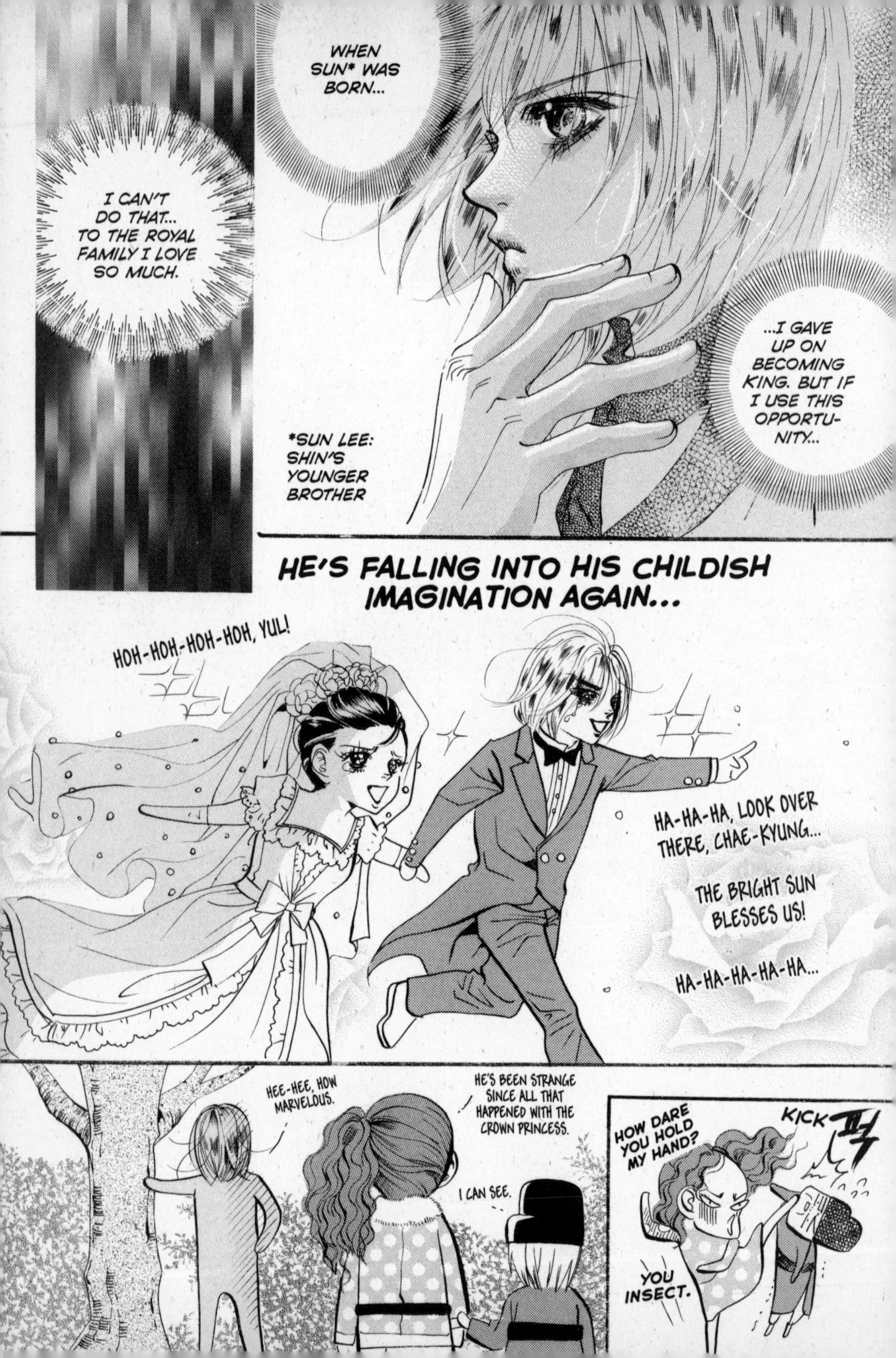

I CAN'T DO THAT... TO THE ROYAL FAMILY I LOVE SO MUCH.
WHEN SUN* WAS BORN...
...I GAVE UP ON BECOMING KING. BUT IF I USE THIS OPPORTU-NITY...
*SUN LEE: SHIN'S YOUNGER BROTHER
HE'S FALLING INTO HIS CHILDISH IMAGINATION AGAIN...
HOH-HOH-HOH-HOH, YUL!
HA-HA-HA, LOOK OVER THERE, CHAE-KYUNG...
THE BRIGHT SUN BLESSES US!
HA-HA-HA-HA-HA...
HEE-HEE, HOW MARVELOUS.
HE'S BEEN STRANGE SINCE ALL THAT HAPPENED WITH THE CROWN PRINCESS.
I CAN SEE.
HOW DARE YOU HOLD MY HAND?
KICK
YOU INSECT.

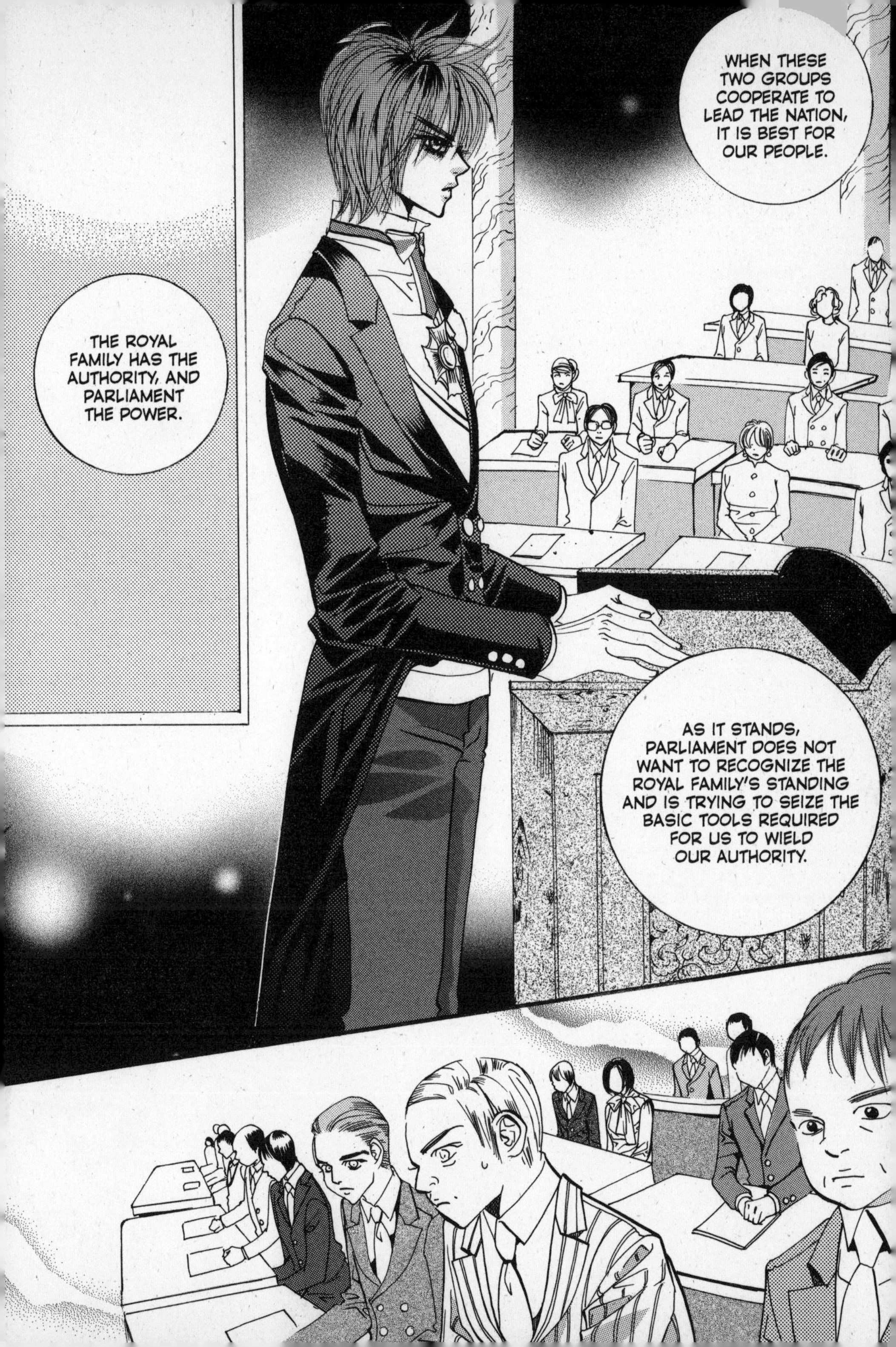
THE ROYAL FAMILY HAS THE AUTHORITY, AND PARLIAMENT THE POWER.
WHEN THESE TWO GROUPS COOPERATE TO LEAD THE NATION, IT IS BEST FOR OUR PEOPLE.
AS IT STANDS, PARLIAMENT DOES NOT WANT TO RECOGNIZE THE ROYAL FAMILY'S STANDING AND IS TRYING TO SEIZE THE BASIC TOOLS REQUIRED FOR US TO WIELD OUR AUTHORITY.

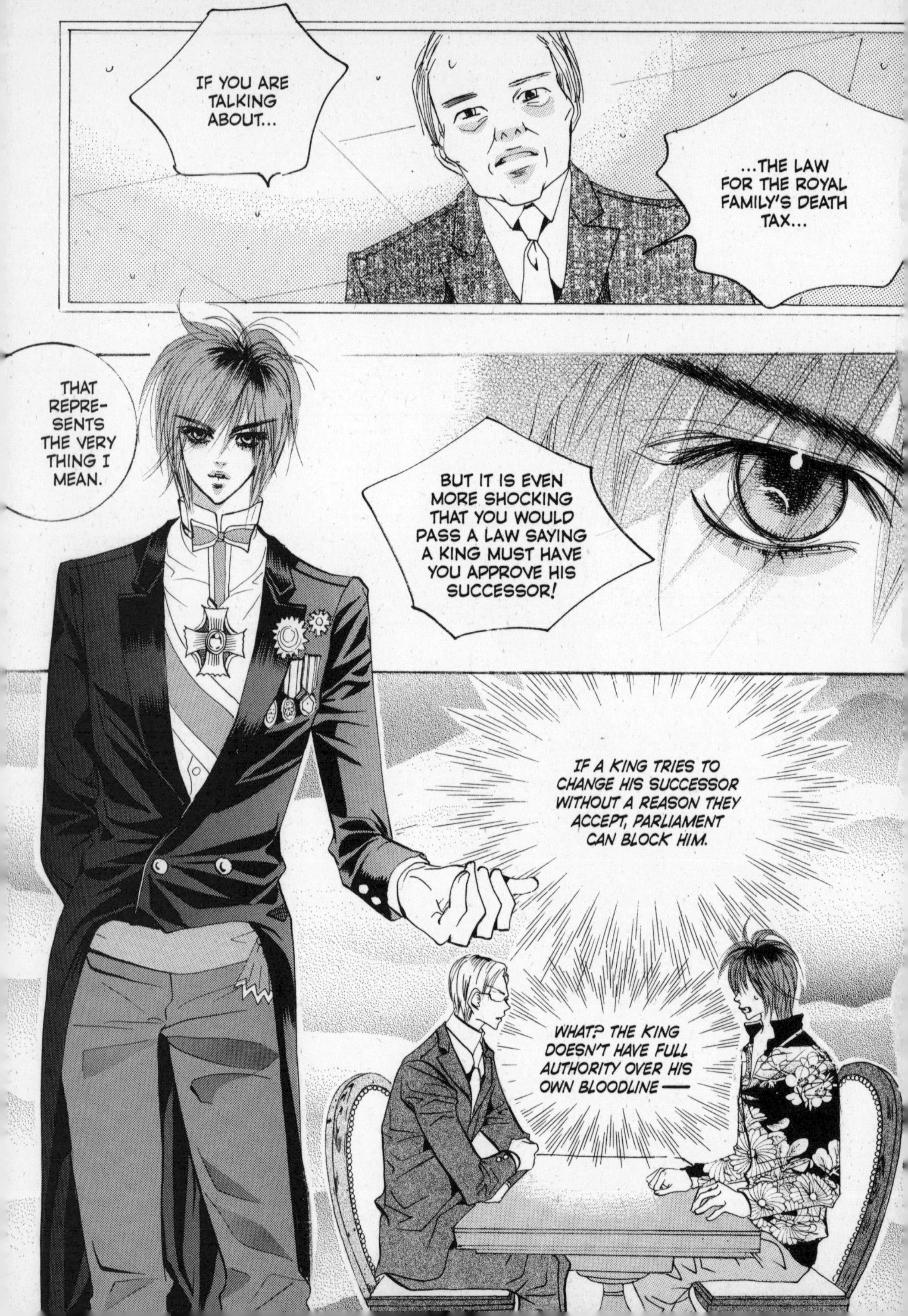
IF YOU ARE TALKING ABOUT...
...THE LAW FOR THE ROYAL FAMILY'S DEATH TAX...
THAT REPRESENTS THE VERY THING I MEAN.
BUT IT IS EVEN MORE SHOCKING THAT YOU WOULD PASS A LAW SAYING A KING MUST HAVE YOU APPROVE HIS SUCCESSOR!
IF A KING TRIES TO CHANGE HIS SUCCESSOR WITHOUT A REASON THEY ACCEPT, PARLIAMENT CAN BLOCK HIM.
WHAT? THE KING DOESN'T HAVE FULL AUTHORITY OVER HIS OWN BLOODLINE—

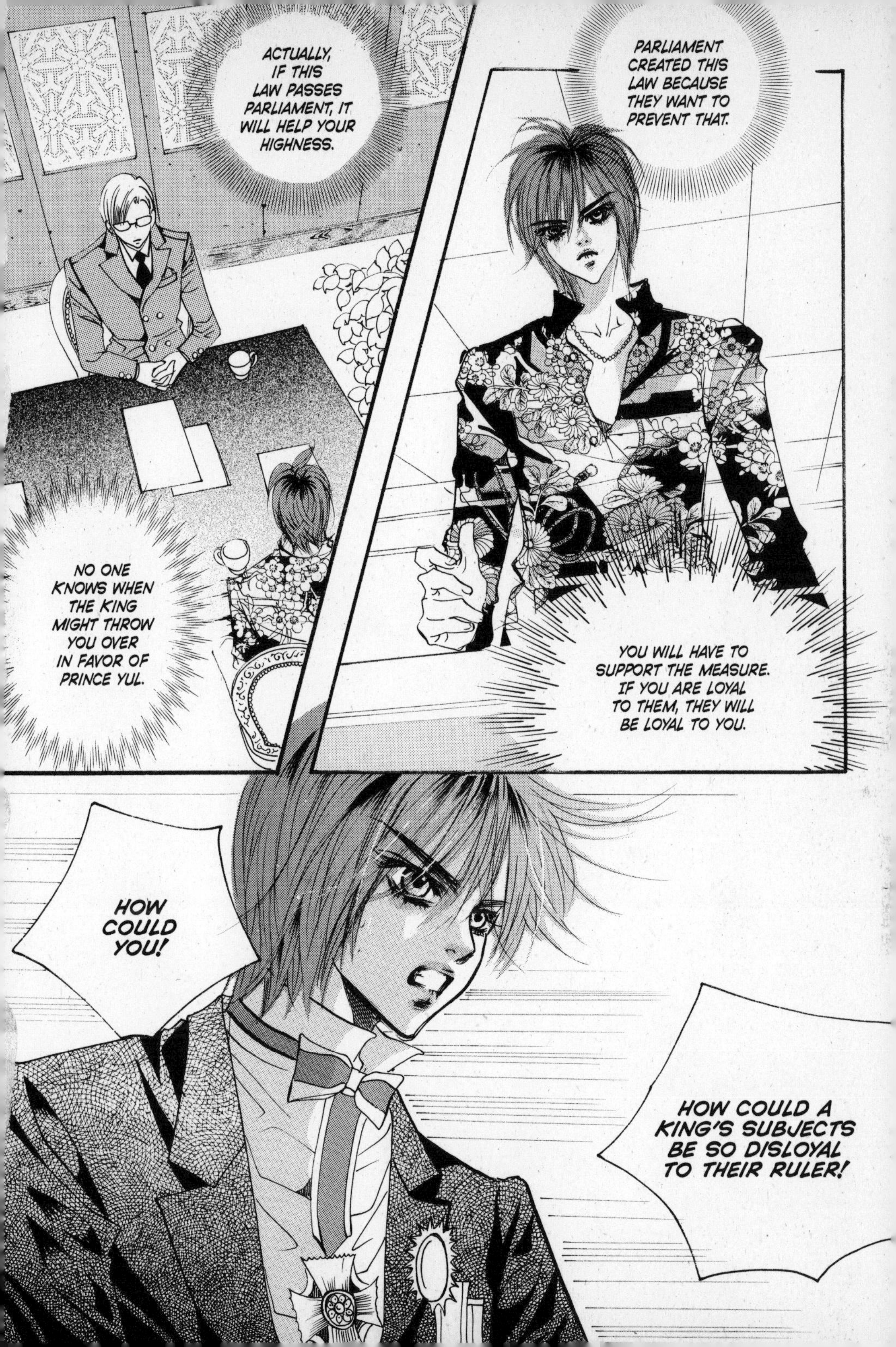
ACTUALLY, IF THIS LAW PASSES PARLIAMENT, IT WILL HELP YOUR HIGHNESS.
NO ONE KNOWS WHEN THE KING MIGHT THROW YOU OVER IN FAVOR OF PRINCE YUL.
PARLIAMENT CREATED THIS LAW BECAUSE THEY WANT TO PREVENT THAT.
YOU WILL HAVE TO SUPPORT THE MEASURE. IF YOU ARE LOYAL TO THEM, THEY WILL BE LOYAL TO YOU.
HOW COULD YOU!
HOW COULD A KING'S SUBJECTS BE SO DISLOYAL TO THEIR RULER!

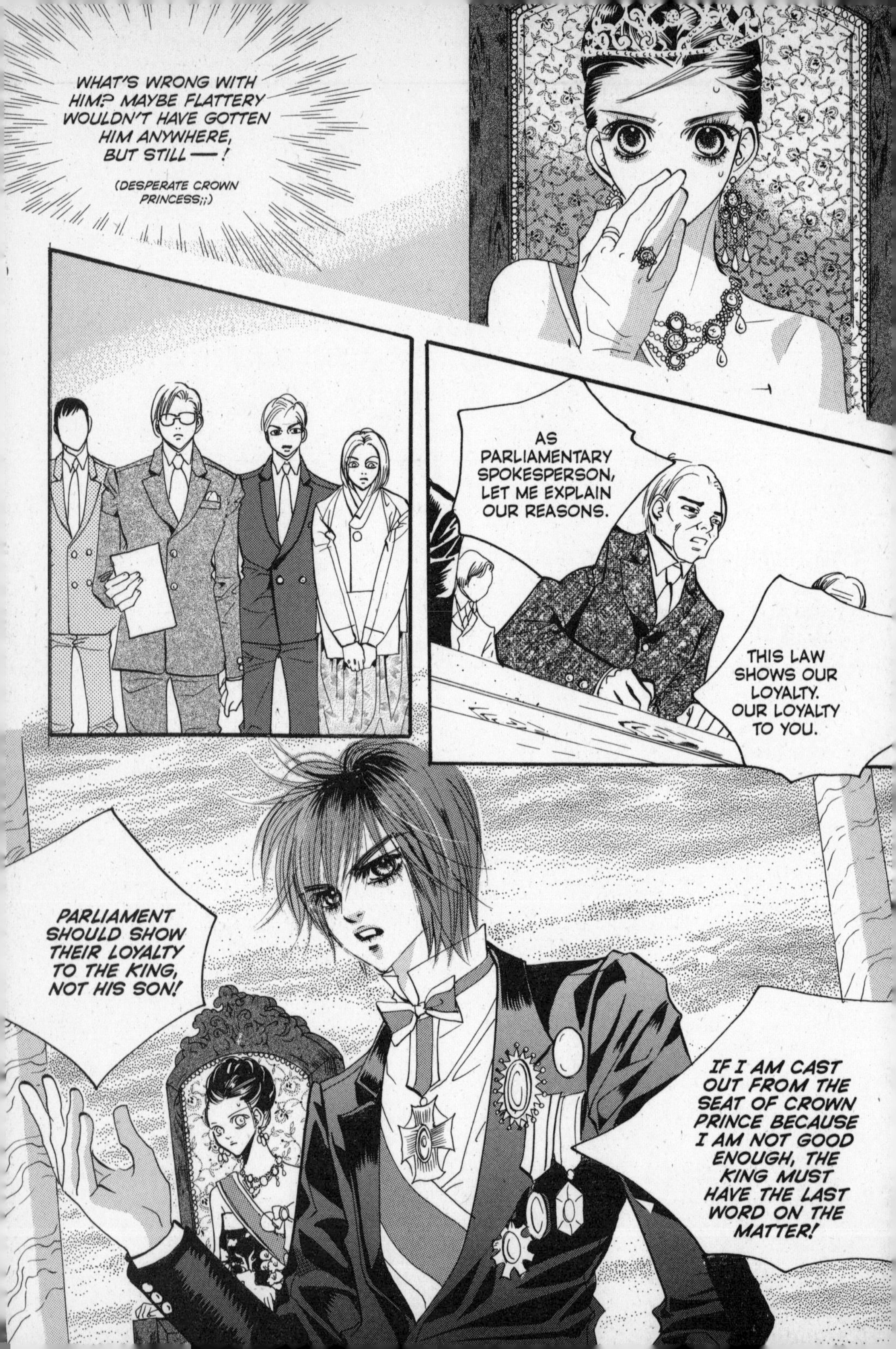
WHAT'S WRONG WITH HIM? MAYBE FLATTERY WOULDN'T HAVE GOTTEN HIM ANYWHERE, BUT STILL—!
(DESPERATE CROWN PRINCESS;;)
AS PARLIAMENTARY SPOKESPERSON, LET ME EXPLAIN OUR REASONS.
THIS LAW SHOWS OUR LOYALTY. OUR LOYALTY TO YOU.
PARLIAMENT SHOULD SHOW THEIR LOYALTY TO THE KING, NOT HIS SON!
IF I AM CAST OUT FROM THE SEAT OF CROWN PRINCE BECAUSE I AM NOT GOOD ENOUGH, THE KING MUST HAVE THE LAST WORD ON THE MATTER!

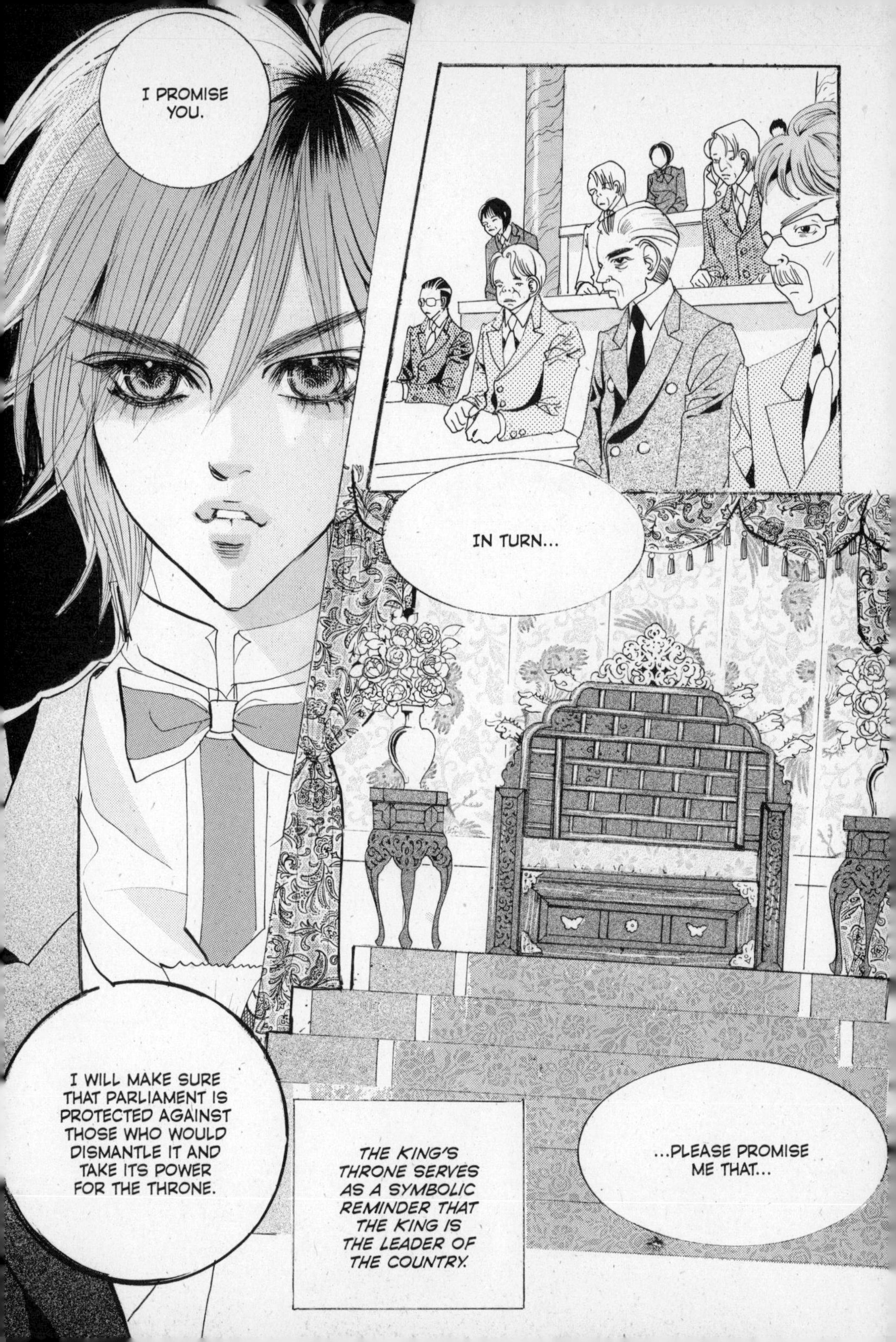

I PROMISE YOU.
I WILL MAKE SURE THAT PARLIAMENT IS PROTECTED AGAINST THOSE WHO WOULD DISMANTLE IT AND TAKE ITS POWER FOR THE THRONE.
IN TURN...
THE KING'S THRONE SERVES AS A SYMBOLIC REMINDER THAT THE KING IS THE LEADER OF THE COUNTRY.
...PLEASE PROMISE ME THAT...

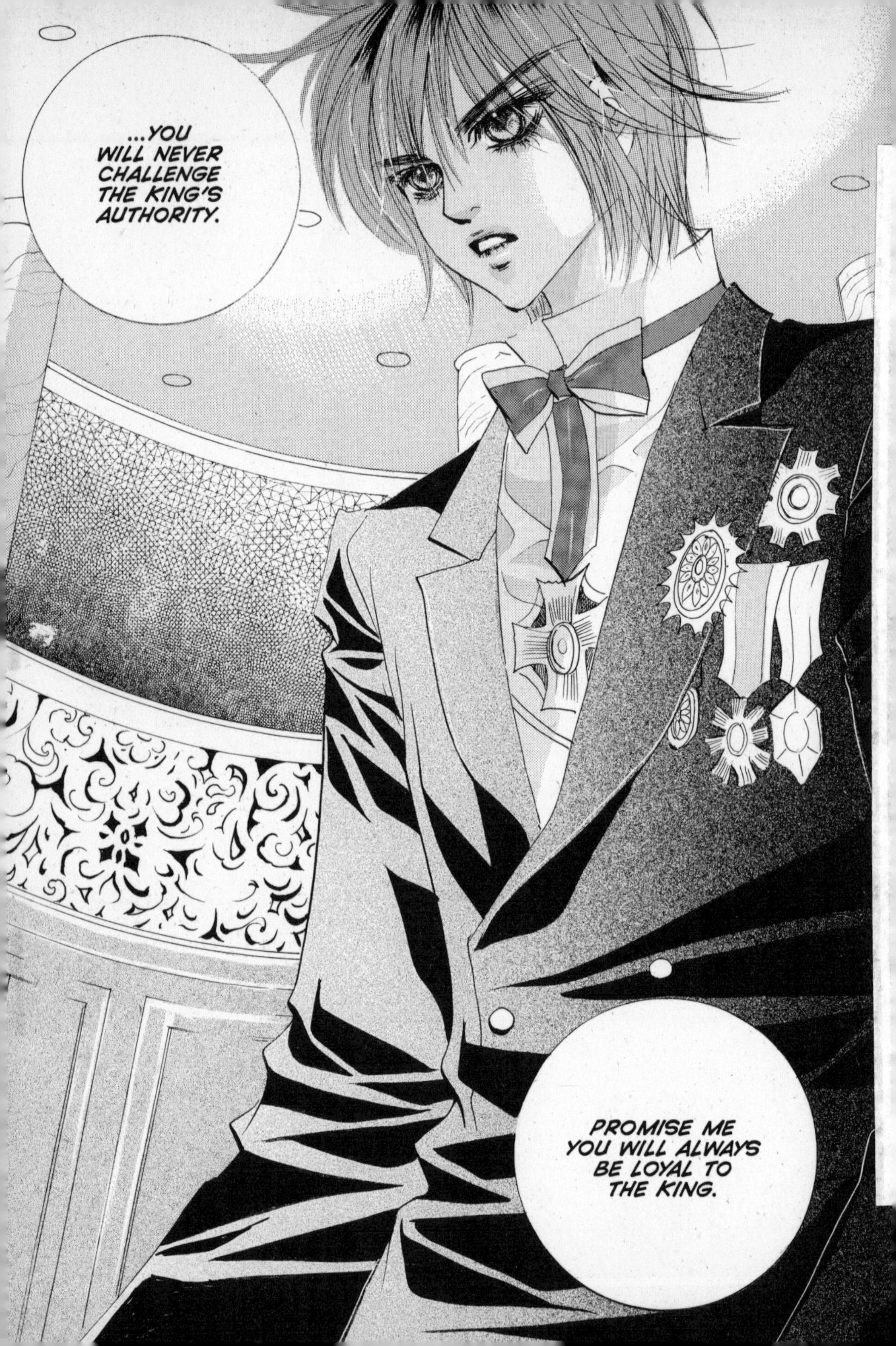
...YOU WILL NEVER CHALLENGE THE KING'S AUTHORITY.
PROMISE ME YOU WILL ALWAYS BE LOYAL TO THE KING.

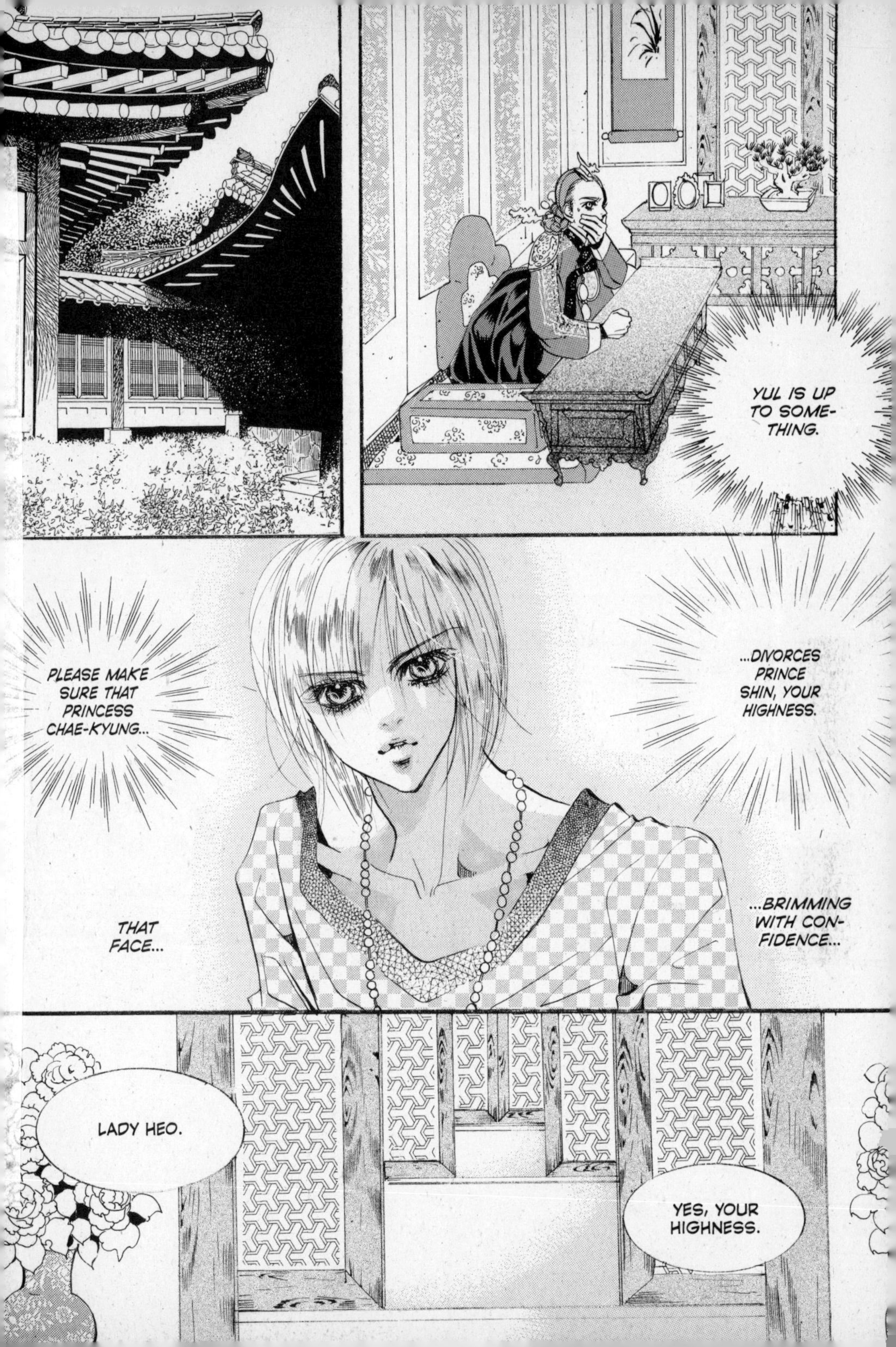
YUL IS UP TO SOME-THING.
PLEASE MAKE SURE THAT PRINCESS CHAE-KYUNG...
...DIVORCES PRINCE SHIN, YOUR HIGHNESS.
THAT FACE...
...BRIMMING WITH CON-FIDENCE...
LADY HEO.
YES, YOUR HIGHNESS.

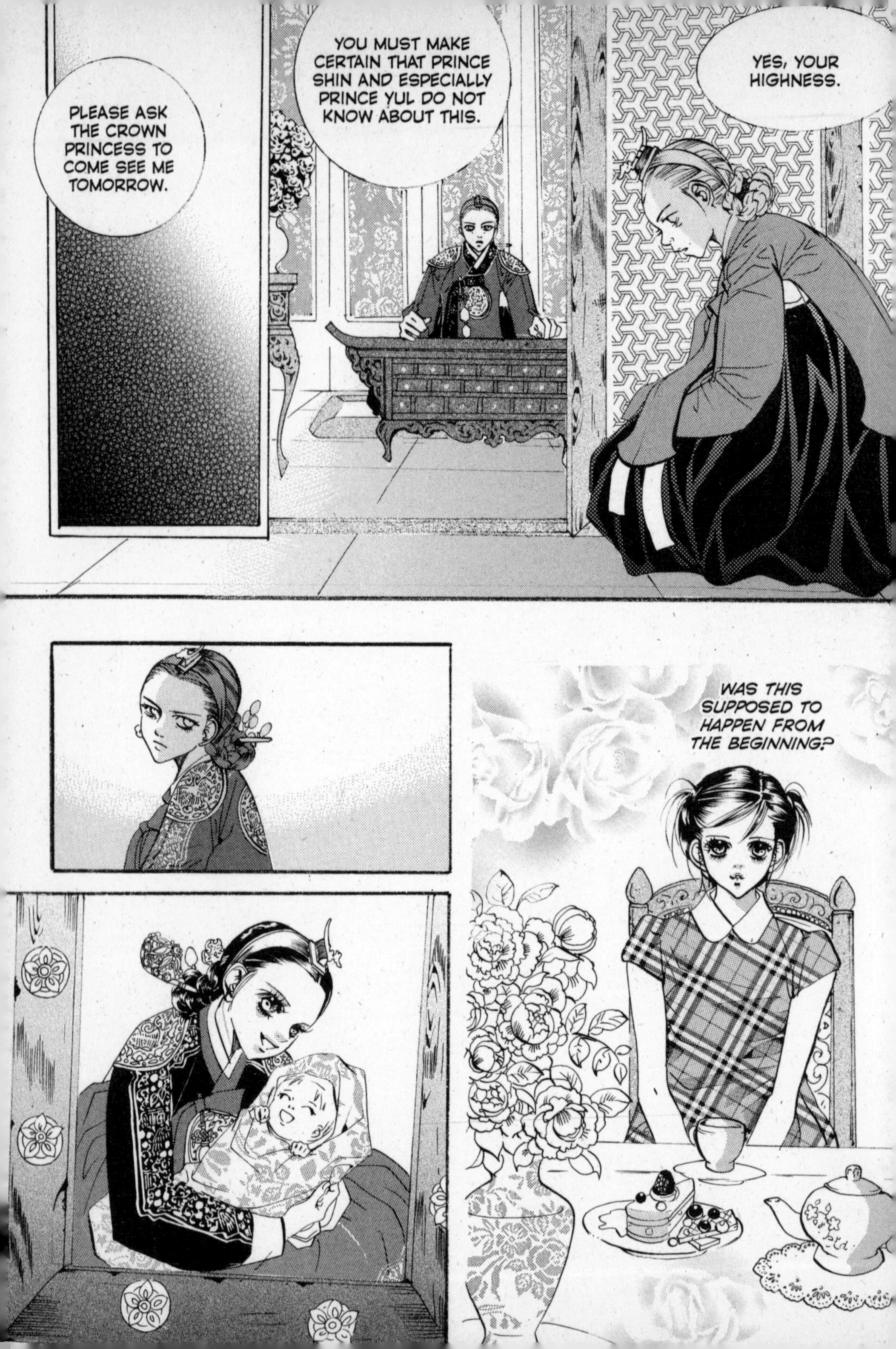
PLEASE ASK THE CROWN PRINCESS TO COME SEE ME TOMORROW.
YOU MUST MAKE CERTAIN THAT PRINCE SHIN AND ESPECIALLY PRINCE YUL DO NOT KNOW ABOUT THIS.
YES, YOUR HIGHNESS.
WAS THIS SUPPOSED TO HAPPEN FROM THE BEGINNING?

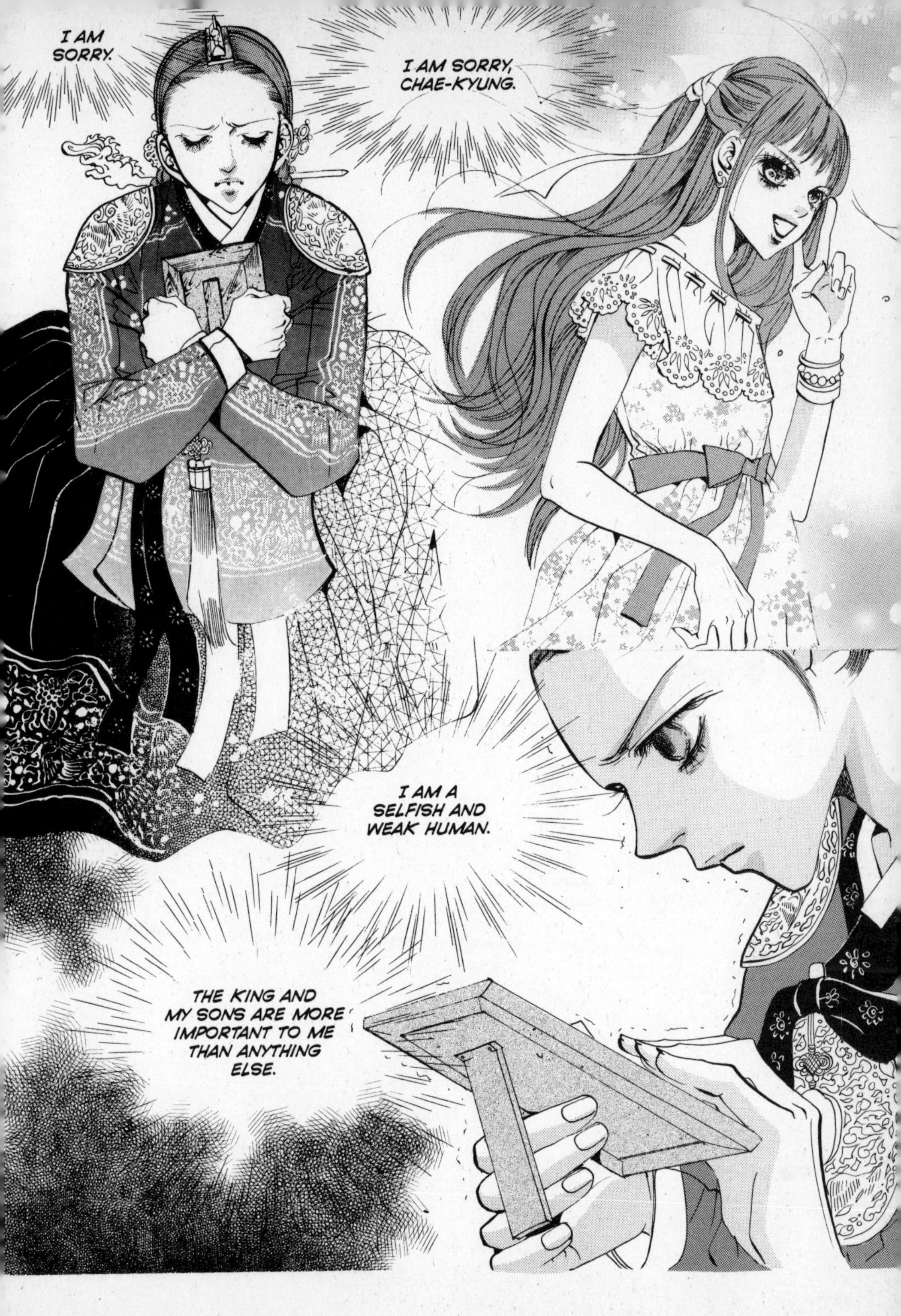
I AM SORRY.
I AM SORRY, CHAE-KYUNG.
I AM A SELFISH AND WEAK HUMAN.
THE KING AND MY SONS ARE MORE IMPORTANT TO ME THAN ANYTHING ELSE.

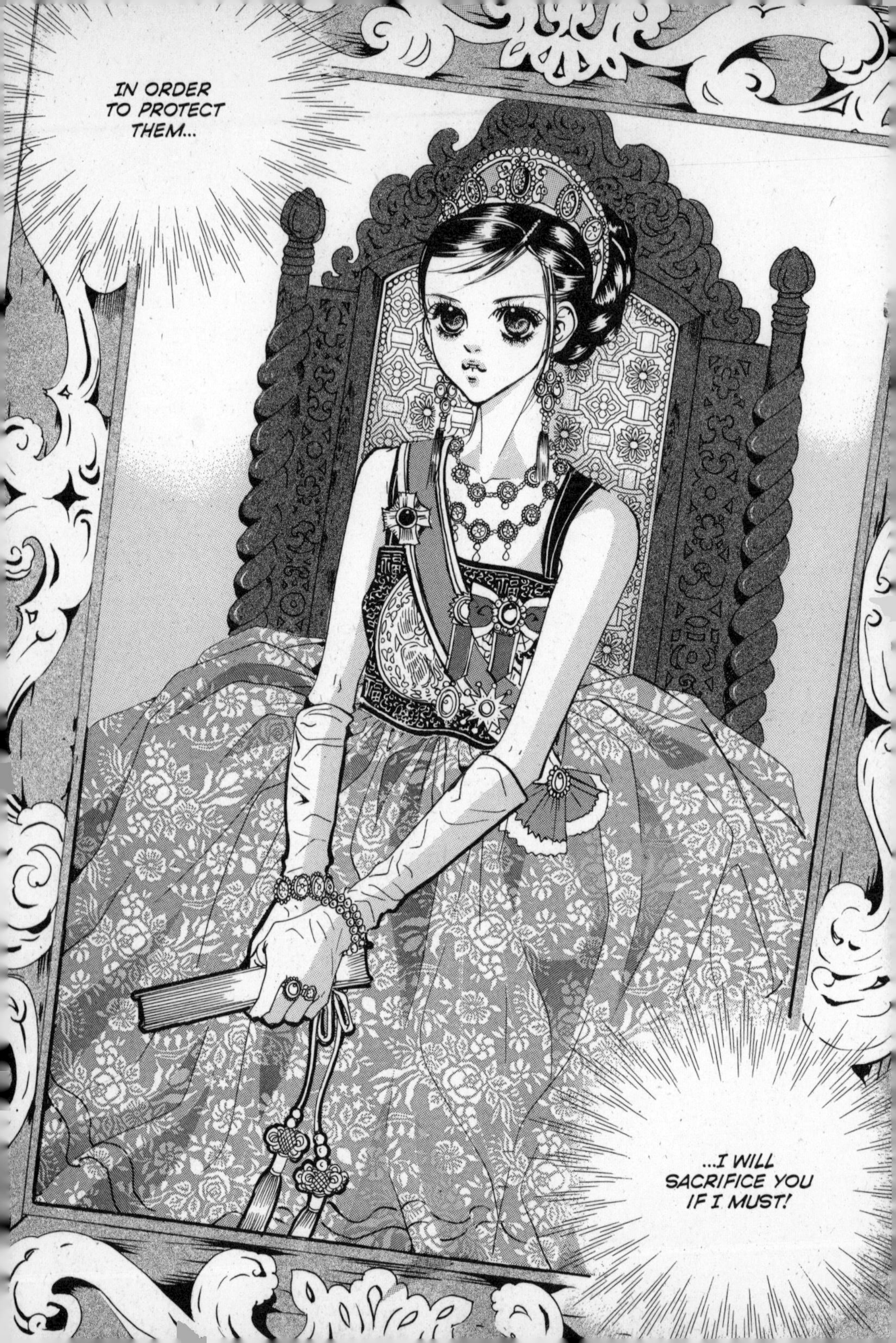
IN ORDER TO PROTECT THEM...
...I WILL SACRIFICE YOU IF I MUST!

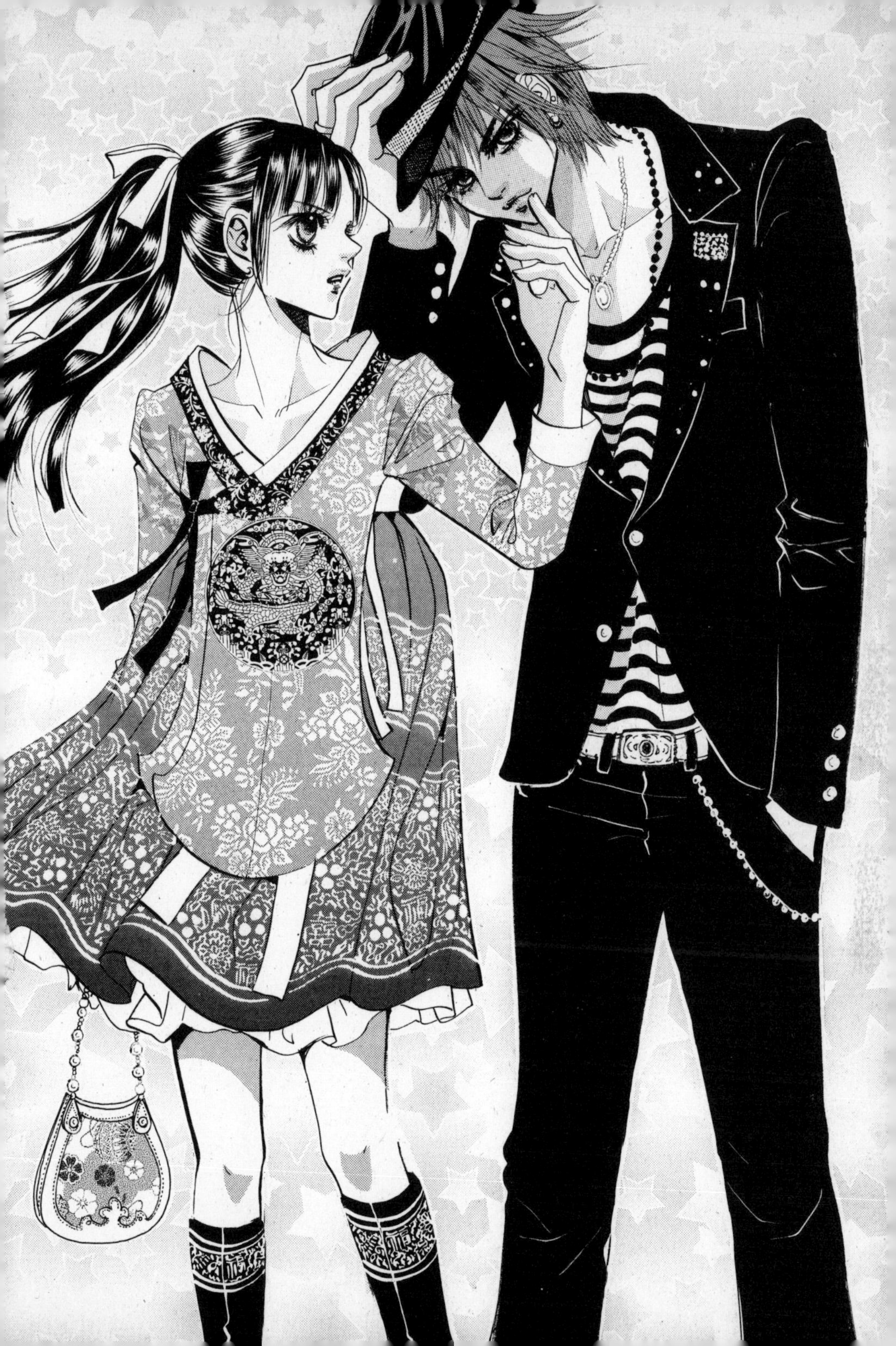

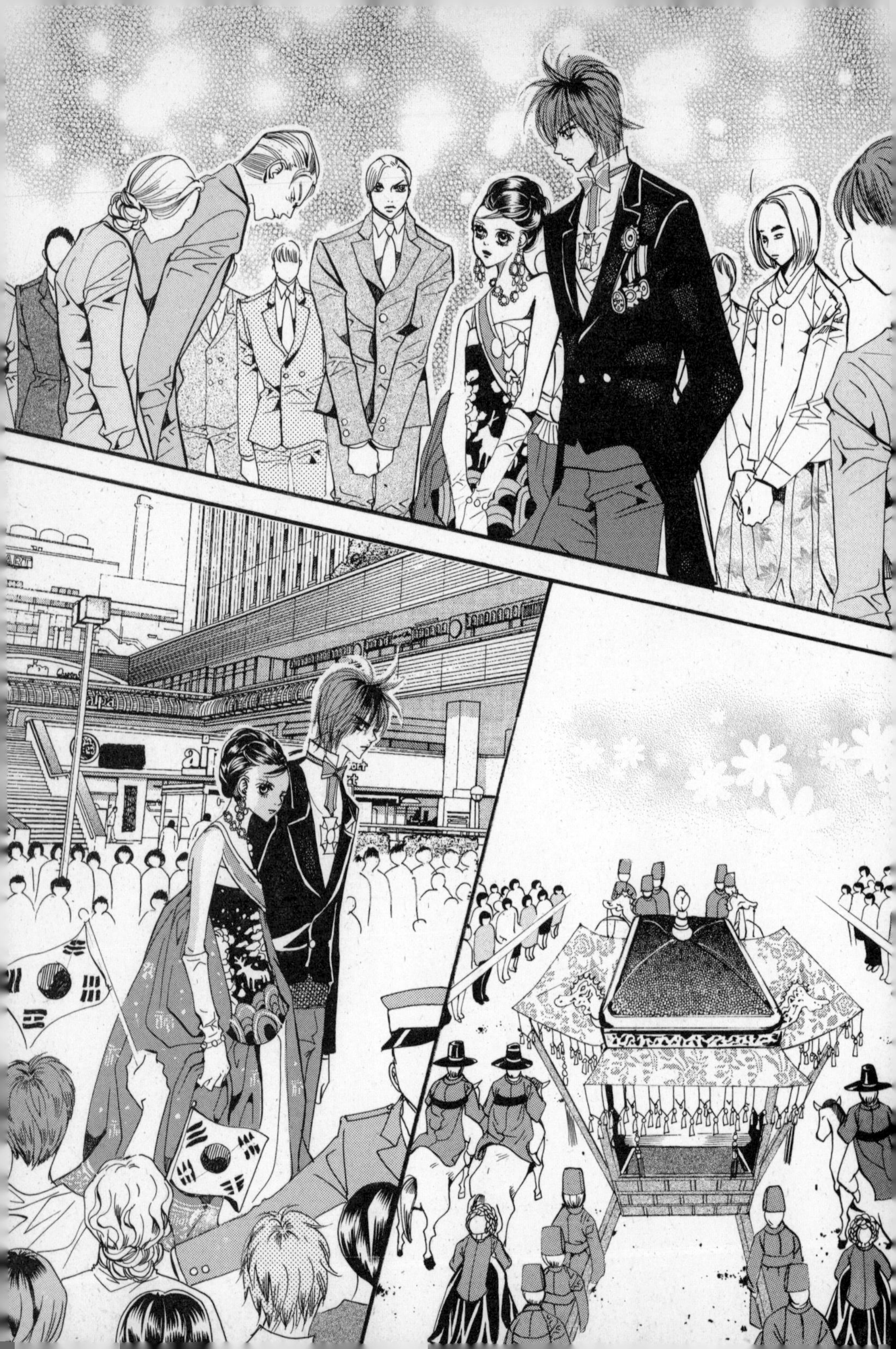

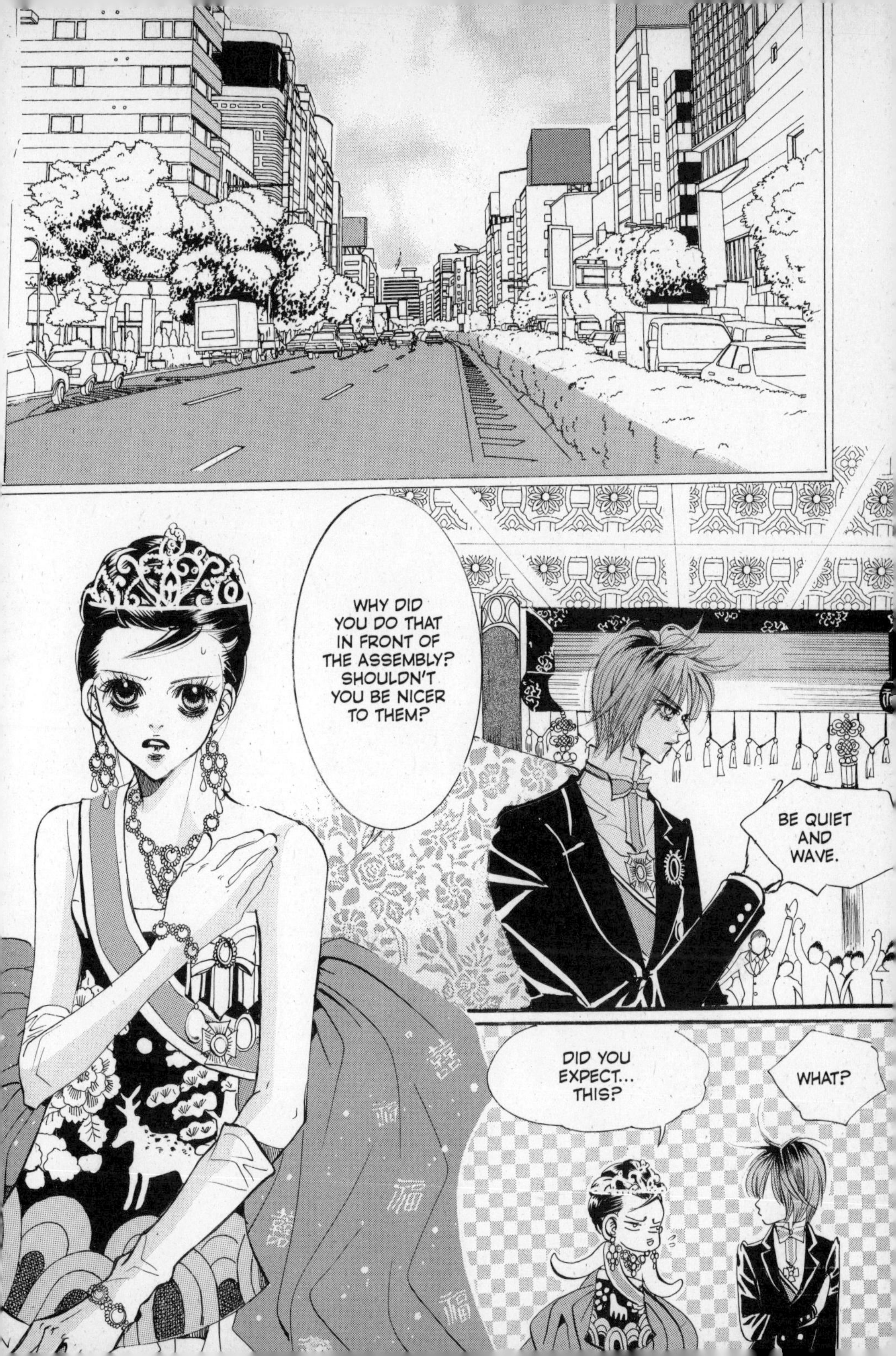

WHY DID YOU DO THAT IN FRONT OF THE ASSEMBLY? SHOULDN'T YOU BE NICER TO THEM?
BE QUIET AND WAVE.
DID YOU EXPECT... THIS?
WHAT?

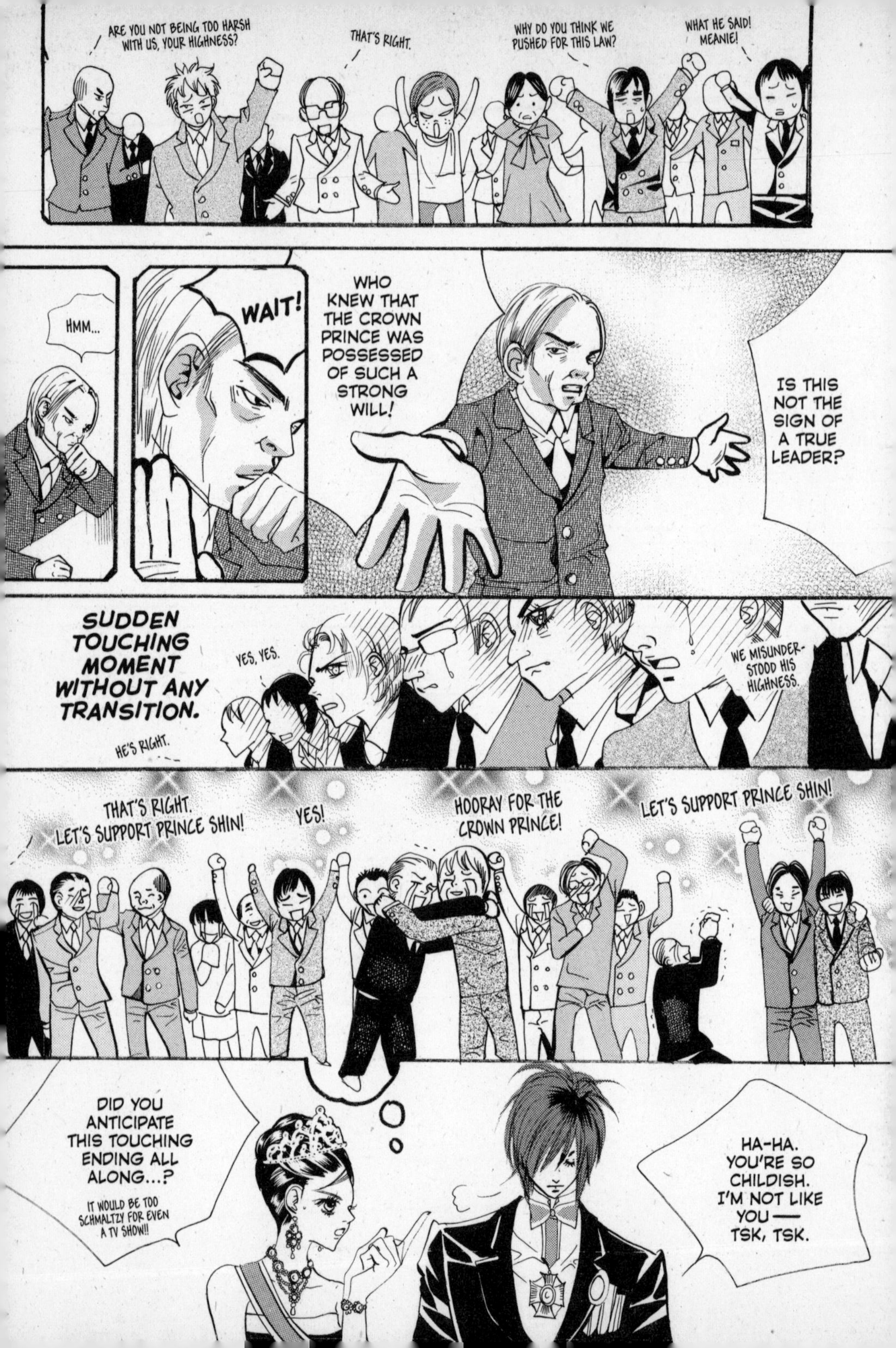
ARE YOU NOT BEING TOO HARSH WITH US, YOUR HIGHNESS?
THAT'S RIGHT.
WHY DO YOU THINK WE PUSHED FOR THIS LAW?
WHAT HE SAID! MEANIE!
HMM...
WAIT!
WHO KNEW THAT THE CROWN PRINCE WAS POSSESSED OF SUCH A STRONG WILL!
IS THIS NOT THE SIGN OF A TRUE LEADER?
SUDDEN TOUCHING MOMENT WITHOUT ANY TRANSITION.
YES, YES.
HE'S RIGHT.
WE MISUNDERSTOOD HIS HIGHNESS.
THAT'S RIGHT. LET'S SUPPORT PRINCE SHIN!
YES!
HOORAY FOR THE CROWN PRINCE!
LET'S SUPPORT PRINCE SHIN!
DID YOU ANTICIPATE THIS TOUCHING ENDING ALL ALONG...?
IT WOULD BE TOO SCHMALTZY FOR EVEN A TV SHOW!!
HA-HA. YOU'RE SO CHILDISH. I'M NOT LIKE YOU— TSK, TSK.

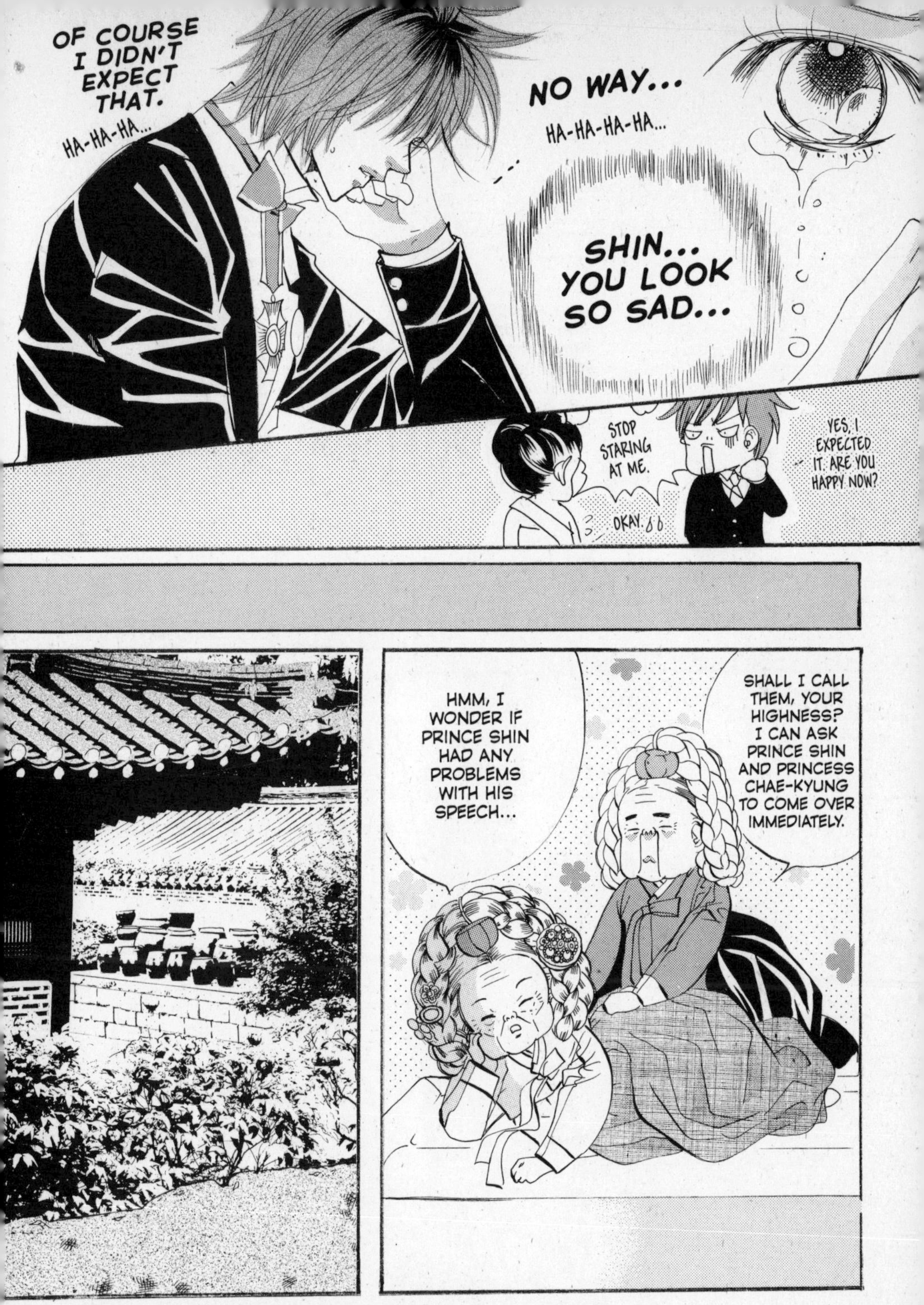
OF COURSE I DIDN'T EXPECT THAT.
HA-HA-HA...
NO WAY...
HA-HA-HA-HA...
...
SHIN... YOU LOOK SO SAD...
STOP STARING AT ME.
OKAY.
YES, I EXPECTED IT. ARE YOU HAPPY NOW?
HMM, I WONDER IF PRINCE SHIN HAD ANY PROBLEMS WITH HIS SPEECH...
SHALL I CALL THEM, YOUR HIGHNESS? I CAN ASK PRINCE SHIN AND PRINCESS CHAE-KYUNG TO COME OVER IMMEDIATELY.

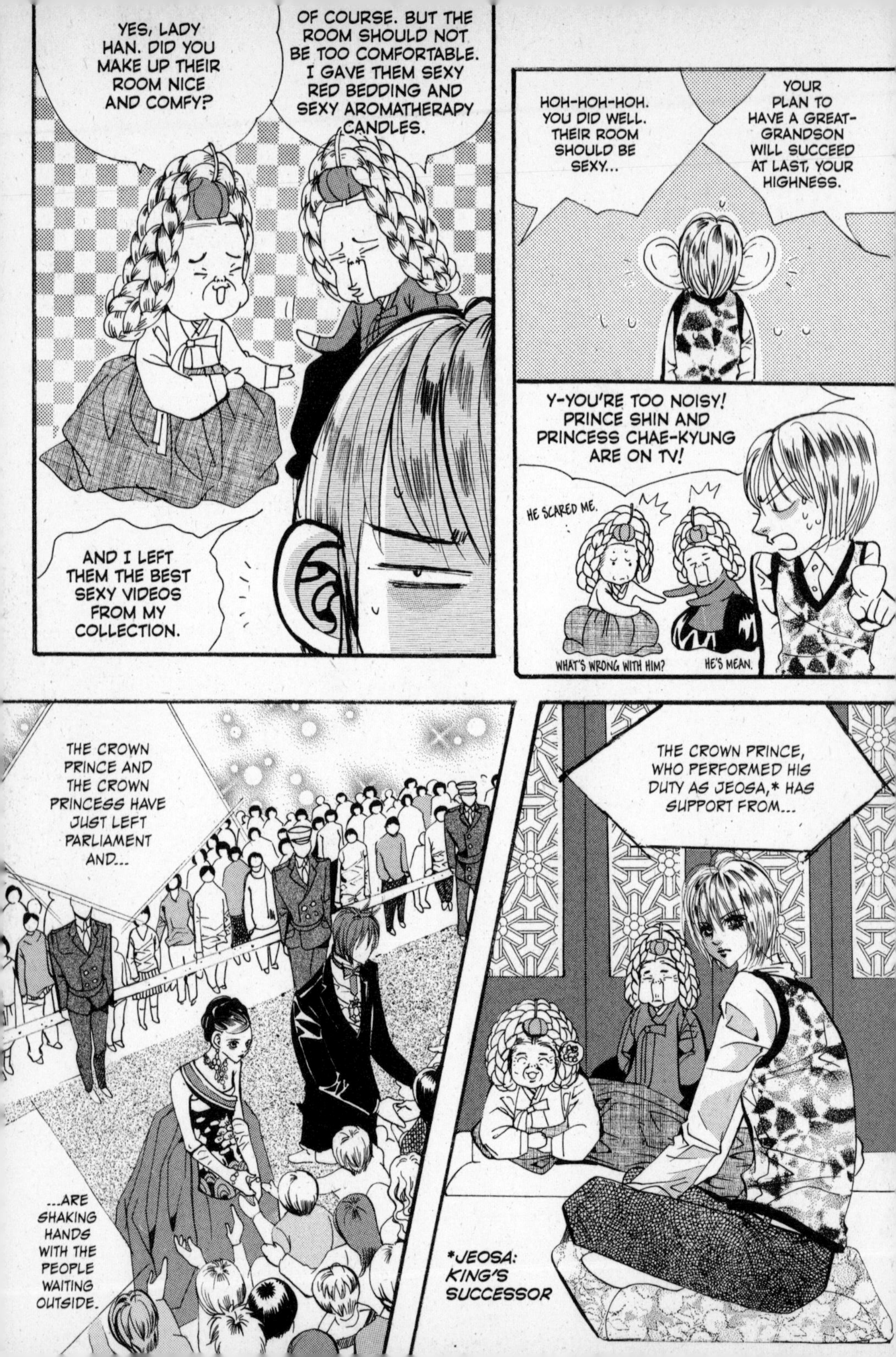
YES, LADY HAN. DID YOU MAKE UP THEIR ROOM NICE AND COMFY?
OF COURSE. BUT THE ROOM SHOULD NOT BE TOO COMFORTABLE. I GAVE THEM SEXY RED BEDDING AND SEXY AROMATHERAPY CANDLES.
AND I LEFT THEM THE BEST SEXY VIDEOS FROM MY COLLECTION.
HOH-HOH-HOH. YOU DID WELL. THEIR ROOM SHOULD BE SEXY...
YOUR PLAN TO HAVE A GREAT-GRANDSON WILL SUCCEED AT LAST, YOUR HIGHNESS.
Y-YOU'RE TOO NOISY! PRINCE SHIN AND PRINCESS CHAE-KYUNG ARE ON TV!
HE SCARED ME.
WHAT'S WRONG WITH HIM?
HE'S MEAN.
THE CROWN PRINCE AND THE CROWN PRINCESS HAVE JUST LEFT PARLIAMENT AND...
...ARE SHAKING HANDS WITH THE PEOPLE WAITING OUTSIDE.
THE CROWN PRINCE, WHO PERFORMED HIS DUTY AS JEOSA,* HAS SUPPORT FROM...
*JEOSA: KING'S SUCCESSOR

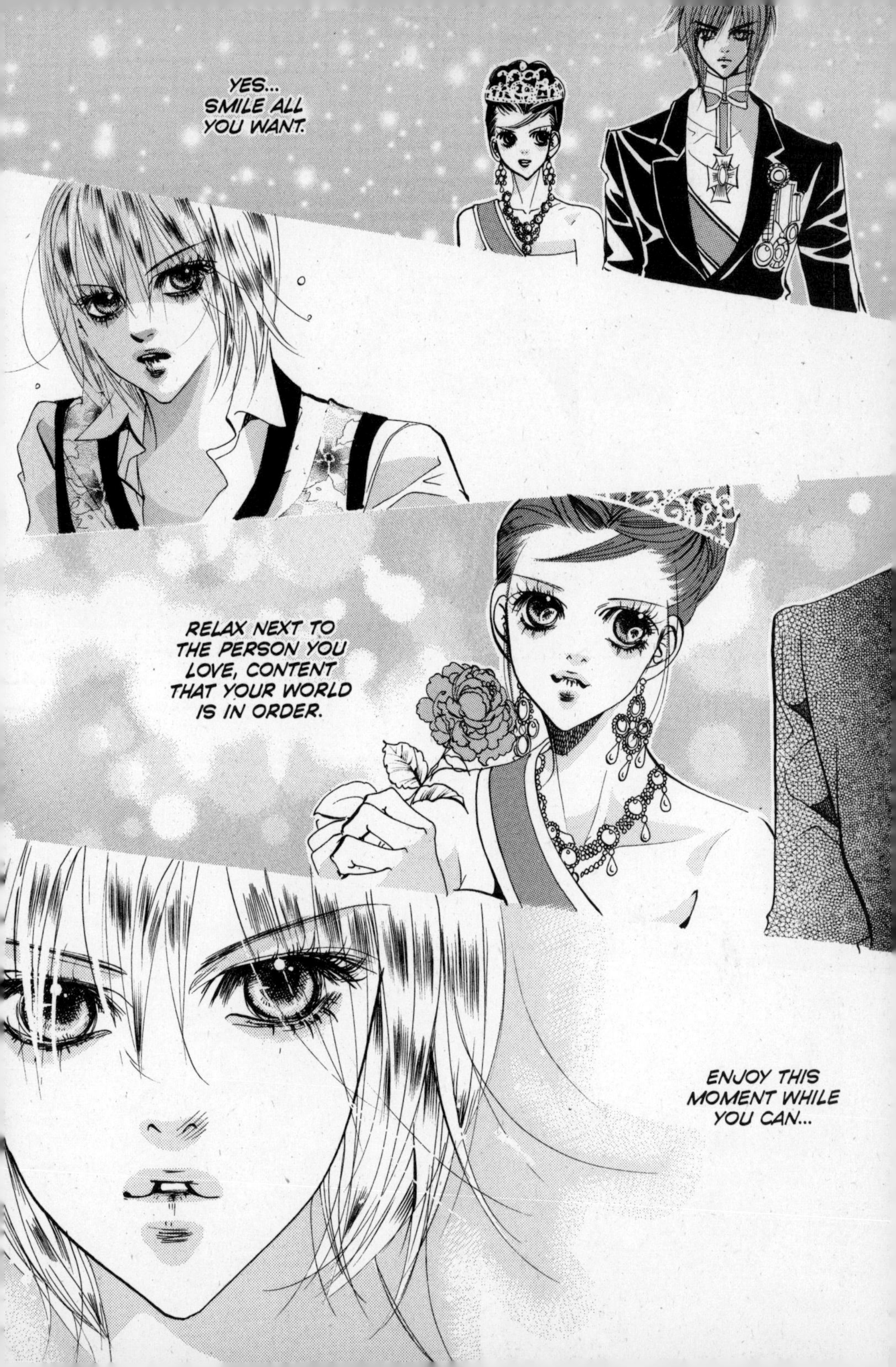
YES... SMILE ALL YOU WANT.
RELAX NEXT TO THE PERSON YOU LOVE, CONTENT THAT YOUR WORLD IS IN ORDER.
ENJOY THIS MOMENT WHILE YOU CAN...

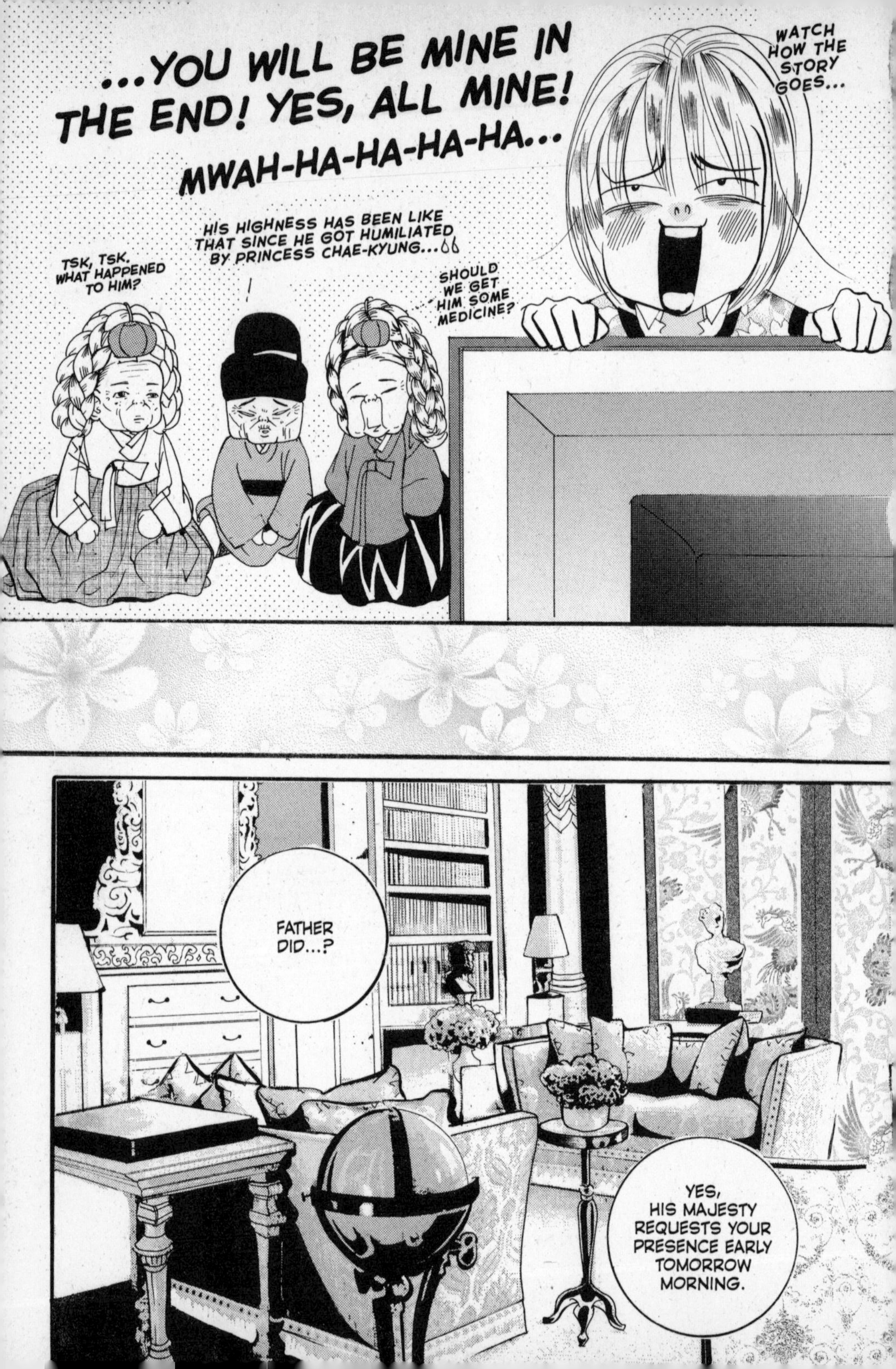
...YOU WILL BE MINE IN THE END! YES, ALL MINE!
MWAH-HA-HA-HA-HA...
WATCH HOW THE STORY GOES...
TSK, TSK. WHAT HAPPENED TO HIM?
HIS HIGHNESS HAS BEEN LIKE THAT SINCE HE GOT HUMILIATED BY PRINCESS CHAE-KYUNG...
SHOULD WE GET HIM SOME MEDICINE?
FATHER DID...?
YES, HIS MAJESTY REQUESTS YOUR PRESENCE EARLY TOMORROW MORNING.

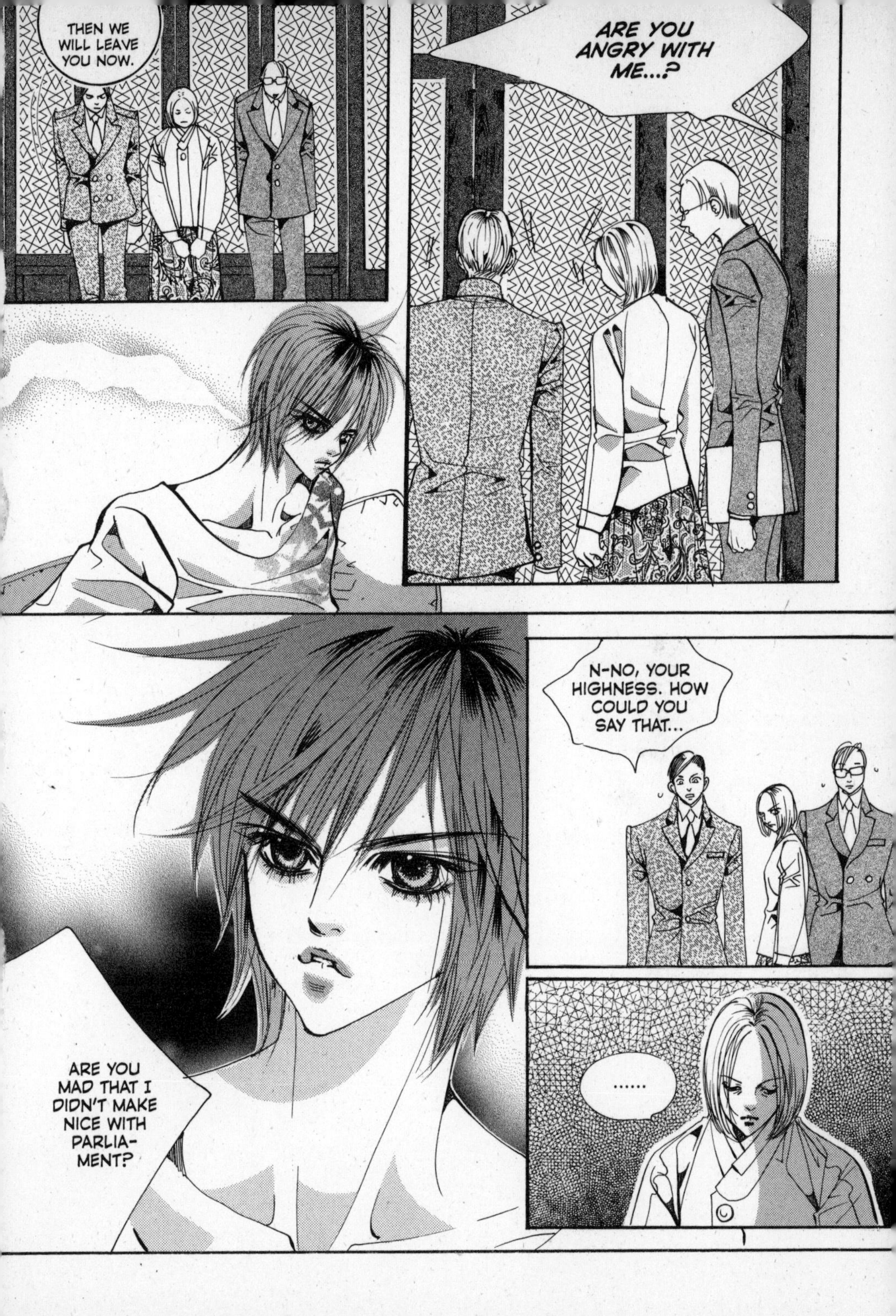
THEN WE WILL LEAVE YOU NOW.
ARE YOU ANGRY WITH ME...?
ARE YOU MAD THAT I DIDN'T MAKE NICE WITH PARLIA-MENT?
N-NO, YOUR HIGHNESS. HOW COULD YOU SAY THAT...
......

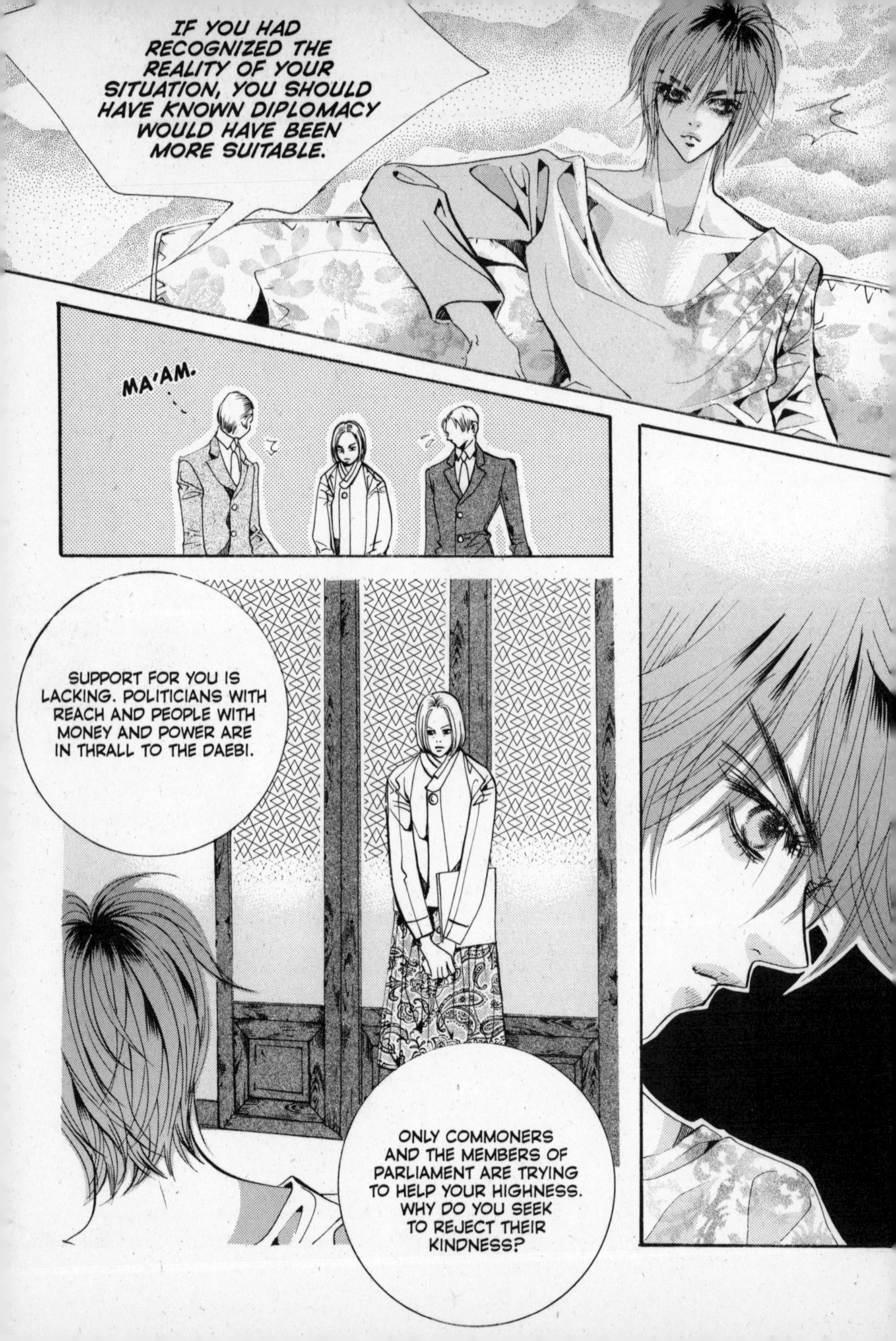
IF YOU HAD RECOGNIZED THE REALITY OF YOUR SITUATION, YOU SHOULD HAVE KNOWN DIPLOMACY WOULD HAVE BEEN MORE SUITABLE.
MA'AM.
SUPPORT FOR YOU IS LACKING. POLITICIANS WITH REACH AND PEOPLE WITH MONEY AND POWER ARE IN THRALL TO THE DAEBI.
ONLY COMMONERS AND THE MEMBERS OF PARLIAMENT ARE TRYING TO HELP YOUR HIGHNESS. WHY DO YOU SEEK TO REJECT THEIR KINDNESS?

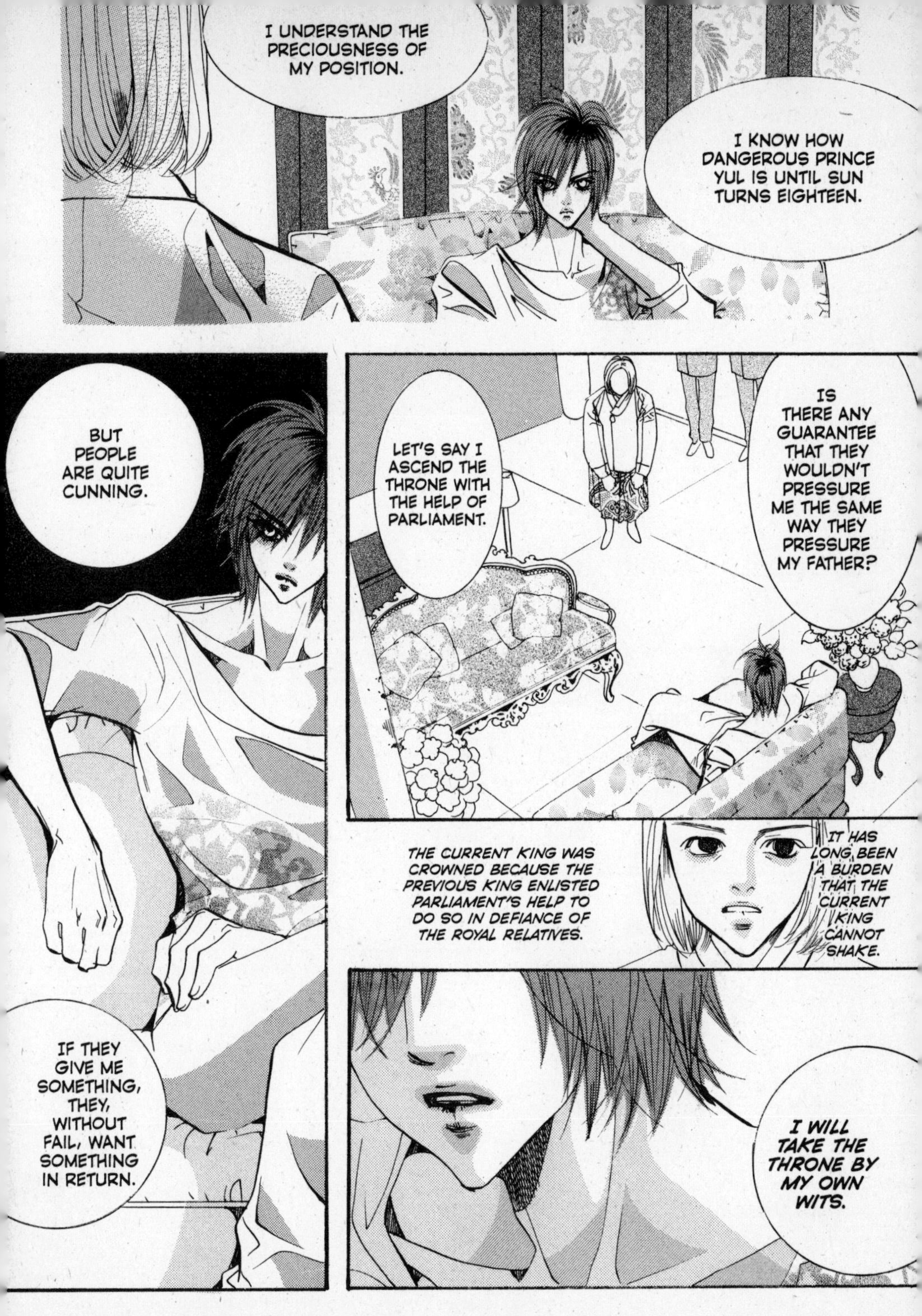
I UNDERSTAND THE PRECIOUSNESS OF MY POSITION.
I KNOW HOW DANGEROUS PRINCE YUL IS UNTIL SUN TURNS EIGHTEEN.
BUT PEOPLE ARE QUITE CUNNING.
IF THEY GIVE ME SOMETHING, THEY, WITHOUT FAIL, WANT SOMETHING IN RETURN.
LET'S SAY I ASCEND THE THRONE WITH THE HELP OF PARLIAMENT.
IS THERE ANY GUARANTEE THAT THEY WOULDN'T PRESSURE ME THE SAME WAY THEY PRESSURE MY FATHER?
THE CURRENT KING WAS CROWNED BECAUSE THE PREVIOUS KING ENLISTED PARLIAMENT'S HELP TO DO SO IN DEFIANCE OF THE ROYAL RELATIVES.
IT HAS LONG BEEN A BURDEN THAT THE CURRENT KING CANNOT SHAKE.
I WILL TAKE THE THRONE BY MY OWN WITS.

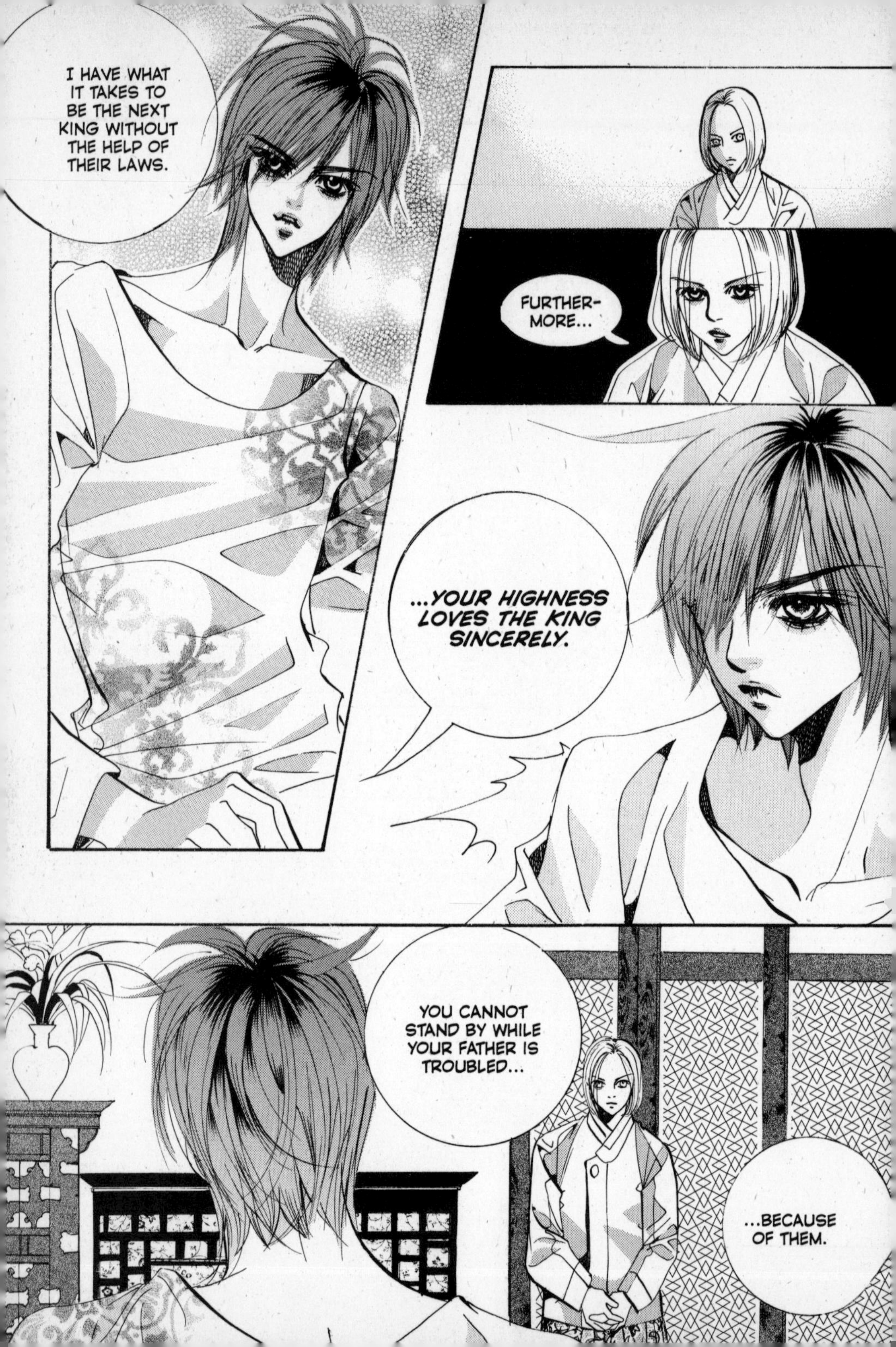
I HAVE WHAT IT TAKES TO BE THE NEXT KING WITHOUT THE HELP OF THEIR LAWS.
FURTHER-MORE...
...YOUR HIGHNESS LOVES THE KING SINCERELY.
YOU CANNOT STAND BY WHILE YOUR FATHER IS TROUBLED...
...BECAUSE OF THEM.

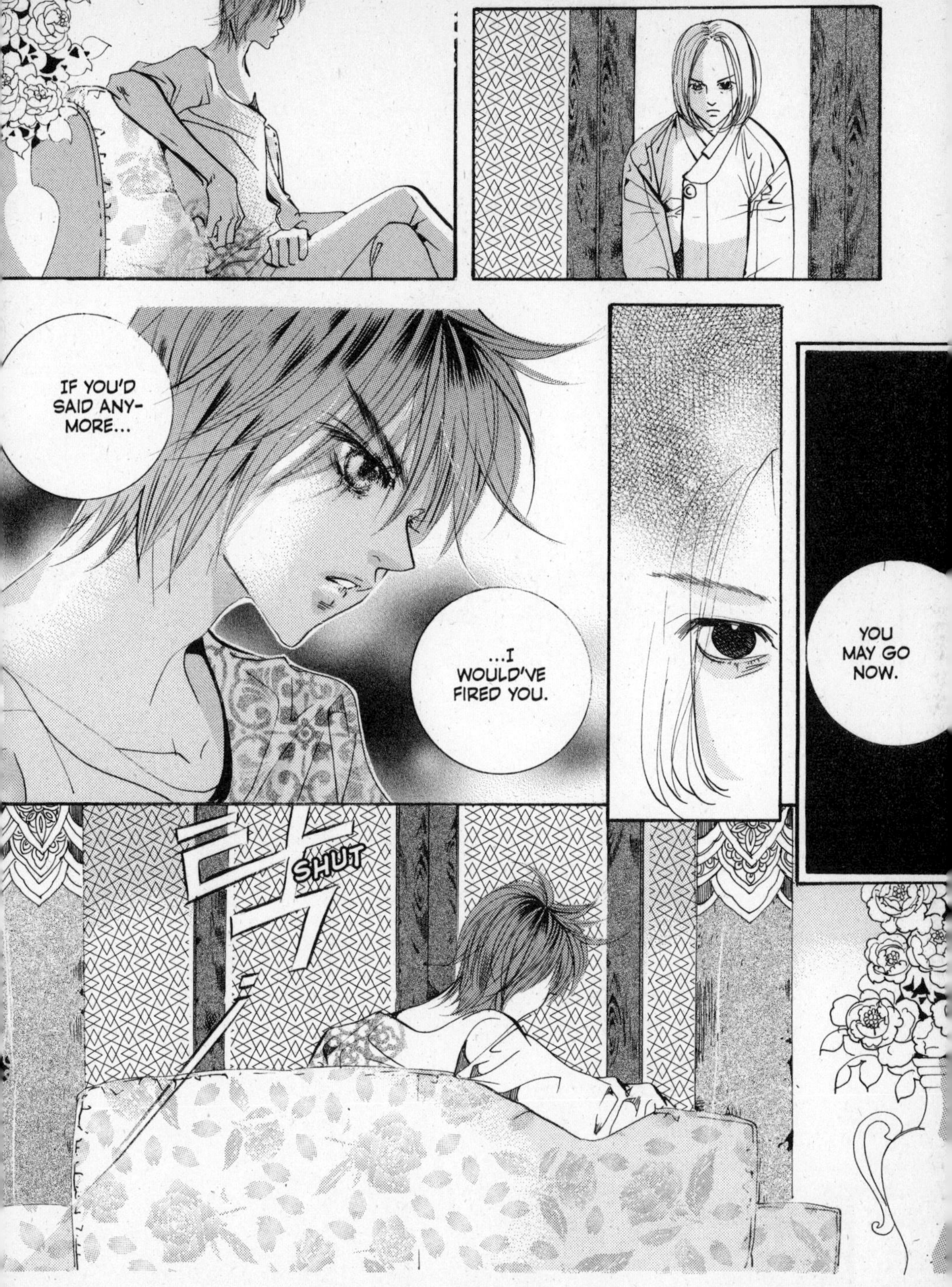
IF YOU'D SAID ANY-MORE...
...I WOULD'VE FIRED YOU.
YOU MAY GO NOW.
SHUT

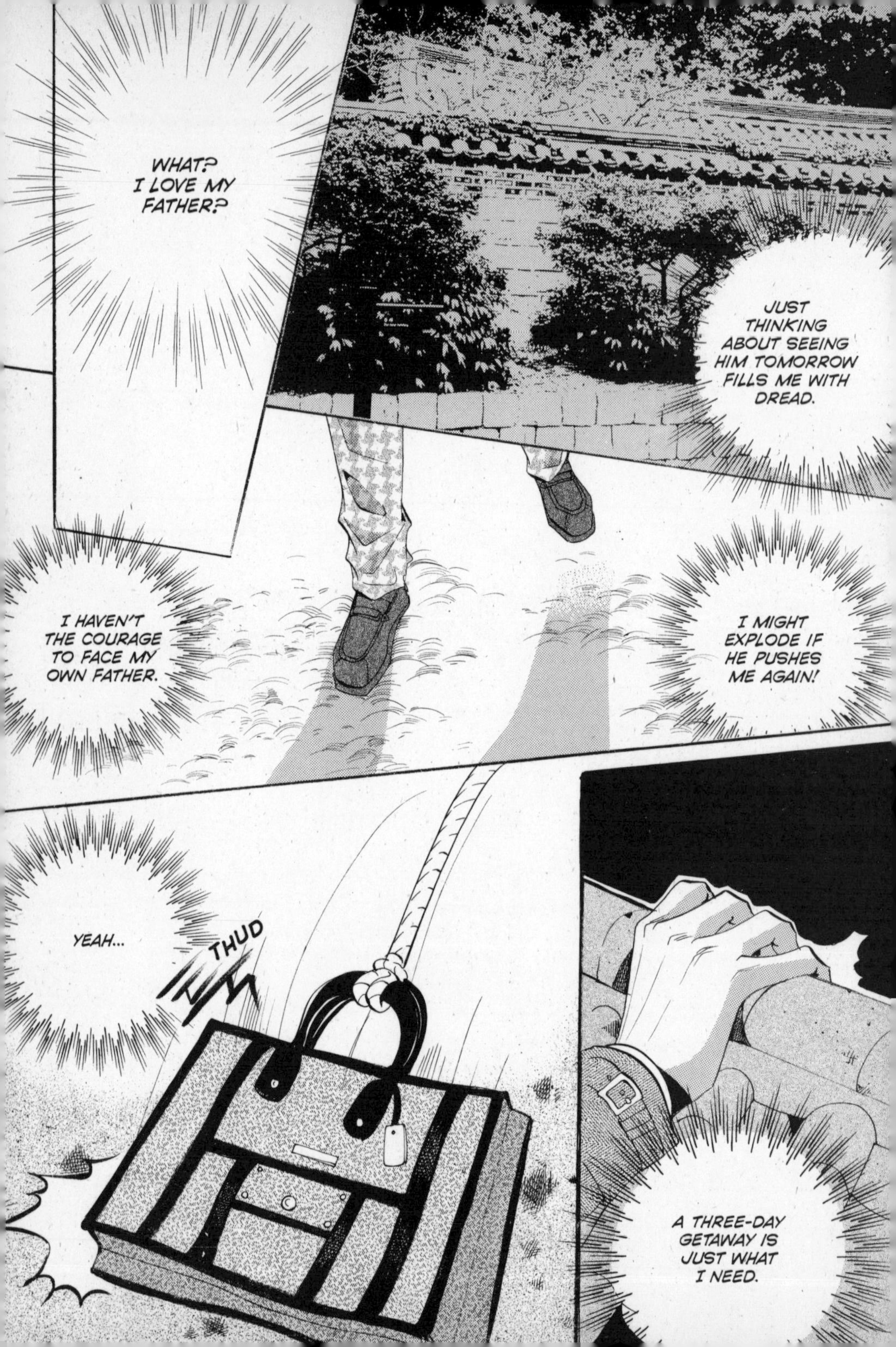
WHAT? I LOVE MY FATHER?
JUST THINKING ABOUT SEEING HIM TOMORROW FILLS ME WITH DREAD.
I HAVEN'T THE COURAGE TO FACE MY OWN FATHER.
I MIGHT EXPLODE IF HE PUSHES ME AGAIN!
YEAH...
THUD
A THREE-DAY GETAWAY IS JUST WHAT I NEED.

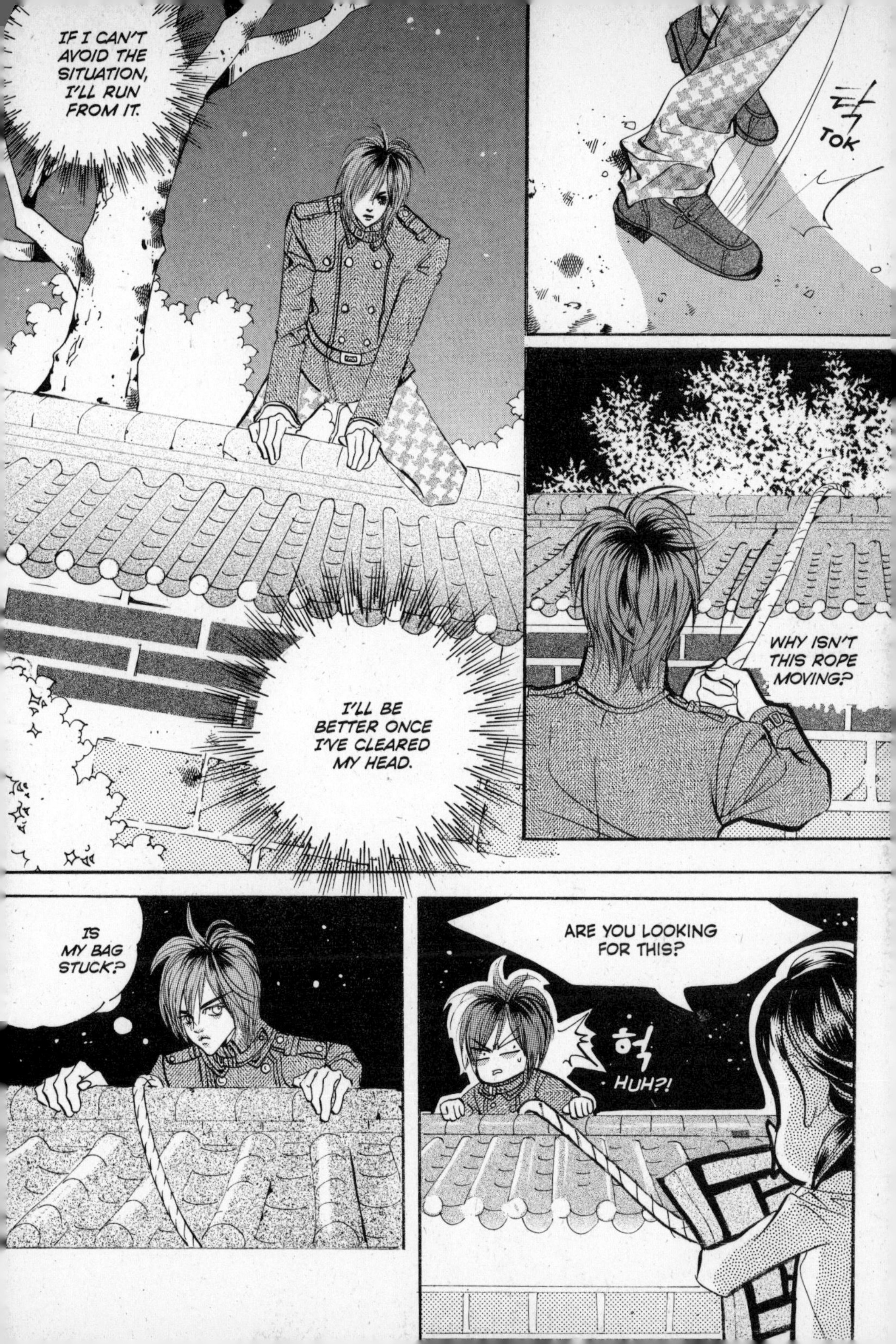
IF I CAN'T AVOID THE SITUATION, I'LL RUN FROM IT.
I'LL BE BETTER ONCE I'VE CLEARED MY HEAD.
탁
TOK
WHY ISN'T THIS ROPE MOVING?
IS MY BAG STUCK?
ARE YOU LOOKING FOR THIS?
헉
HUH?!

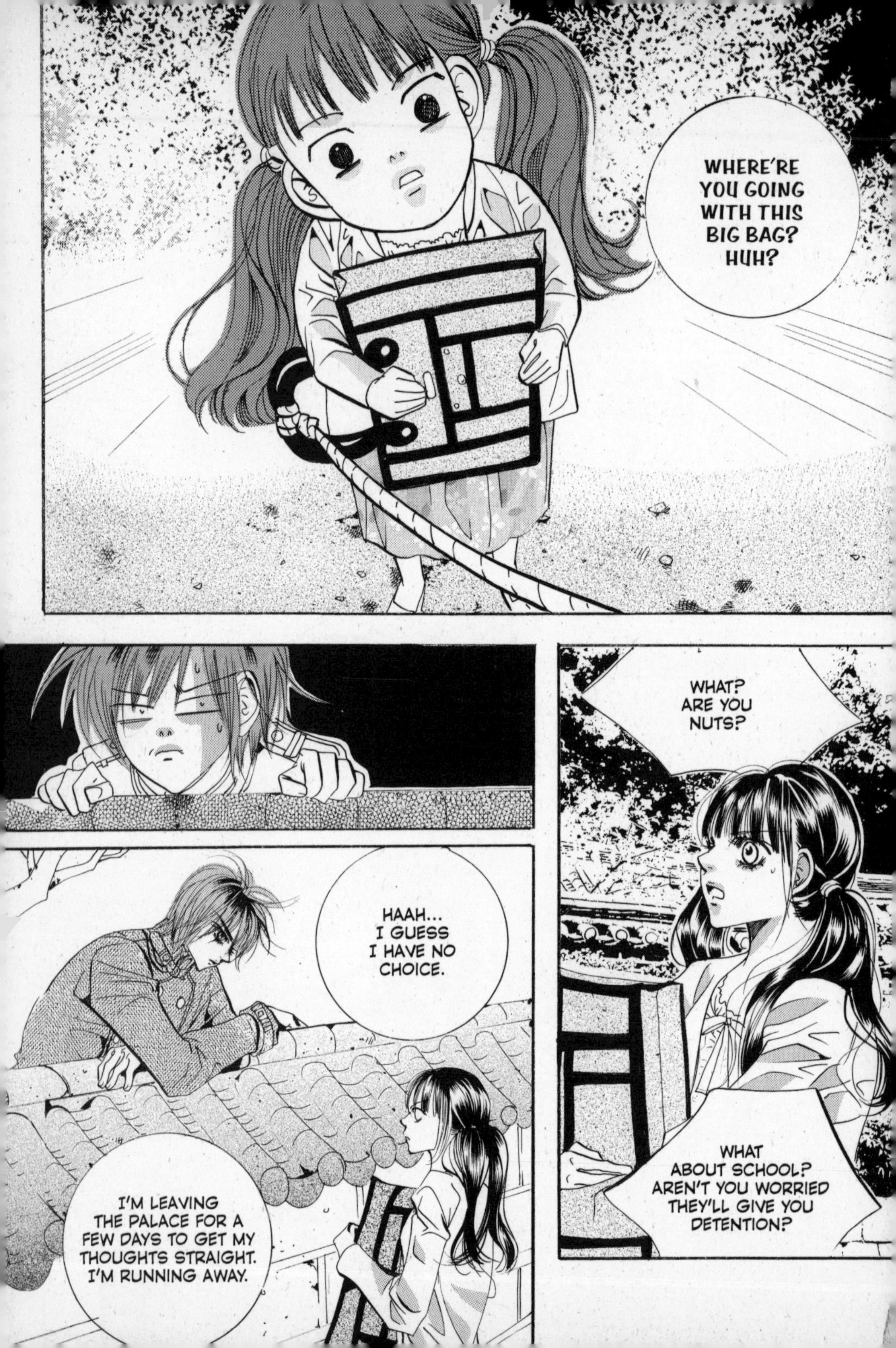
WHERE'RE YOU GOING WITH THIS BIG BAG? HUH?
HAAH... I GUESS I HAVE NO CHOICE.
I'M LEAVING THE PALACE FOR A FEW DAYS TO GET MY THOUGHTS STRAIGHT. I'M RUNNING AWAY.
WHAT? ARE YOU NUTS?
WHAT ABOUT SCHOOL? AREN'T YOU WORRIED THEY'LL GIVE YOU DETENTION?

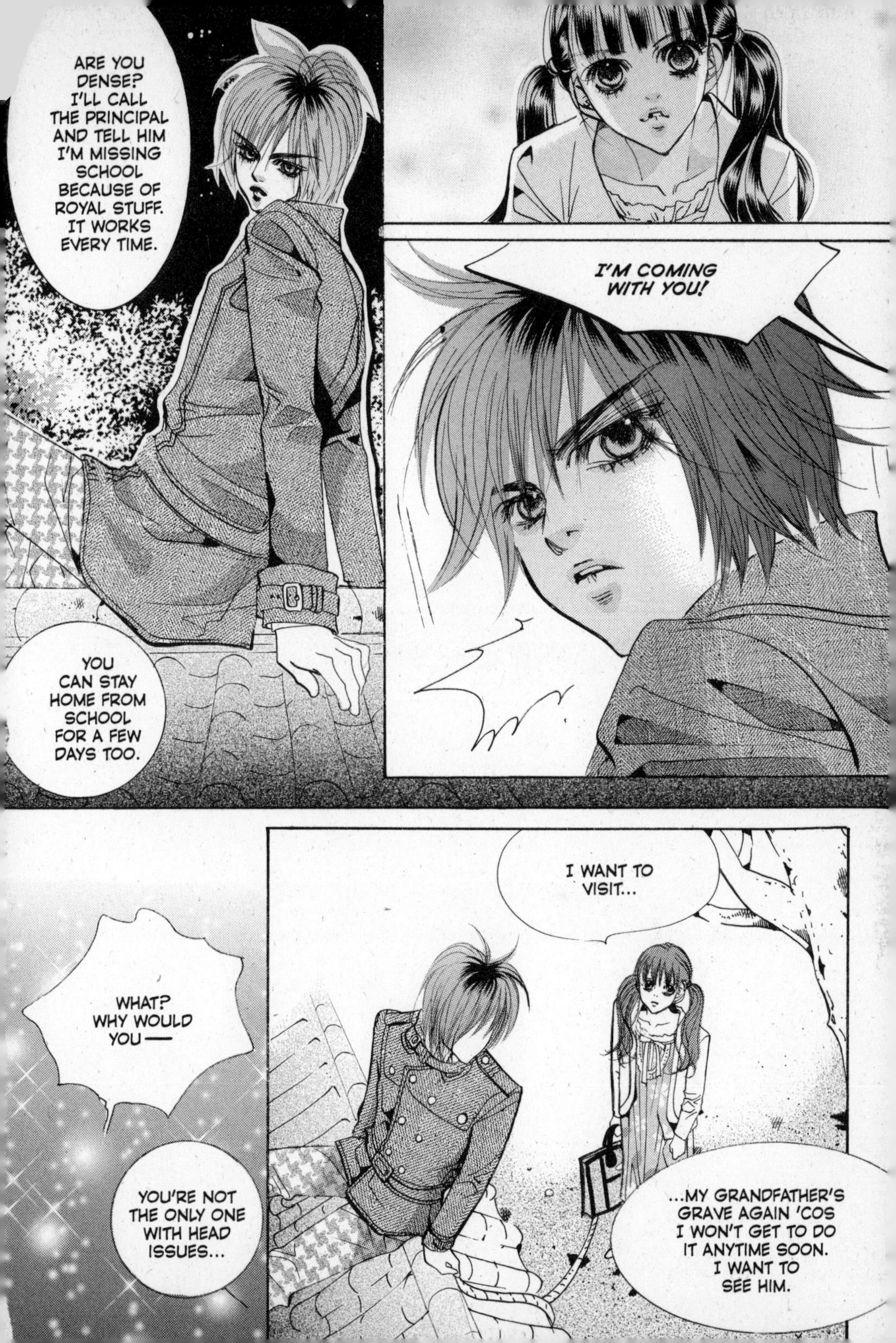
ARE YOU DENSE? I'LL CALL THE PRINCIPAL AND TELL HIM I'M MISSING SCHOOL BECAUSE OF ROYAL STUFF. IT WORKS EVERY TIME.
YOU CAN STAY HOME FROM SCHOOL FOR A FEW DAYS TOO.
I'M COMING WITH YOU!
WHAT? WHY WOULD YOU—
YOU'RE NOT THE ONLY ONE WITH HEAD ISSUES...
I WANT TO VISIT...
...MY GRANDFATHER'S GRAVE AGAIN 'COS I WON'T GET TO DO IT ANYTIME SOON. I WANT TO SEE HIM.

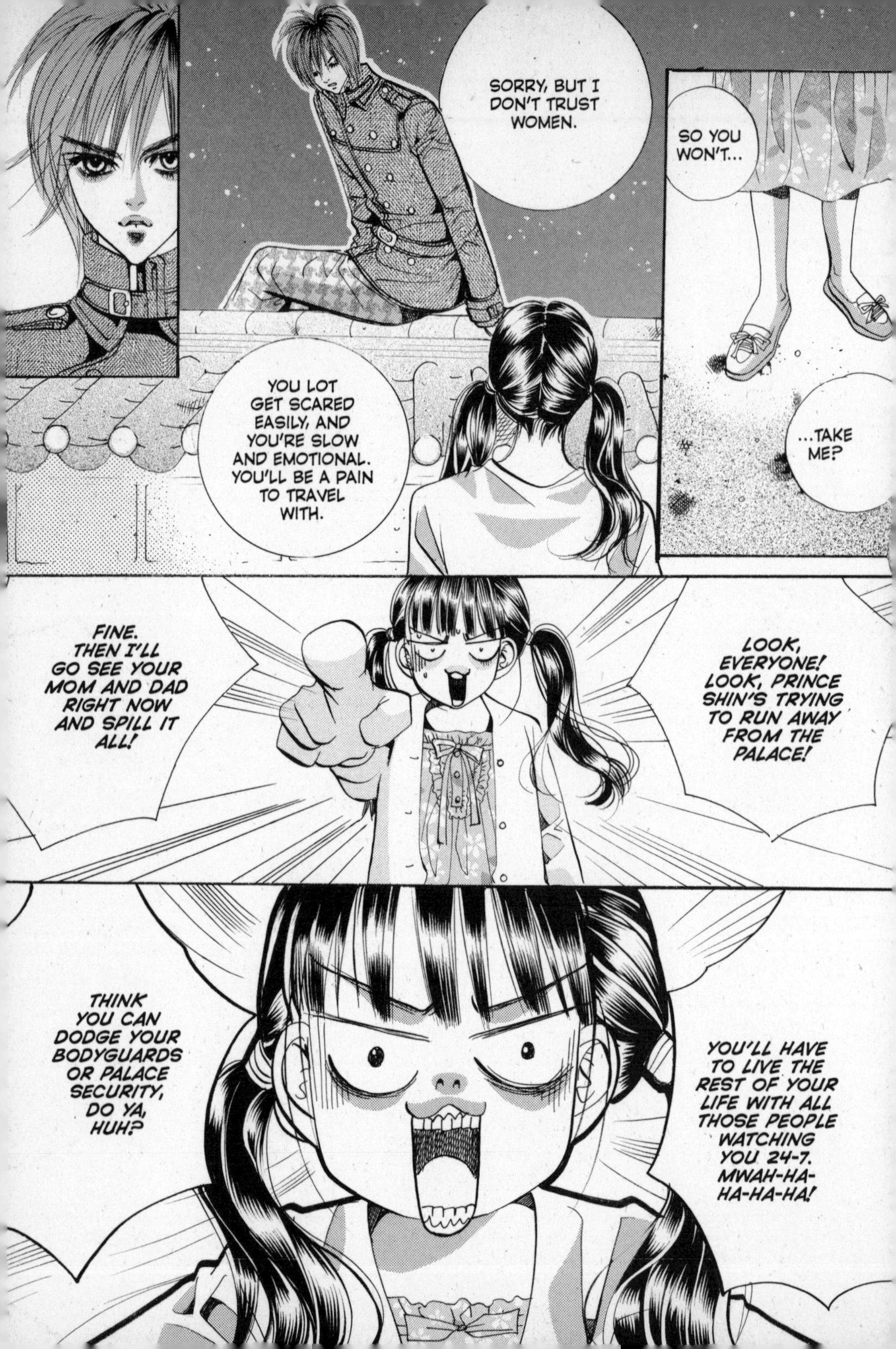
SORRY, BUT I DON'T TRUST WOMEN.
YOU LOT GET SCARED EASILY, AND YOU'RE SLOW AND EMOTIONAL. YOU'LL BE A PAIN TO TRAVEL WITH.
SO YOU WON'T...
...TAKE ME?
FINE. THEN I'LL GO SEE YOUR MOM AND DAD RIGHT NOW AND SPILL IT ALL!
LOOK, EVERYONE! LOOK, PRINCE SHIN'S TRYING TO RUN AWAY FROM THE PALACE!
THINK YOU CAN DODGE YOUR BODYGUARDS OR PALACE SECURITY, DO YA, HUH?
YOU'LL HAVE TO LIVE THE REST OF YOUR LIFE WITH ALL THOSE PEOPLE WATCHING YOU 24-7. MWAH-HA-HA-HA-HA!

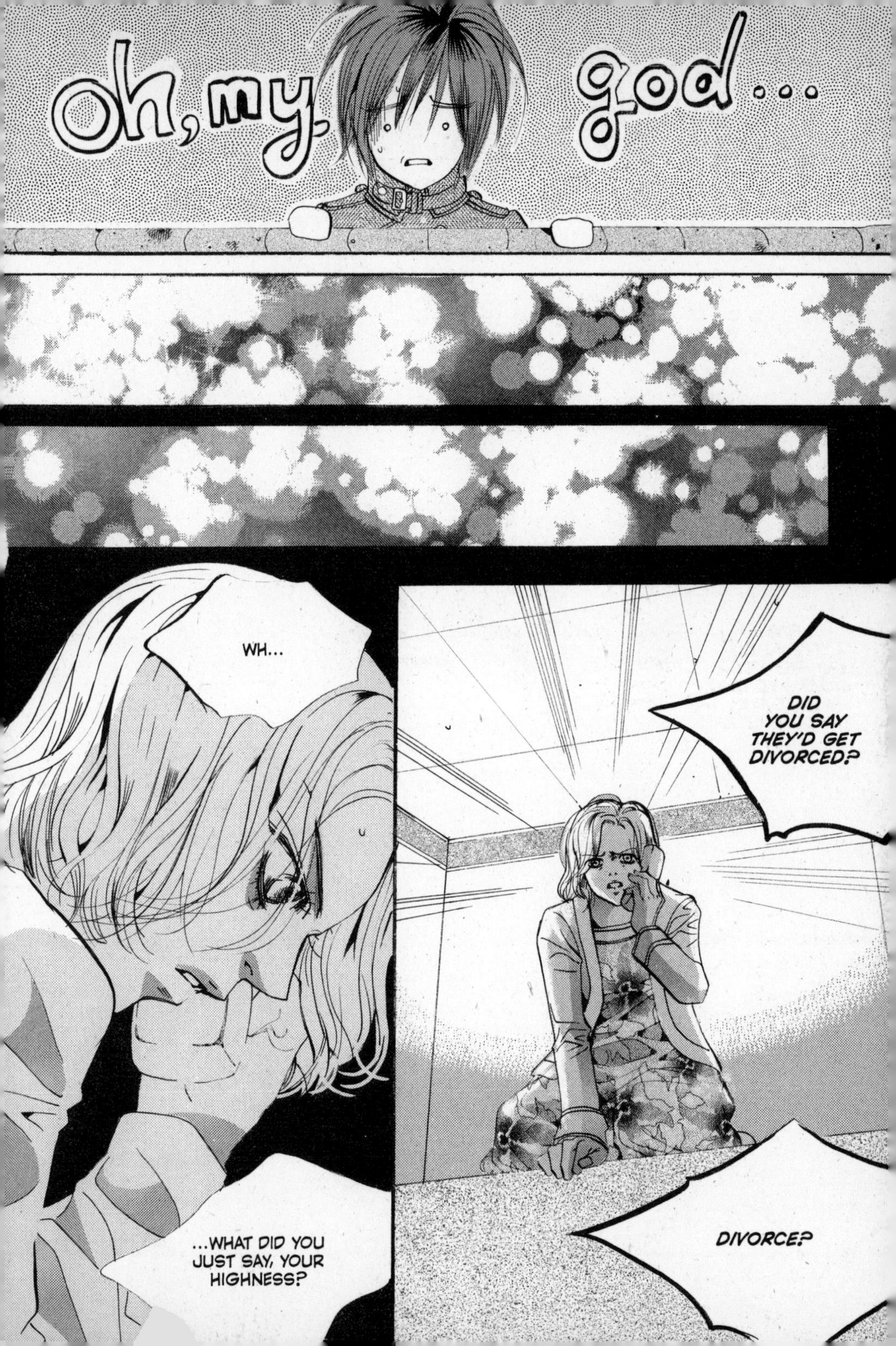
Oh, my god...
WH...
...WHAT DID YOU JUST SAY, YOUR HIGHNESS?
DID YOU SAY THEY'D GET DIVORCED?
DIVORCE?

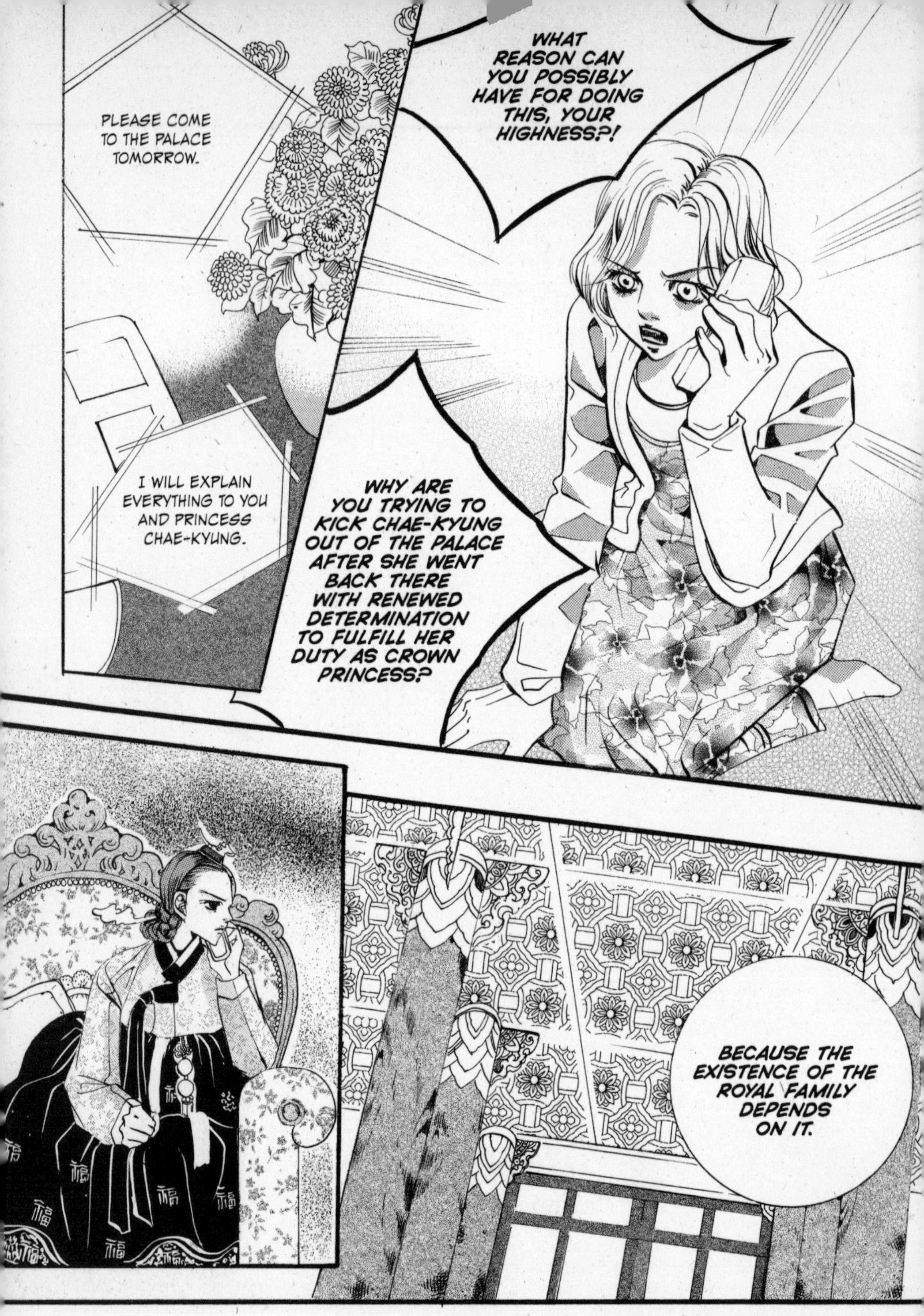
PLEASE COME TO THE PALACE TOMORROW.
I WILL EXPLAIN EVERYTHING TO YOU AND PRINCESS CHAE-KYUNG.
WHAT REASON CAN YOU POSSIBLY HAVE FOR DOING THIS, YOUR HIGHNESS?!
WHY ARE YOU TRYING TO KICK CHAE-KYUNG OUT OF THE PALACE AFTER SHE WENT BACK THERE WITH RENEWED DETERMINATION TO FULFILL HER DUTY AS CROWN PRINCESS?
BECAUSE THE EXISTENCE OF THE ROYAL FAMILY DEPENDS ON IT.

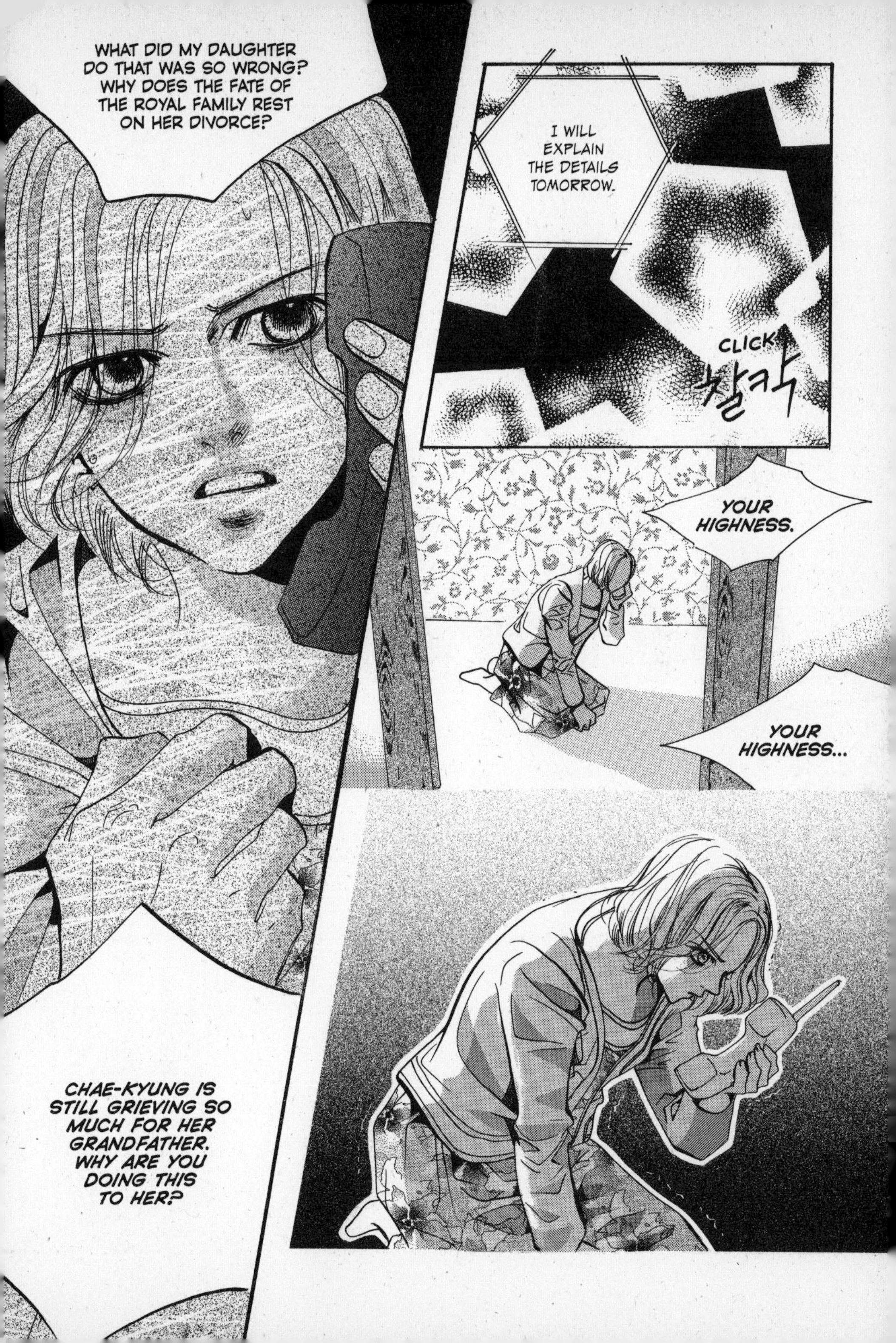
WHAT DID MY DAUGHTER DO THAT WAS SO WRONG? WHY DOES THE FATE OF THE ROYAL FAMILY REST ON HER DIVORCE?
CHAE-KYUNG IS STILL GRIEVING SO MUCH FOR HER GRANDFATHER. WHY ARE YOU DOING THIS TO HER?
I WILL EXPLAIN THE DETAILS TOMORROW.
CLICK
찰칵
YOUR HIGHNESS.
YOUR HIGHNESS...

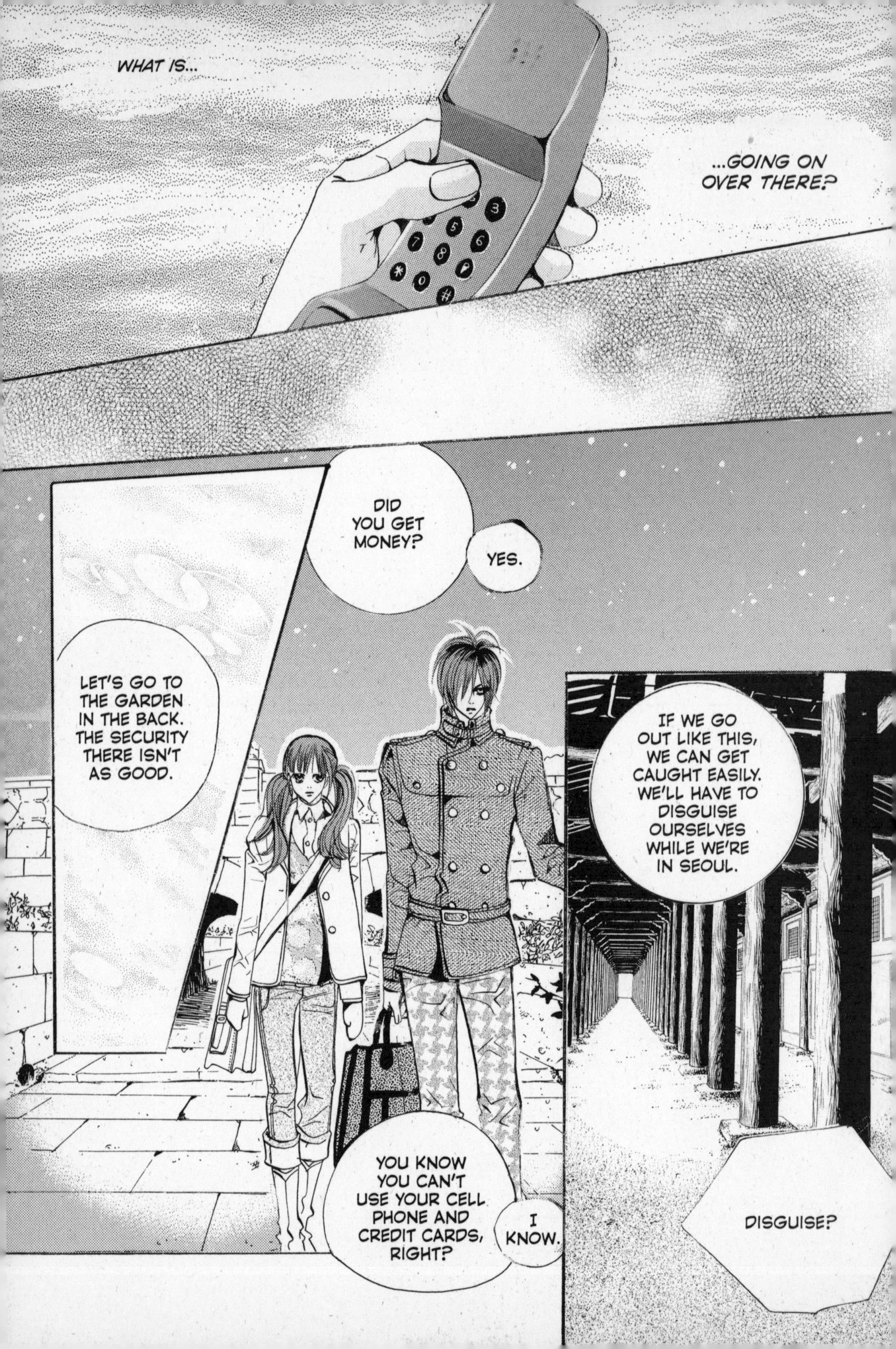
WHAT IS...
...GOING ON OVER THERE?
DID YOU GET MONEY?
YES.
LET'S GO TO THE GARDEN IN THE BACK. THE SECURITY THERE ISN'T AS GOOD.
YOU KNOW YOU CAN'T USE YOUR CELL PHONE AND CREDIT CARDS, RIGHT?
I KNOW.
IF WE GO OUT LIKE THIS, WE CAN GET CAUGHT EASILY. WE'LL HAVE TO DISGUISE OURSELVES WHILE WE'RE IN SEOUL.
DISGUISE?

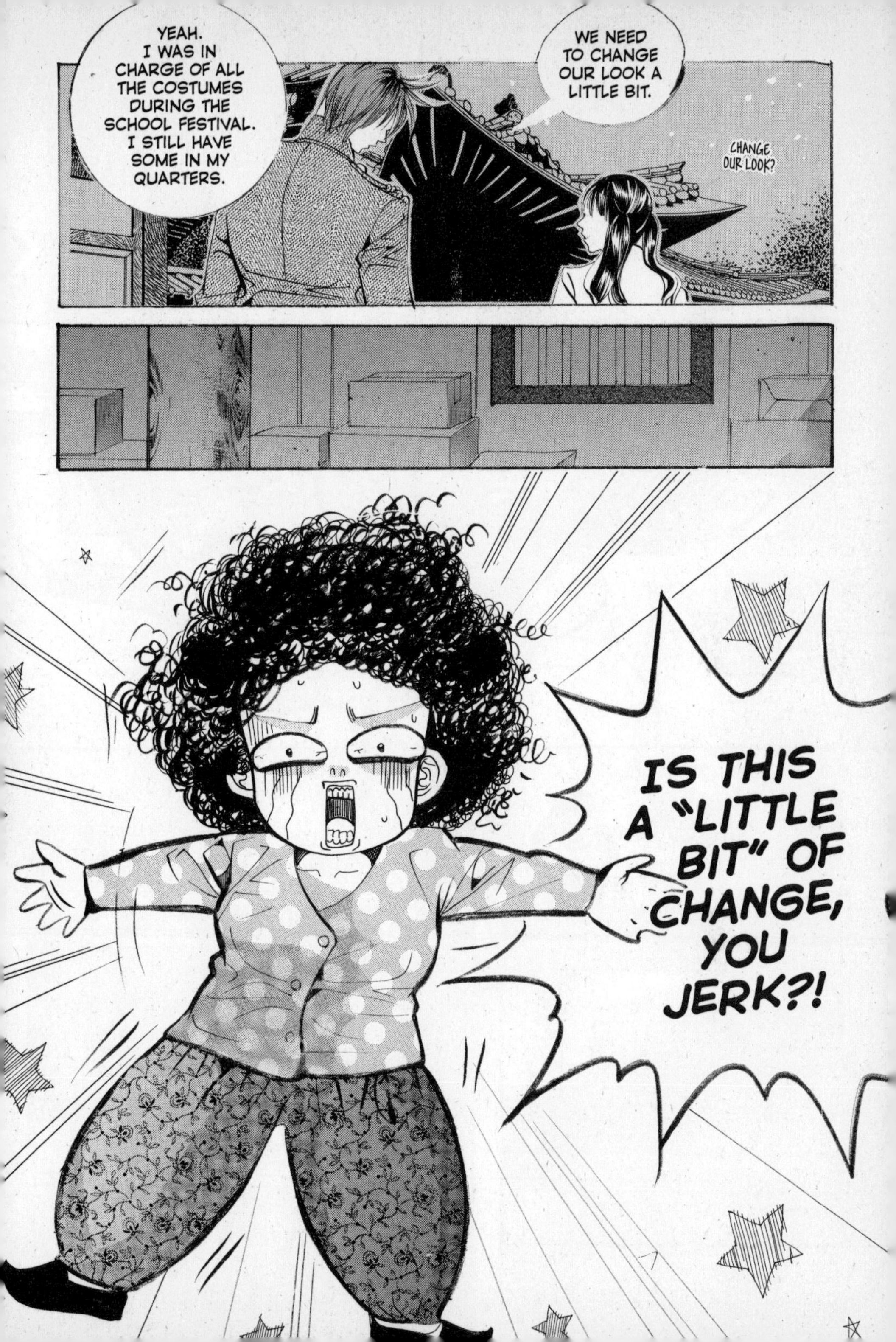
YEAH. I WAS IN CHARGE OF ALL THE COSTUMES DURING THE SCHOOL FESTIVAL. I STILL HAVE SOME IN MY QUARTERS.
WE NEED TO CHANGE OUR LOOK A LITTLE BIT.
CHANGE OUR LOOK?
IS THIS A "LITTLE BIT" OF CHANGE, YOU JERK?!

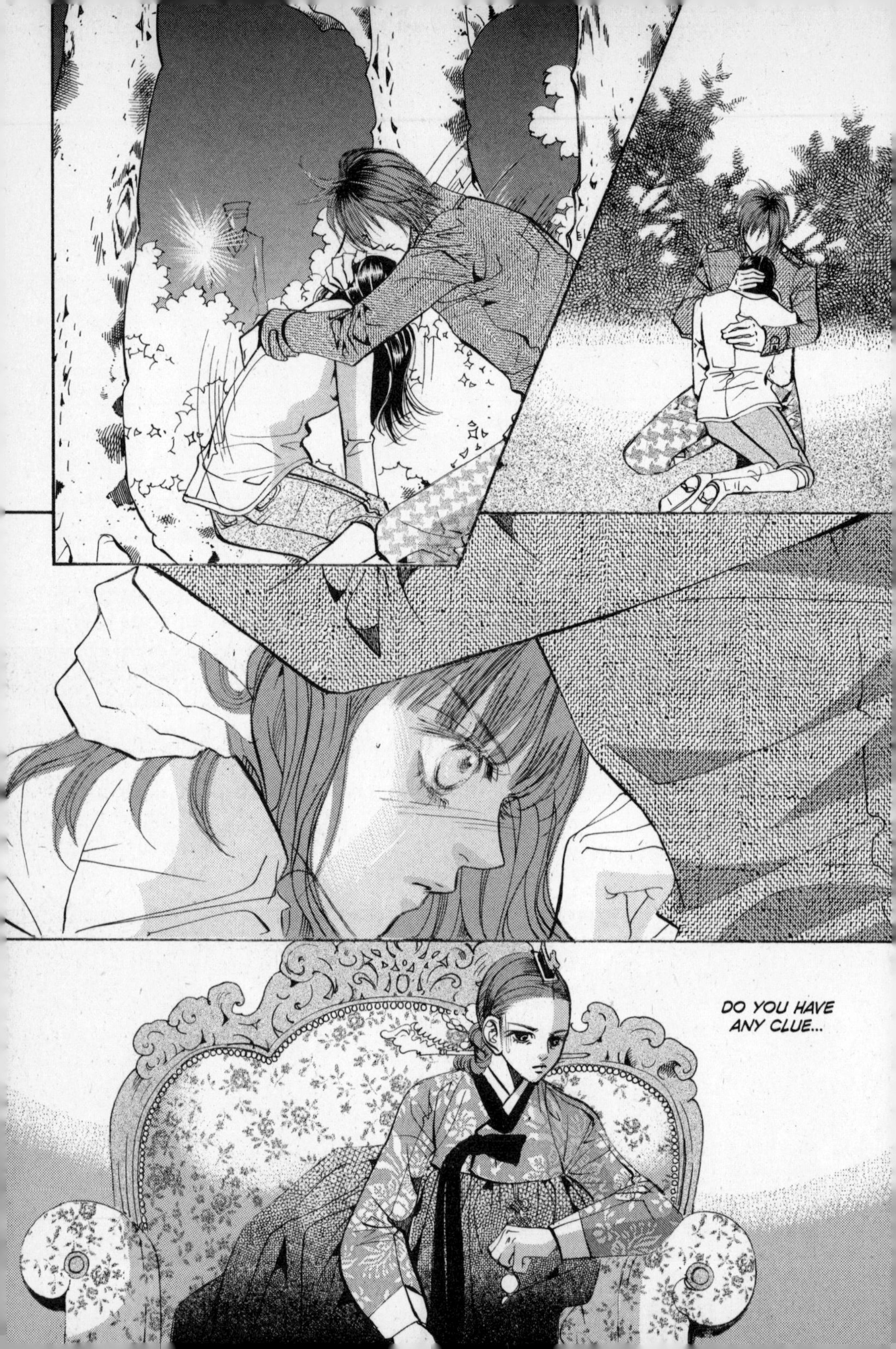
DO YOU HAVE
ANY CLUE...

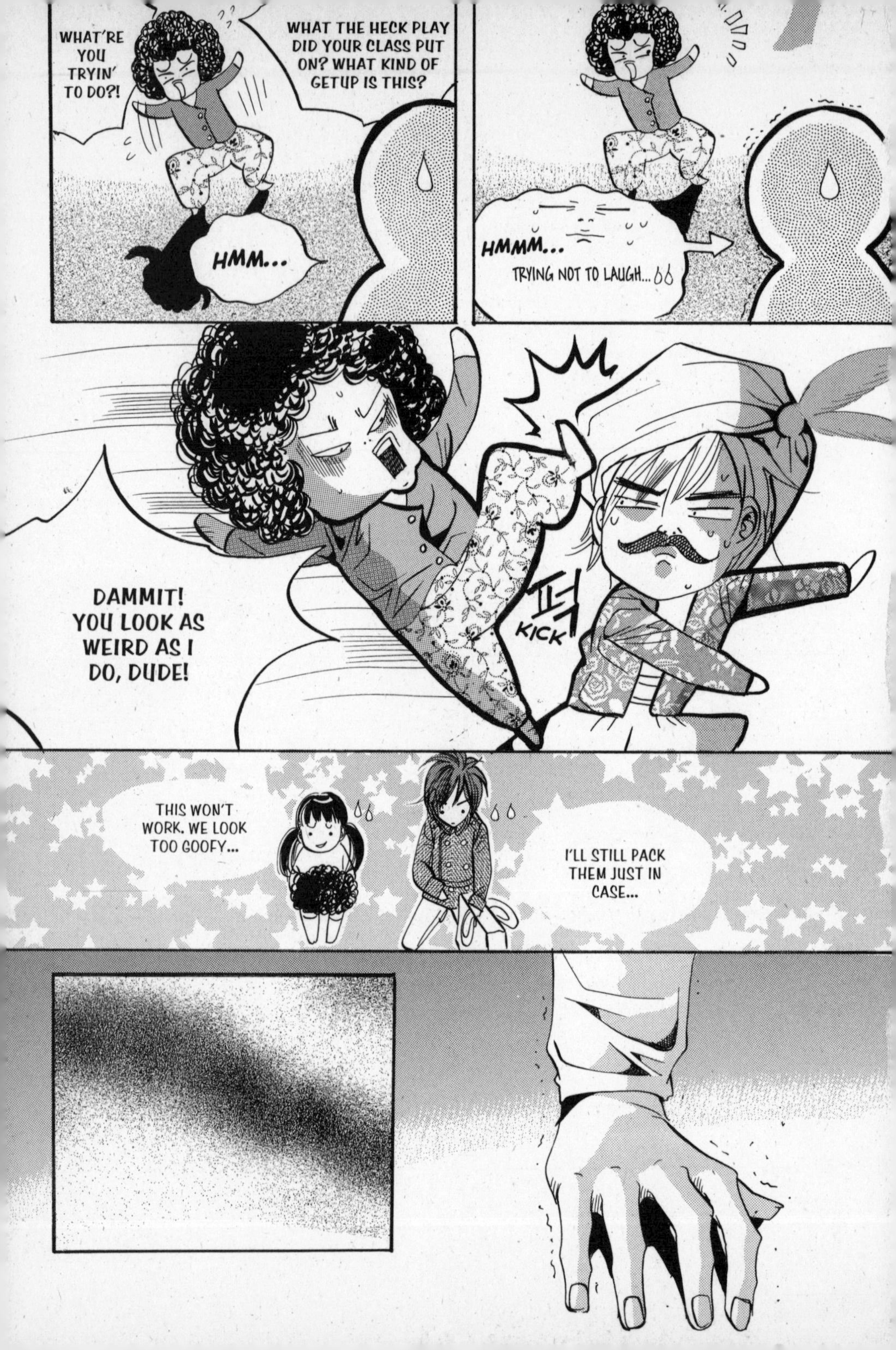
WHAT'RE YOU TRYIN' TO DO?!
WHAT THE HECK PLAY DID YOUR CLASS PUT ON? WHAT KIND OF GETUP IS THIS?
HMM...
HMMM...
TRYING NOT TO LAUGH...
DAMMIT! YOU LOOK AS WEIRD AS I DO, DUDE!
퍽
KICK
THIS WON'T WORK. WE LOOK TOO GOOFY...
I'LL STILL PACK THEM JUST IN CASE...

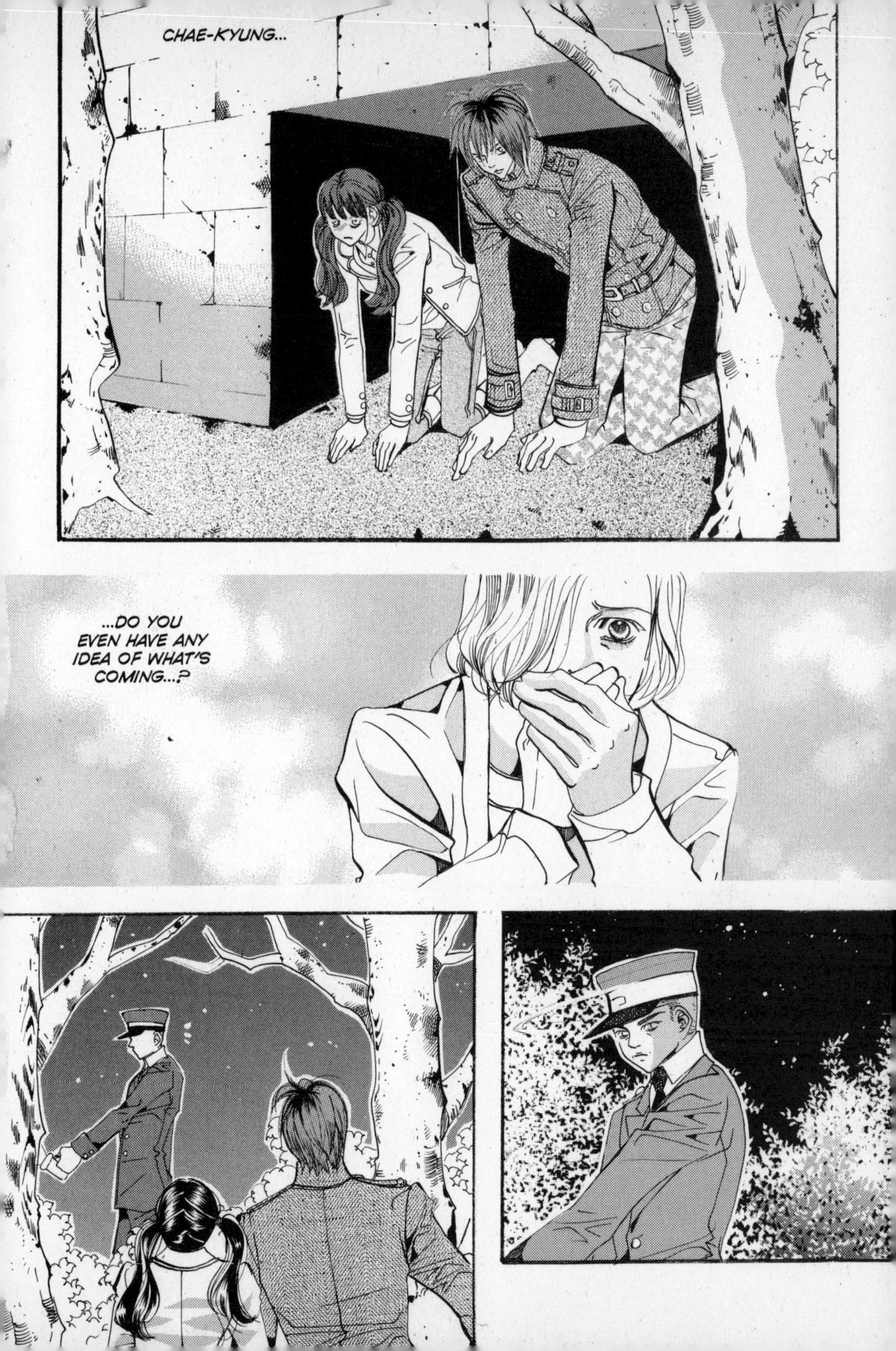
CHAE-KYUNG...
...DO YOU EVEN HAVE ANY IDEA OF WHAT'S COMING...?

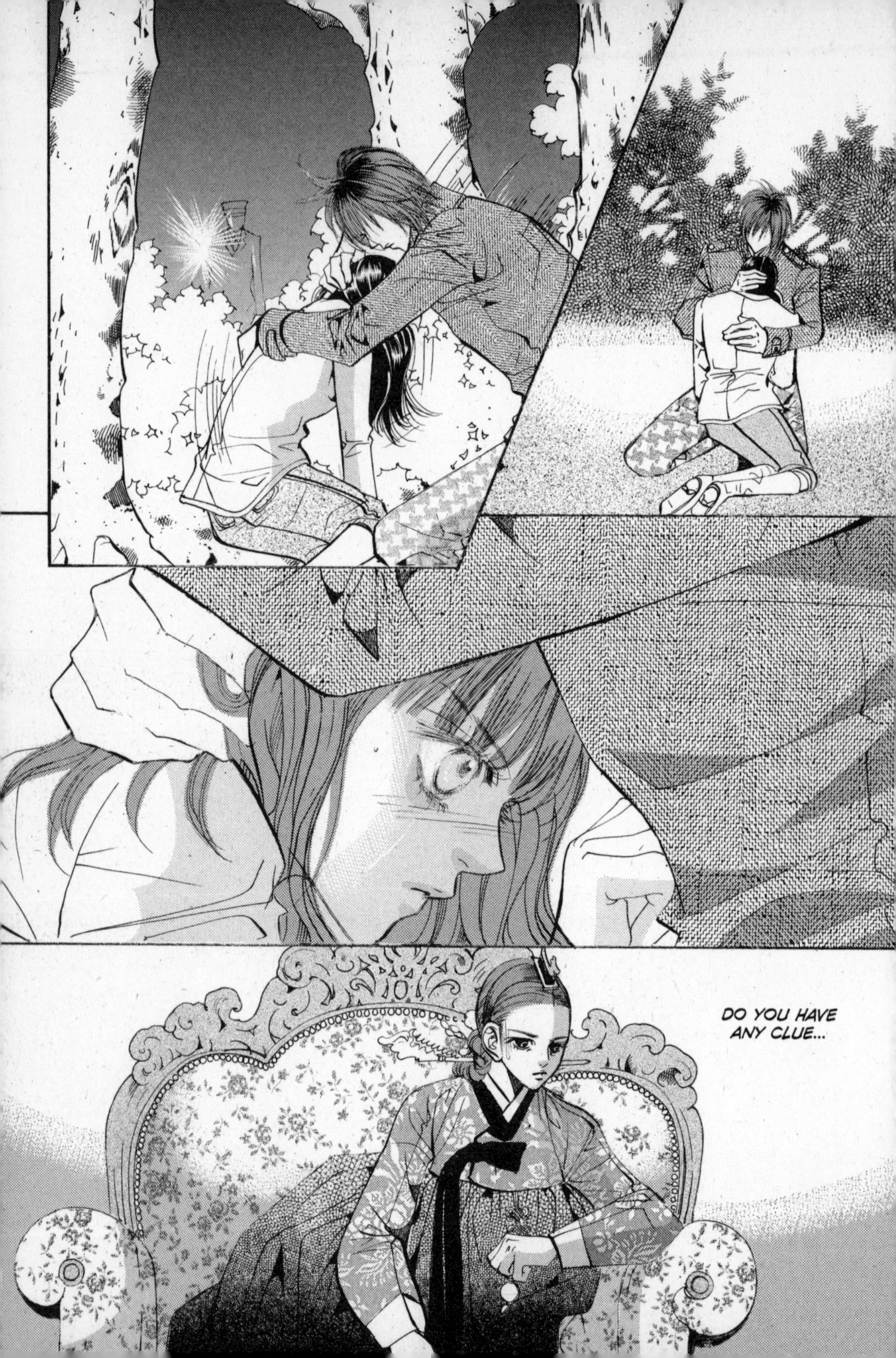
DO YOU HAVE
ANY CLUE...

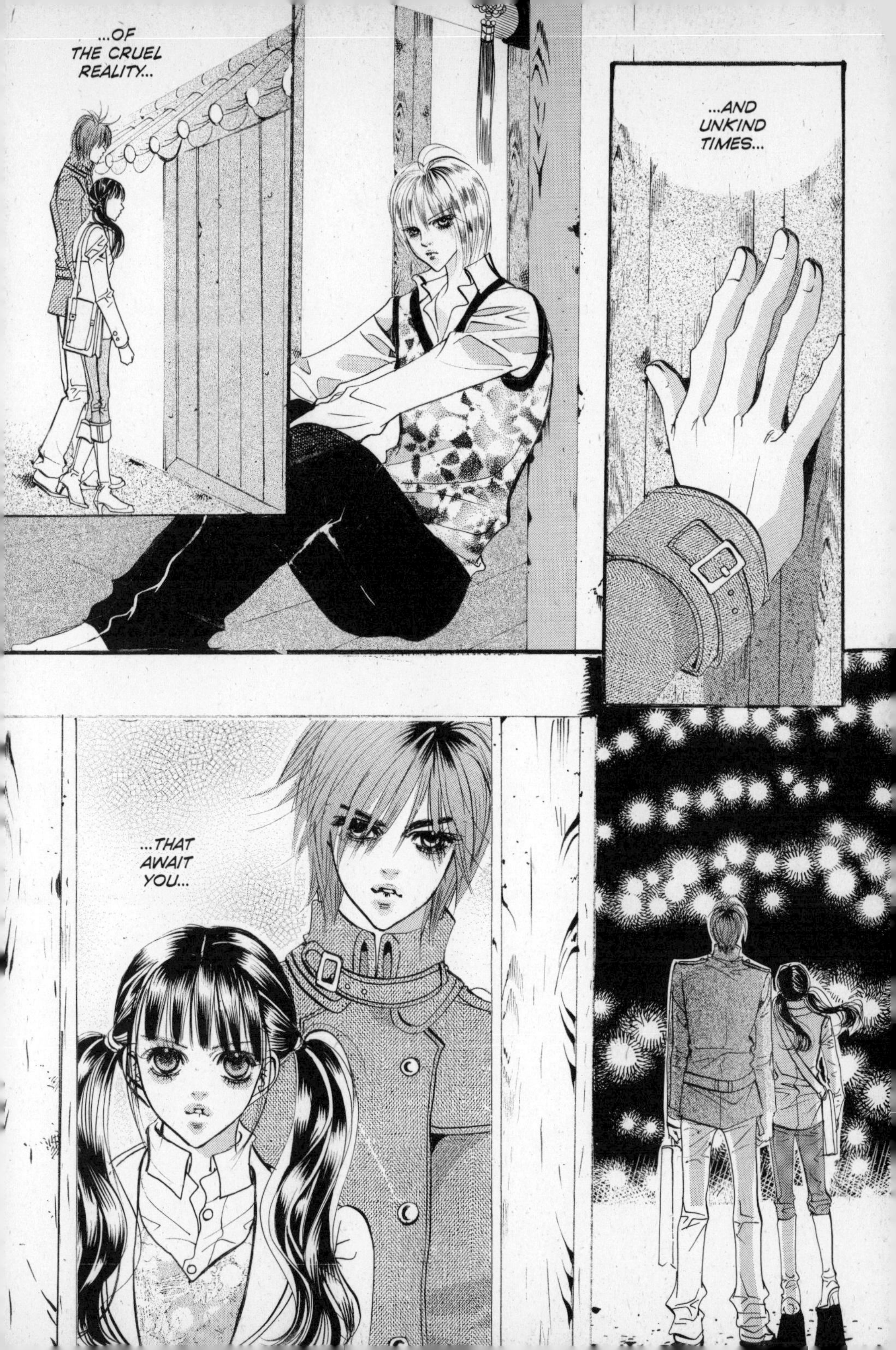
...OF THE CRUEL REALITY...
...AND UNKIND TIMES...
...THAT AWAIT YOU...

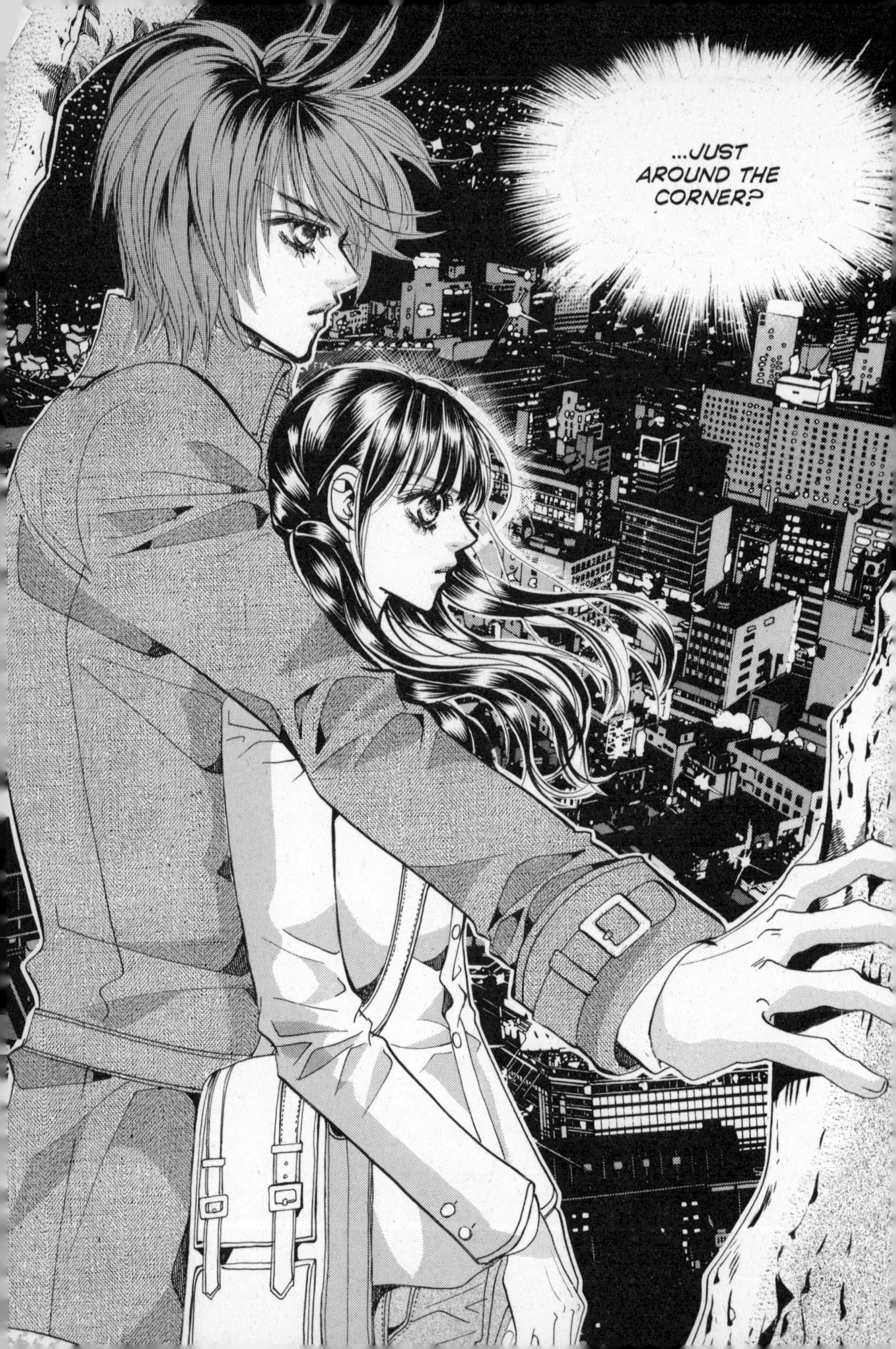
...JUST AROUND THE CORNER?

The Royal Palace

Goong

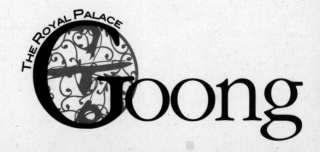

BEAUTY PARK PERSONALLY DESCRIBES HER CHARACTERS.
PART 1

(SHE DOESN'T FEEL GUILTY ABOUT CALLING HERSELF "BEAUTY" ANYMORE.)

CHAE-KYUNG SHIN (18 YEARS OLD)
NICKNAME: KOREAN BLOOD SAUSAGE

CHAE-KYUNG IS THE CHARACTER THAT WAS INSPIRED BY FRIENDS OF MINE OR CHARACTERS THAT I LIKED FROM COMICS, NOVELS, MOVIES, AND TV SHOWS. SHE'S CLUMSY, JUST LIKE ME.

THERE'S A RUMOR THAT THE CREATOR IS THE MODEL FOR HER APPEARANCE. APPARENTLY, THE CREATOR PUTS A MIRROR BESIDE HER WHEN SHE DRAWS CHAE-KYUNG, WHOSE BIG EYES, SHARP NOSE, AND BEAUTIFUL LIPS ARE JUST LIKE HER CREATOR'S. WHEN PEOPLE WANTED TO MAKE GOONG INTO A TV SHOW, THE CREATOR WROTE, "THE CREATOR OF GOONG IS GOING TO PLAY CHAE-KYUNG ON THE TV SHOW." SHE HAS BEEN INVESTIGATED FOR SPREADING LIES ONLINE. TSK, TSK. POOR CHAE-KYUNG.

SHIN LEE (18 YEARS OLD)
NICKNAME: SHIN RAMEN

I GOT THE IDEA FOR SHIN FROM THE OLD CONVENTION OF PRINCES WHO COULD NEVER GET THEIR FATHER'S APPROVAL. SOME EXAMPLES ARE PRINCE SA-DOH AND PRINCE SO-HYUN... ESPECIALLY THE FORMER, WHO WAS KILLED BY HIS OWN FATHER, KING YOUNG-JO. PEOPLE SAY HIS IMAGE WAS DISTORTED BY HIS WIFE'S BOOK. HE WAS CONFIDENT AND SMART, BUT HE WAS LONELY BECAUSE HE WASN'T LOVED BY HIS FATHER. I HOPE I CAN PRESENT SHIN JUST LIKE THAT.

YUL LEE (18 YEARS OLD)
NICKNAME: FLOWER YUL

YUL'S ORIGIN STARTED WITH LOSS. HE LOST HIS FATHER, HIS POSITION AS THE ROYAL GRANDSON, AND HIS FIANCÉE. ON TOP OF THAT, HE HAD TO LEAVE THE PALACE. THAT'S WHY I FEEL BAD FOR HIM AND HAVE MORE LOVE FOR HIM. MY PREFERENCES ARE WEIRD, I GUESS. I LIKE A MAN WHO'S DARK AND MEAN BECAUSE HE FEELS INFERIOR OVER ONE WHO'S ALL HEALTHY AND HAPPY. YUL, GET AWAY FROM CHAE-KYUNG AND MI-ROO AND COME TO ME. I WISH YOU WOULD APPEAR IN A DIRTY COMIC. I APOLOGIZE TO THE READERS WHO LOVE YUL...

DAEBI (40 YEARS OLD)

I THINK I WROTE SOMETHING SIMILAR TO THIS BEFORE. THE MODEL FOR THE DAEBI IS DAEBI INSOO, THE MOTHER OF KING SUNG-JONG. DAEBI INSOO WAS VERY STRICT ABOUT EDUCATING HER CHILDREN. WHEN HER HUSBAND DIED AS CROWN PRINCE, SHE HAD TO LIVE OUTSIDE THE PALACE WITH HER CHILDREN, BUT SHE MAINTAINED A DESIRE TO MAKE ONE OF HER SONS KING. SHE TOLD MYUNG-HUI HAN, "EVEN THOUGH I COULD NOT BE A QUEEN, I WOULD LIKE TO BE A DAEBI." THE DAEBI IN GOONG IS JUST LIKE DAEBI INSOO. SHE'LL DO ANYTHING TO MAKE YUL THE NEXT MONARCH. SHE DOESN'T GIVE A DAMN ABOUT OTHER PEOPLE'S SUFFERING OR SADNESS AND JUST RUNS TOWARD HER GOAL. BUT I STILL CAN'T HATE HER BECAUSE ALL OF US HAVE SIMILAR AMBITIONS SOMEWHERE INSIDE US.

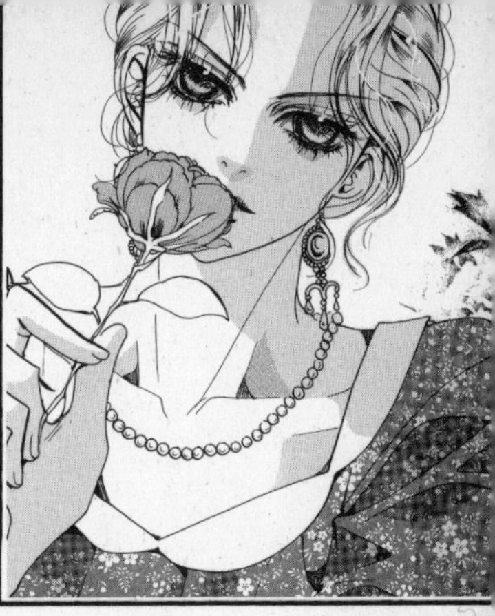

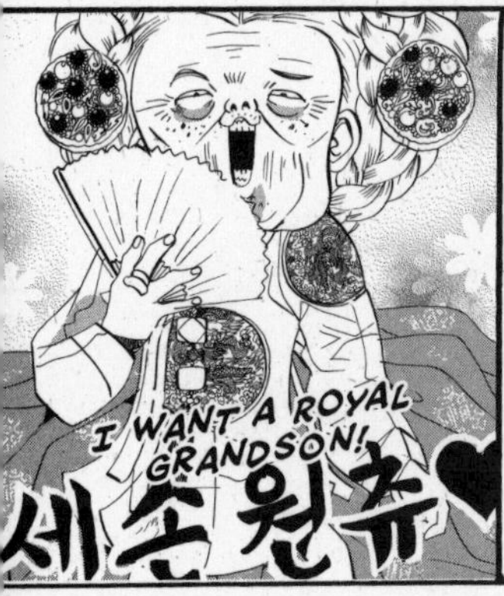
I WANT A ROYAL GRANDSON!
세손원츄♥

THE QUEEN MOTHER (65 YEARS OLD)

MY LATE GRANDMOTHER WAS SO SKINNY AND WEAK. SHE LOOKED TOO DELICATE. THAT'S WHY THE OLD LADIES IN MY BOOKS ARE CHUBBY AND CHATTY. SHE AND LADY HAN SEEM PRETTY CRAZY, BUT SHE'S SAD ABOUT WHAT'S GOING ON IN THE ROYAL FAMILY. I HEARD SHE WAS TRYING TO UNIFY THE ROYAL FAMILY, BUT I CAN'T REALLY SEE THAT. ANYWAY, I LIKE A WARM AND FUNNY GRANDMOTHER MORE THAN A SERIOUS ONE. (I'M JUST SAYING...)

THE QUEEN (39 YEARS OLD)

EVERYONE HAS THEIR EYE ON HER BECAUSE SHE GAVE BIRTH RECENTLY. HER STRICT CHARACTER IS FALLING APART AS A RESULT OF THE INTERNAL POWER STRUGGLES IN THE ROYAL FAMILY. SHE'S TRYING TO KICK CHAE-KYUNG OUT OF THE PALACE, BUT I CAN SYMPATHIZE WITH WHAT MOTIVATES HER. MOST PEOPLE WOULD DO THE SAME THING IN HER POSITION. WE'LL JUST HAVE TO BLAME DESTINY FOR BEING CRUEL. PEOPLE HAVE STARTED HATING HER, BUT PLEASE DON'T DO THAT. SHE'S HAVING A HARD TIME. IT'S TOUGH TO HAVE A BABY AT HER AGE, AFTER ALL.

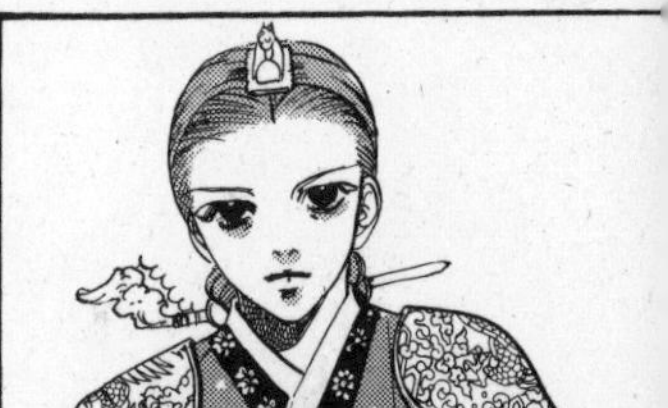

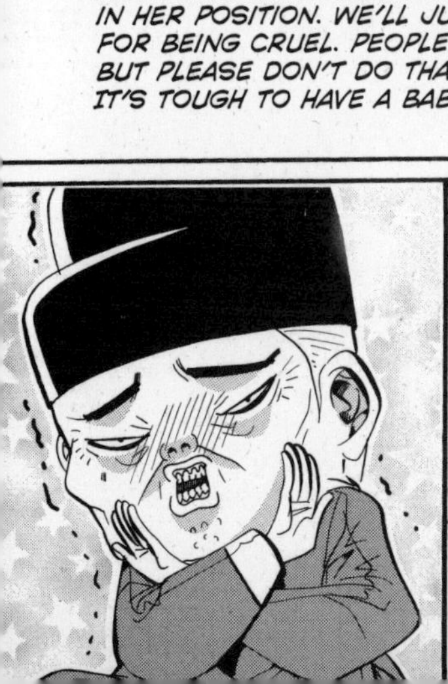

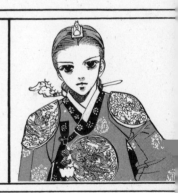

EUNUCH KONG (AGE UNKNOWN. THERE'S A RUMOR HIS NAME APPEARS IN OLD HISTORY BOOKS.)

HE'S THE SYMBOL OF NONSENSE AND CHEESINESS, BUT HE'S ALSO ONE OF MY THREE FAVORITE CHARACTERS. HIS WRINKLES ARE GROWING IN NUMBER BECAUSE HE'S FRETTING OVER AN UNREQUITED LOVE. HE'LL STILL DO ANYTHING FOR YUL. HE'S JUST BEEN A CRAZY OLD MAN SO FAR, BUT HE'LL HAVE AN IMPORTANT ROLE TOWARD THE END OF THE STORY. PLEASE KEEP READING TO FIND OUT WHAT OUR EUNUCH KONG GETS UP TO IN THE FUTURE.

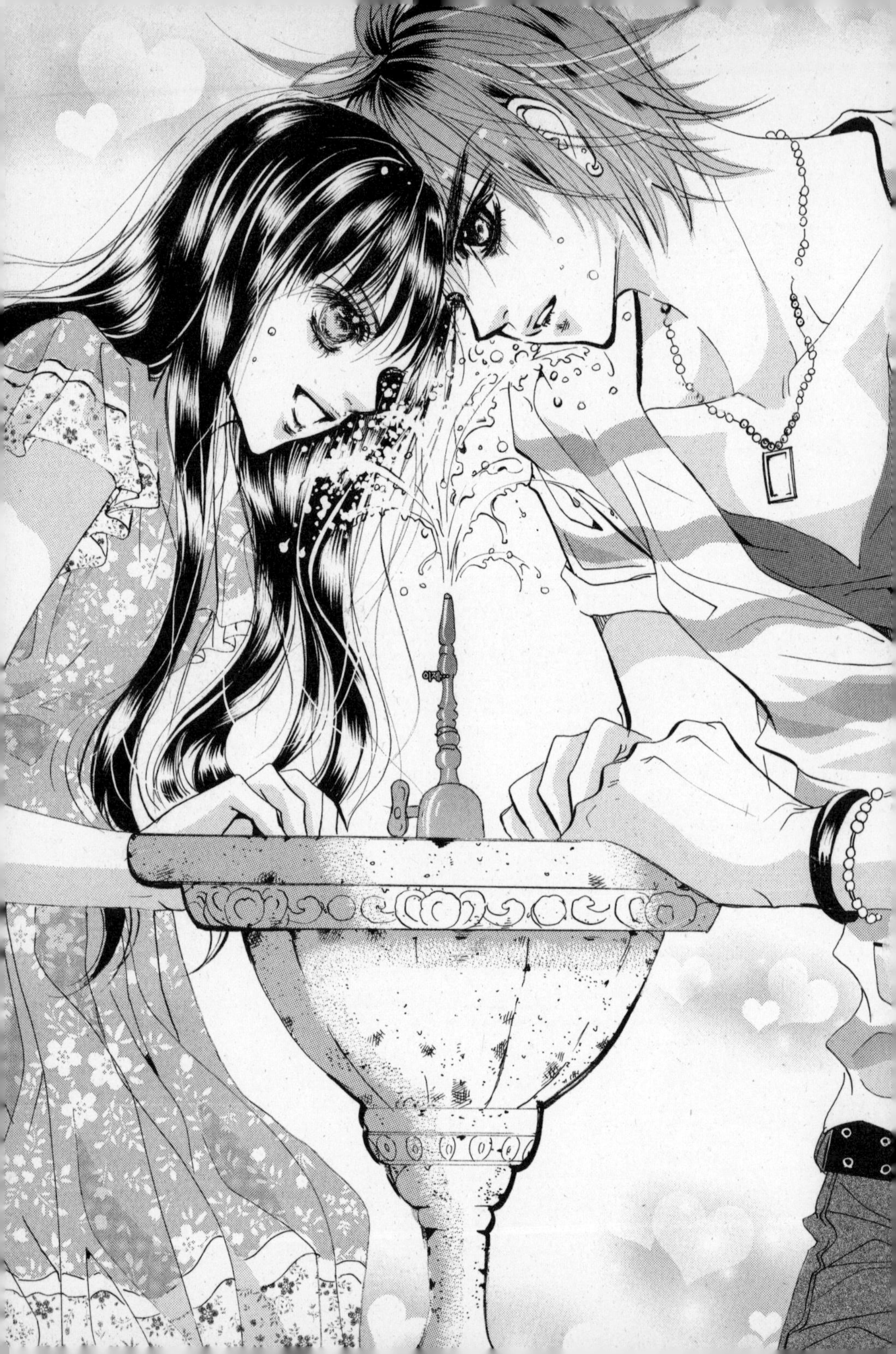
이제...

THE ROYAL PALACE

Goong

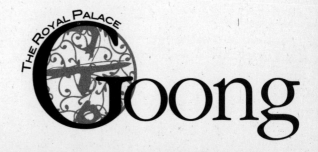

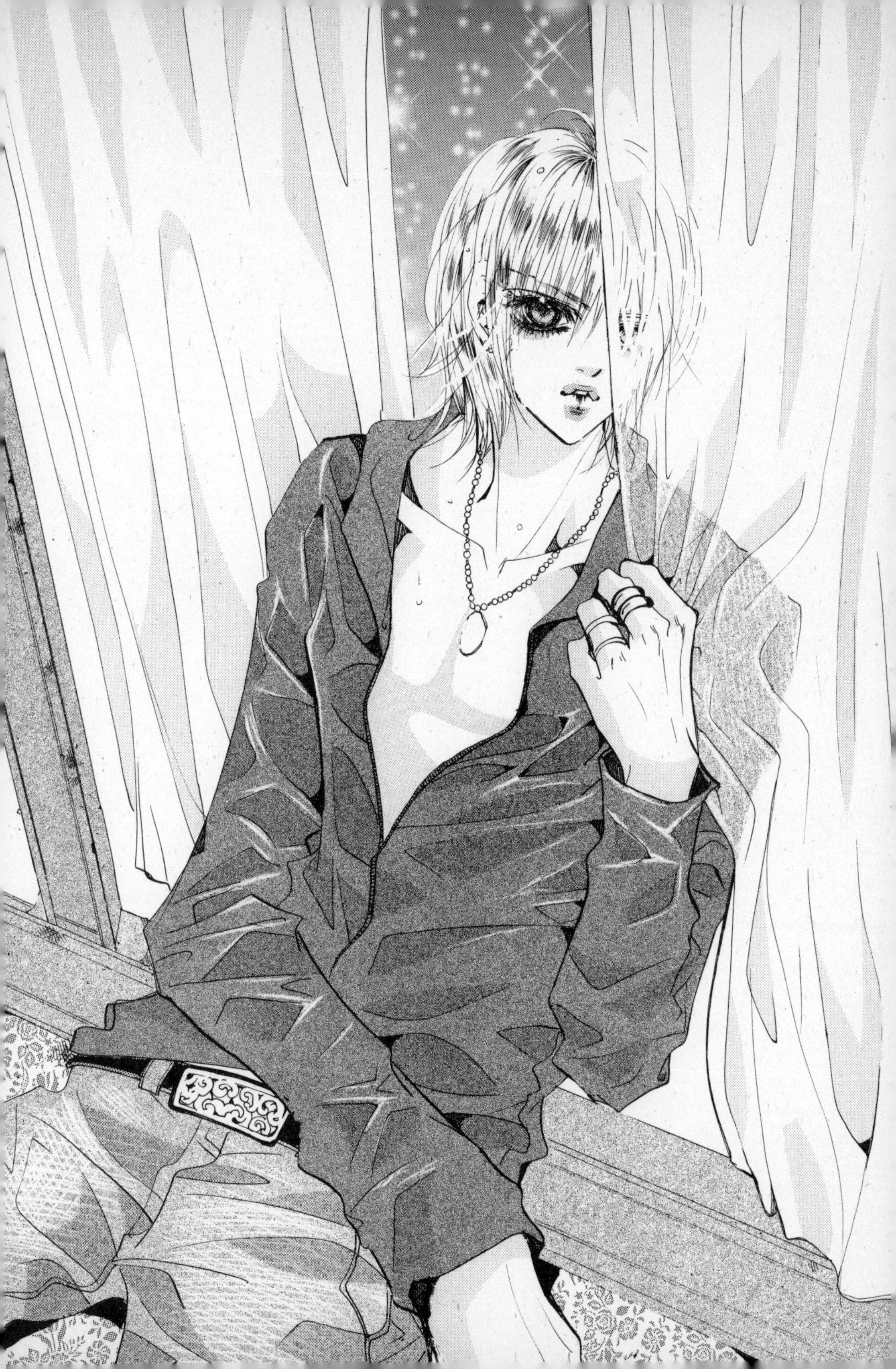

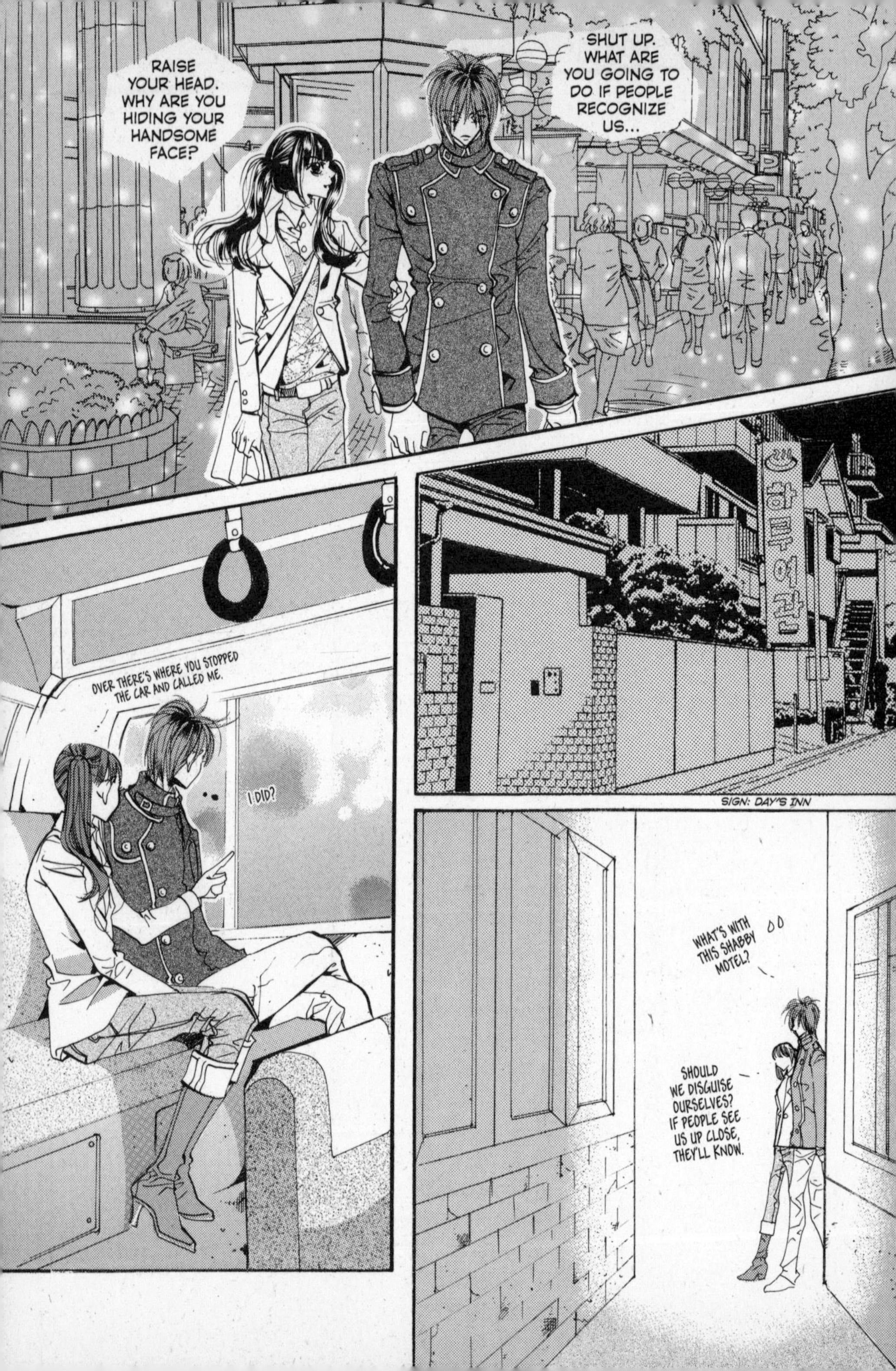
RAISE YOUR HEAD. WHY ARE YOU HIDING YOUR HANDSOME FACE?
SHUT UP. WHAT ARE YOU GOING TO DO IF PEOPLE RECOGNIZE US...
OVER THERE'S WHERE YOU STOPPED THE CAR AND CALLED ME.
I DID?
SIGN: DAY'S INN
WHAT'S WITH THIS SHABBY MOTEL?
SHOULD WE DISGUISE OURSELVES? IF PEOPLE SEE US UP CLOSE, THEY'LL KNOW.

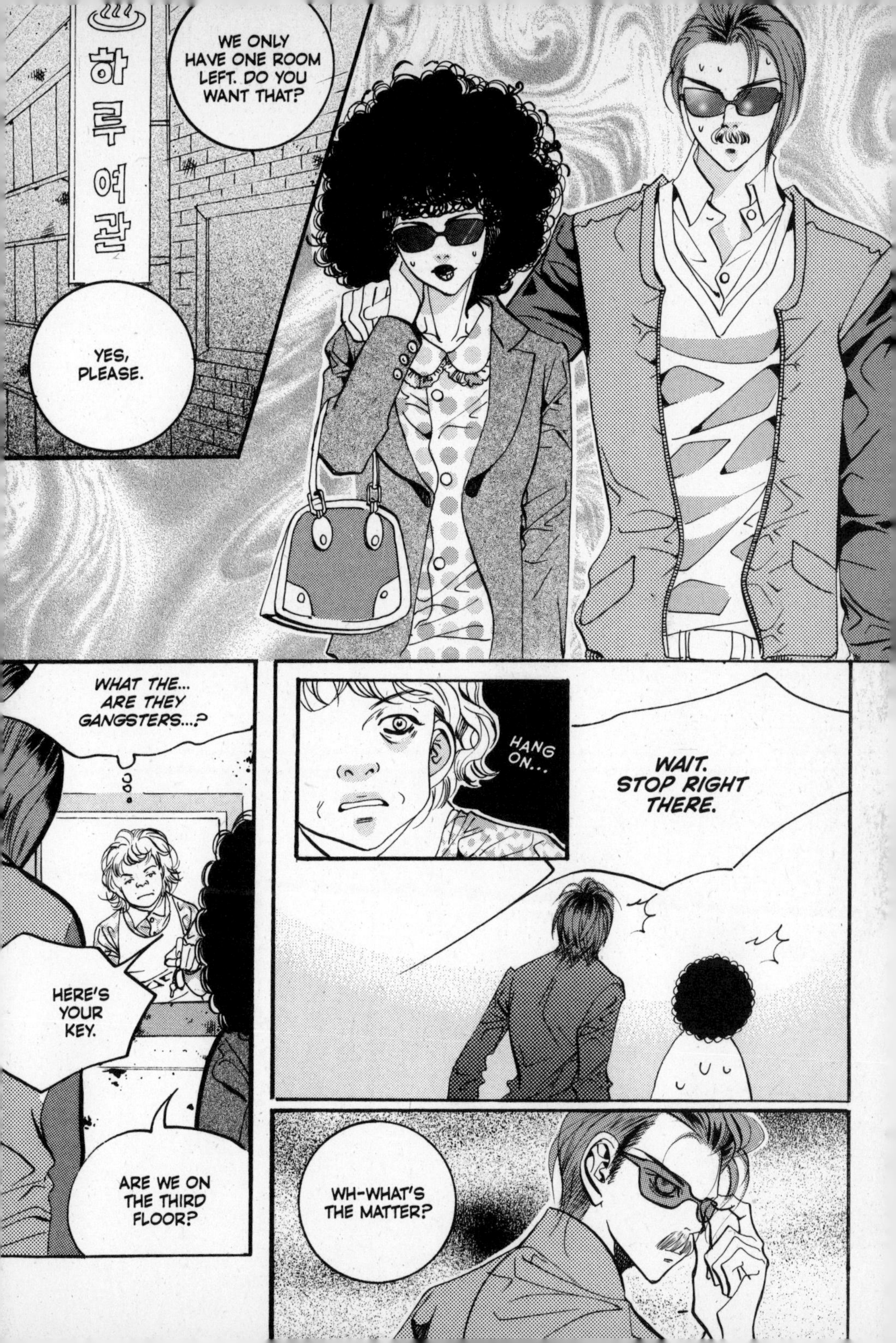
하루 여관
WE ONLY HAVE ONE ROOM LEFT. DO YOU WANT THAT?
YES, PLEASE.
WHAT THE... ARE THEY GANGSTERS...?
HERE'S YOUR KEY.
ARE WE ON THE THIRD FLOOR?
HANG ON...
WAIT. STOP RIGHT THERE.
WH-WHAT'S THE MATTER?

WE PROVIDE A SPECIAL "SERVICE" FOR COUPLES.

TAKE A LOOK AT THE NICE VIDEO ON TOP OF THE TV IN YOUR ROOM. ♡

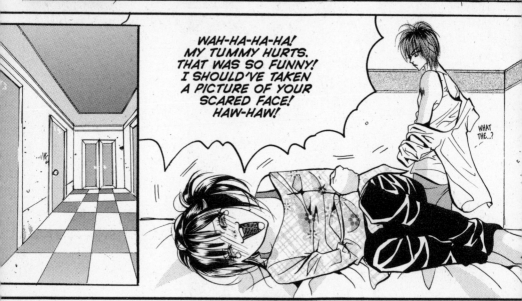

WAH-HA-HA-HA! MY TUMMY HURTS. THAT WAS SO FUNNY! I SHOULD'VE TAKEN A PICTURE OF YOUR SCARED FACE! HAW-HAW!

WHAT THE...?

OH, WHAT DO YOU WANT TO DO ABOUT DINNER? MOST PLACES WILL BE CLOSED BY NOW. SHOULD WE JUST EAT AT THE RESTAURANT DOWNSTAIRS?

I SAW IT ON THE WAY UP. IT LOOKED NASTY.

I BROUGHT SOME SNACKS JUST IN CASE. I HAVE YOUR FAVORITE CHIPS, COOKIES, AND INSTANT RAMEN.

REALLY? WANNA WATCH THAT VIDEO WHILE WE EAT?

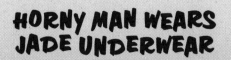

HORNY MAN WEARS JADE UNDERWEAR

STARRING: BEAUTY PARK, HORNYMAN SAK

DIRECTOR: DOGGY INSIDE

AHH, DON'T DO THIS. YOU'RE A HORNY MAN, AHHHH...

COME HERE. HAVE FUN IN MY ARMS BEFORE HE COMES BACK. HEE-HEE-HEE.

UNH, WHY ARE YOU DOING THIS...

¥‰✚✖◊▢¢!

KABOOM°

WHAT THE...? IT'S A DIRTY MOVIE.

AND THOUGH YOU CLEARLY CAN'T TAKE YOUR EYES OFF OF IT, I HAVE NO INTEREST IN WATCHING IT UNLESS I CAN DO WHAT'S ON IT.

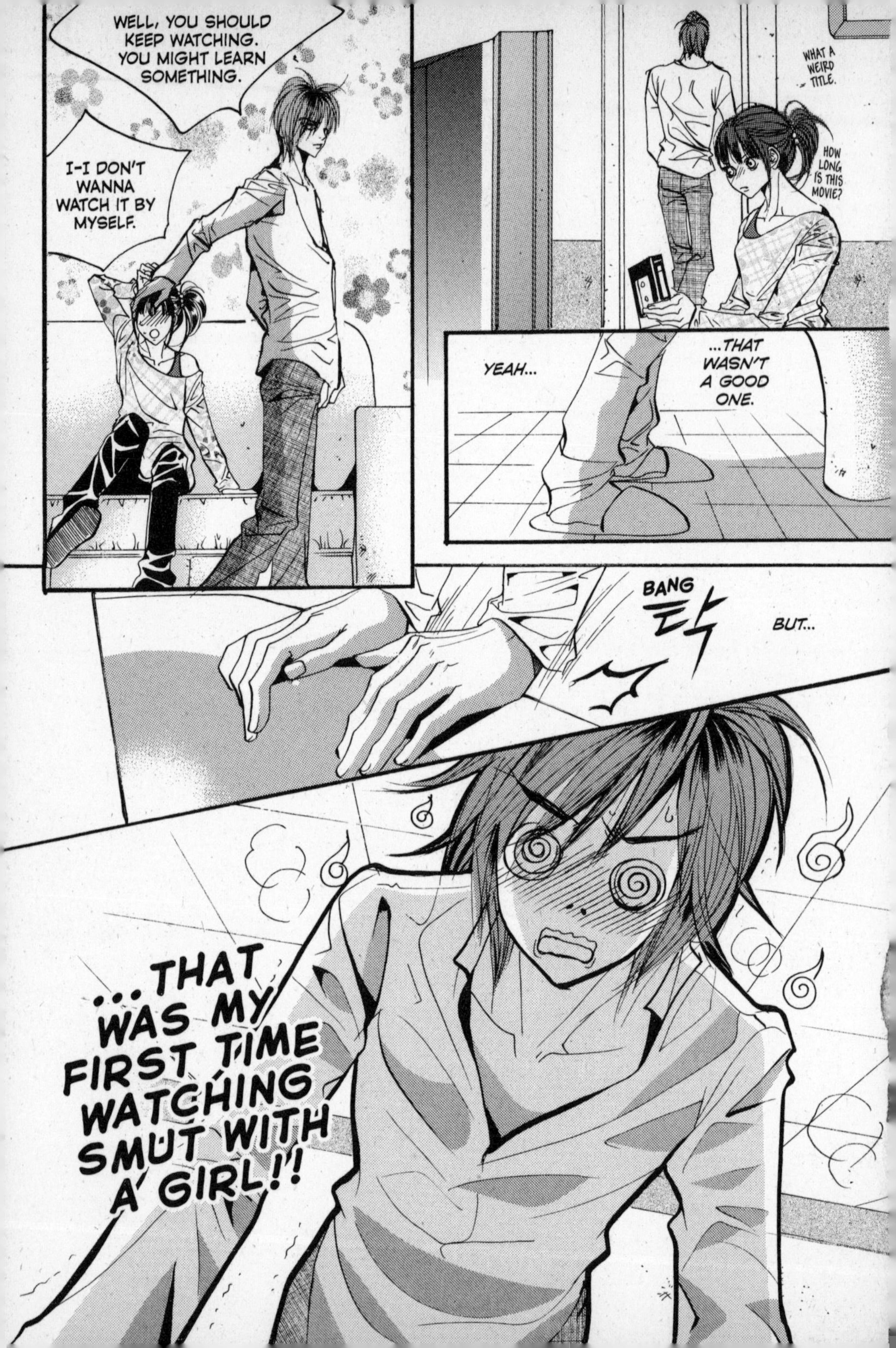
WELL, YOU SHOULD KEEP WATCHING. YOU MIGHT LEARN SOMETHING.
I-I DON'T WANNA WATCH IT BY MYSELF.
WHAT A WEIRD TITLE.
HOW LONG IS THIS MOVIE?
YEAH...
...THAT WASN'T A GOOD ONE.
BANG
탁
BUT...
...THAT WAS MY FIRST TIME WATCHING SMUT WITH A GIRL!!

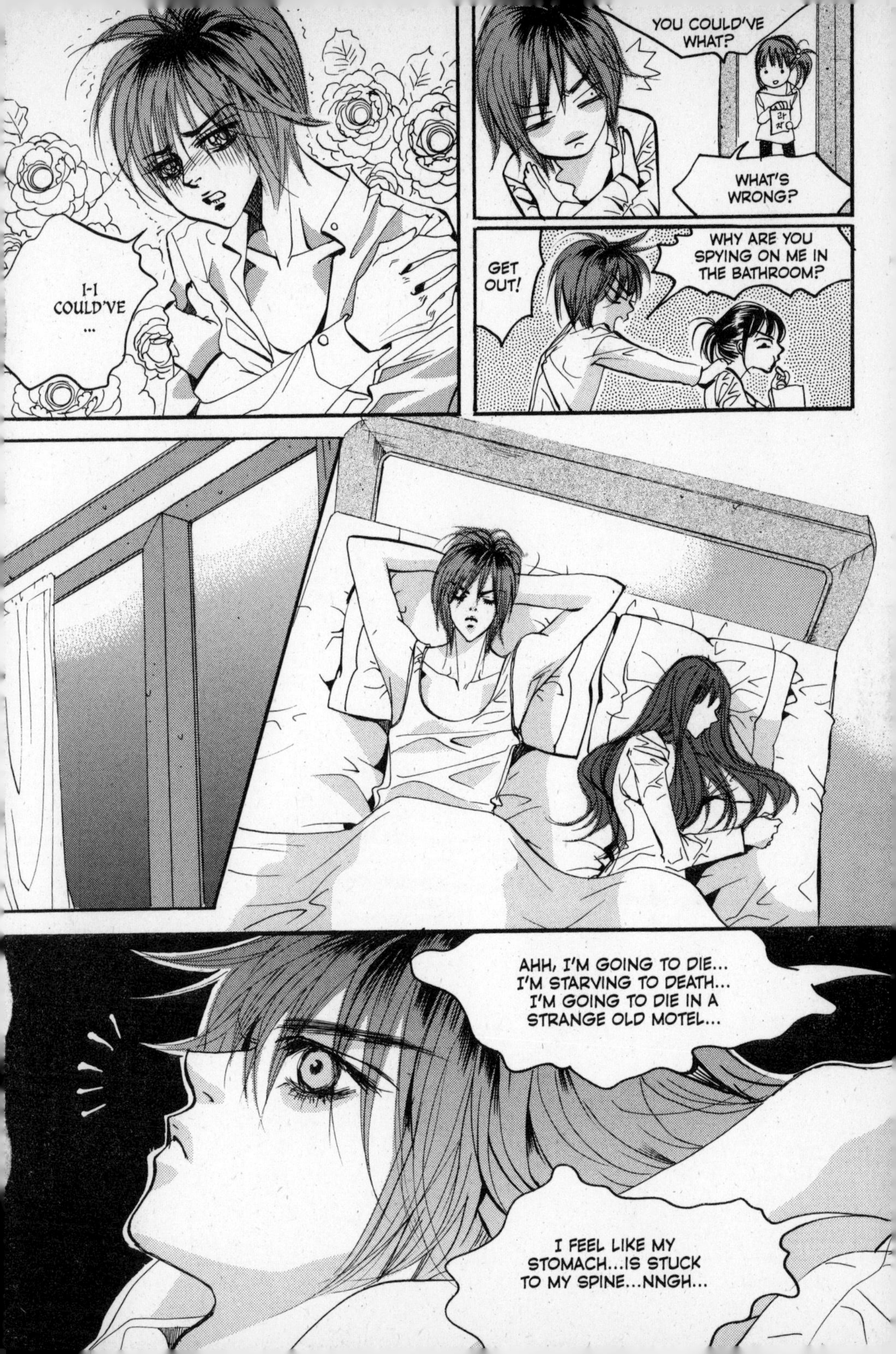
I-I COULD'VE ...
YOU COULD'VE WHAT?
WHAT'S WRONG?
WHY ARE YOU SPYING ON ME IN THE BATHROOM?
GET OUT!
AHH, I'M GOING TO DIE... I'M STARVING TO DEATH... I'M GOING TO DIE IN A STRANGE OLD MOTEL...
I FEEL LIKE MY STOMACH...IS STUCK TO MY SPINE...NNGH...

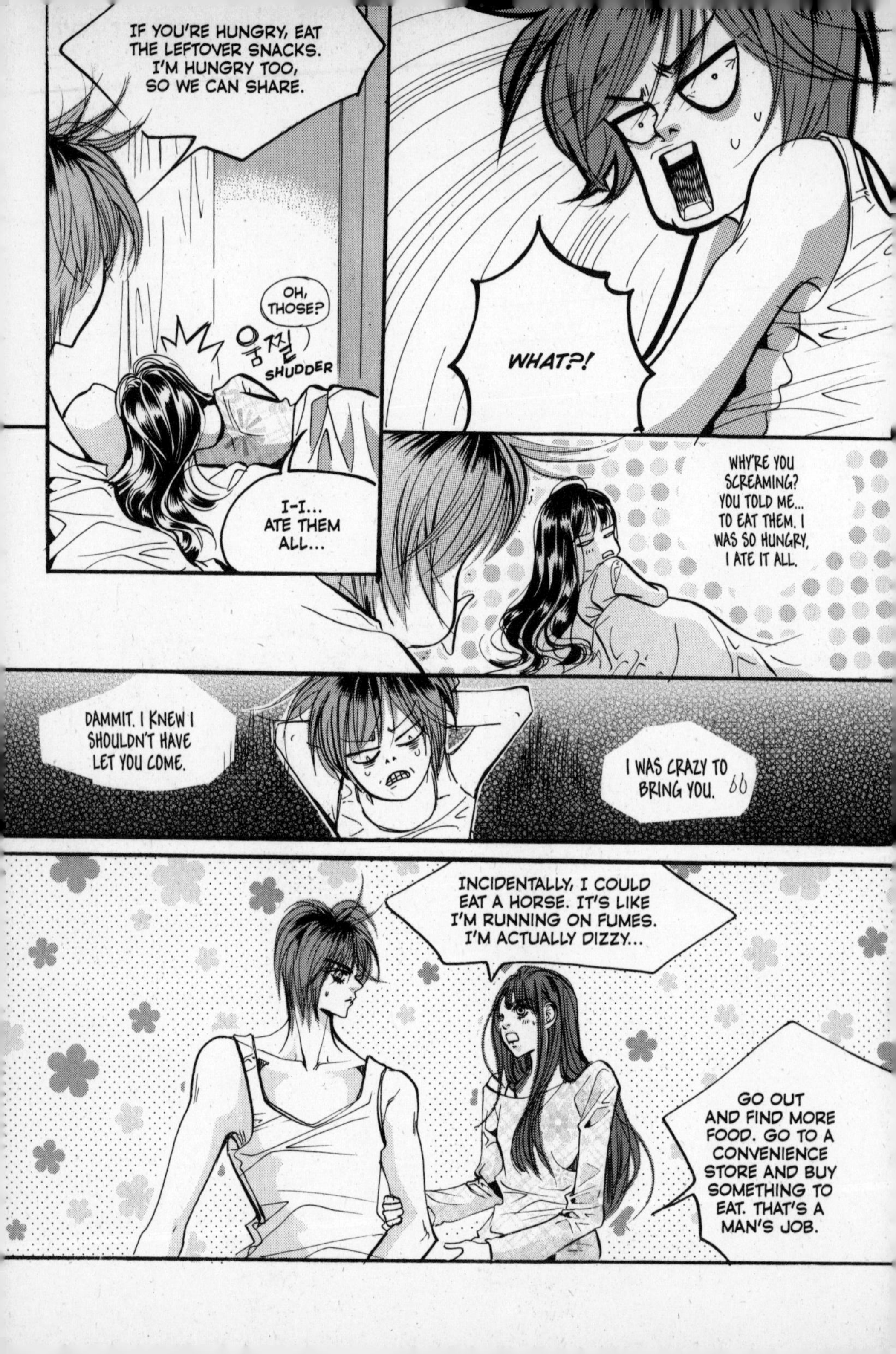
IF YOU'RE HUNGRY, EAT THE LEFTOVER SNACKS. I'M HUNGRY TOO, SO WE CAN SHARE.
OH, THOSE?
움찔
SHUDDER
I-I... ATE THEM ALL...
WHAT?!
WHY'RE YOU SCREAMING? YOU TOLD ME... TO EAT THEM. I WAS SO HUNGRY, I ATE IT ALL.
DAMMIT. I KNEW I SHOULDN'T HAVE LET YOU COME.
I WAS CRAZY TO BRING YOU.
INCIDENTALLY, I COULD EAT A HORSE. IT'S LIKE I'M RUNNING ON FUMES. I'M ACTUALLY DIZZY...
GO OUT AND FIND MORE FOOD. GO TO A CONVENIENCE STORE AND BUY SOMETHING TO EAT. THAT'S A MAN'S JOB.

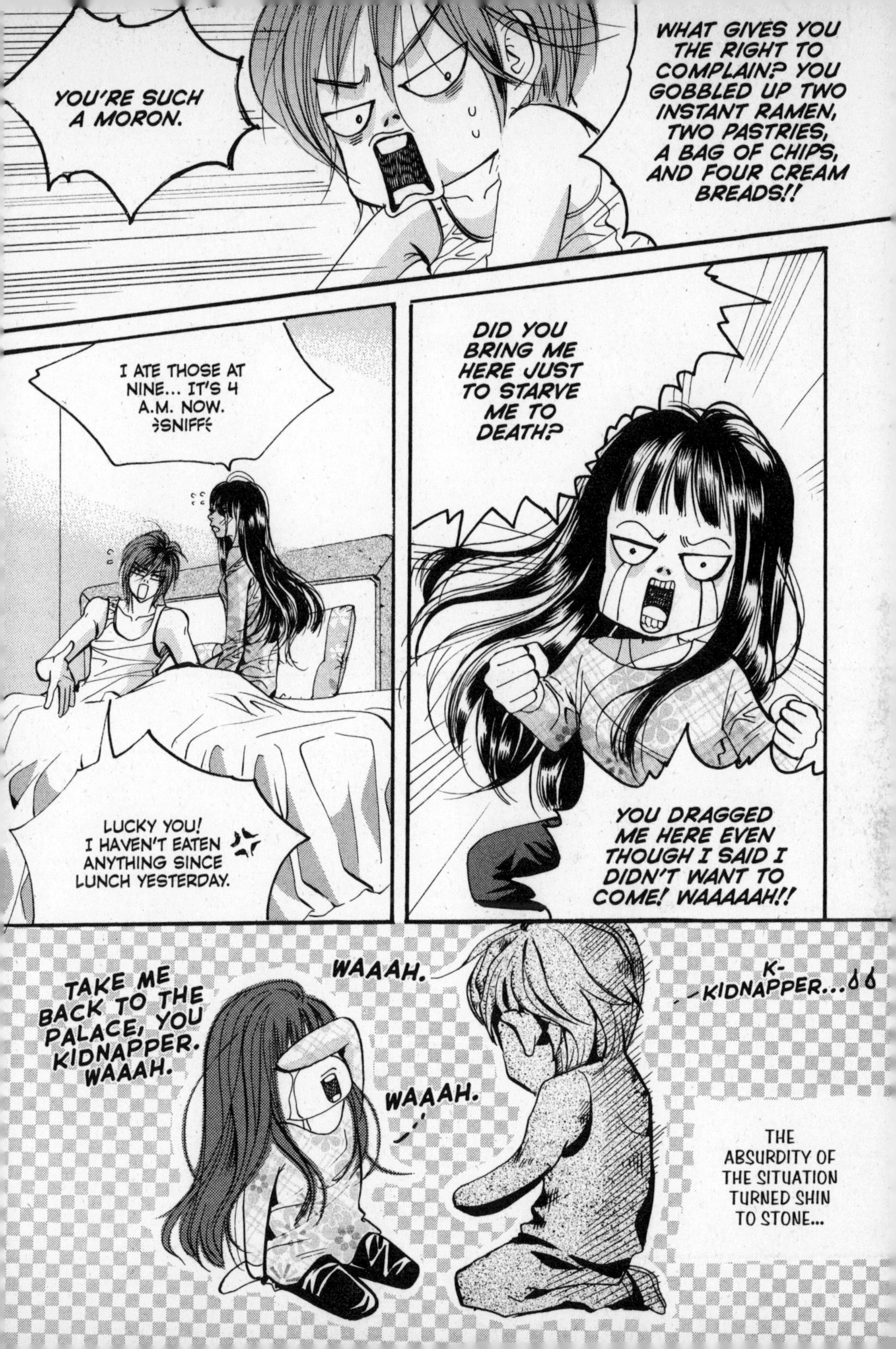

YOU'RE SUCH A MORON.
WHAT GIVES YOU THE RIGHT TO COMPLAIN? YOU GOBBLED UP TWO INSTANT RAMEN, TWO PASTRIES, A BAG OF CHIPS, AND FOUR CREAM BREADS!!
I ATE THOSE AT NINE... IT'S 4 A.M. NOW. SNIFF
LUCKY YOU! I HAVEN'T EATEN ANYTHING SINCE LUNCH YESTERDAY.
DID YOU BRING ME HERE JUST TO STARVE ME TO DEATH?
YOU DRAGGED ME HERE EVEN THOUGH I SAID I DIDN'T WANT TO COME! WAAAAAH!!
TAKE ME BACK TO THE PALACE, YOU KIDNAPPER. WAAAH.
WAAAH.
WAAAH.
K-KIDNAPPER...
THE ABSURDITY OF THE SITUATION TURNED SHIN TO STONE...

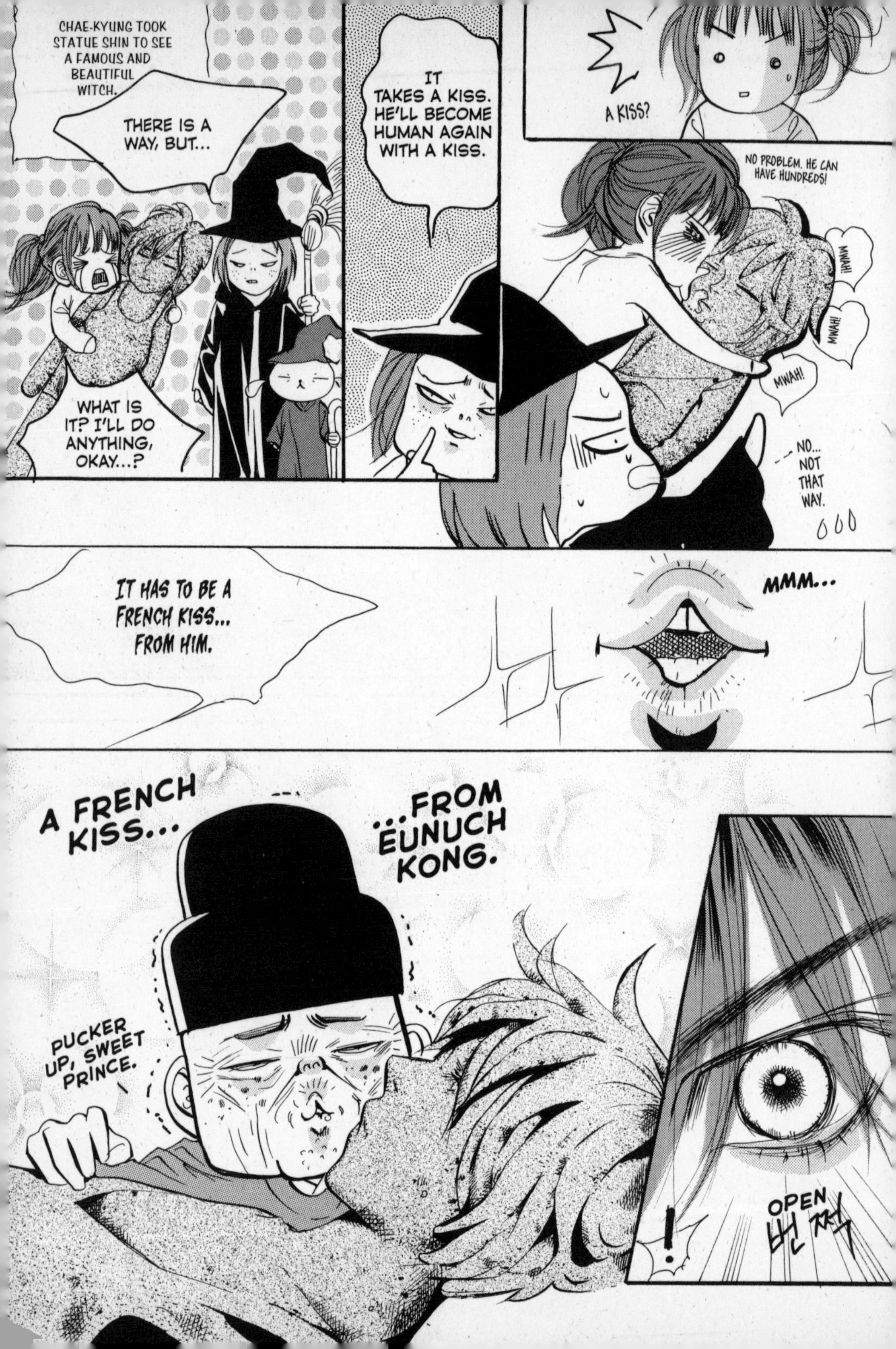
CHAE-KYUNG TOOK STATUE SHIN TO SEE A FAMOUS AND BEAUTIFUL WITCH.
THERE IS A WAY, BUT...
WHAT IS IT? I'LL DO ANYTHING, OKAY...?
IT TAKES A KISS. HE'LL BECOME HUMAN AGAIN WITH A KISS.
A KISS?
NO PROBLEM. HE CAN HAVE HUNDREDS!
MWAH!
MWAH!
MWAH!
NO... NOT THAT WAY.
IT HAS TO BE A FRENCH KISS... FROM HIM.
MMM...
A FRENCH KISS...
...FROM EUNUCH KONG.
PUCKER UP, SWEET PRINCE.
!
OPEN
번쩍

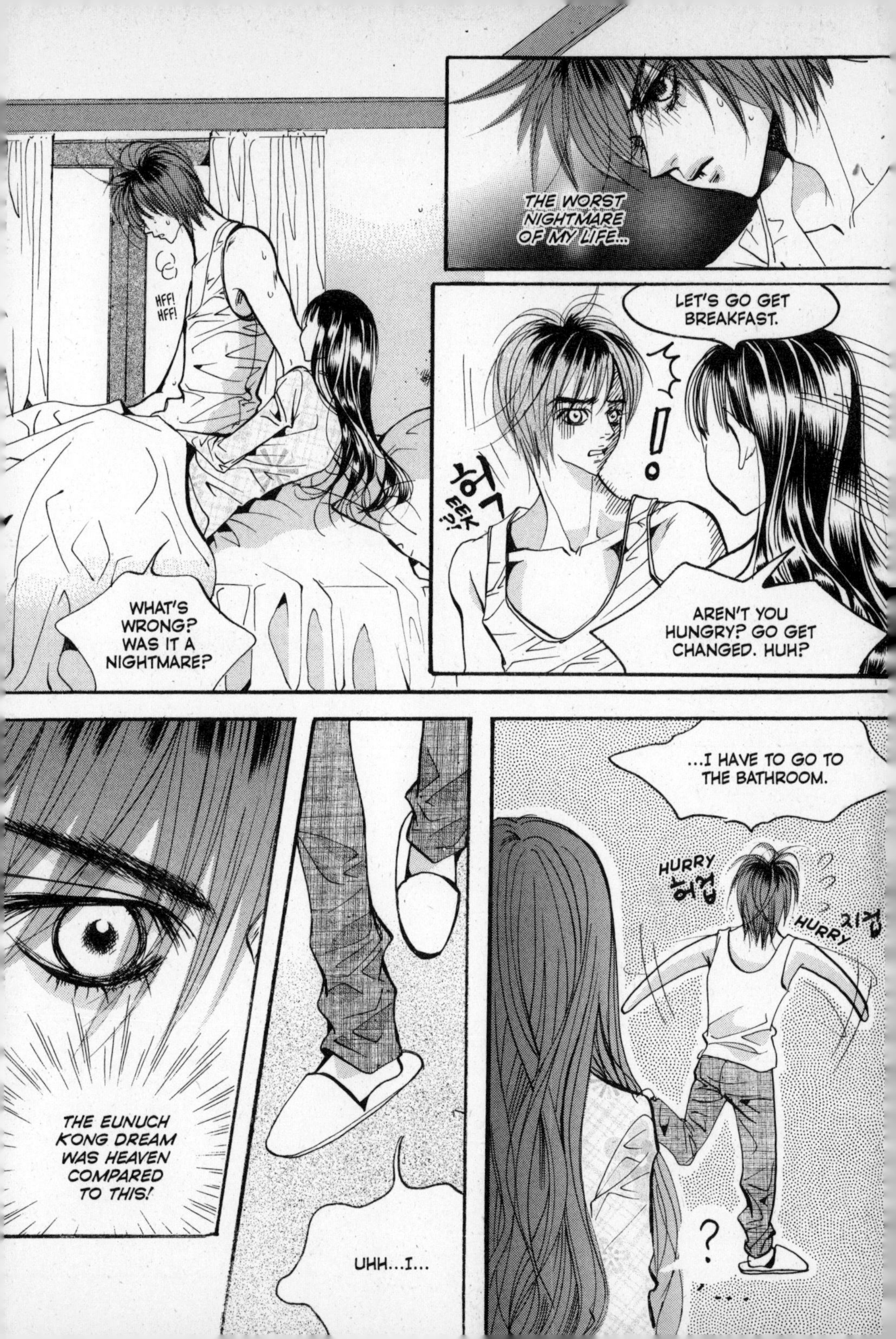
HFF! HFF!
WHAT'S WRONG? WAS IT A NIGHTMARE?
THE WORST NIGHTMARE OF MY LIFE...
LET'S GO GET BREAKFAST.
헉 EEK?!
!
AREN'T YOU HUNGRY? GO GET CHANGED. HUH?
THE EUNUCH KONG DREAM WAS HEAVEN COMPARED TO THIS!
UHH...I...
...I HAVE TO GO TO THE BATHROOM.
HURRY 허겁
HURRY 지겁
?
...

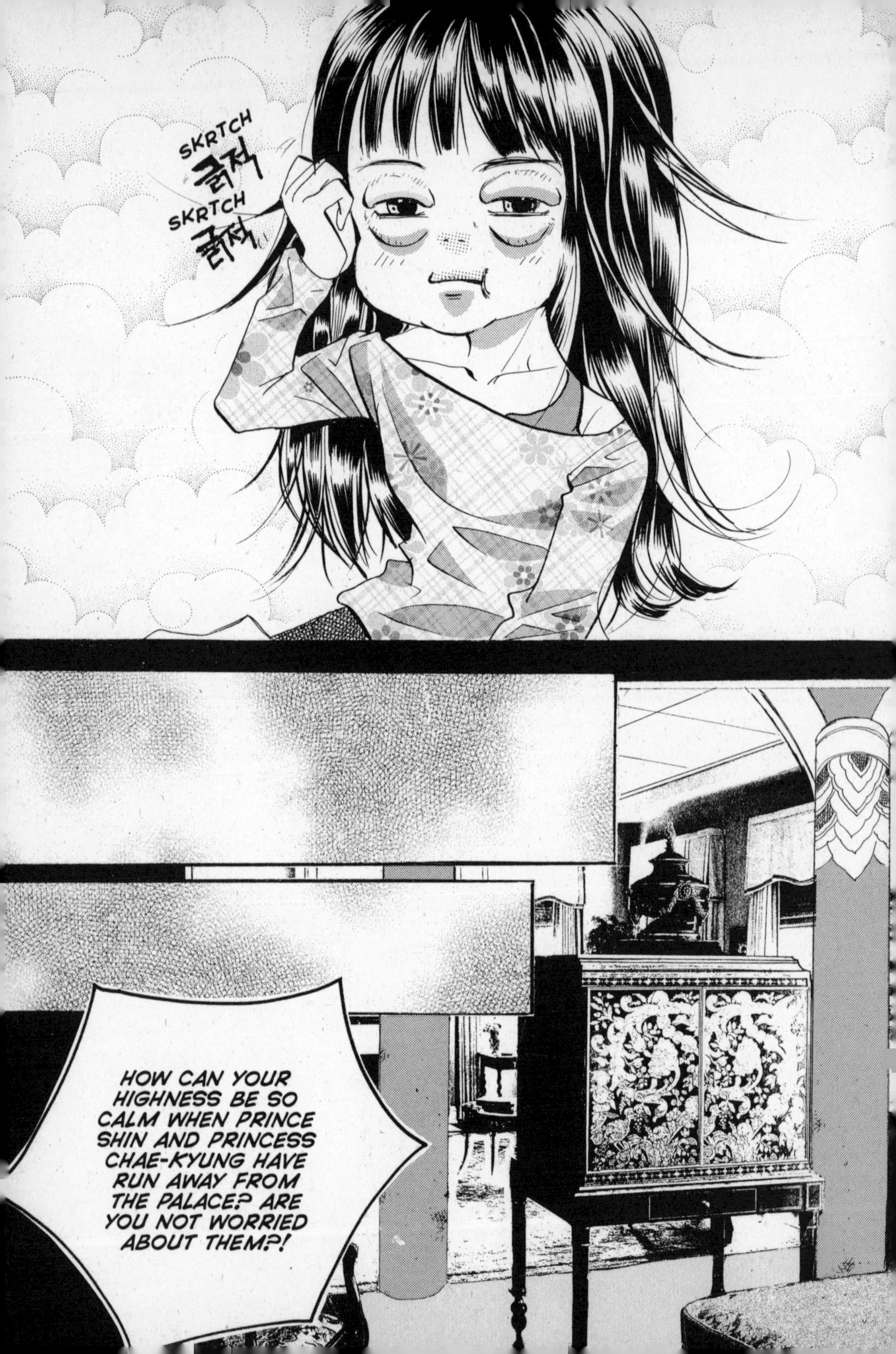
SKRTCH
긁적
SKRTCH
긁적
HOW CAN YOUR HIGHNESS BE SO CALM WHEN PRINCE SHIN AND PRINCESS CHAE-KYUNG HAVE RUN AWAY FROM THE PALACE? ARE YOU NOT WORRIED ABOUT THEM?!

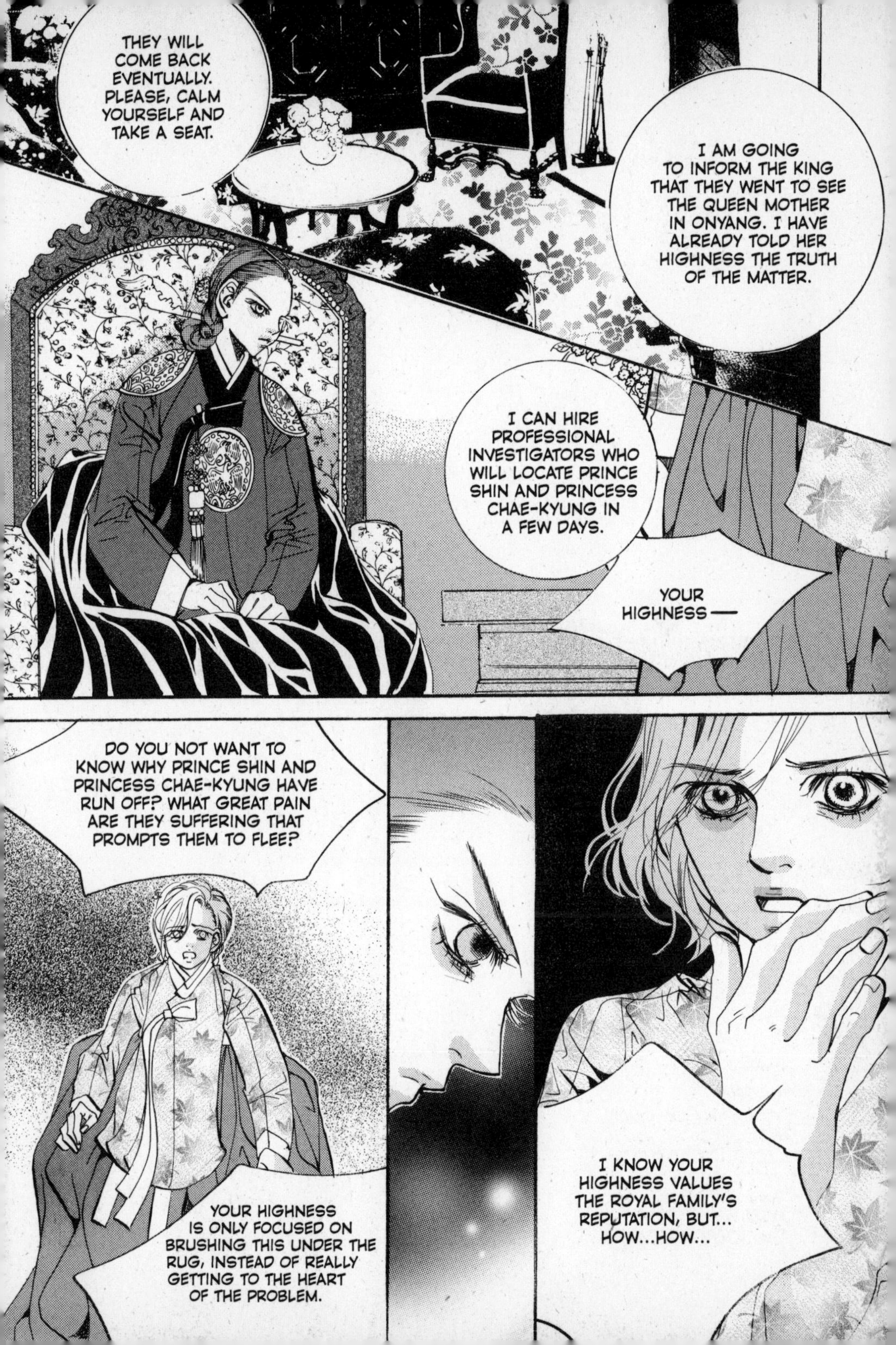
THEY WILL COME BACK EVENTUALLY. PLEASE, CALM YOURSELF AND TAKE A SEAT.
I AM GOING TO INFORM THE KING THAT THEY WENT TO SEE THE QUEEN MOTHER IN ONYANG. I HAVE ALREADY TOLD HER HIGHNESS THE TRUTH OF THE MATTER.
I CAN HIRE PROFESSIONAL INVESTIGATORS WHO WILL LOCATE PRINCE SHIN AND PRINCESS CHAE-KYUNG IN A FEW DAYS.
YOUR HIGHNESS—
DO YOU NOT WANT TO KNOW WHY PRINCE SHIN AND PRINCESS CHAE-KYUNG HAVE RUN OFF? WHAT GREAT PAIN ARE THEY SUFFERING THAT PROMPTS THEM TO FLEE?
YOUR HIGHNESS IS ONLY FOCUSED ON BRUSHING THIS UNDER THE RUG, INSTEAD OF REALLY GETTING TO THE HEART OF THE PROBLEM.
I KNOW YOUR HIGHNESS VALUES THE ROYAL FAMILY'S REPUTATION, BUT... HOW...HOW...

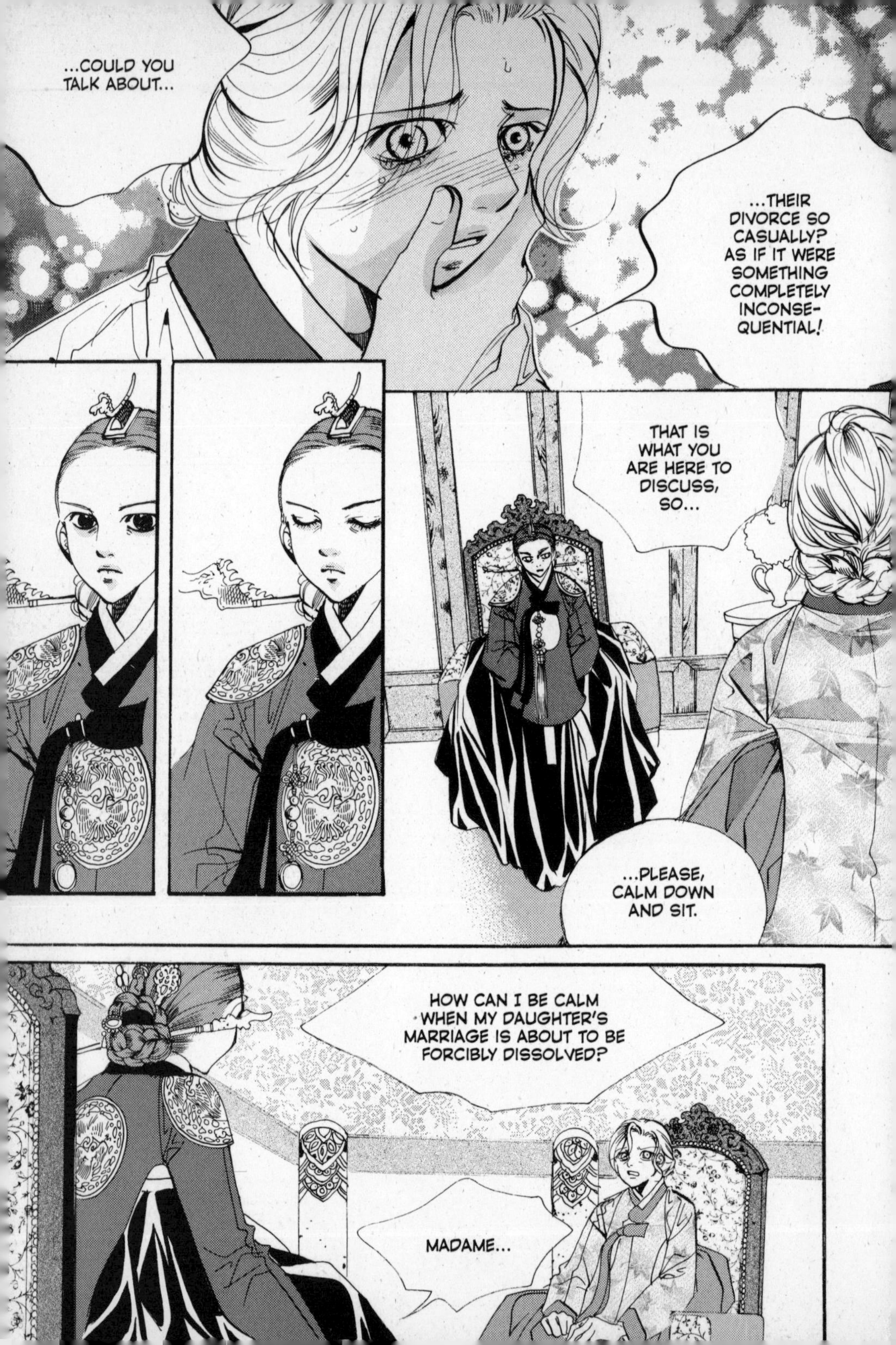
...COULD YOU TALK ABOUT...
...THEIR DIVORCE SO CASUALLY? AS IF IT WERE SOMETHING COMPLETELY INCONSE-QUENTIAL!
THAT IS WHAT YOU ARE HERE TO DISCUSS, SO...
...PLEASE, CALM DOWN AND SIT.
HOW CAN I BE CALM WHEN MY DAUGHTER'S MARRIAGE IS ABOUT TO BE FORCIBLY DISSOLVED?
MADAME...

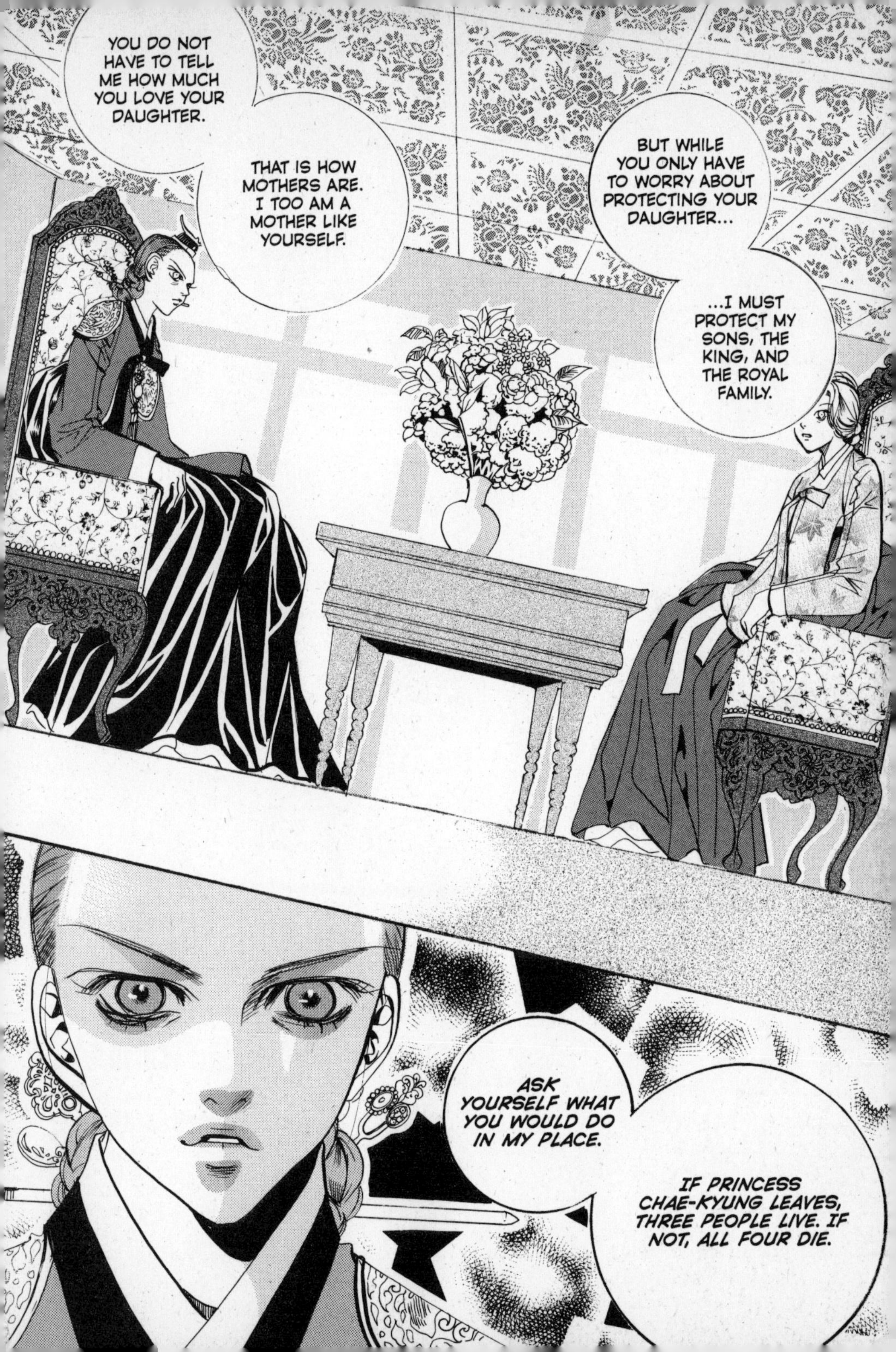
YOU DO NOT HAVE TO TELL ME HOW MUCH YOU LOVE YOUR DAUGHTER.
THAT IS HOW MOTHERS ARE. I TOO AM A MOTHER LIKE YOURSELF.
BUT WHILE YOU ONLY HAVE TO WORRY ABOUT PROTECTING YOUR DAUGHTER...
...I MUST PROTECT MY SONS, THE KING, AND THE ROYAL FAMILY.
ASK YOURSELF WHAT YOU WOULD DO IN MY PLACE.
IF PRINCESS CHAE-KYUNG LEAVES, THREE PEOPLE LIVE. IF NOT, ALL FOUR DIE.

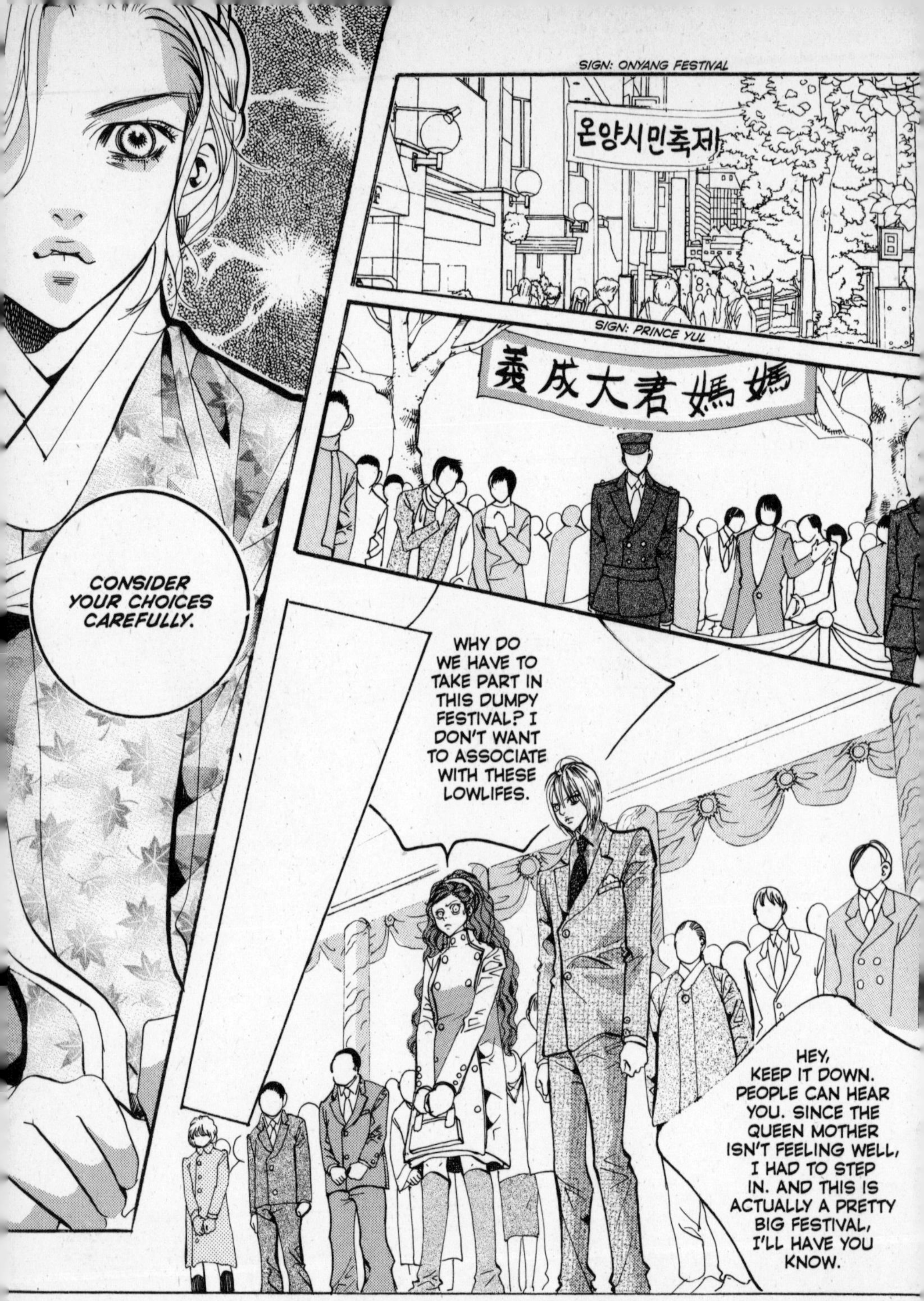
CONSIDER YOUR CHOICES CAREFULLY.
SIGN: ONYANG FESTIVAL
온양시민축제
SIGN: PRINCE YUL
義成大君媽媽
WHY DO WE HAVE TO TAKE PART IN THIS DUMPY FESTIVAL? I DON'T WANT TO ASSOCIATE WITH THESE LOWLIFES.
HEY, KEEP IT DOWN. PEOPLE CAN HEAR YOU. SINCE THE QUEEN MOTHER ISN'T FEELING WELL, I HAD TO STEP IN. AND THIS IS ACTUALLY A PRETTY BIG FESTIVAL, I'LL HAVE YOU KNOW.

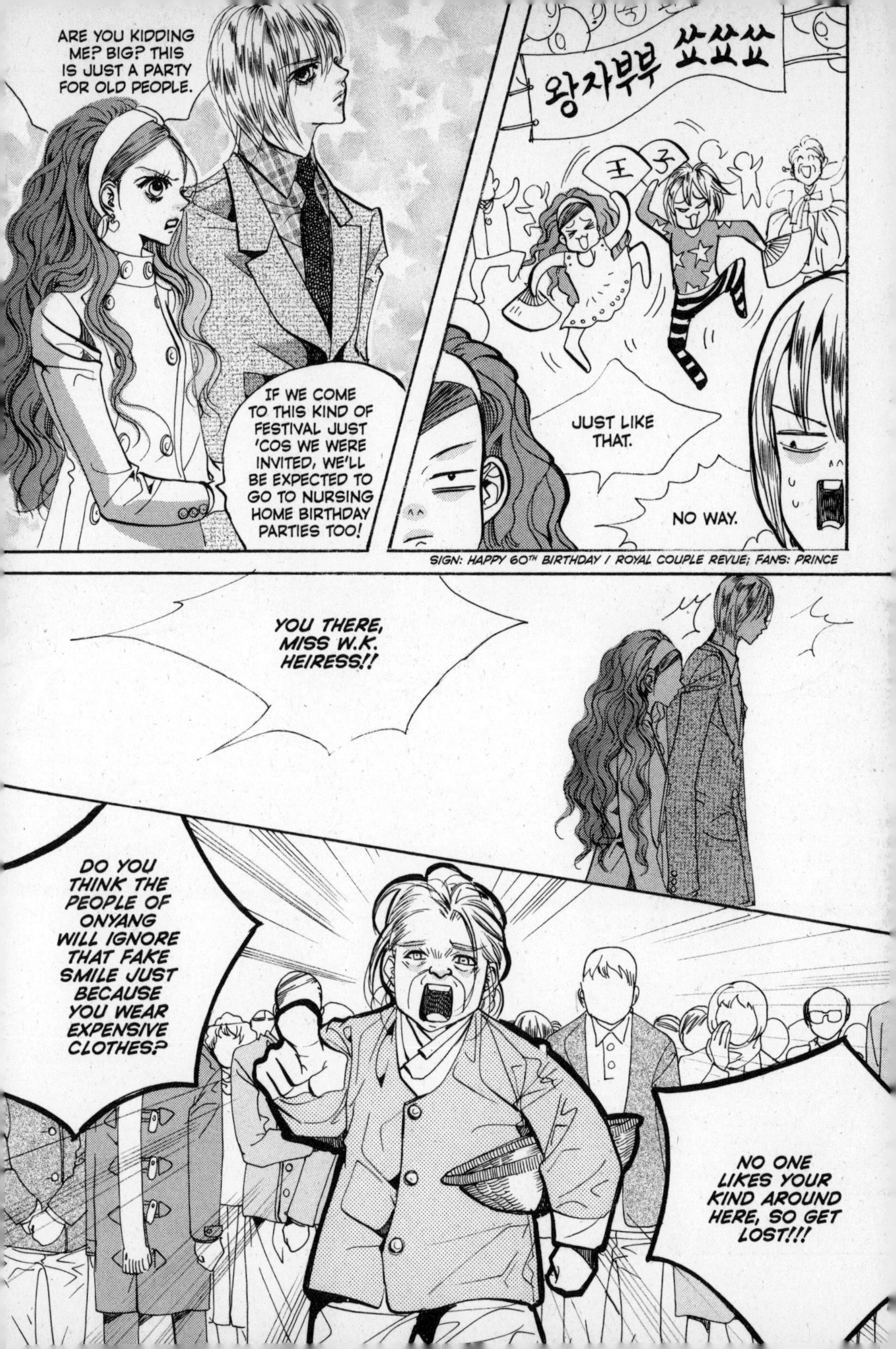
ARE YOU KIDDING ME? BIG? THIS IS JUST A PARTY FOR OLD PEOPLE.
IF WE COME TO THIS KIND OF FESTIVAL JUST 'COS WE WERE INVITED, WE'LL BE EXPECTED TO GO TO NURSING HOME BIRTHDAY PARTIES TOO!
왕자부부 쑈쑈쑈
王
子
JUST LIKE THAT.
NO WAY.
SIGN: HAPPY 60TH BIRTHDAY / ROYAL COUPLE REVUE; FANS: PRINCE
YOU THERE, MISS W.K. HEIRESS!!
DO YOU THINK THE PEOPLE OF ONYANG WILL IGNORE THAT FAKE SMILE JUST BECAUSE YOU WEAR EXPENSIVE CLOTHES?
NO ONE LIKES YOUR KIND AROUND HERE, SO GET LOST!!!

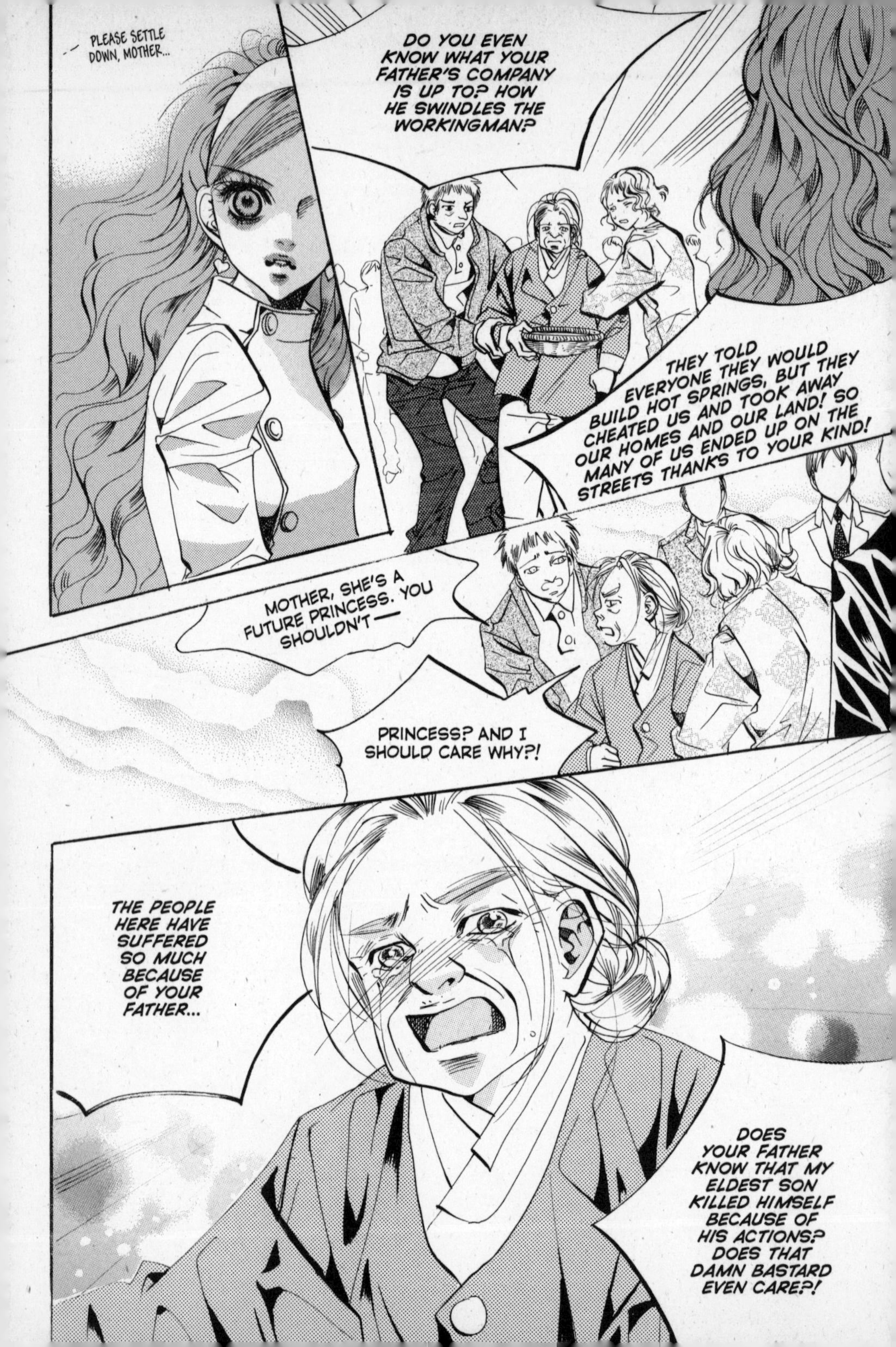
PLEASE SETTLE DOWN, MOTHER...
DO YOU EVEN KNOW WHAT YOUR FATHER'S COMPANY IS UP TO? HOW HE SWINDLES THE WORKINGMAN?
THEY TOLD EVERYONE THEY WOULD BUILD HOT SPRINGS, BUT THEY CHEATED US AND TOOK AWAY OUR HOMES AND OUR LAND! SO MANY OF US ENDED UP ON THE STREETS THANKS TO YOUR KIND!
MOTHER, SHE'S A FUTURE PRINCESS. YOU SHOULDN'T—
PRINCESS? AND I SHOULD CARE WHY?!
THE PEOPLE HERE HAVE SUFFERED SO MUCH BECAUSE OF YOUR FATHER...
DOES YOUR FATHER KNOW THAT MY ELDEST SON KILLED HIMSELF BECAUSE OF HIS ACTIONS? DOES THAT DAMN BASTARD EVEN CARE?!

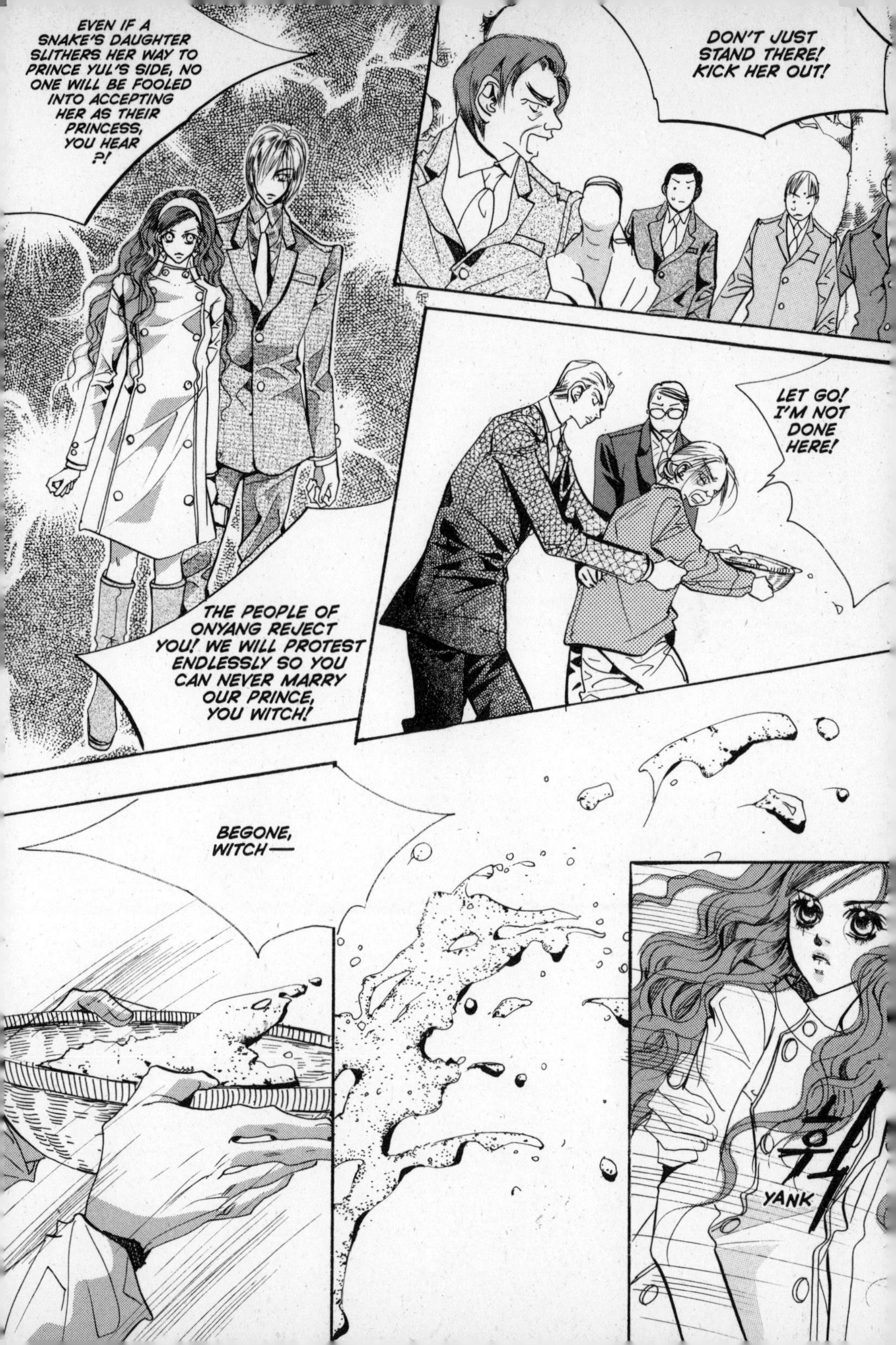
EVEN IF A SNAKE'S DAUGHTER SLITHERS HER WAY TO PRINCE YUL'S SIDE, NO ONE WILL BE FOOLED INTO ACCEPTING HER AS THEIR PRINCESS, YOU HEAR ?!
THE PEOPLE OF ONYANG REJECT YOU! WE WILL PROTEST ENDLESSLY SO YOU CAN NEVER MARRY OUR PRINCE, YOU WITCH!
DON'T JUST STAND THERE! KICK HER OUT!
LET GO! I'M NOT DONE HERE!
BEGONE, WITCH—
YANK

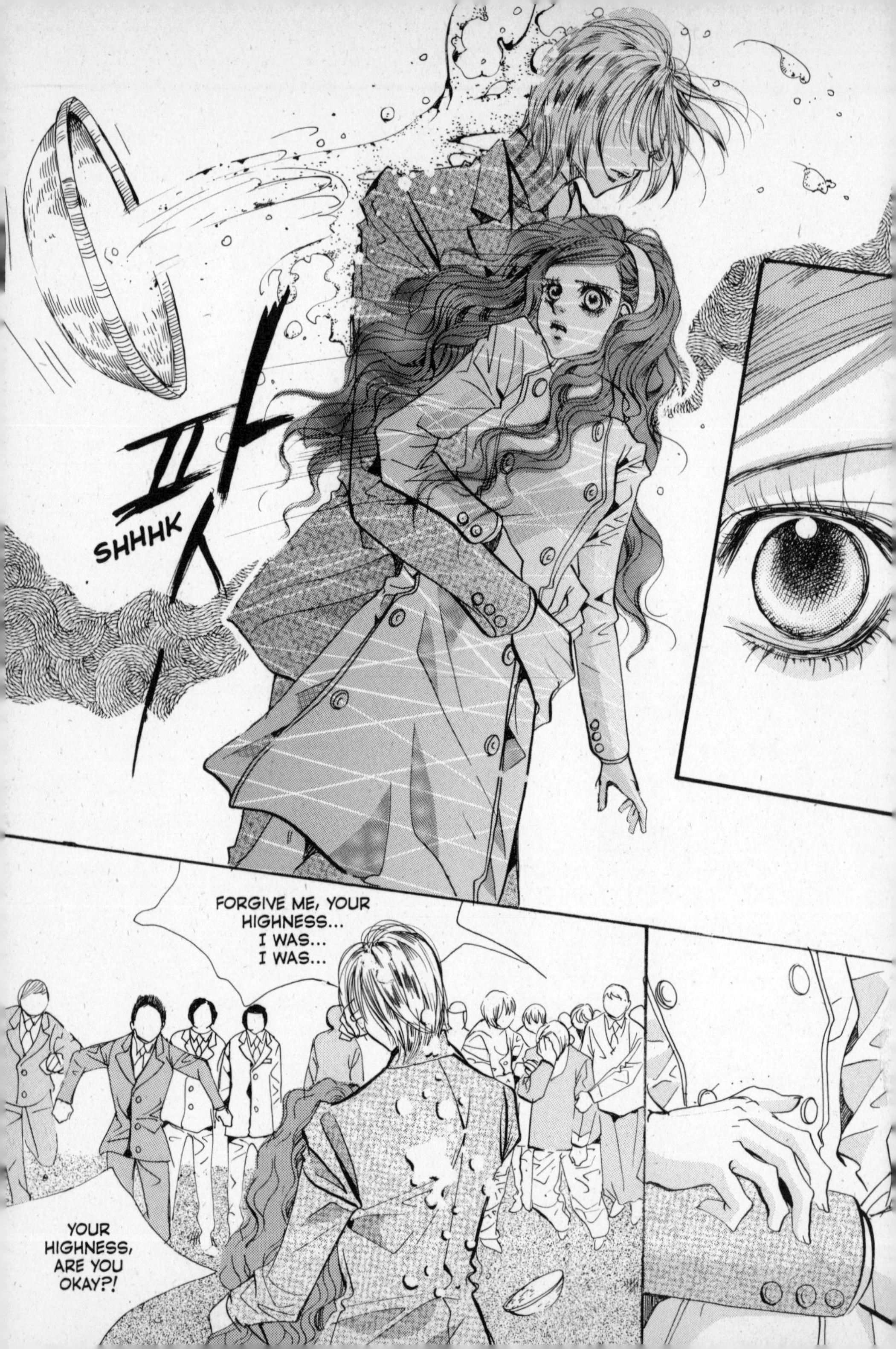
SHHHK
FORGIVE ME, YOUR HIGHNESS... I WAS... I WAS...
YOUR HIGHNESS, ARE YOU OKAY?!

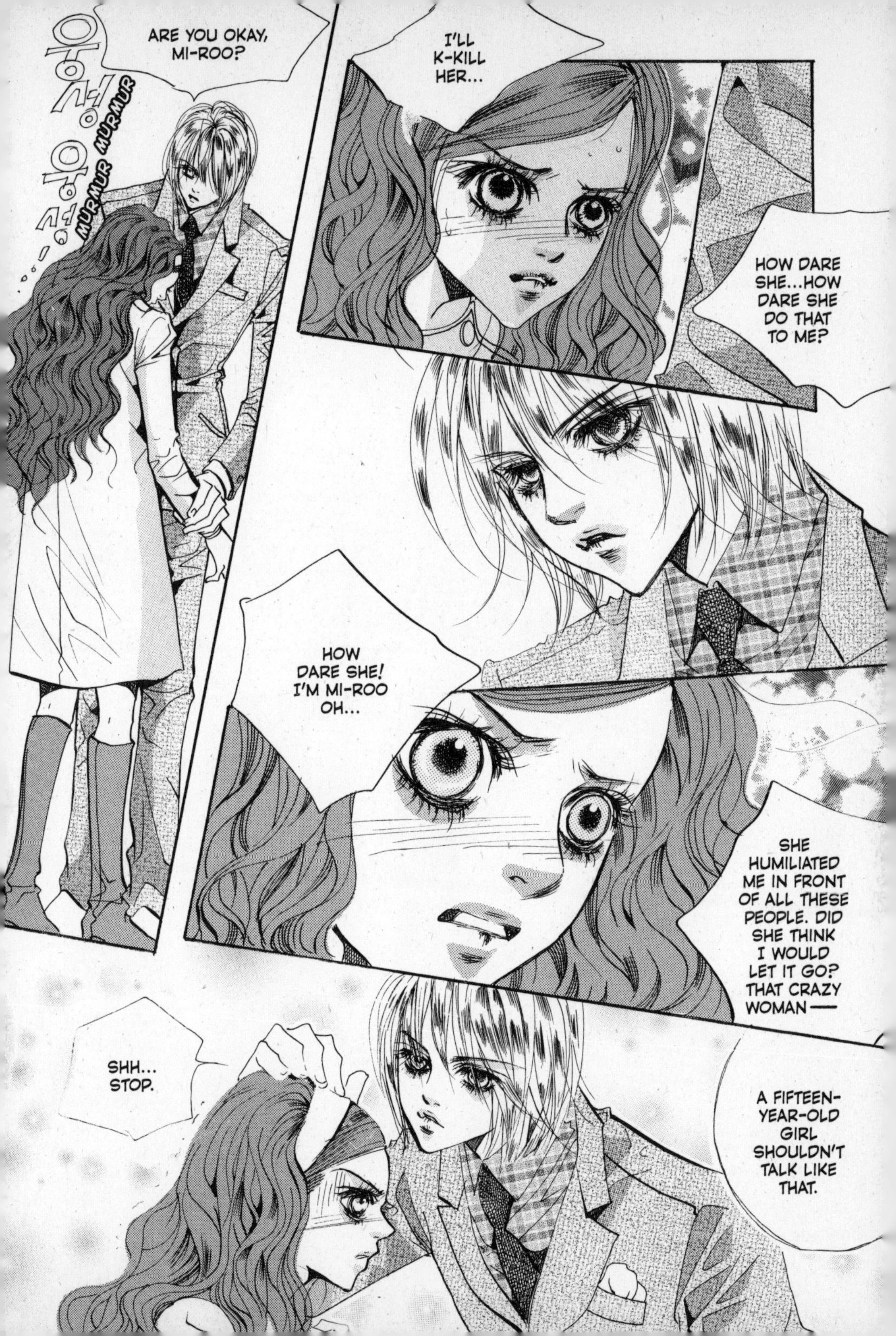
ARE YOU OKAY, MI-ROO?
웅성웅성...
MURMUR MURMUR
I'LL K-KILL HER...
HOW DARE SHE...HOW DARE SHE DO THAT TO ME?
HOW DARE SHE! I'M MI-ROO OH...
SHE HUMILIATED ME IN FRONT OF ALL THESE PEOPLE. DID SHE THINK I WOULD LET IT GO? THAT CRAZY WOMAN—
SHH... STOP.
A FIFTEEN-YEAR-OLD GIRL SHOULDN'T TALK LIKE THAT.

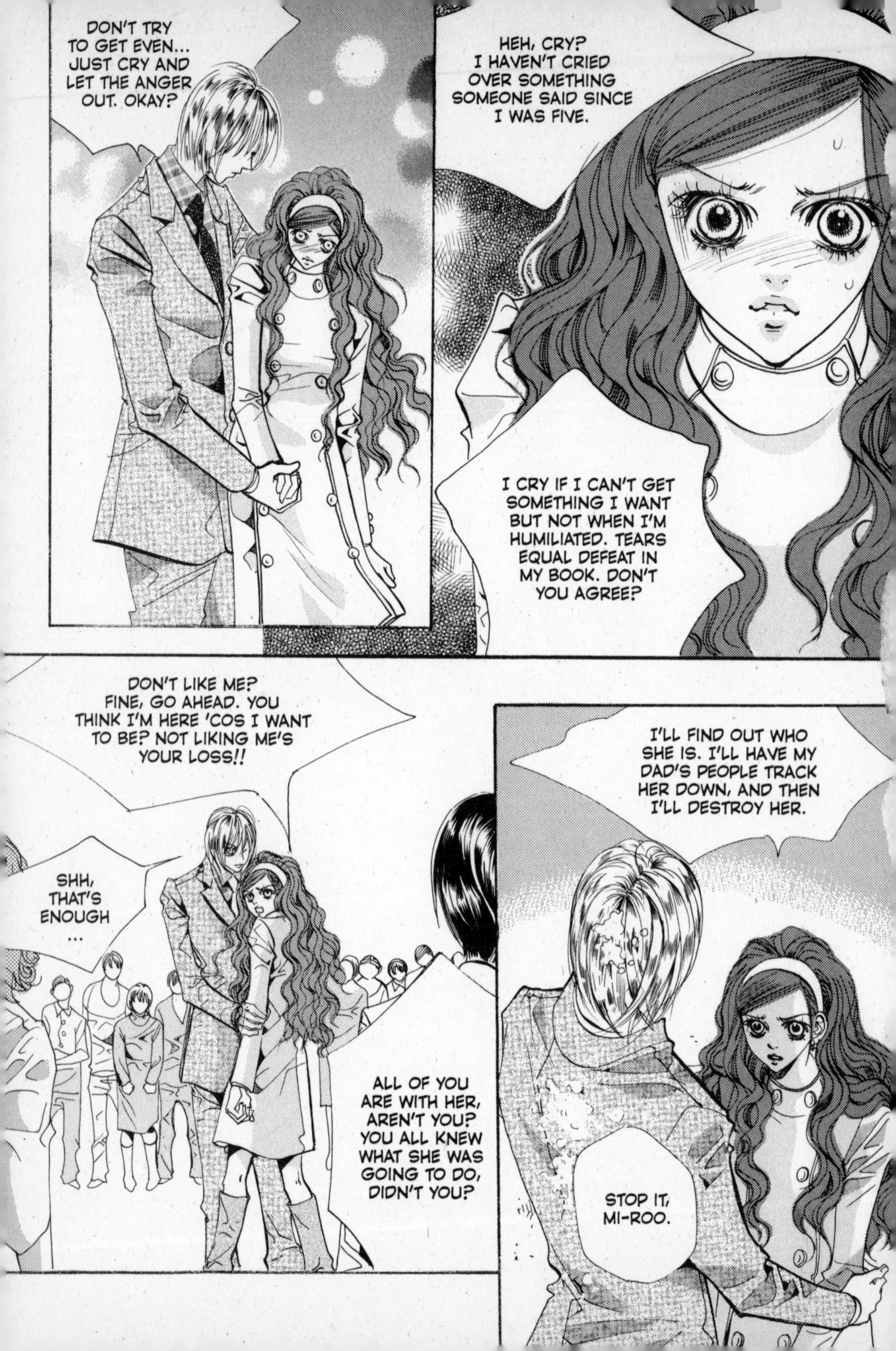
DON'T TRY TO GET EVEN... JUST CRY AND LET THE ANGER OUT. OKAY?
HEH, CRY? I HAVEN'T CRIED OVER SOMETHING SOMEONE SAID SINCE I WAS FIVE.
I CRY IF I CAN'T GET SOMETHING I WANT BUT NOT WHEN I'M HUMILIATED. TEARS EQUAL DEFEAT IN MY BOOK. DON'T YOU AGREE?
DON'T LIKE ME? FINE, GO AHEAD. YOU THINK I'M HERE 'COS I WANT TO BE? NOT LIKING ME'S YOUR LOSS!!
SHH, THAT'S ENOUGH ...
ALL OF YOU ARE WITH HER, AREN'T YOU? YOU ALL KNEW WHAT SHE WAS GOING TO DO, DIDN'T YOU?
I'LL FIND OUT WHO SHE IS. I'LL HAVE MY DAD'S PEOPLE TRACK HER DOWN, AND THEN I'LL DESTROY HER.
STOP IT, MI-ROO.

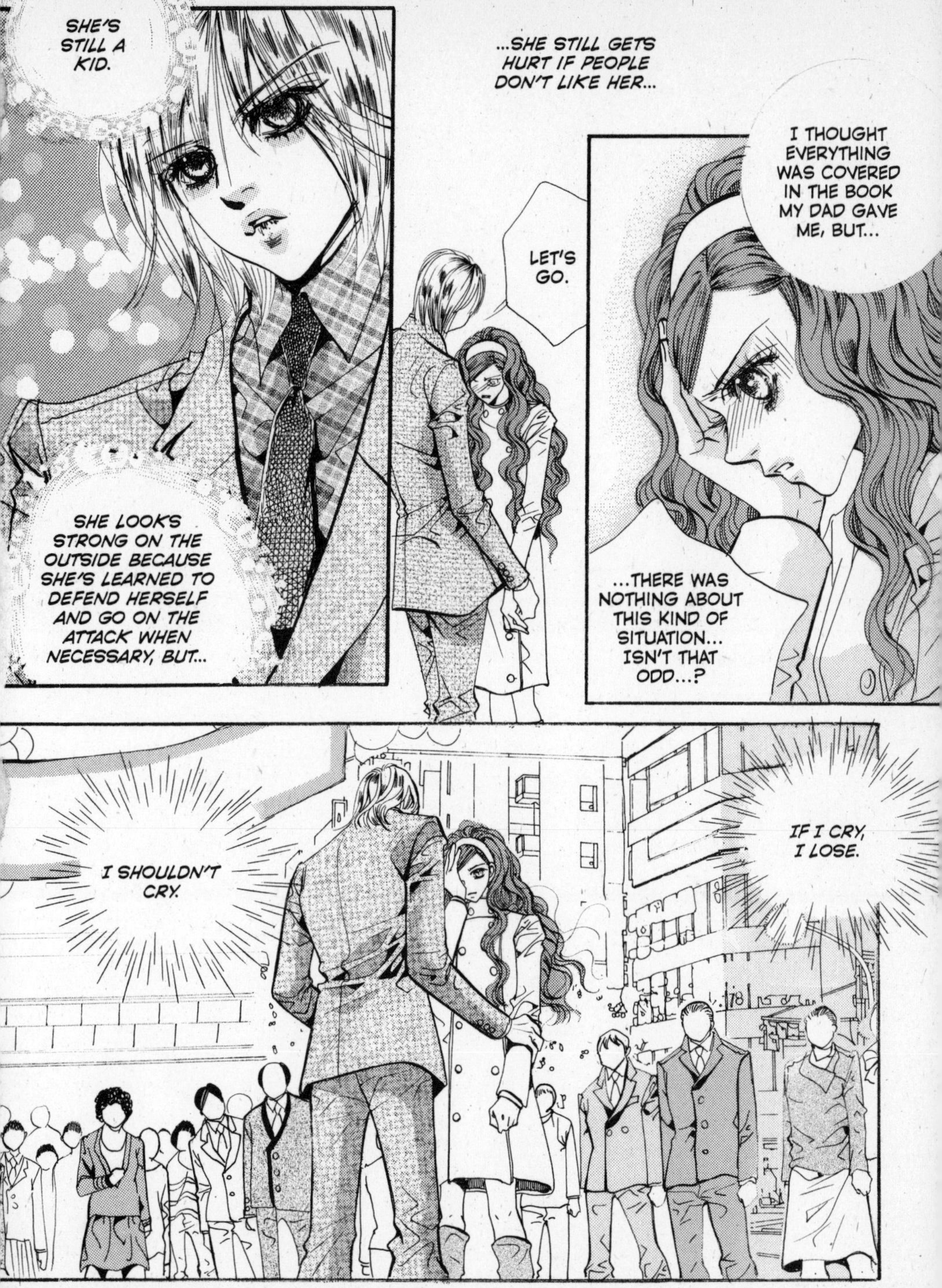

SHE'S STILL A KID.
SHE LOOKS STRONG ON THE OUTSIDE BECAUSE SHE'S LEARNED TO DEFEND HERSELF AND GO ON THE ATTACK WHEN NECESSARY, BUT...
...SHE STILL GETS HURT IF PEOPLE DON'T LIKE HER...
LET'S GO.
I THOUGHT EVERYTHING WAS COVERED IN THE BOOK MY DAD GAVE ME, BUT...
...THERE WAS NOTHING ABOUT THIS KIND OF SITUATION... ISN'T THAT ODD...?
I SHOULDN'T CRY.
IF I CRY, I LOSE.

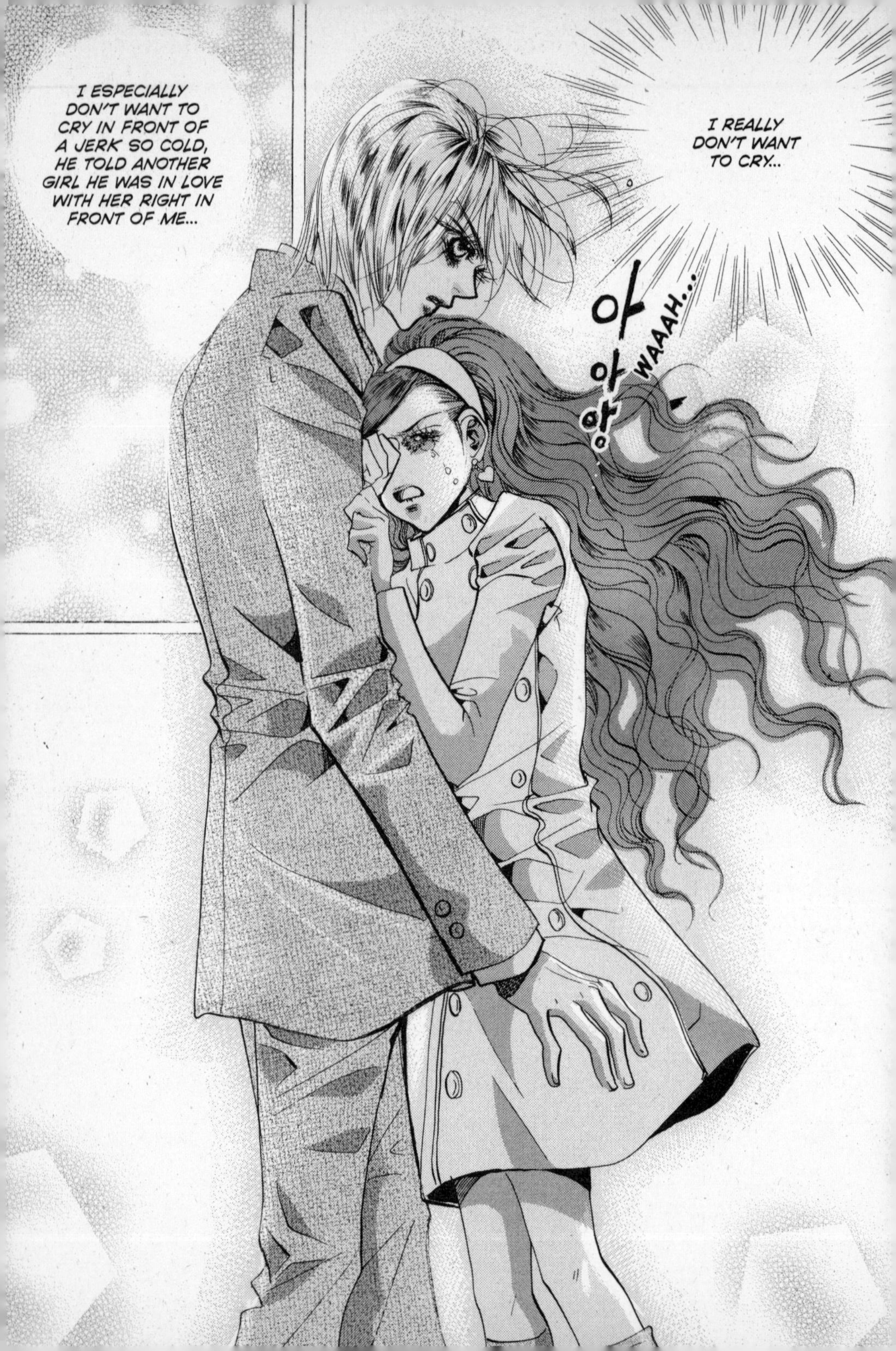
I ESPECIALLY DON'T WANT TO CRY IN FRONT OF A JERK SO COLD, HE TOLD ANOTHER GIRL HE WAS IN LOVE WITH HER RIGHT IN FRONT OF ME...
I REALLY DON'T WANT TO CRY...
아아앙
WAAAH...

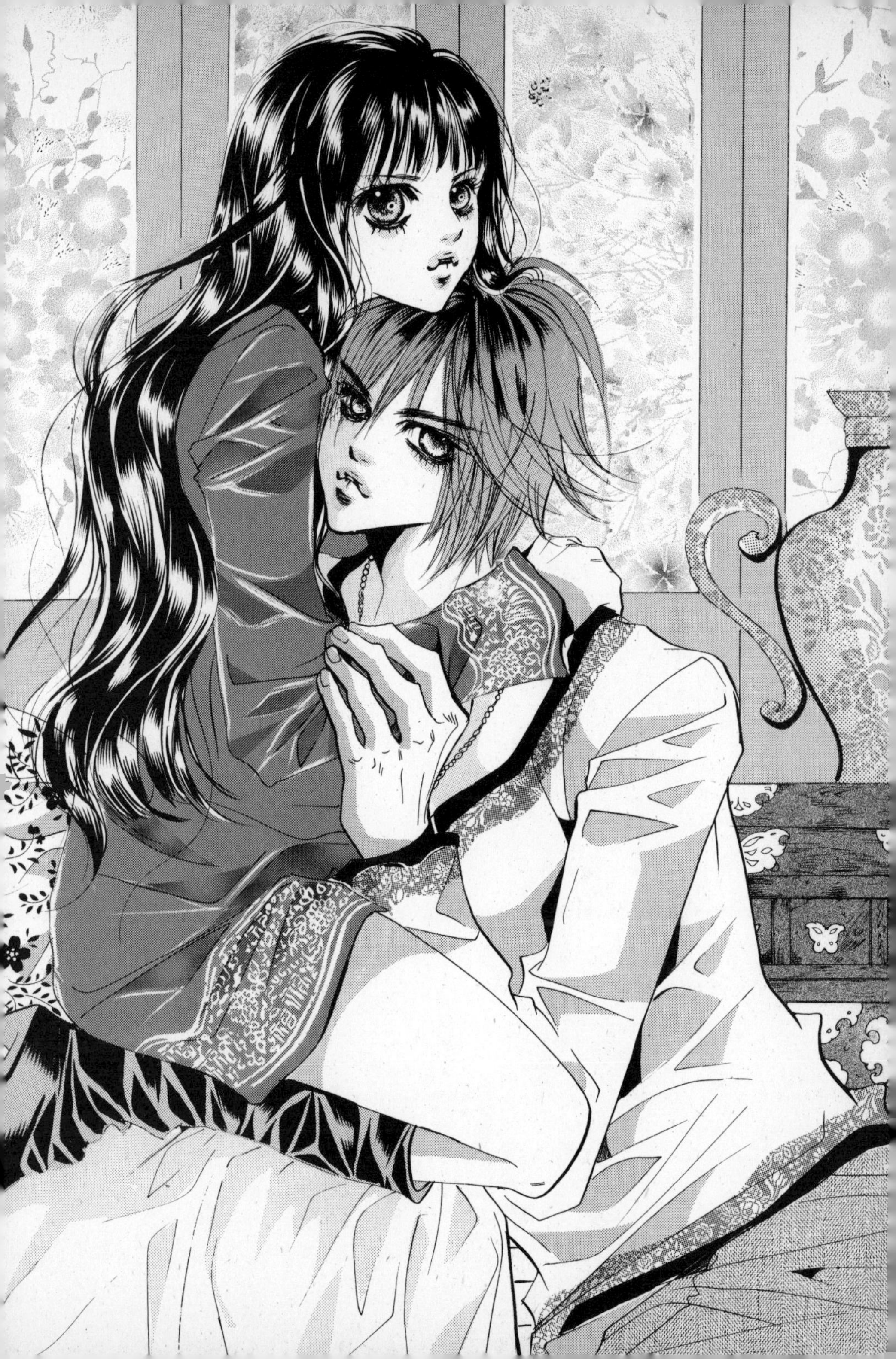

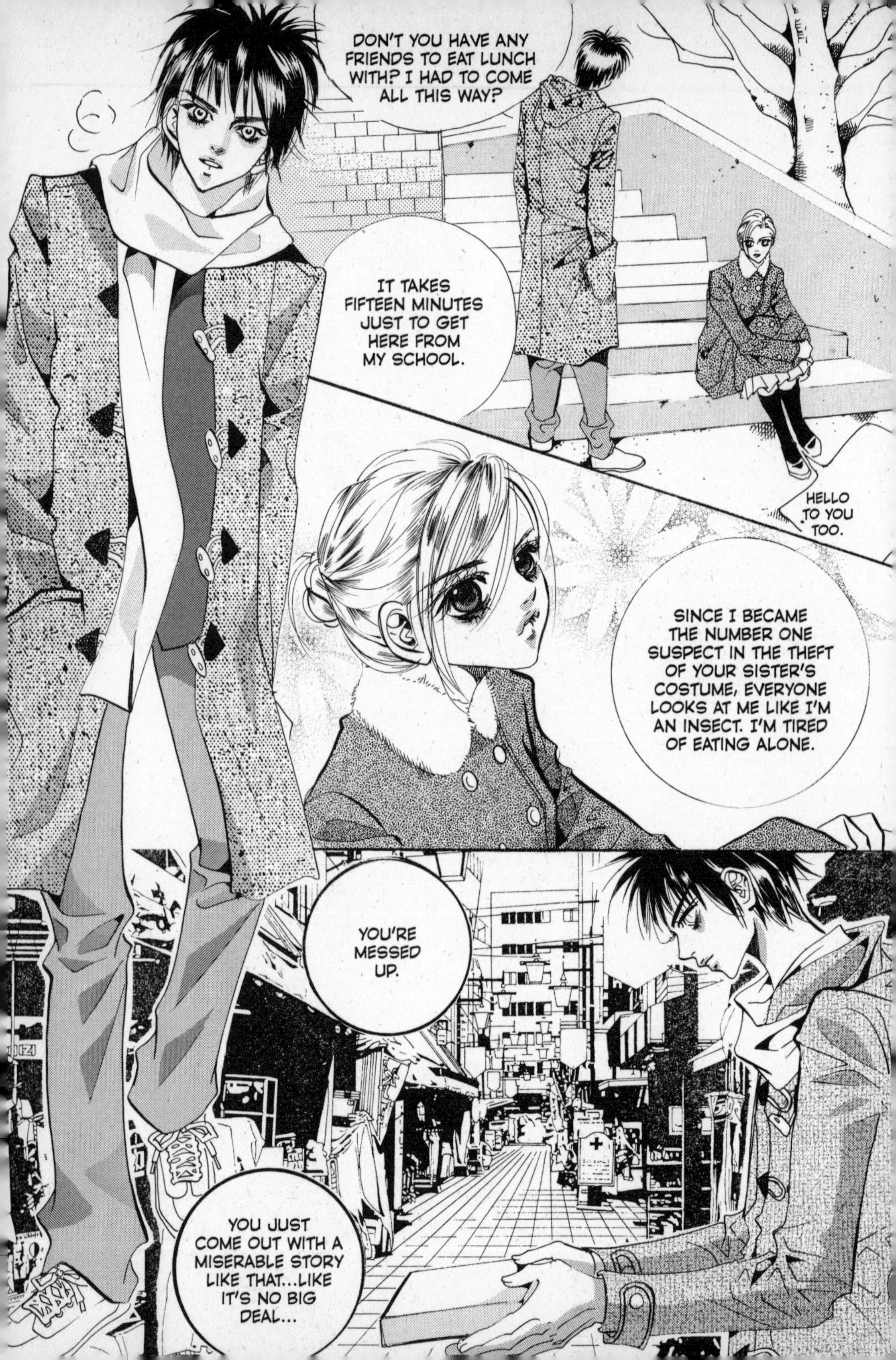

DON'T YOU HAVE ANY FRIENDS TO EAT LUNCH WITH? I HAD TO COME ALL THIS WAY?
IT TAKES FIFTEEN MINUTES JUST TO GET HERE FROM MY SCHOOL.
HELLO TO YOU TOO.
SINCE I BECAME THE NUMBER ONE SUSPECT IN THE THEFT OF YOUR SISTER'S COSTUME, EVERYONE LOOKS AT ME LIKE I'M AN INSECT. I'M TIRED OF EATING ALONE.
YOU'RE MESSED UP.
YOU JUST COME OUT WITH A MISERABLE STORY LIKE THAT...LIKE IT'S NO BIG DEAL...

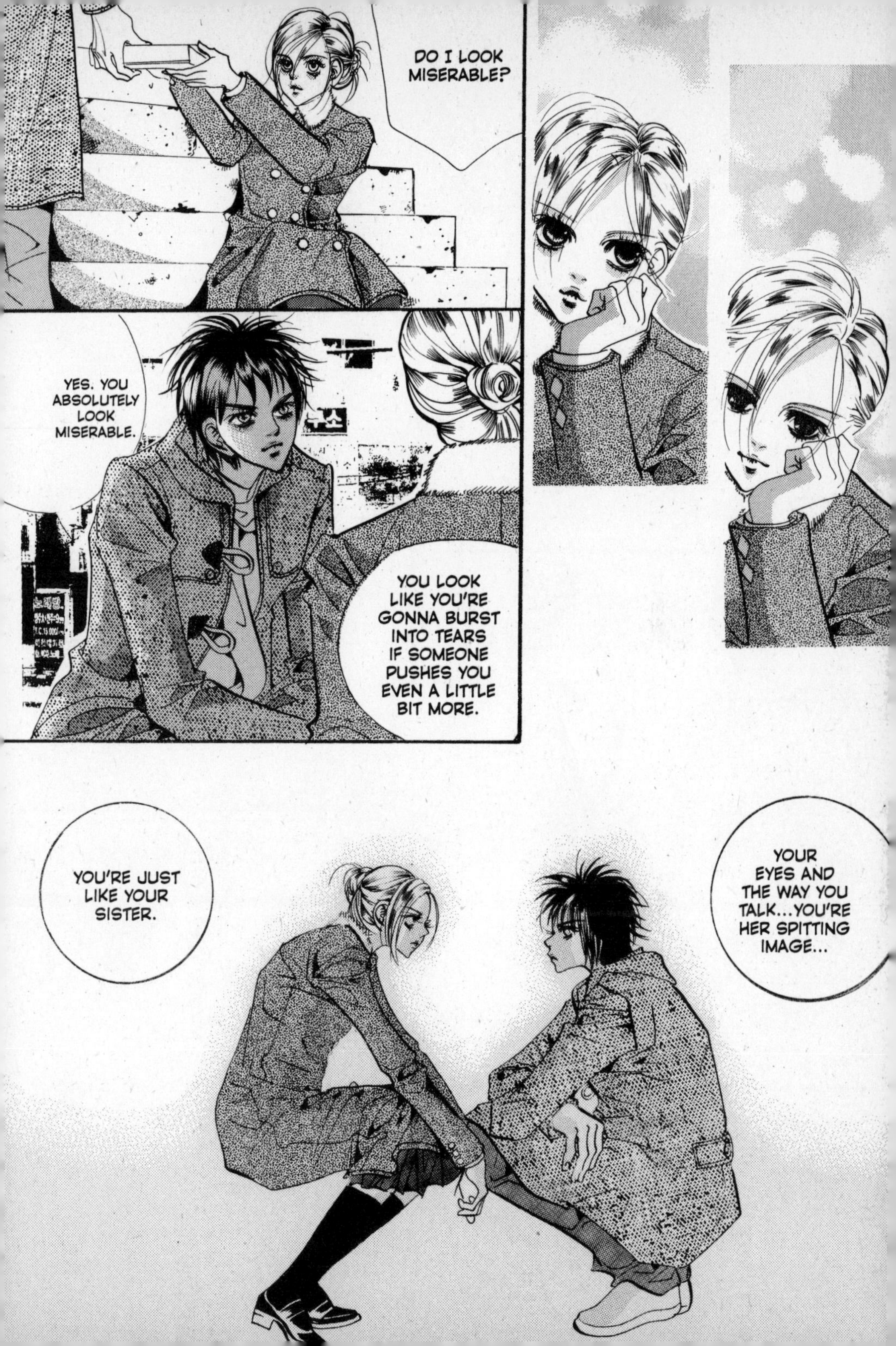
DO I LOOK MISERABLE?
YES. YOU ABSOLUTELY LOOK MISERABLE.
YOU LOOK LIKE YOU'RE GONNA BURST INTO TEARS IF SOMEONE PUSHES YOU EVEN A LITTLE BIT MORE.
YOU'RE JUST LIKE YOUR SISTER.
YOUR EYES AND THE WAY YOU TALK...YOU'RE HER SPITTING IMAGE...

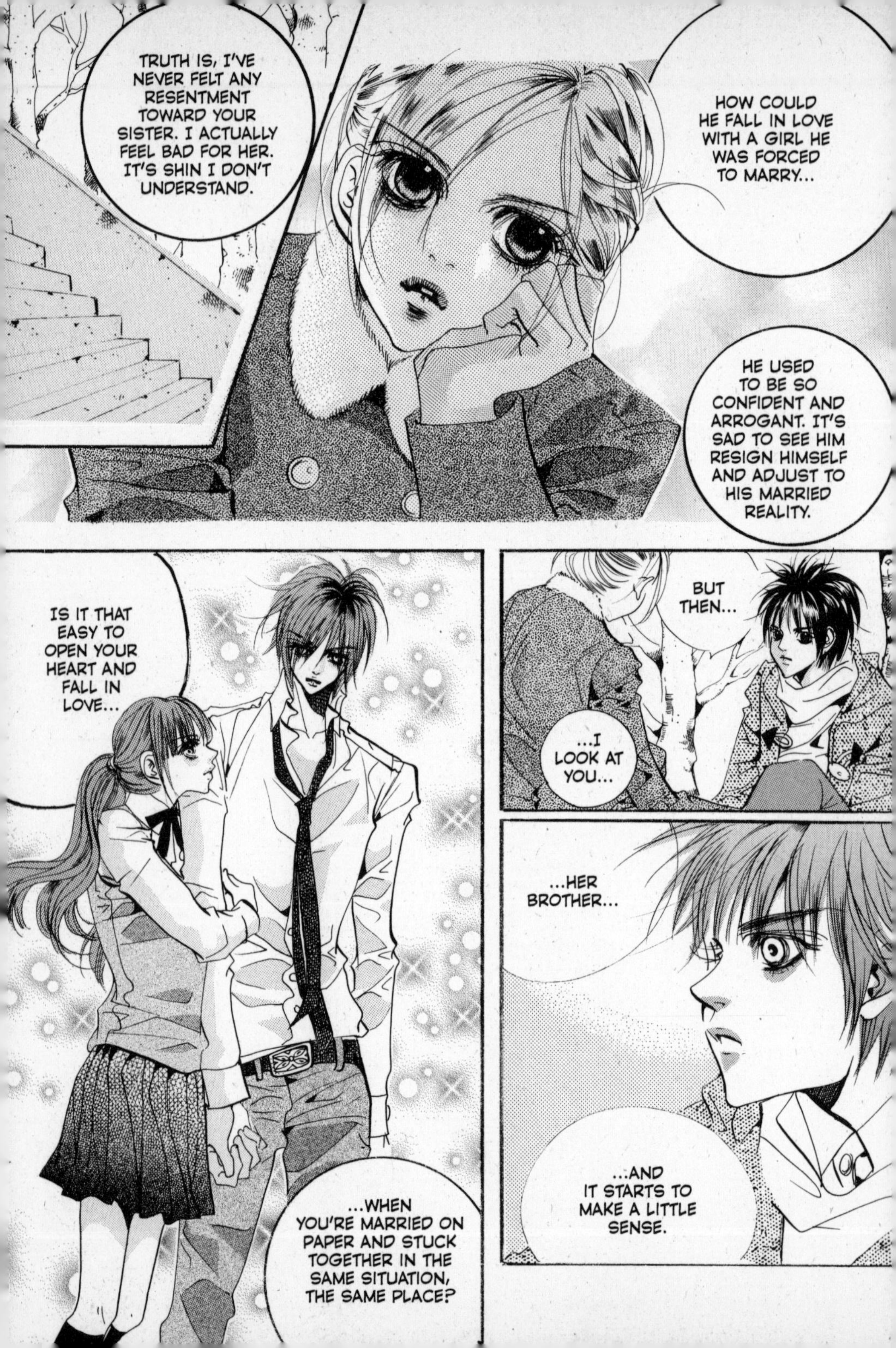
TRUTH IS, I'VE NEVER FELT ANY RESENTMENT TOWARD YOUR SISTER. I ACTUALLY FEEL BAD FOR HER. IT'S SHIN I DON'T UNDERSTAND.
HOW COULD HE FALL IN LOVE WITH A GIRL HE WAS FORCED TO MARRY...
HE USED TO BE SO CONFIDENT AND ARROGANT. IT'S SAD TO SEE HIM RESIGN HIMSELF AND ADJUST TO HIS MARRIED REALITY.
IS IT THAT EASY TO OPEN YOUR HEART AND FALL IN LOVE...
...WHEN YOU'RE MARRIED ON PAPER AND STUCK TOGETHER IN THE SAME SITUATION, THE SAME PLACE?
BUT THEN...
...I LOOK AT YOU...
...HER BROTHER...
...AND IT STARTS TO MAKE A LITTLE SENSE.

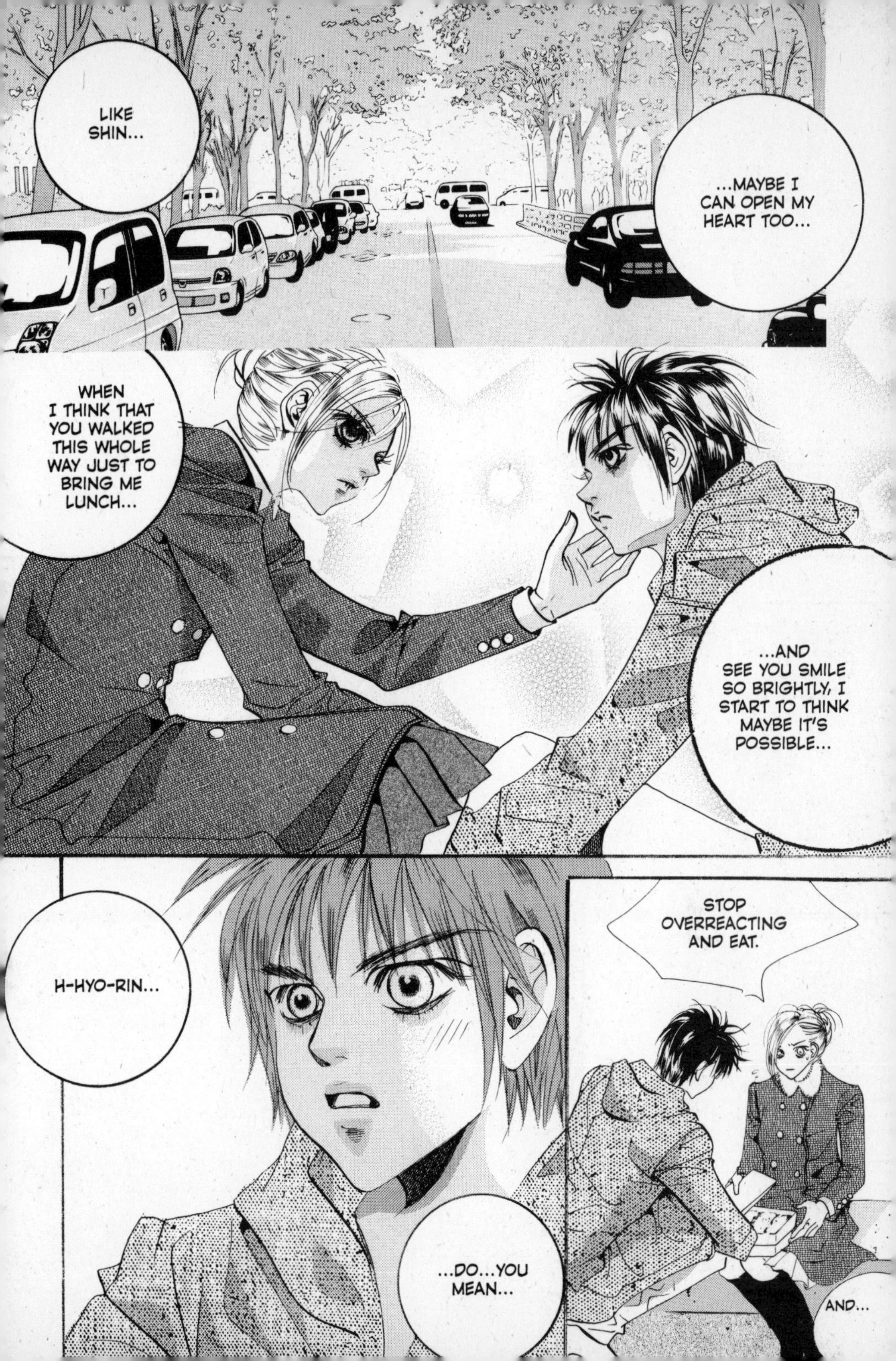
LIKE SHIN...
...MAYBE I CAN OPEN MY HEART TOO...
WHEN I THINK THAT YOU WALKED THIS WHOLE WAY JUST TO BRING ME LUNCH...
...AND SEE YOU SMILE SO BRIGHTLY, I START TO THINK MAYBE IT'S POSSIBLE...
H-HYO-RIN...
...DO...YOU MEAN...
STOP OVERREACTING AND EAT.
AND...

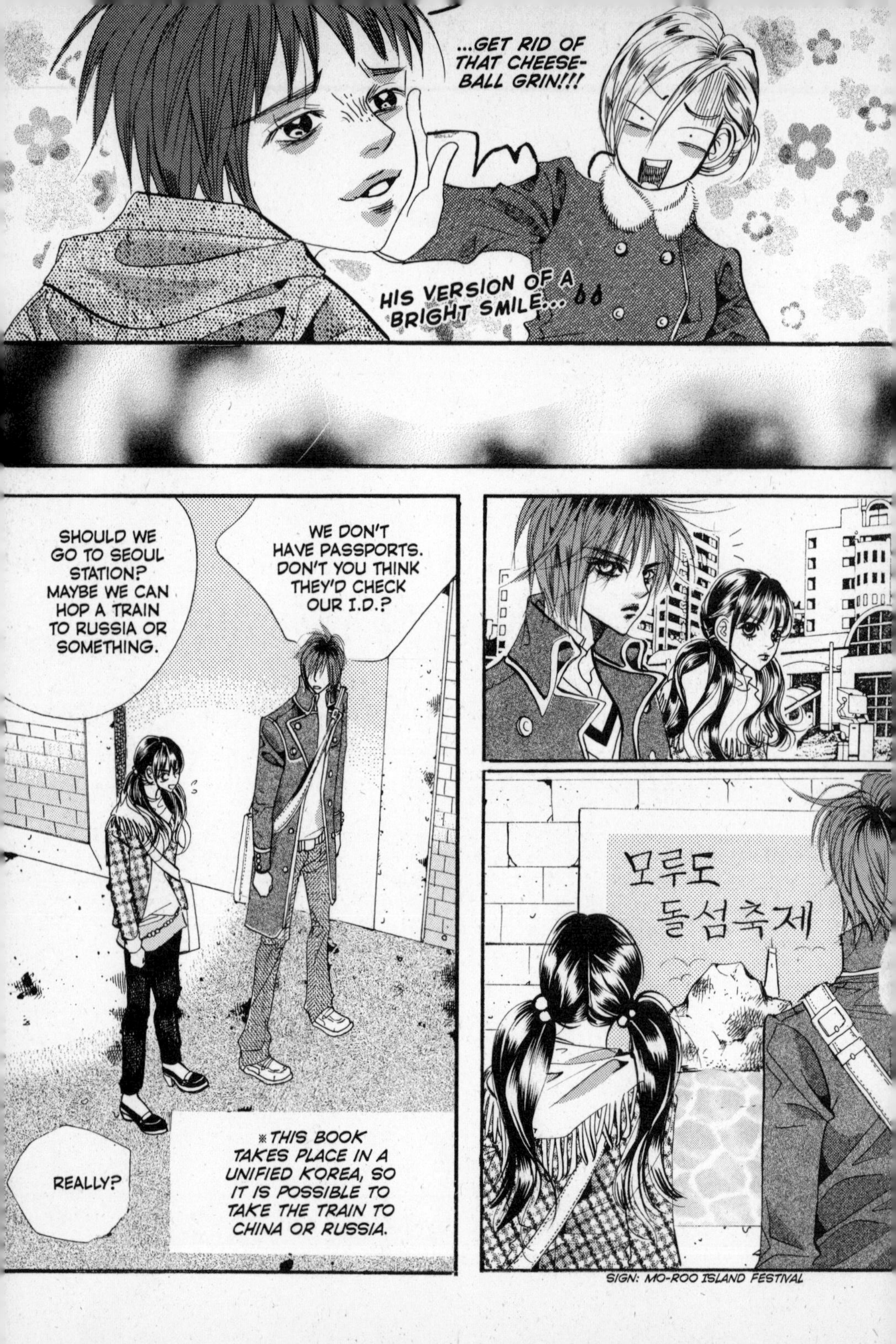
...GET RID OF THAT CHEESE-BALL GRIN!!!
HIS VERSION OF A BRIGHT SMILE...
SHOULD WE GO TO SEOUL STATION? MAYBE WE CAN HOP A TRAIN TO RUSSIA OR SOMETHING.
WE DON'T HAVE PASSPORTS. DON'T YOU THINK THEY'D CHECK OUR I.D.?
REALLY?
※THIS BOOK TAKES PLACE IN A UNIFIED KOREA, SO IT IS POSSIBLE TO TAKE THE TRAIN TO CHINA OR RUSSIA.
모루도
돌섬축제
SIGN: MO-ROO ISLAND FESTIVAL

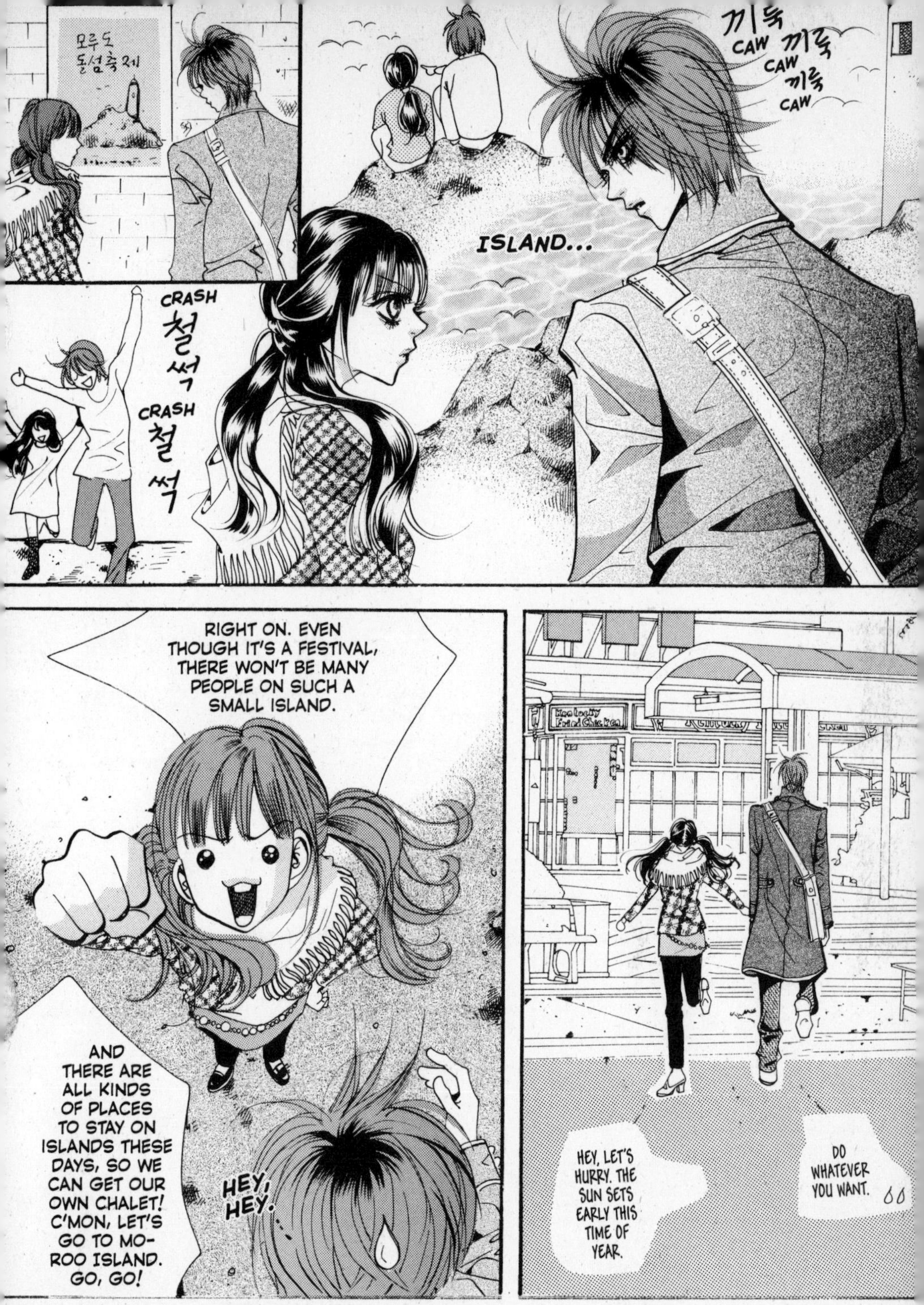
모루도
돌섬축제
끼룩
CAW
끼룩
CAW
끼룩
CAW
ISLAND...
CRASH
철썩
CRASH
철썩
RIGHT ON. EVEN THOUGH IT'S A FESTIVAL, THERE WON'T BE MANY PEOPLE ON SUCH A SMALL ISLAND.
AND THERE ARE ALL KINDS OF PLACES TO STAY ON ISLANDS THESE DAYS, SO WE CAN GET OUR OWN CHALET! C'MON, LET'S GO TO MO-ROO ISLAND. GO, GO!
HEY, HEY.
HEY, LET'S HURRY. THE SUN SETS EARLY THIS TIME OF YEAR.
DO WHATEVER YOU WANT.

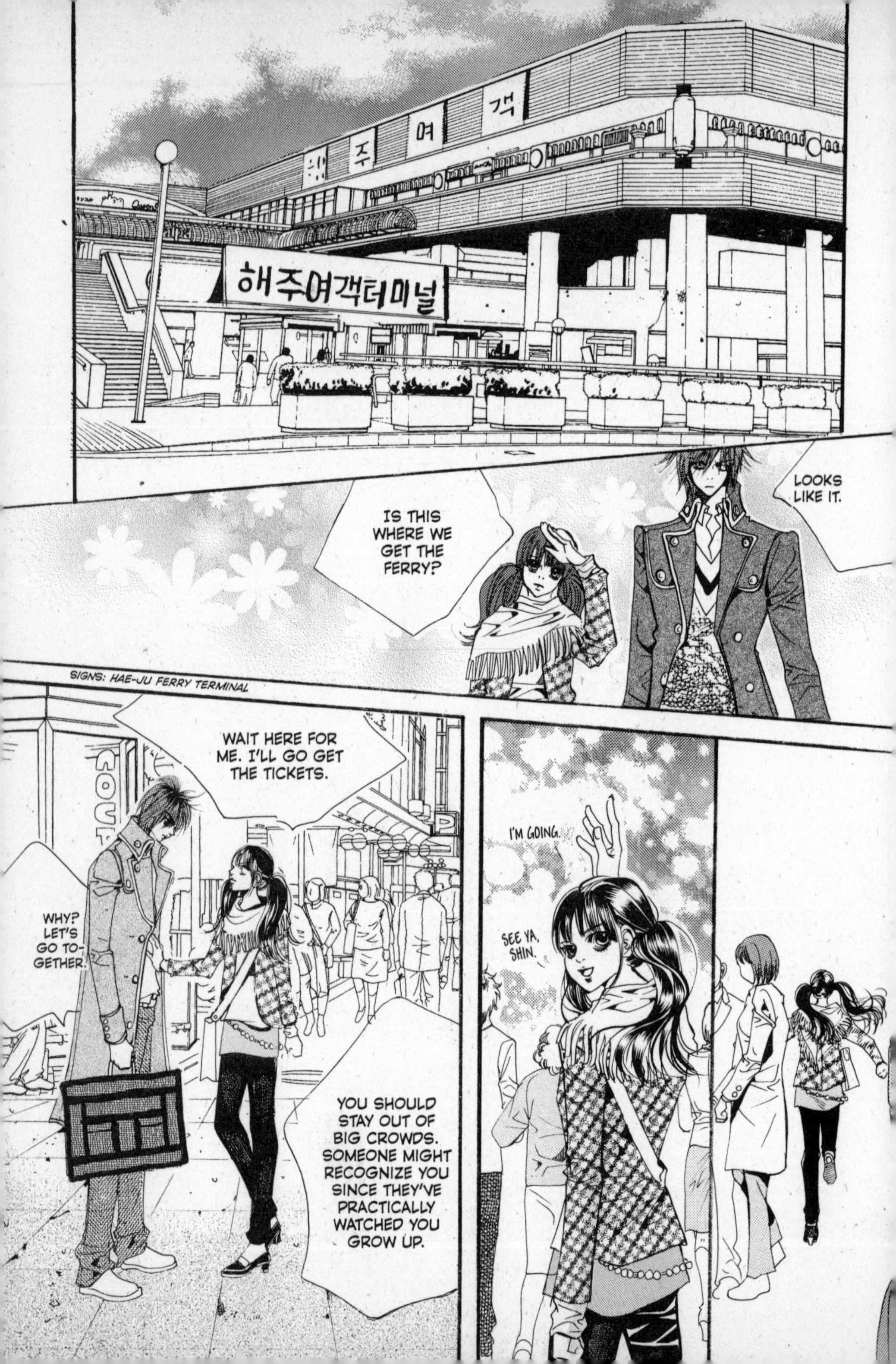
해주여객터미널
IS THIS WHERE WE GET THE FERRY?
LOOKS LIKE IT.
SIGNS: HAE-JU FERRY TERMINAL
WAIT HERE FOR ME. I'LL GO GET THE TICKETS.
WHY? LET'S GO TO-GETHER.
YOU SHOULD STAY OUT OF BIG CROWDS. SOMEONE MIGHT RECOGNIZE YOU SINCE THEY'VE PRACTICALLY WATCHED YOU GROW UP.
I'M GOING.
SEE YA, SHIN.

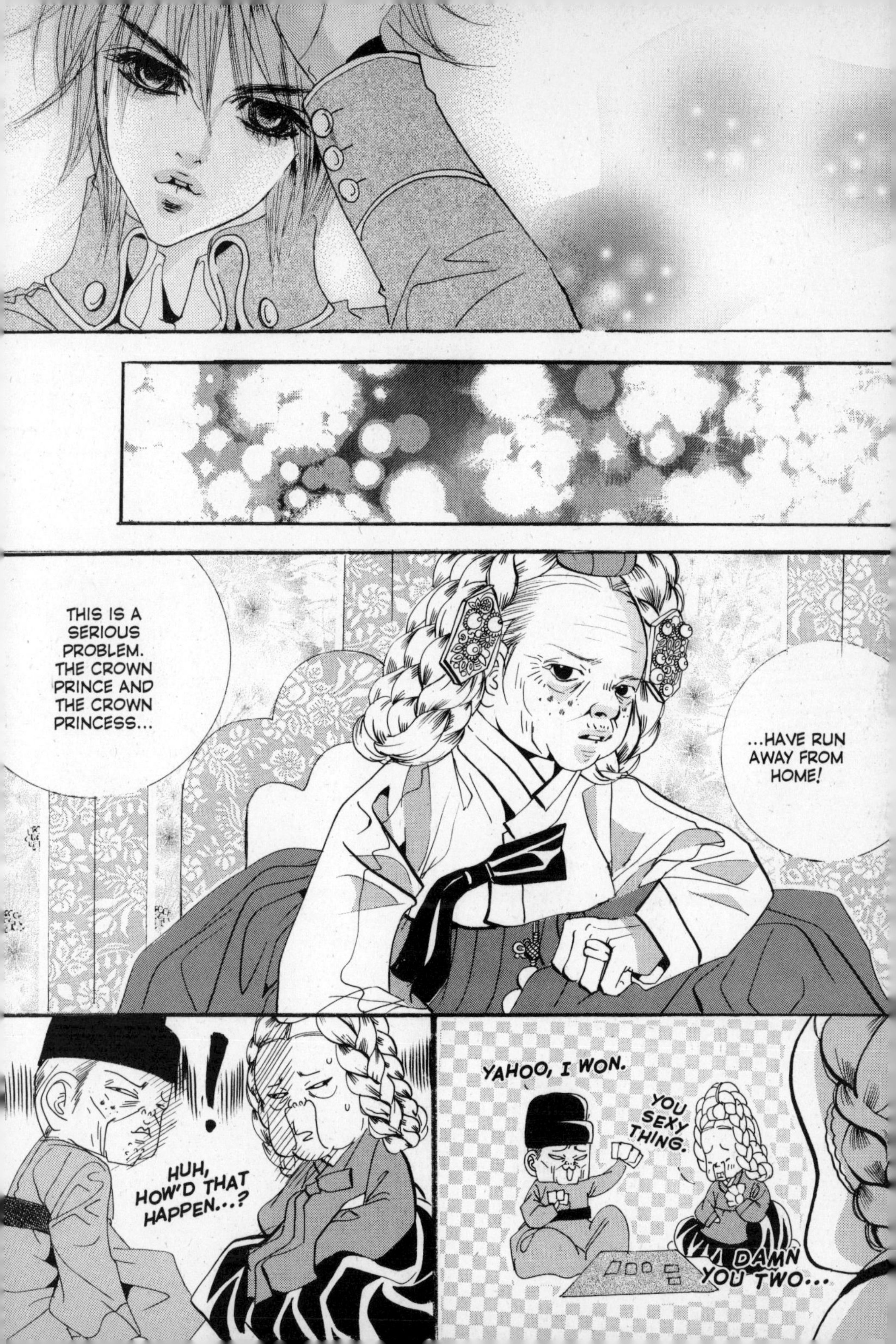
THIS IS A SERIOUS PROBLEM. THE CROWN PRINCE AND THE CROWN PRINCESS...
...HAVE RUN AWAY FROM HOME!
!
HUH, HOW'D THAT HAPPEN...?
YAHOO, I WON.
YOU SEXY THING.
DAMN YOU TWO...

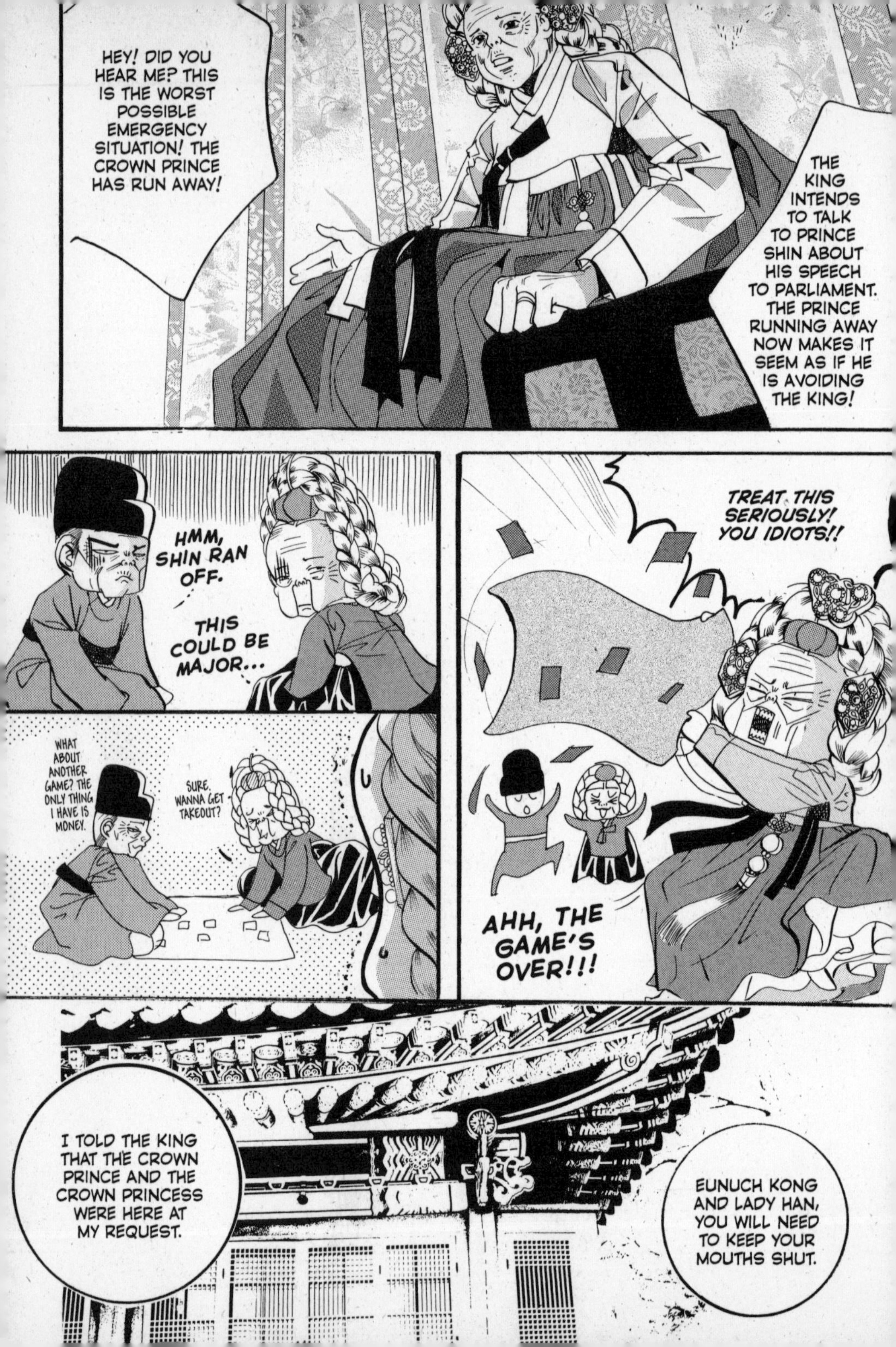
HEY! DID YOU HEAR ME? THIS IS THE WORST POSSIBLE EMERGENCY SITUATION! THE CROWN PRINCE HAS RUN AWAY!
THE KING INTENDS TO TALK TO PRINCE SHIN ABOUT HIS SPEECH TO PARLIAMENT. THE PRINCE RUNNING AWAY NOW MAKES IT SEEM AS IF HE IS AVOIDING THE KING!
HMM, SHIN RAN OFF.
THIS COULD BE MAJOR...
WHAT ABOUT ANOTHER GAME? THE ONLY THING I HAVE IS MONEY.
SURE. WANNA GET TAKEOUT?
TREAT THIS SERIOUSLY! YOU IDIOTS!!
AHH, THE GAME'S OVER!!!
I TOLD THE KING THAT THE CROWN PRINCE AND THE CROWN PRINCESS WERE HERE AT MY REQUEST.
EUNUCH KONG AND LADY HAN, YOU WILL NEED TO KEEP YOUR MOUTHS SHUT.

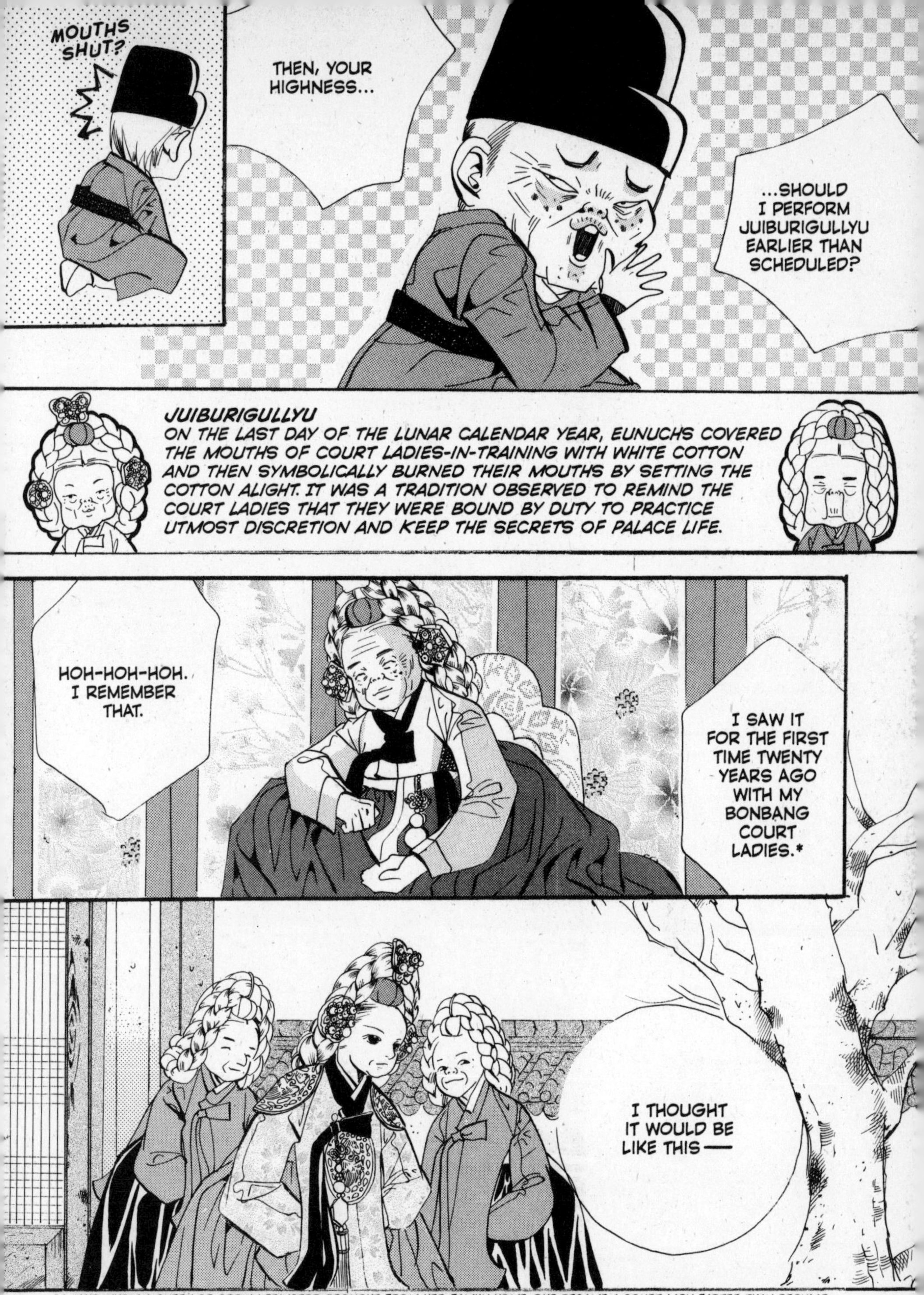
MOUTHS SHUT?
THEN, YOUR HIGHNESS...
...SHOULD I PERFORM JUIBURIGULLYU EARLIER THAN SCHEDULED?
JUIBURIGULLYU
ON THE LAST DAY OF THE LUNAR CALENDAR YEAR, EUNUCHS COVERED THE MOUTHS OF COURT LADIES-IN-TRAINING WITH WHITE COTTON AND THEN SYMBOLICALLY BURNED THEIR MOUTHS BY SETTING THE COTTON ALIGHT. IT WAS A TRADITION OBSERVED TO REMIND THE COURT LADIES THAT THEY WERE BOUND BY DUTY TO PRACTICE UTMOST DISCRETION AND KEEP THE SECRETS OF PALACE LIFE.
HOH-HOH-HOH. I REMEMBER THAT.
I SAW IT FOR THE FIRST TIME TWENTY YEARS AGO WITH MY BONBANG COURT LADIES.*
I THOUGHT IT WOULD BE LIKE THIS—

*A MAID WHOM A QUEEN OR CROWN PRINCESS BROUGHT FROM HER FAMILY HOME. SHE BECAME A COURT LADY FASTER THAN REGULAR MAIDS IN THE PALACE. IF A QUEEN OR CROWN PRINCESS NEEDED SOMEONE TO CARRY OUT A SECRET MISSION, A BONBANG COURT LADY WOULD HAVE BEEN HER FIRST CHOICE. THIS COURT LADY WAS NOT ONLY A SERVANT, BUT ALSO AN ADVISOR AND A CONFIDANTE.

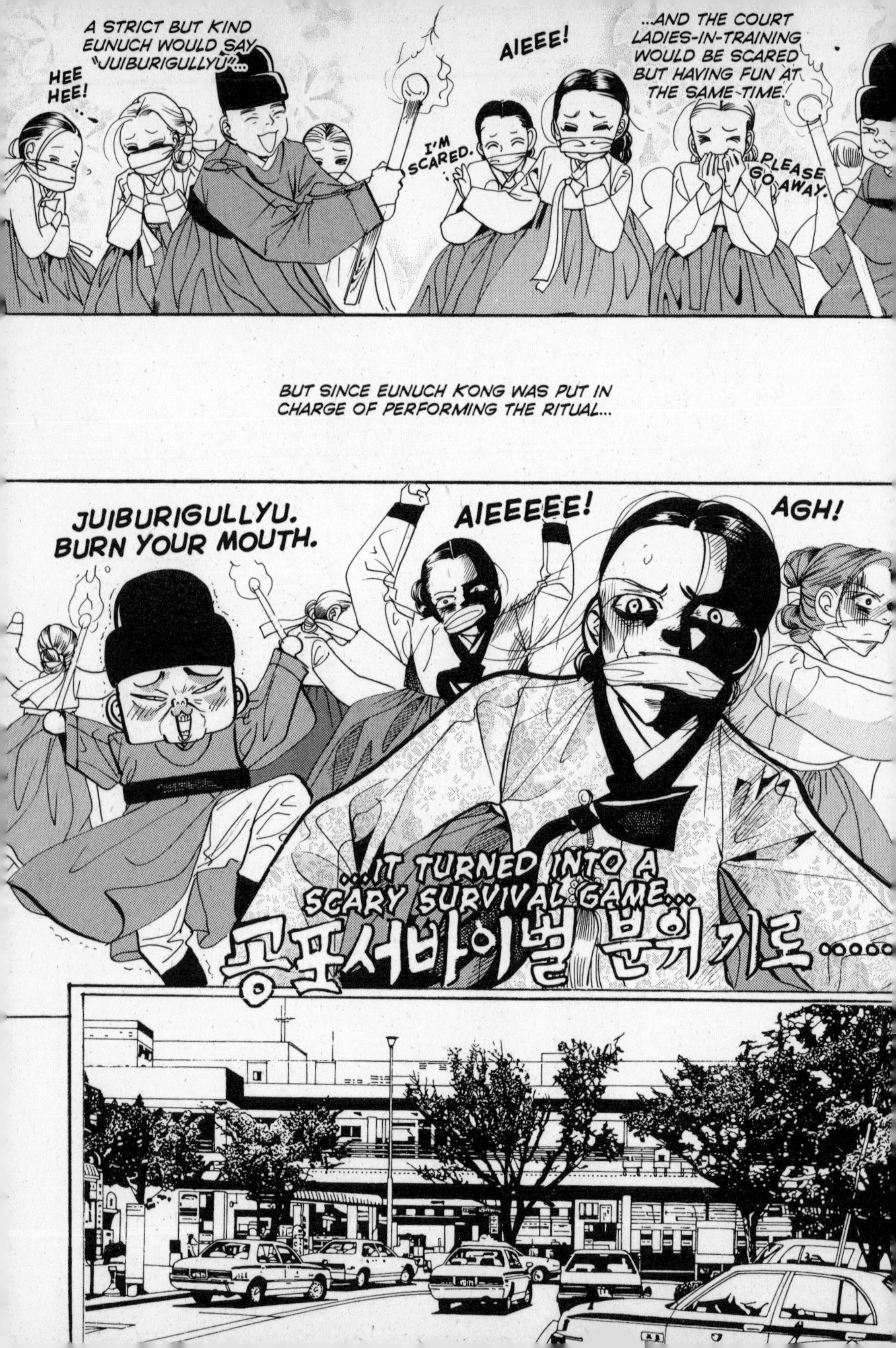
HEE HEE!
A STRICT BUT KIND EUNUCH WOULD SAY "JUIBURIGULLYU"...
I'M SCARED.
AIEEE!
...AND THE COURT LADIES-IN-TRAINING WOULD BE SCARED BUT HAVING FUN AT THE SAME TIME.
PLEASE GO AWAY.
BUT SINCE EUNUCH KONG WAS PUT IN CHARGE OF PERFORMING THE RITUAL...
JUIBURIGULLYU. BURN YOUR MOUTH.
AIEEEEE!
AGH!
...IT TURNED INTO A SCARY SURVIVAL GAME...
공포서바이벌 분위기로......

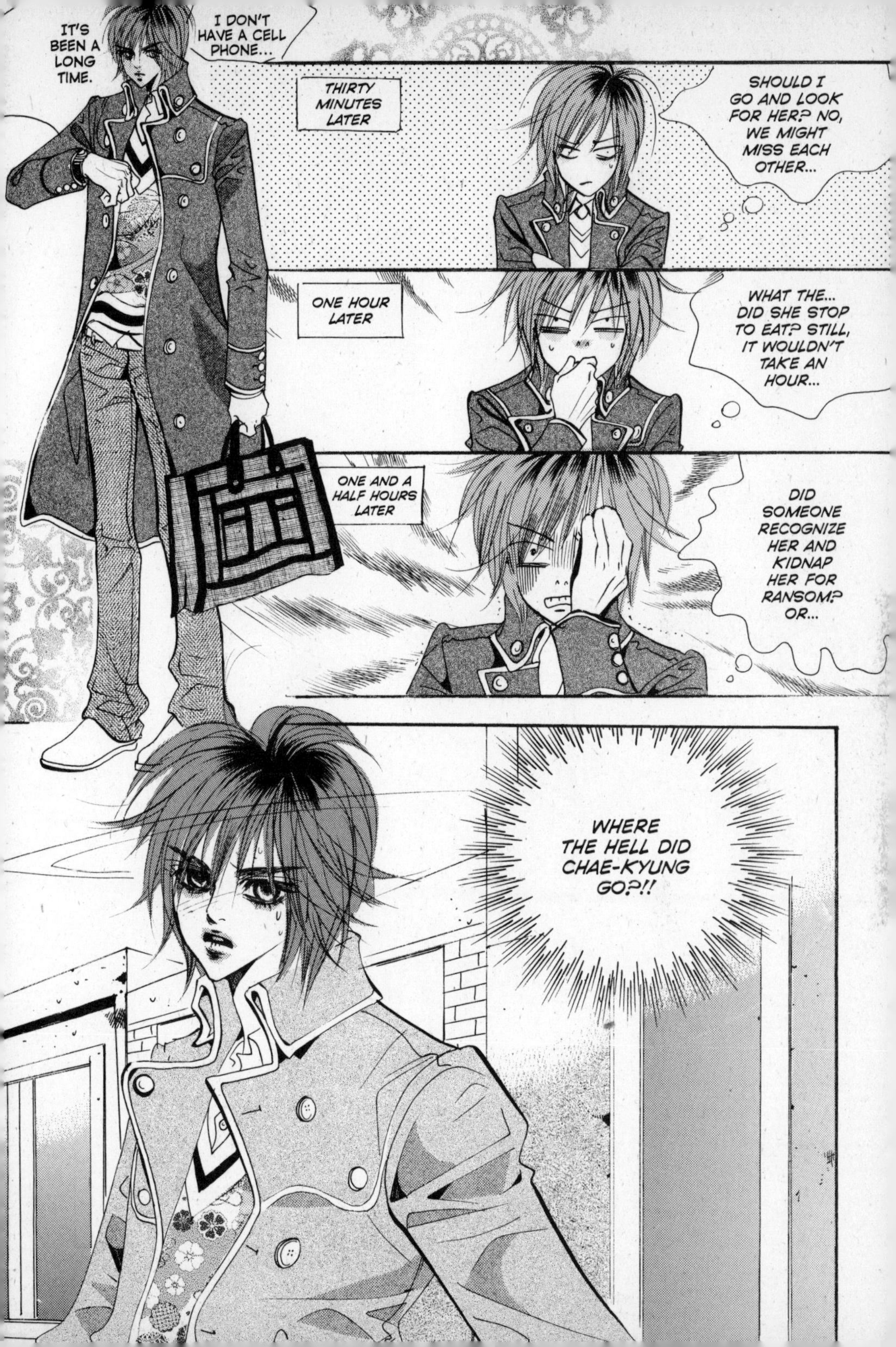
IT'S BEEN A LONG TIME.
I DON'T HAVE A CELL PHONE...
THIRTY MINUTES LATER
SHOULD I GO AND LOOK FOR HER? NO, WE MIGHT MISS EACH OTHER...
ONE HOUR LATER
WHAT THE... DID SHE STOP TO EAT? STILL, IT WOULDN'T TAKE AN HOUR...
ONE AND A HALF HOURS LATER
DID SOMEONE RECOGNIZE HER AND KIDNAP HER FOR RANSOM? OR...
WHERE THE HELL DID CHAE-KYUNG GO?!!

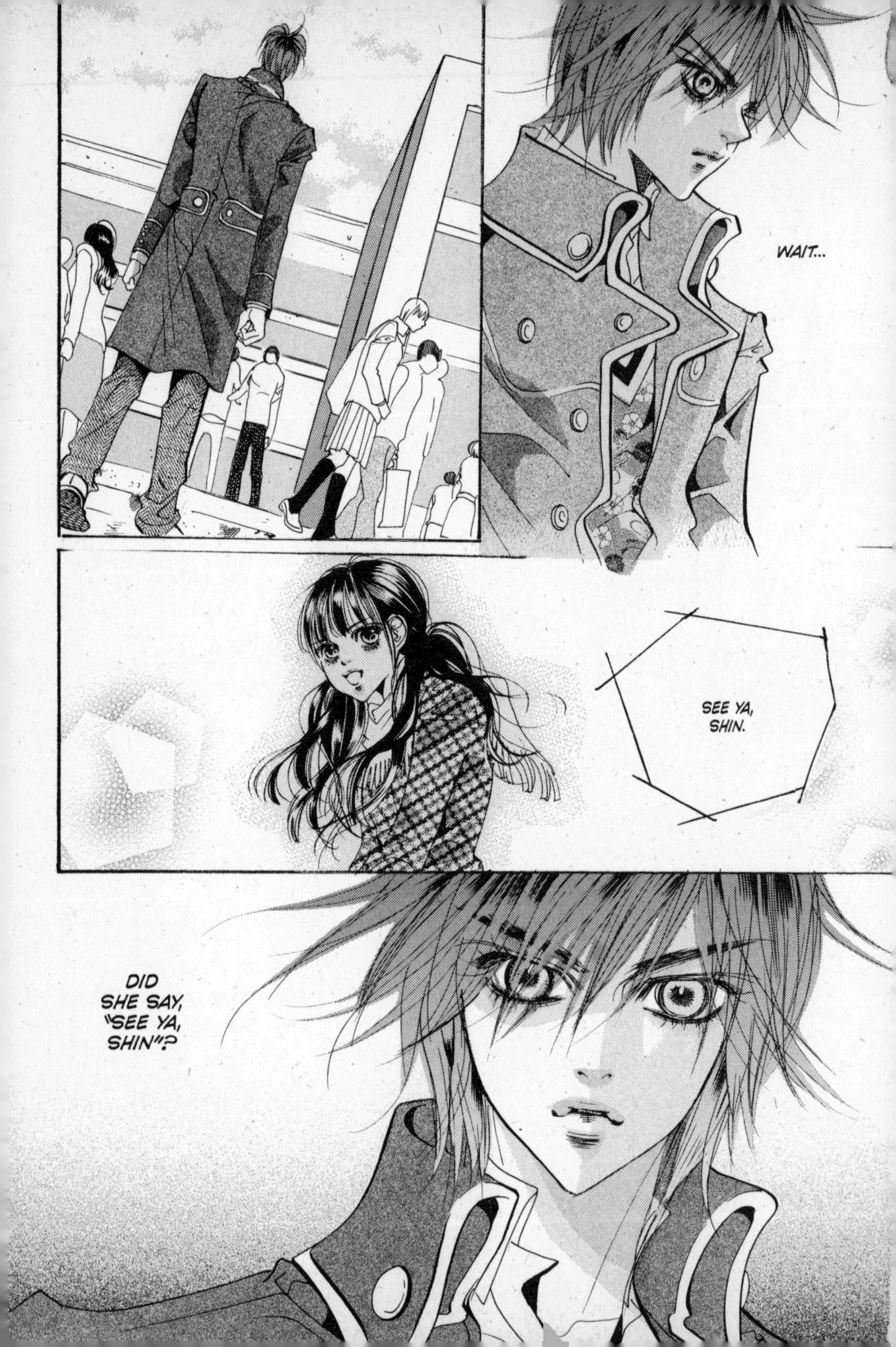
WAIT...
SEE YA, SHIN.
DID SHE SAY, "SEE YA, SHIN"?

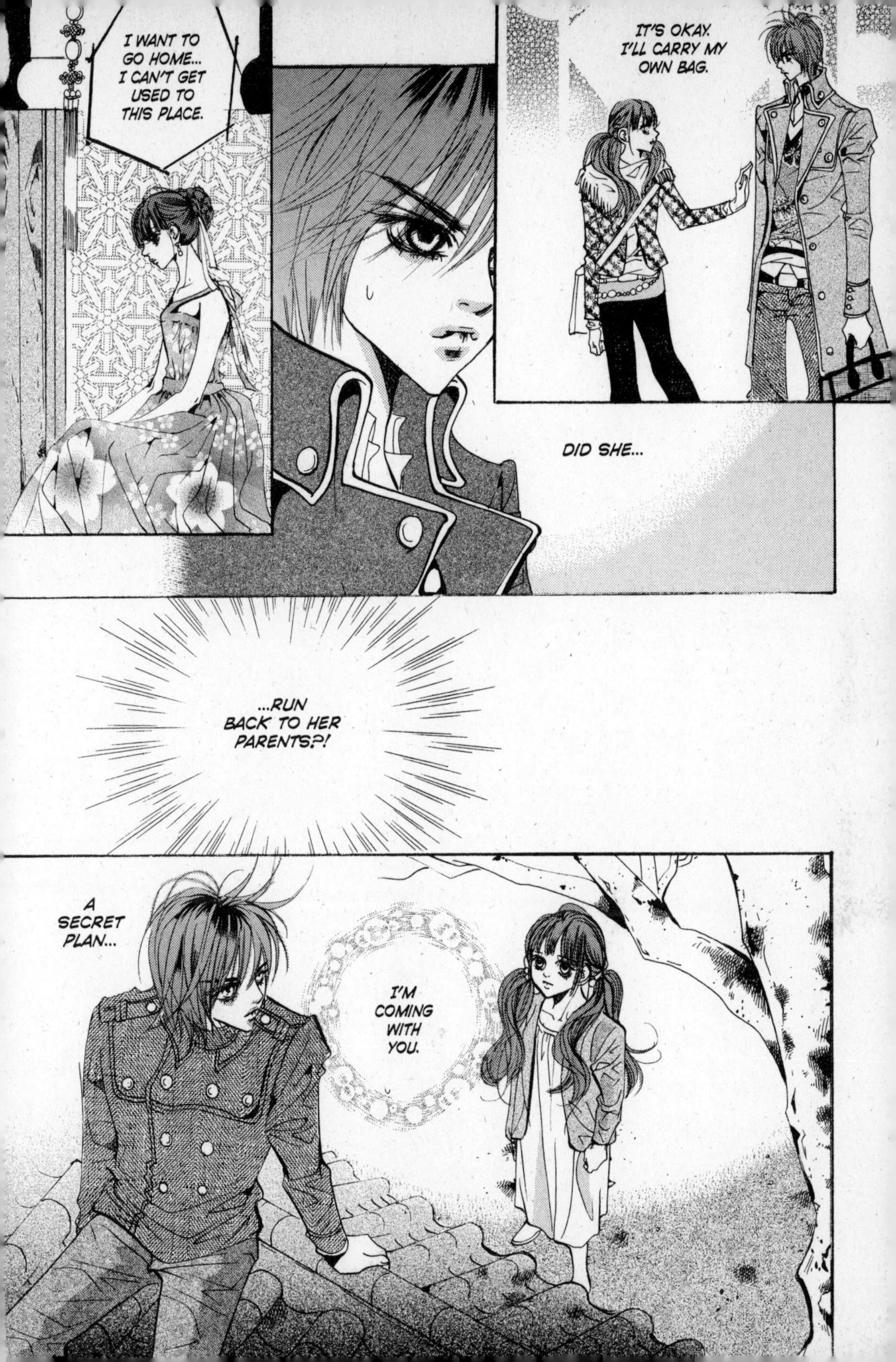
I WANT TO GO HOME... I CAN'T GET USED TO THIS PLACE.
IT'S OKAY. I'LL CARRY MY OWN BAG.
DID SHE...
...RUN BACK TO HER PARENTS?!
A SECRET PLAN...
I'M COMING WITH YOU.

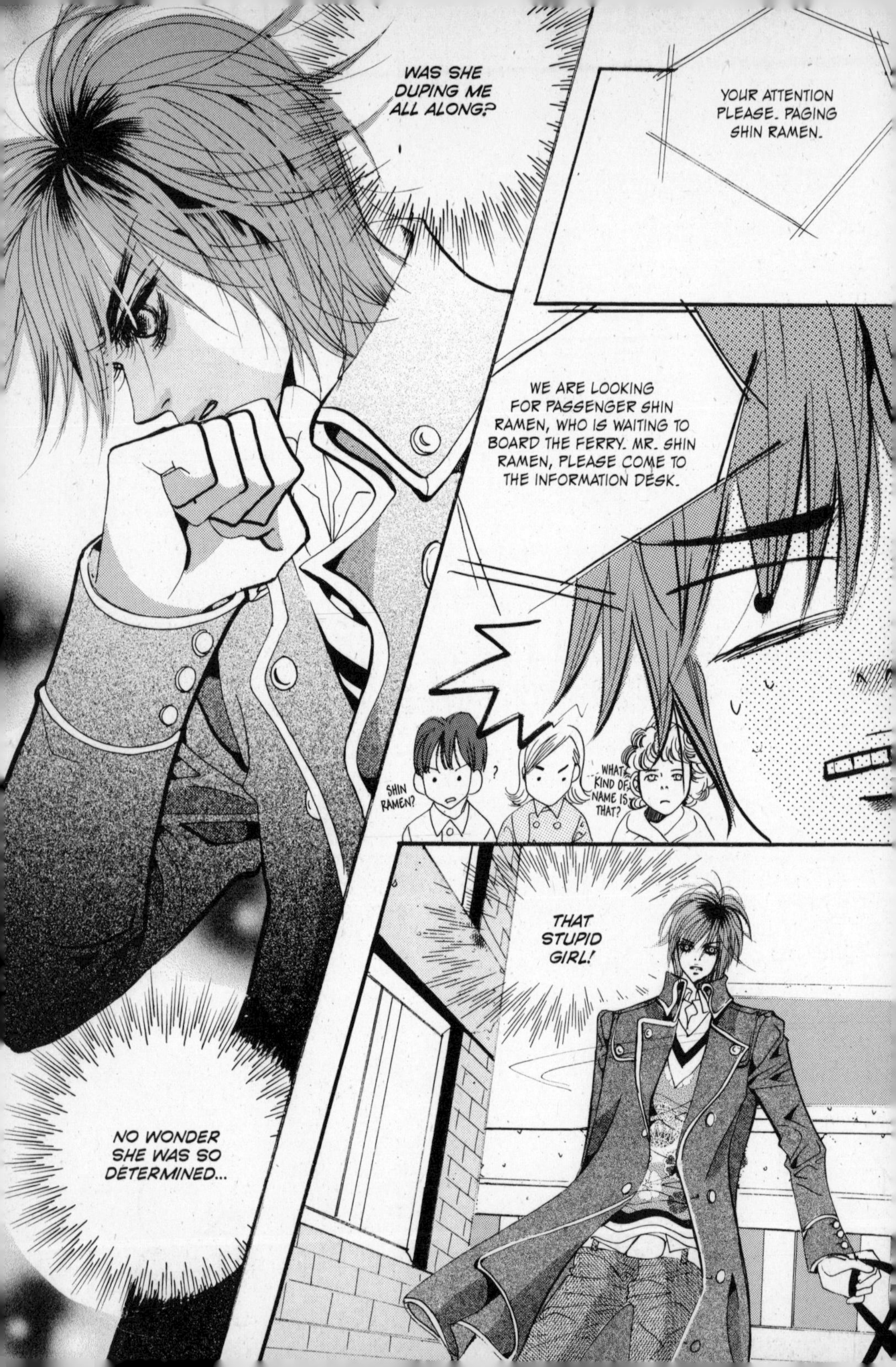
WAS SHE DUPING ME ALL ALONG?
NO WONDER SHE WAS SO DETERMINED...
YOUR ATTENTION PLEASE. PAGING SHIN RAMEN.
WE ARE LOOKING FOR PASSENGER SHIN RAMEN, WHO IS WAITING TO BOARD THE FERRY. MR. SHIN RAMEN, PLEASE COME TO THE INFORMATION DESK.
SHIN RAMEN?
?
WHAT KIND OF NAME IS THAT?
THAT STUPID GIRL!

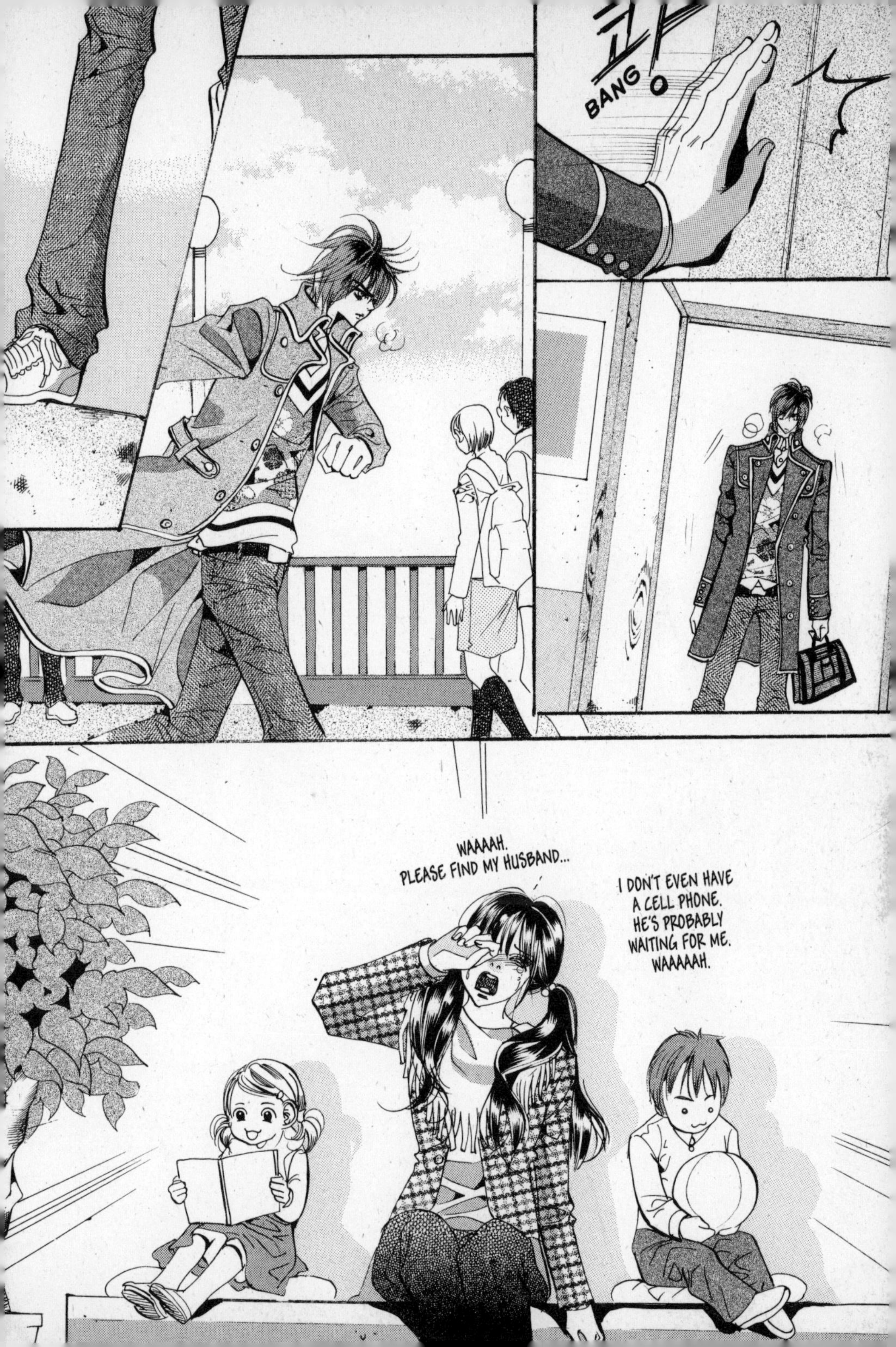
쾅
BANG
WAAAAH.
PLEASE FIND MY HUSBAND...
I DON'T EVEN HAVE
A CELL PHONE.
HE'S PROBABLY
WAITING FOR ME.
WAAAAAH.

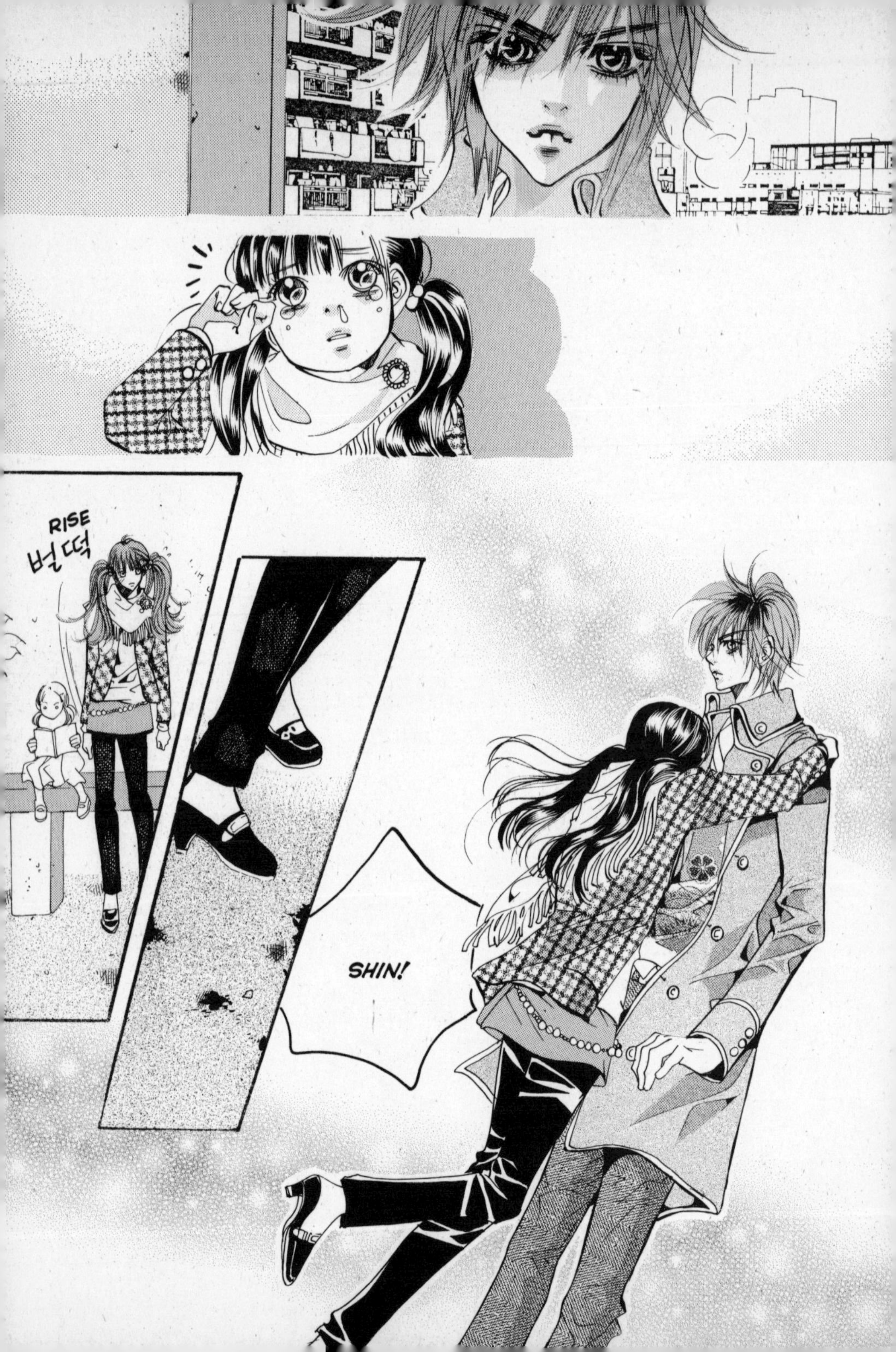

RISE
벌떡
SHIN!

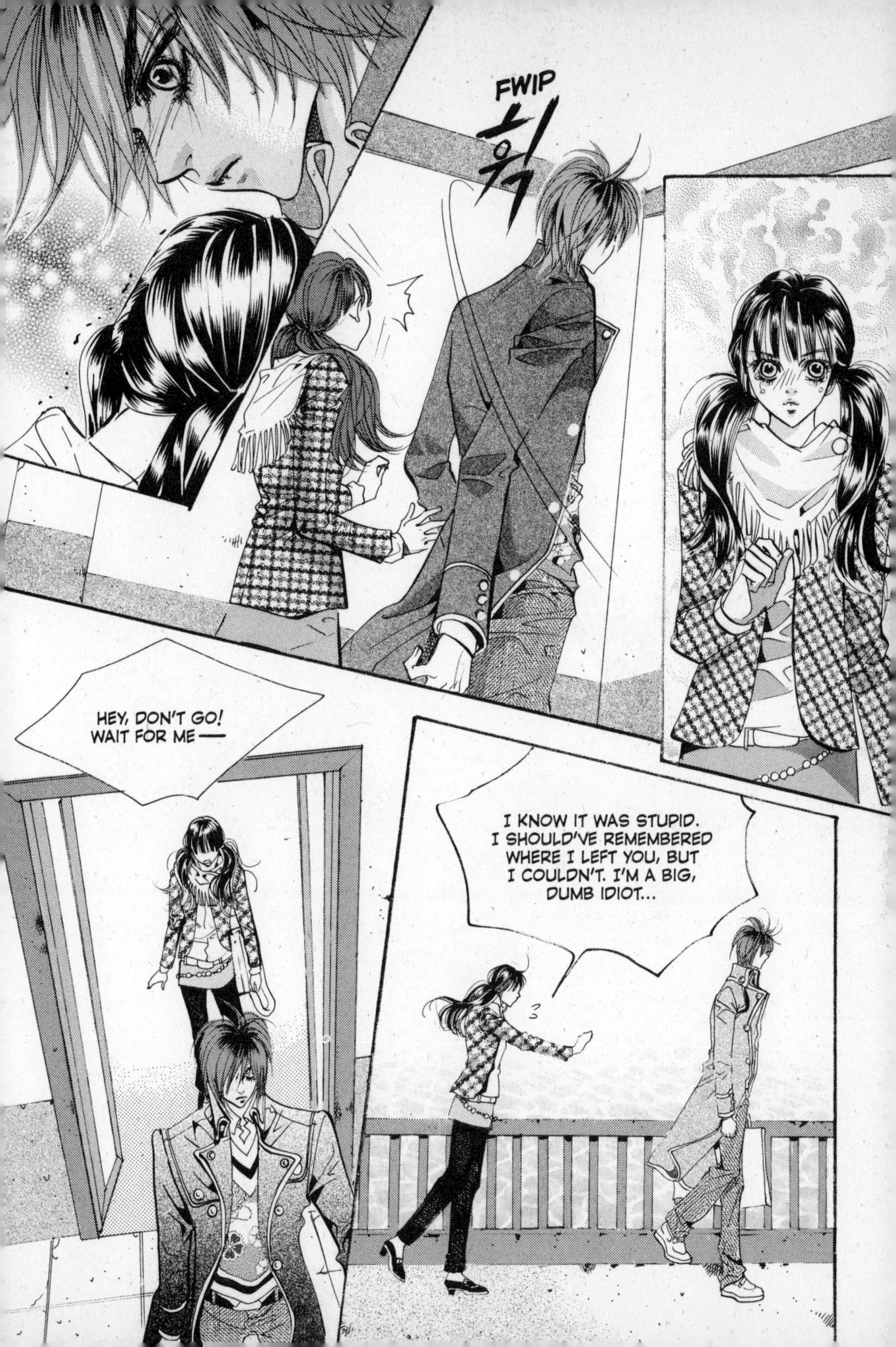
FWIP
HEY, DON'T GO! WAIT FOR ME—
I KNOW IT WAS STUPID. I SHOULD'VE REMEMBERED WHERE I LEFT YOU, BUT I COULDN'T. I'M A BIG, DUMB IDIOT...

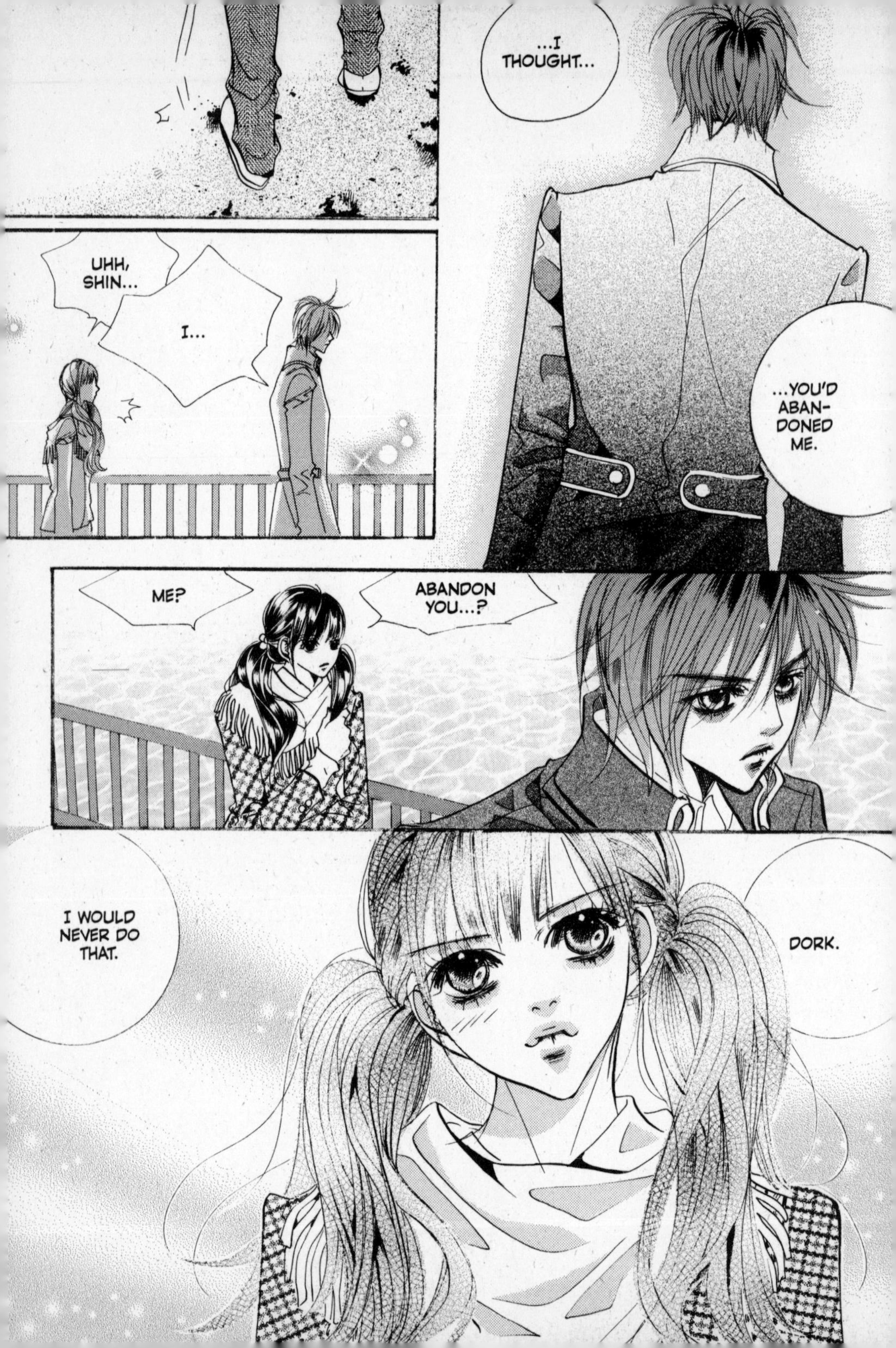

...I THOUGHT...
UHH, SHIN...
I...
...YOU'D ABAN-DONED ME.
ME?
ABANDON YOU...?
I WOULD NEVER DO THAT.
DORK.

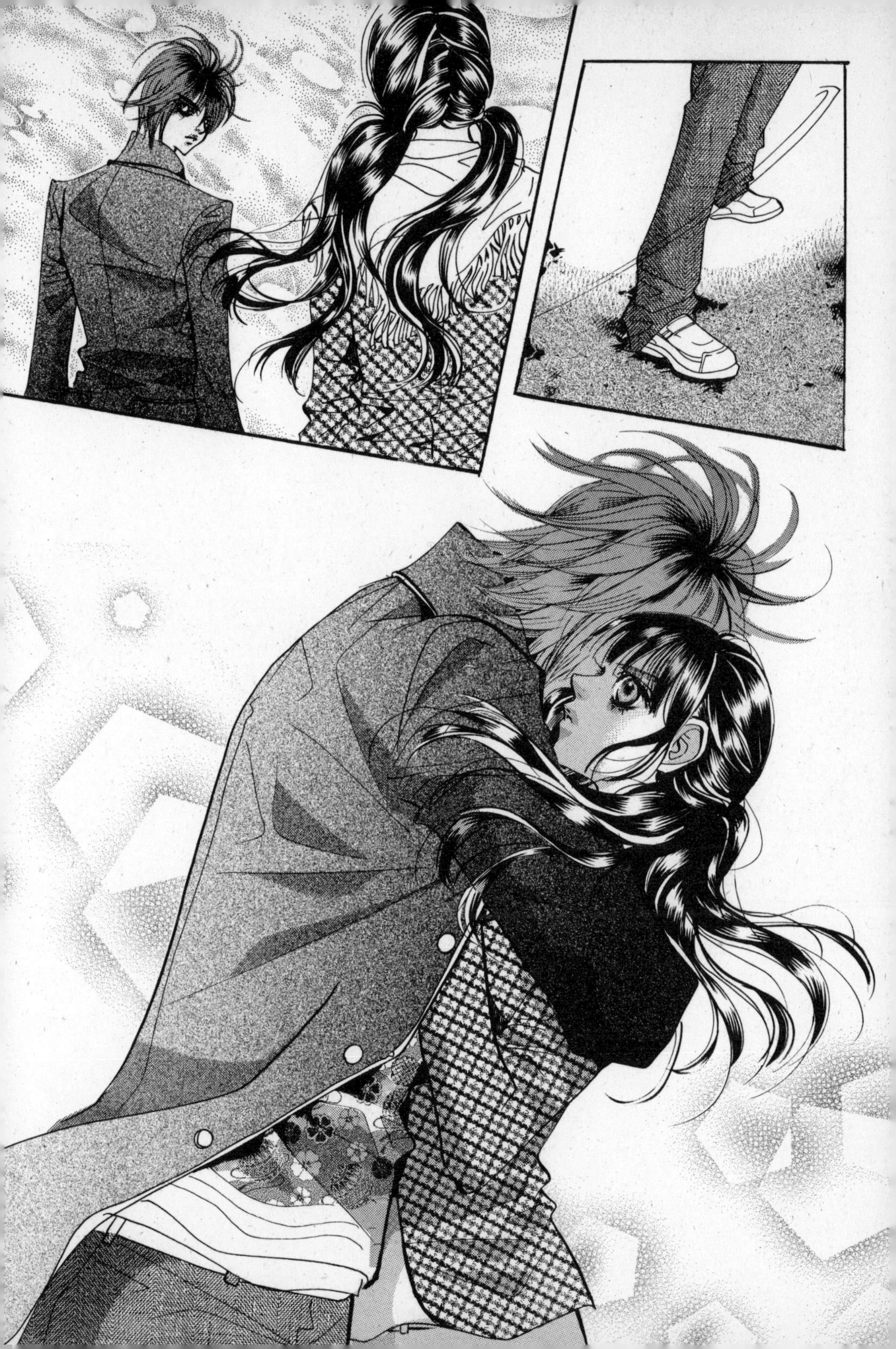

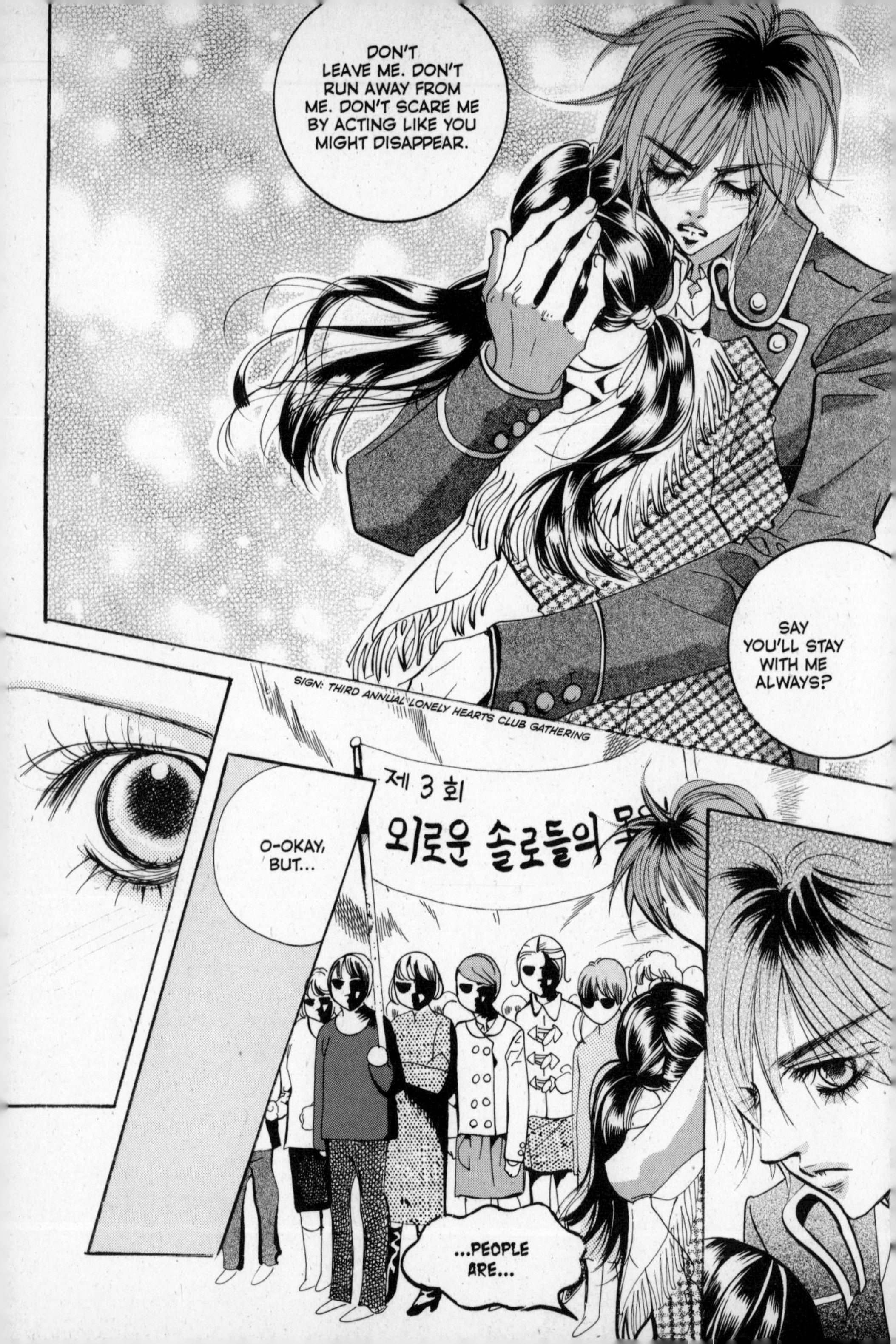
DON'T LEAVE ME. DON'T RUN AWAY FROM ME. DON'T SCARE ME BY ACTING LIKE YOU MIGHT DISAPPEAR.
SAY YOU'LL STAY WITH ME ALWAYS?
O-OKAY, BUT...
SIGN: THIRD ANNUAL LONELY HEARTS CLUB GATHERING
제 3 회
외로운 솔로들의
...PEOPLE ARE...

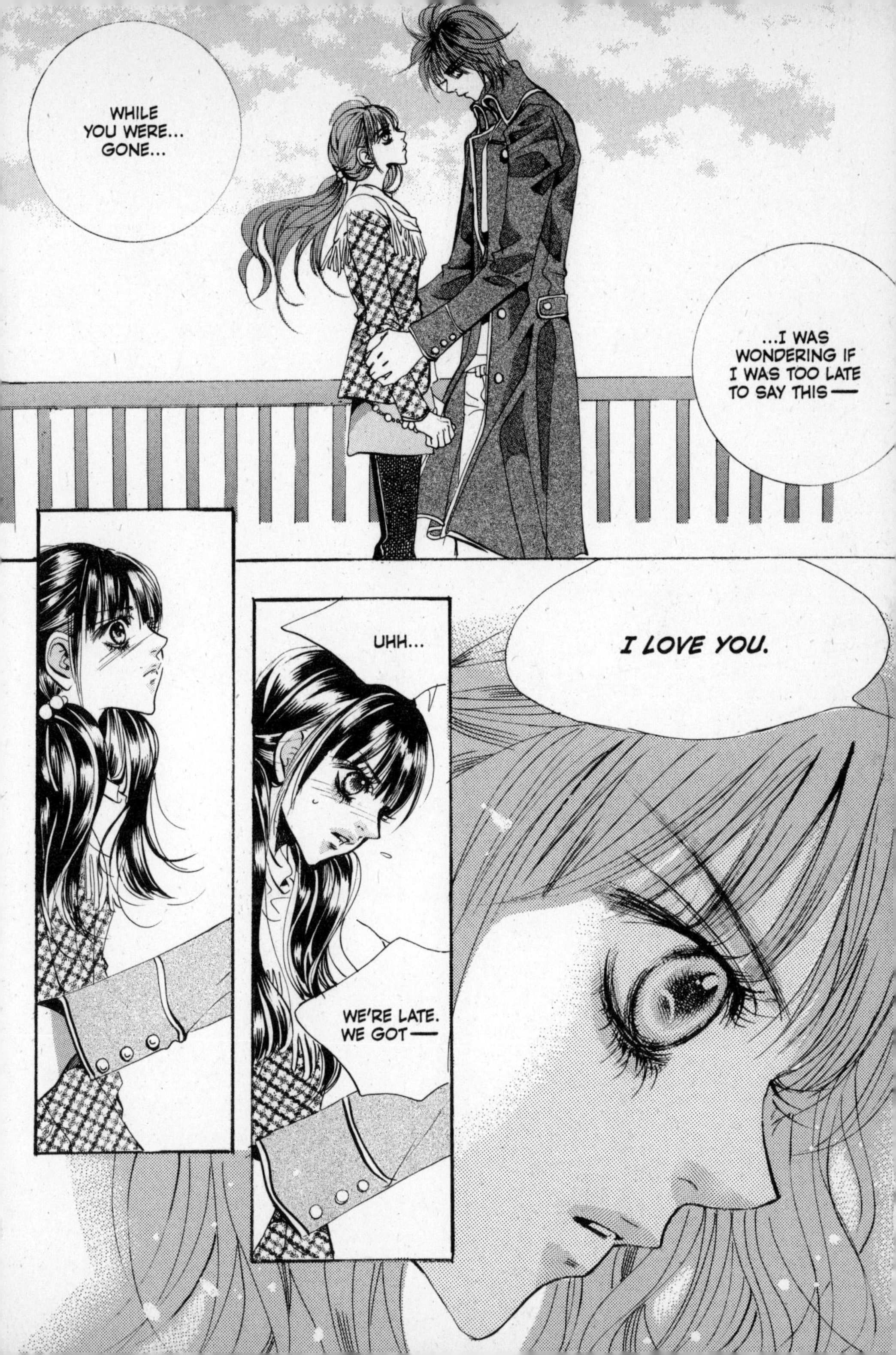
WHILE YOU WERE... GONE...
...I WAS WONDERING IF I WAS TOO LATE TO SAY THIS—
UHH...
WE'RE LATE. WE GOT—
I LOVE YOU.

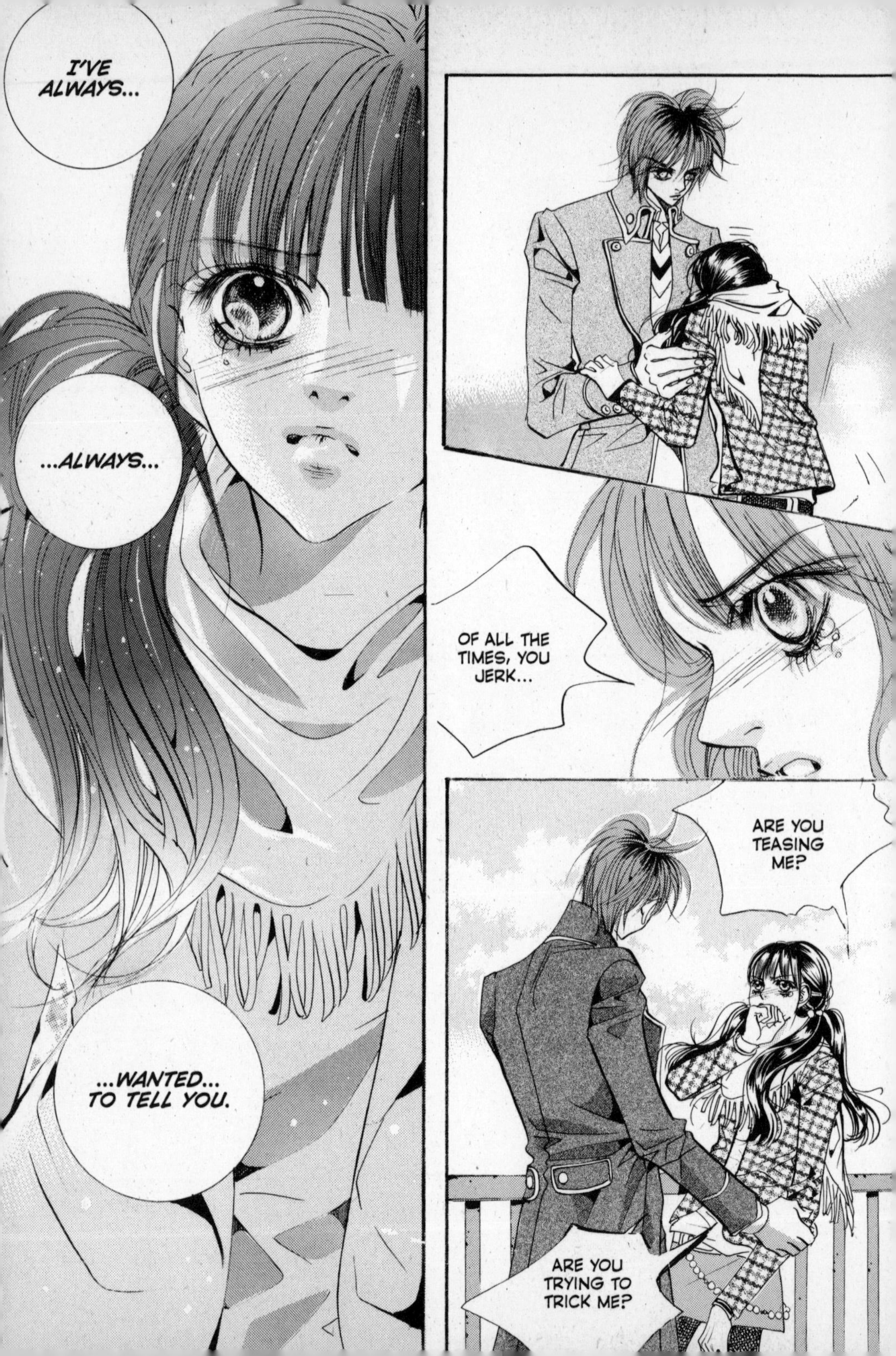
I'VE ALWAYS...
...ALWAYS...
...WANTED... TO TELL YOU.
OF ALL THE TIMES, YOU JERK...
ARE YOU TEASING ME?
ARE YOU TRYING TO TRICK ME?

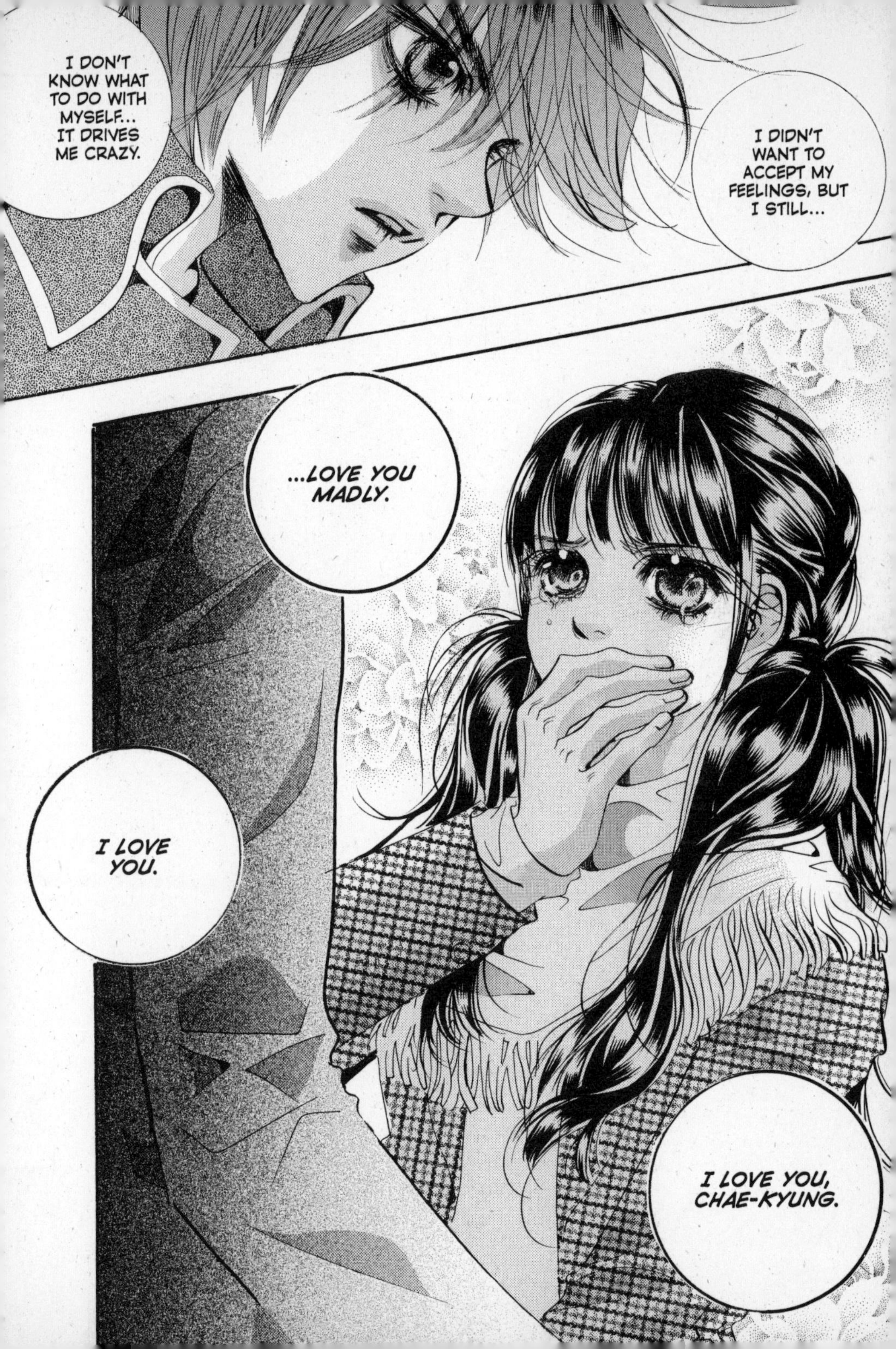
I DON'T KNOW WHAT TO DO WITH MYSELF... IT DRIVES ME CRAZY.
I DIDN'T WANT TO ACCEPT MY FEELINGS, BUT I STILL...
...LOVE YOU MADLY.
I LOVE YOU.
I LOVE YOU, CHAE-KYUNG.

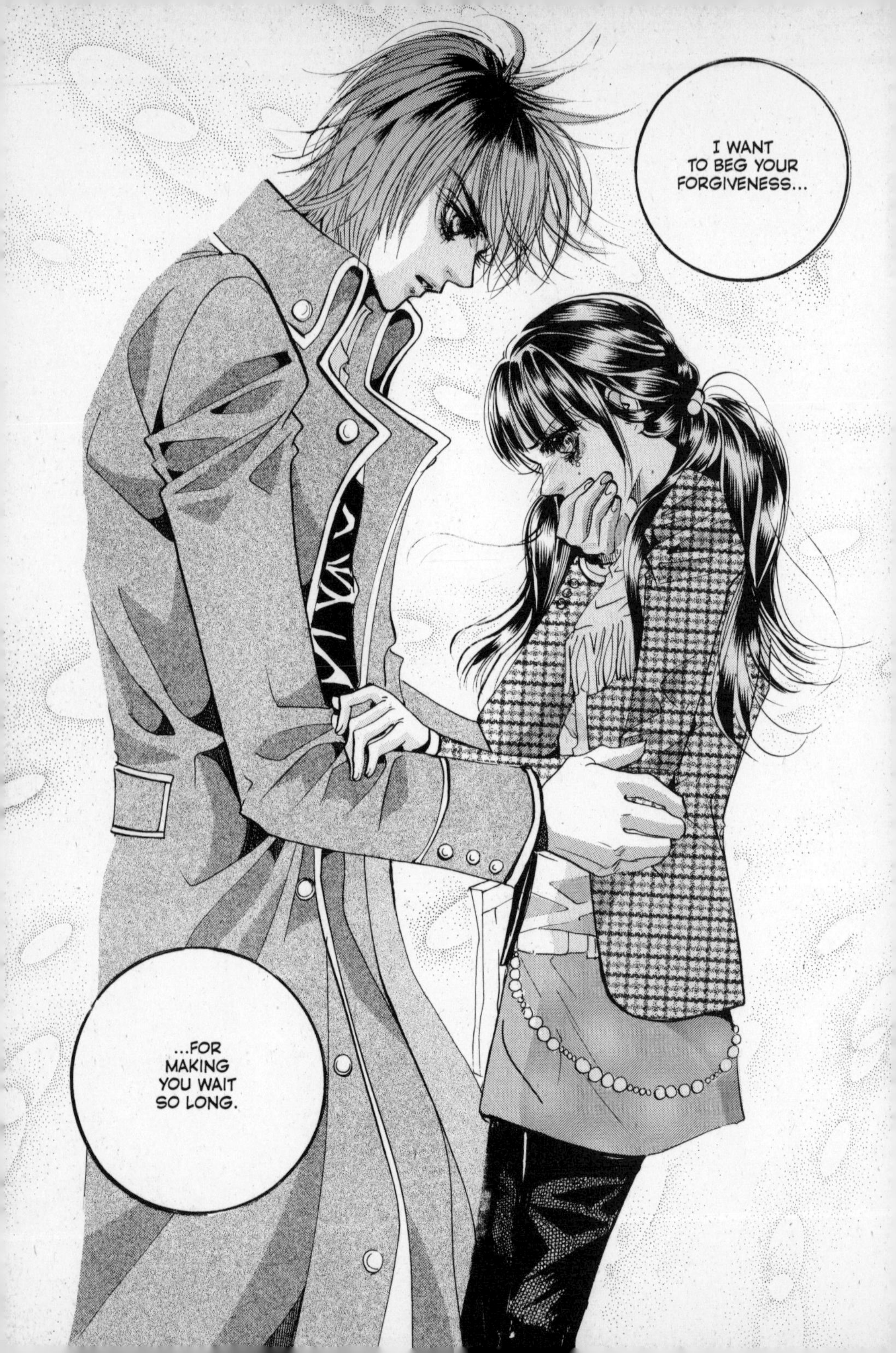
I WANT TO BEG YOUR FORGIVENESS...
...FOR MAKING YOU WAIT SO LONG.

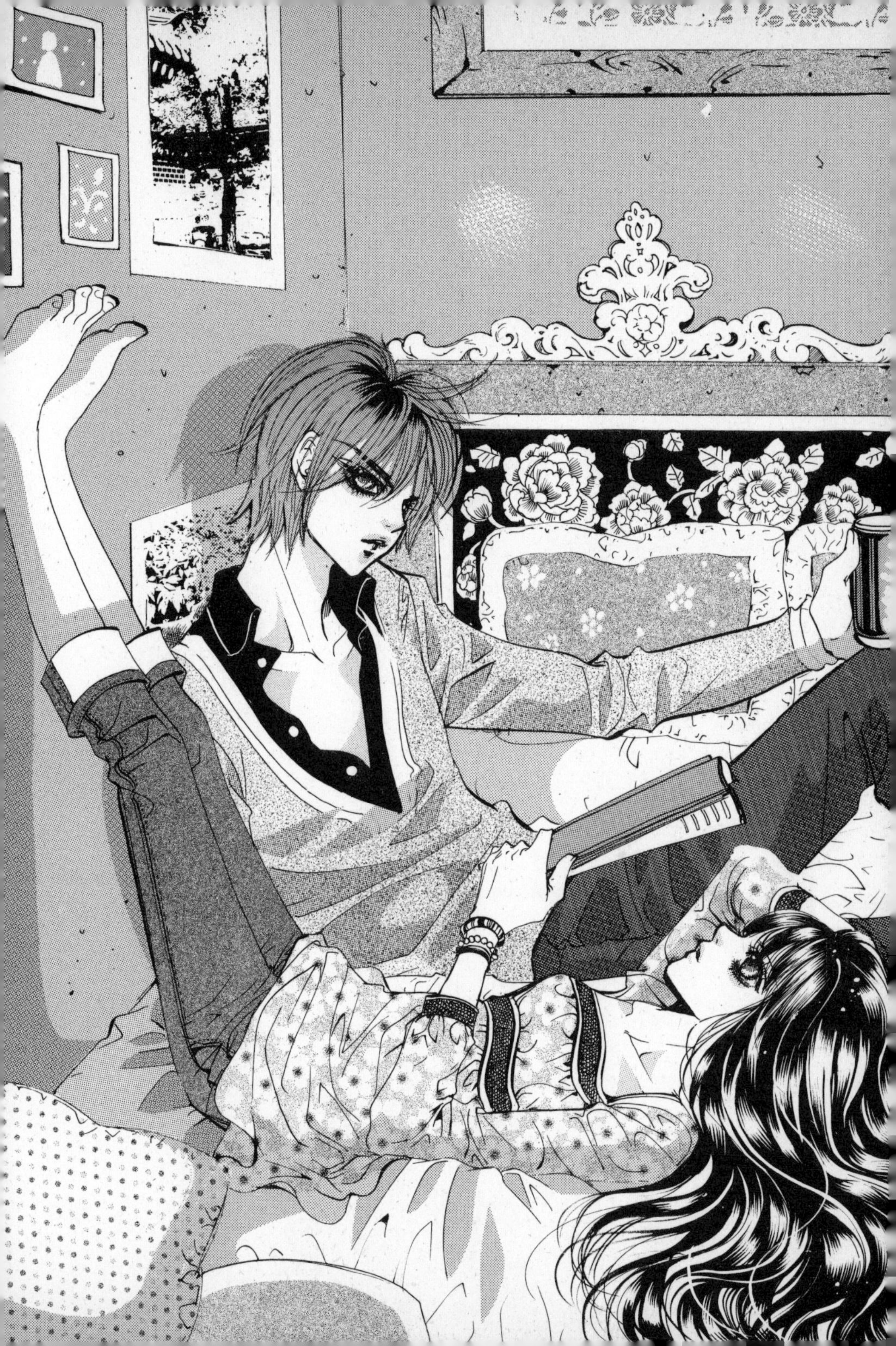

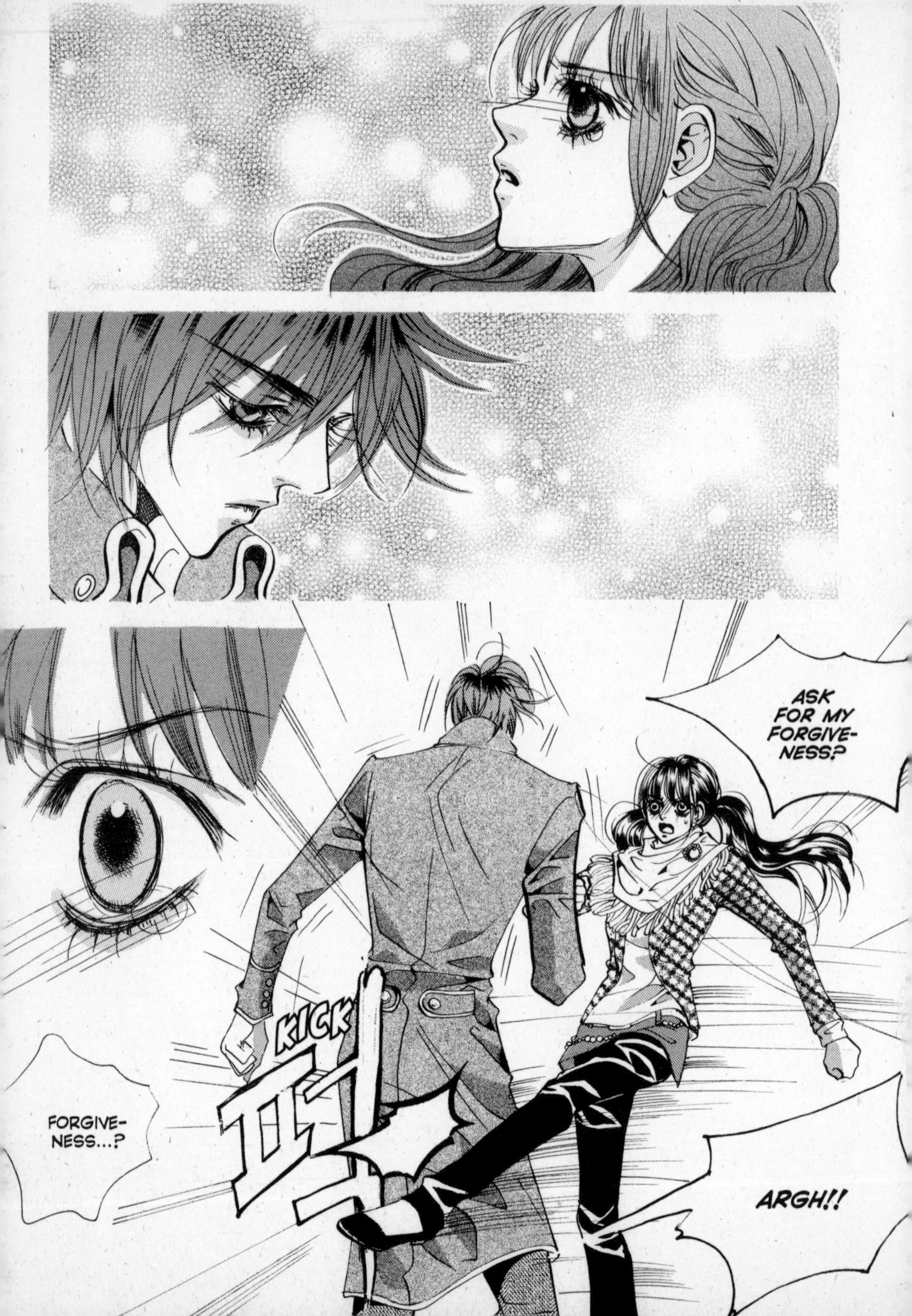
ASK FOR MY FORGIVE-NESS?
FORGIVE-NESS...?
KICK
ARGH!!

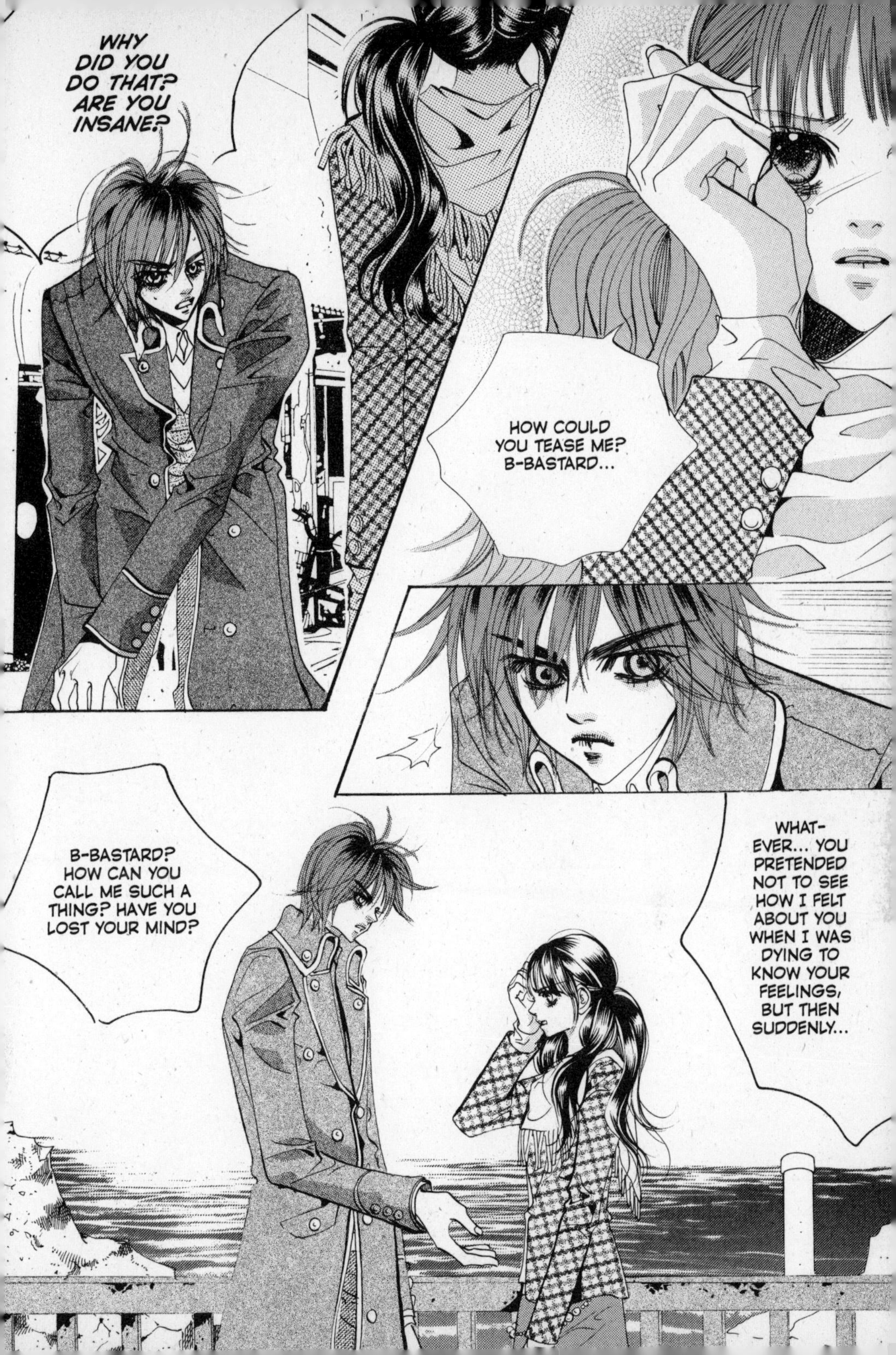
WHY DID YOU DO THAT? ARE YOU INSANE?
HOW COULD YOU TEASE ME? B-BASTARD...
B-BASTARD? HOW CAN YOU CALL ME SUCH A THING? HAVE YOU LOST YOUR MIND?
WHAT-EVER... YOU PRETENDED NOT TO SEE HOW I FELT ABOUT YOU WHEN I WAS DYING TO KNOW YOUR FEELINGS, BUT THEN SUDDENLY...

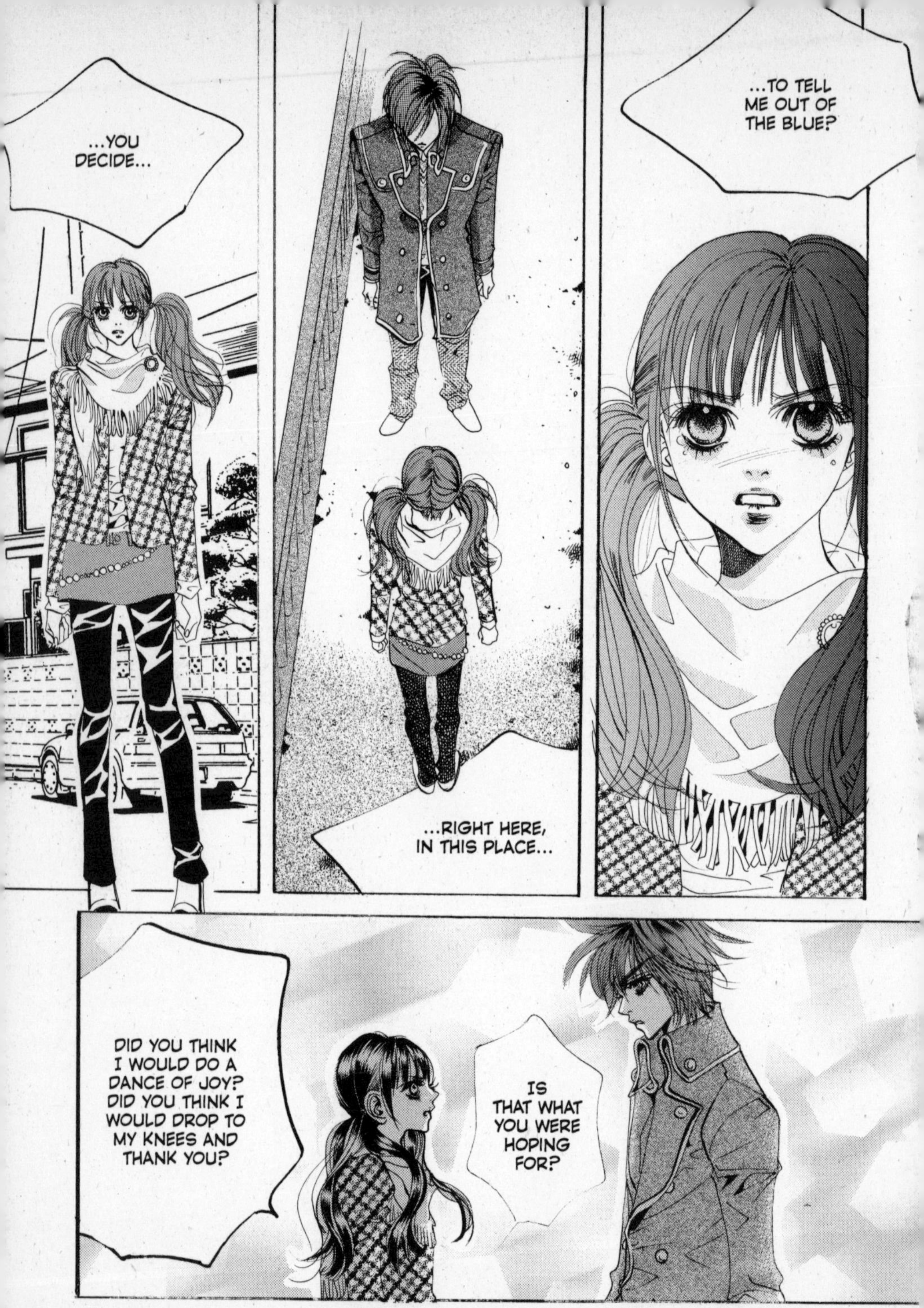
...YOU DECIDE...
...RIGHT HERE, IN THIS PLACE...
...TO TELL ME OUT OF THE BLUE?
DID YOU THINK I WOULD DO A DANCE OF JOY? DID YOU THINK I WOULD DROP TO MY KNEES AND THANK YOU?
IS THAT WHAT YOU WERE HOPING FOR?

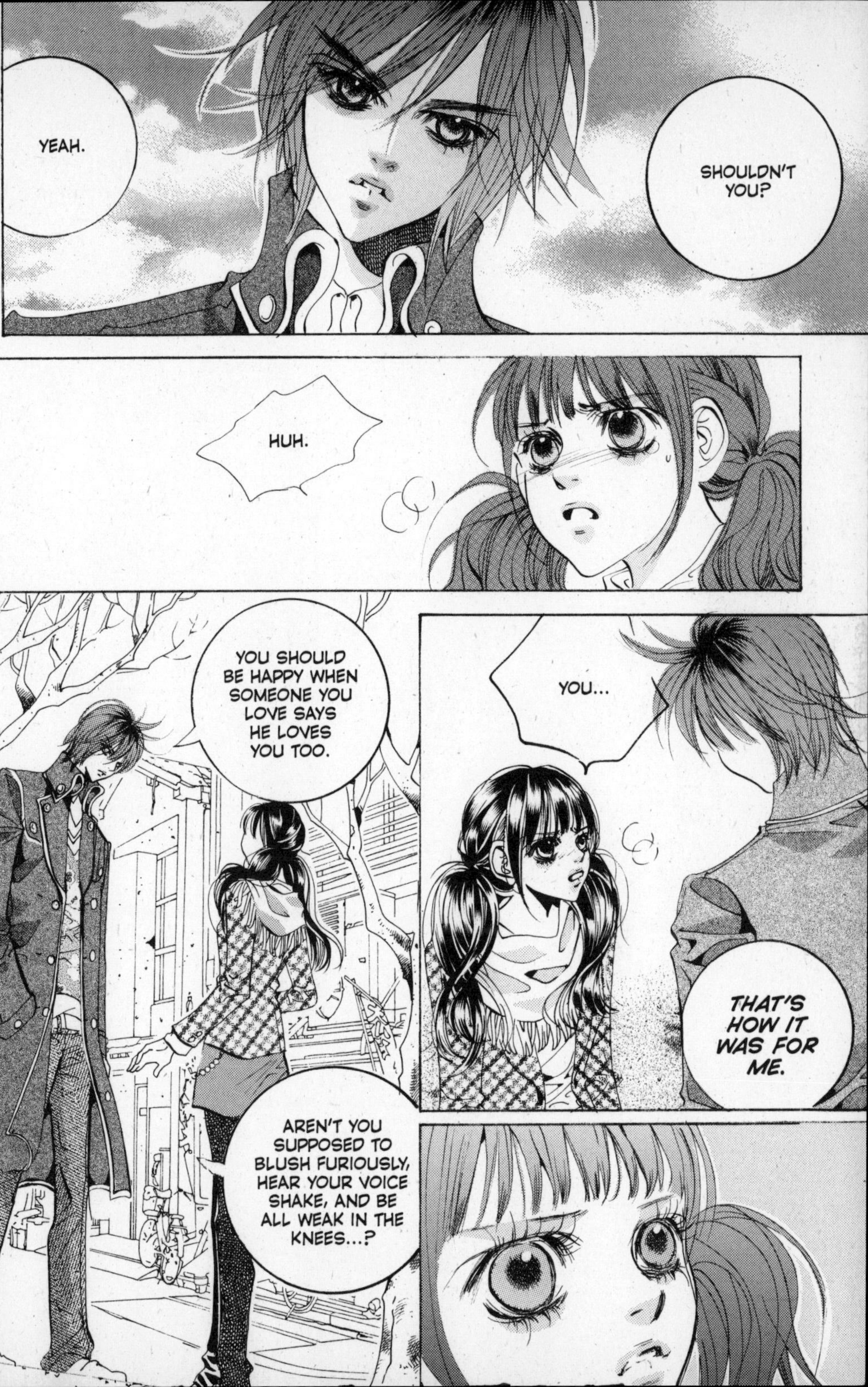
YEAH.
SHOULDN'T YOU?
HUH.
YOU SHOULD BE HAPPY WHEN SOMEONE YOU LOVE SAYS HE LOVES YOU TOO.
AREN'T YOU SUPPOSED TO BLUSH FURIOUSLY, HEAR YOUR VOICE SHAKE, AND BE ALL WEAK IN THE KNEES...?
YOU...
THAT'S HOW IT WAS FOR ME.

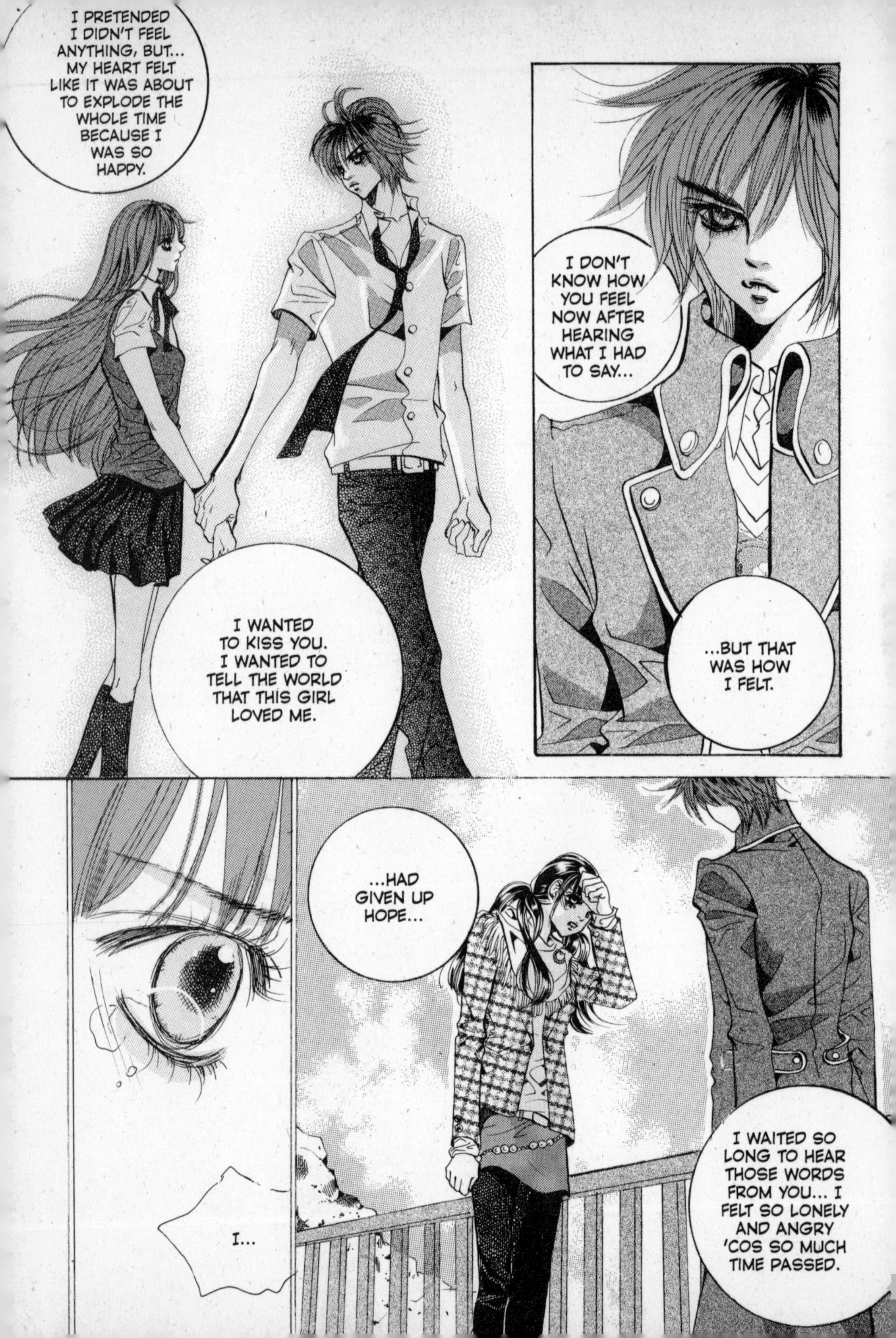
I PRETENDED I DIDN'T FEEL ANYTHING, BUT... MY HEART FELT LIKE IT WAS ABOUT TO EXPLODE THE WHOLE TIME BECAUSE I WAS SO HAPPY.
I WANTED TO KISS YOU. I WANTED TO TELL THE WORLD THAT THIS GIRL LOVED ME.
I DON'T KNOW HOW YOU FEEL NOW AFTER HEARING WHAT I HAD TO SAY...
...BUT THAT WAS HOW I FELT.
I...
...HAD GIVEN UP HOPE...
I WAITED SO LONG TO HEAR THOSE WORDS FROM YOU... I FELT SO LONELY AND ANGRY 'COS SO MUCH TIME PASSED.

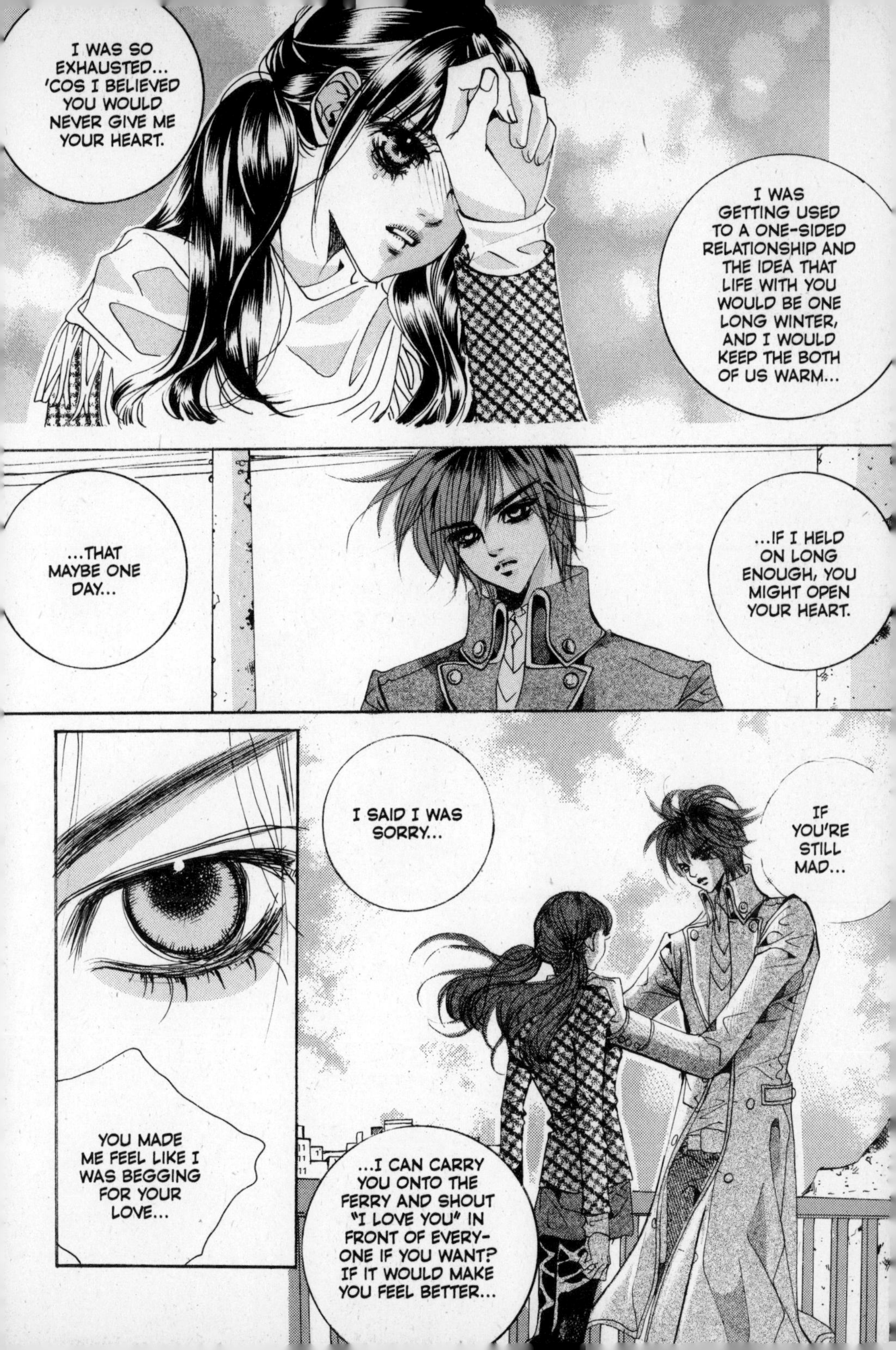
I WAS SO EXHAUSTED... 'COS I BELIEVED YOU WOULD NEVER GIVE ME YOUR HEART.
I WAS GETTING USED TO A ONE-SIDED RELATIONSHIP AND THE IDEA THAT LIFE WITH YOU WOULD BE ONE LONG WINTER, AND I WOULD KEEP THE BOTH OF US WARM...
...THAT MAYBE ONE DAY...
...IF I HELD ON LONG ENOUGH, YOU MIGHT OPEN YOUR HEART.
YOU MADE ME FEEL LIKE I WAS BEGGING FOR YOUR LOVE...
I SAID I WAS SORRY...
IF YOU'RE STILL MAD...
...I CAN CARRY YOU ONTO THE FERRY AND SHOUT "I LOVE YOU" IN FRONT OF EVERY-ONE IF YOU WANT? IF IT WOULD MAKE YOU FEEL BETTER...

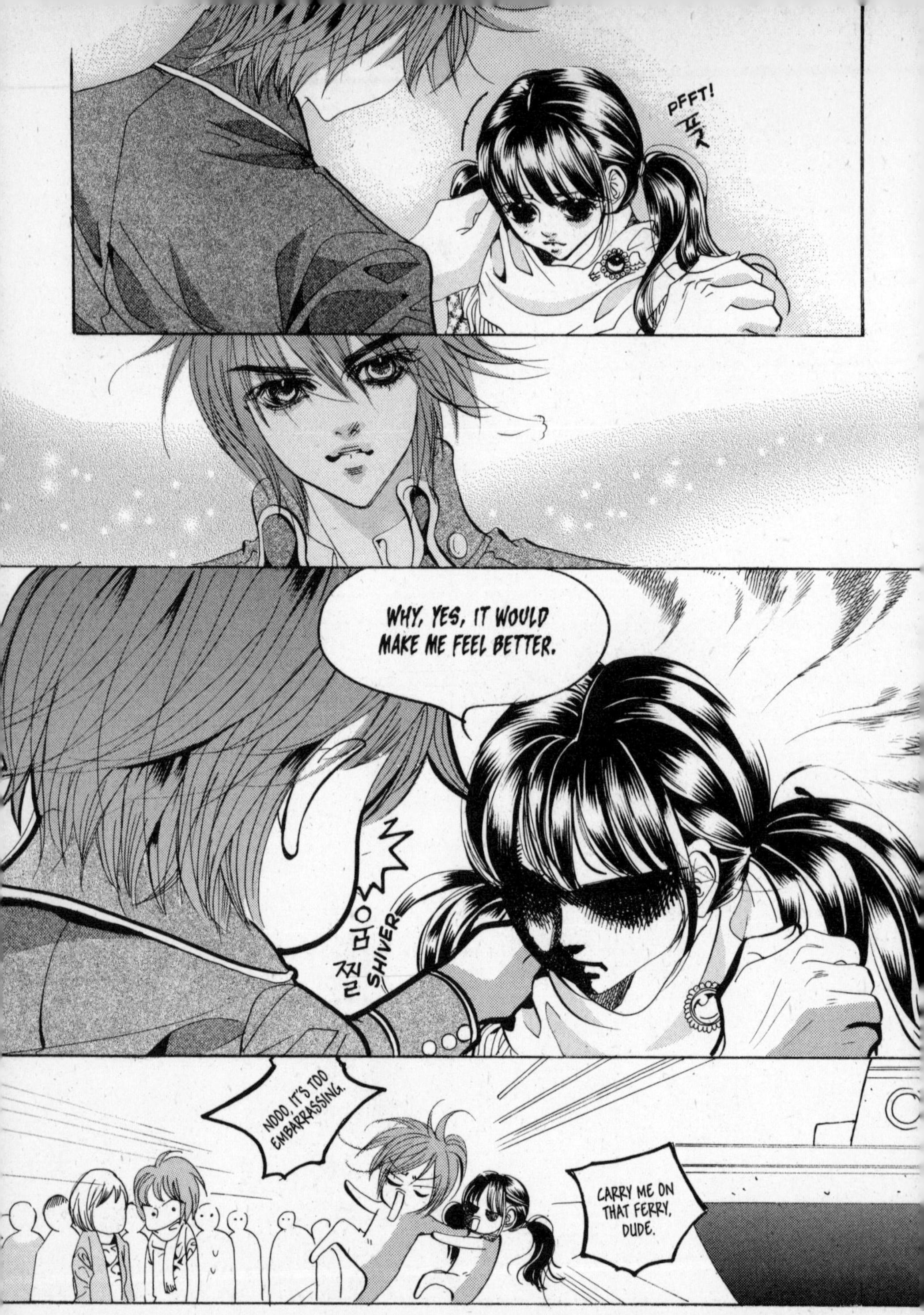
PFFT!
푹
WHY, YES, IT WOULD MAKE ME FEEL BETTER.
SHIVER
찌릿
NOOO, IT'S TOO EMBARRASSING.
CARRY ME ON THAT FERRY, DUDE.

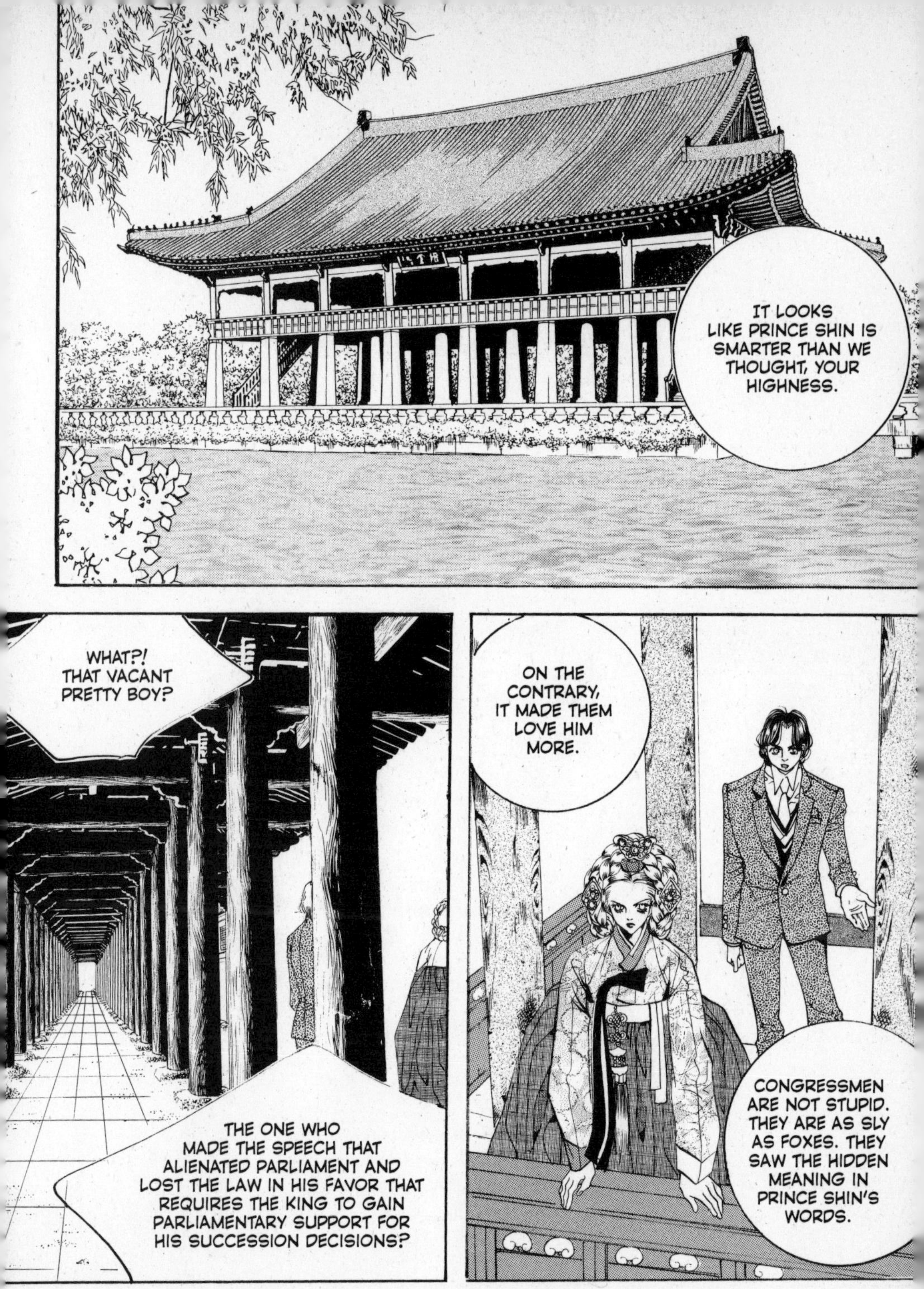
IT LOOKS LIKE PRINCE SHIN IS SMARTER THAN WE THOUGHT, YOUR HIGHNESS.
WHAT?! THAT VACANT PRETTY BOY?
THE ONE WHO MADE THE SPEECH THAT ALIENATED PARLIAMENT AND LOST THE LAW IN HIS FAVOR THAT REQUIRES THE KING TO GAIN PARLIAMENTARY SUPPORT FOR HIS SUCCESSION DECISIONS?
ON THE CONTRARY, IT MADE THEM LOVE HIM MORE.
CONGRESSMEN ARE NOT STUPID. THEY ARE AS SLY AS FOXES. THEY SAW THE HIDDEN MEANING IN PRINCE SHIN'S WORDS.

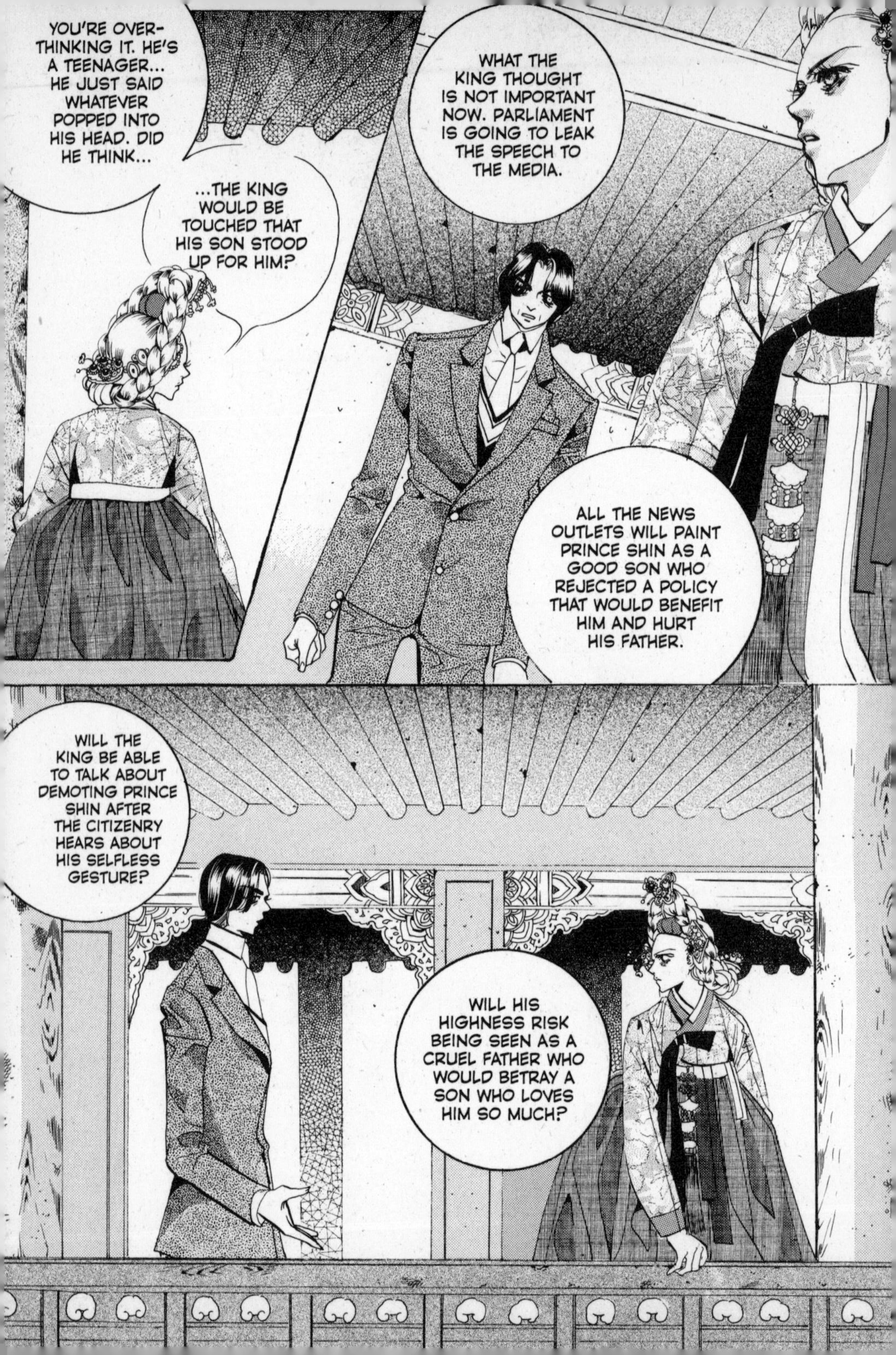
YOU'RE OVER-THINKING IT. HE'S A TEENAGER... HE JUST SAID WHATEVER POPPED INTO HIS HEAD. DID HE THINK...
...THE KING WOULD BE TOUCHED THAT HIS SON STOOD UP FOR HIM?
WHAT THE KING THOUGHT IS NOT IMPORTANT NOW. PARLIAMENT IS GOING TO LEAK THE SPEECH TO THE MEDIA.
ALL THE NEWS OUTLETS WILL PAINT PRINCE SHIN AS A GOOD SON WHO REJECTED A POLICY THAT WOULD BENEFIT HIM AND HURT HIS FATHER.
WILL THE KING BE ABLE TO TALK ABOUT DEMOTING PRINCE SHIN AFTER THE CITIZENRY HEARS ABOUT HIS SELFLESS GESTURE?
WILL HIS HIGHNESS RISK BEING SEEN AS A CRUEL FATHER WHO WOULD BETRAY A SON WHO LOVES HIM SO MUCH?

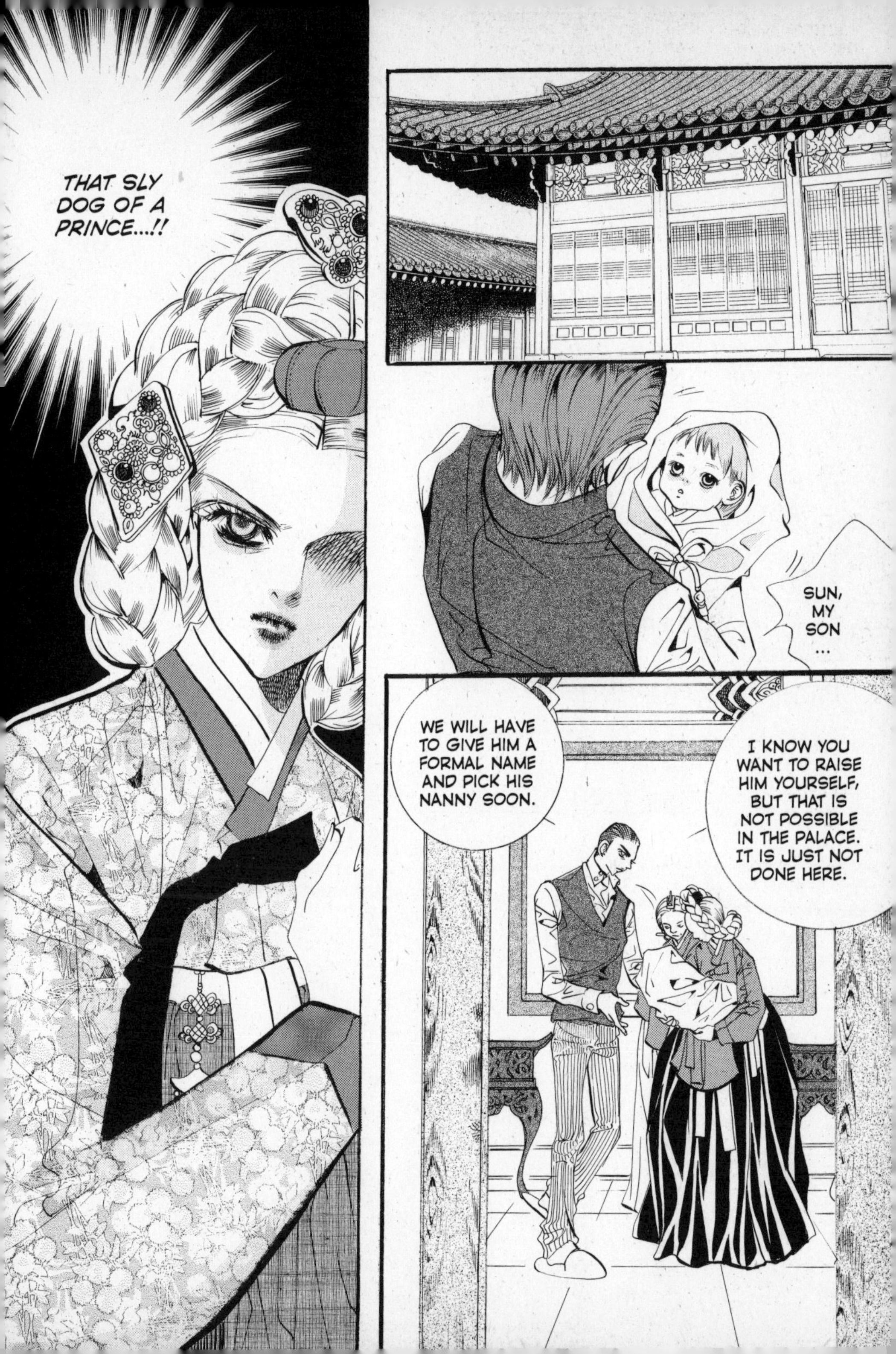
THAT SLY DOG OF A PRINCE...!!
SUN, MY SON ...
WE WILL HAVE TO GIVE HIM A FORMAL NAME AND PICK HIS NANNY SOON.
I KNOW YOU WANT TO RAISE HIM YOURSELF, BUT THAT IS NOT POSSIBLE IN THE PALACE. IT IS JUST NOT DONE HERE.

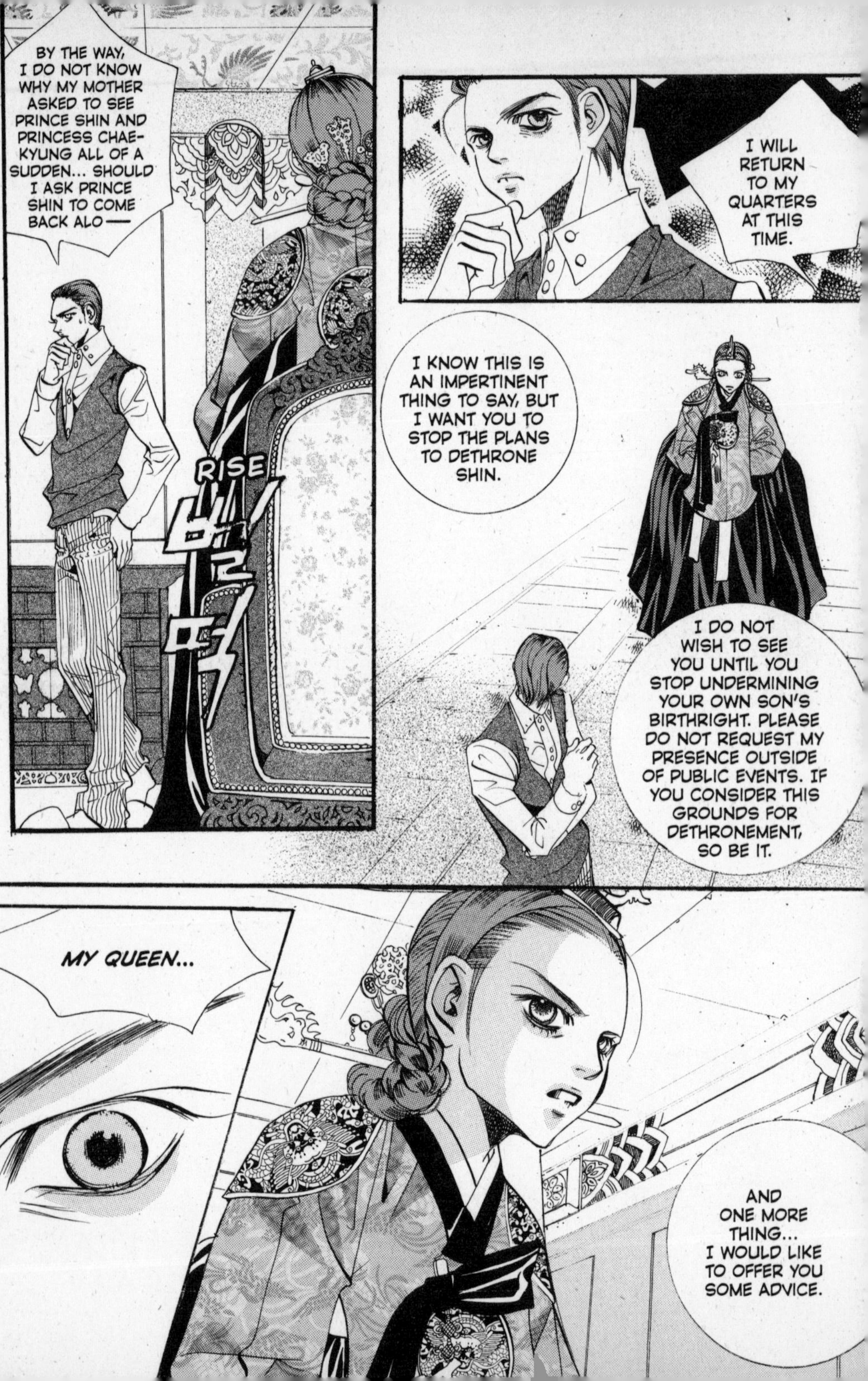
BY THE WAY, I DO NOT KNOW WHY MY MOTHER ASKED TO SEE PRINCE SHIN AND PRINCESS CHAE-KYUNG ALL OF A SUDDEN... SHOULD I ASK PRINCE SHIN TO COME BACK ALO—
RISE
벌떡
I WILL RETURN TO MY QUARTERS AT THIS TIME.
I KNOW THIS IS AN IMPERTINENT THING TO SAY, BUT I WANT YOU TO STOP THE PLANS TO DETHRONE SHIN.
I DO NOT WISH TO SEE YOU UNTIL YOU STOP UNDERMINING YOUR OWN SON'S BIRTHRIGHT. PLEASE DO NOT REQUEST MY PRESENCE OUTSIDE OF PUBLIC EVENTS. IF YOU CONSIDER THIS GROUNDS FOR DETHRONEMENT, SO BE IT.
MY QUEEN...
AND ONE MORE THING... I WOULD LIKE TO OFFER YOU SOME ADVICE.

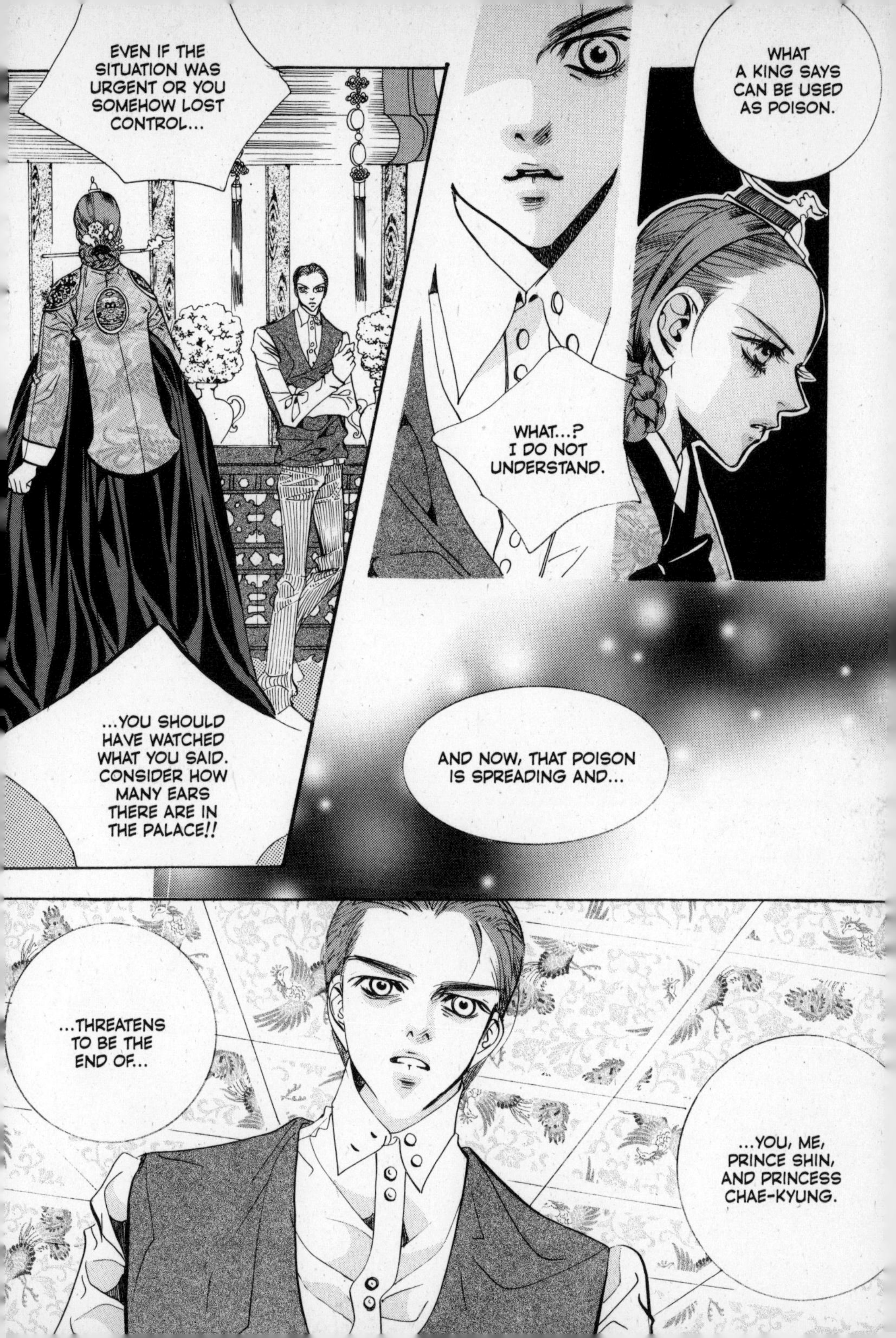
EVEN IF THE SITUATION WAS URGENT OR YOU SOMEHOW LOST CONTROL...
...YOU SHOULD HAVE WATCHED WHAT YOU SAID. CONSIDER HOW MANY EARS THERE ARE IN THE PALACE!!
WHAT...? I DO NOT UNDERSTAND.
WHAT A KING SAYS CAN BE USED AS POISON.
AND NOW, THAT POISON IS SPREADING AND...
...THREATENS TO BE THE END OF...
...YOU, ME, PRINCE SHIN, AND PRINCESS CHAE-KYUNG.

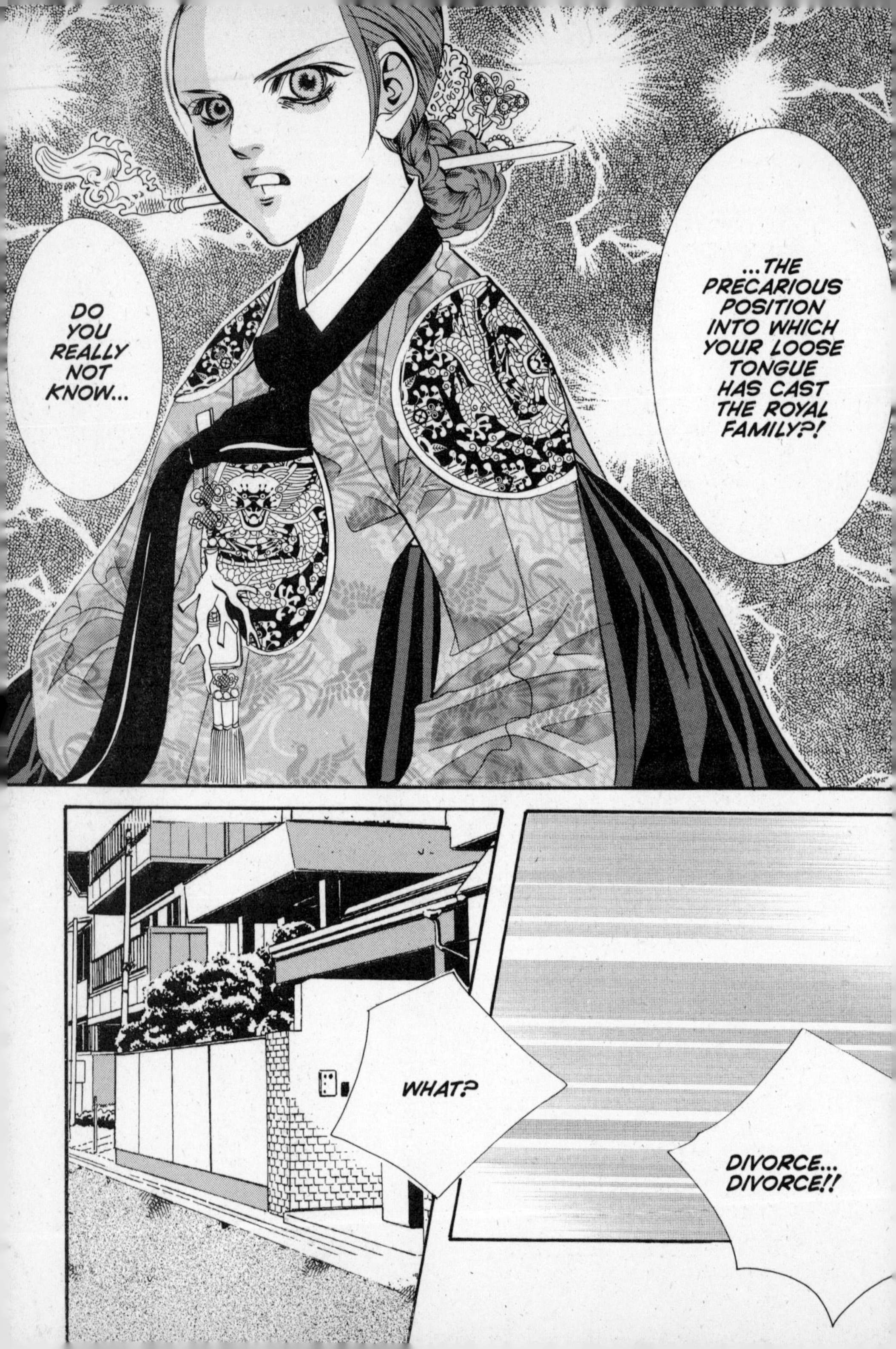
DO YOU REALLY NOT KNOW...
...THE PRECARIOUS POSITION INTO WHICH YOUR LOOSE TONGUE HAS CAST THE ROYAL FAMILY?!
WHAT?
DIVORCE... DIVORCE!!

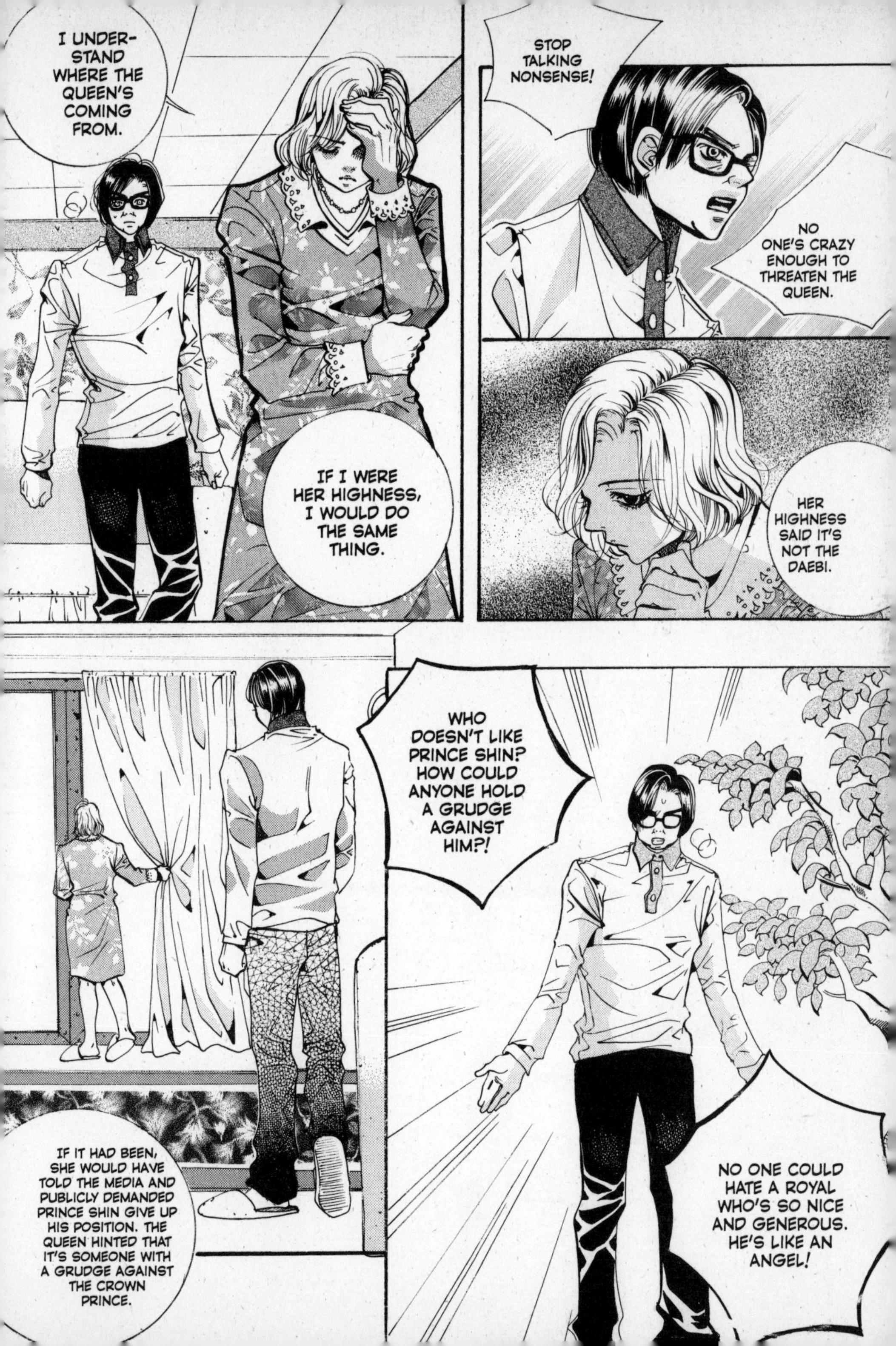
I UNDER-STAND WHERE THE QUEEN'S COMING FROM.
IF I WERE HER HIGHNESS, I WOULD DO THE SAME THING.
STOP TALKING NONSENSE!
NO ONE'S CRAZY ENOUGH TO THREATEN THE QUEEN.
HER HIGHNESS SAID IT'S NOT THE DAEBI.
IF IT HAD BEEN, SHE WOULD HAVE TOLD THE MEDIA AND PUBLICLY DEMANDED PRINCE SHIN GIVE UP HIS POSITION. THE QUEEN HINTED THAT IT'S SOMEONE WITH A GRUDGE AGAINST THE CROWN PRINCE.
WHO DOESN'T LIKE PRINCE SHIN? HOW COULD ANYONE HOLD A GRUDGE AGAINST HIM?!
NO ONE COULD HATE A ROYAL WHO'S SO NICE AND GENEROUS. HE'S LIKE AN ANGEL!

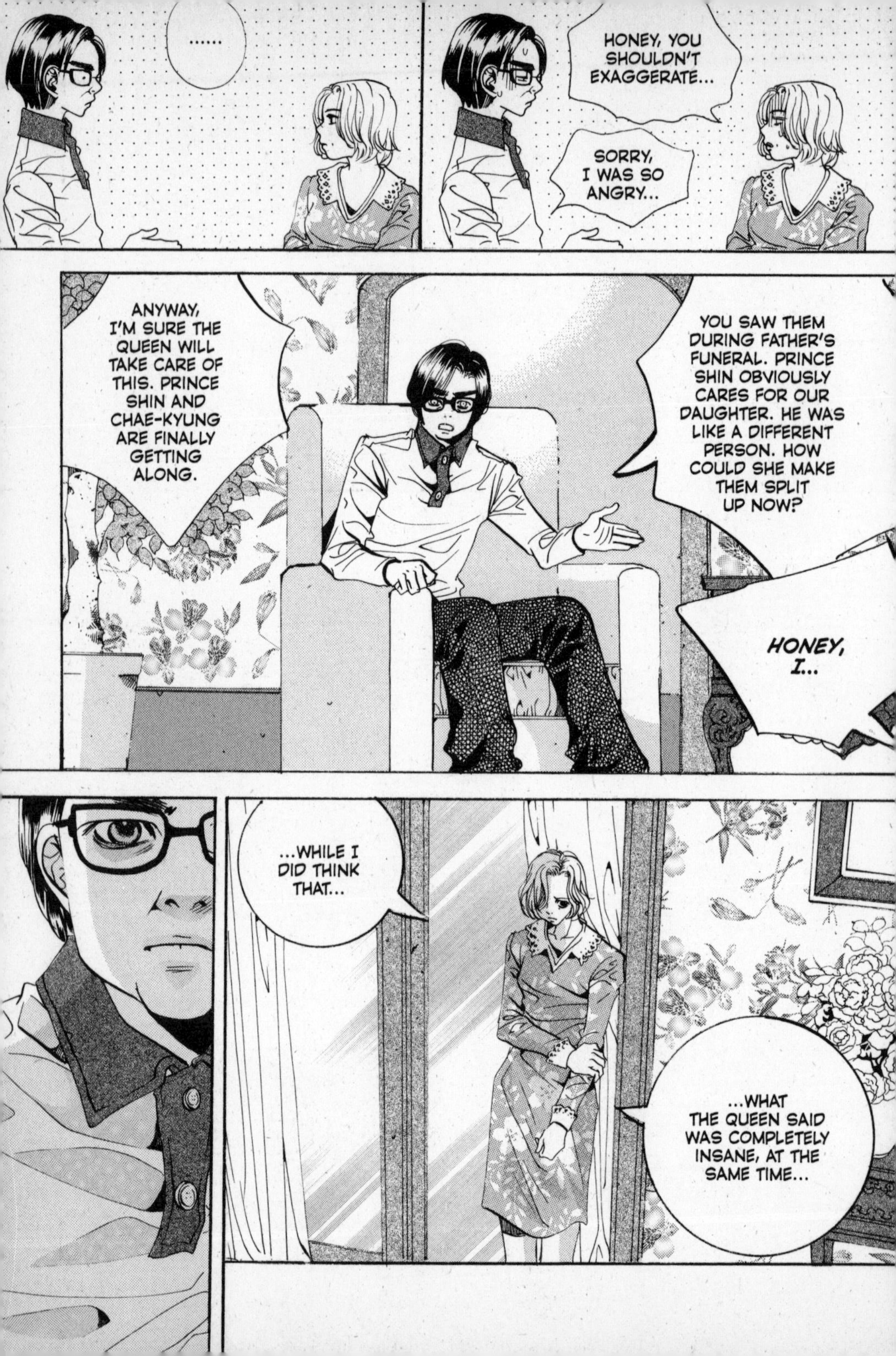
......
HONEY, YOU SHOULDN'T EXAGGERATE...
SORRY, I WAS SO ANGRY...
ANYWAY, I'M SURE THE QUEEN WILL TAKE CARE OF THIS. PRINCE SHIN AND CHAE-KYUNG ARE FINALLY GETTING ALONG.
YOU SAW THEM DURING FATHER'S FUNERAL. PRINCE SHIN OBVIOUSLY CARES FOR OUR DAUGHTER. HE WAS LIKE A DIFFERENT PERSON. HOW COULD SHE MAKE THEM SPLIT UP NOW?
HONEY, I...
...WHILE I DID THINK THAT...
...WHAT THE QUEEN SAID WAS COMPLETELY INSANE, AT THE SAME TIME...

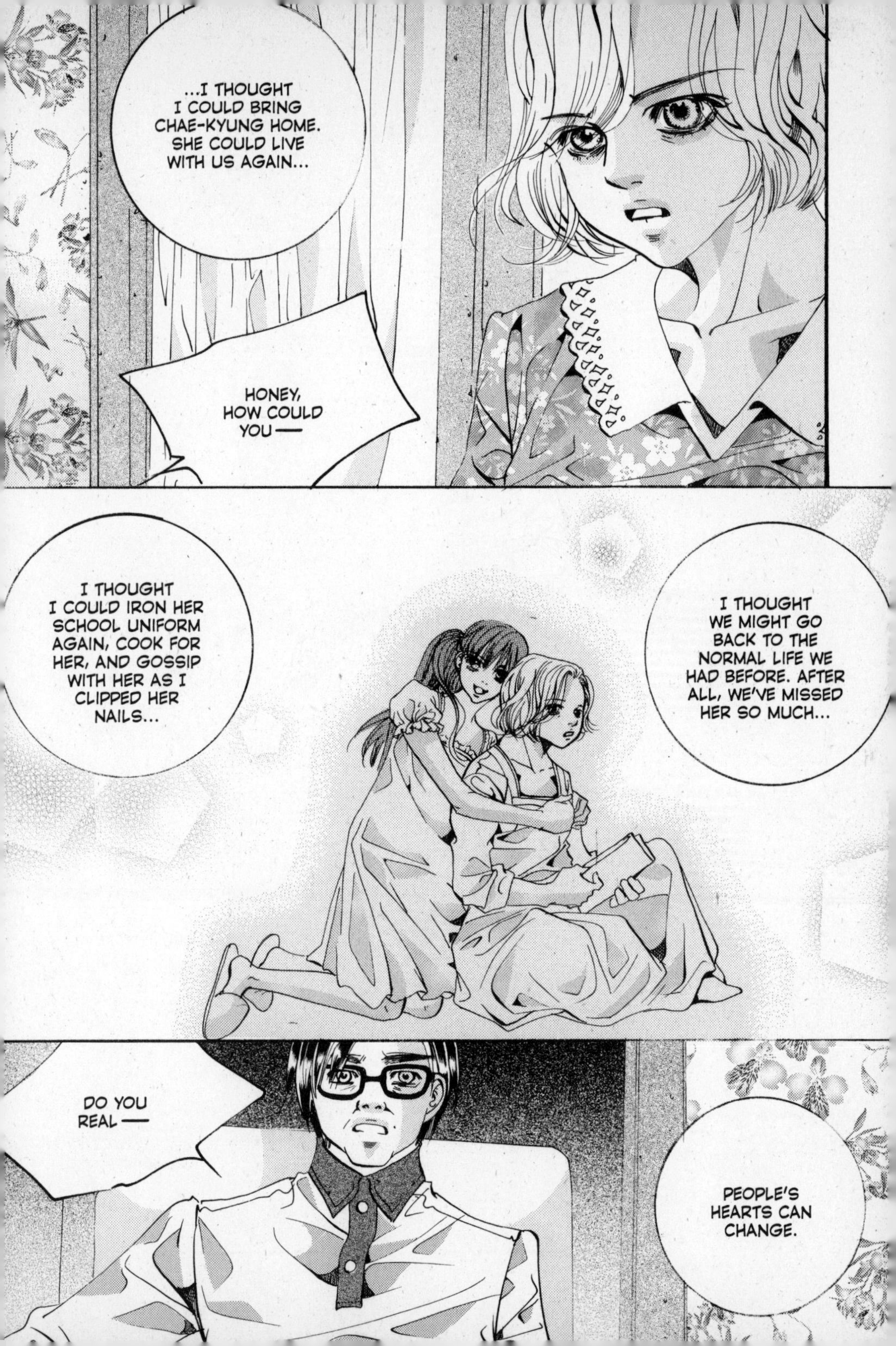
...I THOUGHT I COULD BRING CHAE-KYUNG HOME. SHE COULD LIVE WITH US AGAIN...
HONEY, HOW COULD YOU—
I THOUGHT I COULD IRON HER SCHOOL UNIFORM AGAIN, COOK FOR HER, AND GOSSIP WITH HER AS I CLIPPED HER NAILS...
I THOUGHT WE MIGHT GO BACK TO THE NORMAL LIFE WE HAD BEFORE. AFTER ALL, WE'VE MISSED HER SO MUCH...
DO YOU REAL—
PEOPLE'S HEARTS CAN CHANGE.

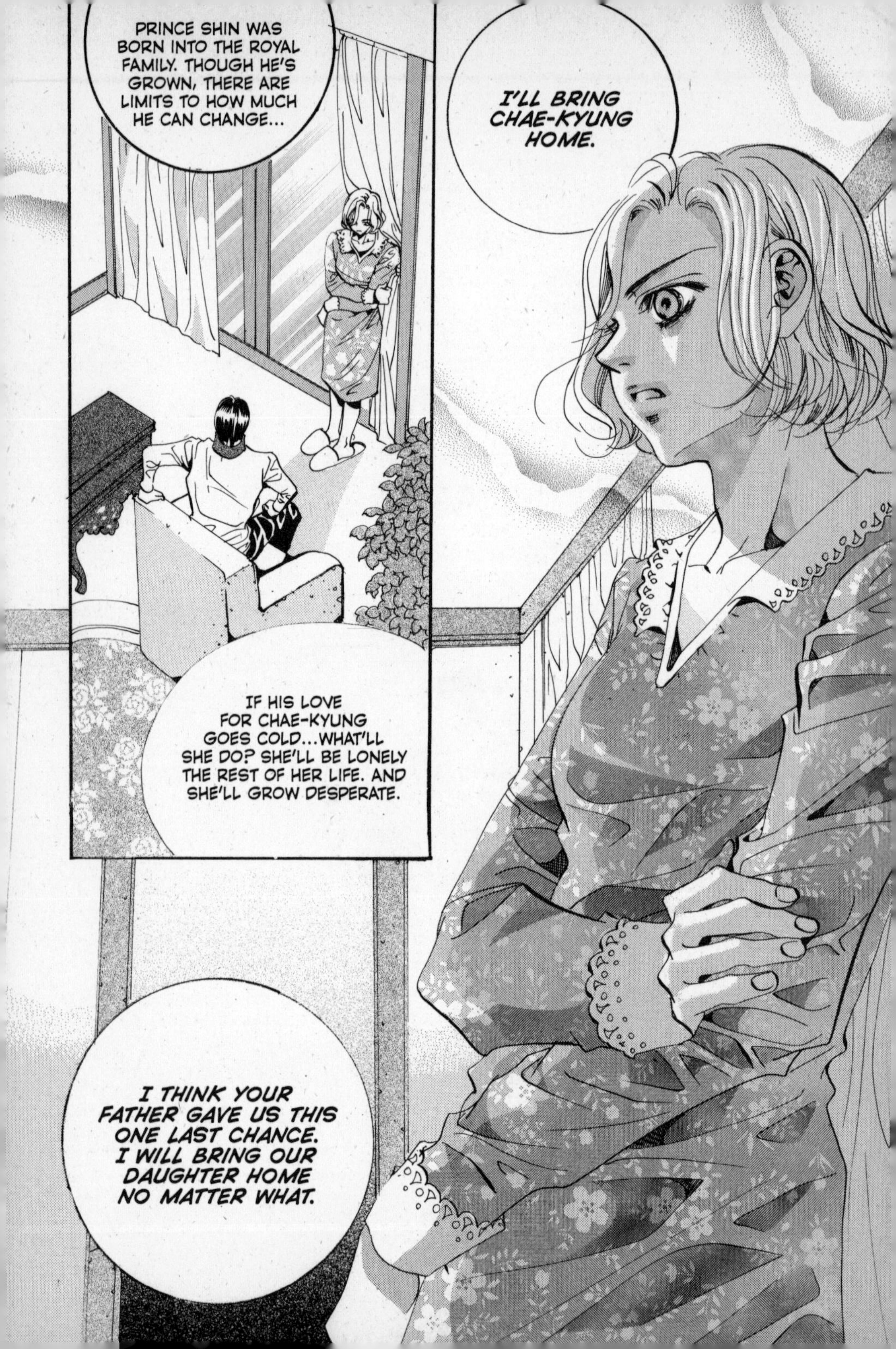
PRINCE SHIN WAS BORN INTO THE ROYAL FAMILY. THOUGH HE'S GROWN, THERE ARE LIMITS TO HOW MUCH HE CAN CHANGE...
IF HIS LOVE FOR CHAE-KYUNG GOES COLD...WHAT'LL SHE DO? SHE'LL BE LONELY THE REST OF HER LIFE. AND SHE'LL GROW DESPERATE.
I'LL BRING CHAE-KYUNG HOME.
I THINK YOUR FATHER GAVE US THIS ONE LAST CHANCE. I WILL BRING OUR DAUGHTER HOME NO MATTER WHAT.

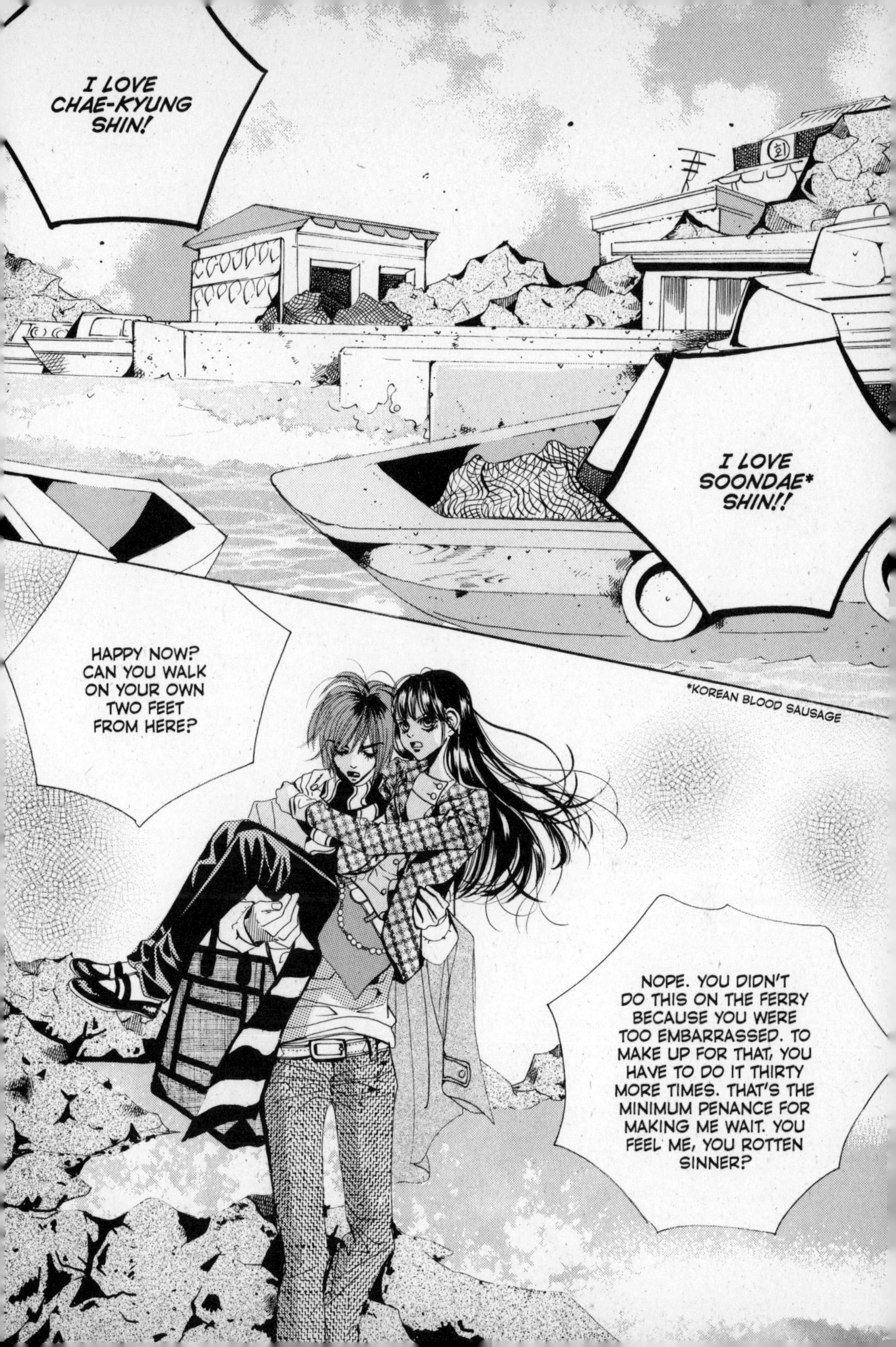
I LOVE CHAE-KYUNG SHIN!
I LOVE SOONDAE* SHIN!!
*KOREAN BLOOD SAUSAGE
HAPPY NOW? CAN YOU WALK ON YOUR OWN TWO FEET FROM HERE?
NOPE. YOU DIDN'T DO THIS ON THE FERRY BECAUSE YOU WERE TOO EMBARRASSED. TO MAKE UP FOR THAT, YOU HAVE TO DO IT THIRTY MORE TIMES. THAT'S THE MINIMUM PENANCE FOR MAKING ME WAIT. YOU FEEL ME, YOU ROTTEN SINNER?

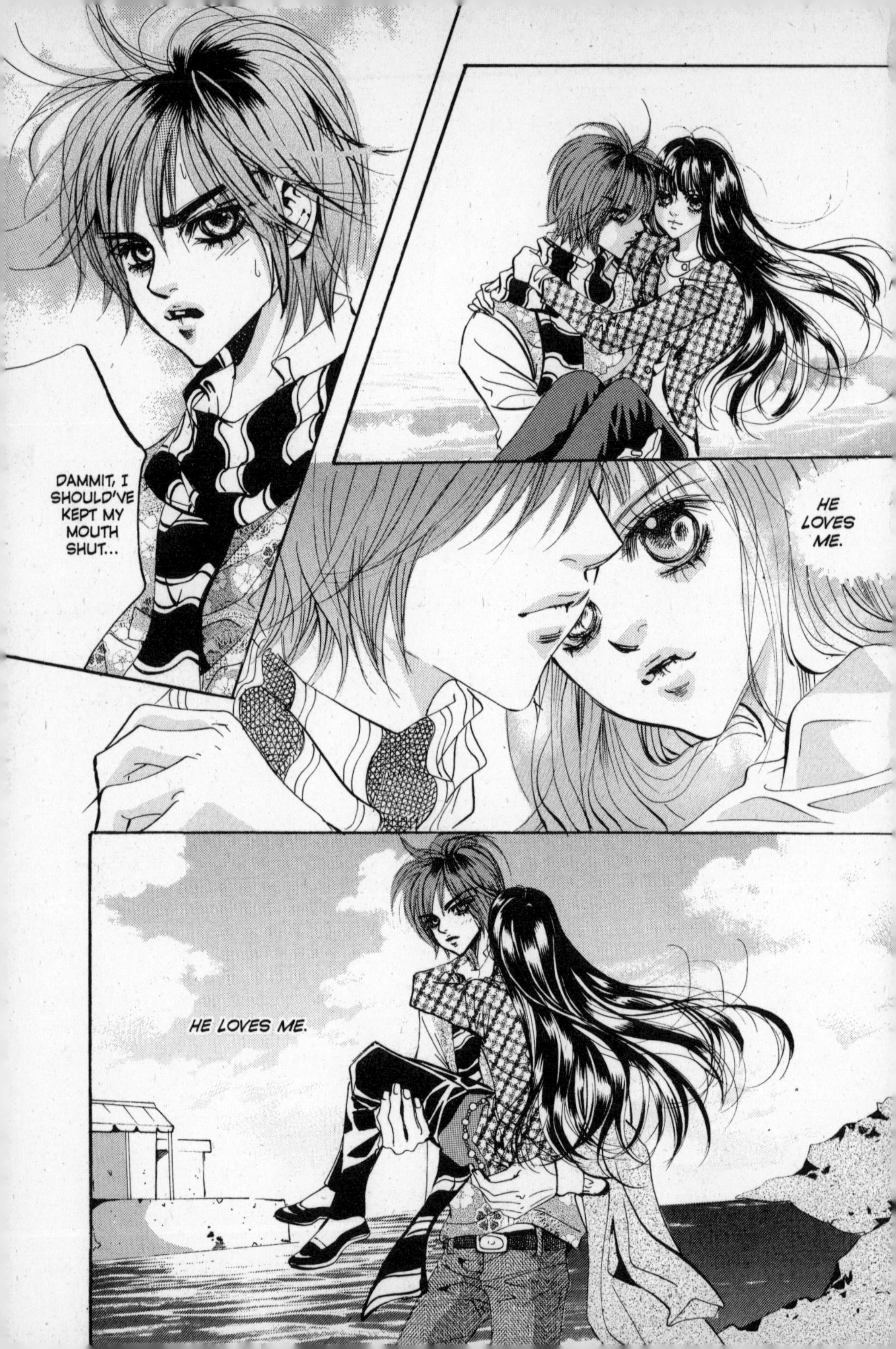
DAMMIT, I SHOULD'VE KEPT MY MOUTH SHUT...
HE LOVES ME.
HE LOVES ME.

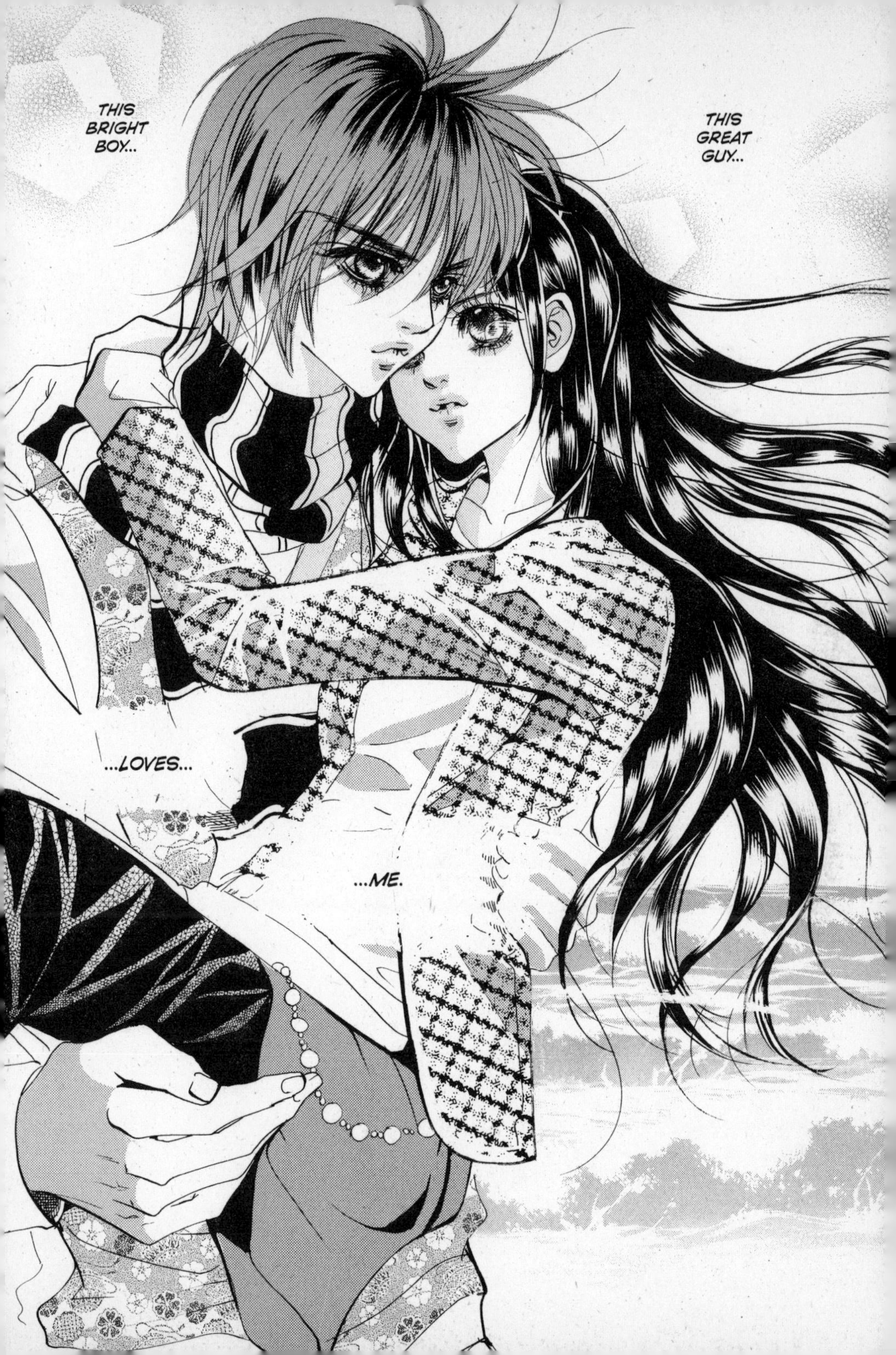
THIS BRIGHT BOY...
THIS GREAT GUY...
...LOVES...
...ME.

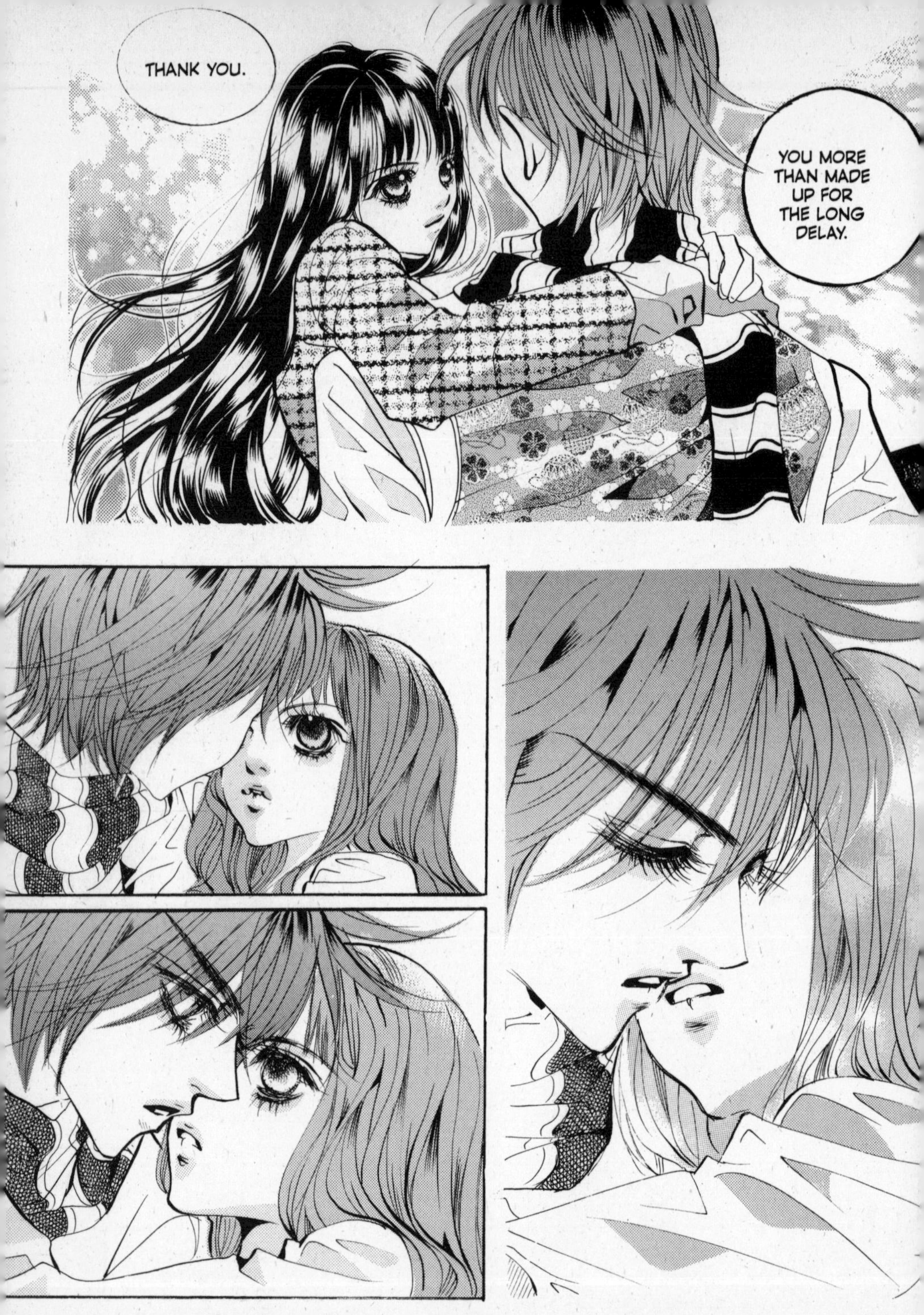
THANK YOU.
YOU MORE THAN MADE UP FOR THE LONG DELAY.

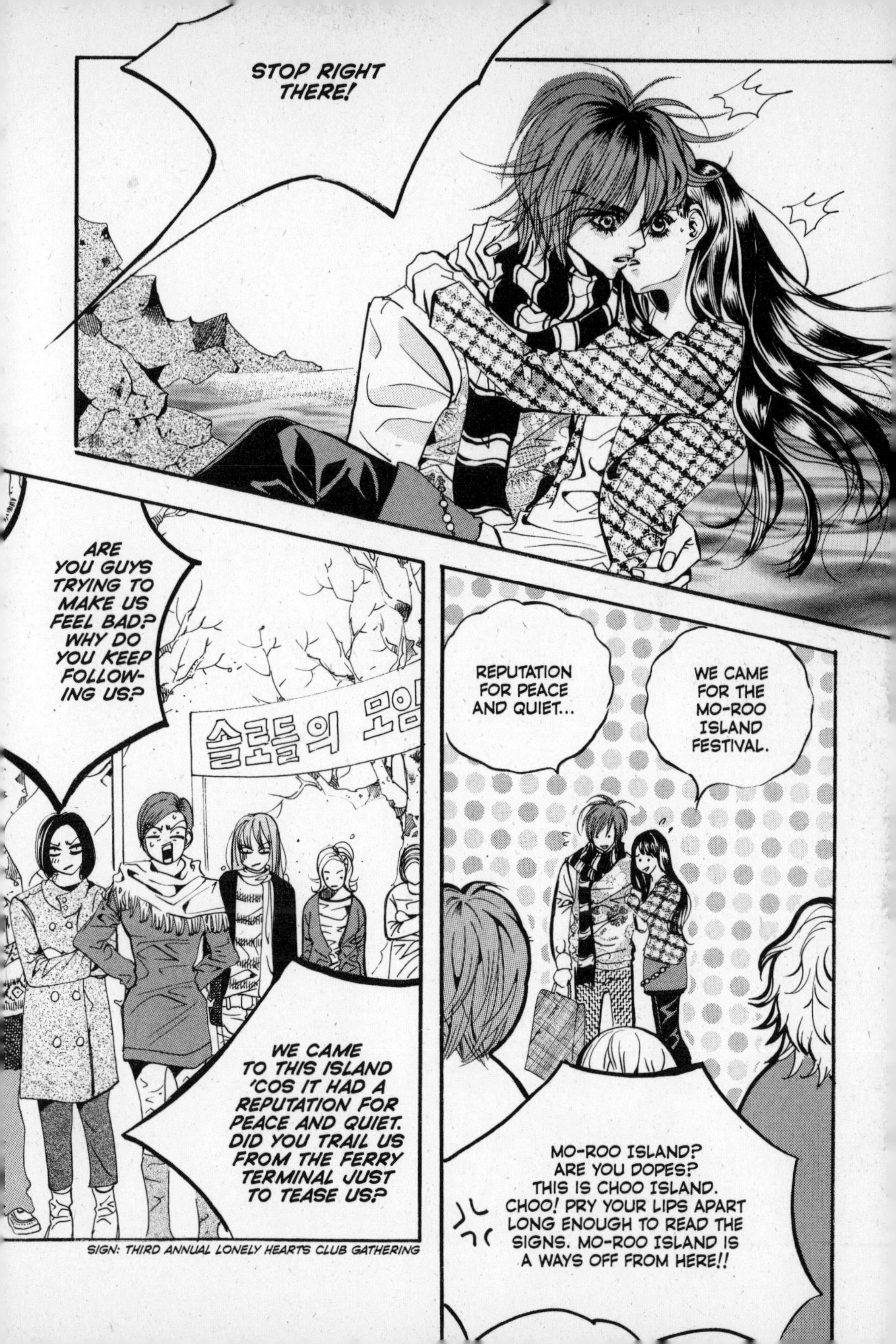
STOP RIGHT THERE!
ARE YOU GUYS TRYING TO MAKE US FEEL BAD? WHY DO YOU KEEP FOLLOW-ING US?
솔로들의 모임
WE CAME TO THIS ISLAND 'COS IT HAD A REPUTATION FOR PEACE AND QUIET. DID YOU TRAIL US FROM THE FERRY TERMINAL JUST TO TEASE US?
SIGN: THIRD ANNUAL LONELY HEARTS CLUB GATHERING
REPUTATION FOR PEACE AND QUIET...
WE CAME FOR THE MO-ROO ISLAND FESTIVAL.
MO-ROO ISLAND? ARE YOU DOPES? THIS IS CHOO ISLAND. CHOO! PRY YOUR LIPS APART LONG ENOUGH TO READ THE SIGNS. MO-ROO ISLAND IS A WAYS OFF FROM HERE!!

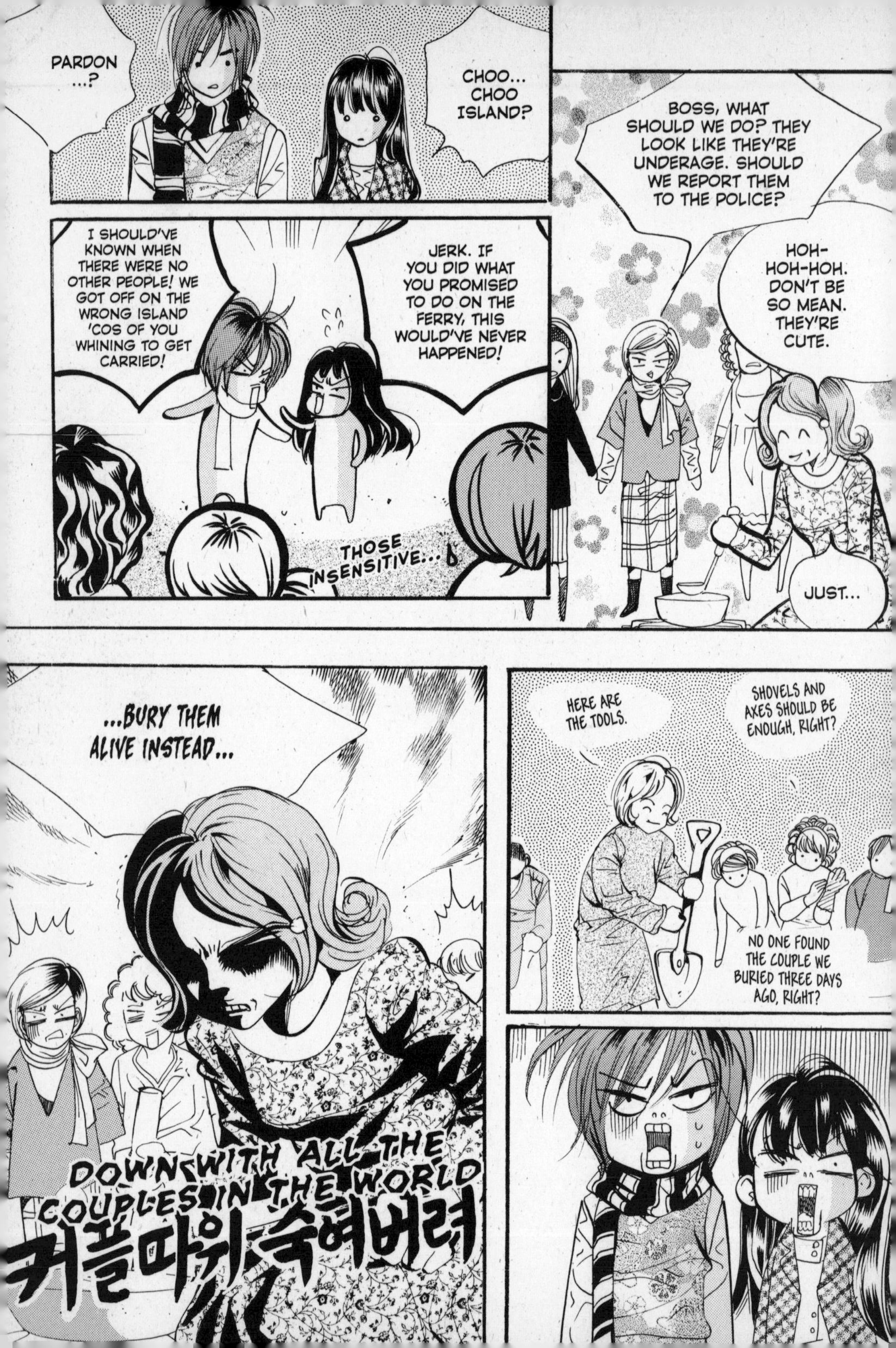
PARDON ...?
CHOO... CHOO ISLAND?
I SHOULD'VE KNOWN WHEN THERE WERE NO OTHER PEOPLE! WE GOT OFF ON THE WRONG ISLAND 'COS OF YOU WHINING TO GET CARRIED!
JERK. IF YOU DID WHAT YOU PROMISED TO DO ON THE FERRY, THIS WOULD'VE NEVER HAPPENED!
THOSE INSENSITIVE...
BOSS, WHAT SHOULD WE DO? THEY LOOK LIKE THEY'RE UNDERAGE. SHOULD WE REPORT THEM TO THE POLICE?
HOH-HOH-HOH. DON'T BE SO MEAN. THEY'RE CUTE.
JUST...
...BURY THEM ALIVE INSTEAD...
DOWN WITH ALL THE COUPLES IN THE WORLD
커플따위 죽여버려
HERE ARE THE TOOLS.
SHOVELS AND AXES SHOULD BE ENOUGH, RIGHT?
NO ONE FOUND THE COUPLE WE BURIED THREE DAYS AGO, RIGHT?

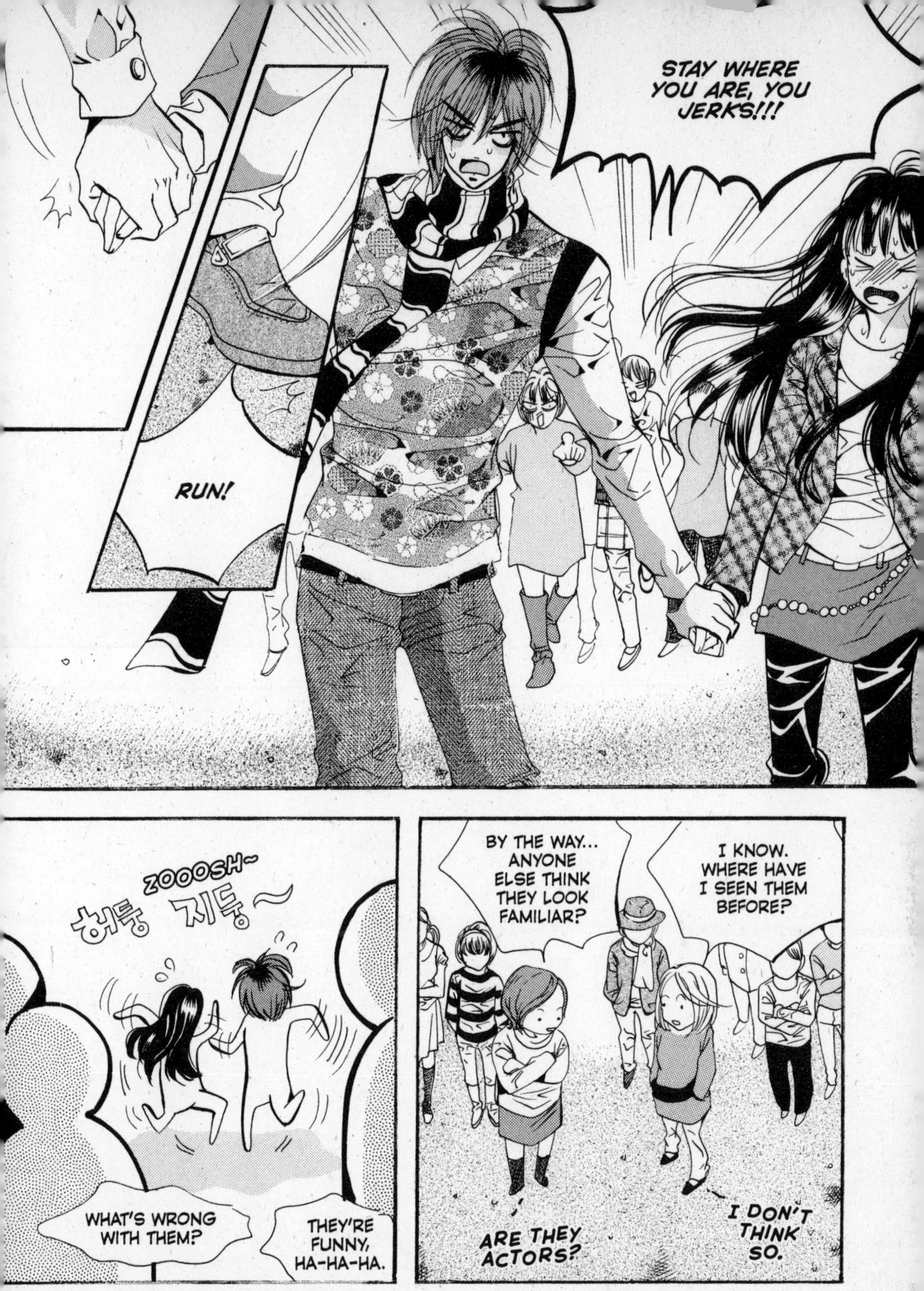
RUN!
STAY WHERE YOU ARE, YOU JERKS!!!
ZOOOSH~
허둥 지둥~
WHAT'S WRONG WITH THEM?
THEY'RE FUNNY, HA-HA-HA.
BY THE WAY... ANYONE ELSE THINK THEY LOOK FAMILIAR?
I KNOW. WHERE HAVE I SEEN THEM BEFORE?
ARE THEY ACTORS?
I DON'T THINK SO.

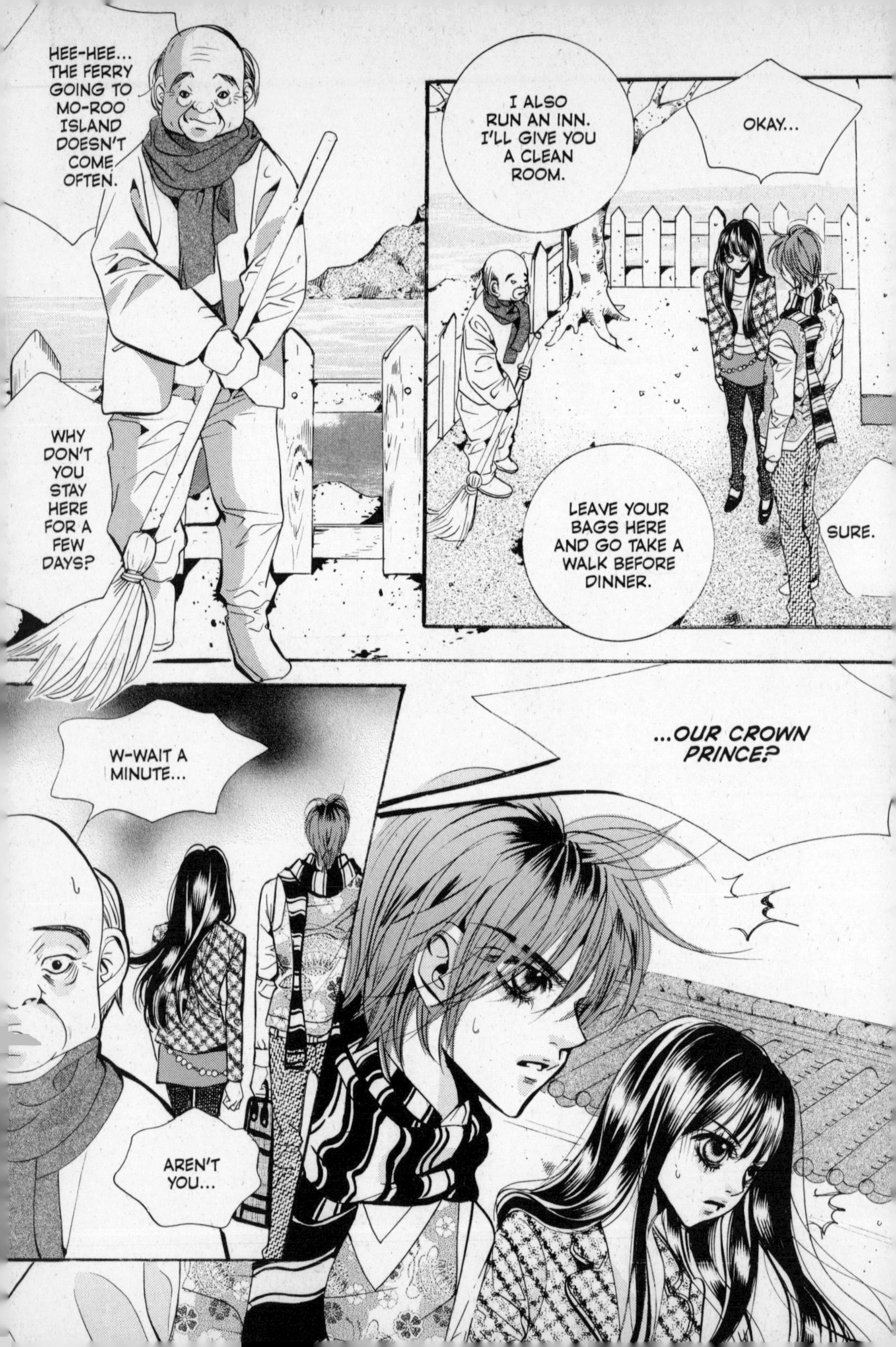
HEE-HEE... THE FERRY GOING TO MO-ROO ISLAND DOESN'T COME OFTEN.
WHY DON'T YOU STAY HERE FOR A FEW DAYS?
I ALSO RUN AN INN. I'LL GIVE YOU A CLEAN ROOM.
OKAY...
LEAVE YOUR BAGS HERE AND GO TAKE A WALK BEFORE DINNER.
SURE.
W-WAIT A MINUTE...
AREN'T YOU...
...OUR CROWN PRINCE?

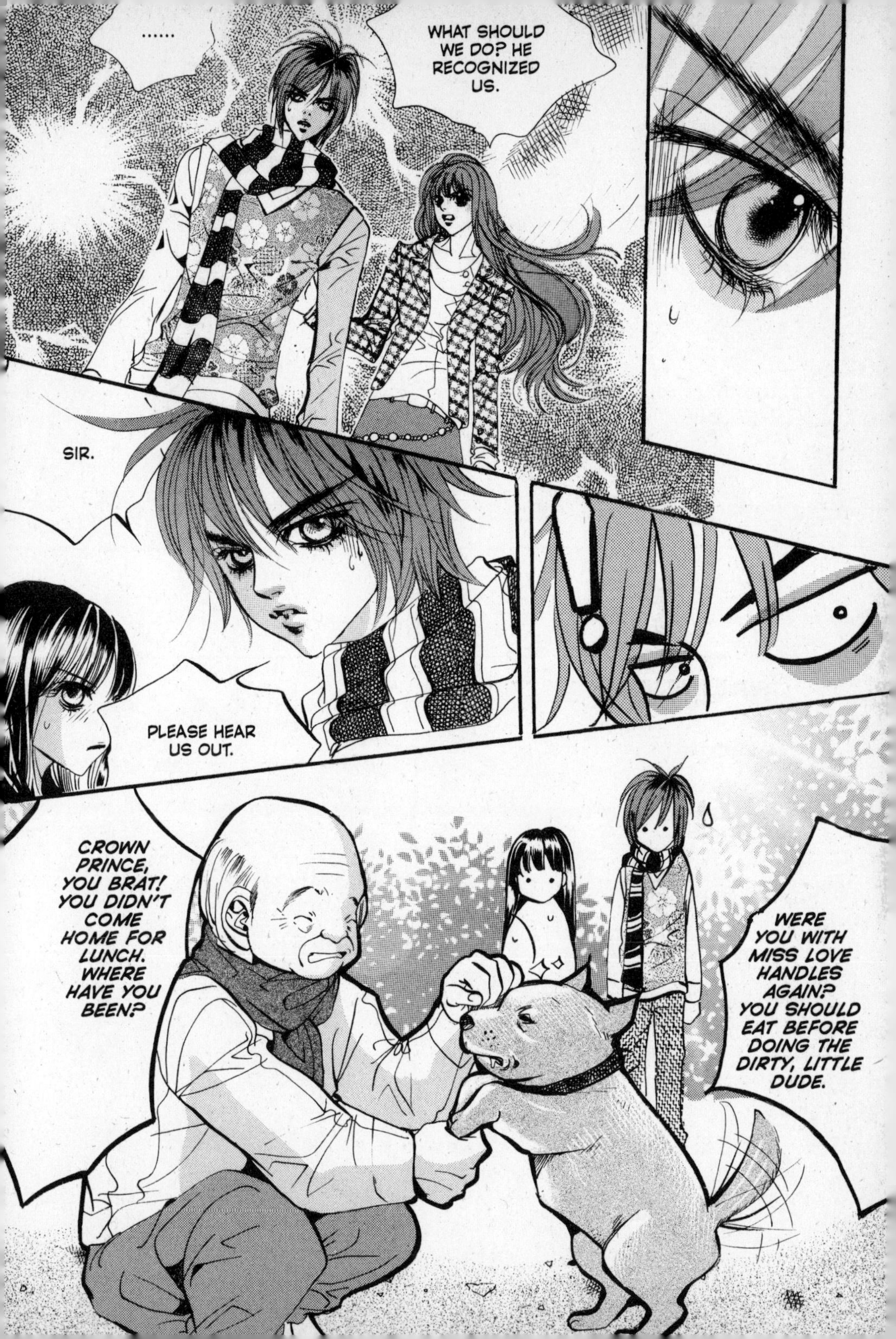
......
WHAT SHOULD WE DO? HE RECOGNIZED US.
SIR.
PLEASE HEAR US OUT.
CROWN PRINCE, YOU BRAT! YOU DIDN'T COME HOME FOR LUNCH. WHERE HAVE YOU BEEN?
WERE YOU WITH MISS LOVE HANDLES AGAIN? YOU SHOULD EAT BEFORE DOING THE DIRTY, LITTLE DUDE.

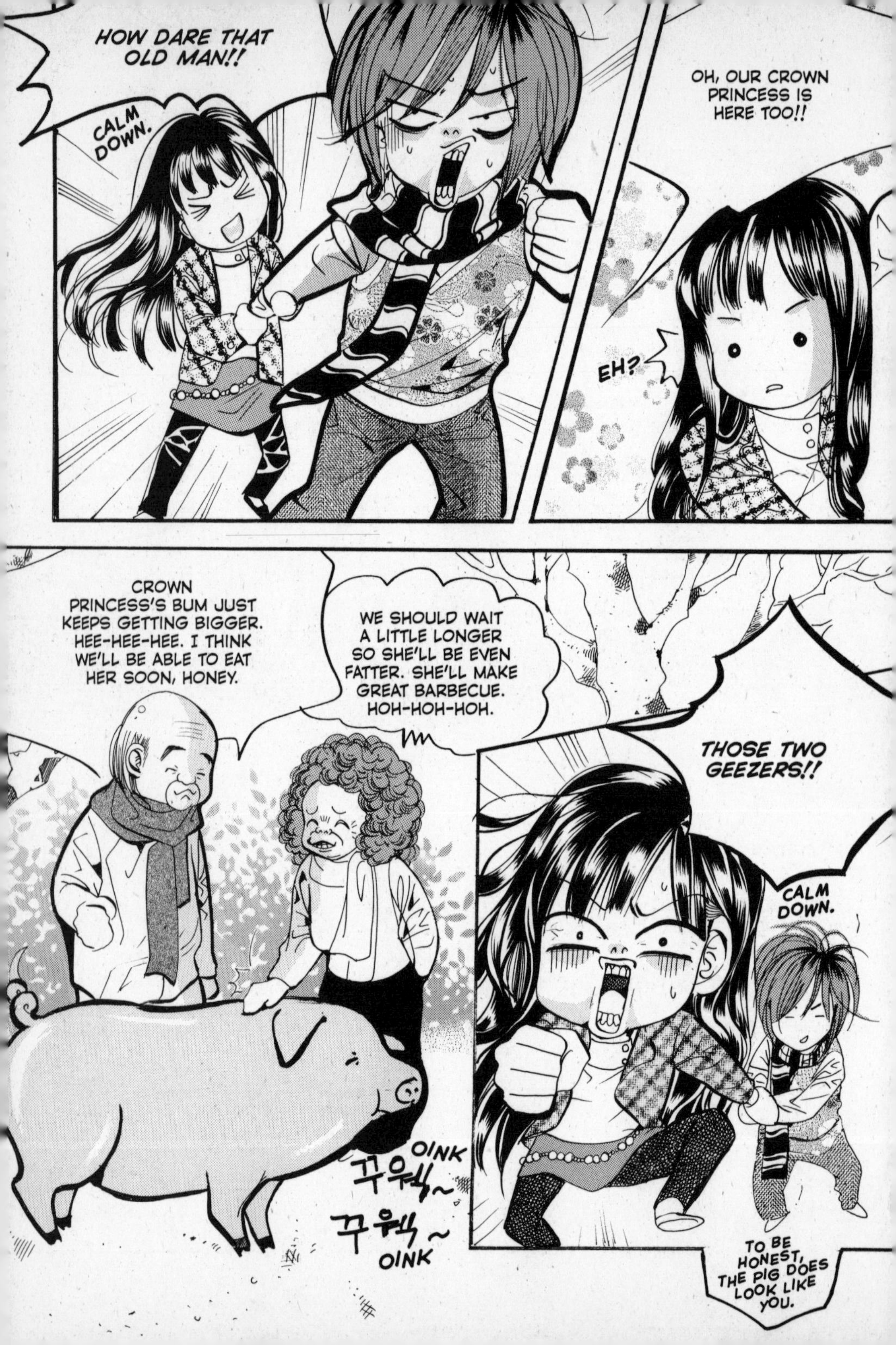
HOW DARE THAT OLD MAN!!
CALM DOWN.
OH, OUR CROWN PRINCESS IS HERE TOO!!
EH?
CROWN PRINCESS'S BUM JUST KEEPS GETTING BIGGER. HEE-HEE-HEE. I THINK WE'LL BE ABLE TO EAT HER SOON, HONEY.
WE SHOULD WAIT A LITTLE LONGER SO SHE'LL BE EVEN FATTER. SHE'LL MAKE GREAT BARBECUE. HOH-HOH-HOH.
OINK
꾸웩~
꾸웩~
OINK
THOSE TWO GEEZERS!!
CALM DOWN.
TO BE HONEST, THE PIG DOES LOOK LIKE YOU.

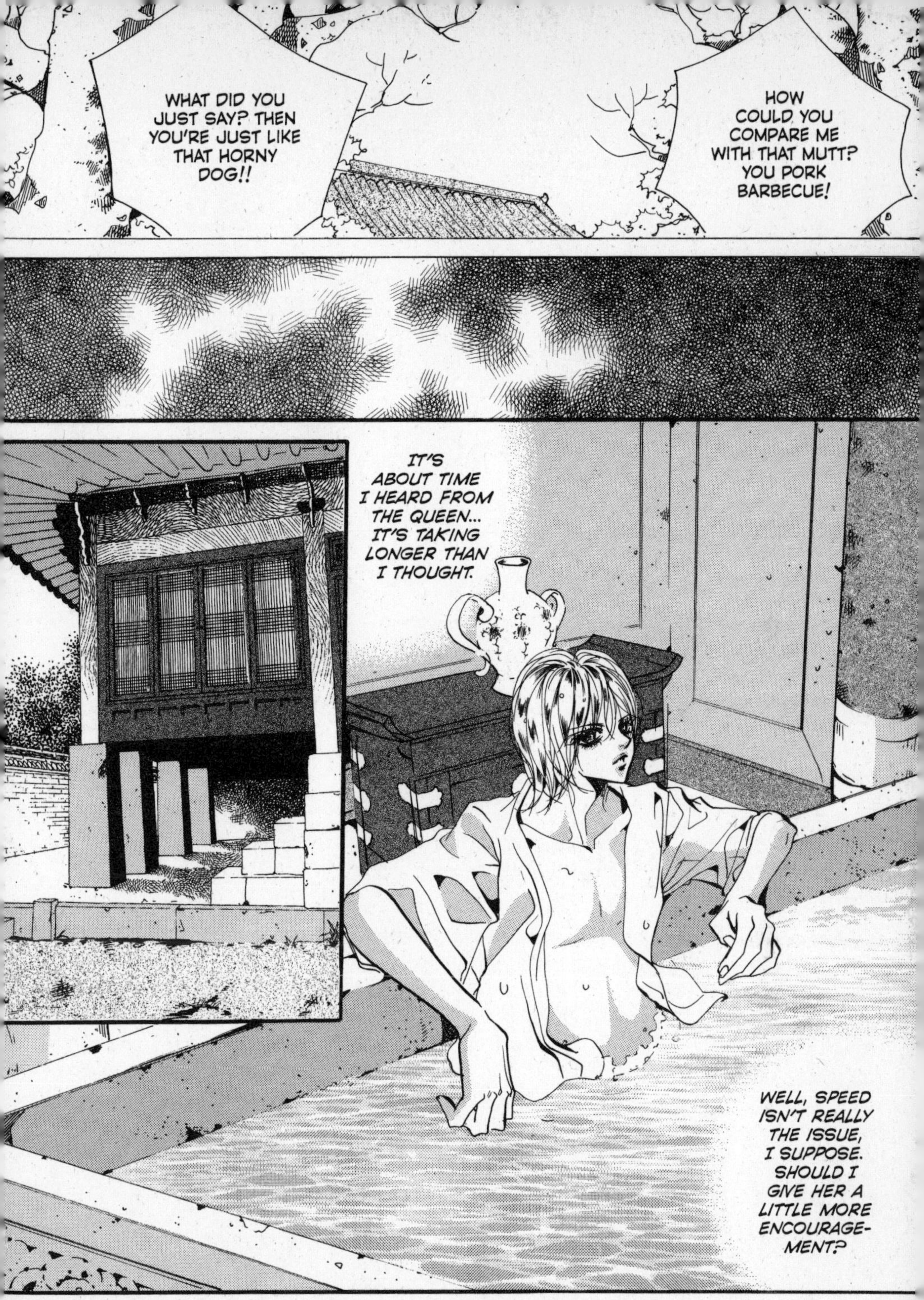
WHAT DID YOU JUST SAY? THEN YOU'RE JUST LIKE THAT HORNY DOG!!
HOW COULD YOU COMPARE ME WITH THAT MUTT? YOU PORK BARBECUE!
IT'S ABOUT TIME I HEARD FROM THE QUEEN... IT'S TAKING LONGER THAN I THOUGHT.
WELL, SPEED ISN'T REALLY THE ISSUE, I SUPPOSE. SHOULD I GIVE HER A LITTLE MORE ENCOURAGE-MENT?

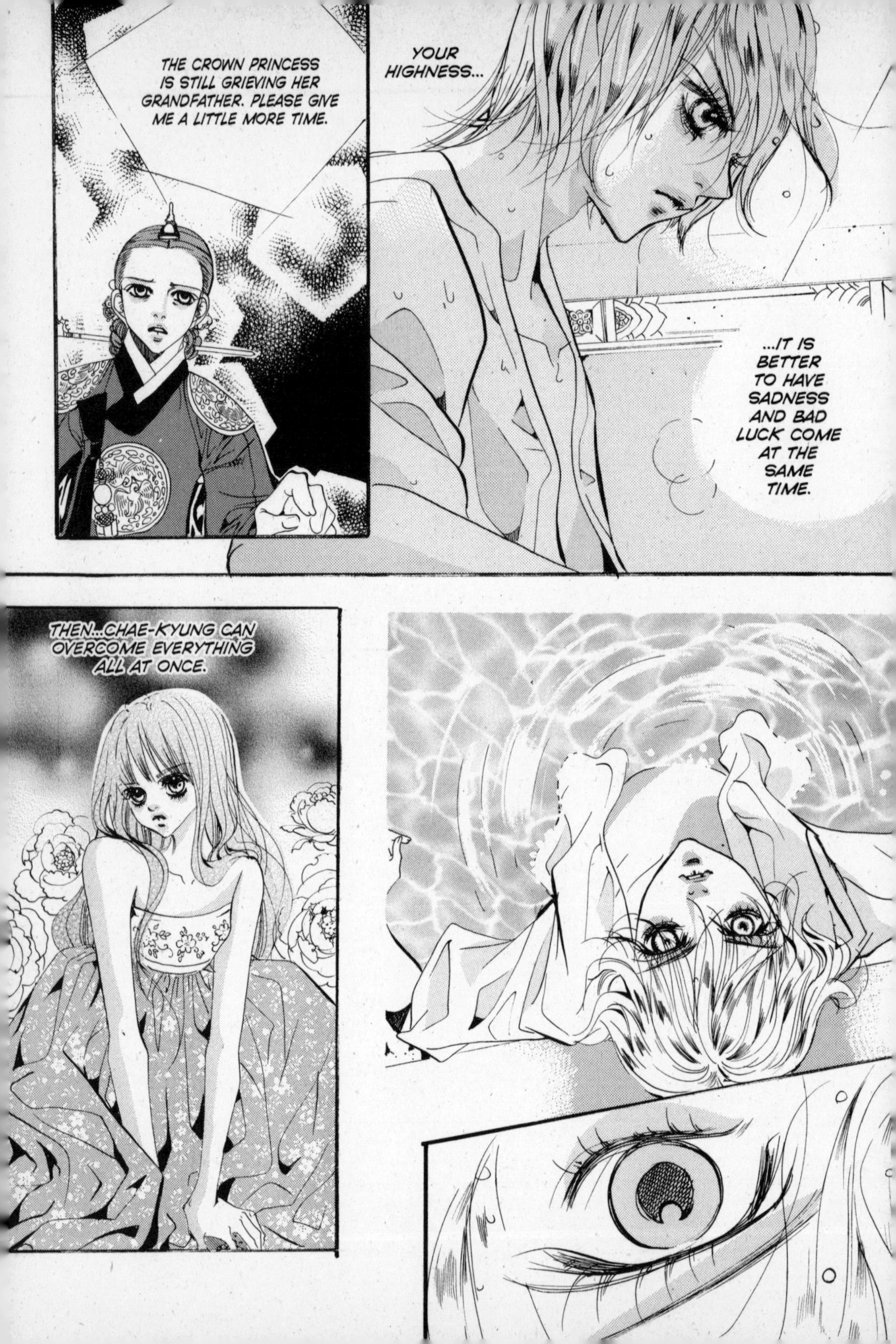
THE CROWN PRINCESS IS STILL GRIEVING HER GRANDFATHER. PLEASE GIVE ME A LITTLE MORE TIME.
YOUR HIGHNESS...
...IT IS BETTER TO HAVE SADNESS AND BAD LUCK COME AT THE SAME TIME.
THEN...CHAE-KYUNG CAN OVERCOME EVERYTHING ALL AT ONCE.

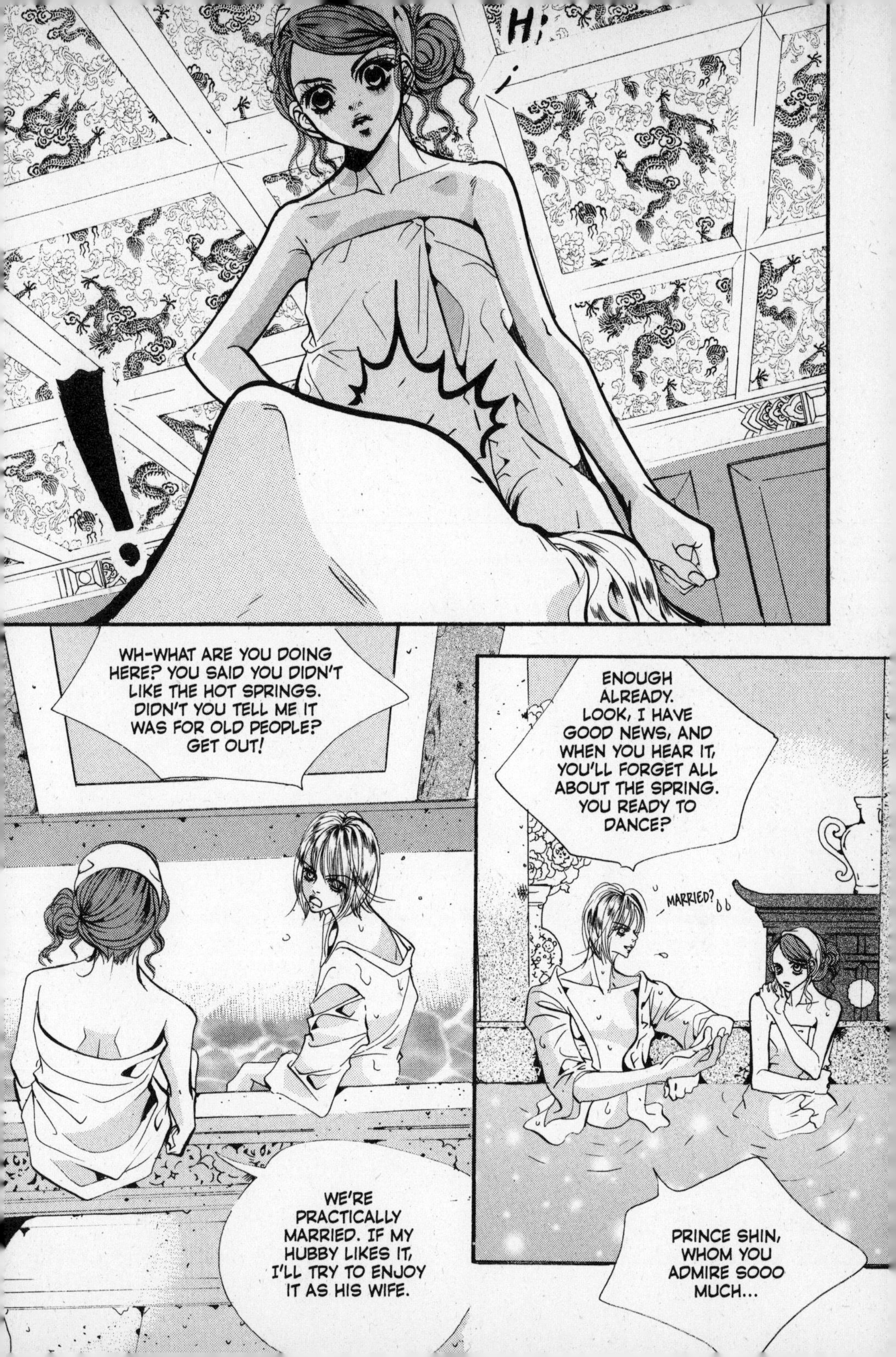
H!
WH-WHAT ARE YOU DOING HERE? YOU SAID YOU DIDN'T LIKE THE HOT SPRINGS. DIDN'T YOU TELL ME IT WAS FOR OLD PEOPLE? GET OUT!
WE'RE PRACTICALLY MARRIED. IF MY HUBBY LIKES IT, I'LL TRY TO ENJOY IT AS HIS WIFE.
ENOUGH ALREADY. LOOK, I HAVE GOOD NEWS, AND WHEN YOU HEAR IT, YOU'LL FORGET ALL ABOUT THE SPRING. YOU READY TO DANCE?
MARRIED?
PRINCE SHIN, WHOM YOU ADMIRE SOOO MUCH...

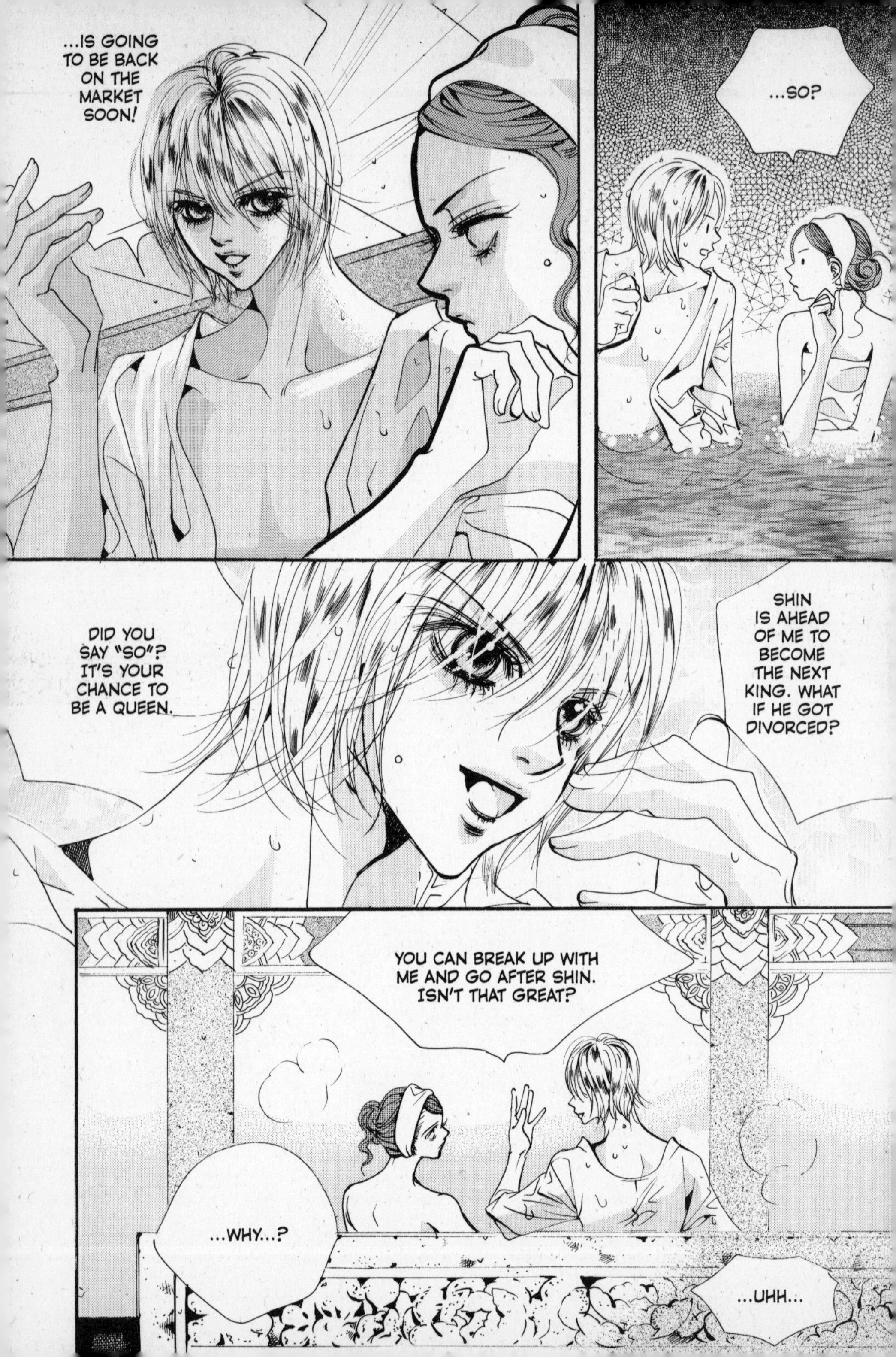
...IS GOING TO BE BACK ON THE MARKET SOON!
...SO?
DID YOU SAY "SO"? IT'S YOUR CHANCE TO BE A QUEEN.
SHIN IS AHEAD OF ME TO BECOME THE NEXT KING. WHAT IF HE GOT DIVORCED?
YOU CAN BREAK UP WITH ME AND GO AFTER SHIN. ISN'T THAT GREAT?
...WHY...?
...UHH...

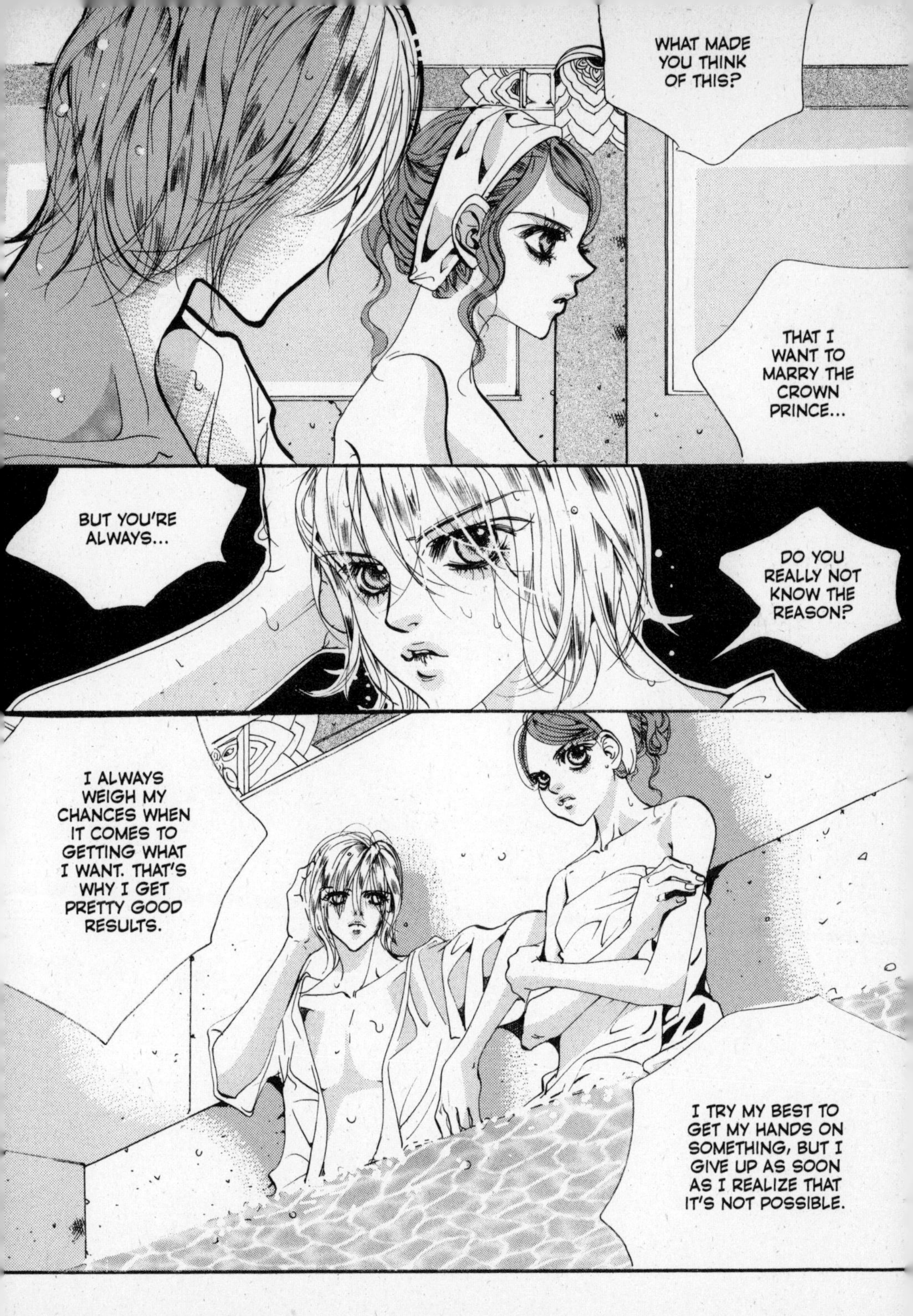
WHAT MADE YOU THINK OF THIS?
THAT I WANT TO MARRY THE CROWN PRINCE...
BUT YOU'RE ALWAYS...
DO YOU REALLY NOT KNOW THE REASON?
I ALWAYS WEIGH MY CHANCES WHEN IT COMES TO GETTING WHAT I WANT. THAT'S WHY I GET PRETTY GOOD RESULTS.
I TRY MY BEST TO GET MY HANDS ON SOMETHING, BUT I GIVE UP AS SOON AS I REALIZE THAT IT'S NOT POSSIBLE.

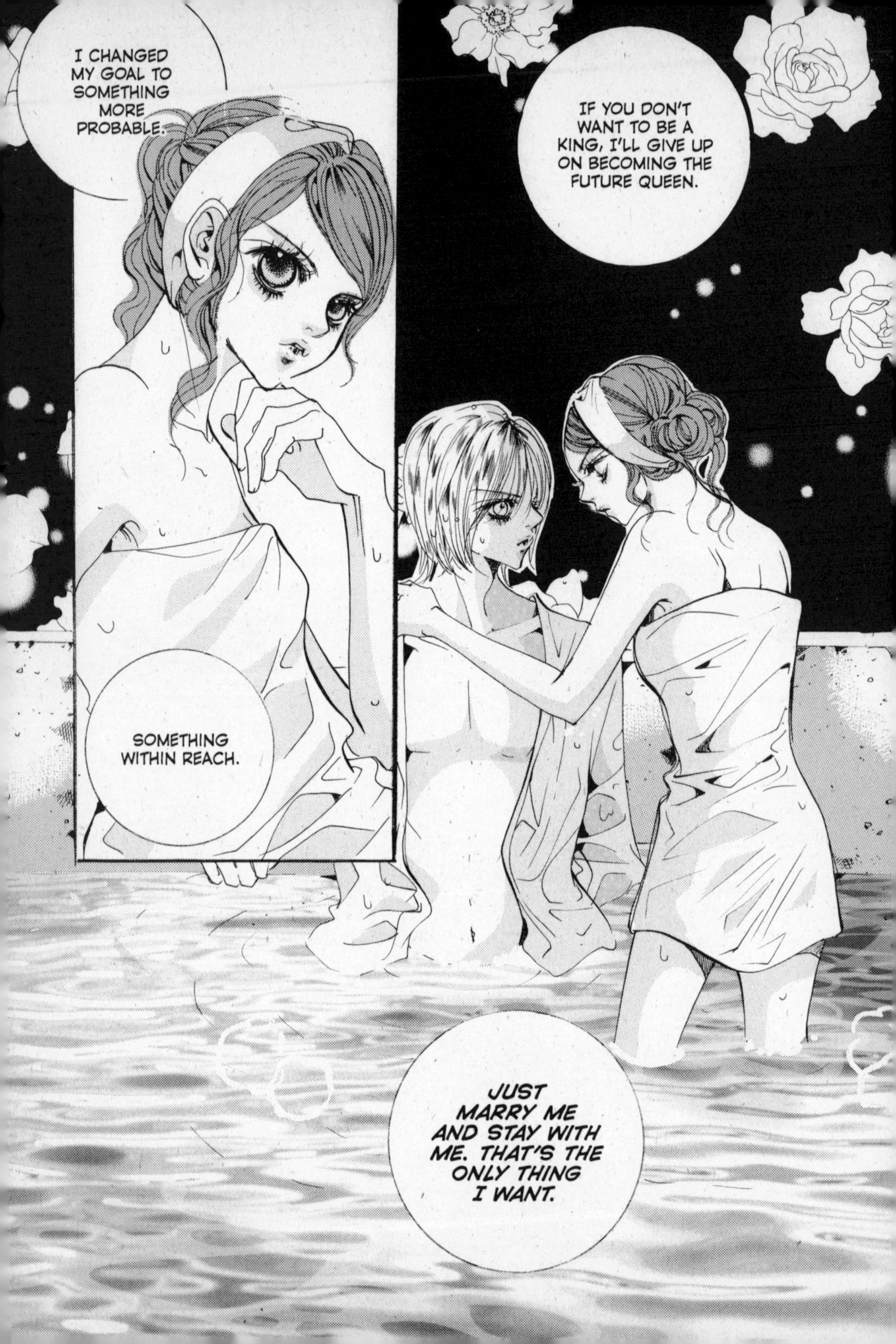
I CHANGED MY GOAL TO SOMETHING MORE PROBABLE.
SOMETHING WITHIN REACH.
IF YOU DON'T WANT TO BE A KING, I'LL GIVE UP ON BECOMING THE FUTURE QUEEN.
JUST MARRY ME AND STAY WITH ME. THAT'S THE ONLY THING I WANT.

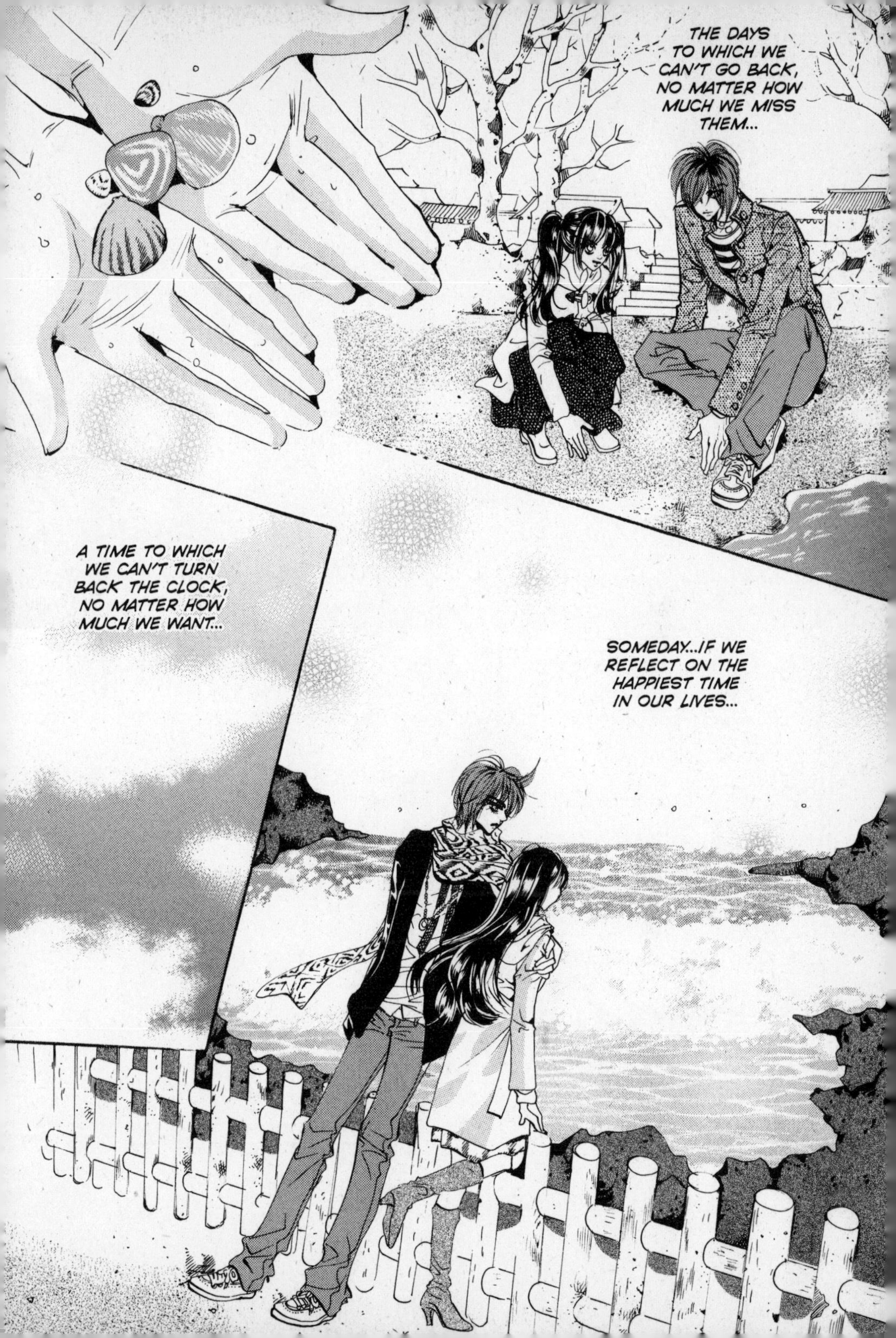
THE DAYS TO WHICH WE CAN'T GO BACK, NO MATTER HOW MUCH WE MISS THEM...
A TIME TO WHICH WE CAN'T TURN BACK THE CLOCK, NO MATTER HOW MUCH WE WANT...
SOMEDAY...IF WE REFLECT ON THE HAPPIEST TIME IN OUR LIVES...

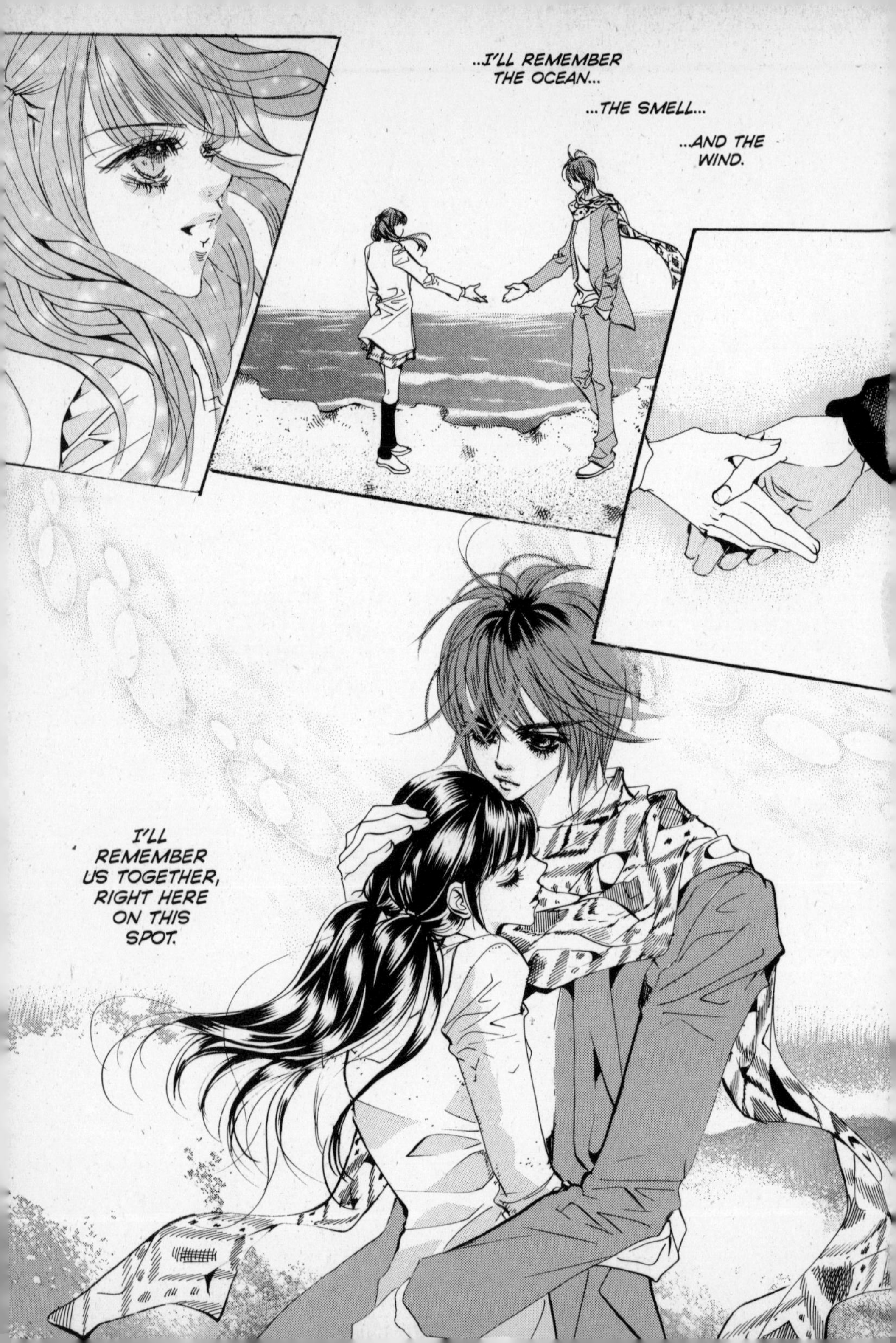
...I'LL REMEMBER THE OCEAN...
...THE SMELL...
...AND THE WIND.
I'LL REMEMBER US TOGETHER, RIGHT HERE ON THIS SPOT.

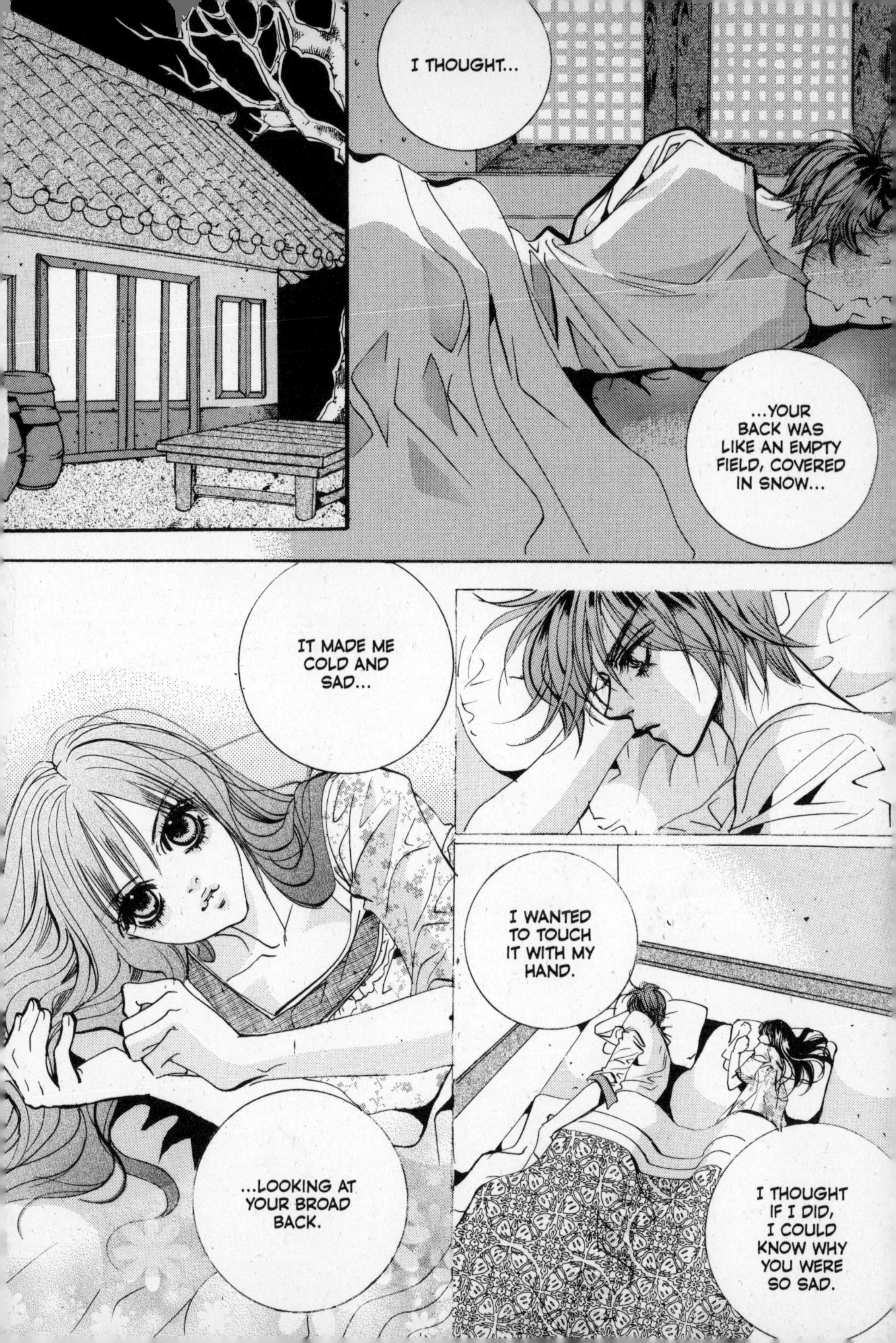
I THOUGHT...
...YOUR BACK WAS LIKE AN EMPTY FIELD, COVERED IN SNOW...
IT MADE ME COLD AND SAD...
...LOOKING AT YOUR BROAD BACK.
I WANTED TO TOUCH IT WITH MY HAND.
I THOUGHT IF I DID, I COULD KNOW WHY YOU WERE SO SAD.

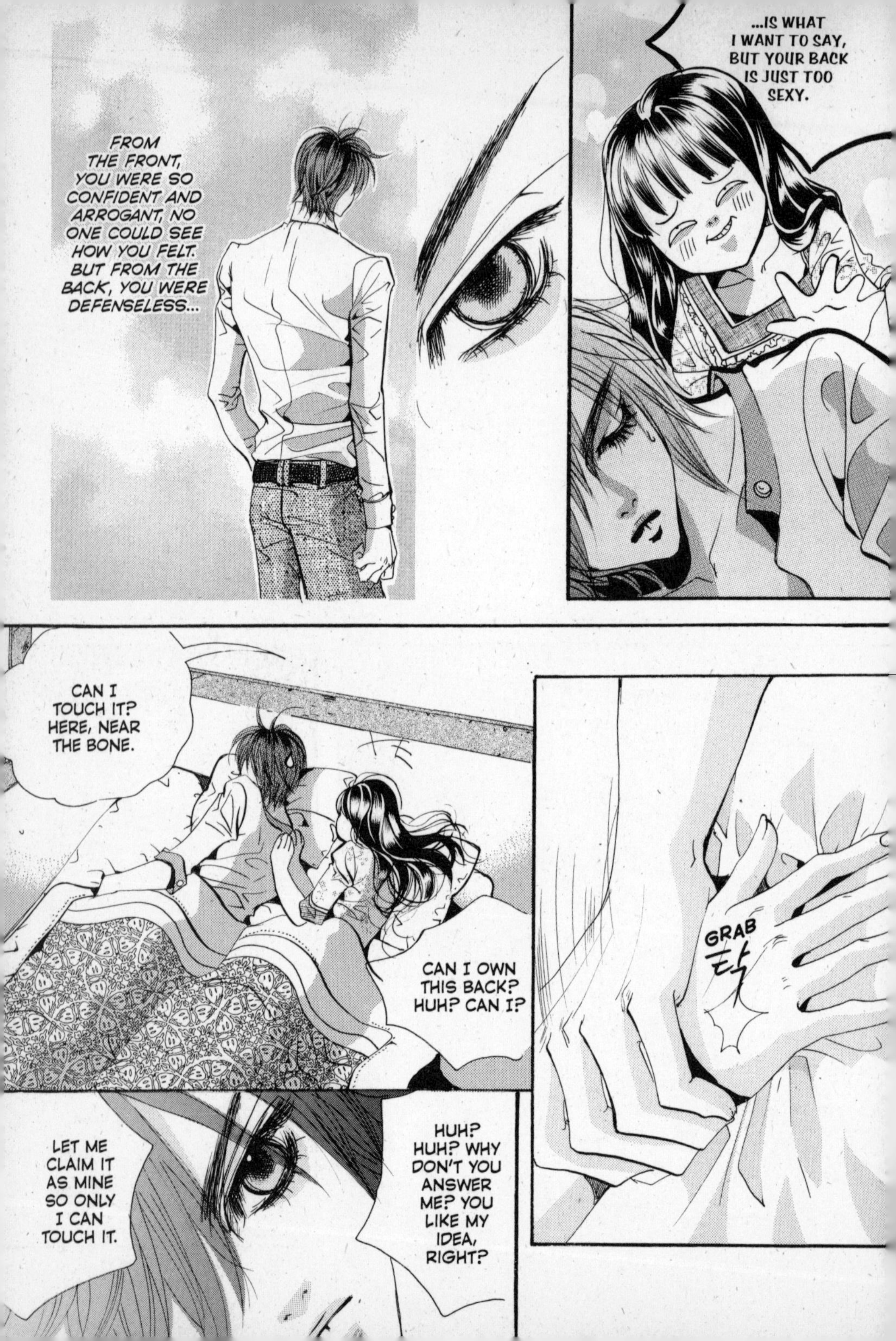
FROM THE FRONT, YOU WERE SO CONFIDENT AND ARROGANT, NO ONE COULD SEE HOW YOU FELT. BUT FROM THE BACK, YOU WERE DEFENSELESS...
...IS WHAT I WANT TO SAY, BUT YOUR BACK IS JUST TOO SEXY.
CAN I TOUCH IT? HERE, NEAR THE BONE.
CAN I OWN THIS BACK? HUH? CAN I?
LET ME CLAIM IT AS MINE SO ONLY I CAN TOUCH IT.
HUH? HUH? WHY DON'T YOU ANSWER ME? YOU LIKE MY IDEA, RIGHT?
GRAB
탁

BADUM BADUM.
BADUM BADUM.

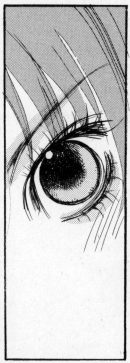

THE
REASON
I DIDN'T
WANT YOU
TO TOUCH
ME WAS...

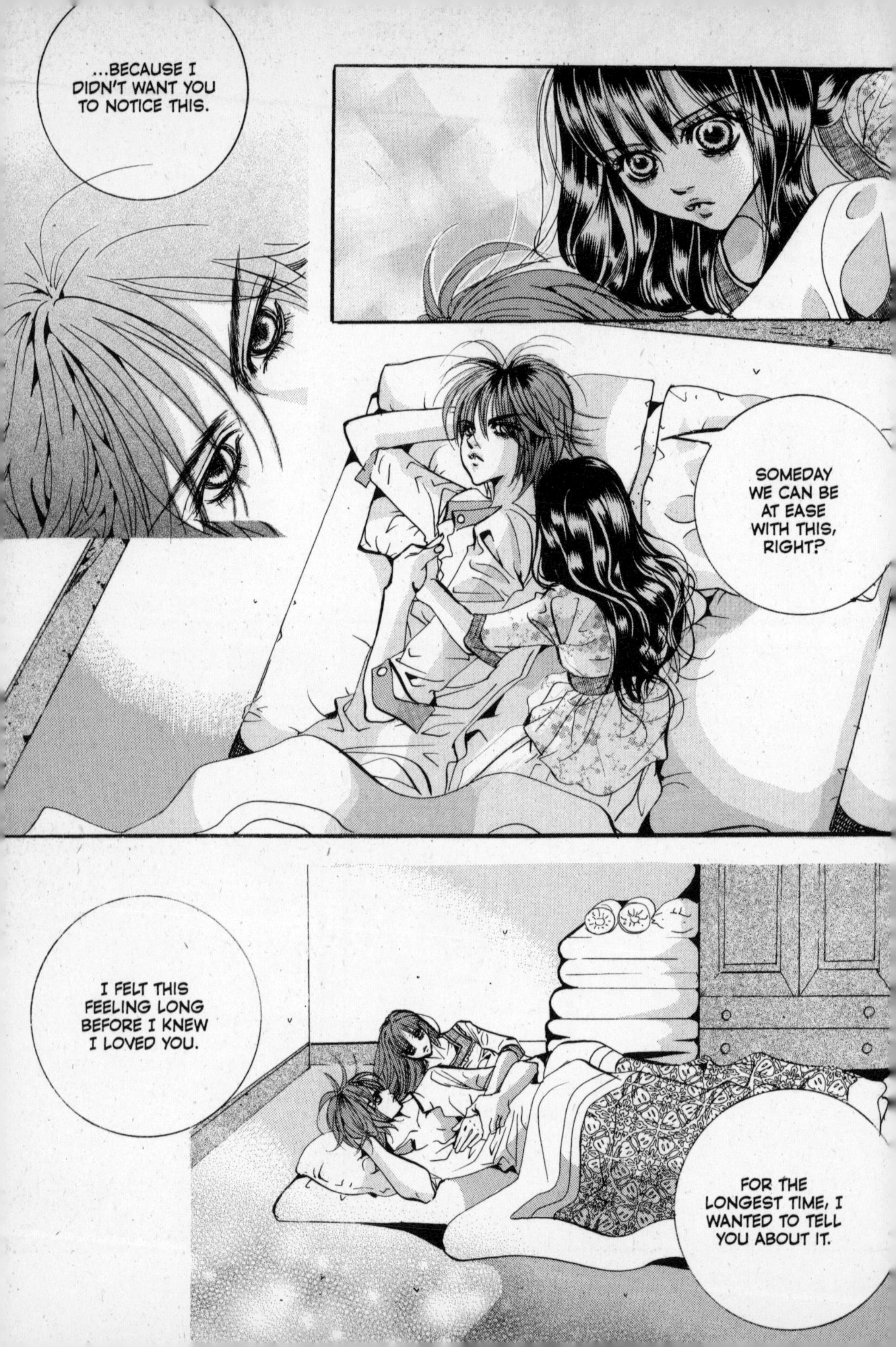
...BECAUSE I DIDN'T WANT YOU TO NOTICE THIS.
SOMEDAY WE CAN BE AT EASE WITH THIS, RIGHT?
I FELT THIS FEELING LONG BEFORE I KNEW I LOVED YOU.
FOR THE LONGEST TIME, I WANTED TO TELL YOU ABOUT IT.

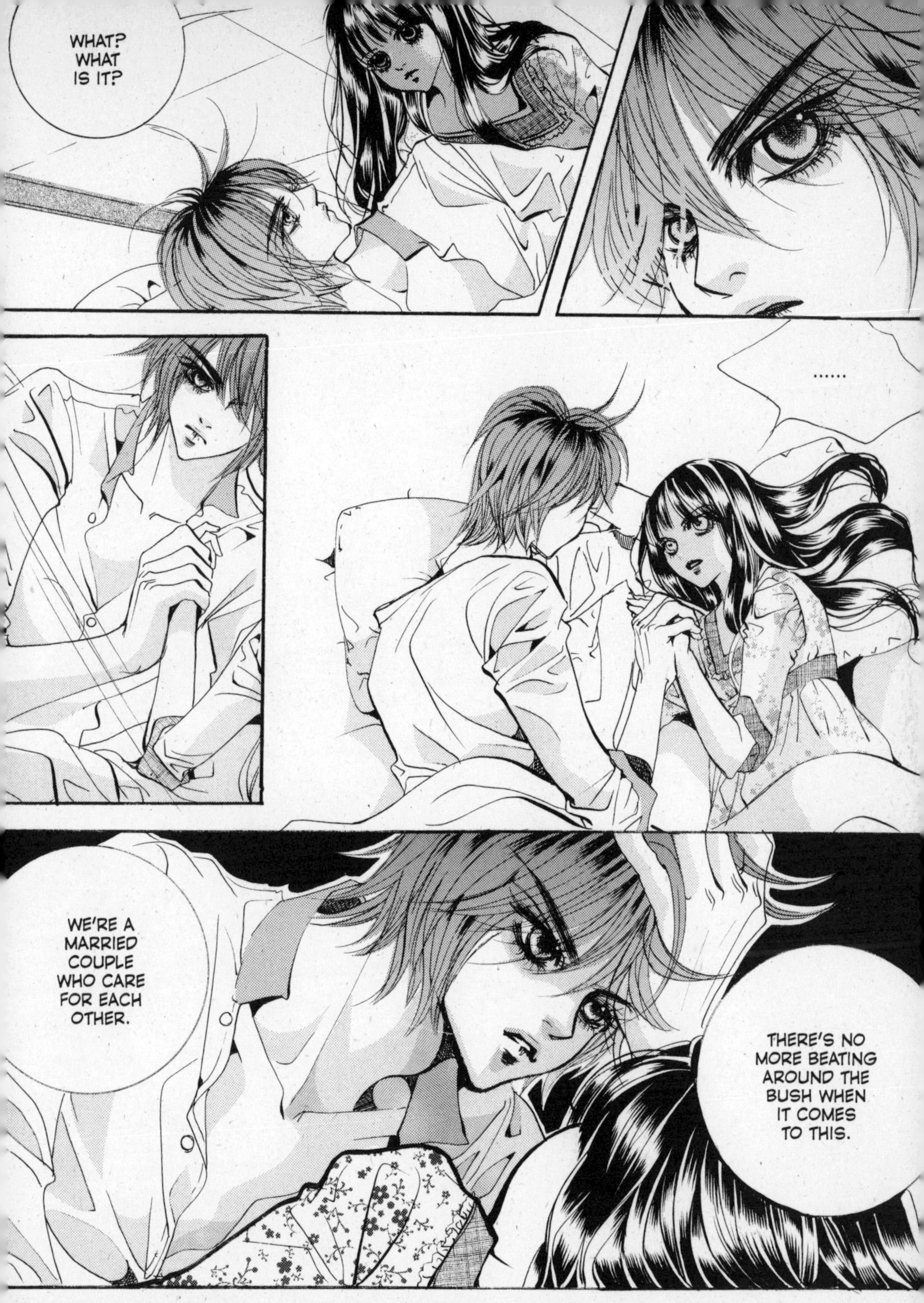
WHAT? WHAT IS IT?
......
WE'RE A MARRIED COUPLE WHO CARE FOR EACH OTHER.
THERE'S NO MORE BEATING AROUND THE BUSH WHEN IT COMES TO THIS.

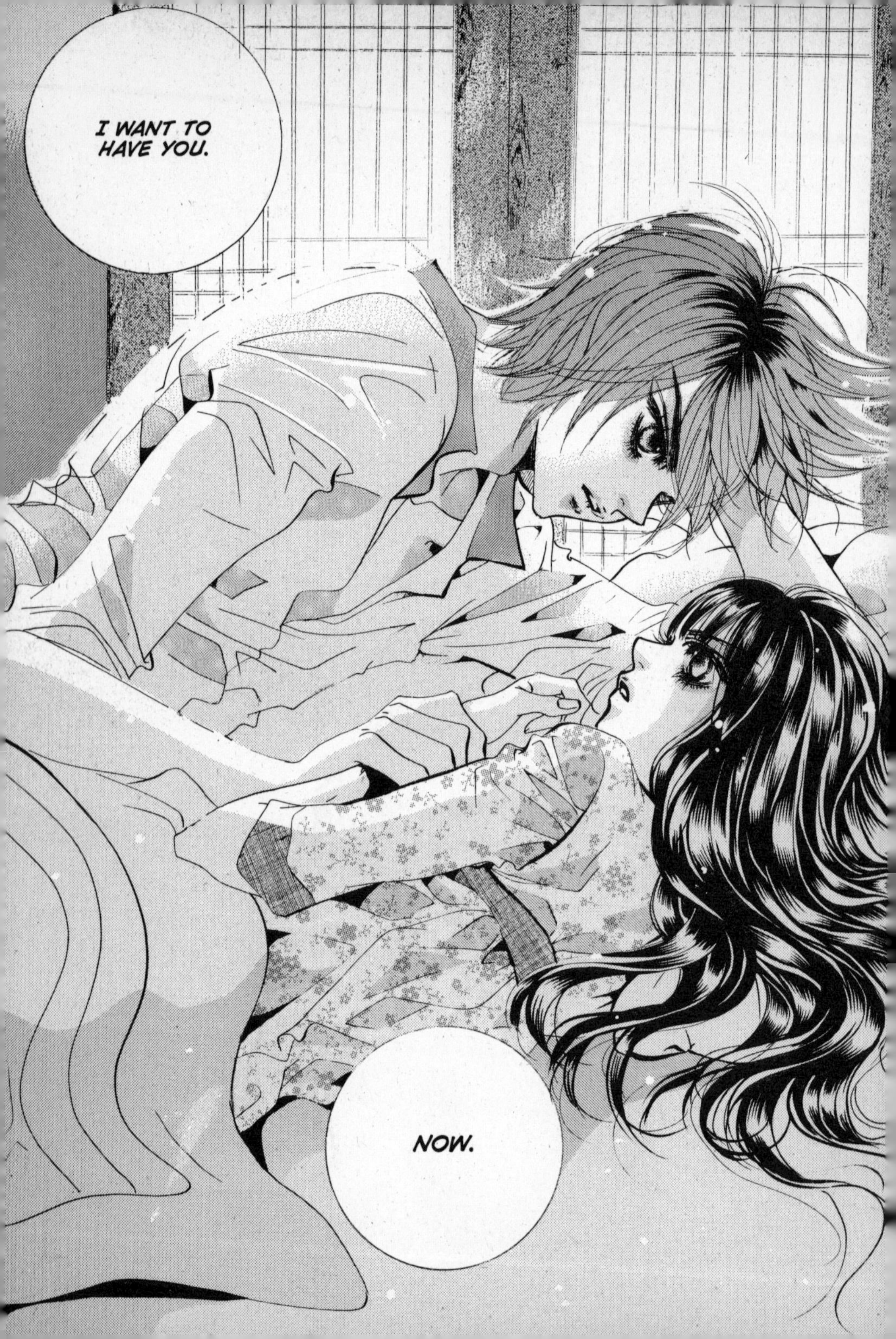
I WANT TO HAVE YOU.
NOW.

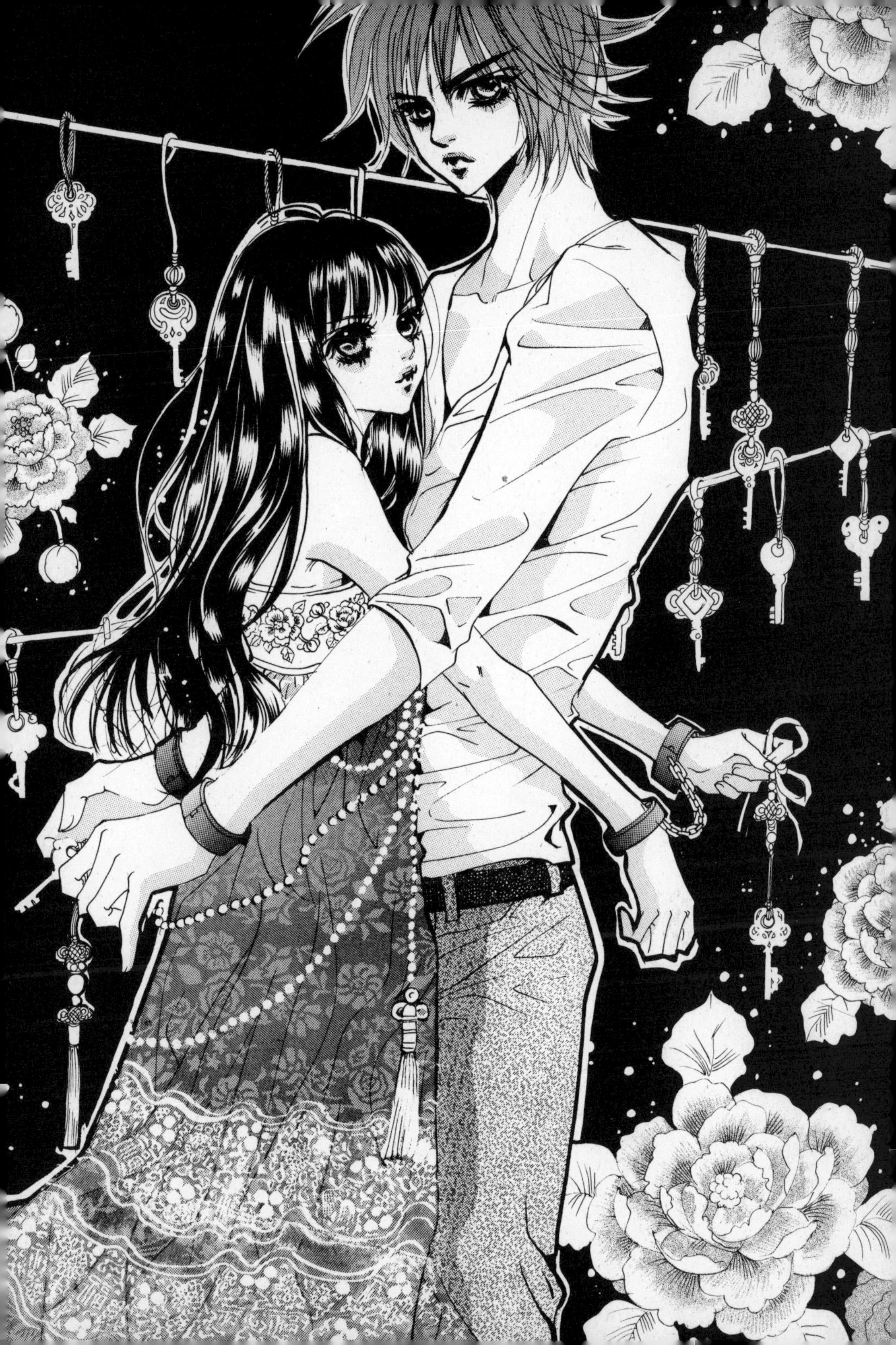

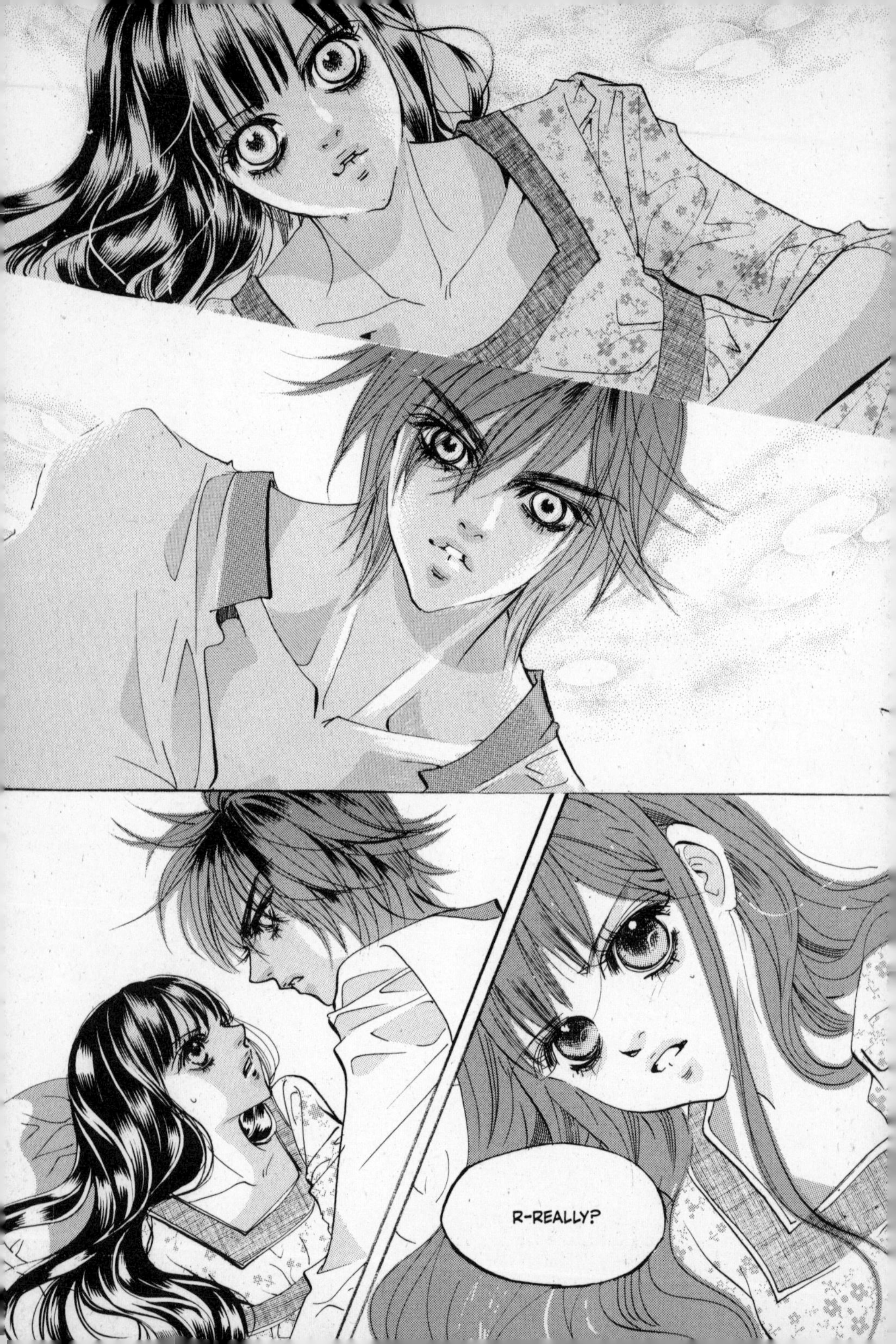
R-REALLY?

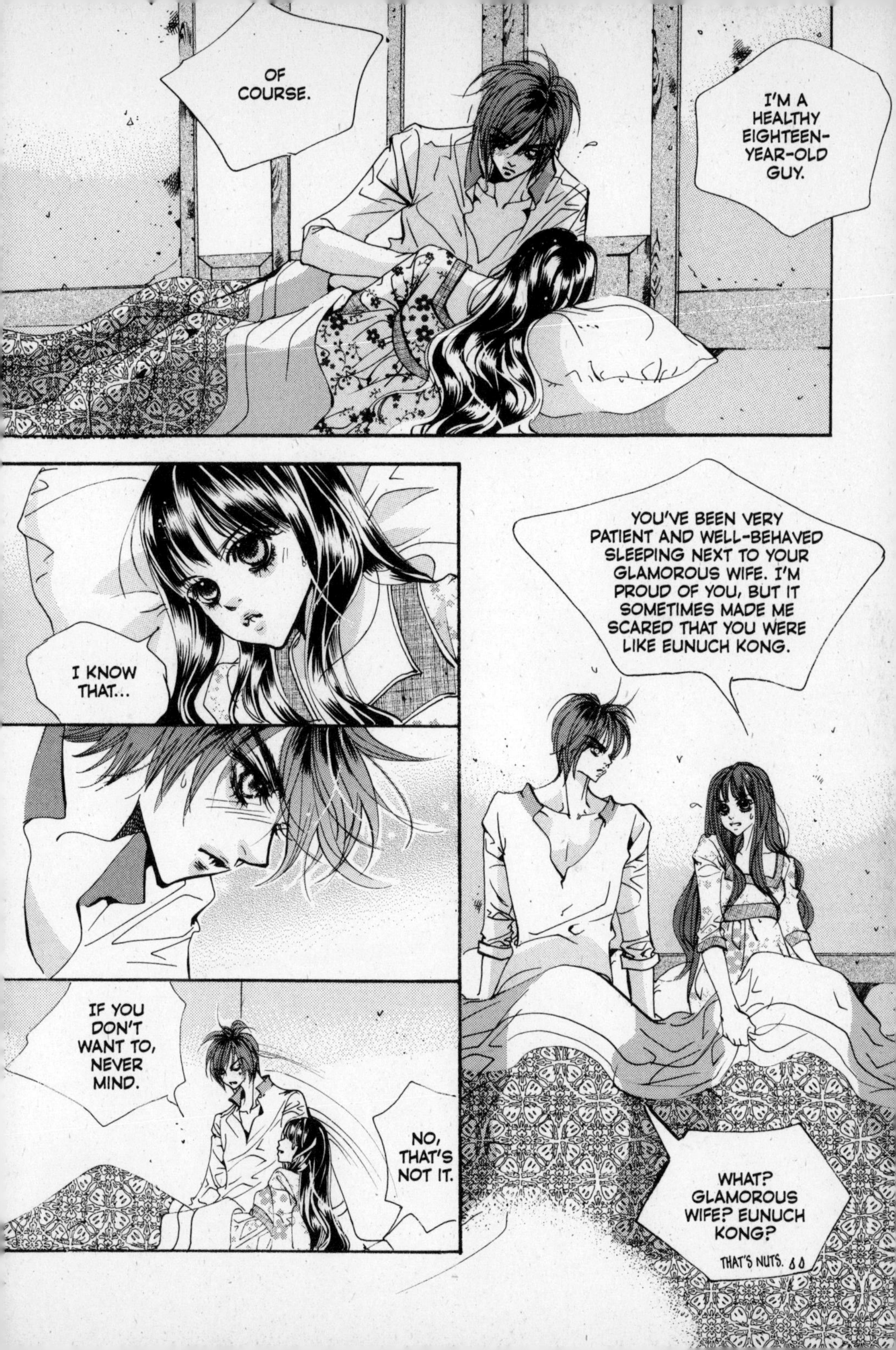
OF COURSE.
I'M A HEALTHY EIGHTEEN-YEAR-OLD GUY.
I KNOW THAT...
IF YOU DON'T WANT TO, NEVER MIND.
NO, THAT'S NOT IT.
YOU'VE BEEN VERY PATIENT AND WELL-BEHAVED SLEEPING NEXT TO YOUR GLAMOROUS WIFE. I'M PROUD OF YOU, BUT IT SOMETIMES MADE ME SCARED THAT YOU WERE LIKE EUNUCH KONG.
WHAT? GLAMOROUS WIFE? EUNUCH KONG?
THAT'S NUTS.

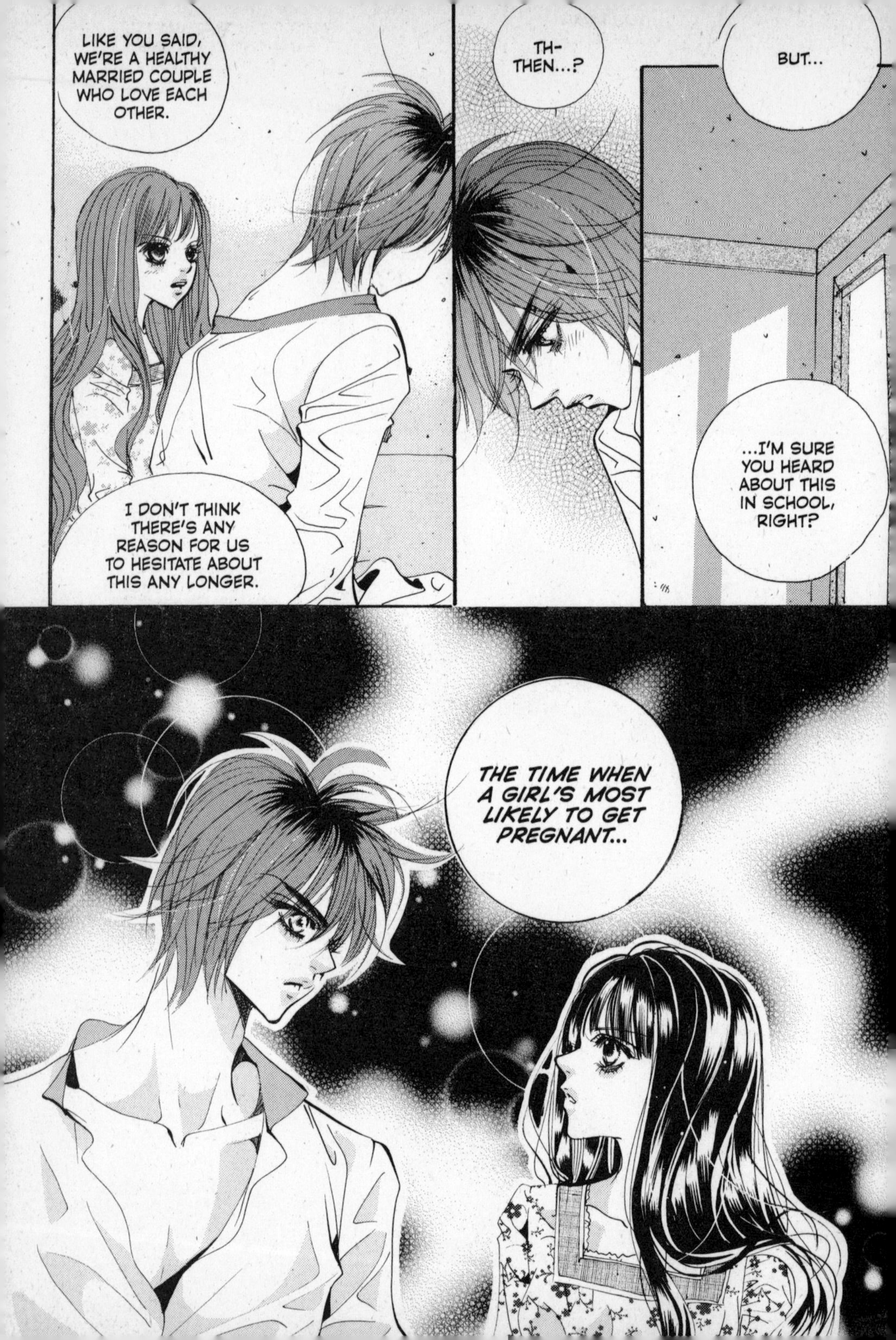
LIKE YOU SAID, WE'RE A HEALTHY MARRIED COUPLE WHO LOVE EACH OTHER.
I DON'T THINK THERE'S ANY REASON FOR US TO HESITATE ABOUT THIS ANY LONGER.
TH- THEN...?
BUT...
...I'M SURE YOU HEARD ABOUT THIS IN SCHOOL, RIGHT?
THE TIME WHEN A GIRL'S MOST LIKELY TO GET PREGNANT...

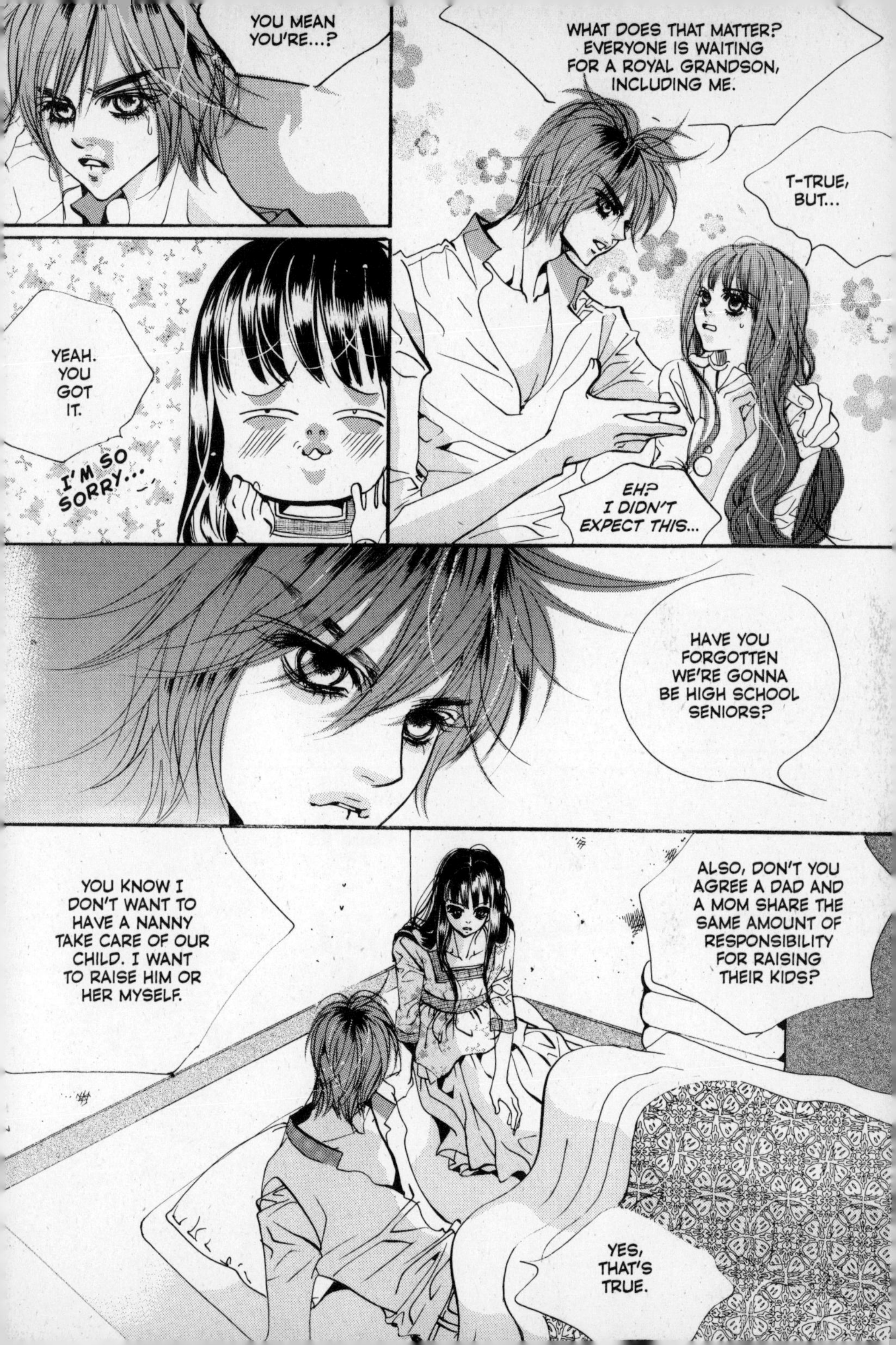

YOU MEAN YOU'RE...?
WHAT DOES THAT MATTER? EVERYONE IS WAITING FOR A ROYAL GRANDSON, INCLUDING ME.
T-TRUE, BUT...
YEAH. YOU GOT IT.
I'M SO SORRY...
EH? I DIDN'T EXPECT THIS...
HAVE YOU FORGOTTEN WE'RE GONNA BE HIGH SCHOOL SENIORS?
YOU KNOW I DON'T WANT TO HAVE A NANNY TAKE CARE OF OUR CHILD. I WANT TO RAISE HIM OR HER MYSELF.
ALSO, DON'T YOU AGREE A DAD AND A MOM SHARE THE SAME AMOUNT OF RESPONSIBILITY FOR RAISING THEIR KIDS?
YES, THAT'S TRUE.

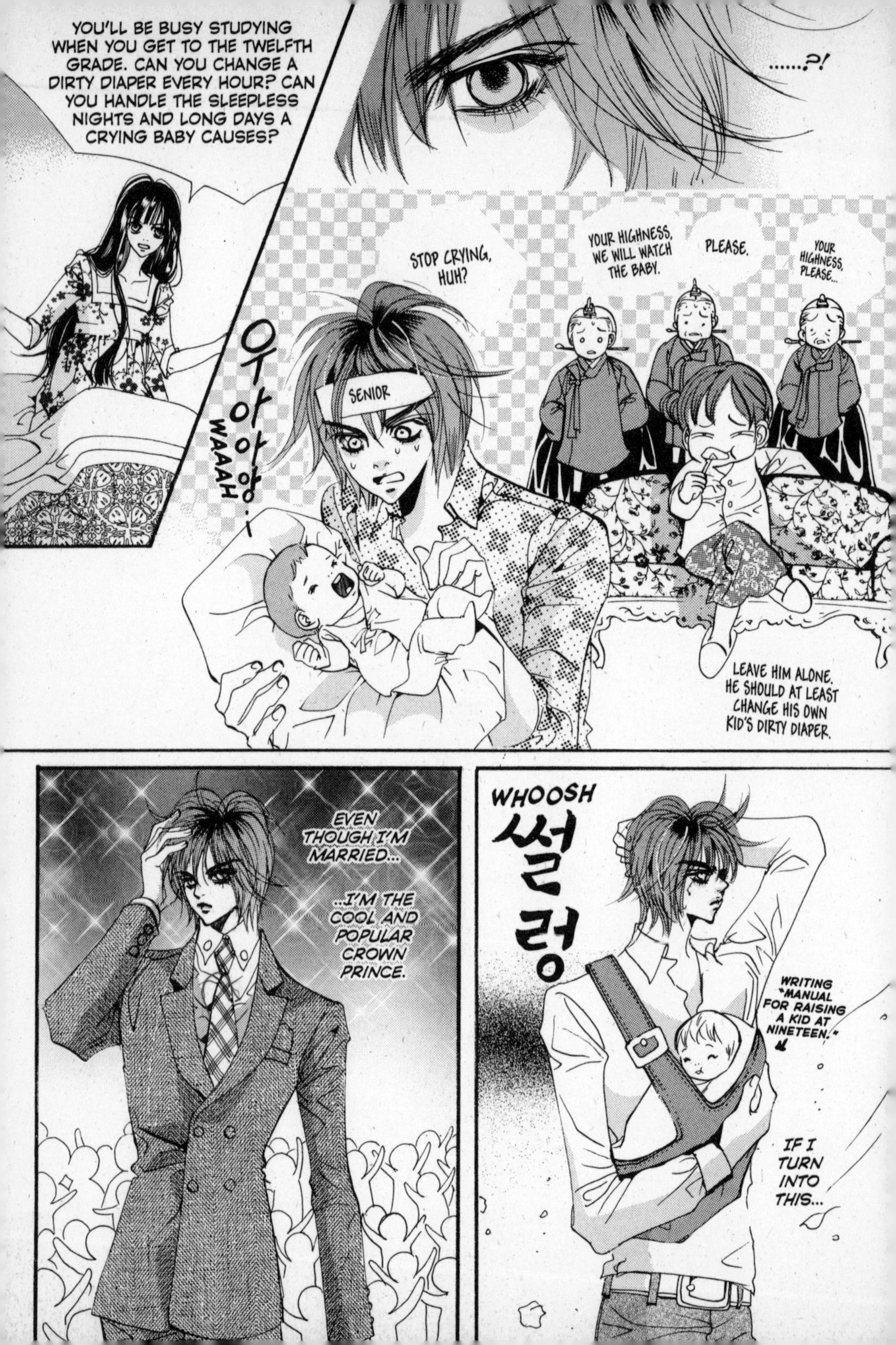
YOU'LL BE BUSY STUDYING WHEN YOU GET TO THE TWELFTH GRADE. CAN YOU CHANGE A DIRTY DIAPER EVERY HOUR? CAN YOU HANDLE THE SLEEPLESS NIGHTS AND LONG DAYS A CRYING BABY CAUSES?
......?!
우아아앙...
WAAAH
SENIOR
STOP CRYING, HUH?
YOUR HIGHNESS, WE WILL WATCH THE BABY.
PLEASE.
YOUR HIGHNESS, PLEASE...
LEAVE HIM ALONE. HE SHOULD AT LEAST CHANGE HIS OWN KID'S DIRTY DIAPER.
EVEN THOUGH I'M MARRIED...
...I'M THE COOL AND POPULAR CROWN PRINCE.
WHOOSH
썰렁
WRITING "MANUAL FOR RAISING A KID AT NINETEEN."
IF I TURN INTO THIS...

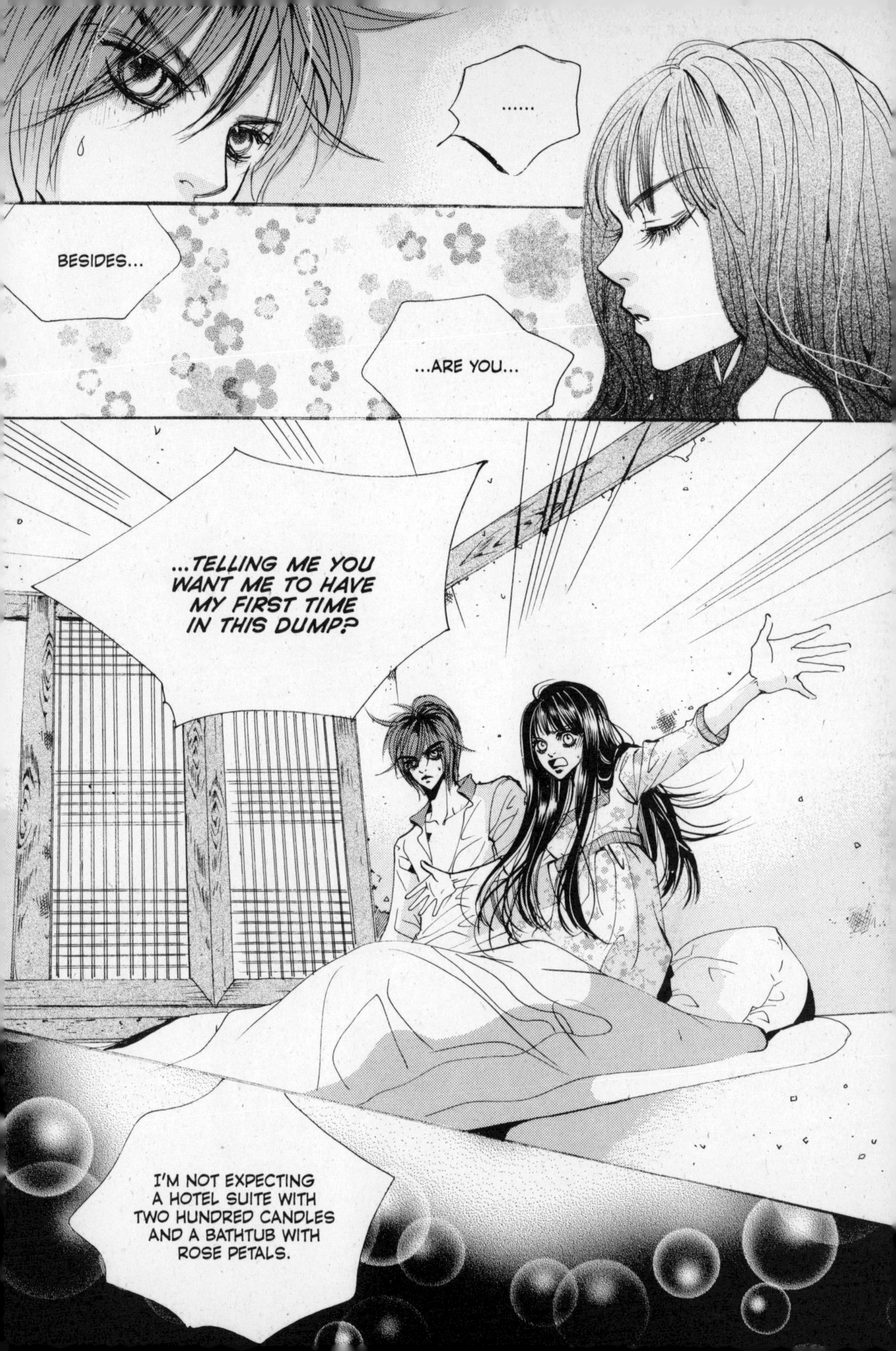
......
BESIDES...
...ARE YOU...
...TELLING ME YOU WANT ME TO HAVE MY FIRST TIME IN THIS DUMP?
I'M NOT EXPECTING A HOTEL SUITE WITH TWO HUNDRED CANDLES AND A BATHTUB WITH ROSE PETALS.

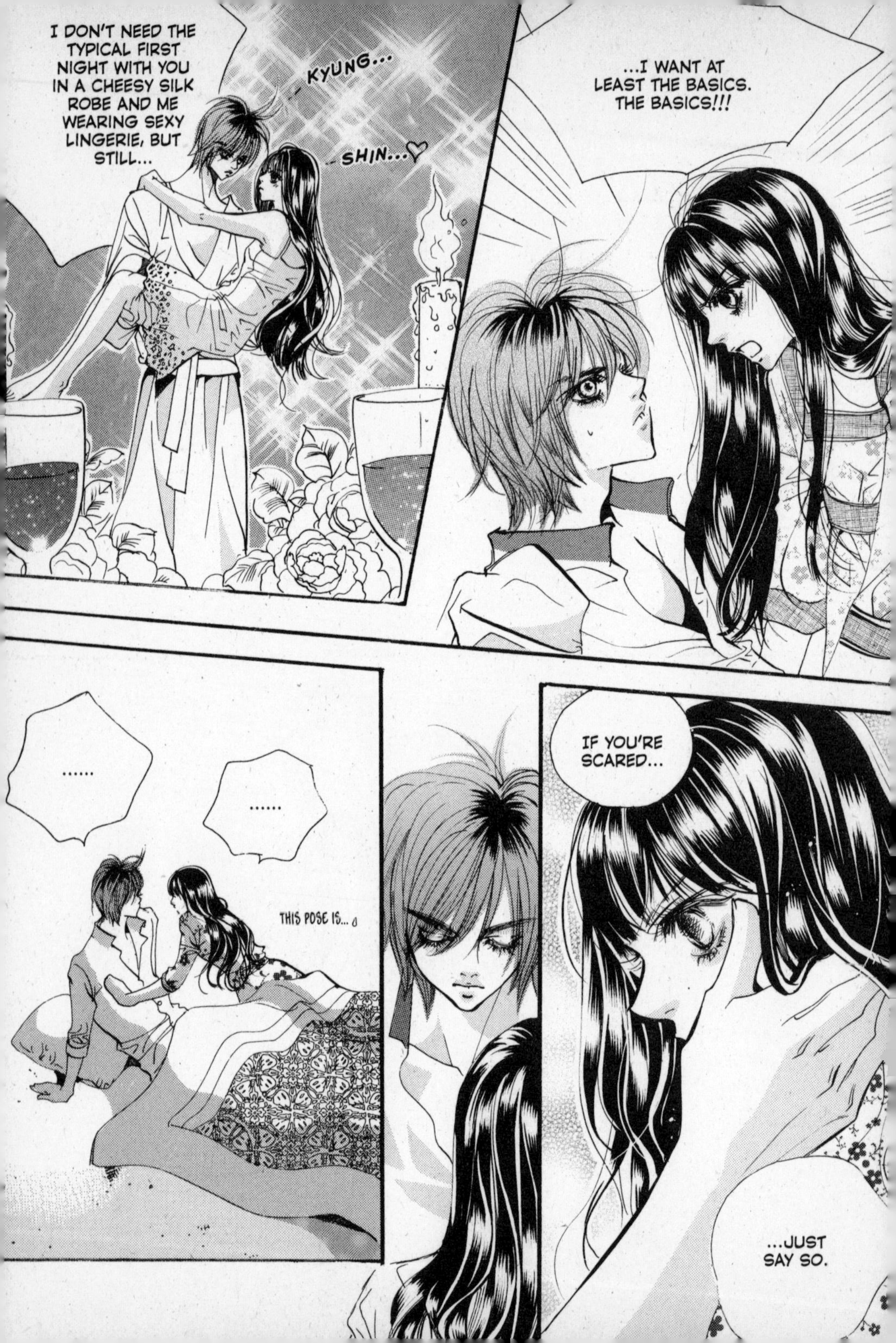
I DON'T NEED THE TYPICAL FIRST NIGHT WITH YOU IN A CHEESY SILK ROBE AND ME WEARING SEXY LINGERIE, BUT STILL...
KYUNG...
SHIN...♡
...I WANT AT LEAST THE BASICS. THE BASICS!!!
......
......
THIS POSE IS...
IF YOU'RE SCARED...
...JUST SAY SO.

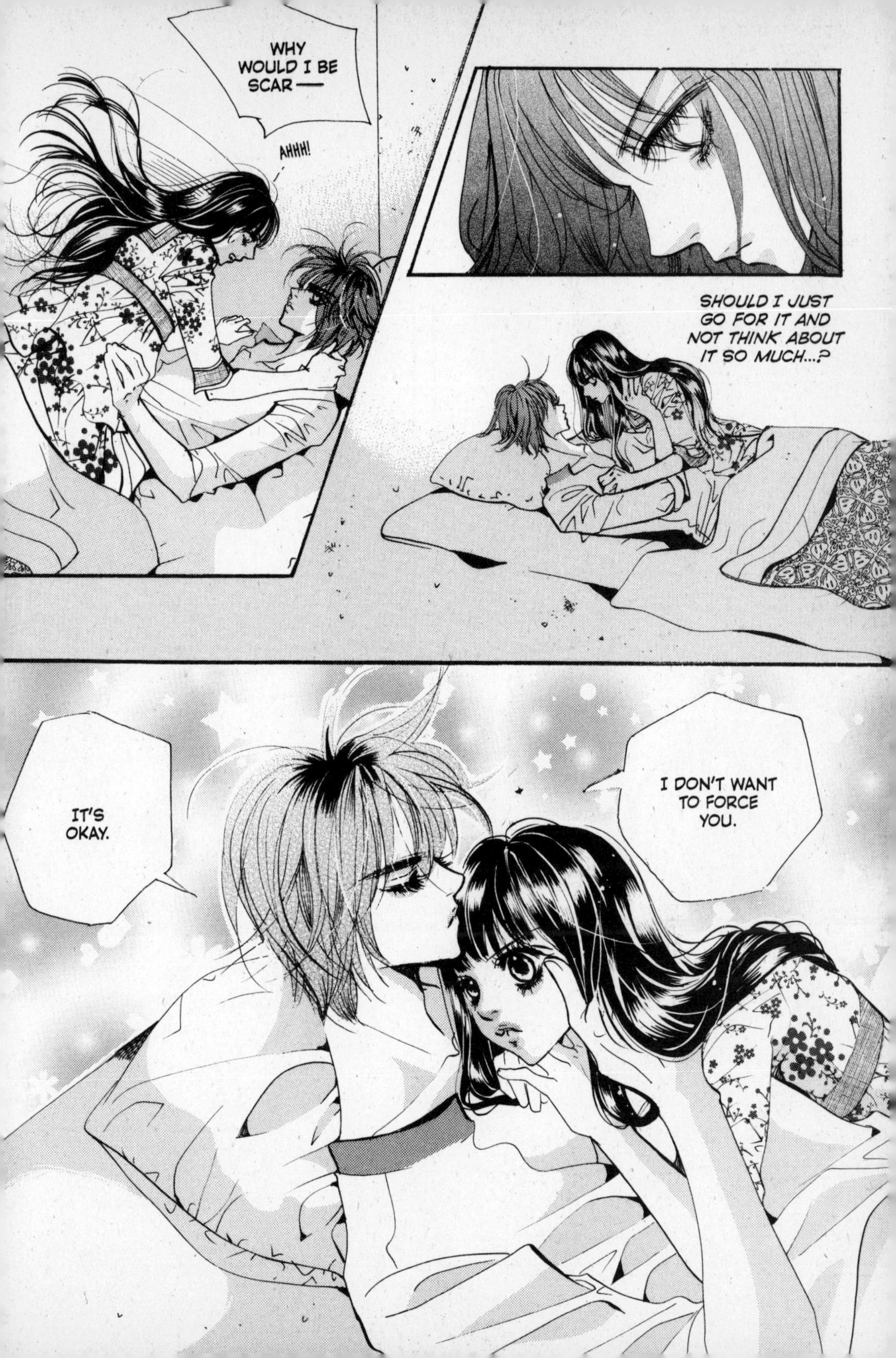
WHY WOULD I BE SCAR—
AHHH!
SHOULD I JUST GO FOR IT AND NOT THINK ABOUT IT SO MUCH...?
IT'S OKAY.
I DON'T WANT TO FORCE YOU.

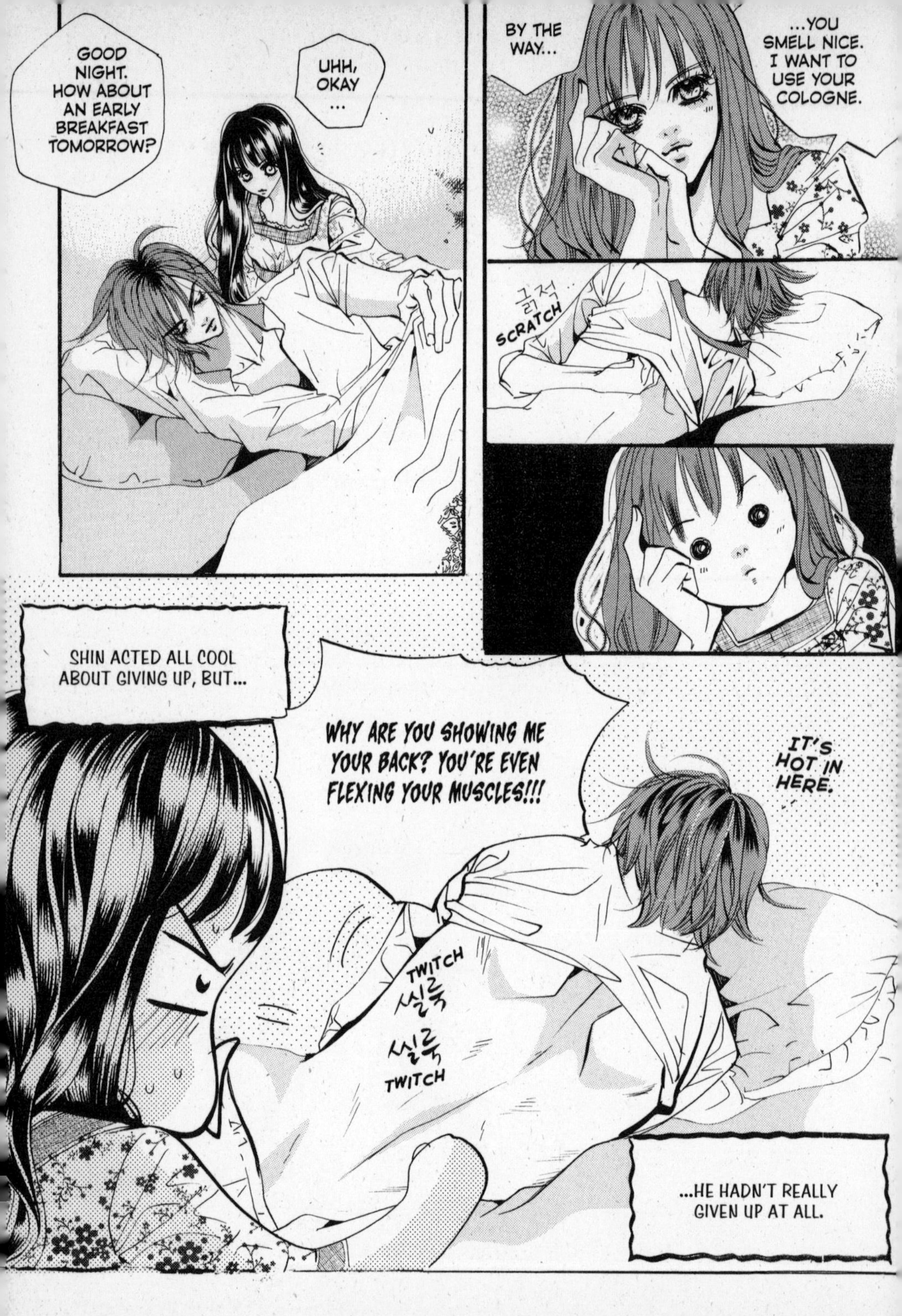
GOOD NIGHT. HOW ABOUT AN EARLY BREAKFAST TOMORROW?
UHH, OKAY ...
BY THE WAY...
...YOU SMELL NICE. I WANT TO USE YOUR COLOGNE.
긁적
SCRATCH
SHIN ACTED ALL COOL ABOUT GIVING UP, BUT...
WHY ARE YOU SHOWING ME YOUR BACK? YOU'RE EVEN FLEXING YOUR MUSCLES!!!
IT'S HOT IN HERE.
TWITCH
실룩
실룩
TWITCH
...HE HADN'T REALLY GIVEN UP AT ALL.

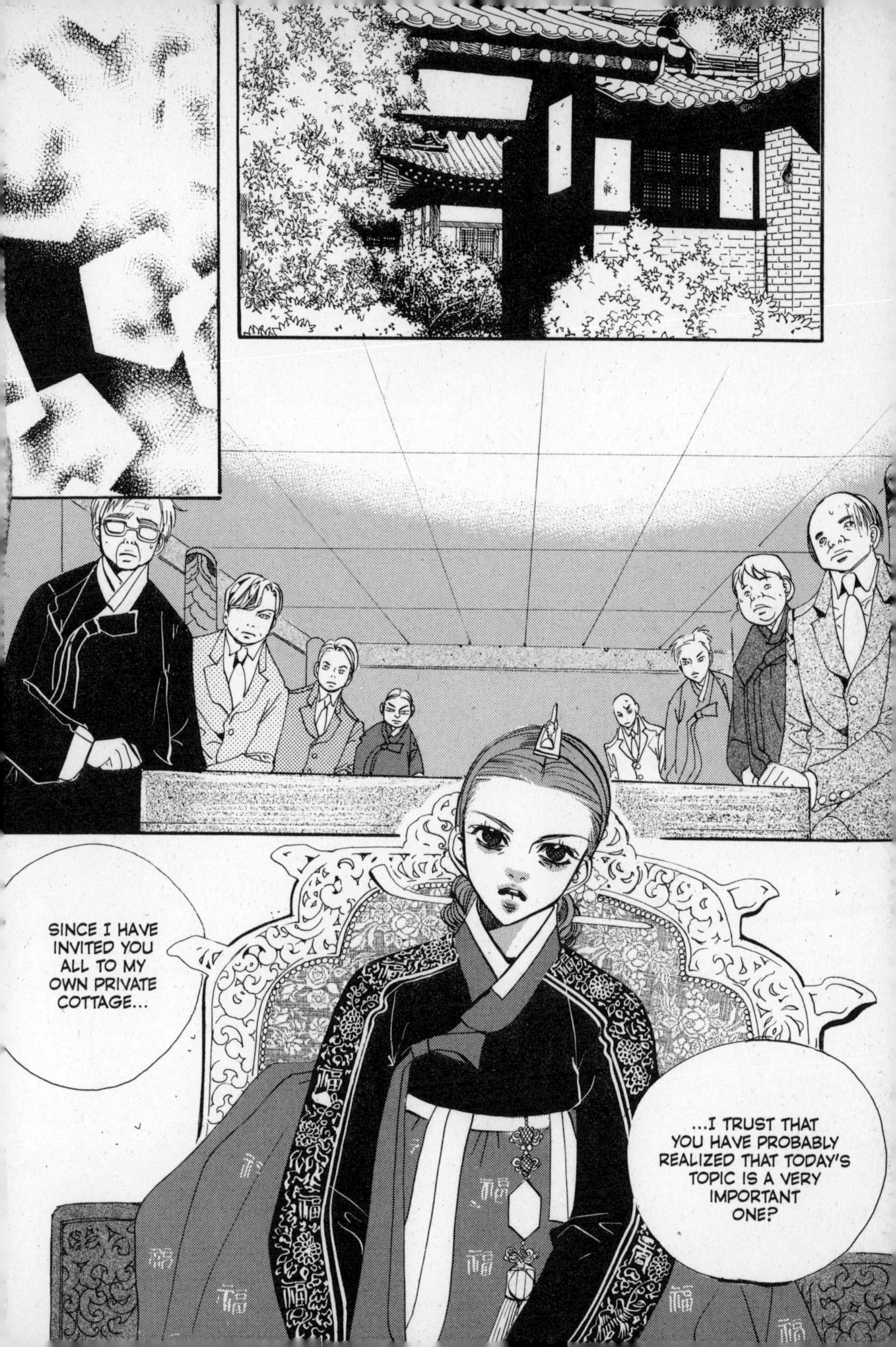
SINCE I HAVE INVITED YOU ALL TO MY OWN PRIVATE COTTAGE...
...I TRUST THAT YOU HAVE PROBABLY REALIZED THAT TODAY'S TOPIC IS A VERY IMPORTANT ONE?

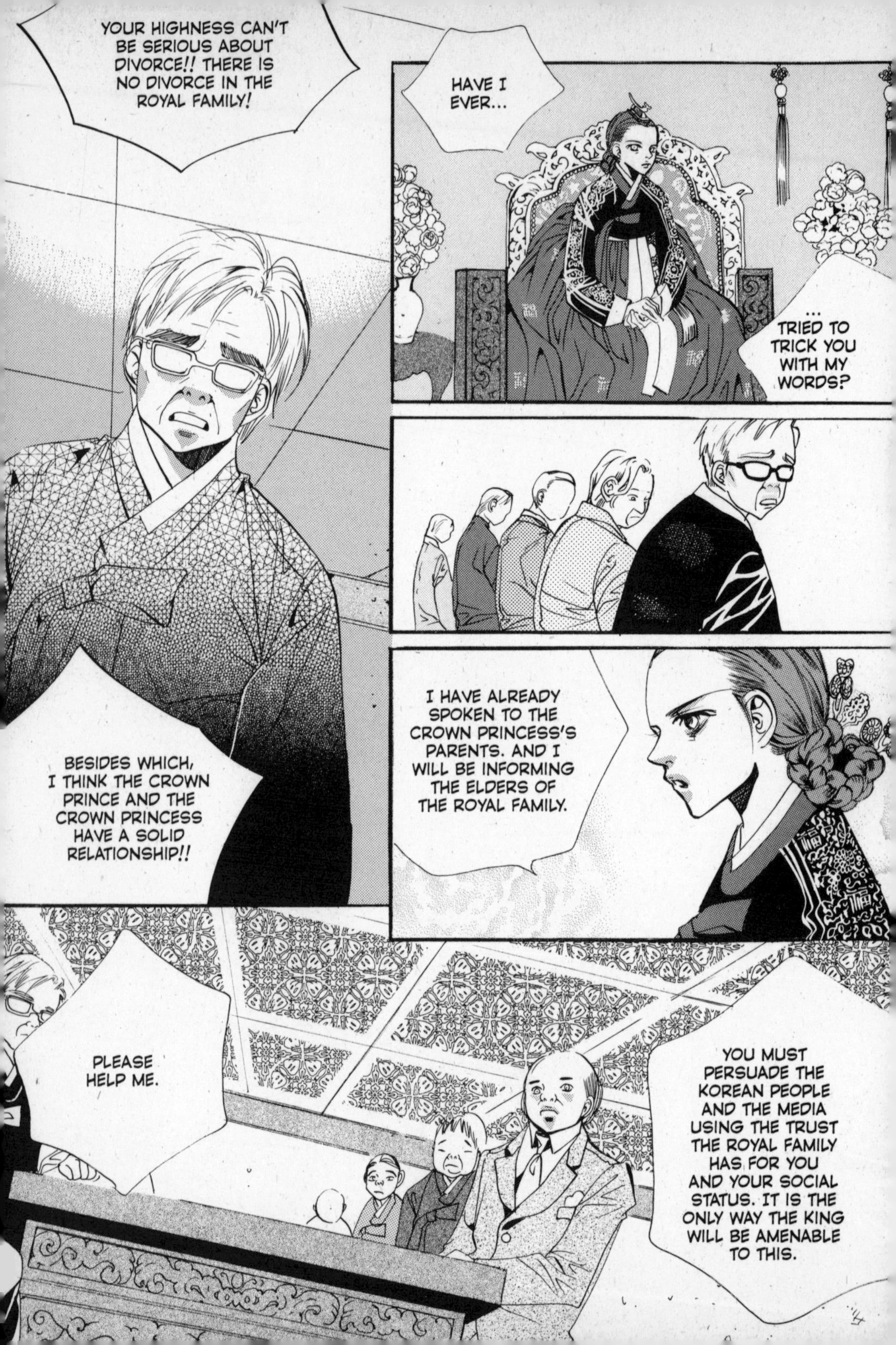
YOUR HIGHNESS CAN'T BE SERIOUS ABOUT DIVORCE!! THERE IS NO DIVORCE IN THE ROYAL FAMILY!
BESIDES WHICH, I THINK THE CROWN PRINCE AND THE CROWN PRINCESS HAVE A SOLID RELATIONSHIP!!
HAVE I EVER...
... TRIED TO TRICK YOU WITH MY WORDS?
I HAVE ALREADY SPOKEN TO THE CROWN PRINCESS'S PARENTS. AND I WILL BE INFORMING THE ELDERS OF THE ROYAL FAMILY.
PLEASE HELP ME.
YOU MUST PERSUADE THE KOREAN PEOPLE AND THE MEDIA USING THE TRUST THE ROYAL FAMILY HAS FOR YOU AND YOUR SOCIAL STATUS. IT IS THE ONLY WAY THE KING WILL BE AMENABLE TO THIS.

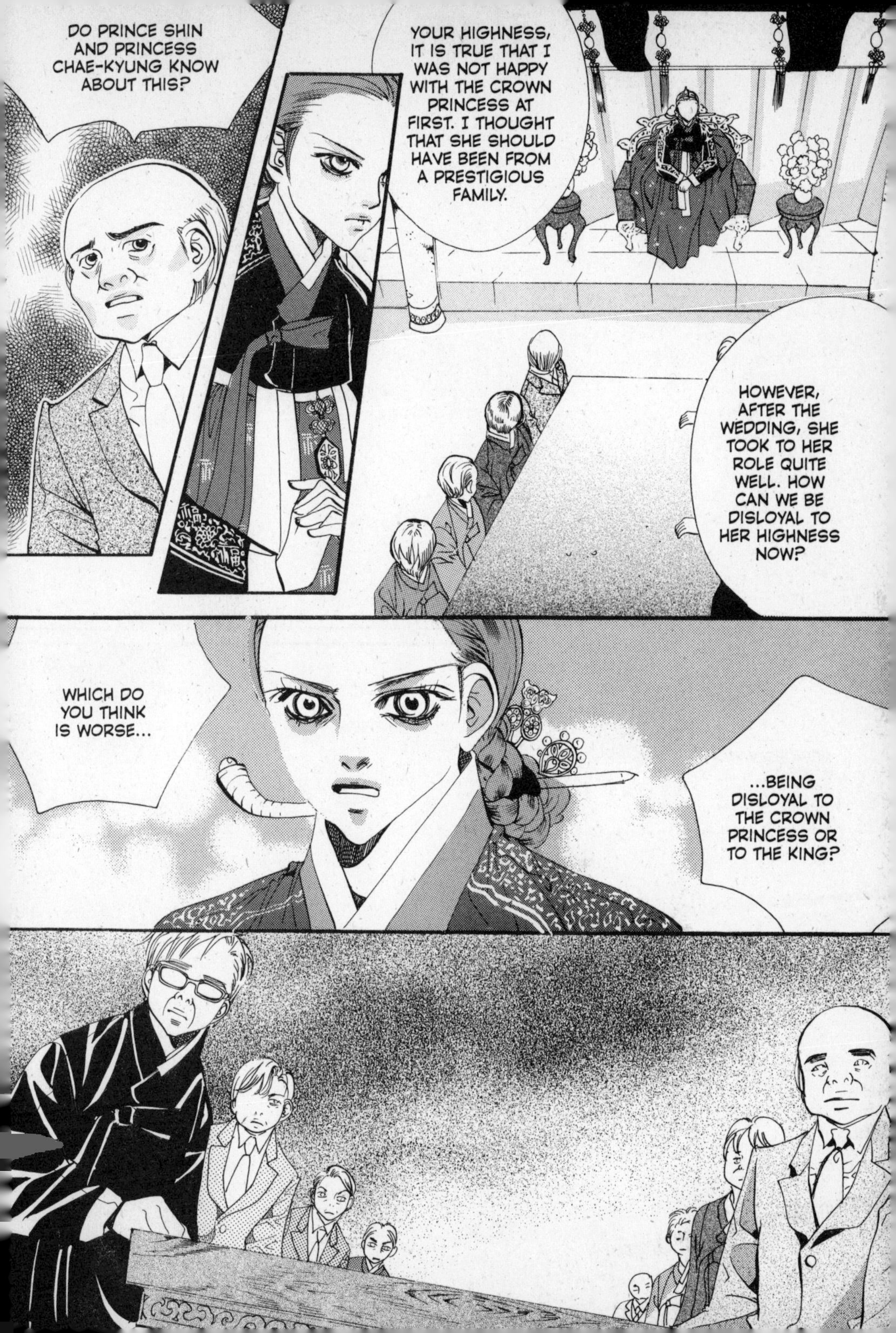
DO PRINCE SHIN AND PRINCESS CHAE-KYUNG KNOW ABOUT THIS?
YOUR HIGHNESS, IT IS TRUE THAT I WAS NOT HAPPY WITH THE CROWN PRINCESS AT FIRST. I THOUGHT THAT SHE SHOULD HAVE BEEN FROM A PRESTIGIOUS FAMILY.
HOWEVER, AFTER THE WEDDING, SHE TOOK TO HER ROLE QUITE WELL. HOW CAN WE BE DISLOYAL TO HER HIGHNESS NOW?
WHICH DO YOU THINK IS WORSE...
...BEING DISLOYAL TO THE CROWN PRINCESS OR TO THE KING?

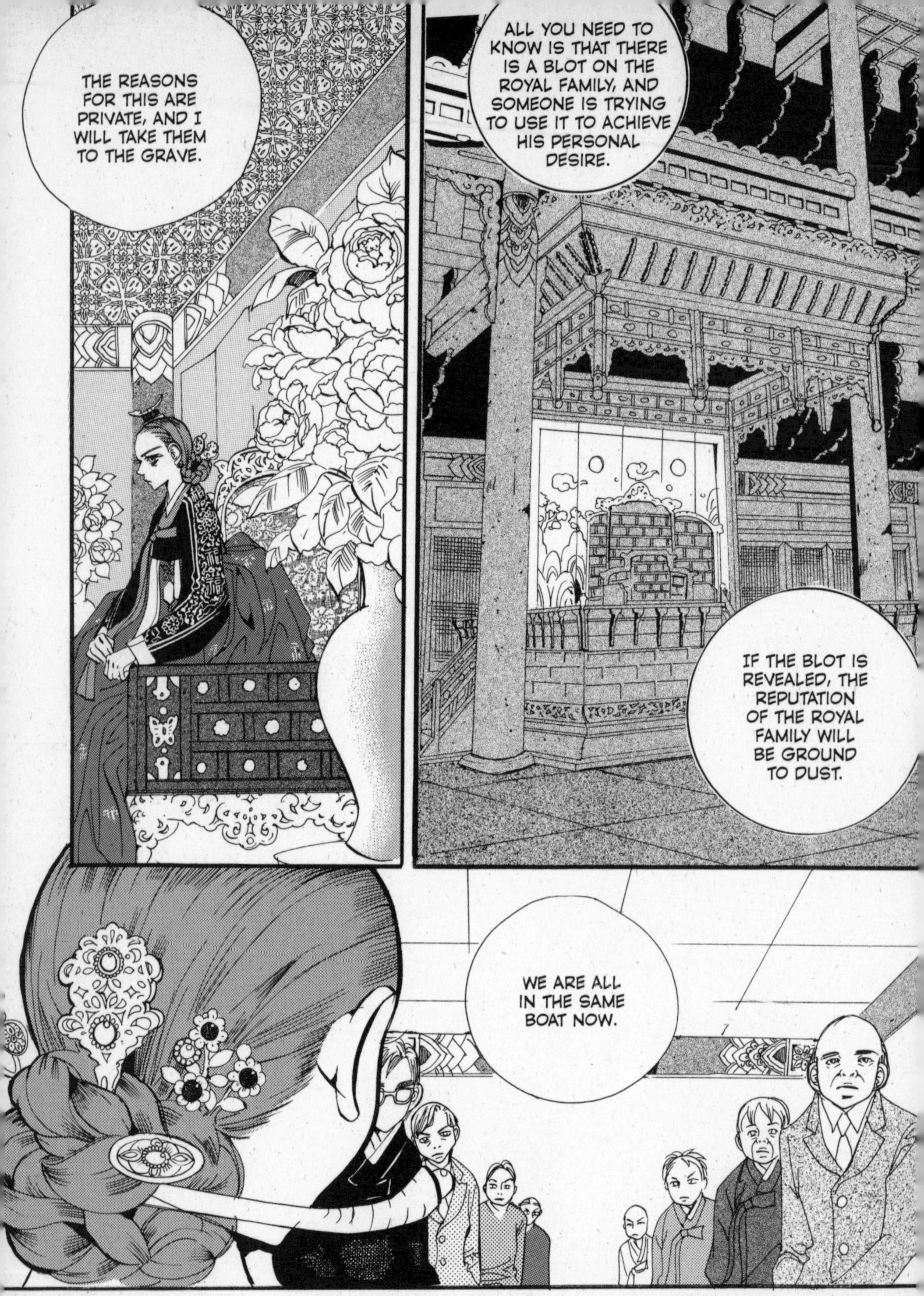
THE REASONS FOR THIS ARE PRIVATE, AND I WILL TAKE THEM TO THE GRAVE.
ALL YOU NEED TO KNOW IS THAT THERE IS A BLOT ON THE ROYAL FAMILY, AND SOMEONE IS TRYING TO USE IT TO ACHIEVE HIS PERSONAL DESIRE.
IF THE BLOT IS REVEALED, THE REPUTATION OF THE ROYAL FAMILY WILL BE GROUND TO DUST.
WE ARE ALL IN THE SAME BOAT NOW.

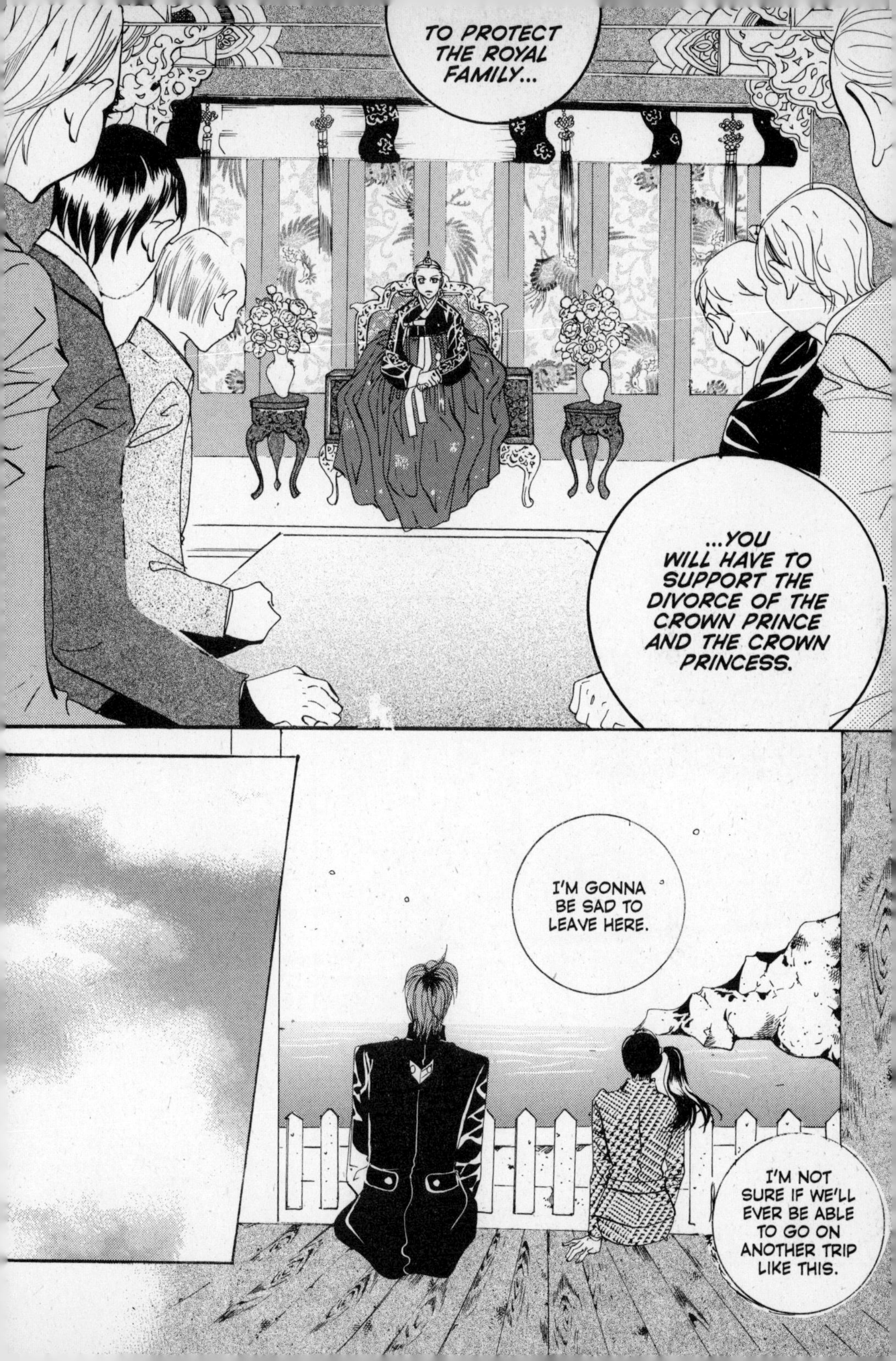
TO PROTECT THE ROYAL FAMILY...
...YOU WILL HAVE TO SUPPORT THE DIVORCE OF THE CROWN PRINCE AND THE CROWN PRINCESS.
I'M GONNA BE SAD TO LEAVE HERE.
I'M NOT SURE IF WE'LL EVER BE ABLE TO GO ON ANOTHER TRIP LIKE THIS.

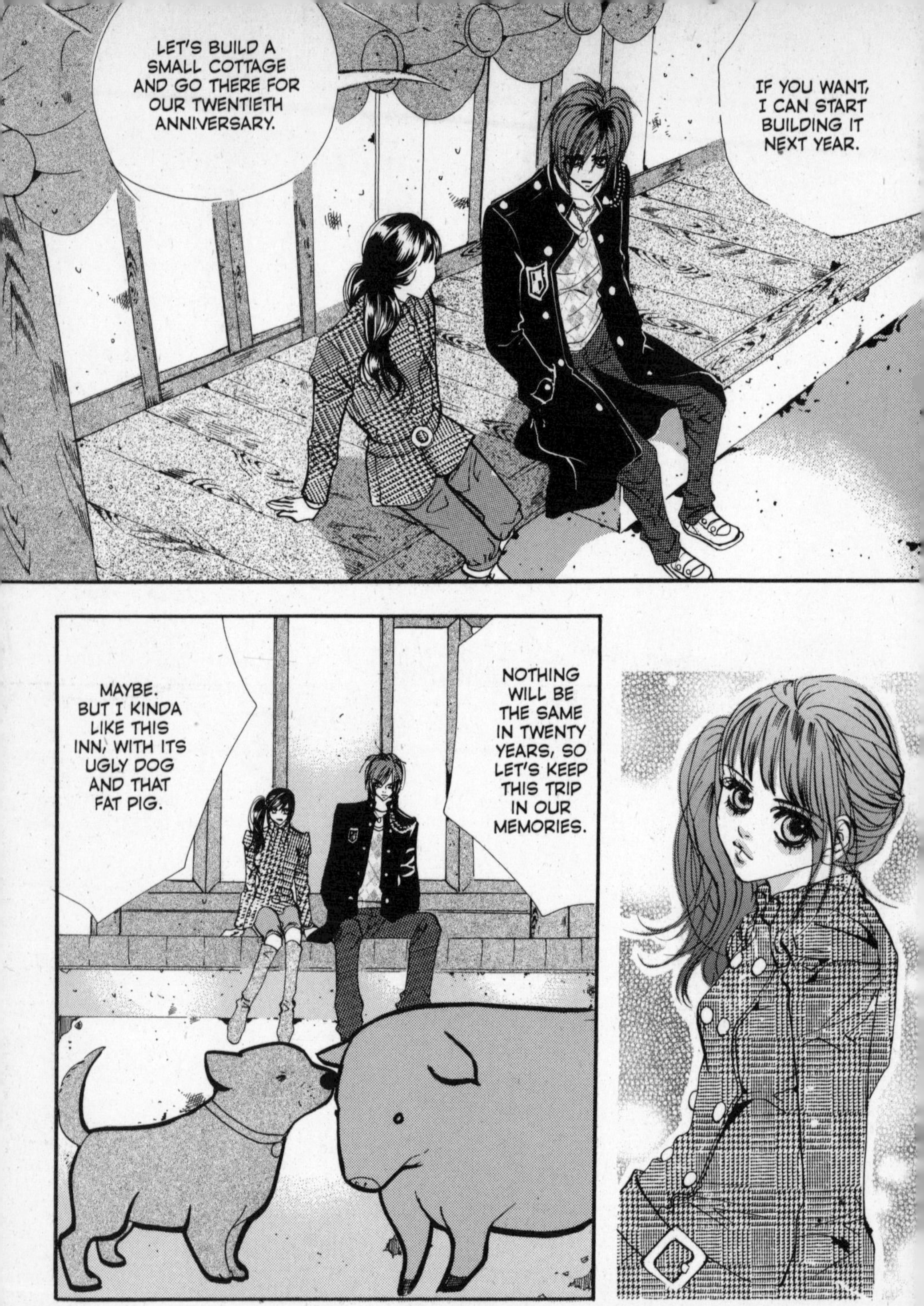
LET'S BUILD A SMALL COTTAGE AND GO THERE FOR OUR TWENTIETH ANNIVERSARY.
IF YOU WANT, I CAN START BUILDING IT NEXT YEAR.
MAYBE. BUT I KINDA LIKE THIS INN, WITH ITS UGLY DOG AND THAT FAT PIG.
NOTHING WILL BE THE SAME IN TWENTY YEARS, SO LET'S KEEP THIS TRIP IN OUR MEMORIES.

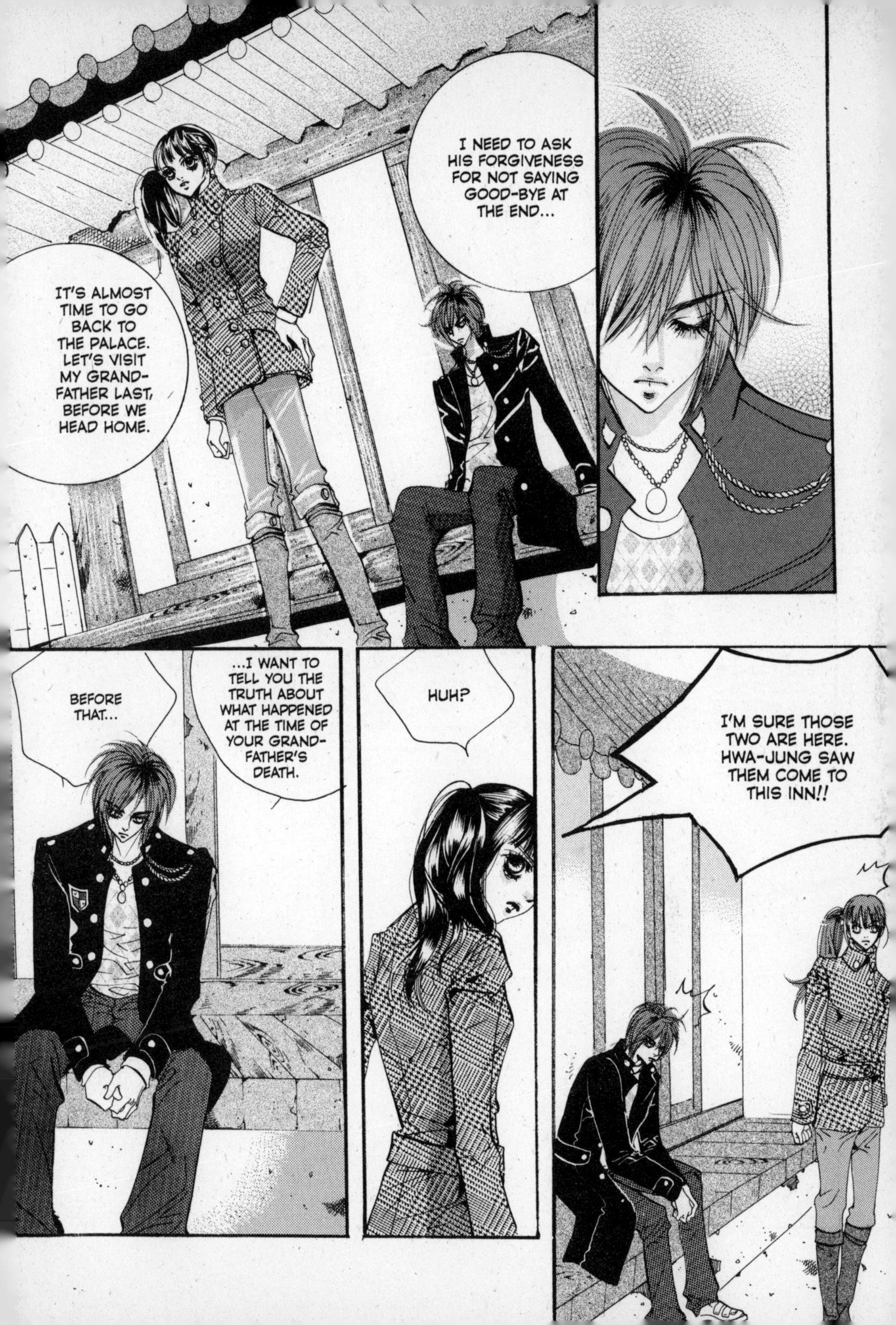

IT'S ALMOST TIME TO GO BACK TO THE PALACE. LET'S VISIT MY GRAND-FATHER LAST, BEFORE WE HEAD HOME.
I NEED TO ASK HIS FORGIVENESS FOR NOT SAYING GOOD-BYE AT THE END...
BEFORE THAT...
...I WANT TO TELL YOU THE TRUTH ABOUT WHAT HAPPENED AT THE TIME OF YOUR GRAND-FATHER'S DEATH.
HUH?
I'M SURE THOSE TWO ARE HERE. HWA-JUNG SAW THEM COME TO THIS INN!!

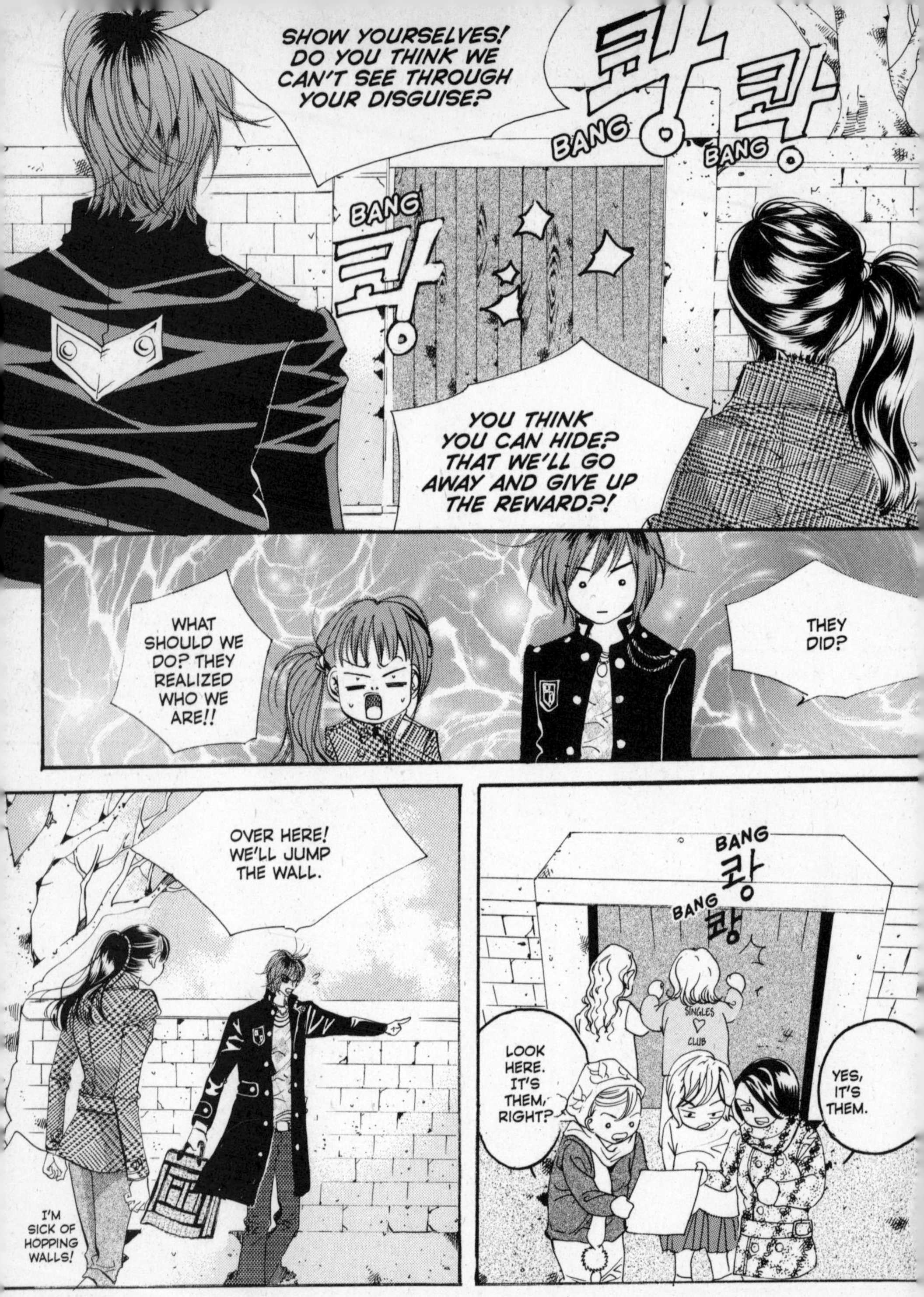

SHOW YOURSELVES! DO YOU THINK WE CAN'T SEE THROUGH YOUR DISGUISE?
쾅 쾅
BANG
BANG
BANG
쾅
YOU THINK YOU CAN HIDE? THAT WE'LL GO AWAY AND GIVE UP THE REWARD?!
WHAT SHOULD WE DO? THEY REALIZED WHO WE ARE!!
THEY DID?
OVER HERE! WE'LL JUMP THE WALL.
I'M SICK OF HOPPING WALLS!
BANG
쾅
BANG
쾅
SINGLES CLUB
LOOK HERE. IT'S THEM, RIGHT?
YES, IT'S THEM.

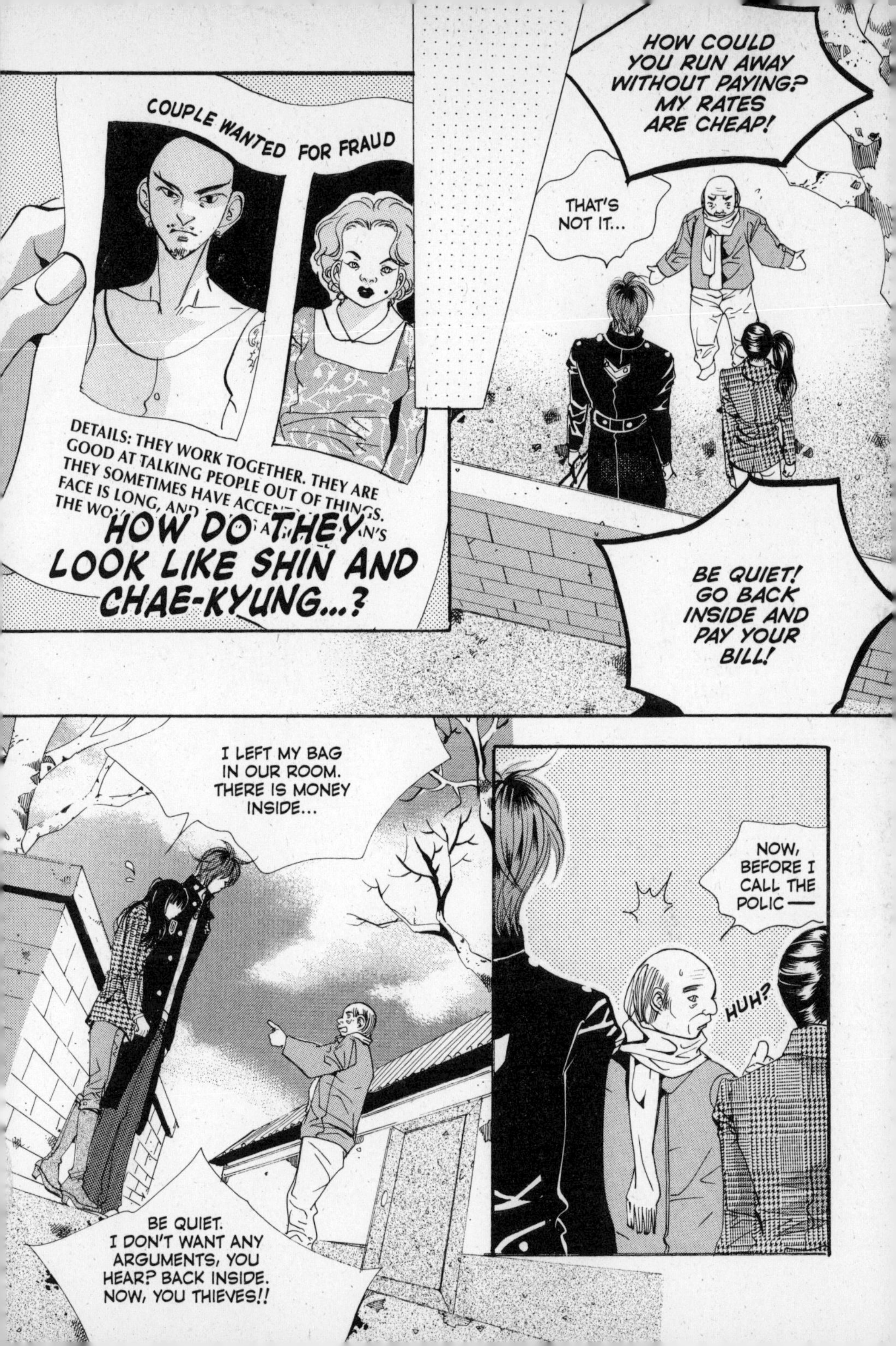
COUPLE WANTED FOR FRAUD
DETAILS: THEY WORK TOGETHER. THEY ARE GOOD AT TALKING PEOPLE OUT OF THINGS.
HOW DO THEY LOOK LIKE SHIN AND CHAE-KYUNG...?
HOW COULD YOU RUN AWAY WITHOUT PAYING? MY RATES ARE CHEAP!
THAT'S NOT IT...
BE QUIET! GO BACK INSIDE AND PAY YOUR BILL!
I LEFT MY BAG IN OUR ROOM. THERE IS MONEY INSIDE...
BE QUIET. I DON'T WANT ANY ARGUMENTS, YOU HEAR? BACK INSIDE. NOW, YOU THIEVES!!
NOW, BEFORE I CALL THE POLIC—
HUH?

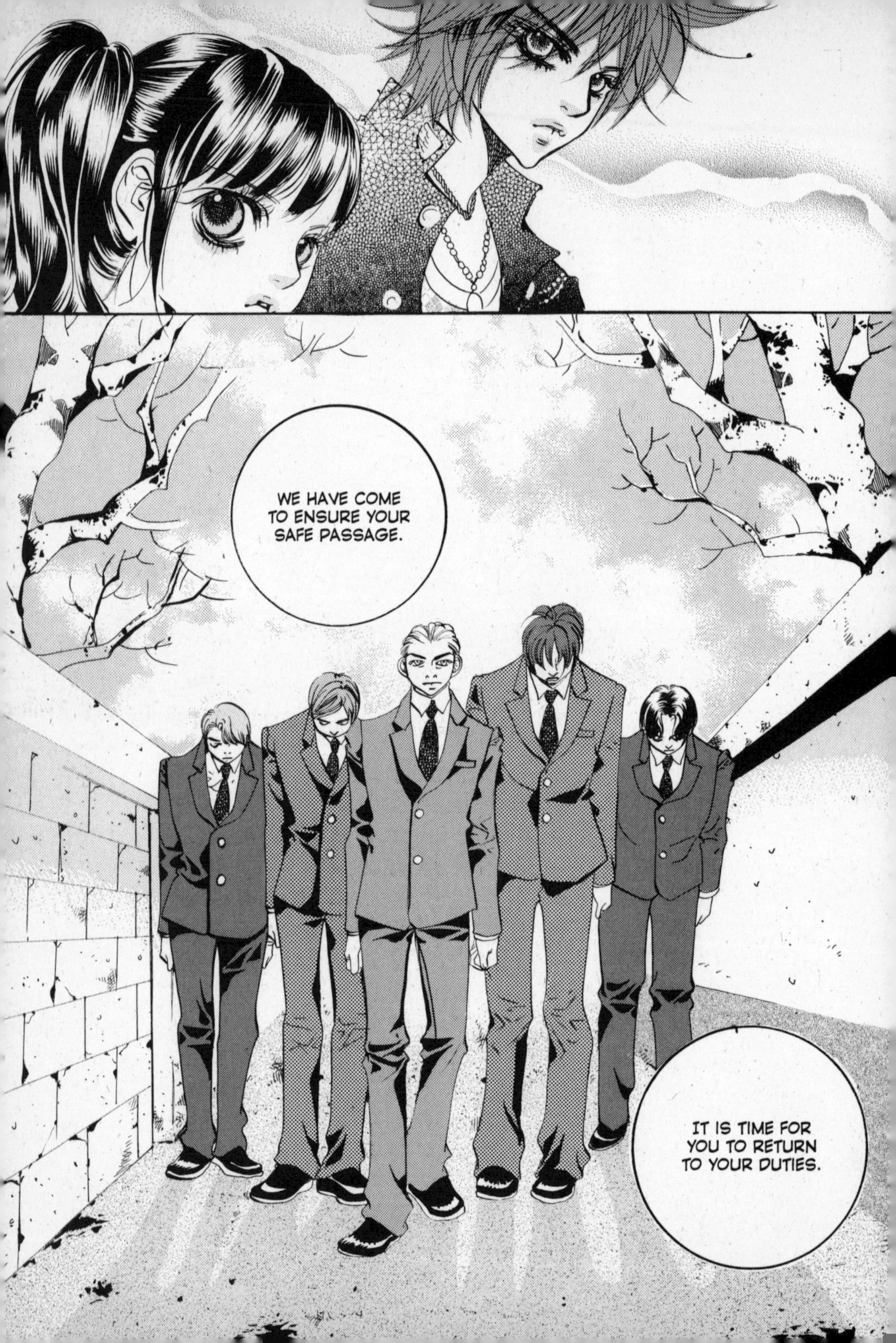
WE HAVE COME TO ENSURE YOUR SAFE PASSAGE.
IT IS TIME FOR YOU TO RETURN TO YOUR DUTIES.

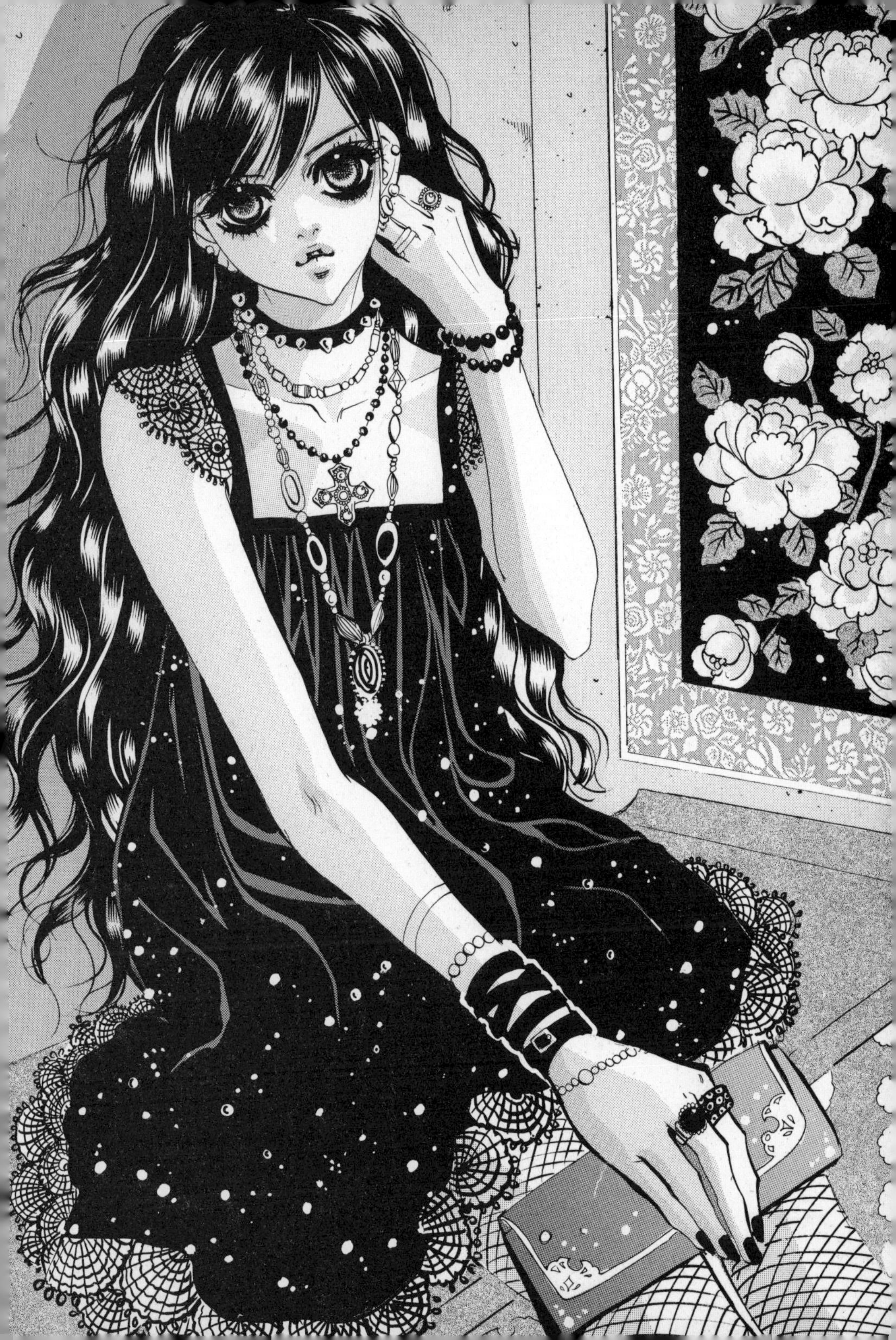

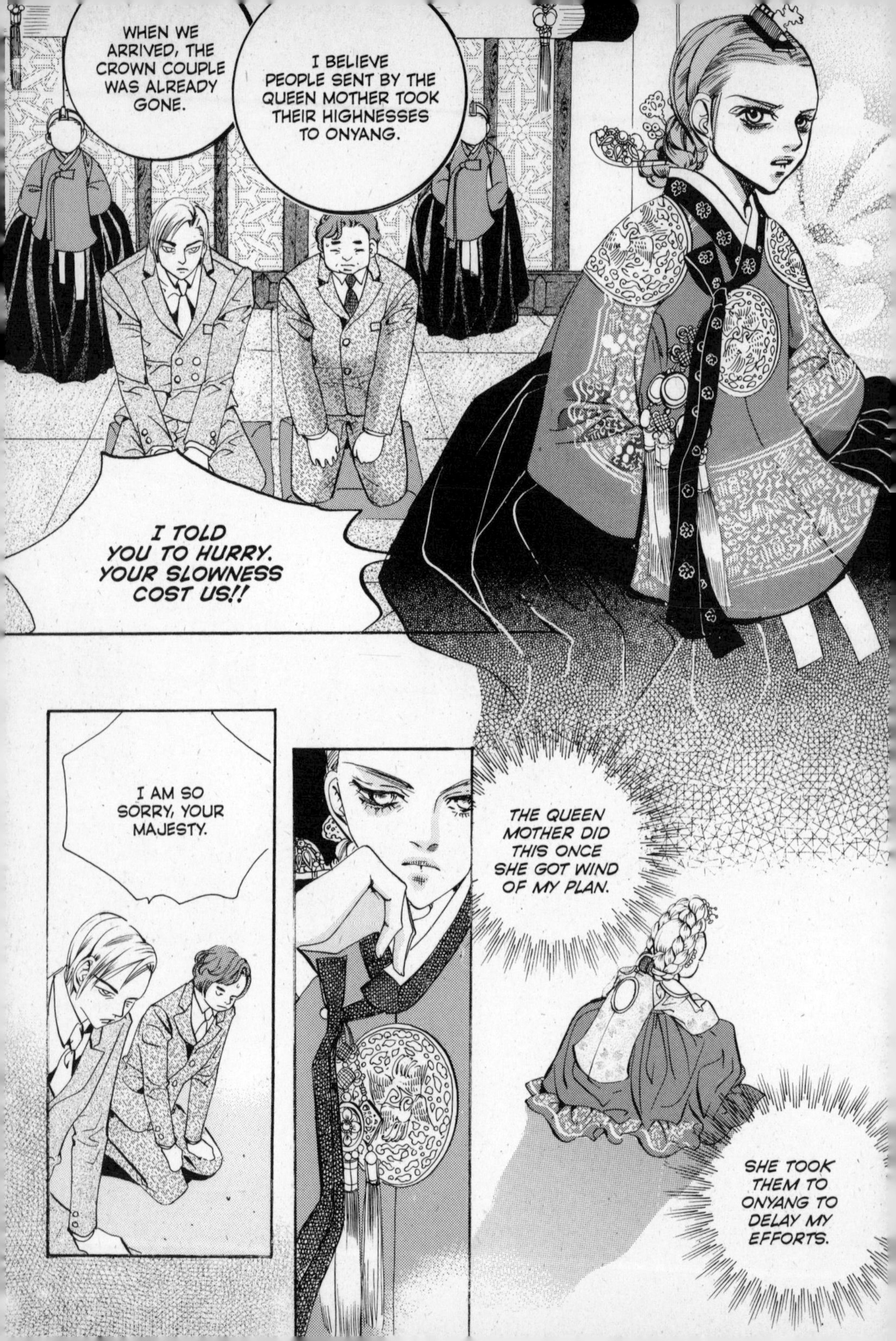
WHEN WE ARRIVED, THE CROWN COUPLE WAS ALREADY GONE.
I BELIEVE PEOPLE SENT BY THE QUEEN MOTHER TOOK THEIR HIGHNESSES TO ONYANG.
I TOLD YOU TO HURRY. YOUR SLOWNESS COST US!!
I AM SO SORRY, YOUR MAJESTY.
THE QUEEN MOTHER DID THIS ONCE SHE GOT WIND OF MY PLAN.
SHE TOOK THEM TO ONYANG TO DELAY MY EFFORTS.

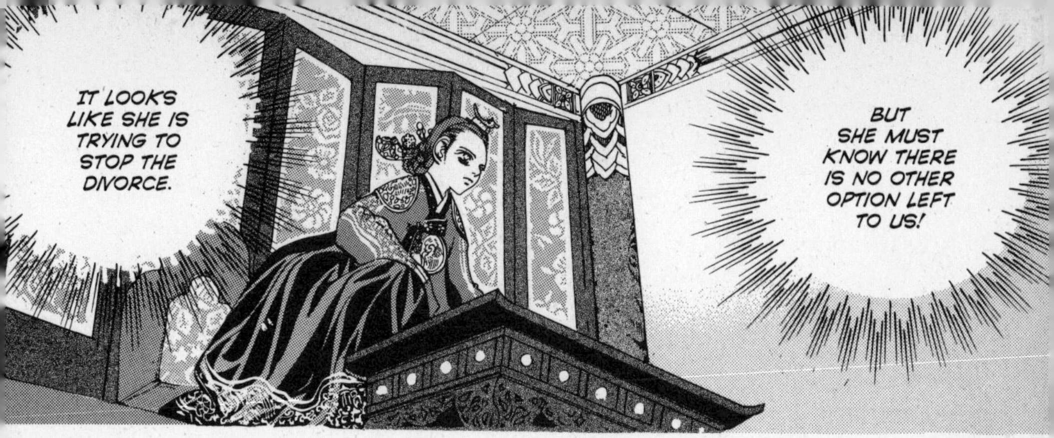
IT LOOKS LIKE SHE IS TRYING TO STOP THE DIVORCE.
BUT SHE MUST KNOW THERE IS NO OTHER OPTION LEFT TO US!
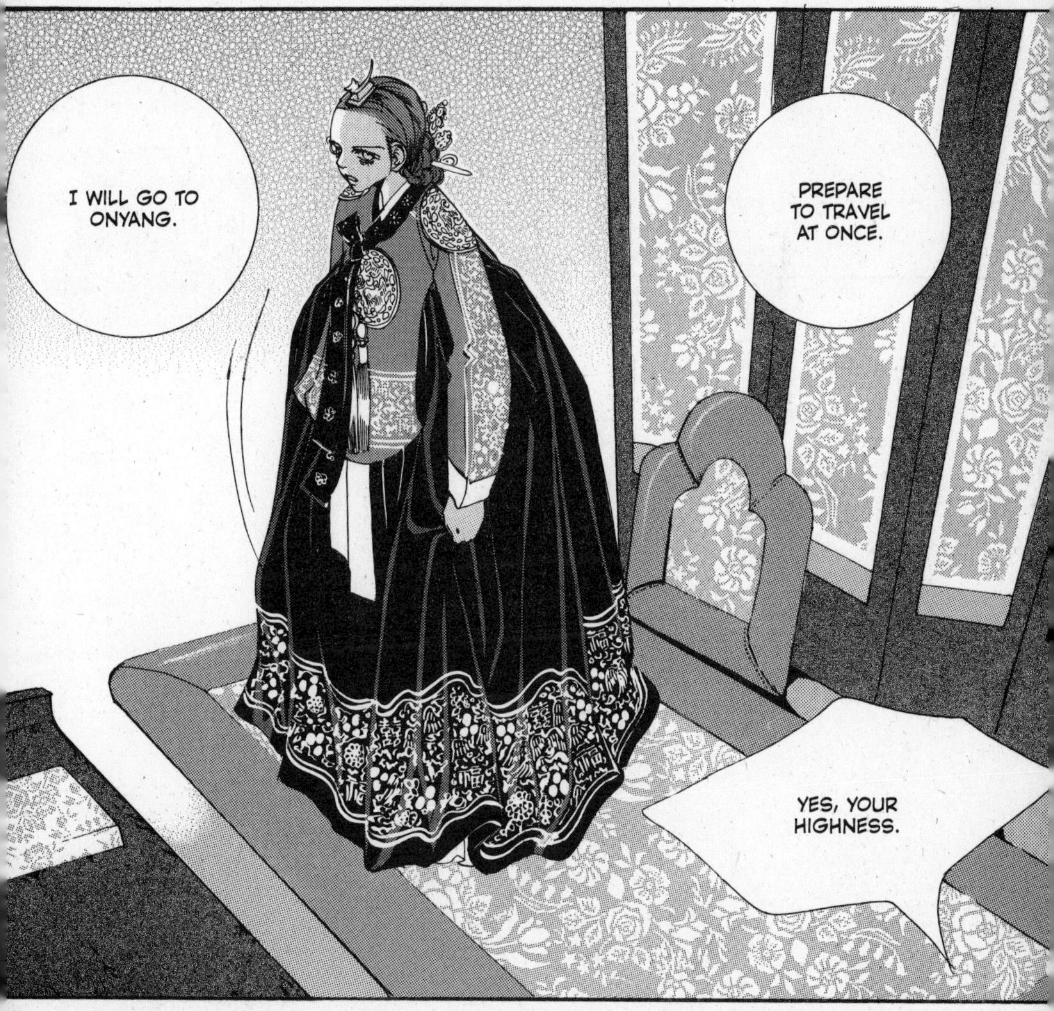
I WILL GO TO ONYANG.
PREPARE TO TRAVEL AT ONCE.
YES, YOUR HIGHNESS.

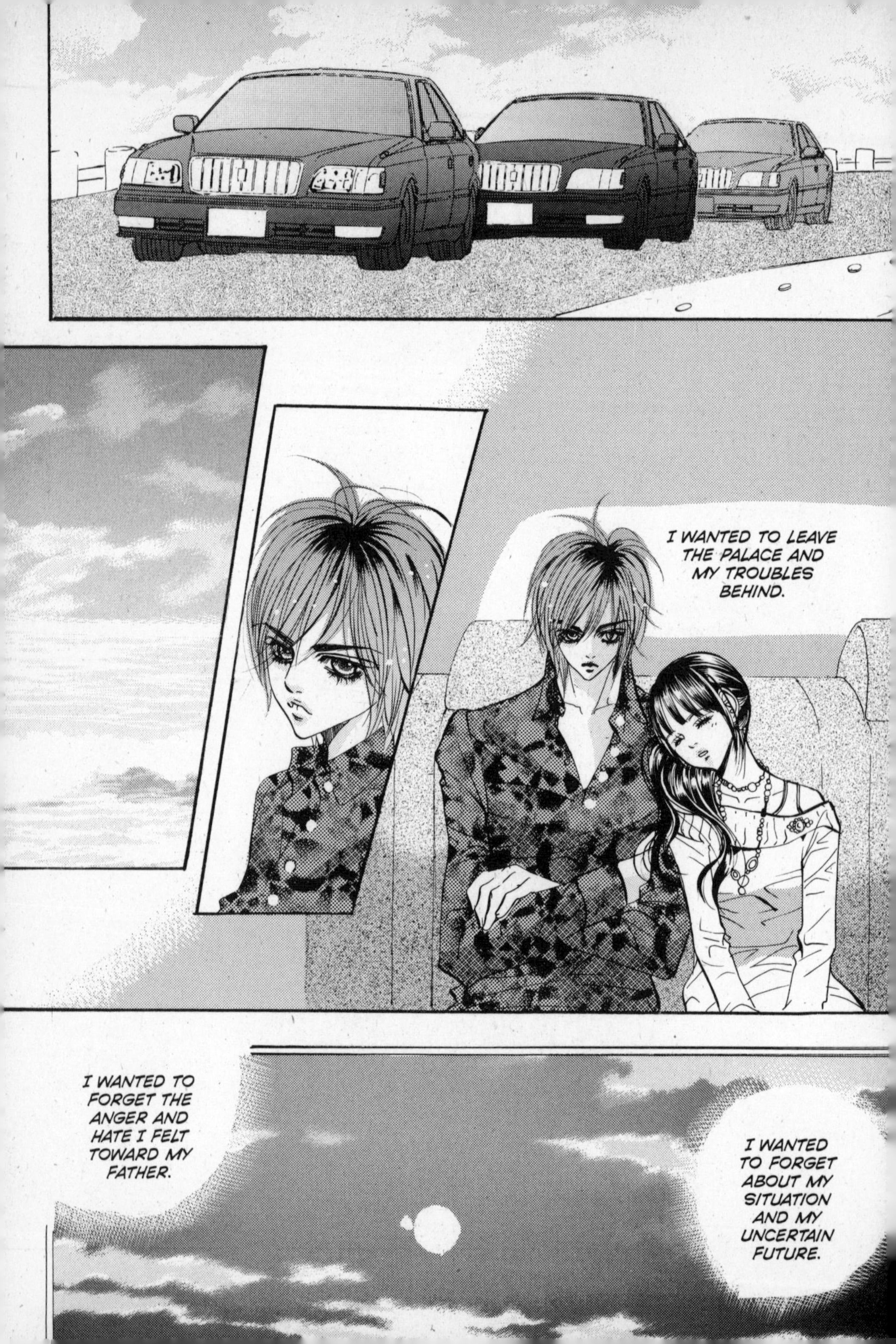
I WANTED TO LEAVE THE PALACE AND MY TROUBLES BEHIND.
I WANTED TO FORGET THE ANGER AND HATE I FELT TOWARD MY FATHER.
I WANTED TO FORGET ABOUT MY SITUATION AND MY UNCERTAIN FUTURE.

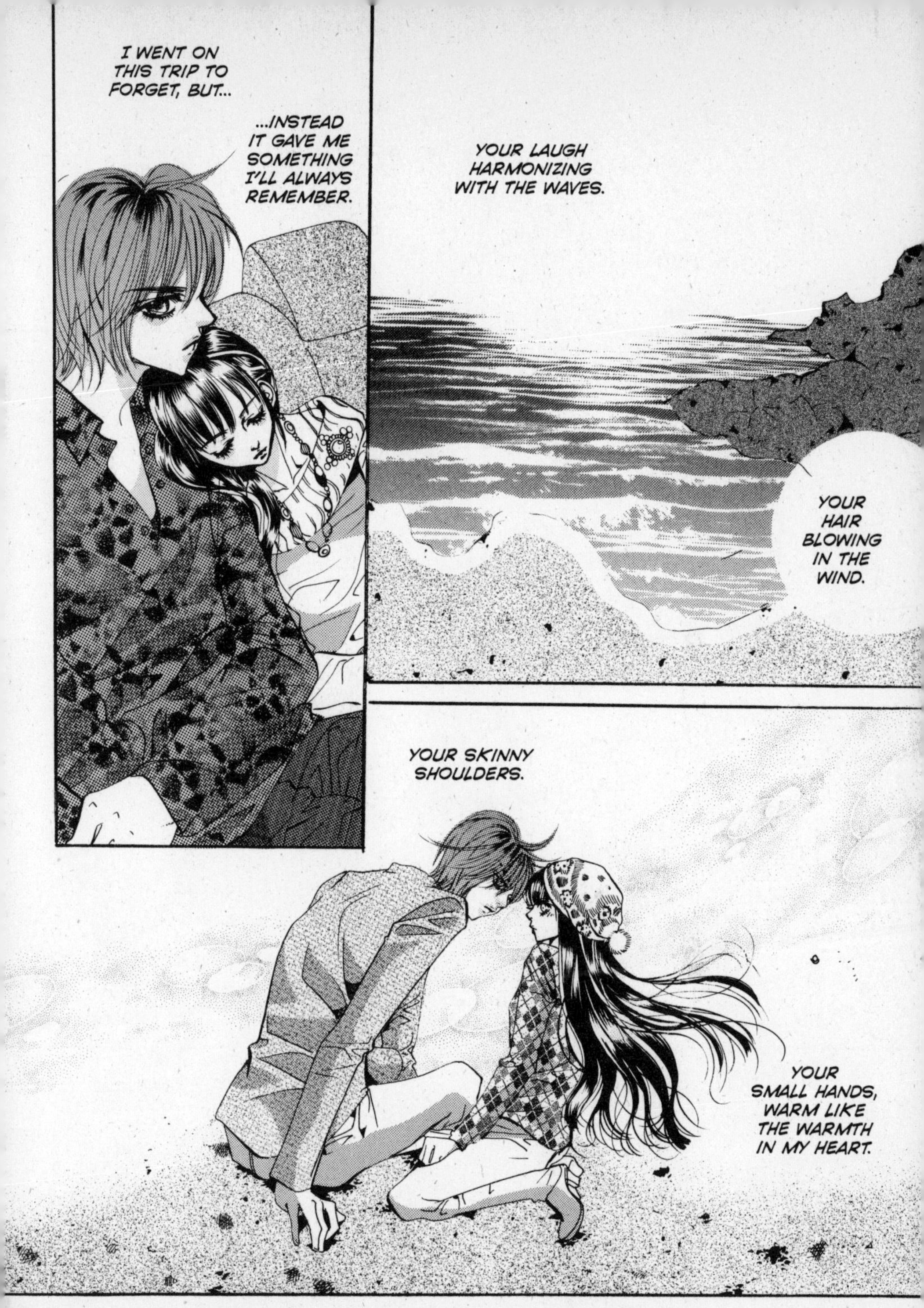
I WENT ON THIS TRIP TO FORGET, BUT...
...INSTEAD IT GAVE ME SOMETHING I'LL ALWAYS REMEMBER.
YOUR LAUGH HARMONIZING WITH THE WAVES.
YOUR HAIR BLOWING IN THE WIND.
YOUR SKINNY SHOULDERS.
YOUR SMALL HANDS, WARM LIKE THE WARMTH IN MY HEART.

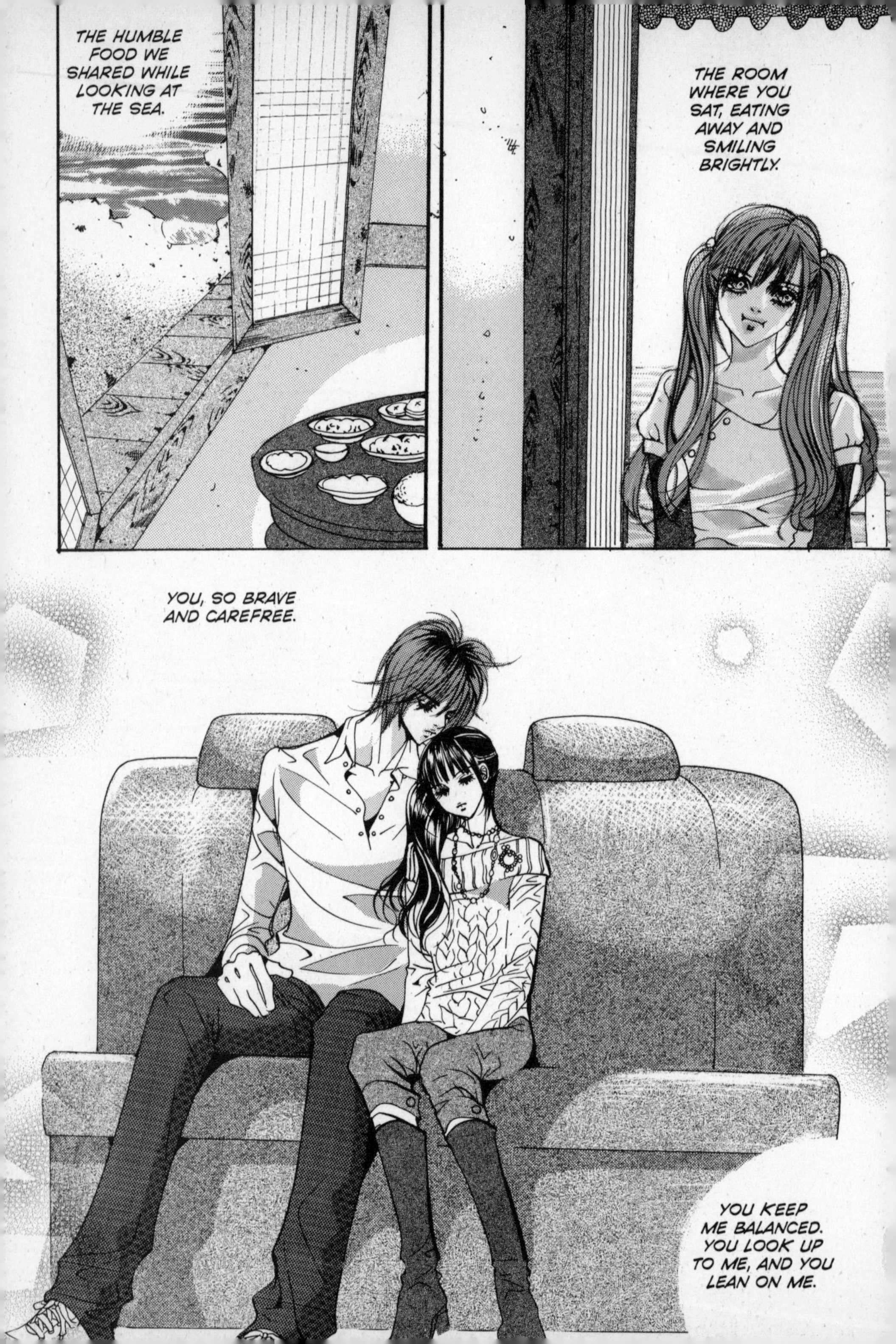
THE HUMBLE FOOD WE SHARED WHILE LOOKING AT THE SEA.
THE ROOM WHERE YOU SAT, EATING AWAY AND SMILING BRIGHTLY.
YOU, SO BRAVE AND CAREFREE.
YOU KEEP ME BALANCED. YOU LOOK UP TO ME, AND YOU LEAN ON ME.

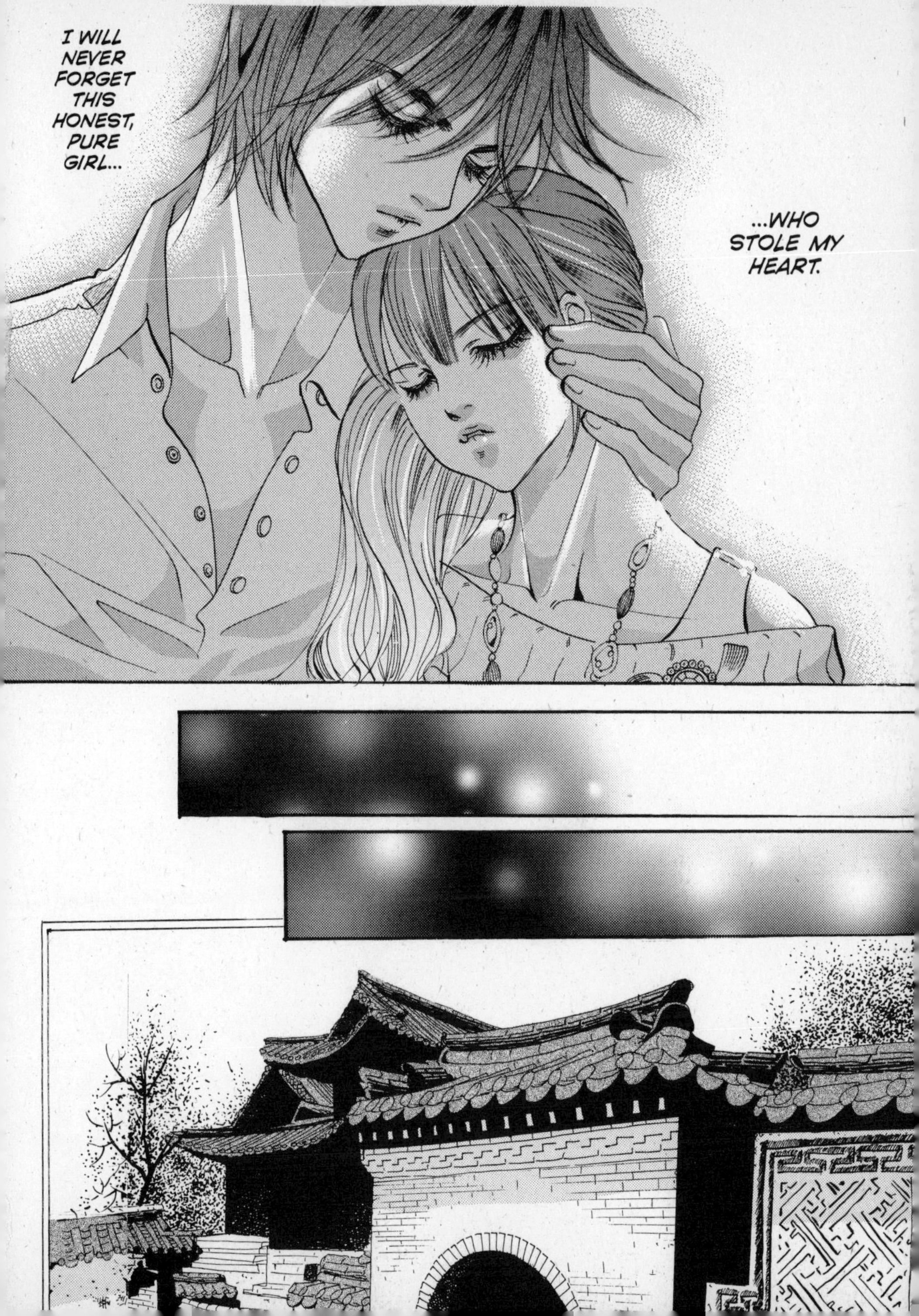
I WILL NEVER FORGET THIS HONEST, PURE GIRL...
...WHO STOLE MY HEART.

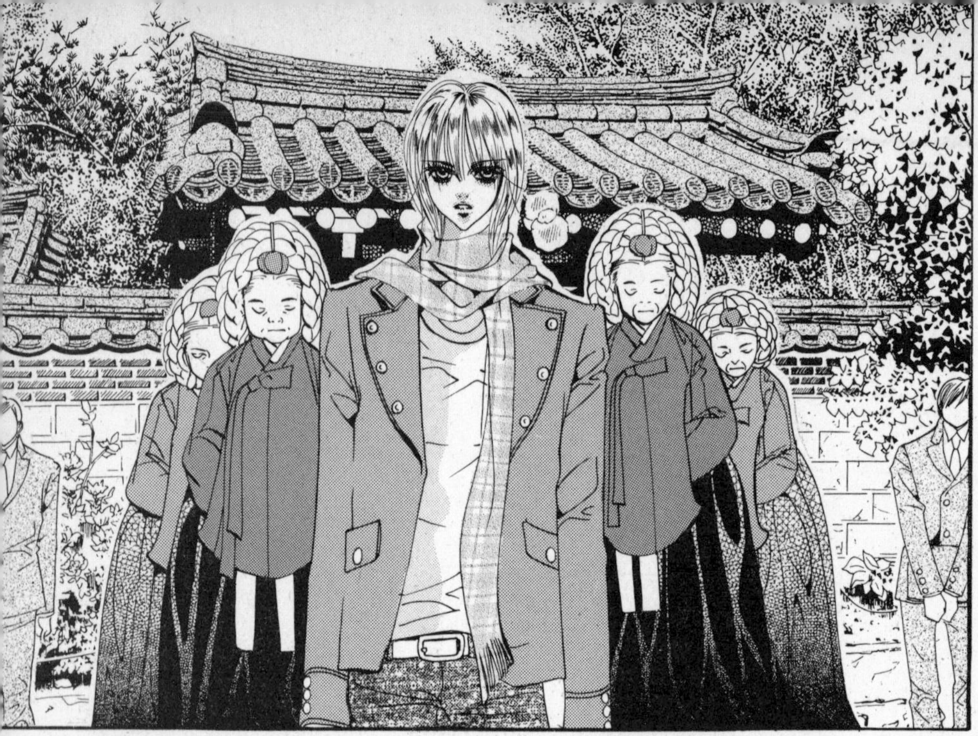
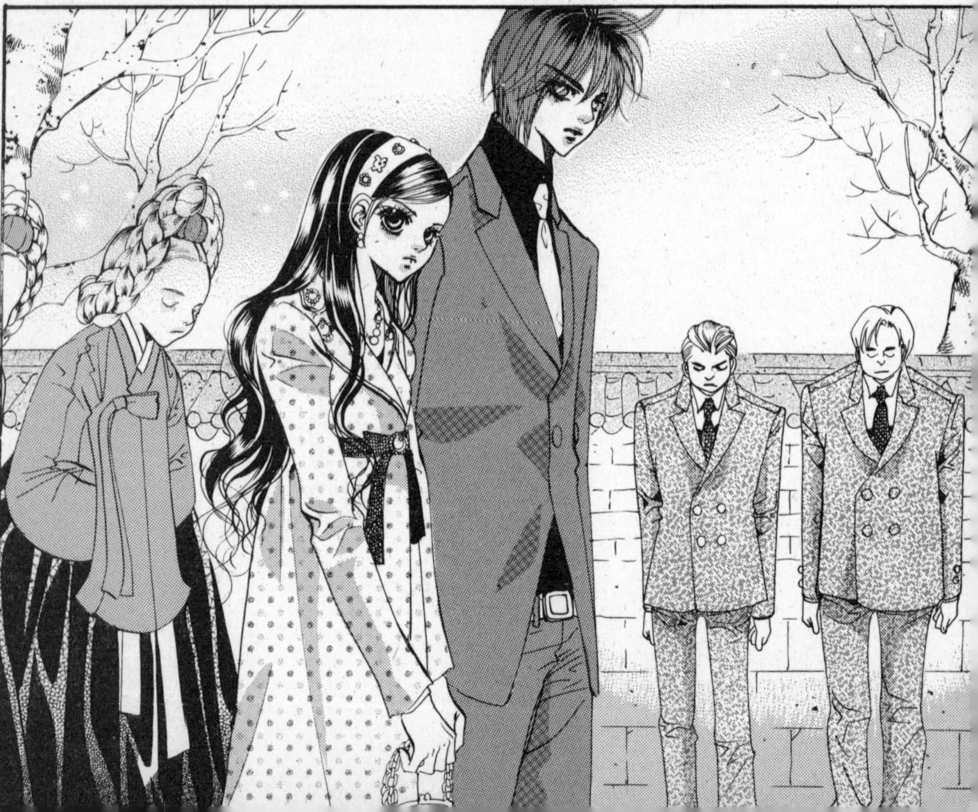

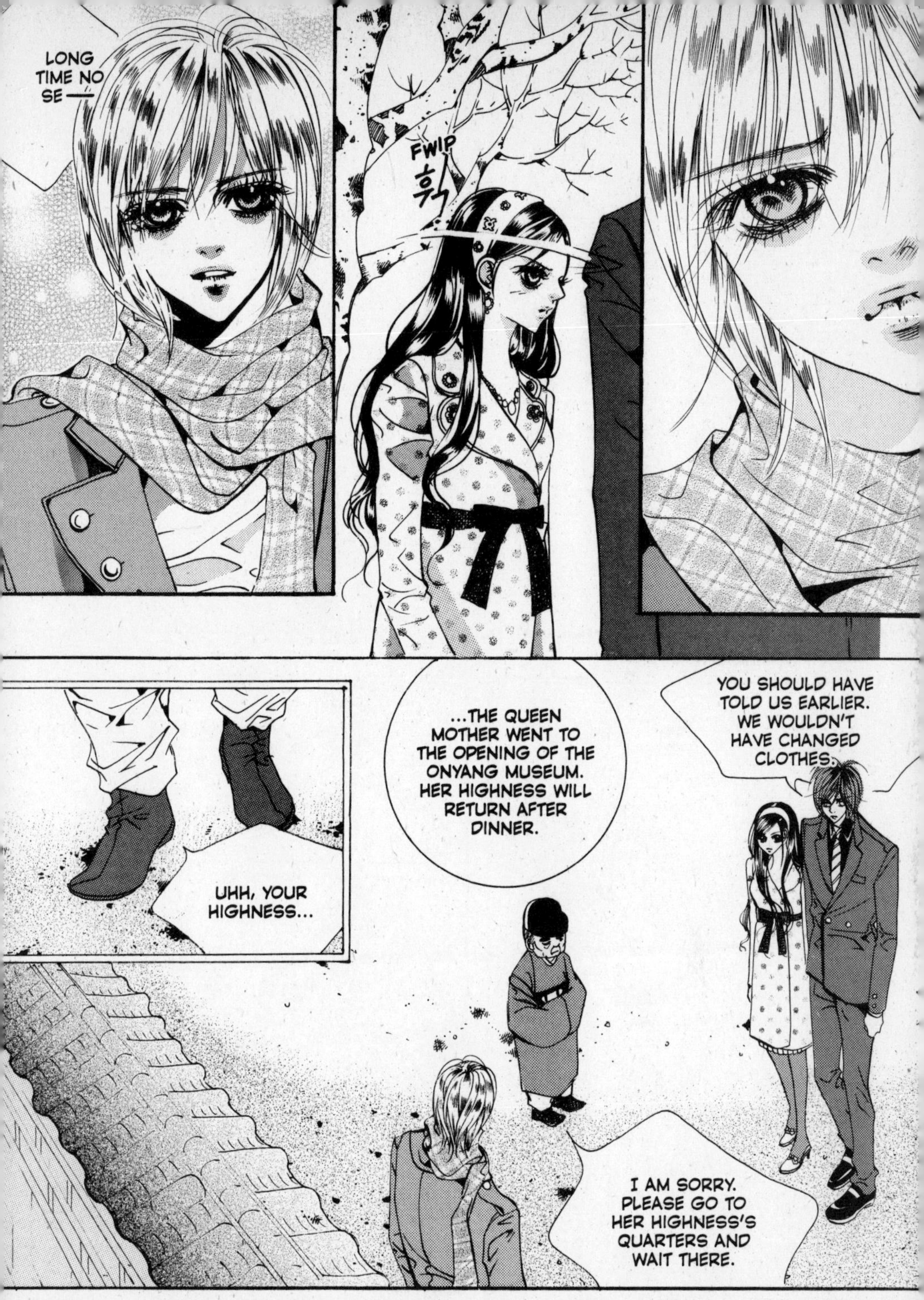
LONG TIME NO SE—
FWIP
훅
UHH, YOUR HIGHNESS...
...THE QUEEN MOTHER WENT TO THE OPENING OF THE ONYANG MUSEUM. HER HIGHNESS WILL RETURN AFTER DINNER.
YOU SHOULD HAVE TOLD US EARLIER. WE WOULDN'T HAVE CHANGED CLOTHES.
I AM SORRY. PLEASE GO TO HER HIGHNESS'S QUARTERS AND WAIT THERE.

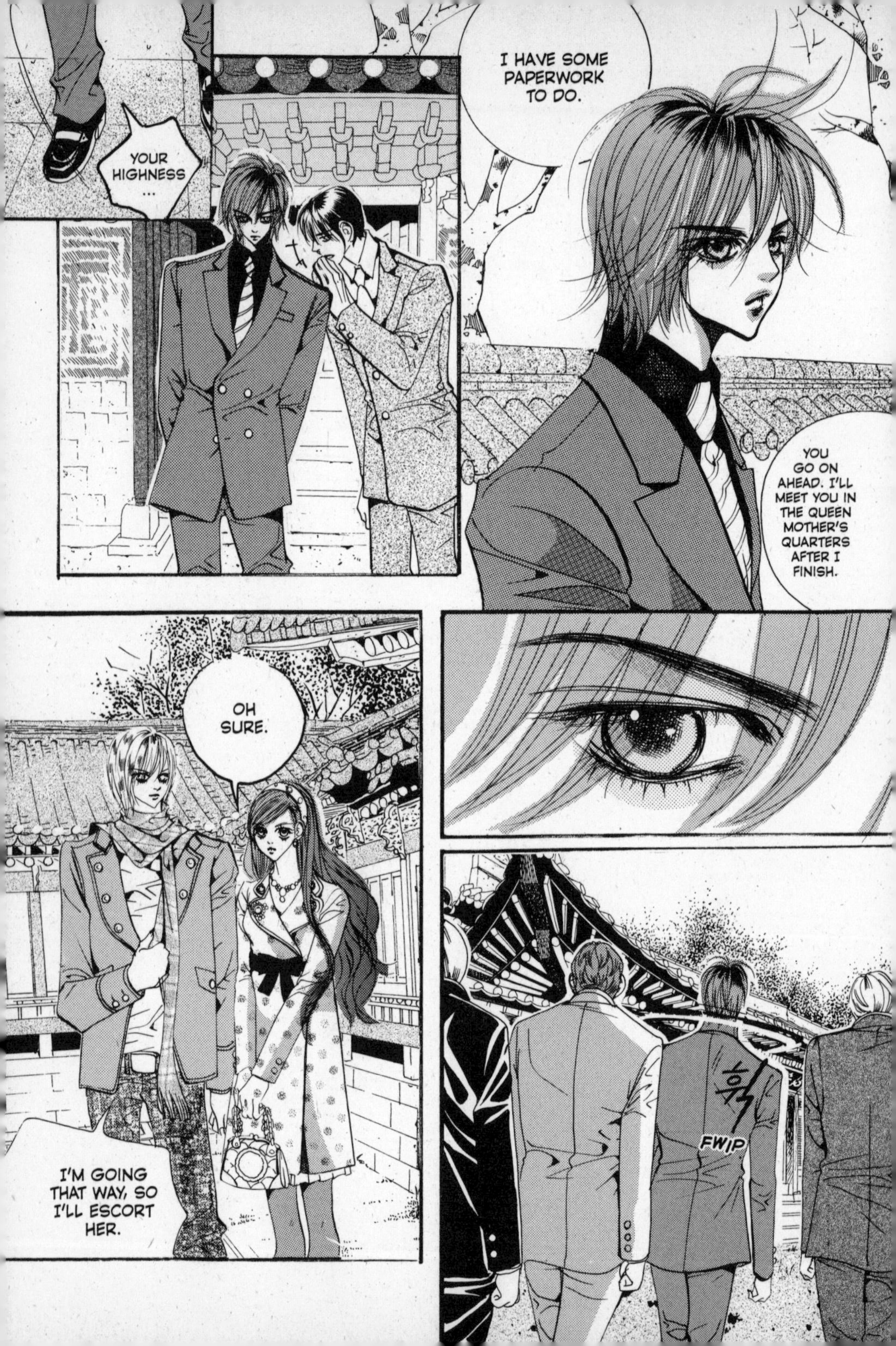
YOUR HIGHNESS ...
I HAVE SOME PAPERWORK TO DO.
YOU GO ON AHEAD. I'LL MEET YOU IN THE QUEEN MOTHER'S QUARTERS AFTER I FINISH.
OH SURE.
I'M GOING THAT WAY, SO I'LL ESCORT HER.
휙
FWIP

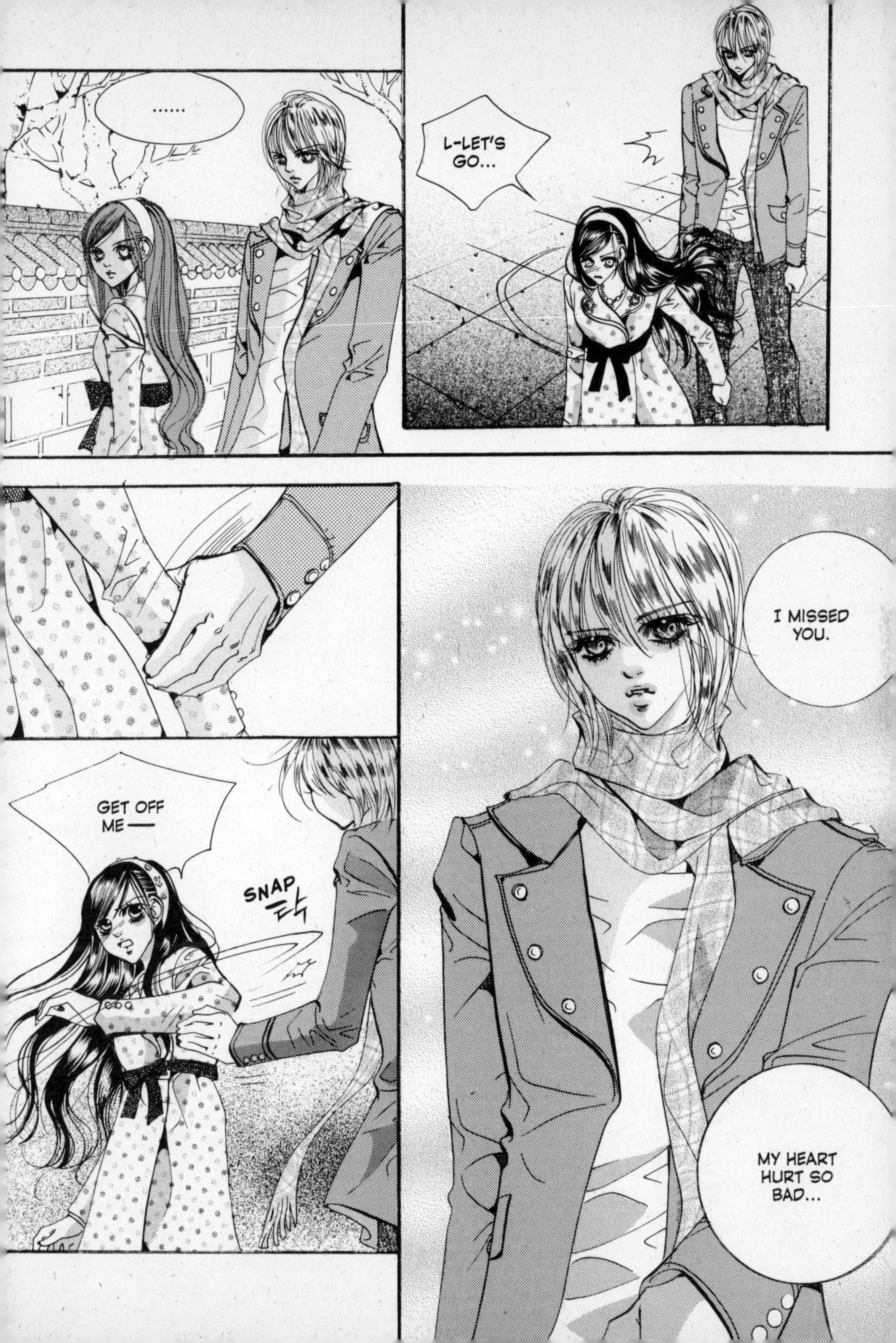
......
L-LET'S GO...
GET OFF ME—
SNAP
탁
I MISSED YOU.
MY HEART HURT SO BAD...

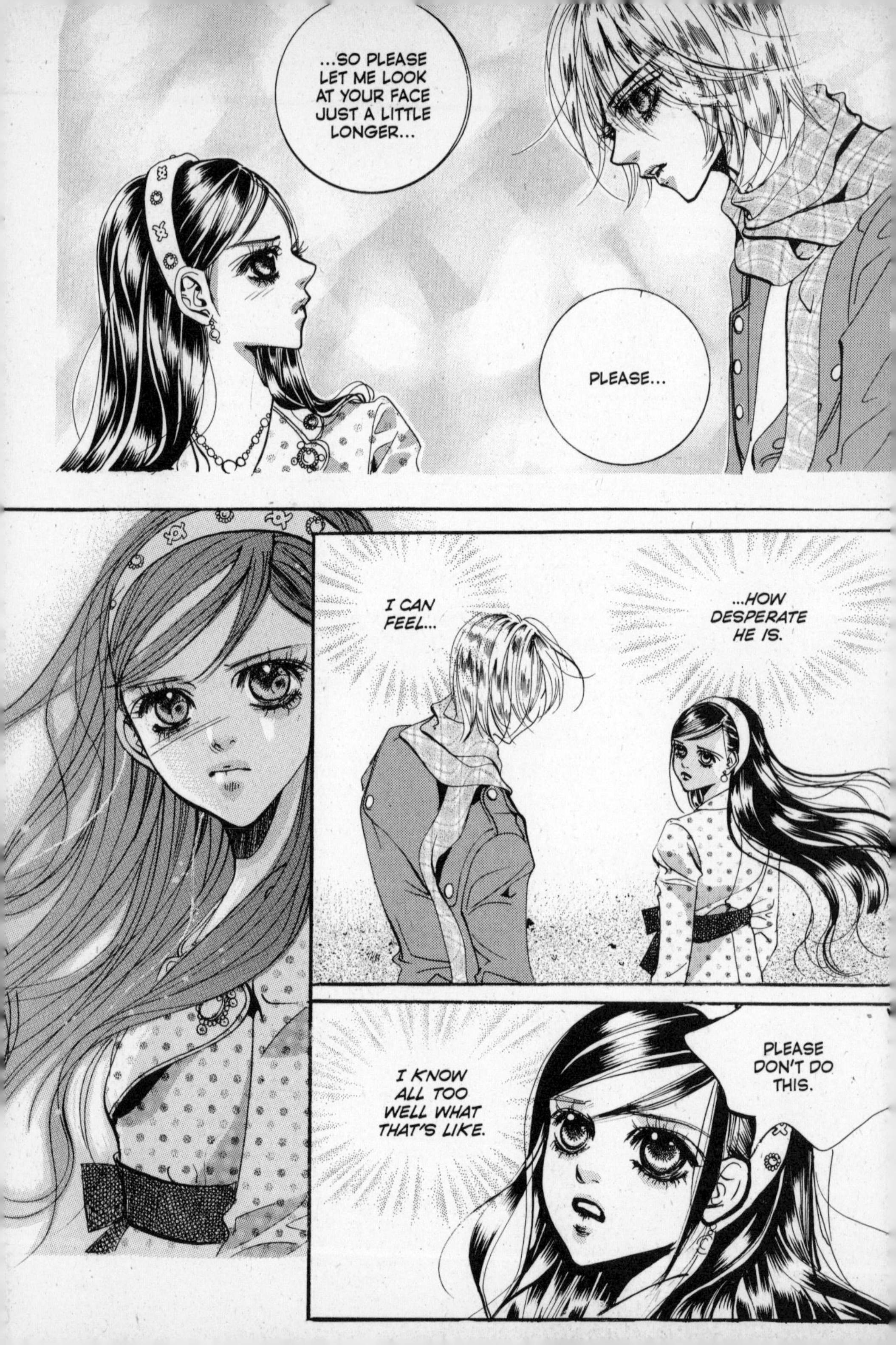
...SO PLEASE LET ME LOOK AT YOUR FACE JUST A LITTLE LONGER...
PLEASE...
I CAN FEEL...
...HOW DESPERATE HE IS.
I KNOW ALL TOO WELL WHAT THAT'S LIKE.
PLEASE DON'T DO THIS.

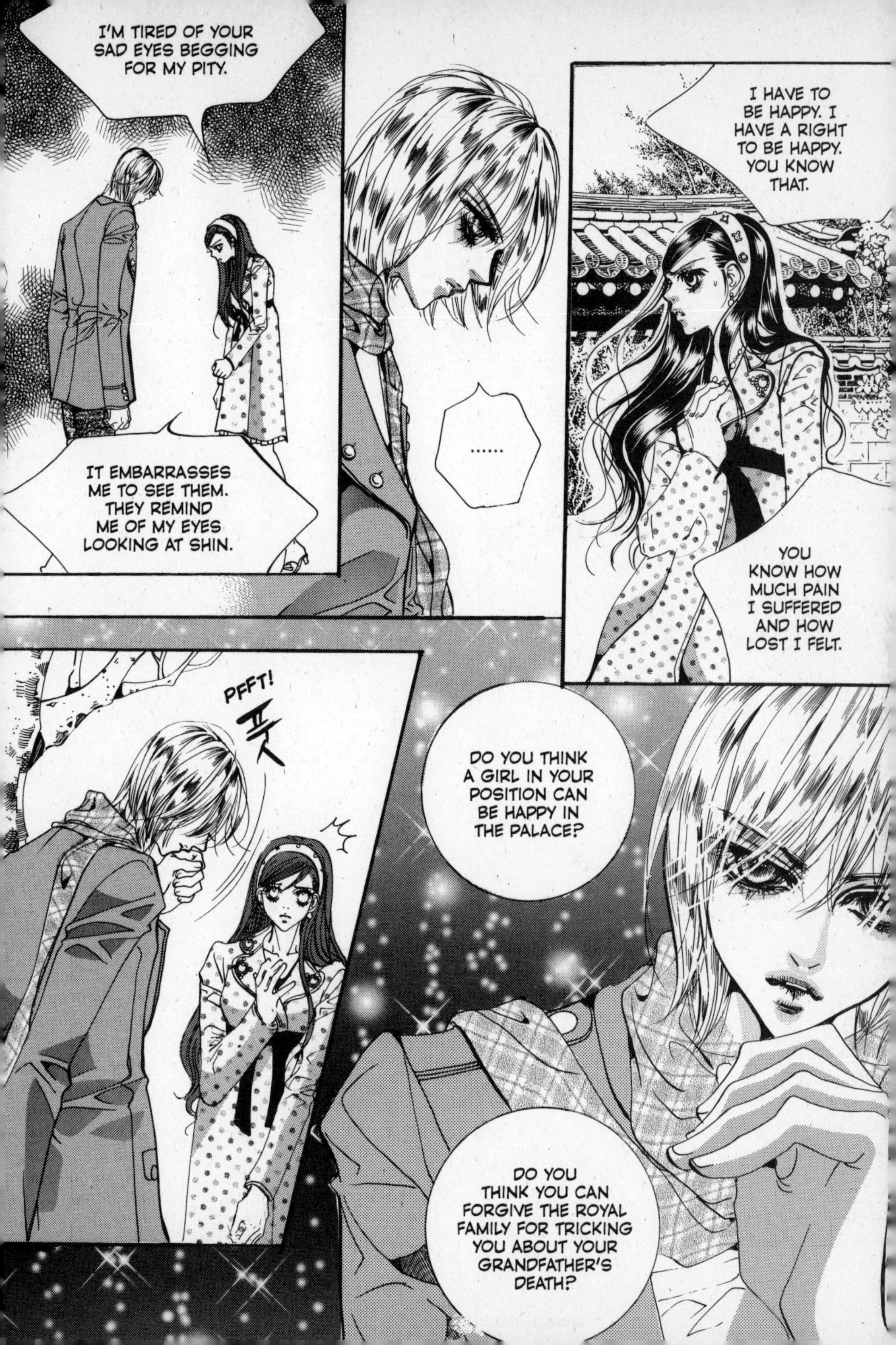
I'M TIRED OF YOUR SAD EYES BEGGING FOR MY PITY.
IT EMBARRASSES ME TO SEE THEM. THEY REMIND ME OF MY EYES LOOKING AT SHIN.
......
I HAVE TO BE HAPPY. I HAVE A RIGHT TO BE HAPPY. YOU KNOW THAT.
YOU KNOW HOW MUCH PAIN I SUFFERED AND HOW LOST I FELT.
PFFT!
DO YOU THINK A GIRL IN YOUR POSITION CAN BE HAPPY IN THE PALACE?
DO YOU THINK YOU CAN FORGIVE THE ROYAL FAMILY FOR TRICKING YOU ABOUT YOUR GRANDFATHER'S DEATH?

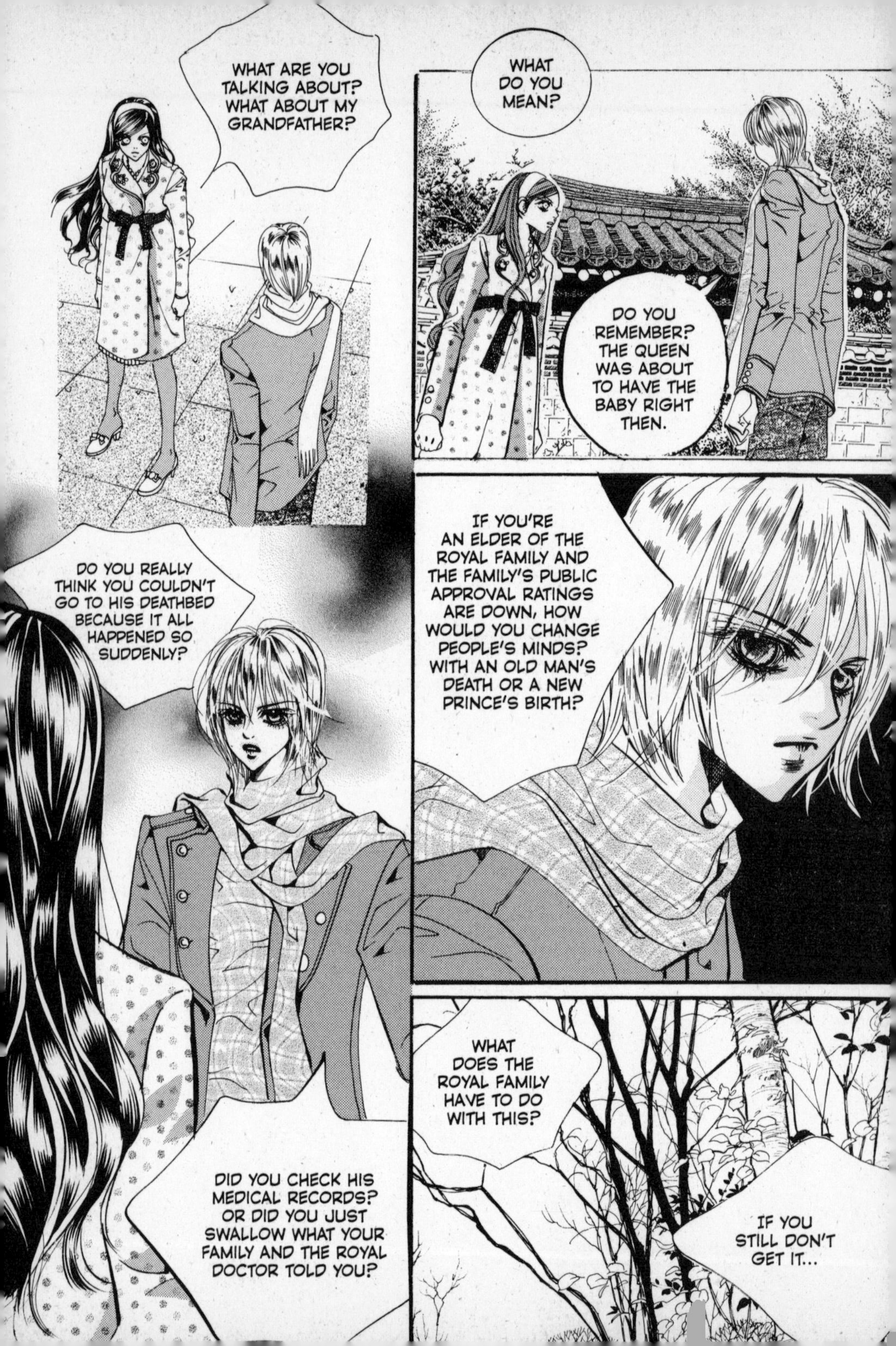
WHAT ARE YOU TALKING ABOUT? WHAT ABOUT MY GRANDFATHER?
WHAT DO YOU MEAN?
DO YOU REMEMBER? THE QUEEN WAS ABOUT TO HAVE THE BABY RIGHT THEN.
DO YOU REALLY THINK YOU COULDN'T GO TO HIS DEATHBED BECAUSE IT ALL HAPPENED SO SUDDENLY?
DID YOU CHECK HIS MEDICAL RECORDS? OR DID YOU JUST SWALLOW WHAT YOUR FAMILY AND THE ROYAL DOCTOR TOLD YOU?
IF YOU'RE AN ELDER OF THE ROYAL FAMILY AND THE FAMILY'S PUBLIC APPROVAL RATINGS ARE DOWN, HOW WOULD YOU CHANGE PEOPLE'S MINDS? WITH AN OLD MAN'S DEATH OR A NEW PRINCE'S BIRTH?
WHAT DOES THE ROYAL FAMILY HAVE TO DO WITH THIS?
IF YOU STILL DON'T GET IT...

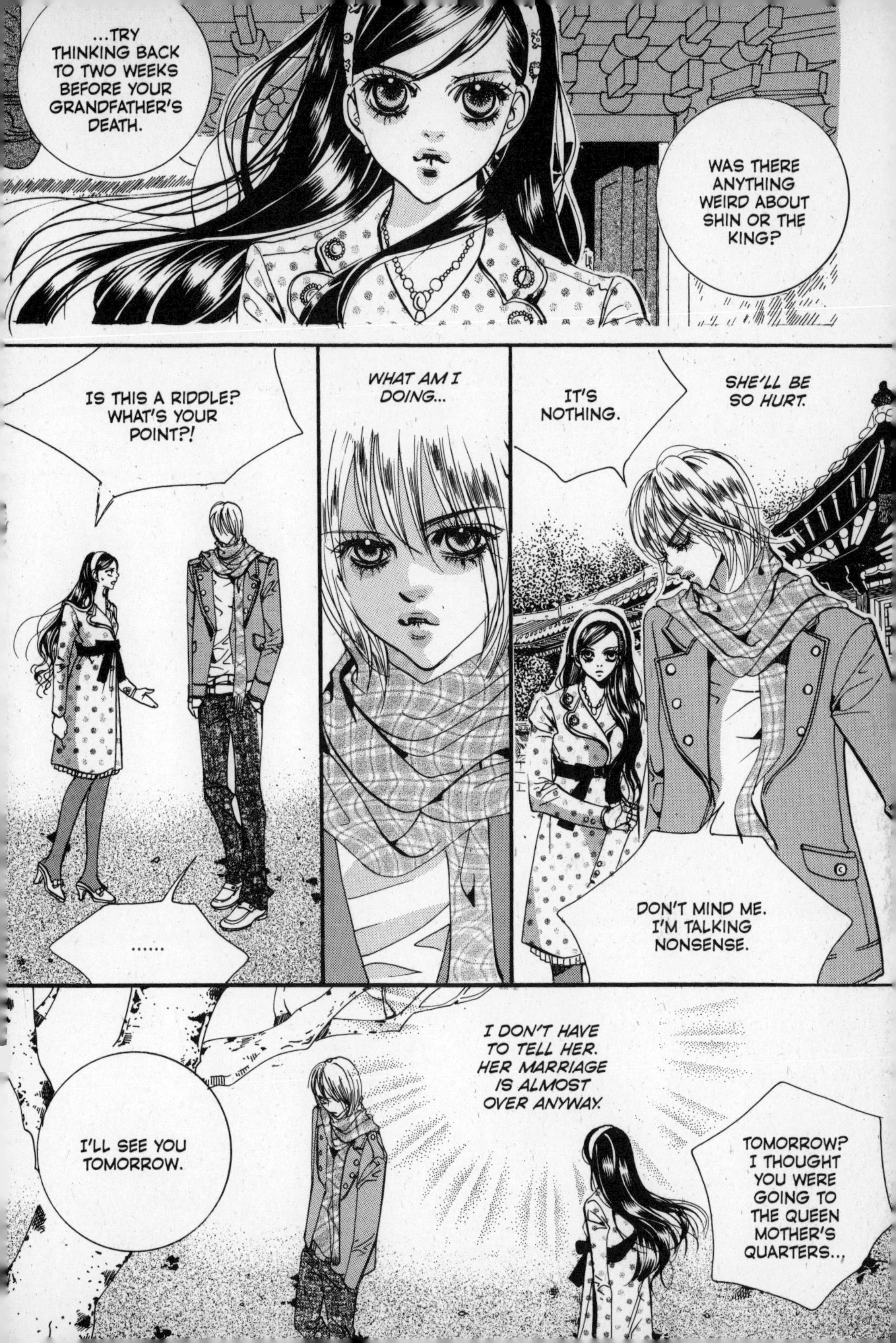
...TRY THINKING BACK TO TWO WEEKS BEFORE YOUR GRANDFATHER'S DEATH.
WAS THERE ANYTHING WEIRD ABOUT SHIN OR THE KING?
IS THIS A RIDDLE? WHAT'S YOUR POINT?!
......
WHAT AM I DOING...
IT'S NOTHING.
SHE'LL BE SO HURT.
DON'T MIND ME. I'M TALKING NONSENSE.
I'LL SEE YOU TOMORROW.
I DON'T HAVE TO TELL HER. HER MARRIAGE IS ALMOST OVER ANYWAY.
TOMORROW? I THOUGHT YOU WERE GOING TO THE QUEEN MOTHER'S QUARTERS...

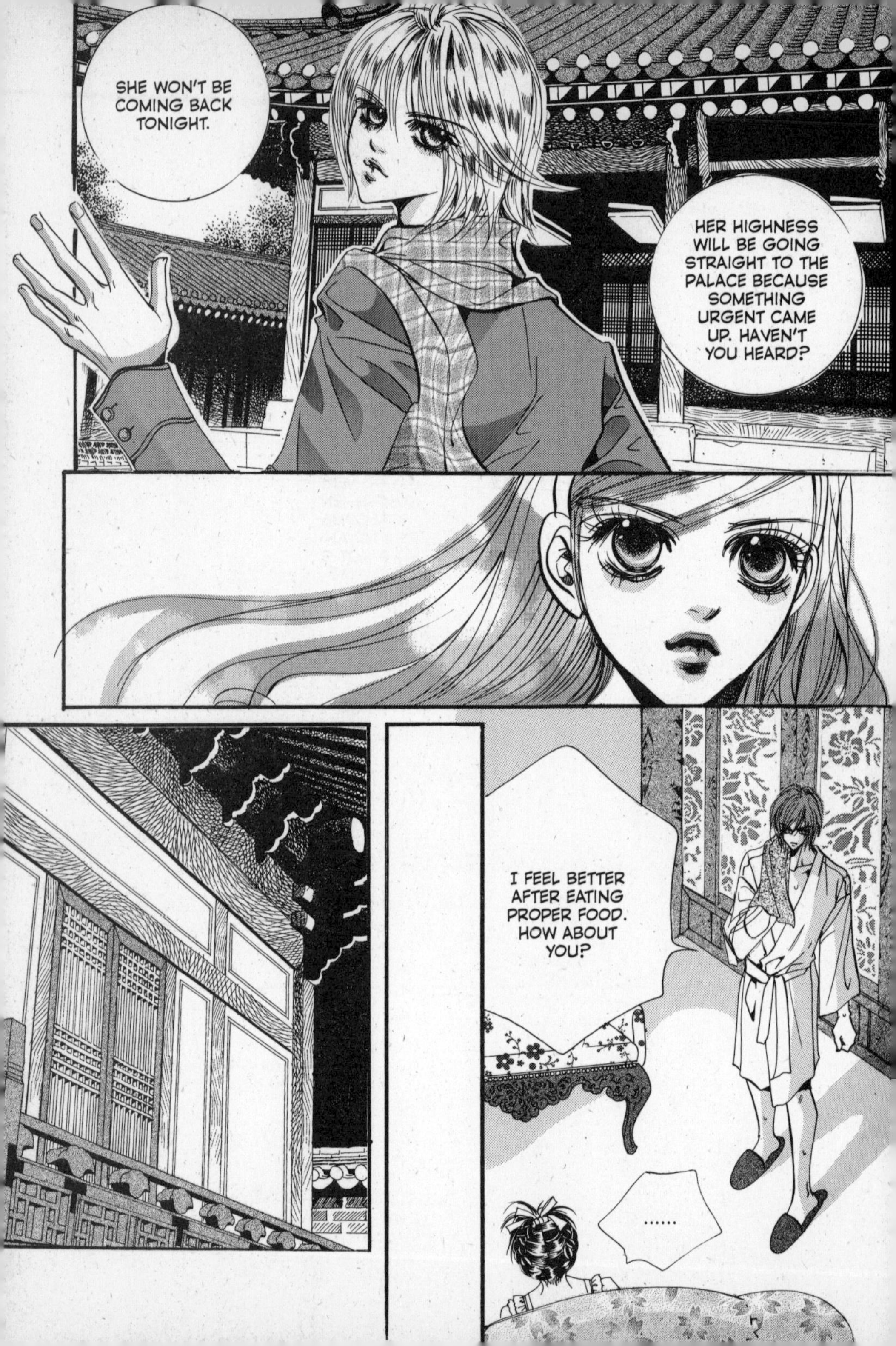
SHE WON'T BE COMING BACK TONIGHT.
HER HIGHNESS WILL BE GOING STRAIGHT TO THE PALACE BECAUSE SOMETHING URGENT CAME UP. HAVEN'T YOU HEARD?
I FEEL BETTER AFTER EATING PROPER FOOD. HOW ABOUT YOU?
......

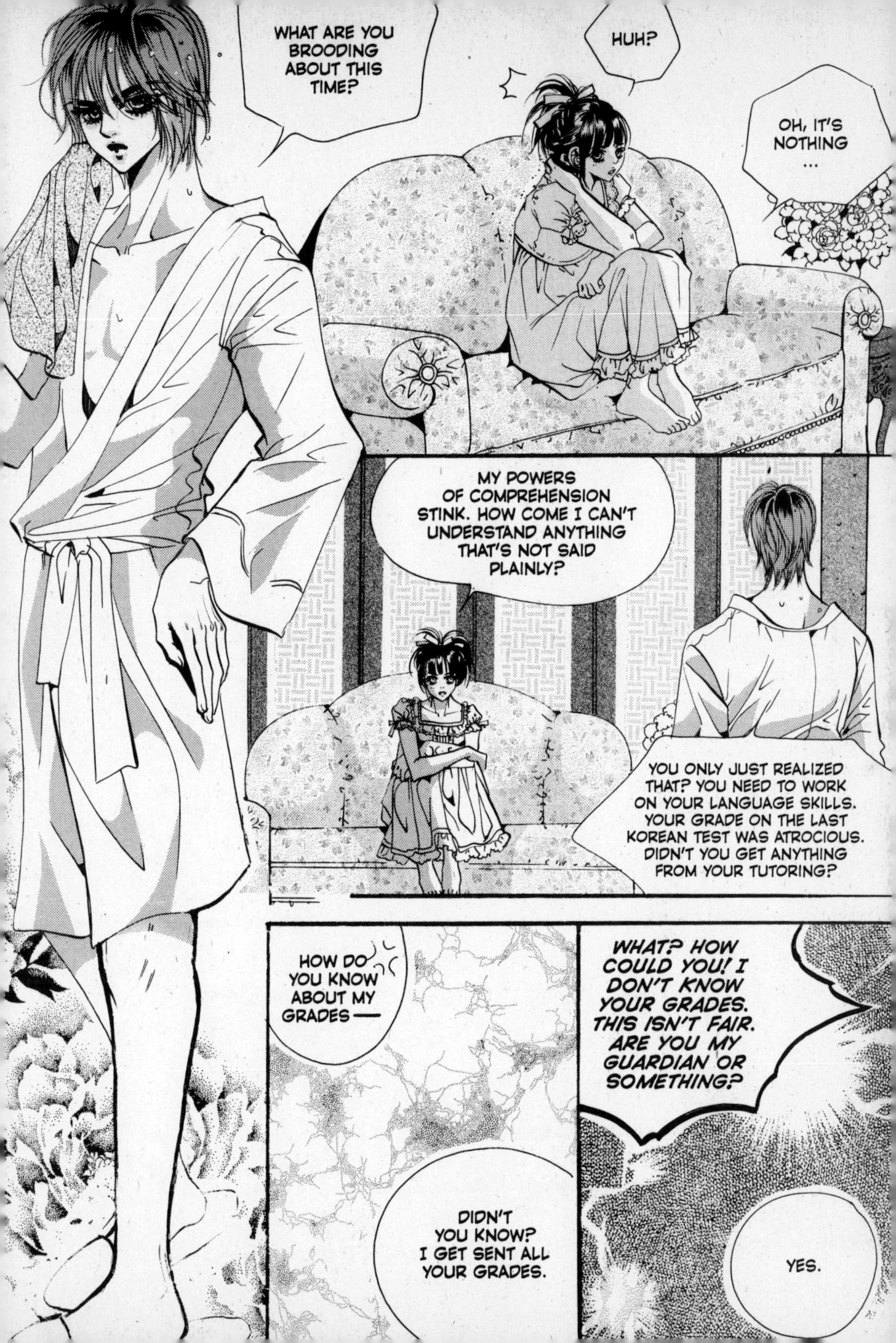
WHAT ARE YOU BROODING ABOUT THIS TIME?
HUH?
OH, IT'S NOTHING ...
MY POWERS OF COMPREHENSION STINK. HOW COME I CAN'T UNDERSTAND ANYTHING THAT'S NOT SAID PLAINLY?
YOU ONLY JUST REALIZED THAT? YOU NEED TO WORK ON YOUR LANGUAGE SKILLS. YOUR GRADE ON THE LAST KOREAN TEST WAS ATROCIOUS. DIDN'T YOU GET ANYTHING FROM YOUR TUTORING?
HOW DO YOU KNOW ABOUT MY GRADES—
DIDN'T YOU KNOW? I GET SENT ALL YOUR GRADES.
WHAT? HOW COULD YOU! I DON'T KNOW YOUR GRADES. THIS ISN'T FAIR. ARE YOU MY GUARDIAN OR SOMETHING?
YES.

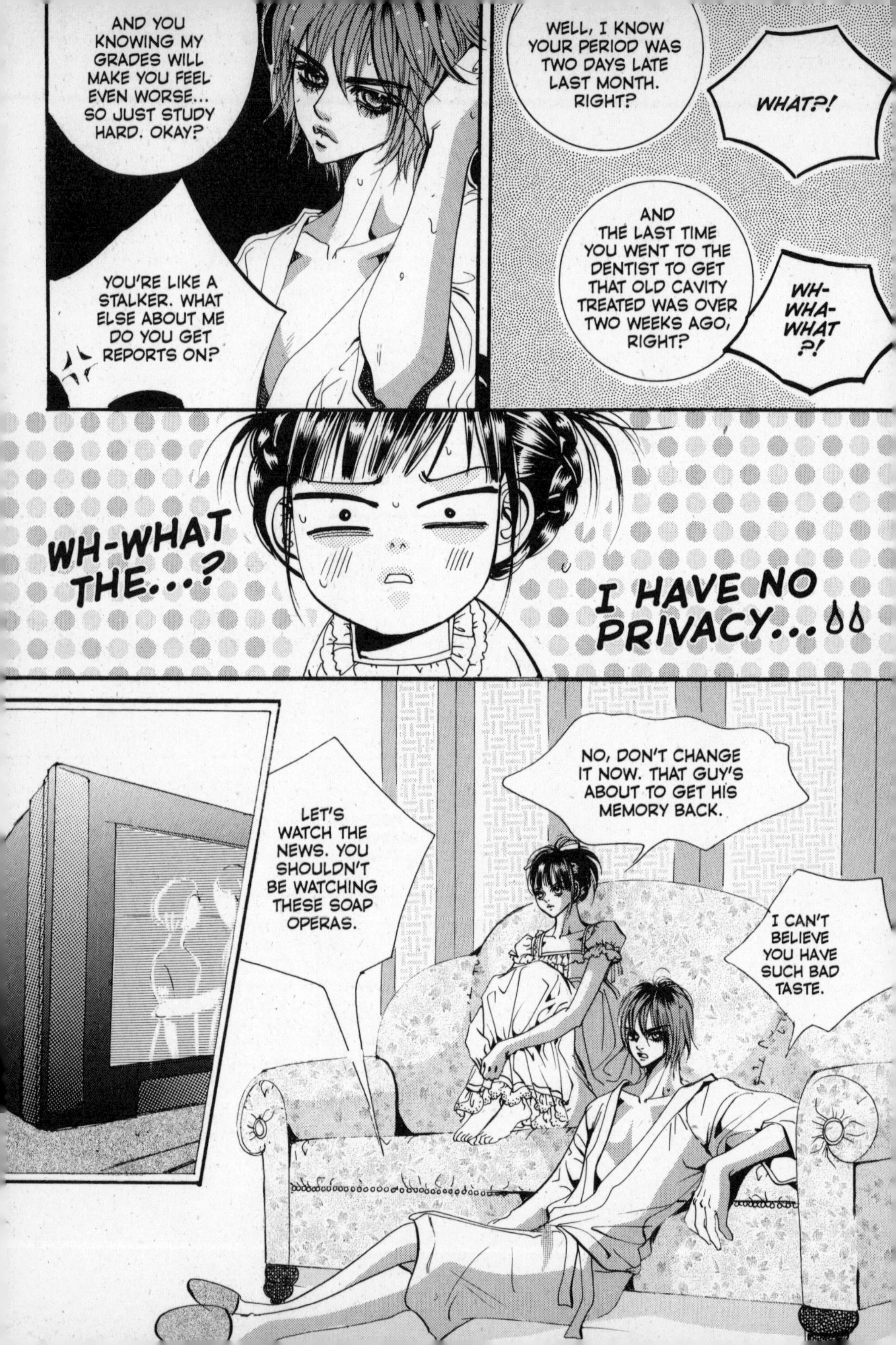
AND YOU KNOWING MY GRADES WILL MAKE YOU FEEL EVEN WORSE... SO JUST STUDY HARD. OKAY?
YOU'RE LIKE A STALKER. WHAT ELSE ABOUT ME DO YOU GET REPORTS ON?
WELL, I KNOW YOUR PERIOD WAS TWO DAYS LATE LAST MONTH. RIGHT?
WHAT?!
AND THE LAST TIME YOU WENT TO THE DENTIST TO GET THAT OLD CAVITY TREATED WAS OVER TWO WEEKS AGO, RIGHT?
WH-WHA-WHAT?!
WH-WHAT THE...?
I HAVE NO PRIVACY...
LET'S WATCH THE NEWS. YOU SHOULDN'T BE WATCHING THESE SOAP OPERAS.
NO, DON'T CHANGE IT NOW. THAT GUY'S ABOUT TO GET HIS MEMORY BACK.
I CAN'T BELIEVE YOU HAVE SUCH BAD TASTE.

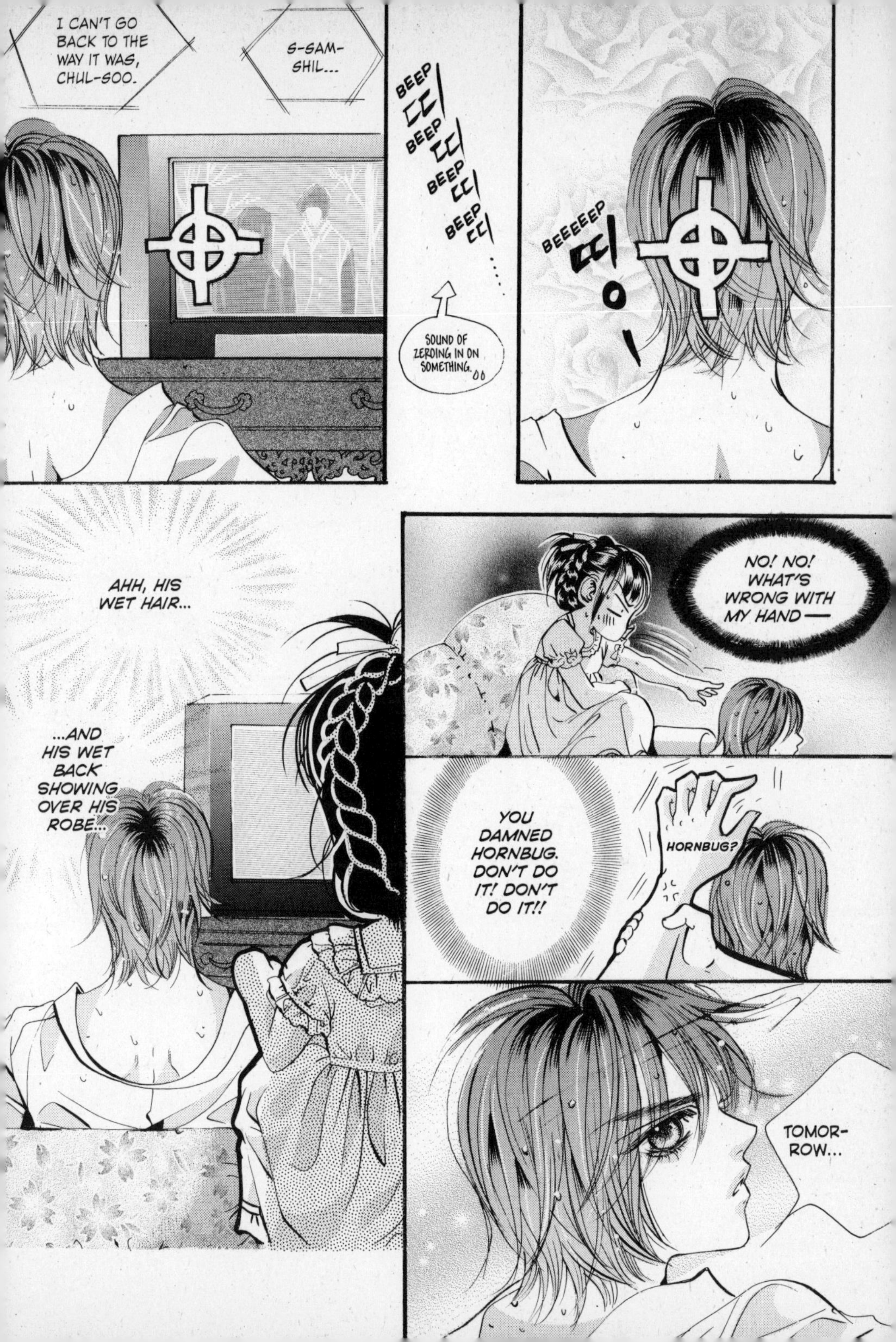
I CAN'T GO BACK TO THE WAY IT WAS, CHUL-SOO.
S-SAM-SHIL...
BEEP BEEP BEEP BEEP
SOUND OF ZEROING IN ON SOMETHING.
BEEEEEP
AHH, HIS WET HAIR...
...AND HIS WET BACK SHOWING OVER HIS ROBE...
NO! NO! WHAT'S WRONG WITH MY HAND—
YOU DAMNED HORNBUG. DON'T DO IT! DON'T DO IT!!
HORNBUG?
TOMOR-ROW...

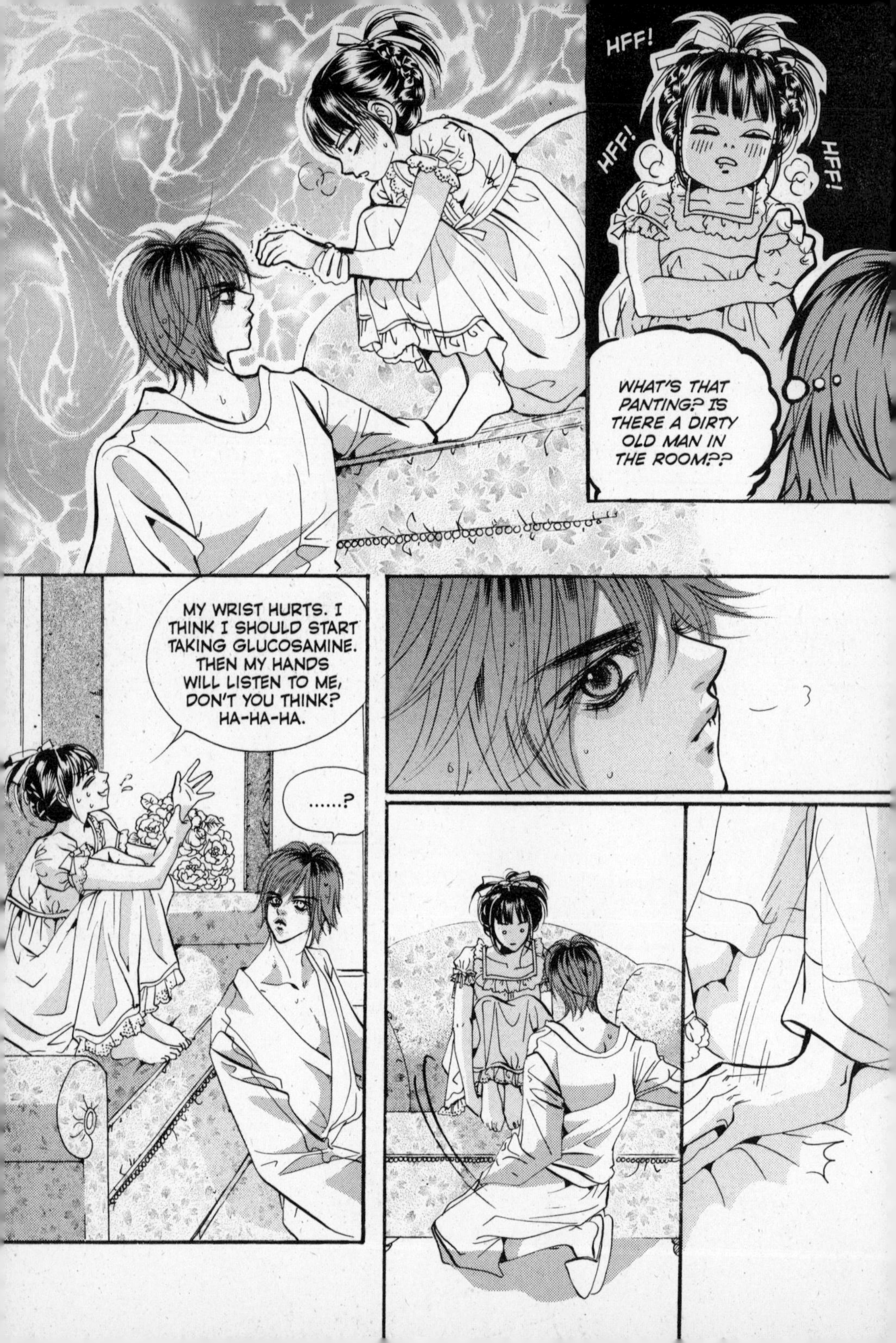
HFF!
HFF!
HFF!
WHAT'S THAT PANTING? IS THERE A DIRTY OLD MAN IN THE ROOM??
MY WRIST HURTS. I THINK I SHOULD START TAKING GLUCOSAMINE. THEN MY HANDS WILL LISTEN TO ME, DON'T YOU THINK? HA-HA-HA.
......?

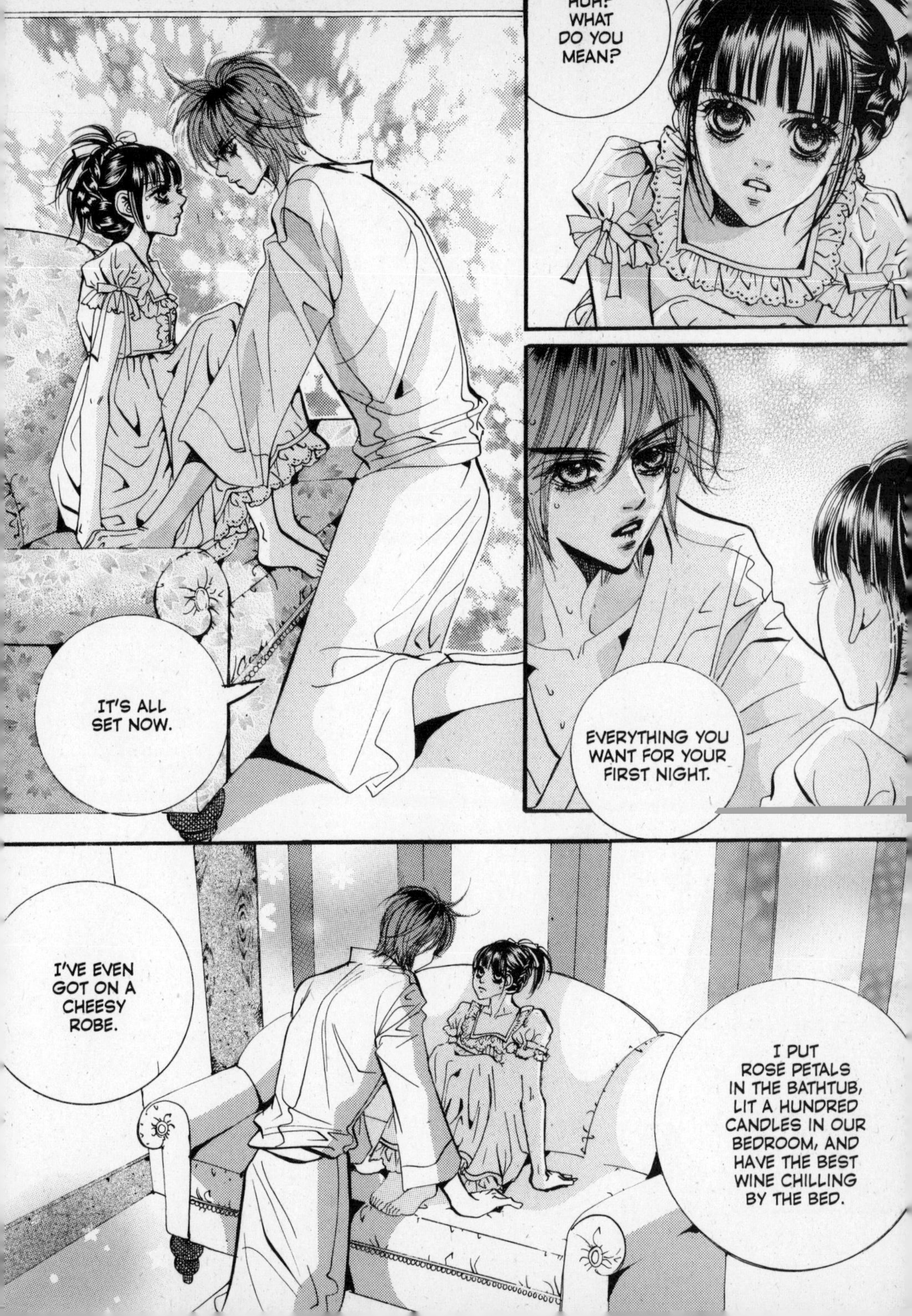
IT'S ALL SET NOW.
HUH? WHAT DO YOU MEAN?
EVERYTHING YOU WANT FOR YOUR FIRST NIGHT.
I'VE EVEN GOT ON A CHEESY ROBE.
I PUT ROSE PETALS IN THE BATHTUB, LIT A HUNDRED CANDLES IN OUR BEDROOM, AND HAVE THE BEST WINE CHILLING BY THE BED.

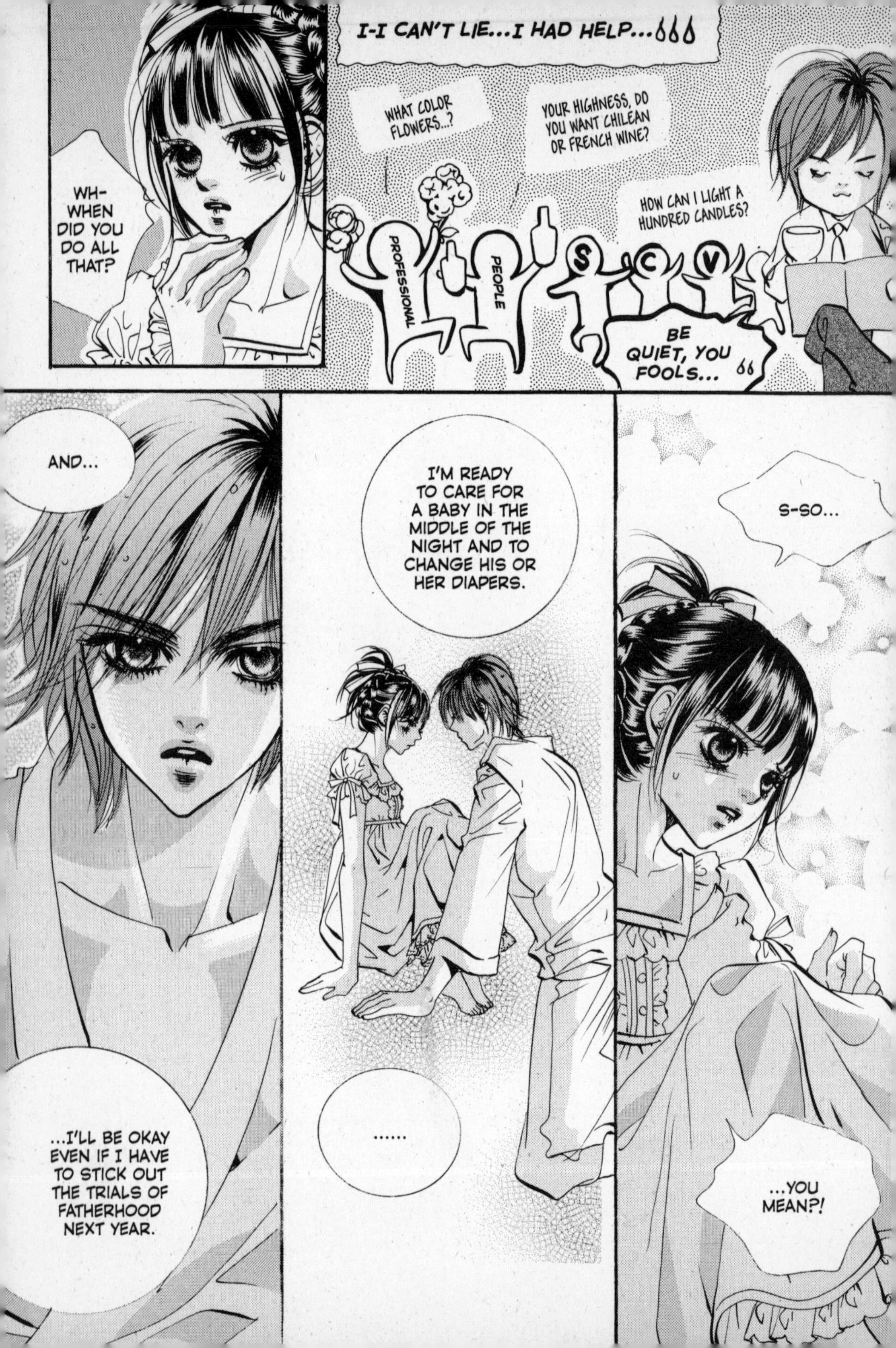
WH-WHEN DID YOU DO ALL THAT?
I-I CAN'T LIE...I HAD HELP...
WHAT COLOR FLOWERS...?
YOUR HIGHNESS, DO YOU WANT CHILEAN OR FRENCH WINE?
HOW CAN I LIGHT A HUNDRED CANDLES?
PROFESSIONAL
PEOPLE
S
C
V
BE QUIET, YOU FOOLS...
AND...
...I'LL BE OKAY EVEN IF I HAVE TO STICK OUT THE TRIALS OF FATHERHOOD NEXT YEAR.
I'M READY TO CARE FOR A BABY IN THE MIDDLE OF THE NIGHT AND TO CHANGE HIS OR HER DIAPERS.
......
S-SO...
...YOU MEAN?!

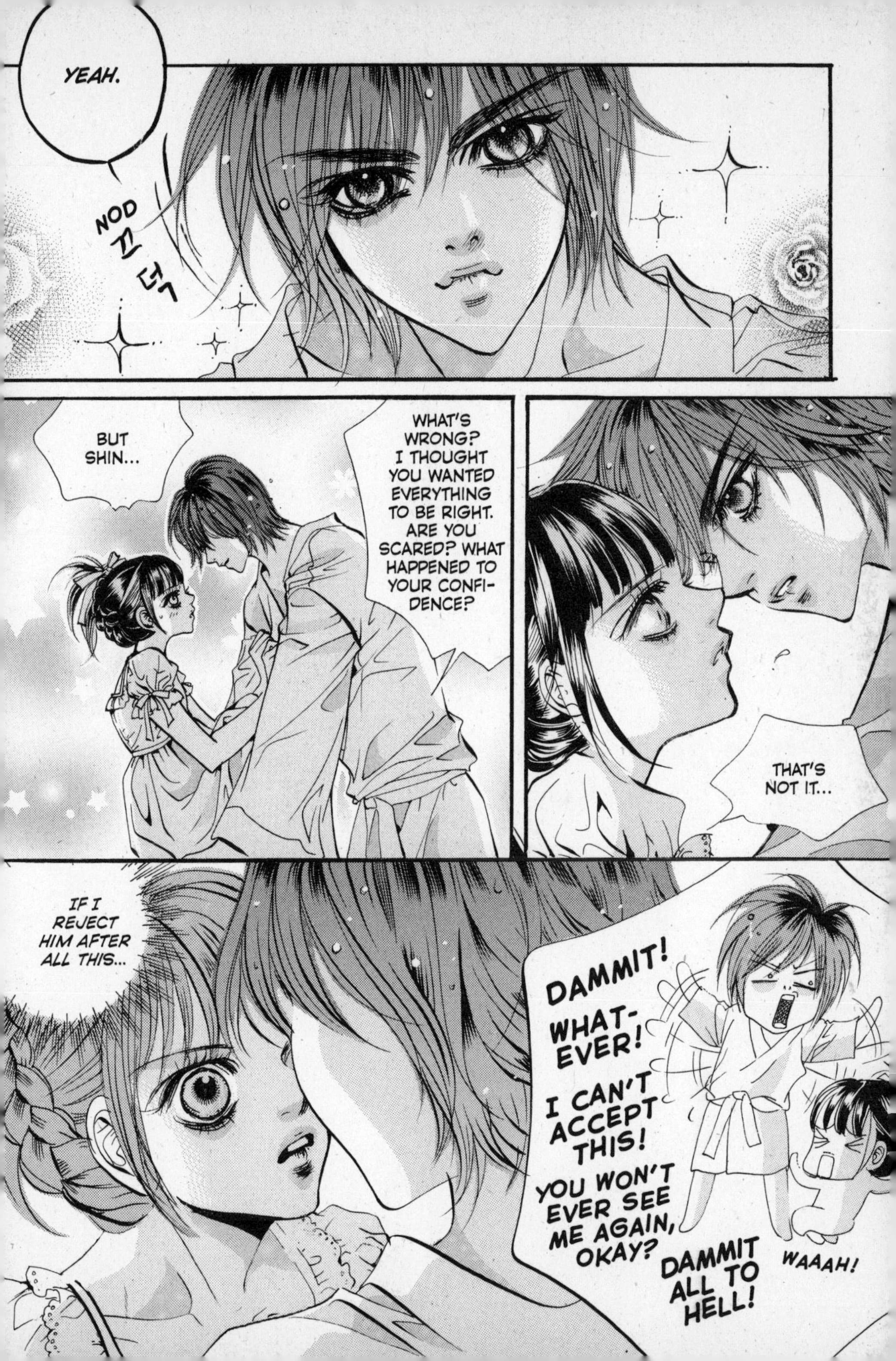
YEAH.
NOD 끄덕
BUT SHIN...
WHAT'S WRONG? I THOUGHT YOU WANTED EVERYTHING TO BE RIGHT. ARE YOU SCARED? WHAT HAPPENED TO YOUR CONFI-DENCE?
THAT'S NOT IT...
IF I REJECT HIM AFTER ALL THIS...
DAMMIT!
WHAT-EVER!
I CAN'T ACCEPT THIS!
YOU WON'T EVER SEE ME AGAIN, OKAY?
DAMMIT ALL TO HELL!
WAAAH!

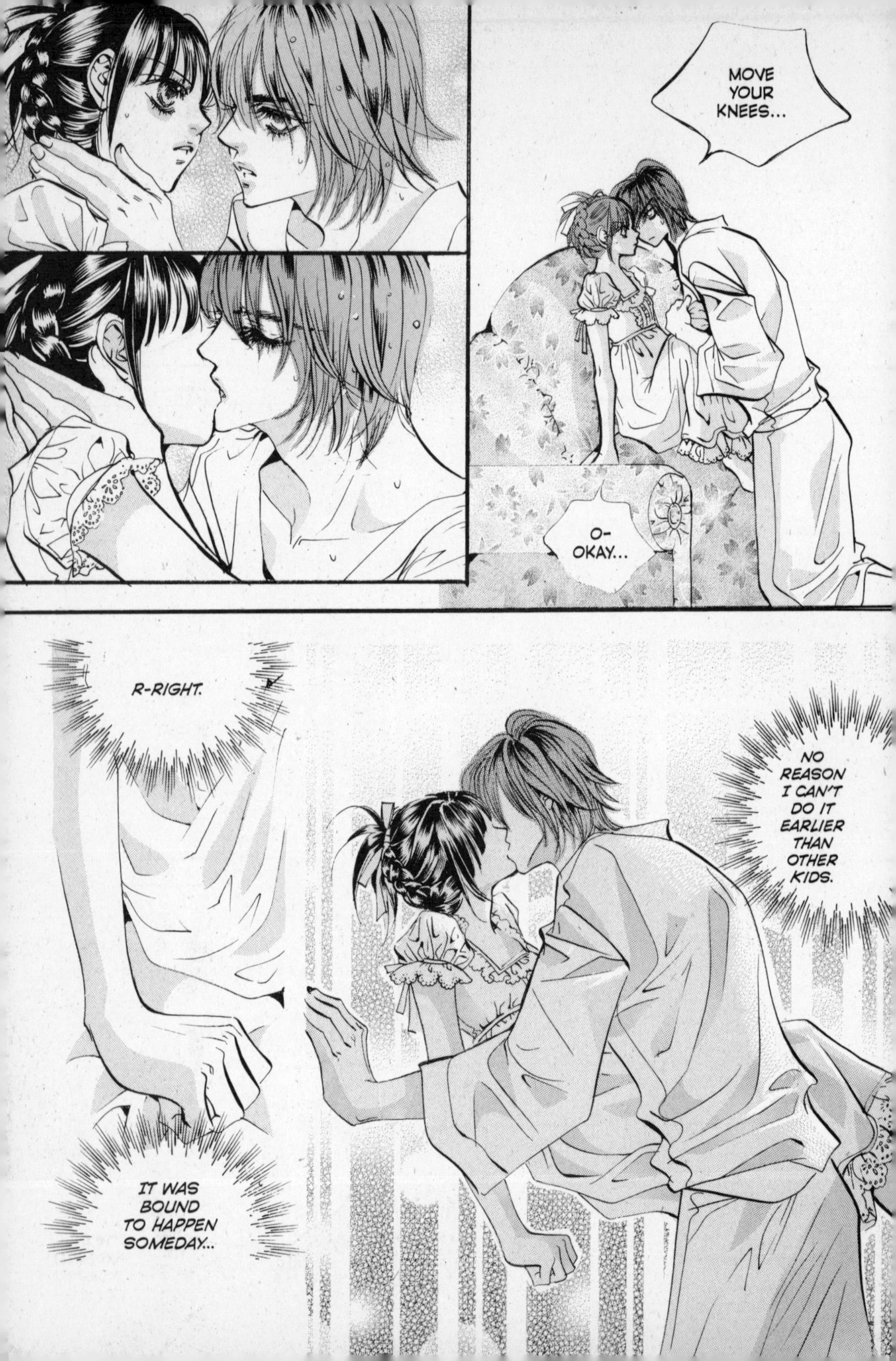
MOVE YOUR KNEES...
O-OKAY...
R-RIGHT.
IT WAS BOUND TO HAPPEN SOMEDAY...
NO REASON I CAN'T DO IT EARLIER THAN OTHER KIDS.

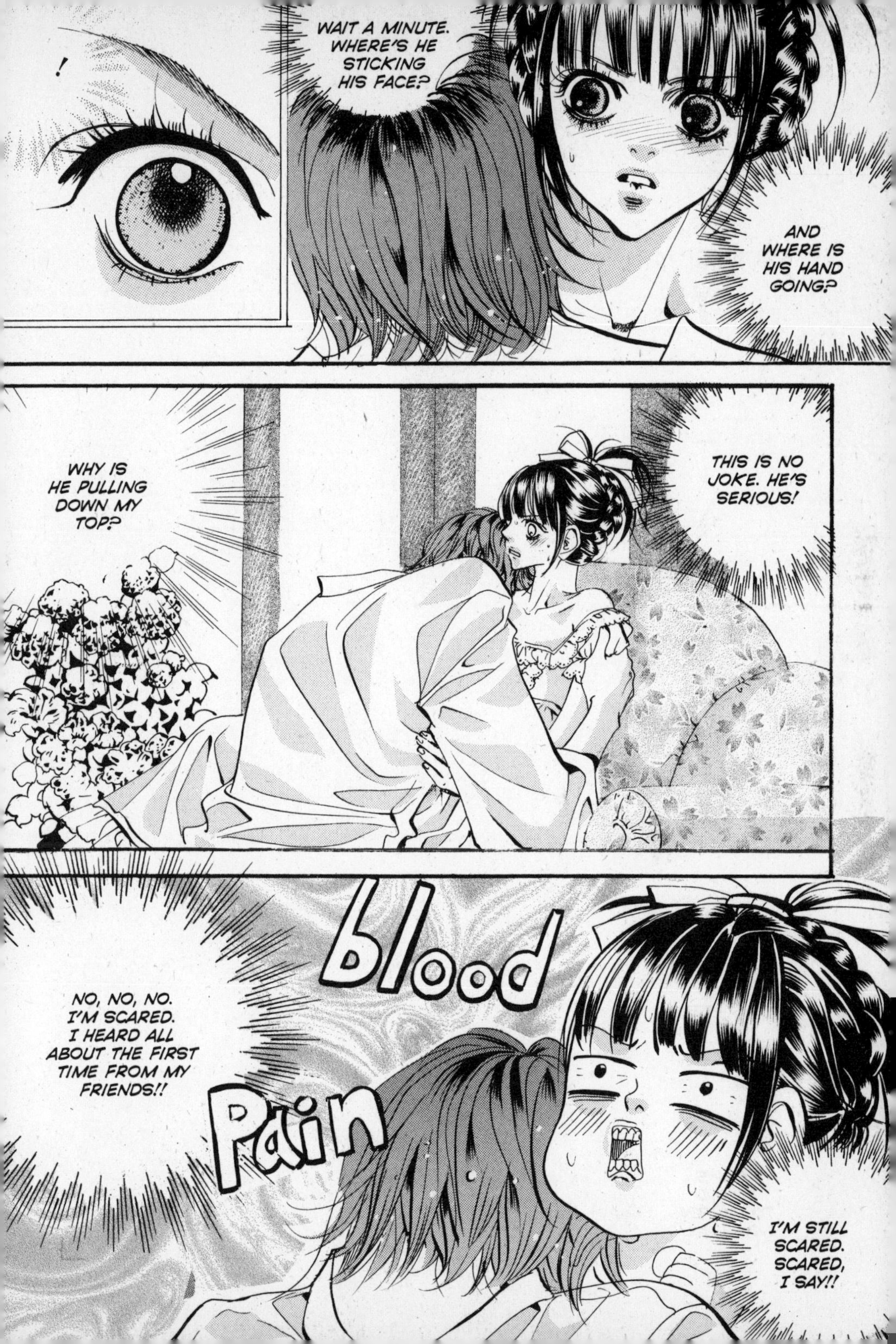
!
WAIT A MINUTE. WHERE'S HE STICKING HIS FACE?
AND WHERE IS HIS HAND GOING?
WHY IS HE PULLING DOWN MY TOP?
THIS IS NO JOKE. HE'S SERIOUS!
NO, NO, NO. I'M SCARED. I HEARD ALL ABOUT THE FIRST TIME FROM MY FRIENDS!!
blood
Pain
I'M STILL SCARED. SCARED, I SAY!!

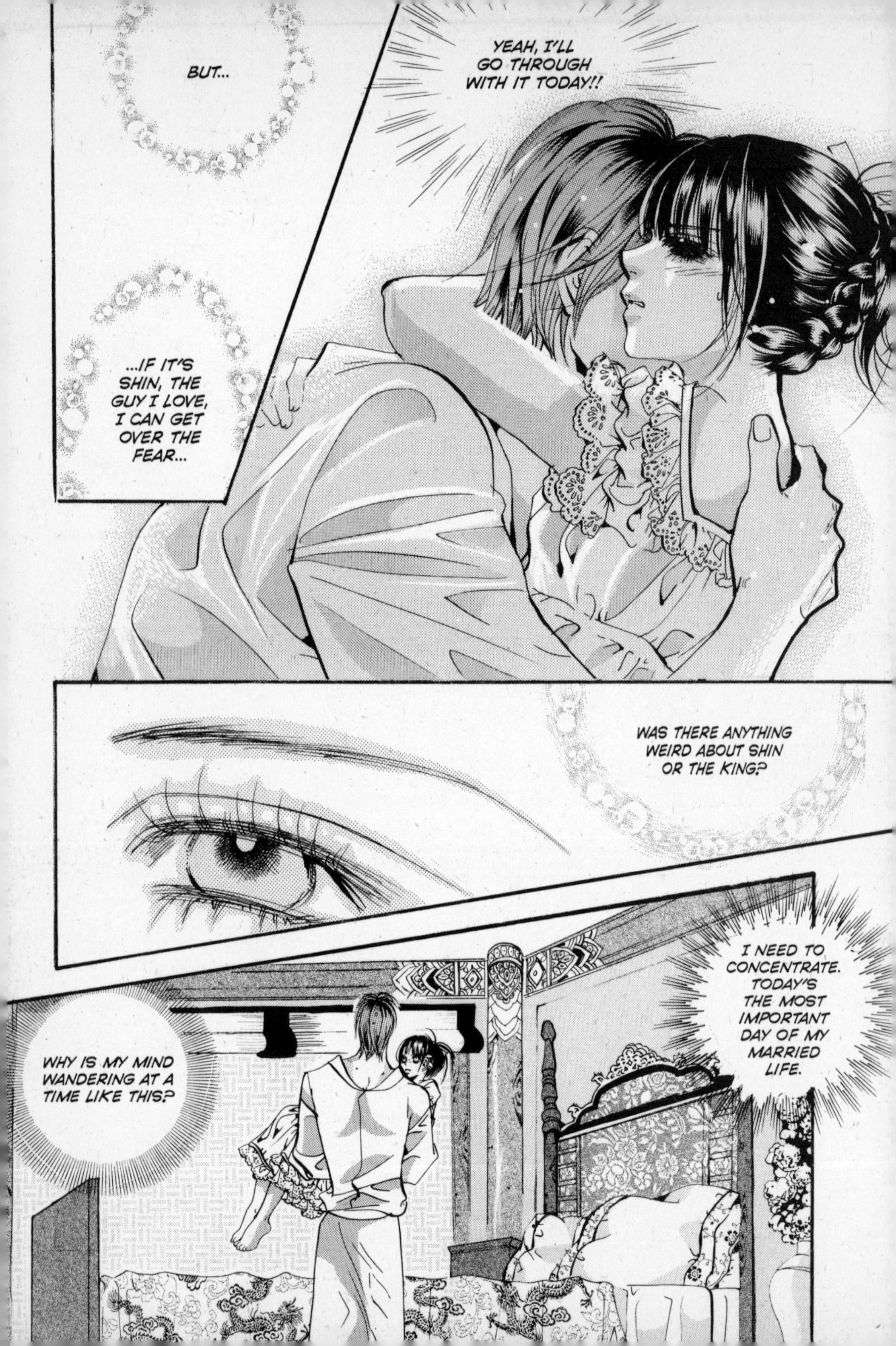
BUT...
...IF IT'S SHIN, THE GUY I LOVE, I CAN GET OVER THE FEAR...
YEAH, I'LL GO THROUGH WITH IT TODAY!!
WAS THERE ANYTHING WEIRD ABOUT SHIN OR THE KING?
WHY IS MY MIND WANDERING AT A TIME LIKE THIS?
I NEED TO CONCENTRATE. TODAY'S THE MOST IMPORTANT DAY OF MY MARRIED LIFE.

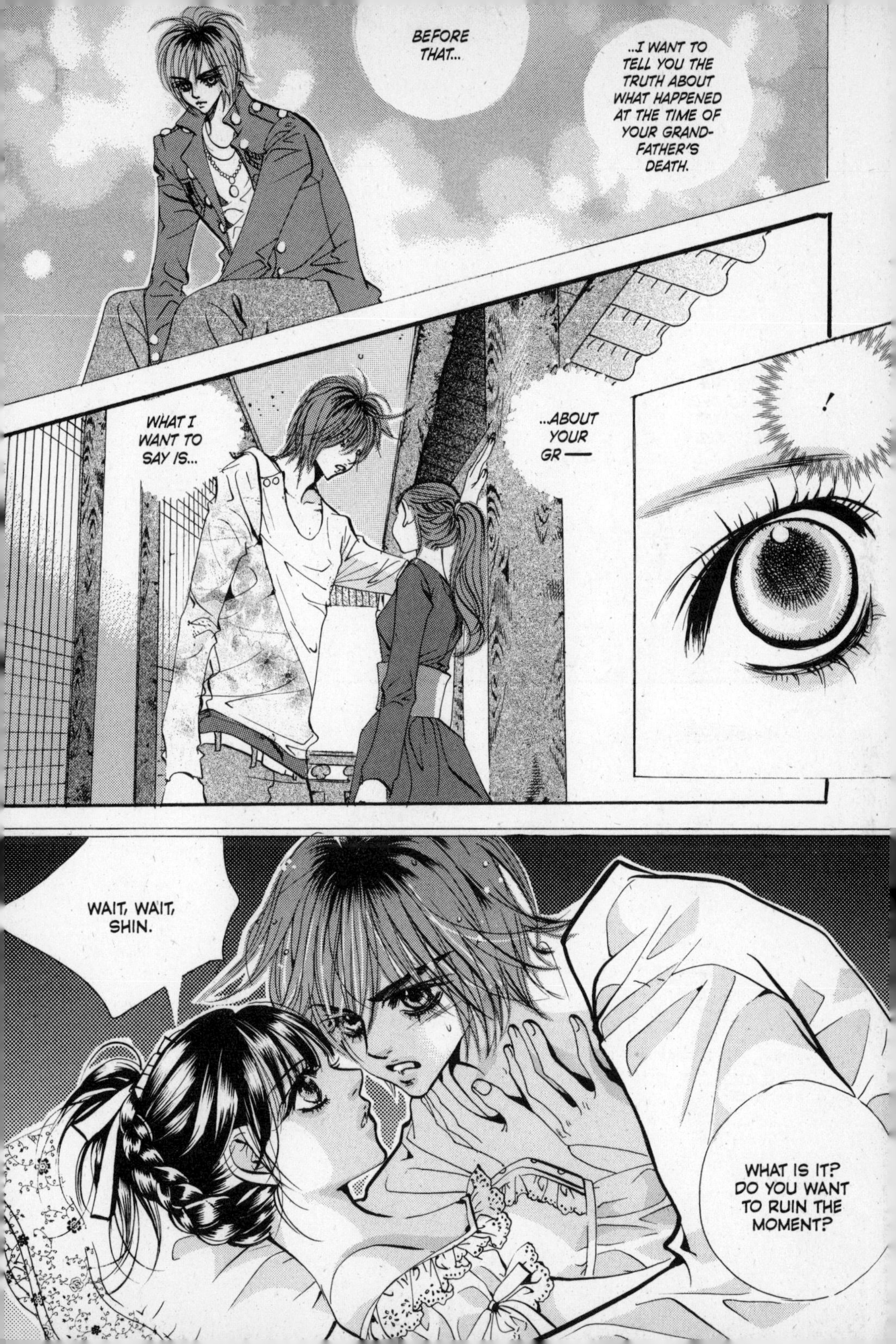
BEFORE THAT...
...I WANT TO TELL YOU THE TRUTH ABOUT WHAT HAPPENED AT THE TIME OF YOUR GRAND-FATHER'S DEATH.
WHAT I WANT TO SAY IS...
...ABOUT YOUR GR—
!
WAIT, WAIT, SHIN.
WHAT IS IT? DO YOU WANT TO RUIN THE MOMENT?

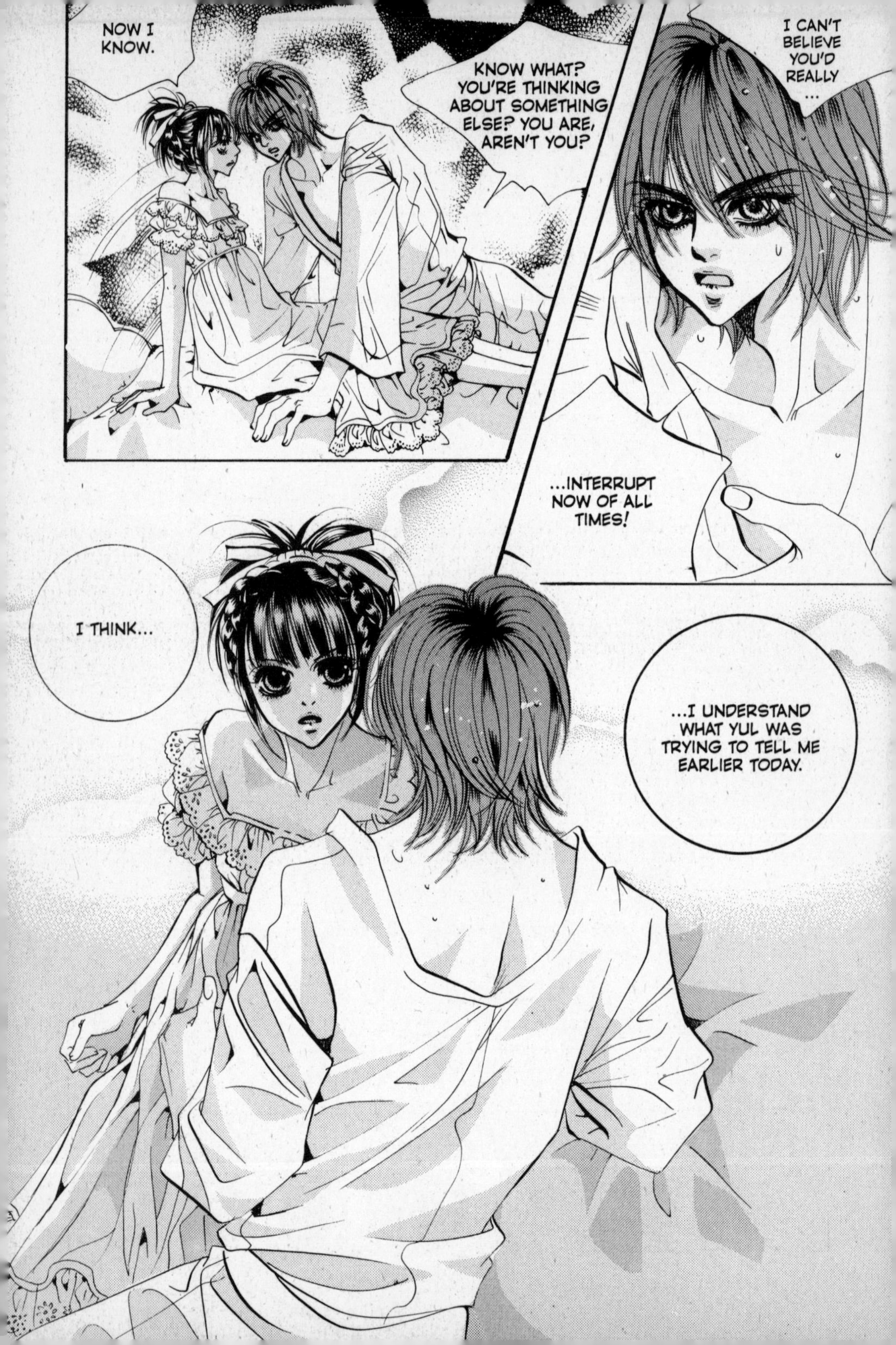
NOW I KNOW.
KNOW WHAT? YOU'RE THINKING ABOUT SOMETHING ELSE? YOU ARE, AREN'T YOU?
I CAN'T BELIEVE YOU'D REALLY ...
...INTERRUPT NOW OF ALL TIMES!
I THINK...
...I UNDERSTAND WHAT YUL WAS TRYING TO TELL ME EARLIER TODAY.

THE ROYAL PALACE

Goong

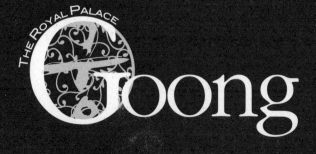

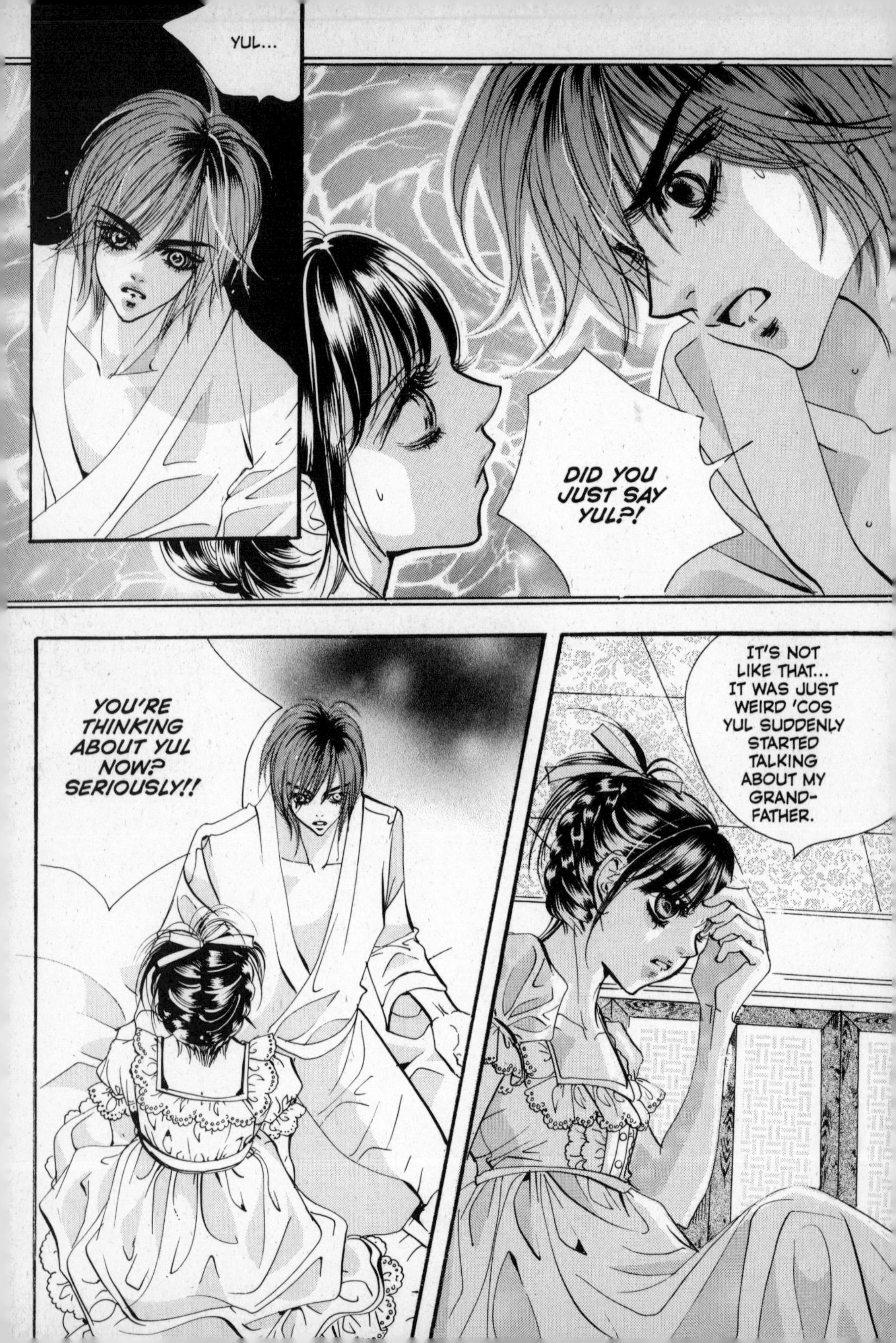
YUL...
DID YOU JUST SAY YUL?!
YOU'RE THINKING ABOUT YUL NOW? SERIOUSLY!!
IT'S NOT LIKE THAT... IT WAS JUST WEIRD 'COS YUL SUDDENLY STARTED TALKING ABOUT MY GRAND-FATHER.

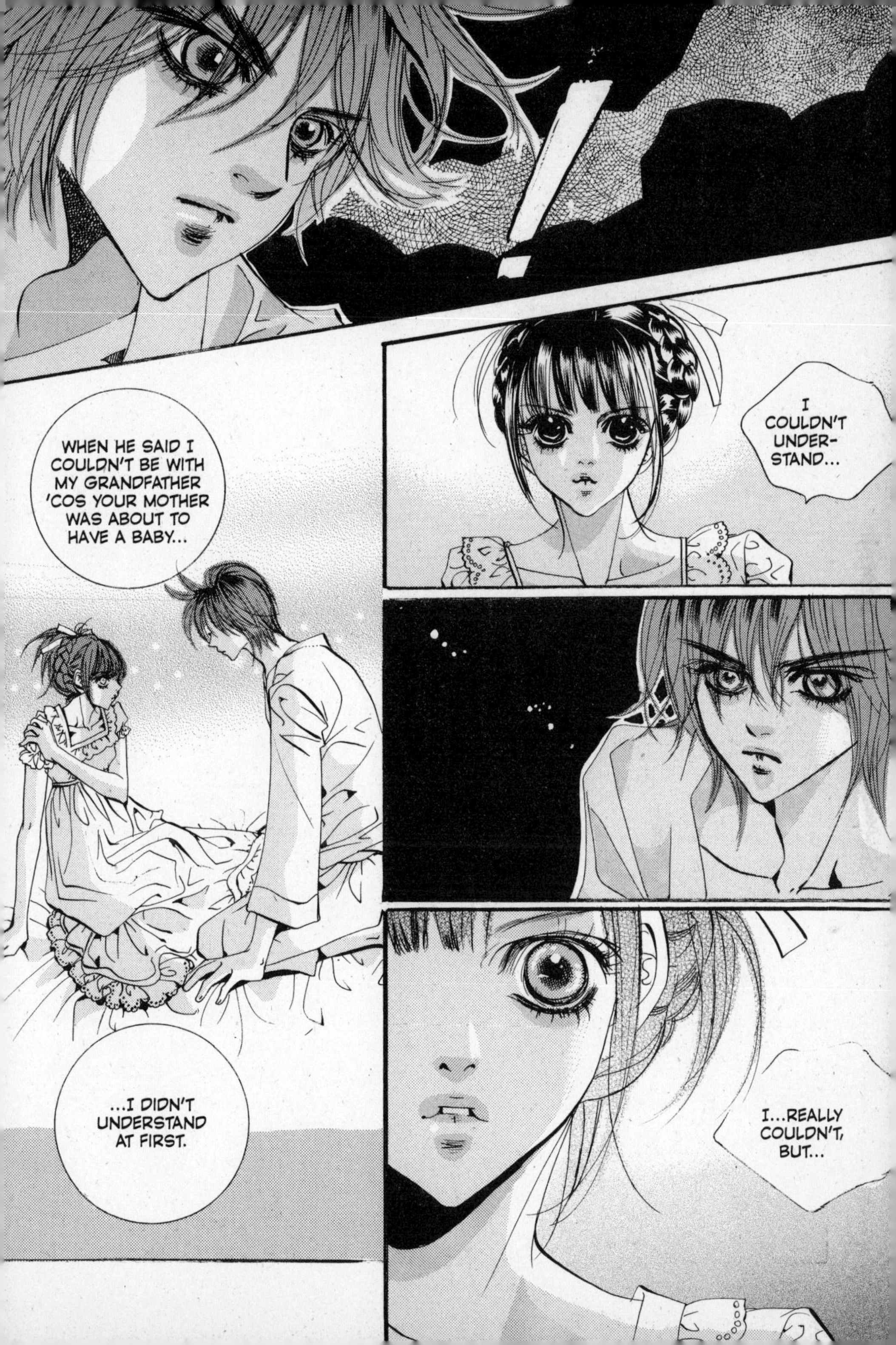
WHEN HE SAID I COULDN'T BE WITH MY GRANDFATHER 'COS YOUR MOTHER WAS ABOUT TO HAVE A BABY...
...I DIDN'T UNDERSTAND AT FIRST.
I COULDN'T UNDER-STAND...
I...REALLY COULDN'T, BUT...

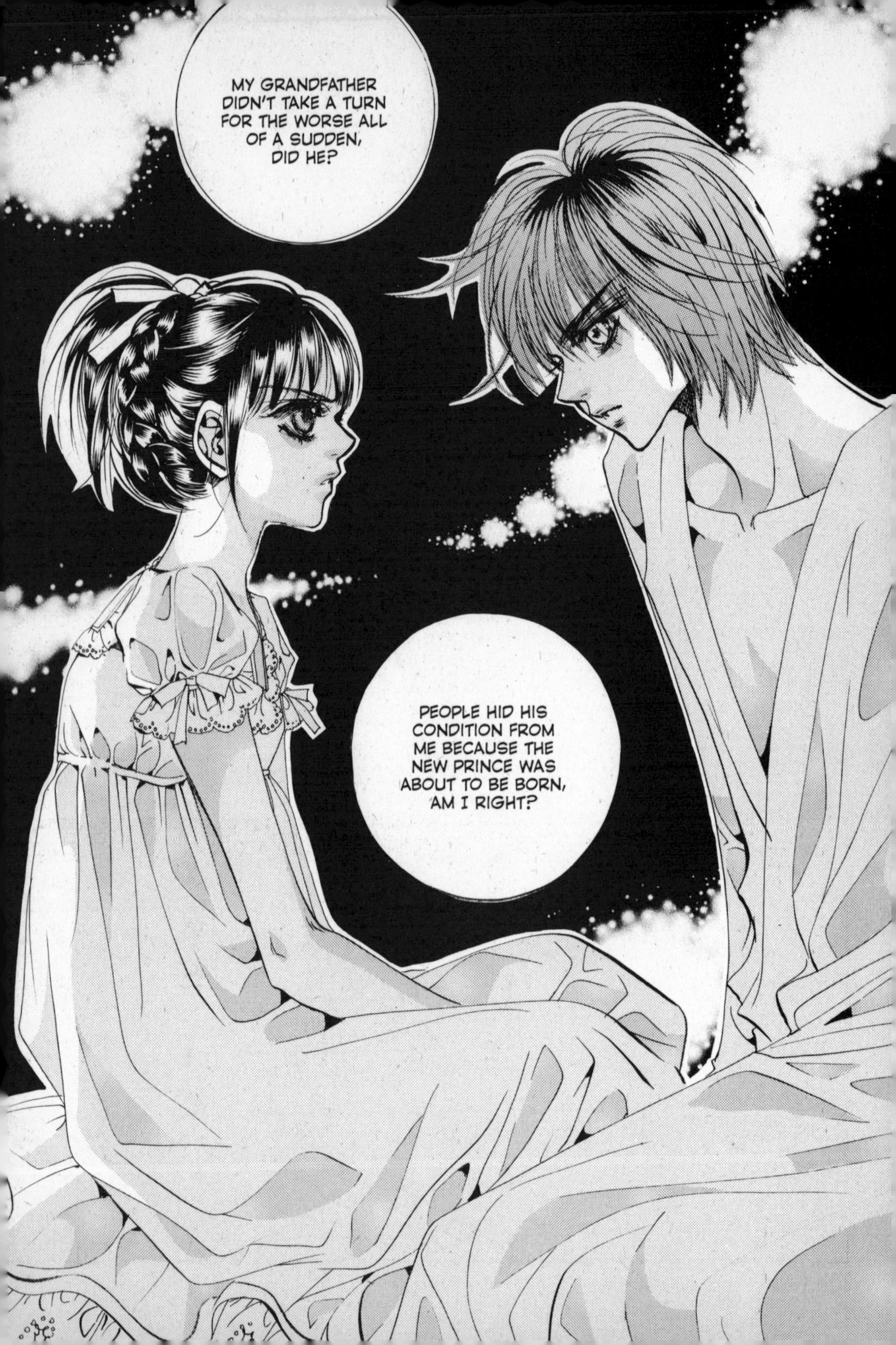
MY GRANDFATHER DIDN'T TAKE A TURN FOR THE WORSE ALL OF A SUDDEN, DID HE?
PEOPLE HID HIS CONDITION FROM ME BECAUSE THE NEW PRINCE WAS ABOUT TO BE BORN, AM I RIGHT?

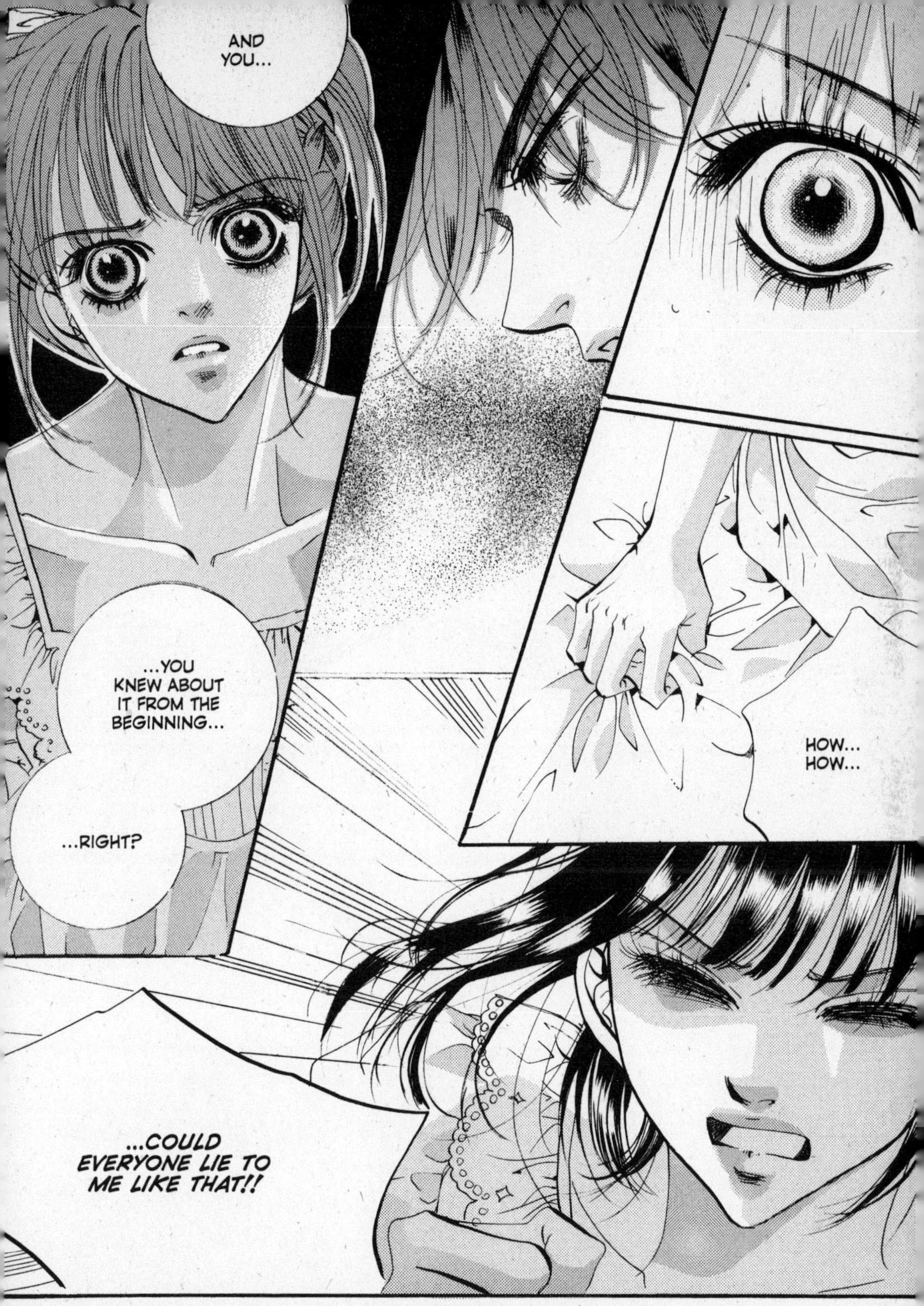
AND YOU...
...YOU KNEW ABOUT IT FROM THE BEGINNING...
...RIGHT?
HOW... HOW...
...COULD EVERYONE LIE TO ME LIKE THAT!!

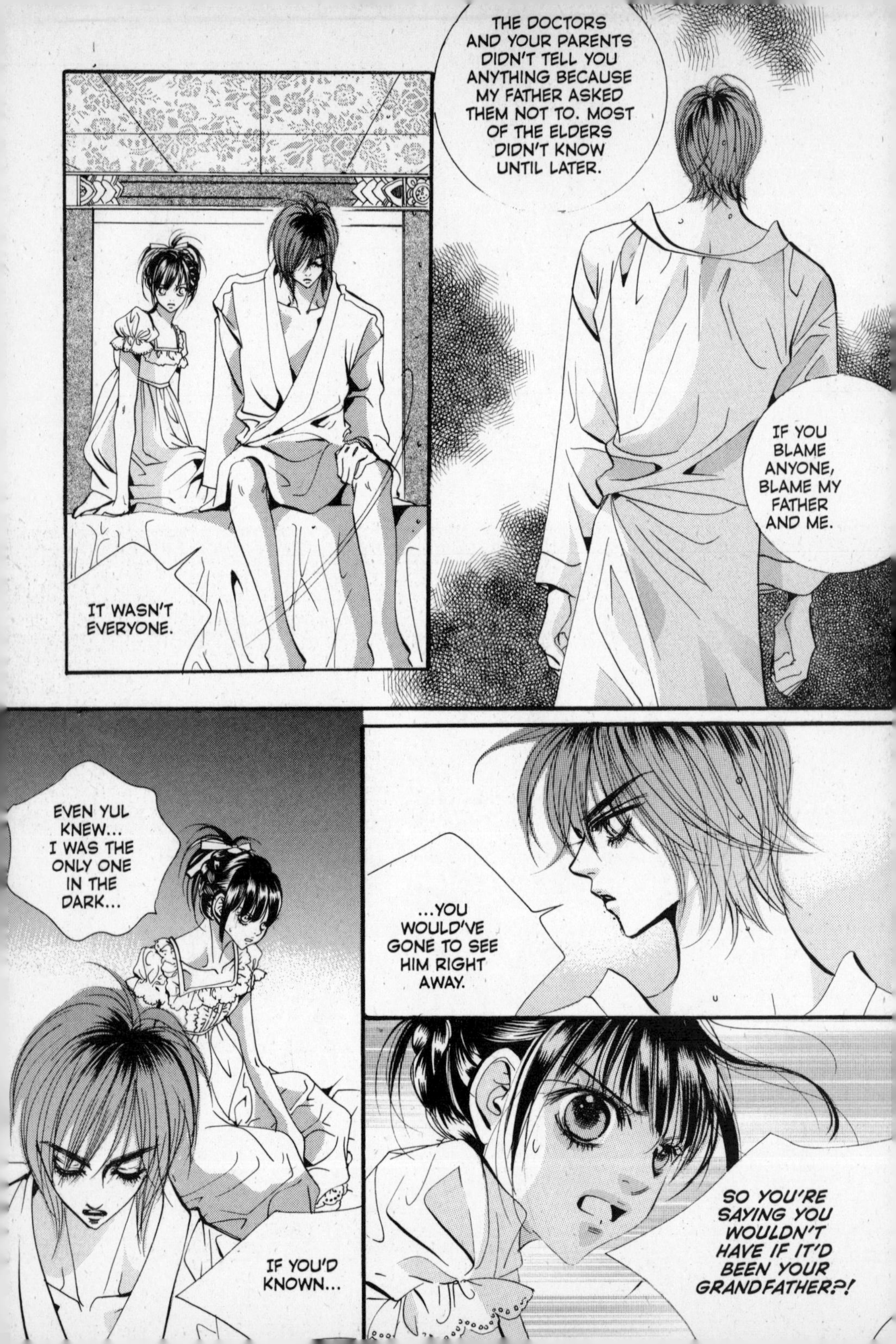
IT WASN'T EVERYONE.
THE DOCTORS AND YOUR PARENTS DIDN'T TELL YOU ANYTHING BECAUSE MY FATHER ASKED THEM NOT TO. MOST OF THE ELDERS DIDN'T KNOW UNTIL LATER.
IF YOU BLAME ANYONE, BLAME MY FATHER AND ME.
EVEN YUL KNEW... I WAS THE ONLY ONE IN THE DARK...
IF YOU'D KNOWN...
...YOU WOULD'VE GONE TO SEE HIM RIGHT AWAY.
SO YOU'RE SAYING YOU WOULDN'T HAVE IF IT'D BEEN YOUR GRANDFATHER?!

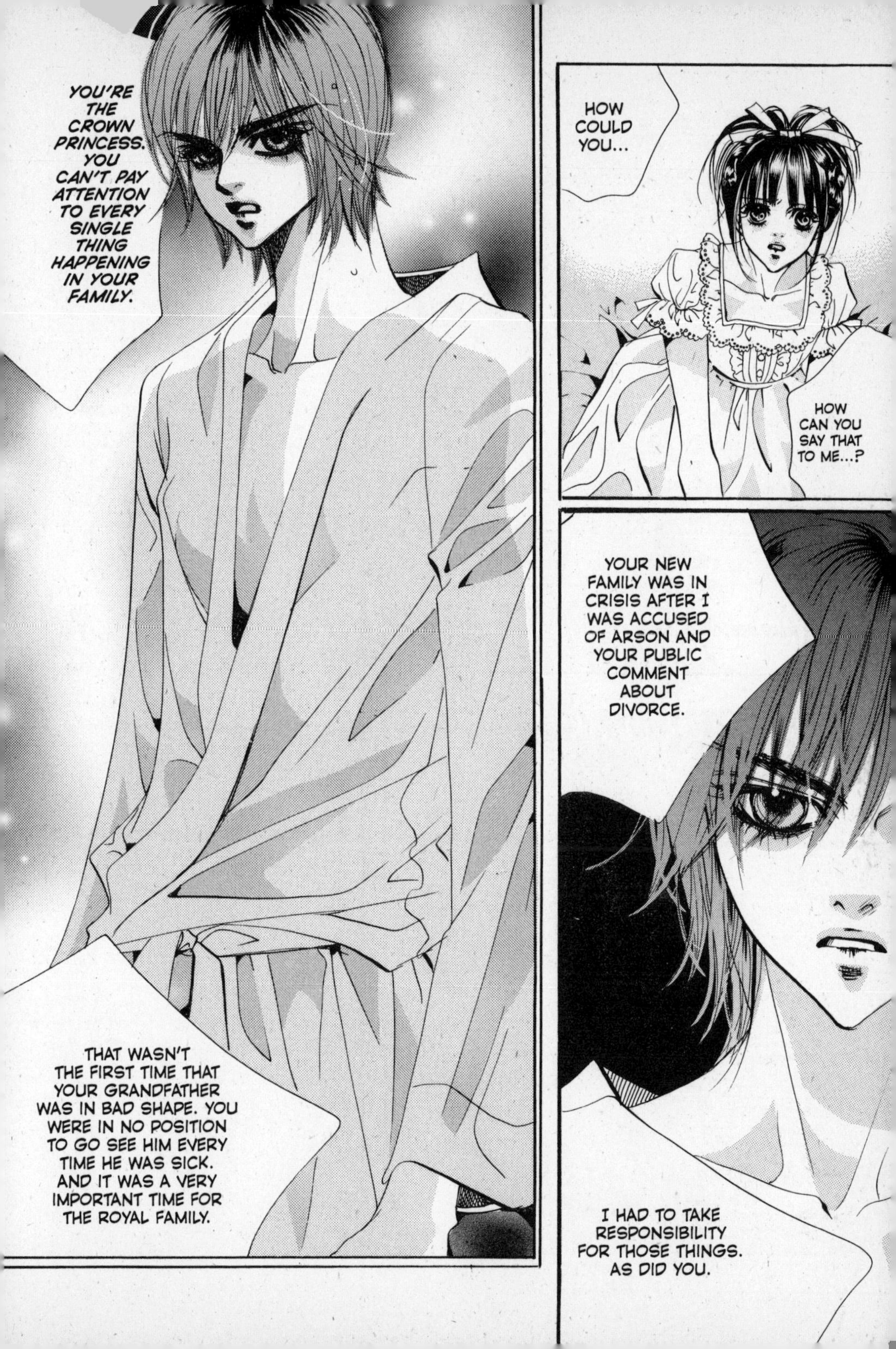
YOU'RE THE CROWN PRINCESS. YOU CAN'T PAY ATTENTION TO EVERY SINGLE THING HAPPENING IN YOUR FAMILY.
THAT WASN'T THE FIRST TIME THAT YOUR GRANDFATHER WAS IN BAD SHAPE. YOU WERE IN NO POSITION TO GO SEE HIM EVERY TIME HE WAS SICK. AND IT WAS A VERY IMPORTANT TIME FOR THE ROYAL FAMILY.
HOW COULD YOU...
HOW CAN YOU SAY THAT TO ME...?
YOUR NEW FAMILY WAS IN CRISIS AFTER I WAS ACCUSED OF ARSON AND YOUR PUBLIC COMMENT ABOUT DIVORCE.
I HAD TO TAKE RESPONSIBILITY FOR THOSE THINGS. AS DID YOU.

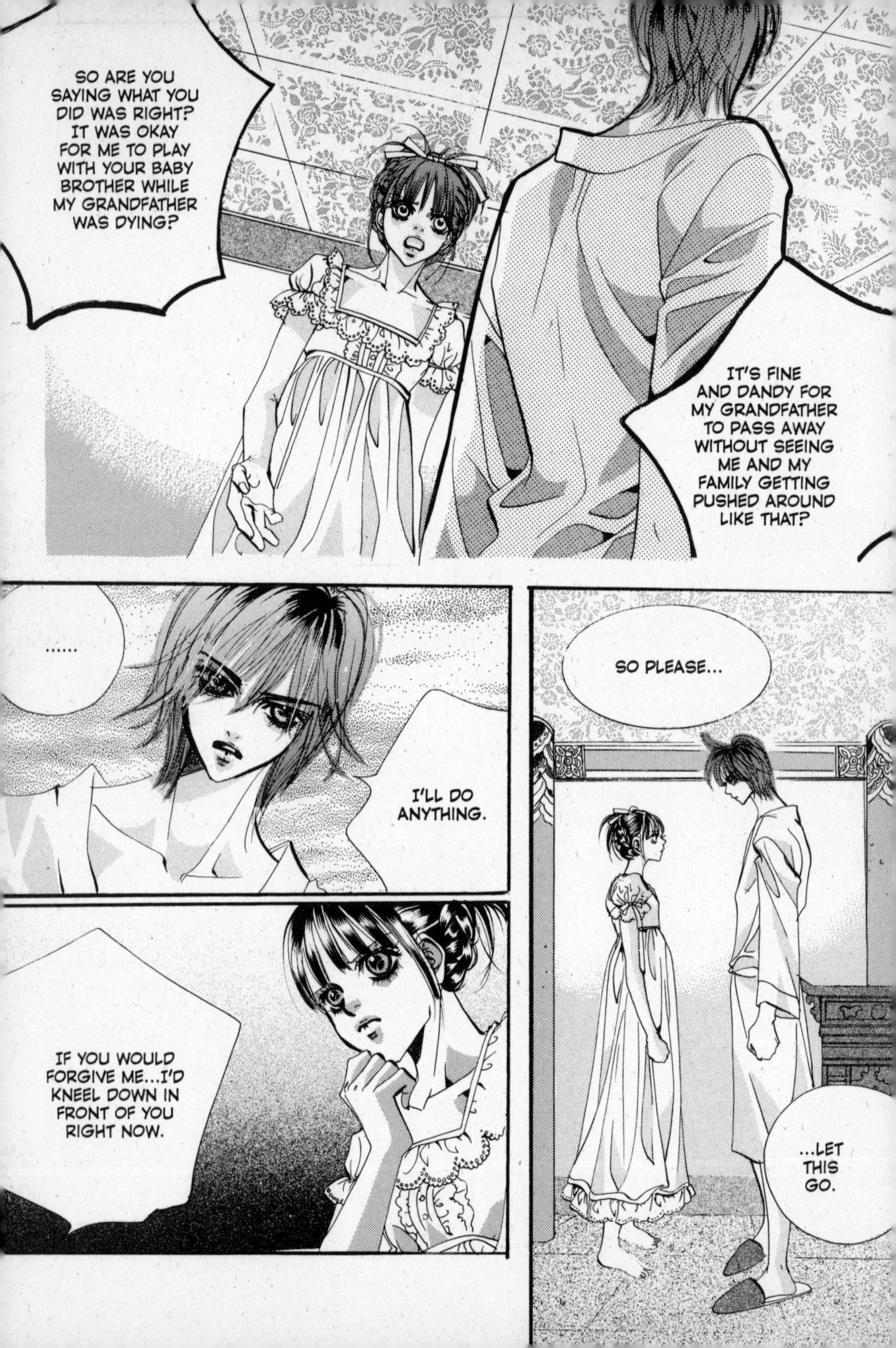
SO ARE YOU SAYING WHAT YOU DID WAS RIGHT? IT WAS OKAY FOR ME TO PLAY WITH YOUR BABY BROTHER WHILE MY GRANDFATHER WAS DYING?
IT'S FINE AND DANDY FOR MY GRANDFATHER TO PASS AWAY WITHOUT SEEING ME AND MY FAMILY GETTING PUSHED AROUND LIKE THAT?
......
I'LL DO ANYTHING.
IF YOU WOULD FORGIVE ME...I'D KNEEL DOWN IN FRONT OF YOU RIGHT NOW.
SO PLEASE...
...LET THIS GO.

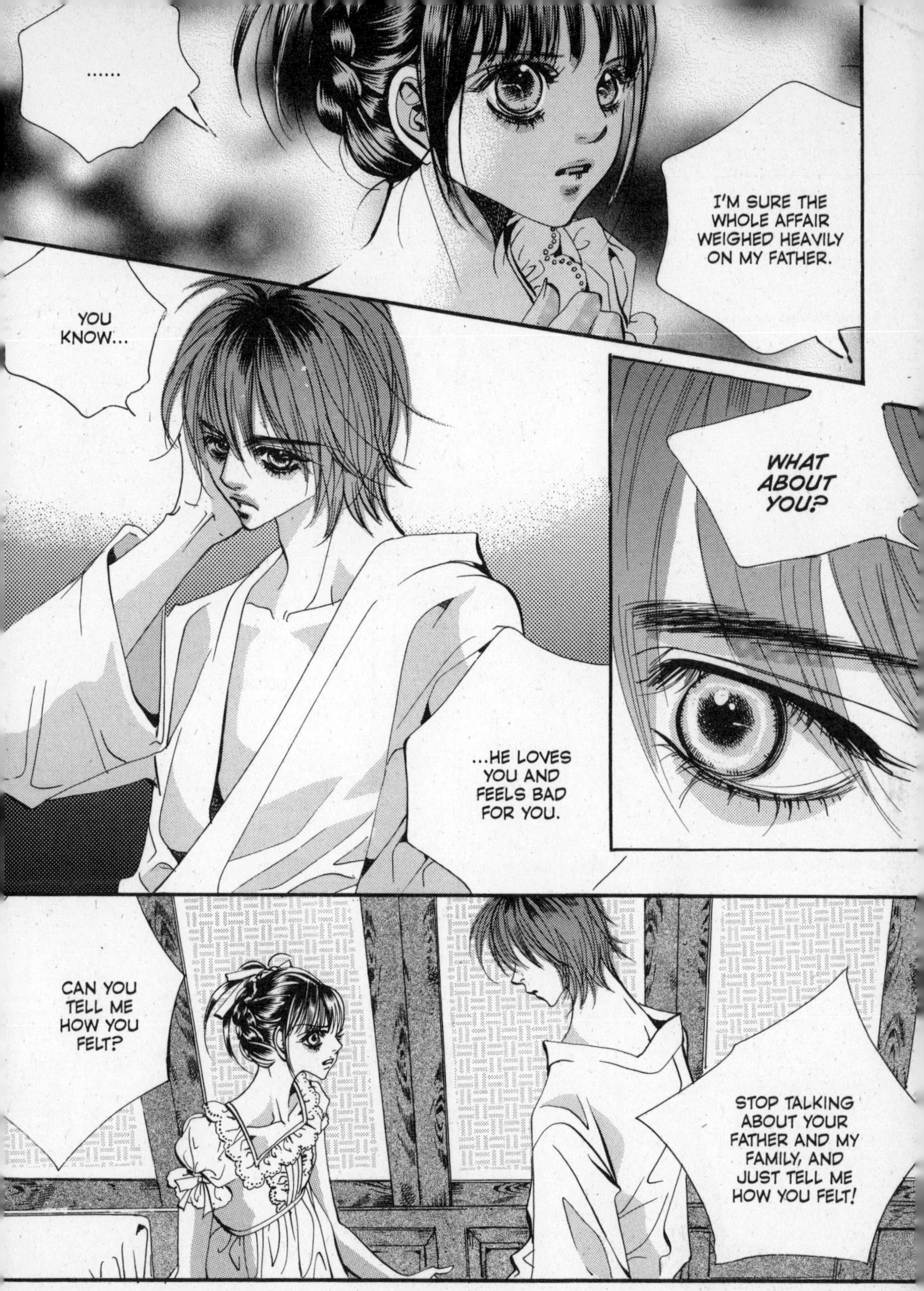
......
I'M SURE THE WHOLE AFFAIR WEIGHED HEAVILY ON MY FATHER.
YOU KNOW...
...HE LOVES YOU AND FEELS BAD FOR YOU.
WHAT ABOUT YOU?
CAN YOU TELL ME HOW YOU FELT?
STOP TALKING ABOUT YOUR FATHER AND MY FAMILY, AND JUST TELL ME HOW YOU FELT!

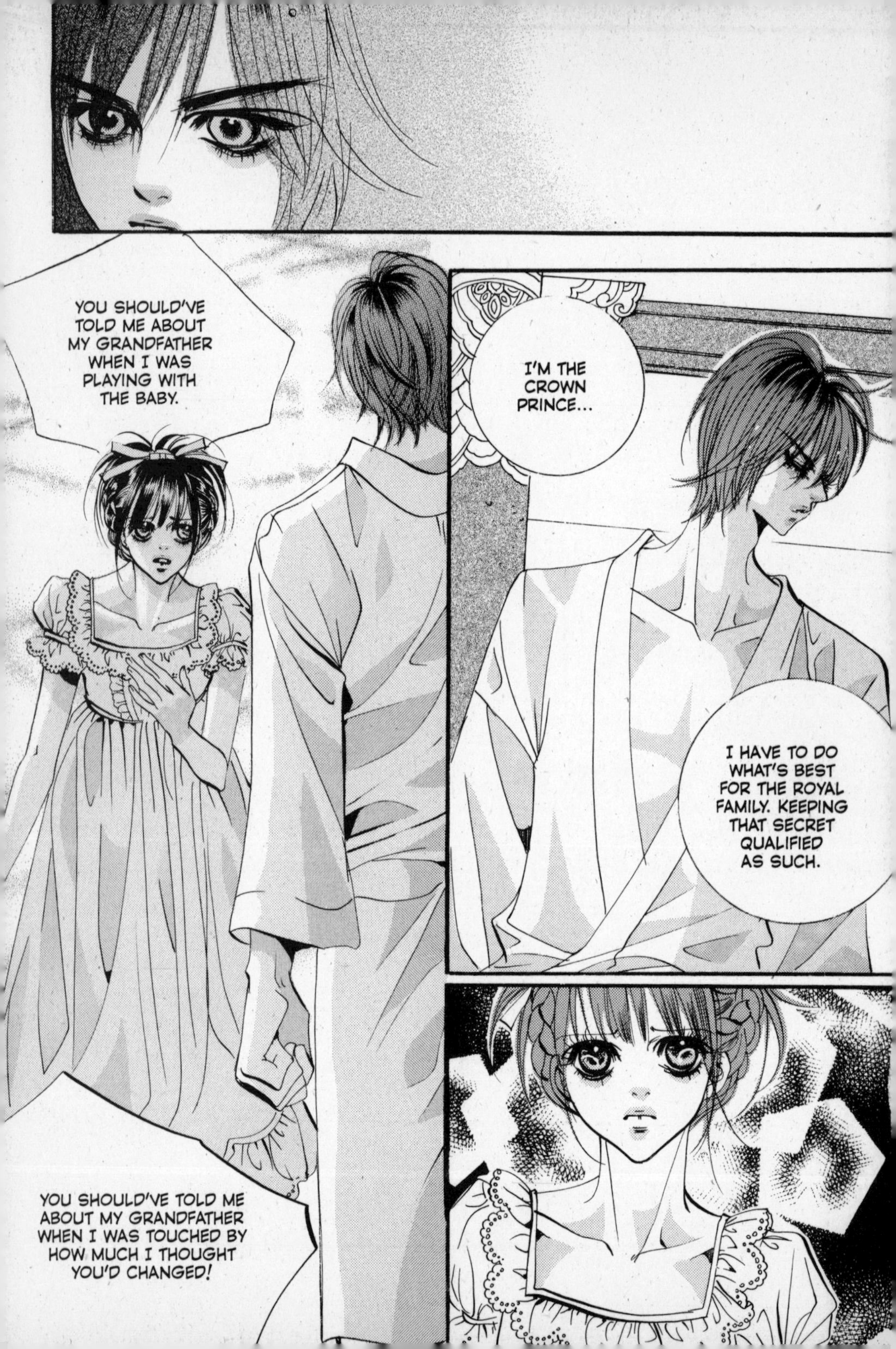
YOU SHOULD'VE TOLD ME ABOUT MY GRANDFATHER WHEN I WAS PLAYING WITH THE BABY.
YOU SHOULD'VE TOLD ME ABOUT MY GRANDFATHER WHEN I WAS TOUCHED BY HOW MUCH I THOUGHT YOU'D CHANGED!
I'M THE CROWN PRINCE...
I HAVE TO DO WHAT'S BEST FOR THE ROYAL FAMILY. KEEPING THAT SECRET QUALIFIED AS SUCH.

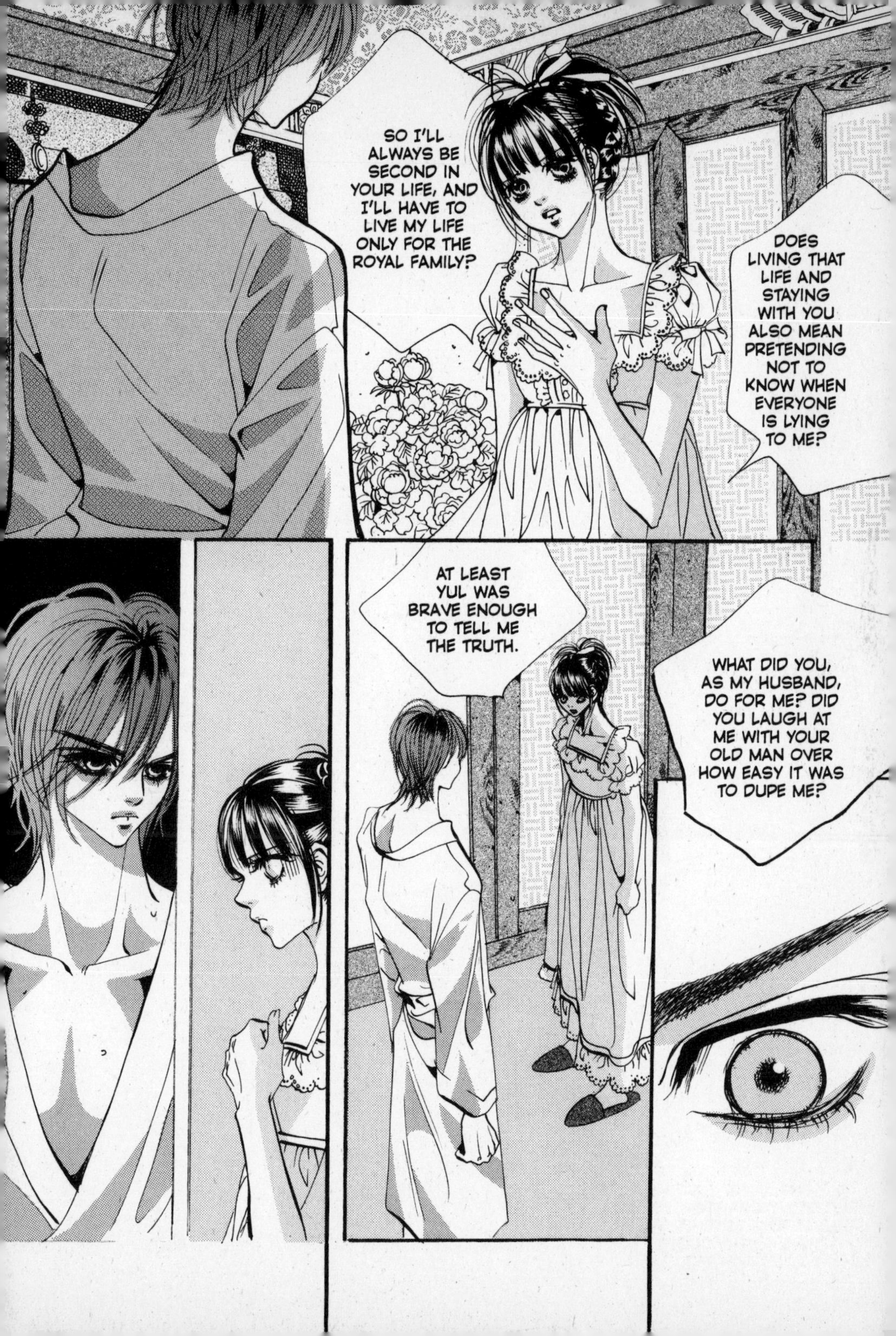
SO I'LL ALWAYS BE SECOND IN YOUR LIFE, AND I'LL HAVE TO LIVE MY LIFE ONLY FOR THE ROYAL FAMILY?
DOES LIVING THAT LIFE AND STAYING WITH YOU ALSO MEAN PRETENDING NOT TO KNOW WHEN EVERYONE IS LYING TO ME?
AT LEAST YUL WAS BRAVE ENOUGH TO TELL ME THE TRUTH.
WHAT DID YOU, AS MY HUSBAND, DO FOR ME? DID YOU LAUGH AT ME WITH YOUR OLD MAN OVER HOW EASY IT WAS TO DUPE ME?

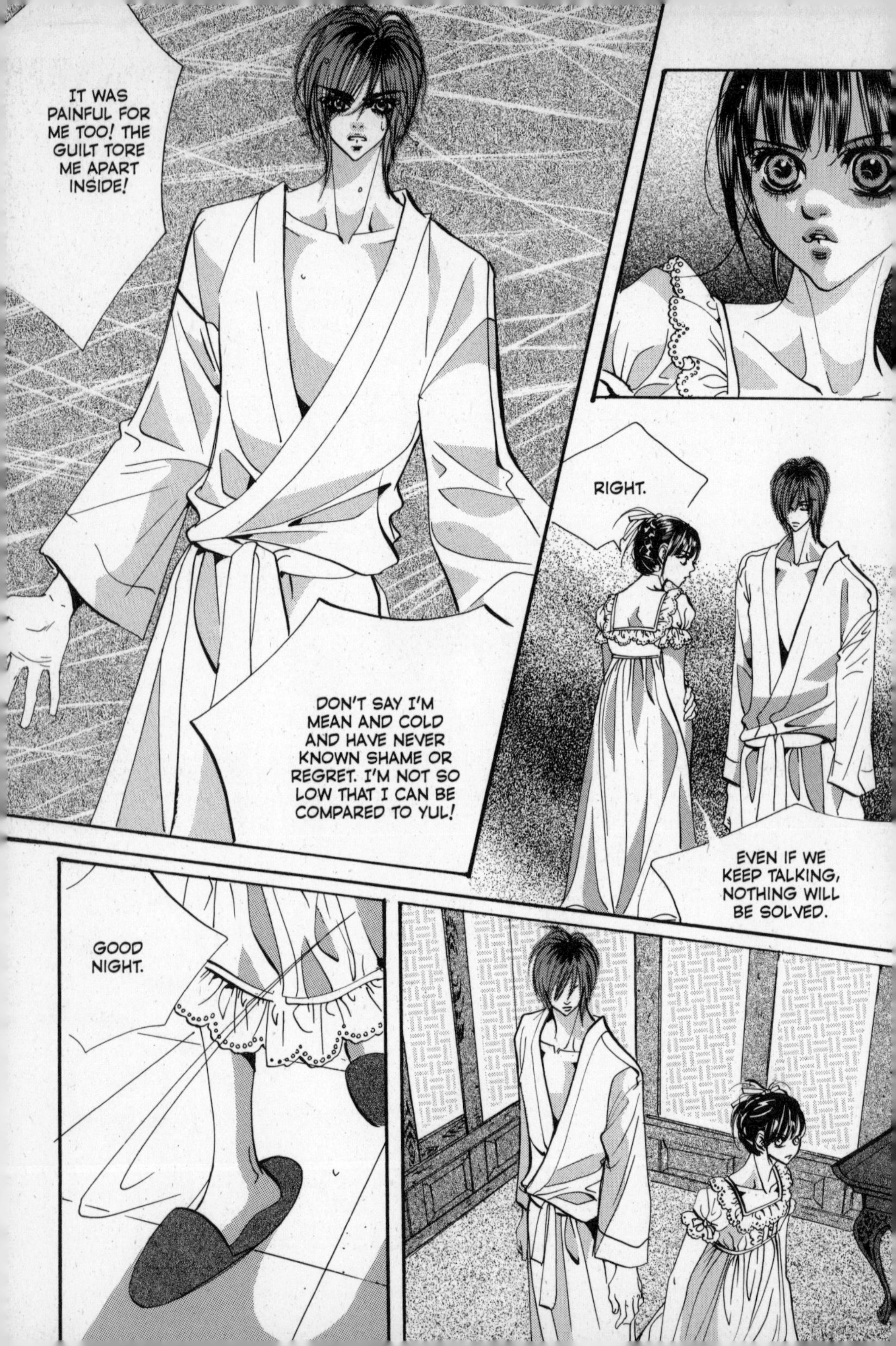
IT WAS PAINFUL FOR ME TOO! THE GUILT TORE ME APART INSIDE!
DON'T SAY I'M MEAN AND COLD AND HAVE NEVER KNOWN SHAME OR REGRET. I'M NOT SO LOW THAT I CAN BE COMPARED TO YUL!
RIGHT.
EVEN IF WE KEEP TALKING, NOTHING WILL BE SOLVED.
GOOD NIGHT.

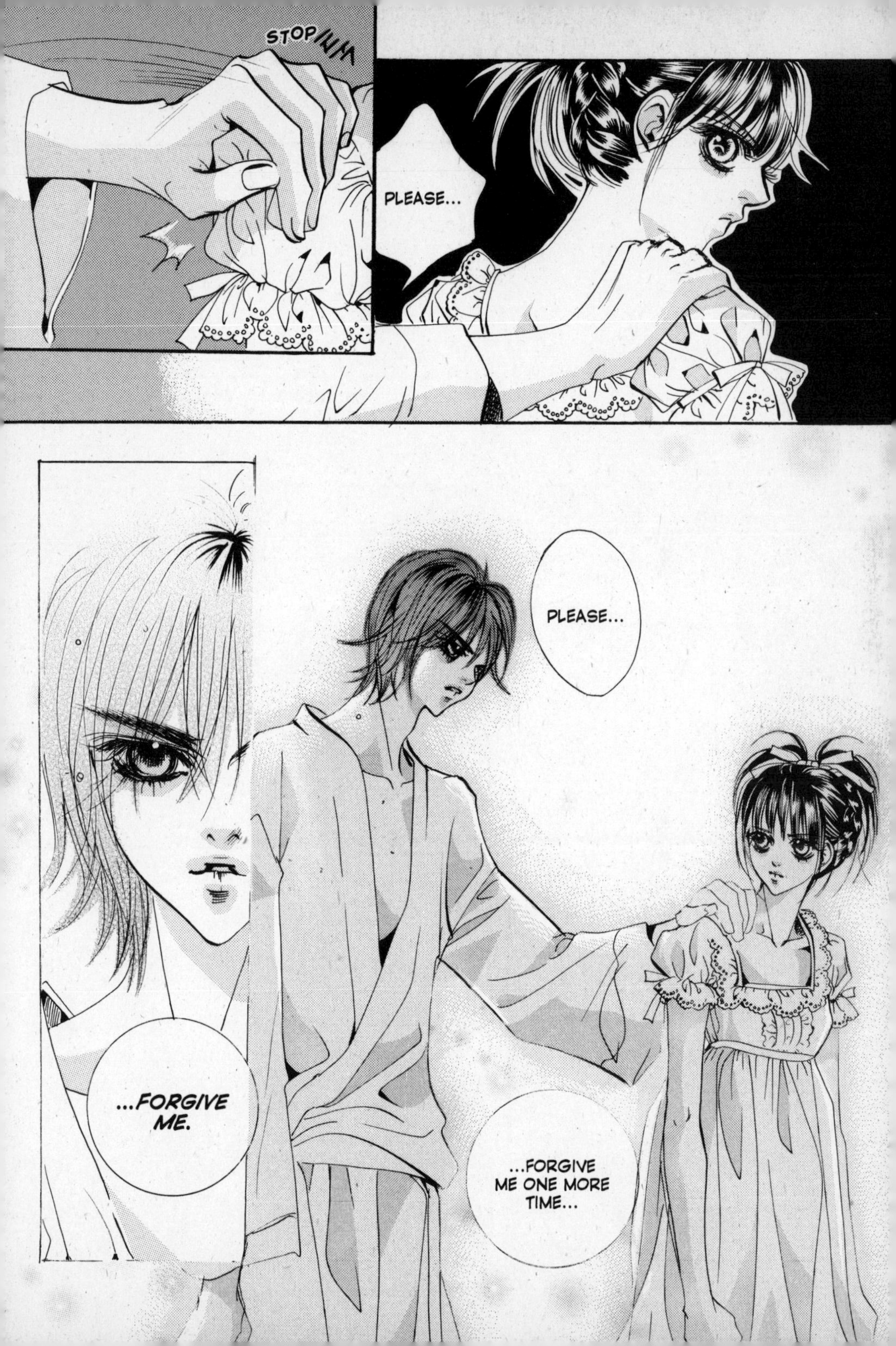
STOP/N/M
PLEASE...
...FORGIVE ME.
PLEASE...
...FORGIVE ME ONE MORE TIME...

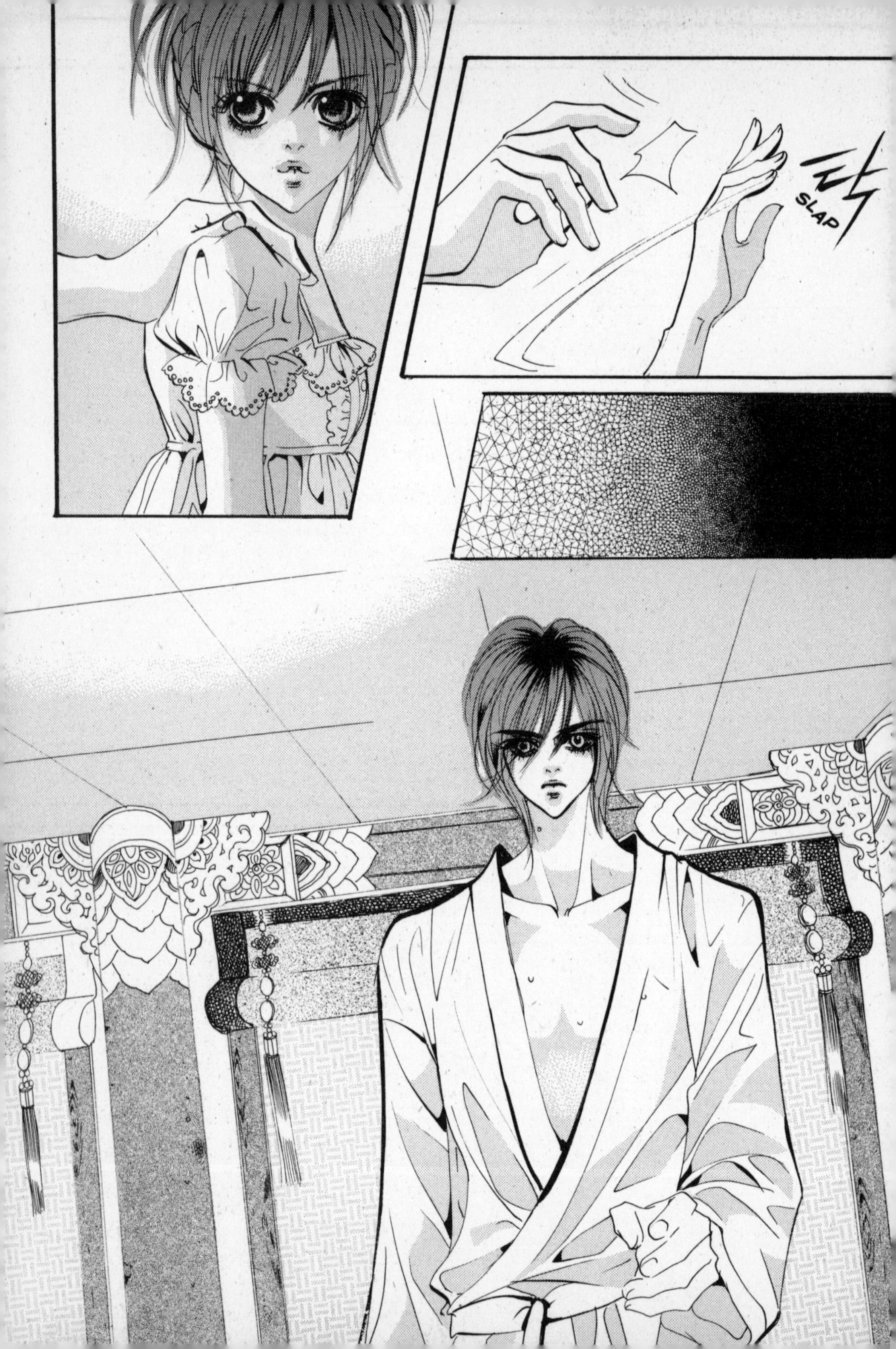
SLAP

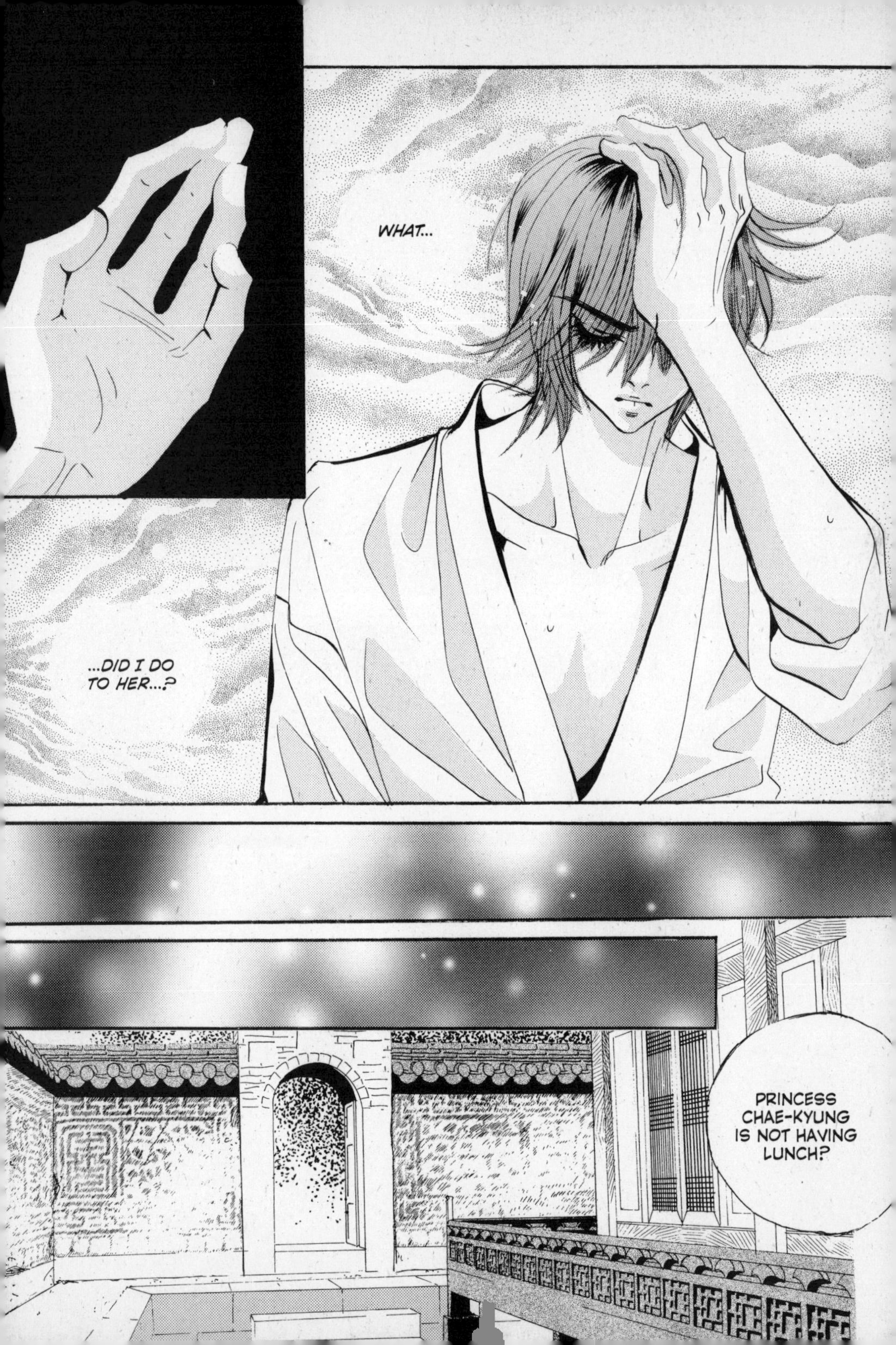
WHAT...
...DID I DO
TO HER...?
PRINCESS
CHAE-KYUNG
IS NOT HAVING
LUNCH?

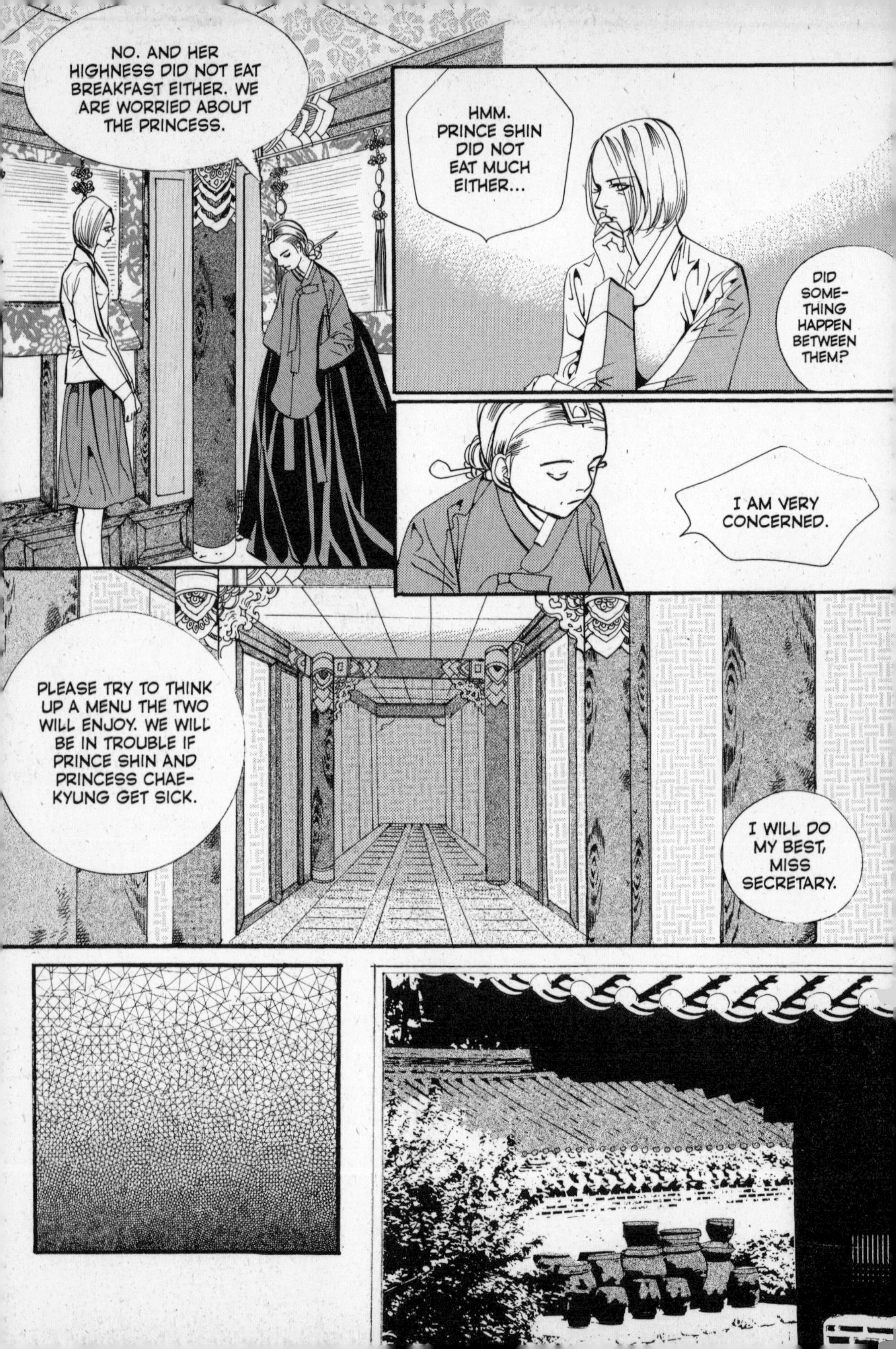
NO. AND HER HIGHNESS DID NOT EAT BREAKFAST EITHER. WE ARE WORRIED ABOUT THE PRINCESS.
HMM. PRINCE SHIN DID NOT EAT MUCH EITHER...
DID SOMETHING HAPPEN BETWEEN THEM?
I AM VERY CONCERNED.
PLEASE TRY TO THINK UP A MENU THE TWO WILL ENJOY. WE WILL BE IN TROUBLE IF PRINCE SHIN AND PRINCESS CHAE-KYUNG GET SICK.
I WILL DO MY BEST, MISS SECRETARY.

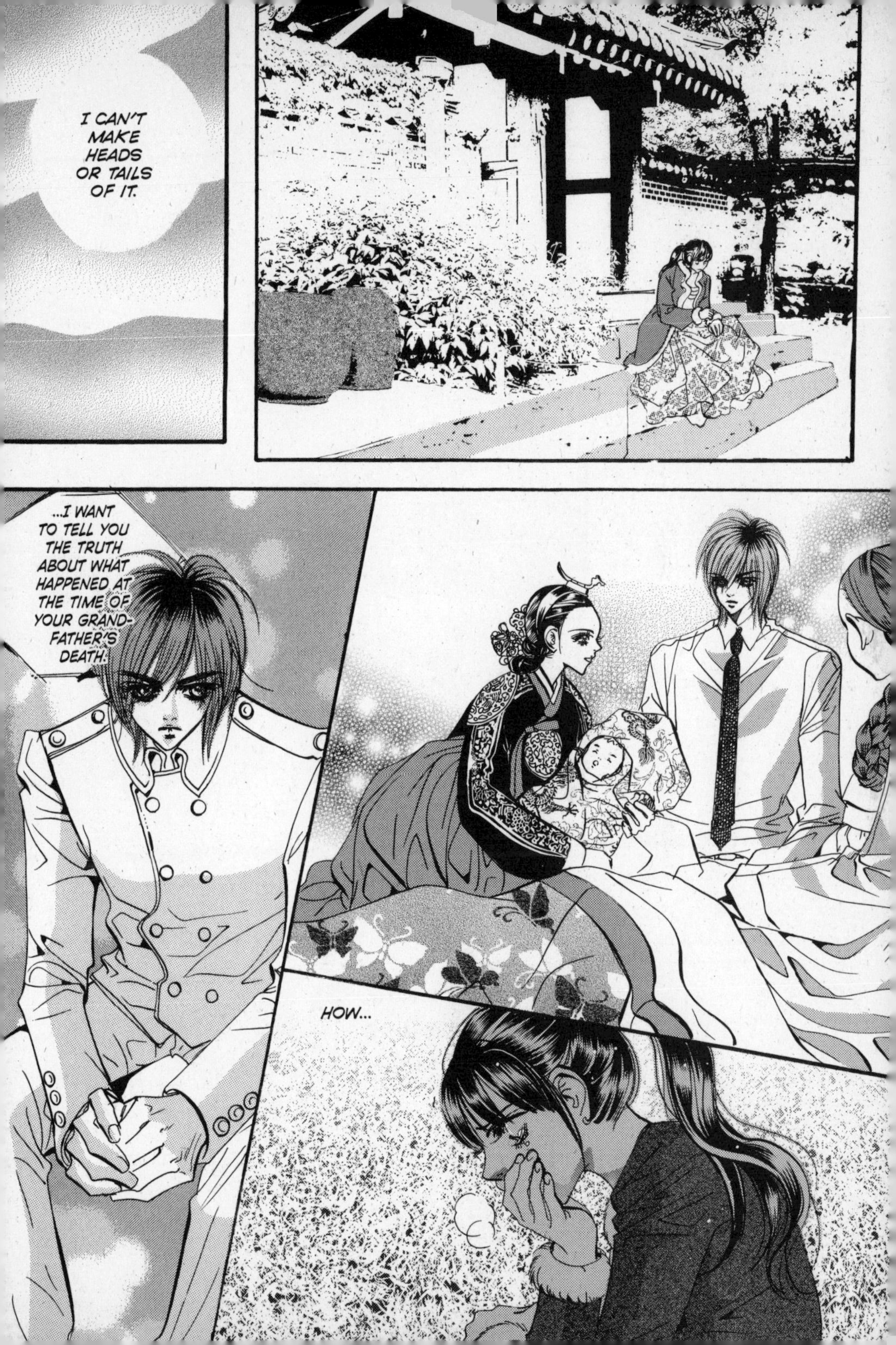
I CAN'T MAKE HEADS OR TAILS OF IT.
...I WANT TO TELL YOU THE TRUTH ABOUT WHAT HAPPENED AT THE TIME OF YOUR GRAND-FATHER'S DEATH.
HOW...

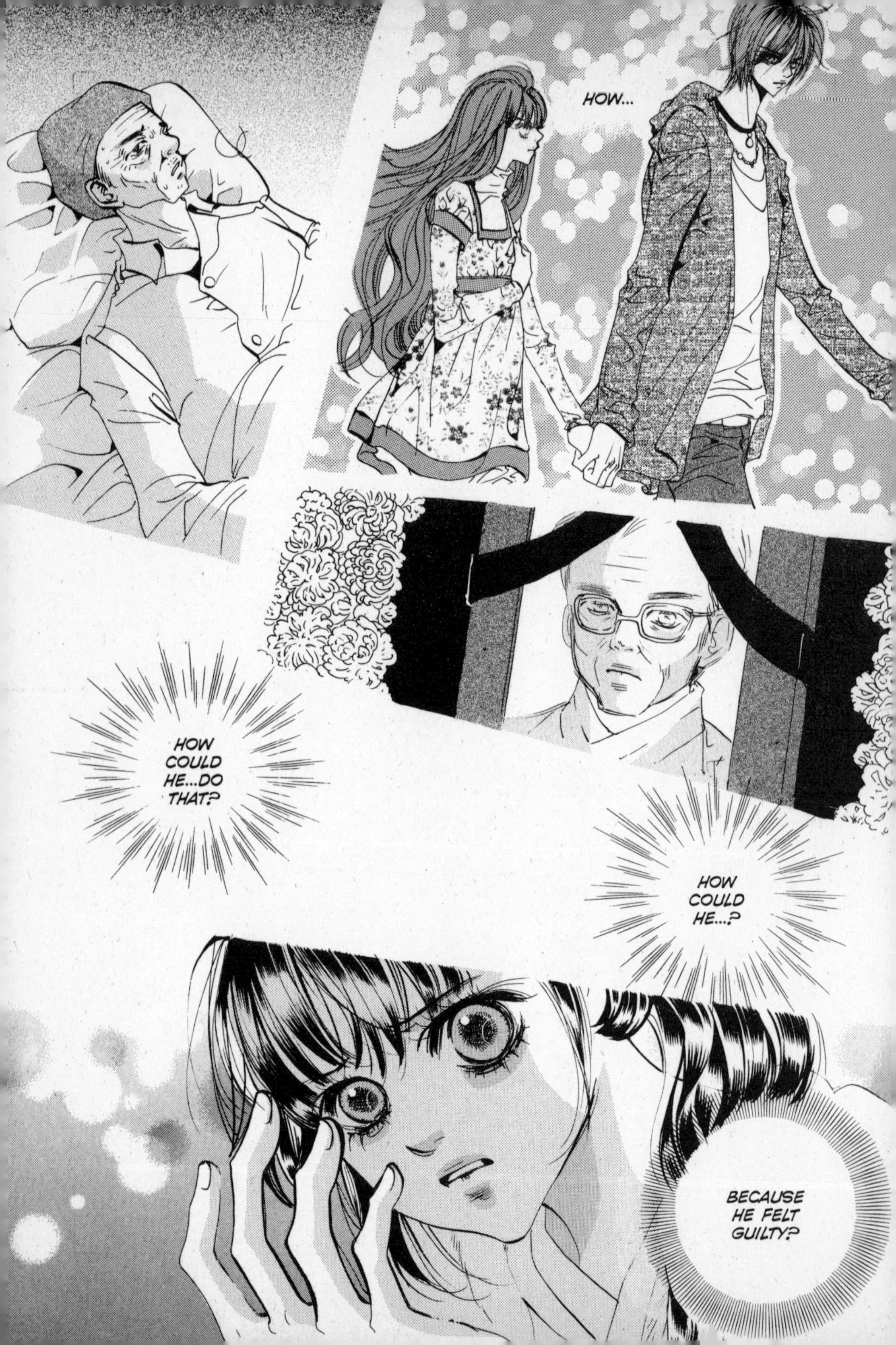
HOW...
HOW COULD HE...DO THAT?
HOW COULD HE...?
BECAUSE HE FELT GUILTY?

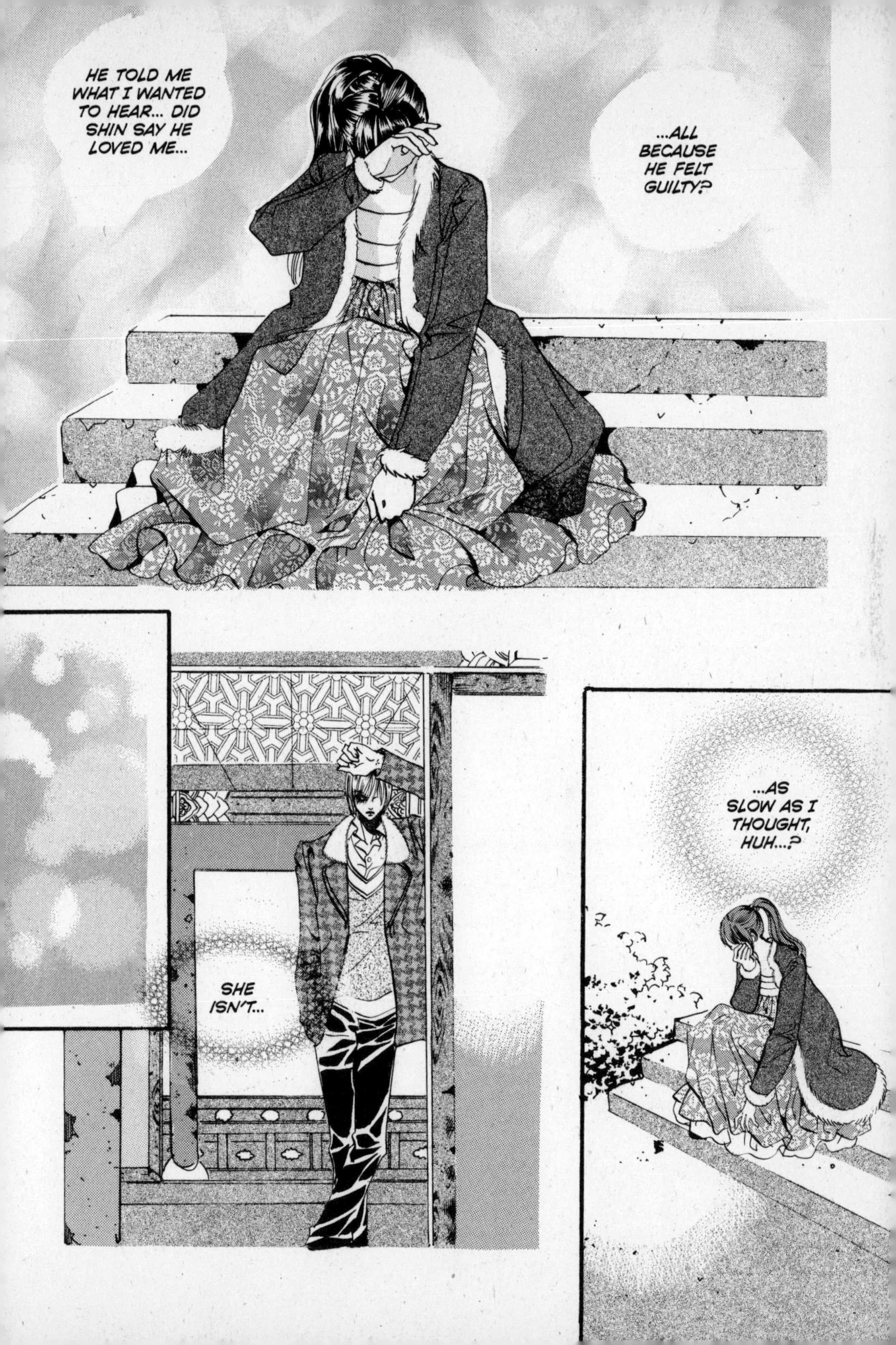
HE TOLD ME WHAT I WANTED TO HEAR... DID SHIN SAY HE LOVED ME...
...ALL BECAUSE HE FELT GUILTY?
SHE ISN'T...
...AS SLOW AS I THOUGHT, HUH...?

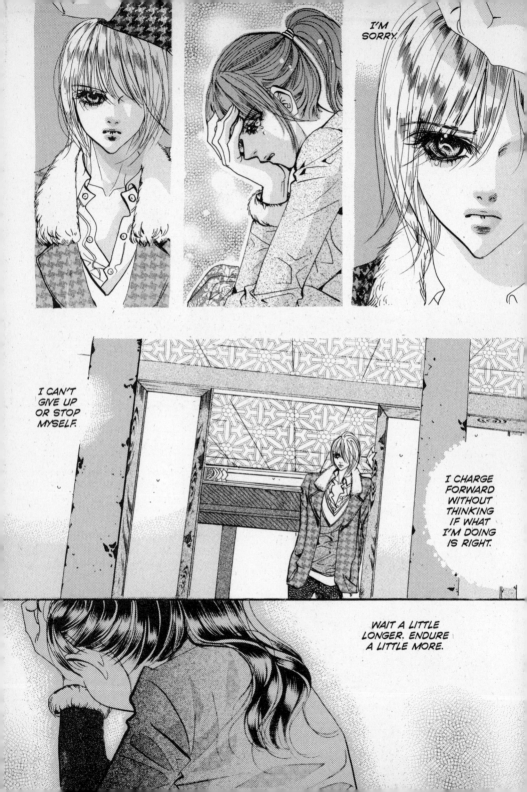

I'M SORRY.

I CAN'T GIVE UP OR STOP MYSELF.

I CHARGE FORWARD WITHOUT THINKING IF WHAT I'M DOING IS RIGHT.

WAIT A LITTLE LONGER. ENDURE A LITTLE MORE.

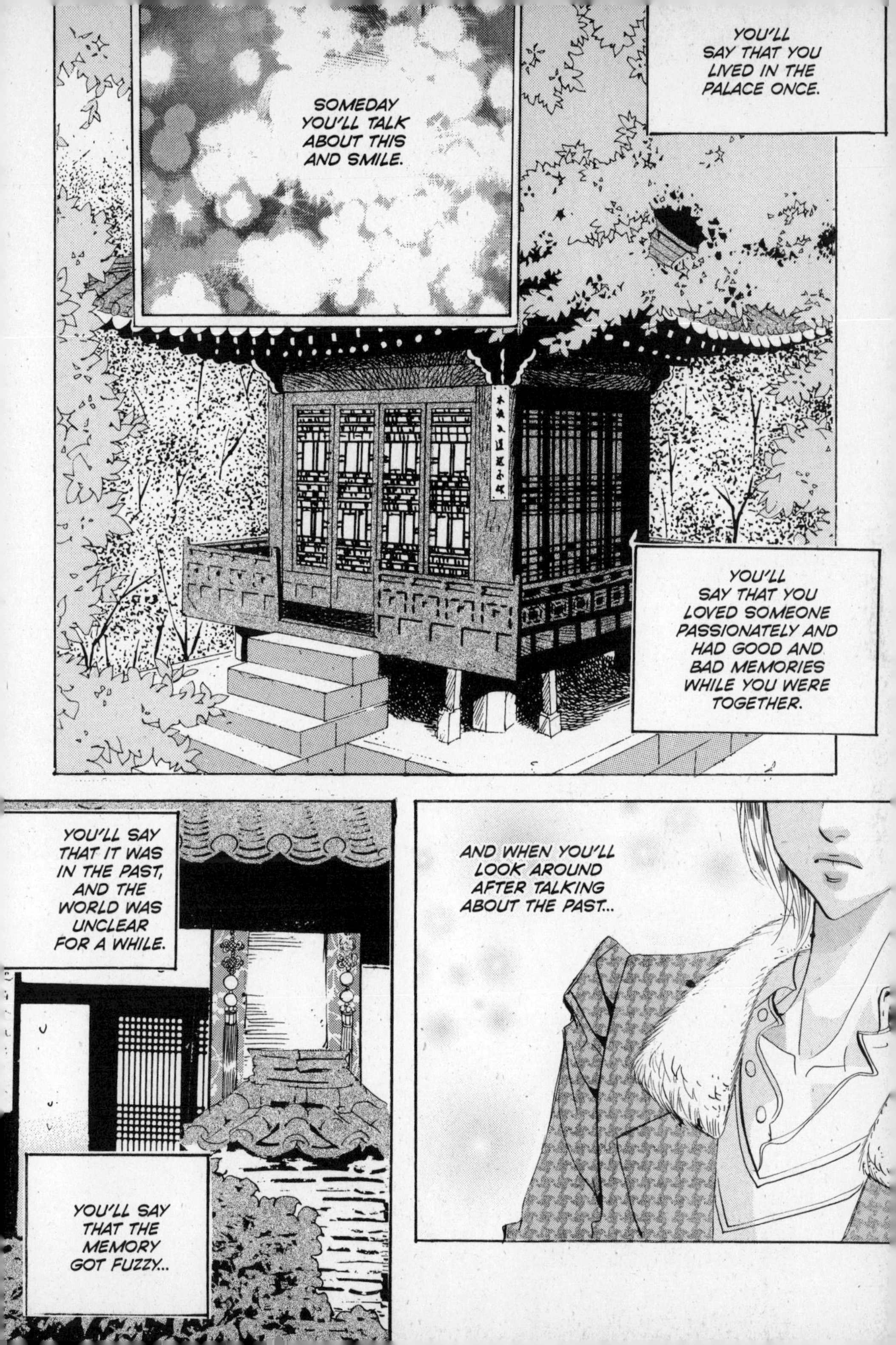
SOMEDAY YOU'LL TALK ABOUT THIS AND SMILE.
YOU'LL SAY THAT YOU LIVED IN THE PALACE ONCE.
YOU'LL SAY THAT YOU LOVED SOMEONE PASSIONATELY AND HAD GOOD AND BAD MEMORIES WHILE YOU WERE TOGETHER.
YOU'LL SAY THAT IT WAS IN THE PAST, AND THE WORLD WAS UNCLEAR FOR A WHILE.
YOU'LL SAY THAT THE MEMORY GOT FUZZY...
AND WHEN YOU'LL LOOK AROUND AFTER TALKING ABOUT THE PAST...

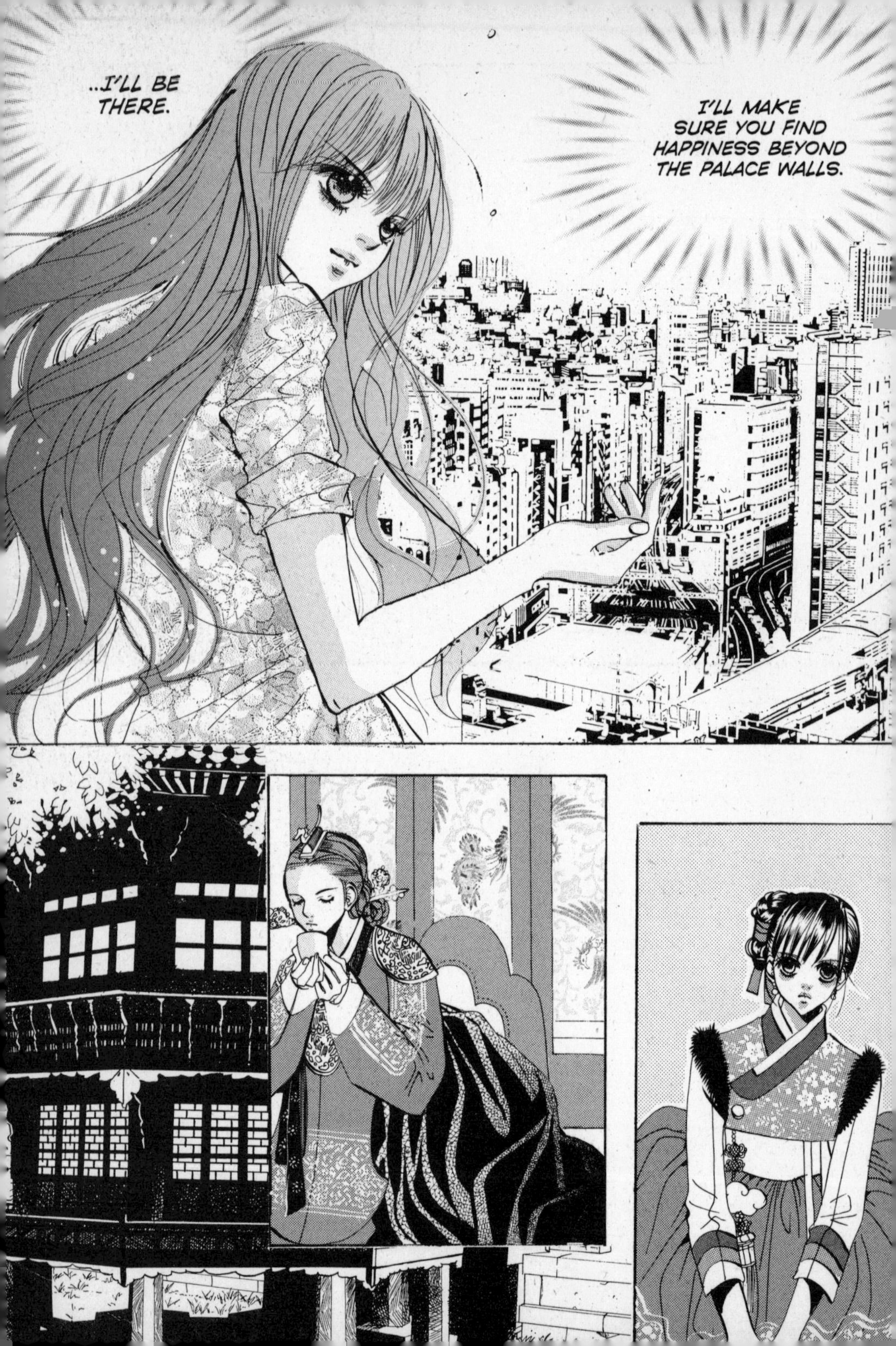
...I'LL BE THERE.
I'LL MAKE SURE YOU FIND HAPPINESS BEYOND THE PALACE WALLS.

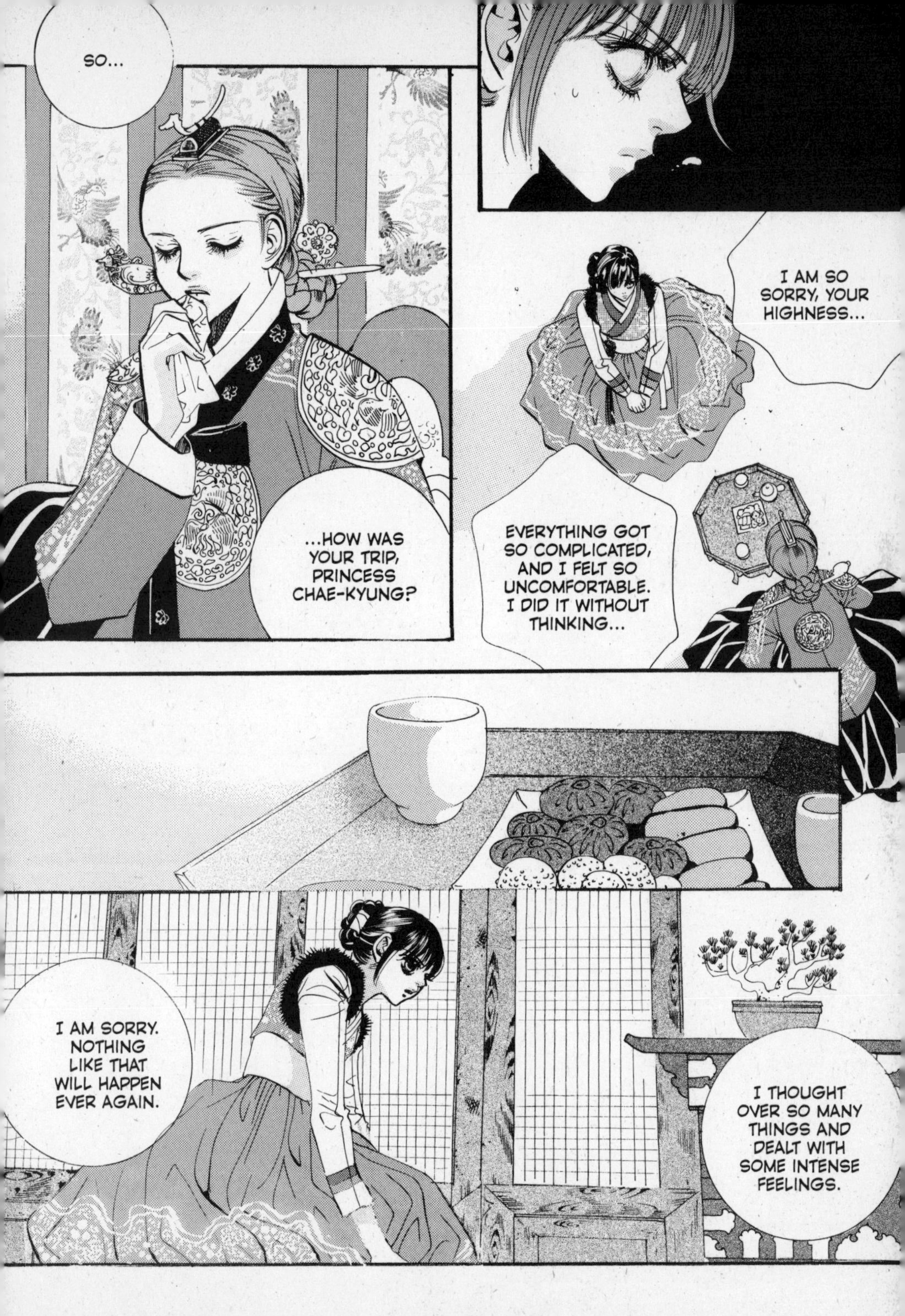
SO...
...HOW WAS YOUR TRIP, PRINCESS CHAE-KYUNG?
I AM SO SORRY, YOUR HIGHNESS...
EVERYTHING GOT SO COMPLICATED, AND I FELT SO UNCOMFORTABLE. I DID IT WITHOUT THINKING...
I AM SORRY. NOTHING LIKE THAT WILL HAPPEN EVER AGAIN.
I THOUGHT OVER SO MANY THINGS AND DEALT WITH SOME INTENSE FEELINGS.

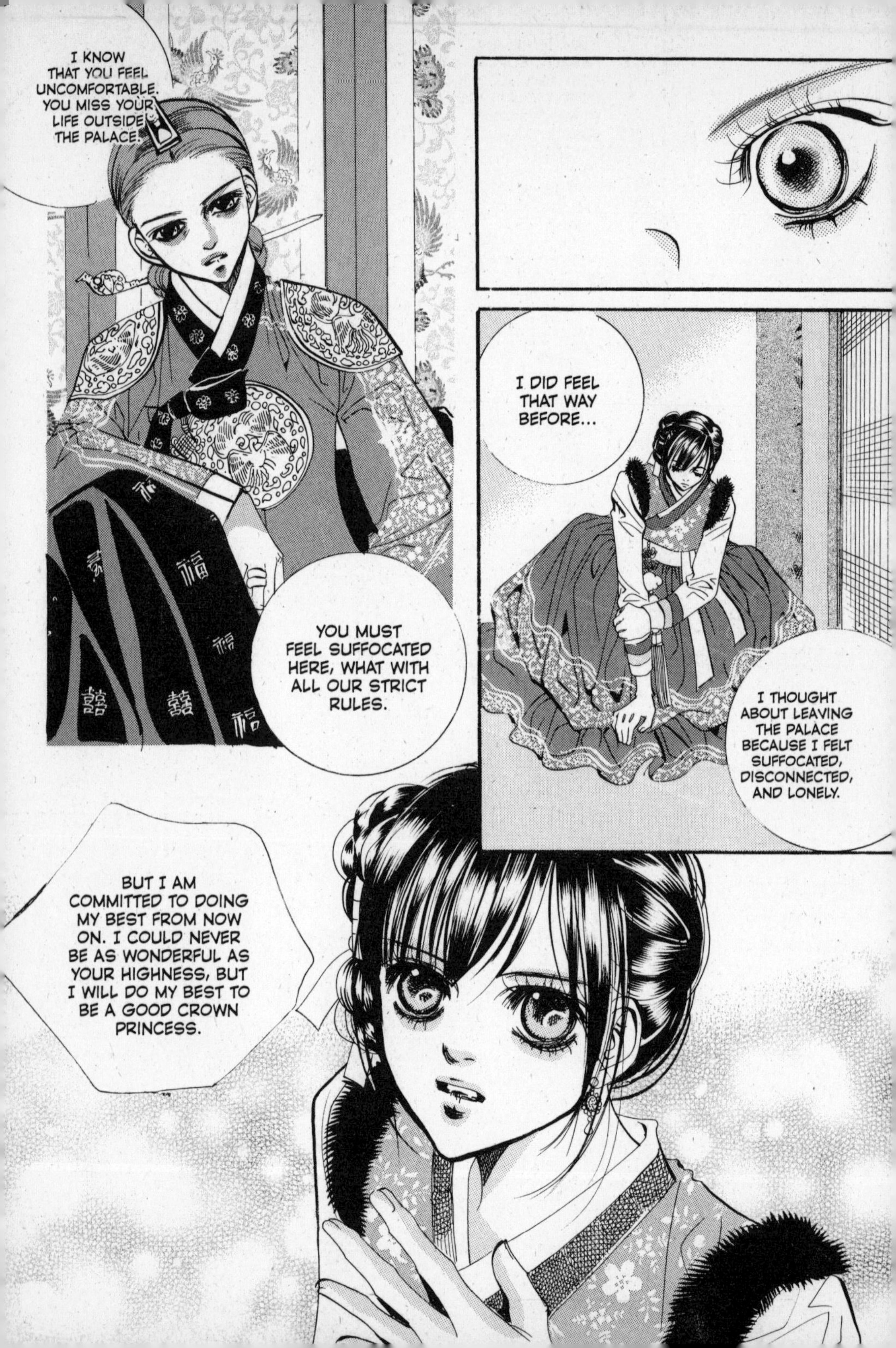
I KNOW THAT YOU FEEL UNCOMFORTABLE. YOU MISS YOUR LIFE OUTSIDE THE PALACE.
YOU MUST FEEL SUFFOCATED HERE, WHAT WITH ALL OUR STRICT RULES.
I DID FEEL THAT WAY BEFORE...
I THOUGHT ABOUT LEAVING THE PALACE BECAUSE I FELT SUFFOCATED, DISCONNECTED, AND LONELY.
BUT I AM COMMITTED TO DOING MY BEST FROM NOW ON. I COULD NEVER BE AS WONDERFUL AS YOUR HIGHNESS, BUT I WILL DO MY BEST TO BE A GOOD CROWN PRINCESS.

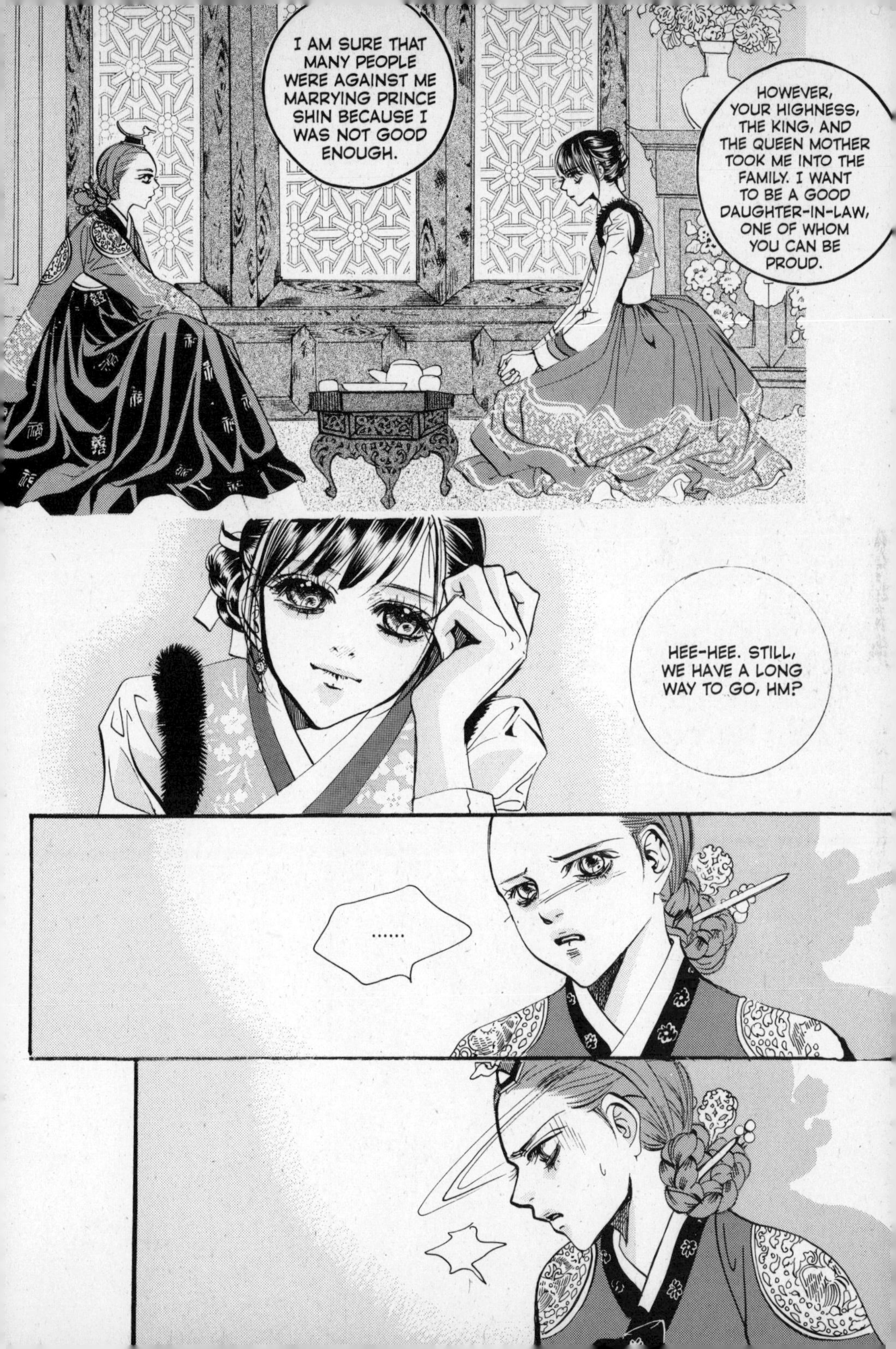
I AM SURE THAT MANY PEOPLE WERE AGAINST ME MARRYING PRINCE SHIN BECAUSE I WAS NOT GOOD ENOUGH.
HOWEVER, YOUR HIGHNESS, THE KING, AND THE QUEEN MOTHER TOOK ME INTO THE FAMILY. I WANT TO BE A GOOD DAUGHTER-IN-LAW, ONE OF WHOM YOU CAN BE PROUD.
HEE-HEE. STILL, WE HAVE A LONG WAY TO GO, HM?
......

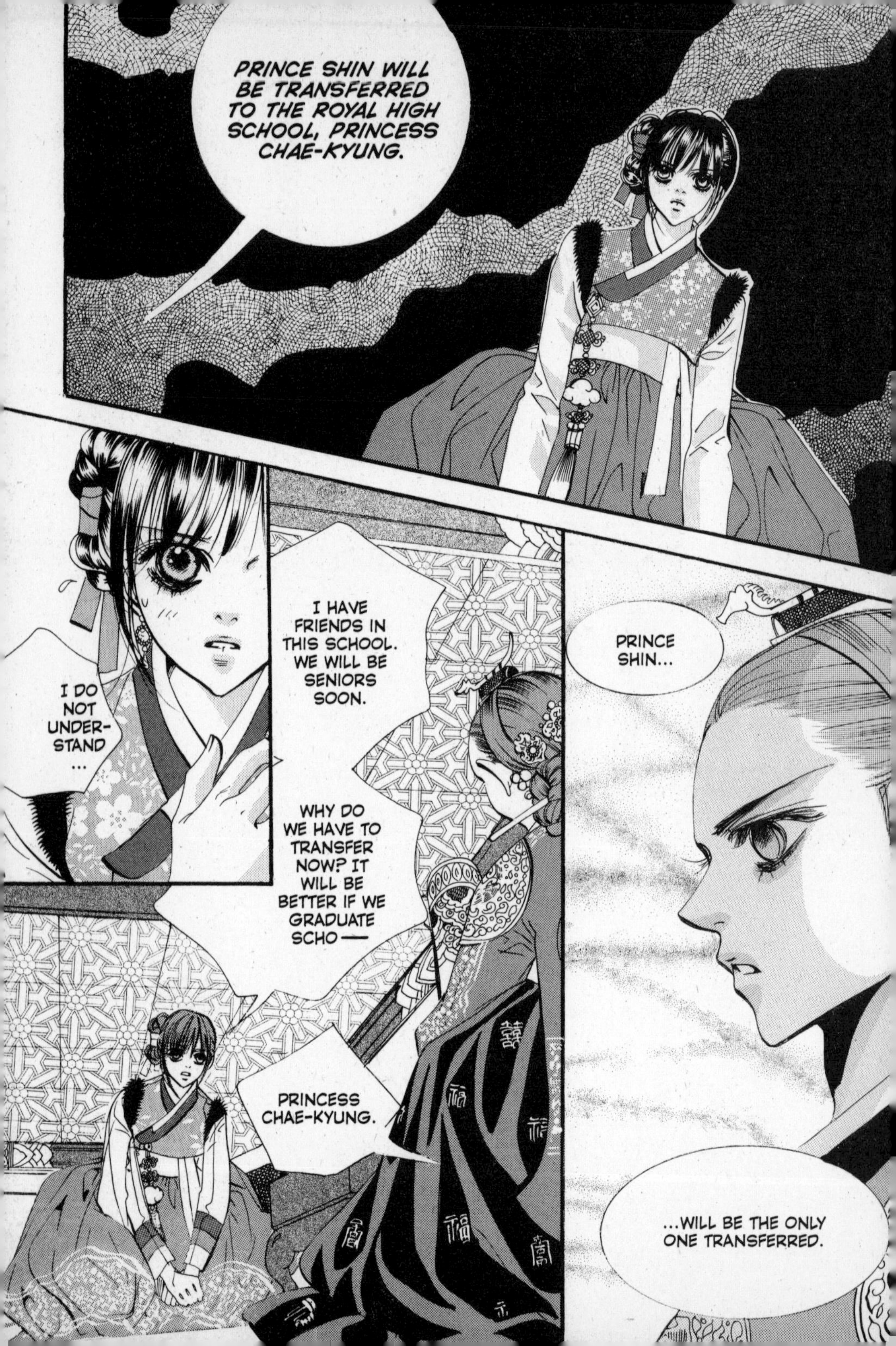
PRINCE SHIN WILL BE TRANSFERRED TO THE ROYAL HIGH SCHOOL, PRINCESS CHAE-KYUNG.
I DO NOT UNDER-STAND ...
I HAVE FRIENDS IN THIS SCHOOL. WE WILL BE SENIORS SOON.
WHY DO WE HAVE TO TRANSFER NOW? IT WILL BE BETTER IF WE GRADUATE SCHO—
PRINCESS CHAE-KYUNG.
PRINCE SHIN...
...WILL BE THE ONLY ONE TRANSFERRED.

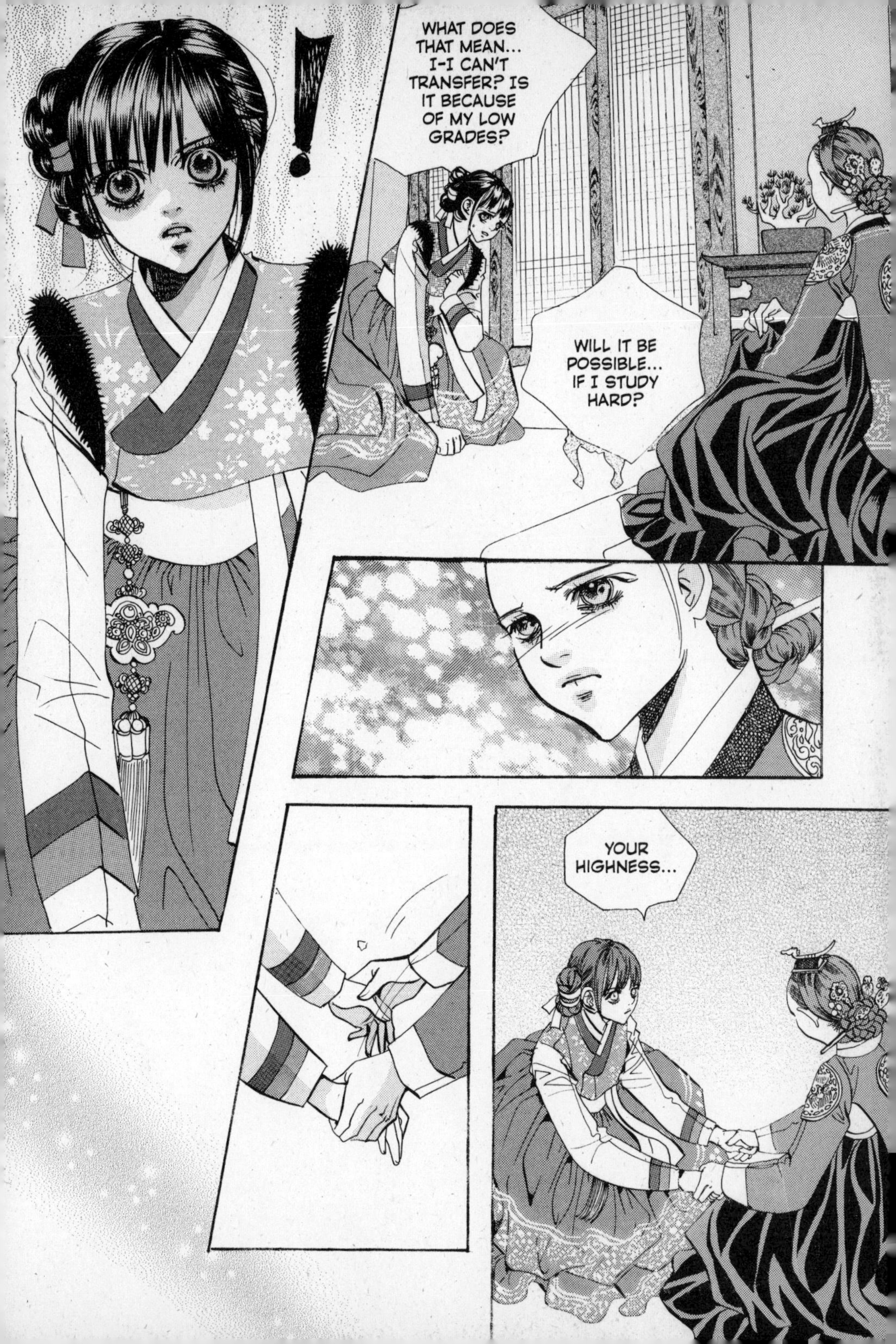
!
WHAT DOES THAT MEAN... I-I CAN'T TRANSFER? IS IT BECAUSE OF MY LOW GRADES?
WILL IT BE POSSIBLE... IF I STUDY HARD?
YOUR HIGHNESS...

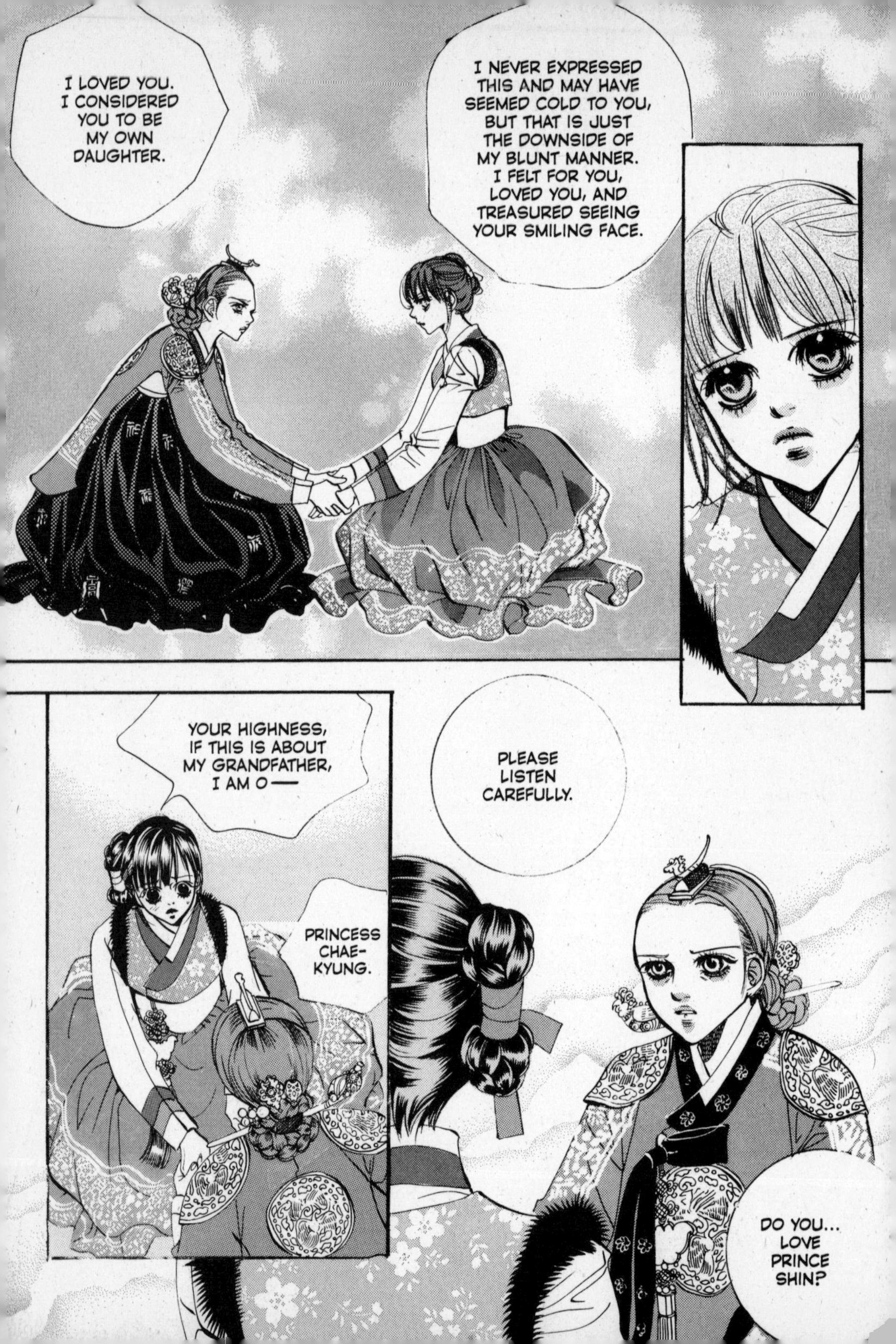
I LOVED YOU. I CONSIDERED YOU TO BE MY OWN DAUGHTER.
I NEVER EXPRESSED THIS AND MAY HAVE SEEMED COLD TO YOU, BUT THAT IS JUST THE DOWNSIDE OF MY BLUNT MANNER. I FELT FOR YOU, LOVED YOU, AND TREASURED SEEING YOUR SMILING FACE.
YOUR HIGHNESS, IF THIS IS ABOUT MY GRANDFATHER, I AM O—
PRINCESS CHAE-KYUNG.
PLEASE LISTEN CAREFULLY.
DO YOU... LOVE PRINCE SHIN?

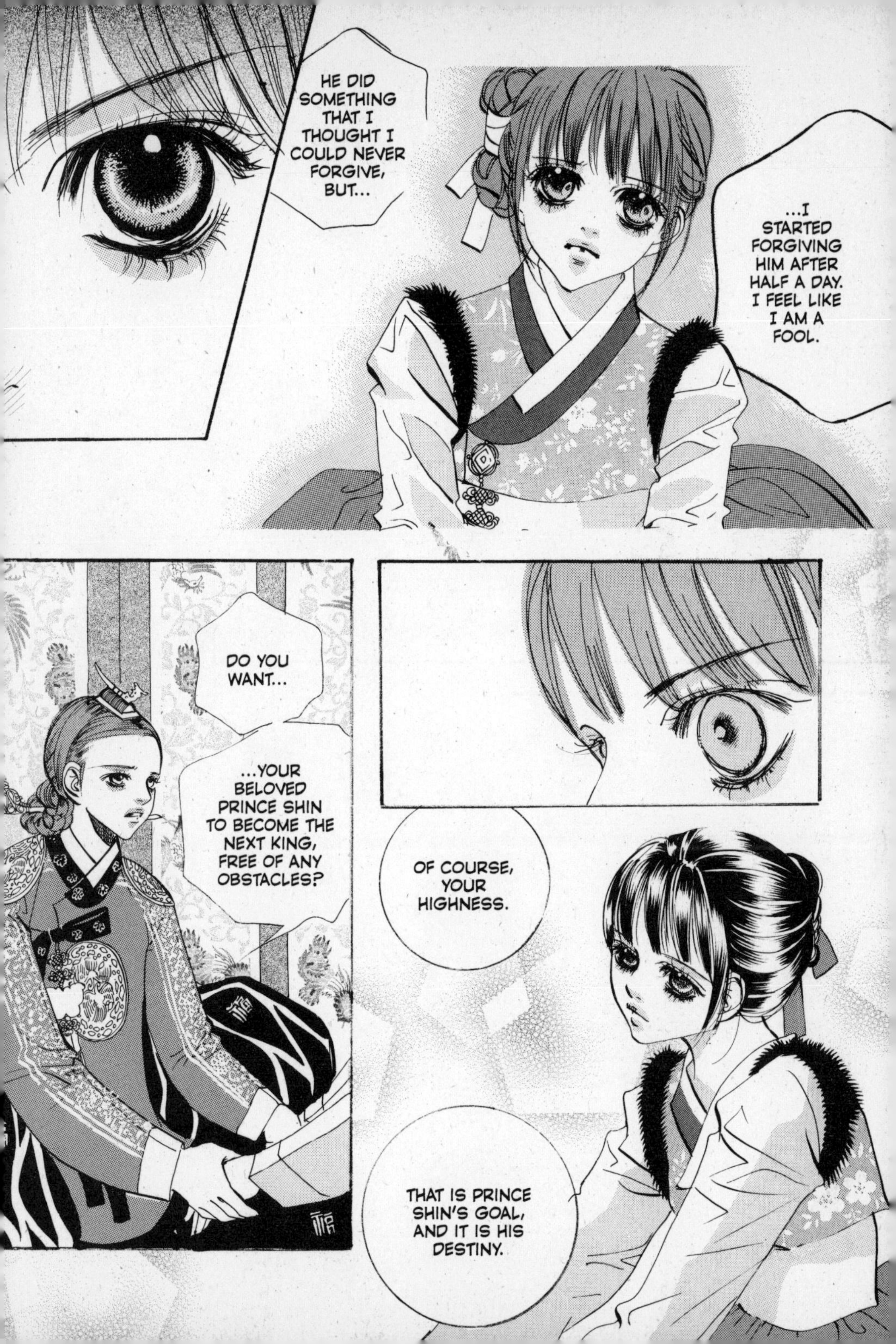
HE DID SOMETHING THAT I THOUGHT I COULD NEVER FORGIVE, BUT...
...I STARTED FORGIVING HIM AFTER HALF A DAY. I FEEL LIKE I AM A FOOL.
DO YOU WANT...
...YOUR BELOVED PRINCE SHIN TO BECOME THE NEXT KING, FREE OF ANY OBSTACLES?
OF COURSE, YOUR HIGHNESS.
THAT IS PRINCE SHIN'S GOAL, AND IT IS HIS DESTINY.

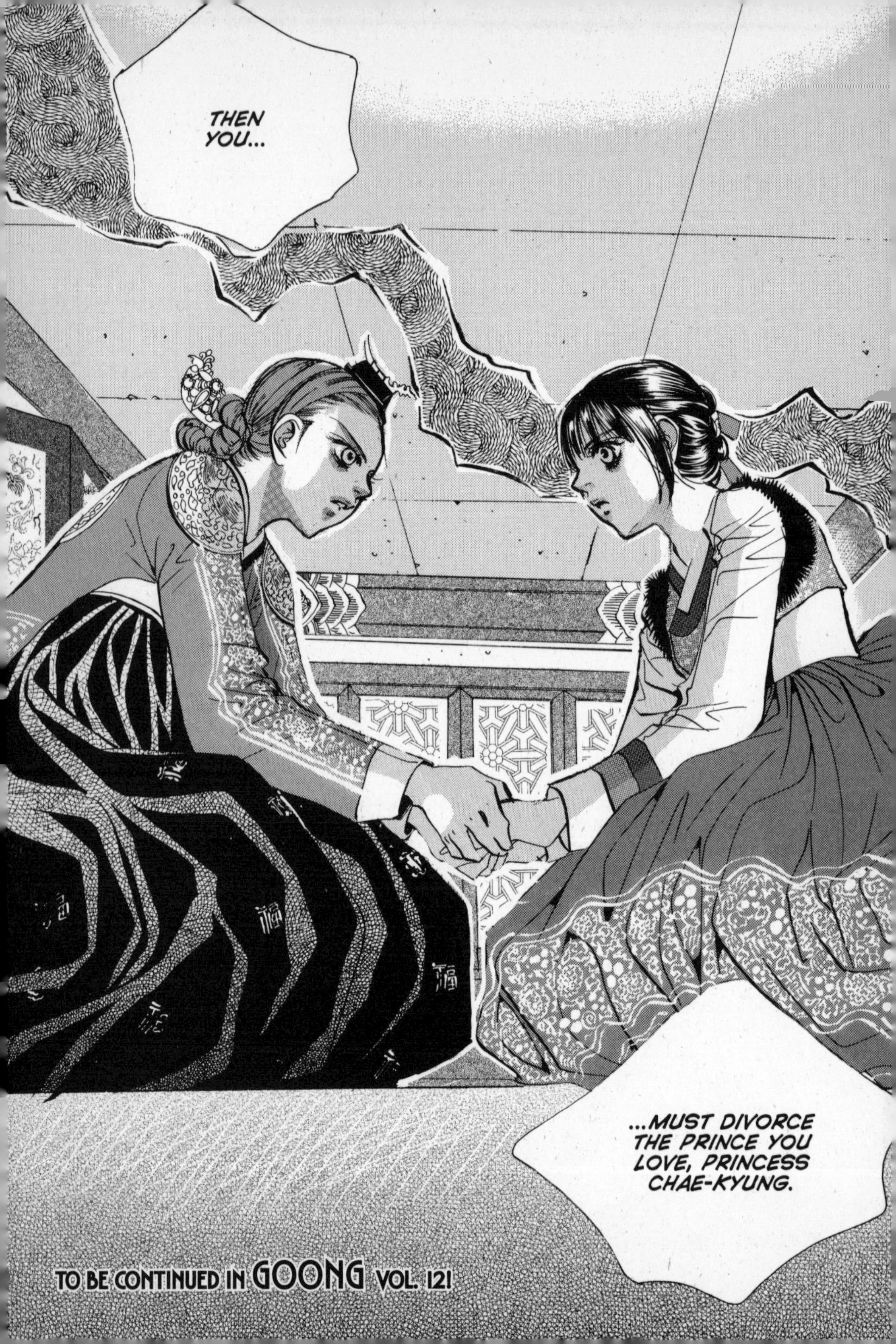
THEN YOU...
...MUST DIVORCE THE PRINCE YOU LOVE, PRINCESS CHAE-KYUNG.
TO BE CONTINUED IN GOONG VOL. 12!

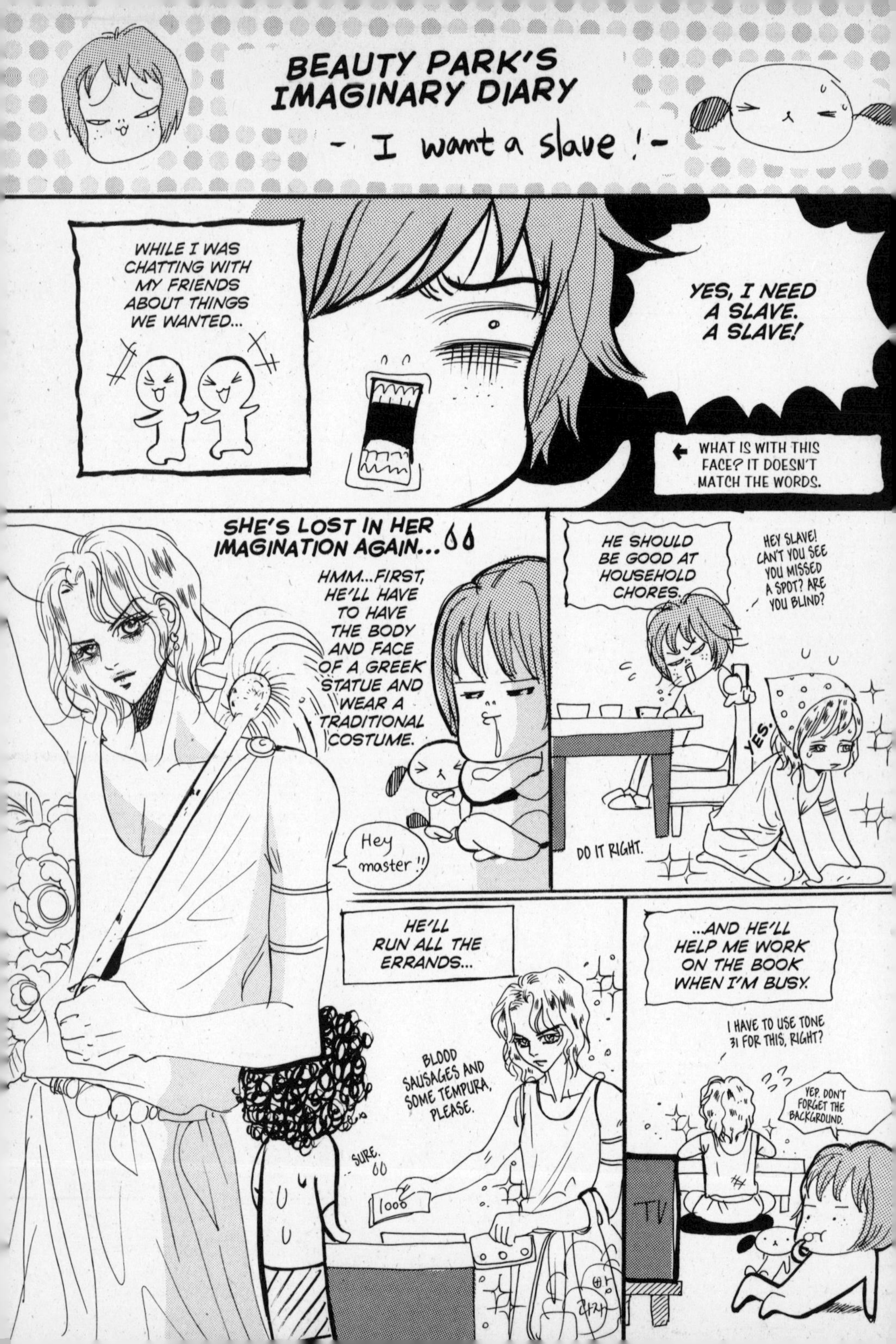
BEAUTY PARK'S IMAGINARY DIARY
- I want a slave! -
WHILE I WAS CHATTING WITH MY FRIENDS ABOUT THINGS WE WANTED...
YES, I NEED A SLAVE. A SLAVE!
← WHAT IS WITH THIS FACE? IT DOESN'T MATCH THE WORDS.
SHE'S LOST IN HER IMAGINATION AGAIN...
HMM...FIRST, HE'LL HAVE TO HAVE THE BODY AND FACE OF A GREEK STATUE AND WEAR A TRADITIONAL COSTUME.
Hey master!!
HE SHOULD BE GOOD AT HOUSEHOLD CHORES.
HEY SLAVE! CAN'T YOU SEE YOU MISSED A SPOT? ARE YOU BLIND?
YES.
DO IT RIGHT.
HE'LL RUN ALL THE ERRANDS...
BLOOD SAUSAGES AND SOME TEMPURA, PLEASE.
SURE.
1000
...AND HE'LL HELP ME WORK ON THE BOOK WHEN I'M BUSY.
I HAVE TO USE TONE 31 FOR THIS, RIGHT?
YEP. DON'T FORGET THE BACKGROUND.
TV

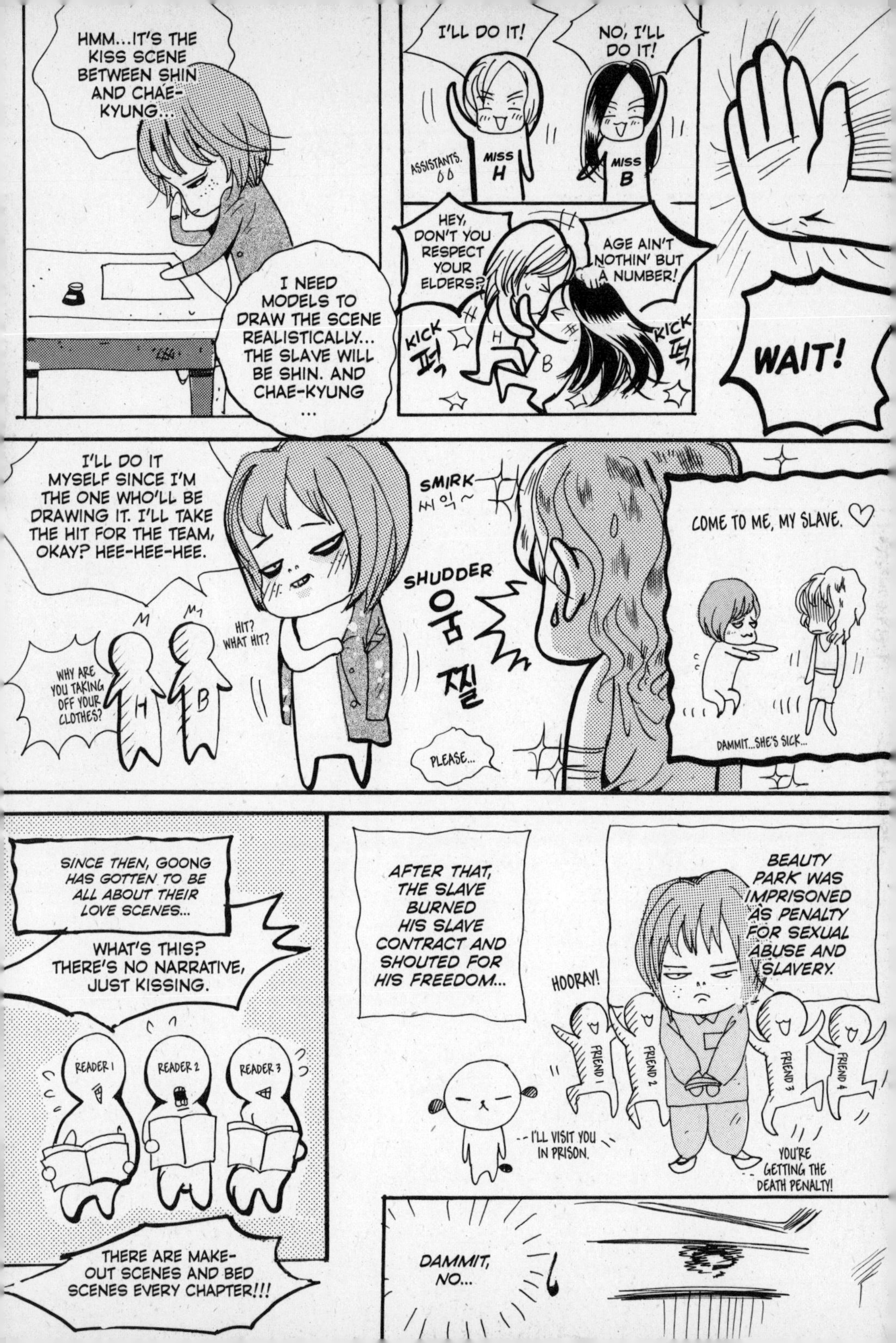

HMM...IT'S THE KISS SCENE BETWEEN SHIN AND CHAE-KYUNG...
I NEED MODELS TO DRAW THE SCENE REALISTICALLY... THE SLAVE WILL BE SHIN. AND CHAE-KYUNG ...
I'LL DO IT!
NO, I'LL DO IT!
ASSISTANTS.
MISS H
MISS B
HEY, DON'T YOU RESPECT YOUR ELDERS?
AGE AIN'T NOTHIN' BUT A NUMBER!
KICK 퍽
KICK 퍽
WAIT!
I'LL DO IT MYSELF SINCE I'M THE ONE WHO'LL BE DRAWING IT. I'LL TAKE THE HIT FOR THE TEAM, OKAY? HEE-HEE-HEE.
HIT? WHAT HIT?
WHY ARE YOU TAKING OFF YOUR CLOTHES?
SMIRK 씨익~
SHUDDER 움찔
PLEASE...
COME TO ME, MY SLAVE. ♡
DAMMIT...SHE'S SICK...
SINCE THEN, GOONG HAS GOTTEN TO BE ALL ABOUT THEIR LOVE SCENES...
WHAT'S THIS? THERE'S NO NARRATIVE, JUST KISSING.
READER 1
READER 2
READER 3
THERE ARE MAKE-OUT SCENES AND BED SCENES EVERY CHAPTER!!!
AFTER THAT, THE SLAVE BURNED HIS SLAVE CONTRACT AND SHOUTED FOR HIS FREEDOM...
BEAUTY PARK WAS IMPRISONED AS PENALTY FOR SEXUAL ABUSE AND SLAVERY.
HOORAY!
FRIEND 1
FRIEND 2
FRIEND 3
FRIEND 4
I'LL VISIT YOU IN PRISON.
YOU'RE GETTING THE DEATH PENALTY!
DAMMIT, NO...

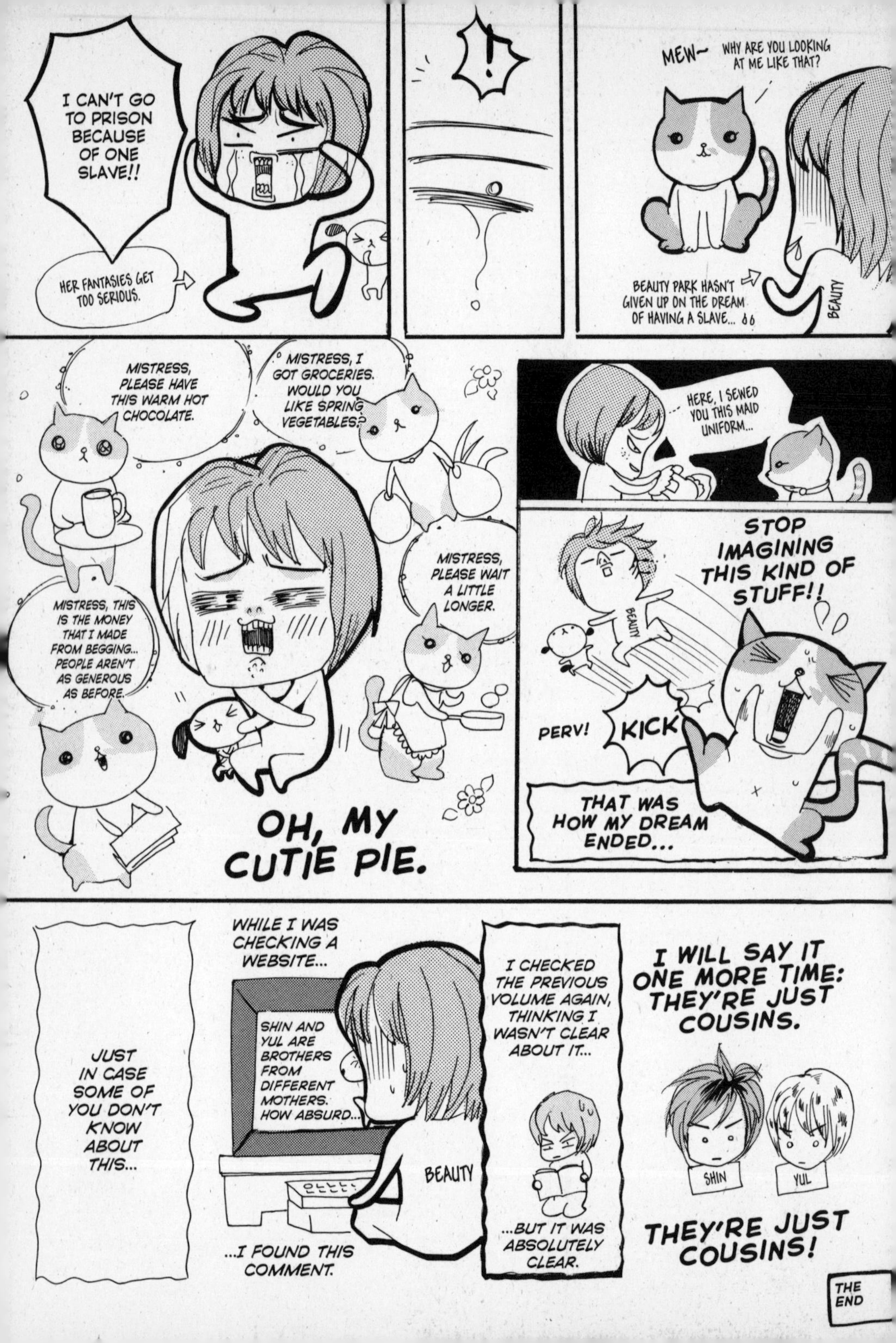
I CAN'T GO TO PRISON BECAUSE OF ONE SLAVE!!
HER FANTASIES GET TOO SERIOUS.
!
MEW~
WHY ARE YOU LOOKING AT ME LIKE THAT?
BEAUTY PARK HASN'T GIVEN UP ON THE DREAM OF HAVING A SLAVE...
BEAUTY
MISTRESS, PLEASE HAVE THIS WARM HOT CHOCOLATE.
MISTRESS, I GOT GROCERIES. WOULD YOU LIKE SPRING VEGETABLES?
MISTRESS, THIS IS THE MONEY THAT I MADE FROM BEGGING... PEOPLE AREN'T AS GENEROUS AS BEFORE.
MISTRESS, PLEASE WAIT A LITTLE LONGER.
OH, MY CUTIE PIE.
HERE, I SEWED YOU THIS MAID UNIFORM...
STOP IMAGINING THIS KIND OF STUFF!!
BEAUTY
PERV!
KICK
THAT WAS HOW MY DREAM ENDED...
JUST IN CASE SOME OF YOU DON'T KNOW ABOUT THIS...
WHILE I WAS CHECKING A WEBSITE...
SHIN AND YUL ARE BROTHERS FROM DIFFERENT MOTHERS. HOW ABSURD...
BEAUTY
...I FOUND THIS COMMENT.
I CHECKED THE PREVIOUS VOLUME AGAIN, THINKING I WASN'T CLEAR ABOUT IT...
...BUT IT WAS ABSOLUTELY CLEAR.
I WILL SAY IT ONE MORE TIME: THEY'RE JUST COUSINS.
SHIN
YUL
THEY'RE JUST COUSINS!
THE END

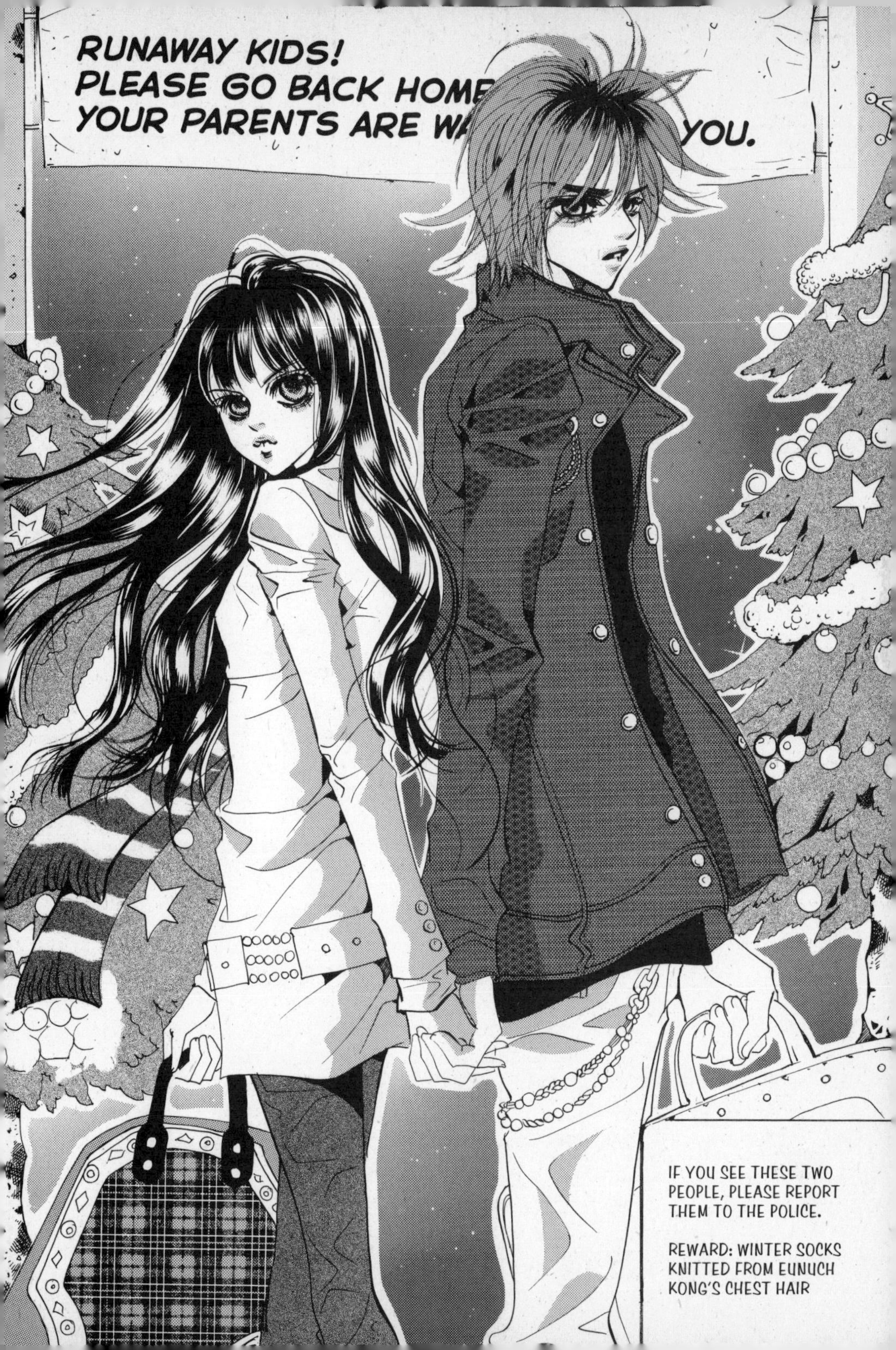
RUNAWAY KIDS!
PLEASE GO BACK HOME
YOUR PARENTS ARE WA
YOU.
IF YOU SEE THESE TWO PEOPLE, PLEASE REPORT THEM TO THE POLICE.
REWARD: WINTER SOCKS KNITTED FROM EUNUCH KONG'S CHEST HAIR

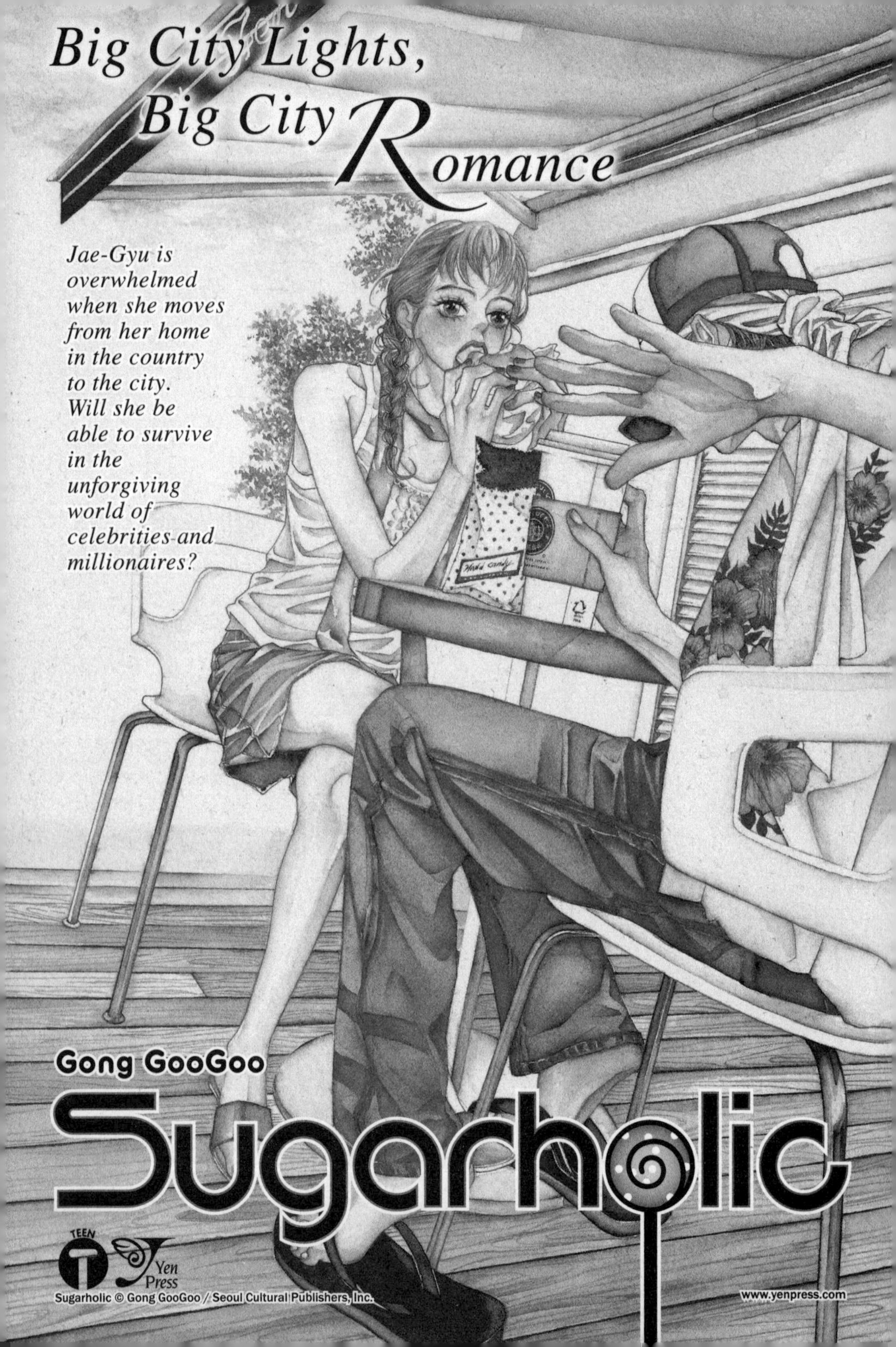
Big City Lights,
Big City Romance
Jae-Gyu is overwhelmed when she moves from her home in the country to the city. Will she be able to survive in the unforgiving world of celebrities and millionaires?
Gong GooGoo
Sugarholic
TEEN
Yen Press
Sugarholic © Gong GooGoo / Seoul Cultural Publishers, Inc.
www.yenpress.com

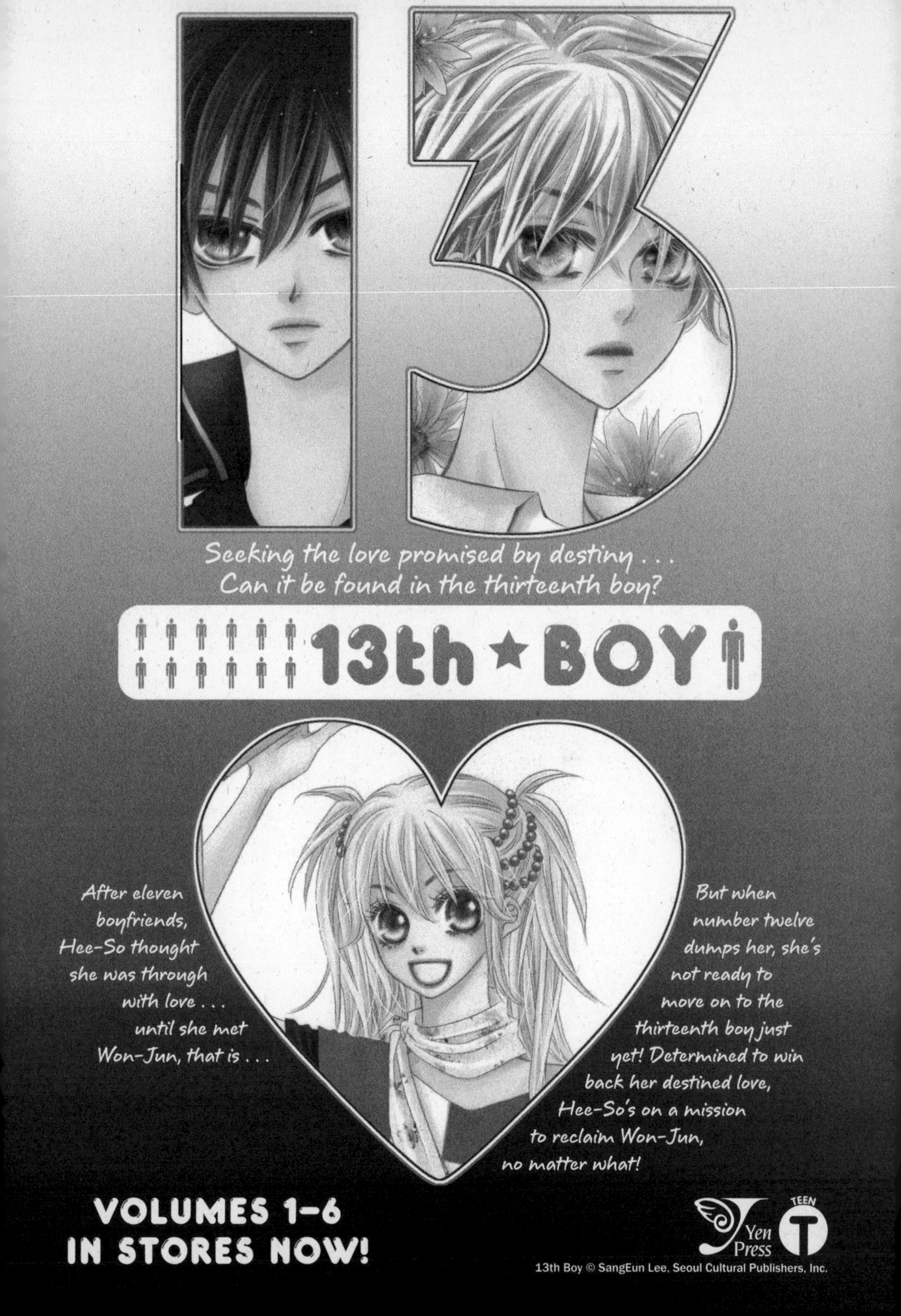

Seeking the love promised by destiny . . .
Can it be found in the thirteenth boy?
13th ★ BOY
After eleven boyfriends, Hee-So thought she was through with love . . . until she met Won-Jun, that is . . .
But when number twelve dumps her, she's not ready to move on to the thirteenth boy just yet! Determined to win back her destined love, Hee-So's on a mission to reclaim Won-Jun, no matter what!
VOLUMES 1–6
IN STORES NOW!
Yen Press
TEEN
T
13th Boy © SangEun Lee, Seoul Cultural Publishers, Inc.

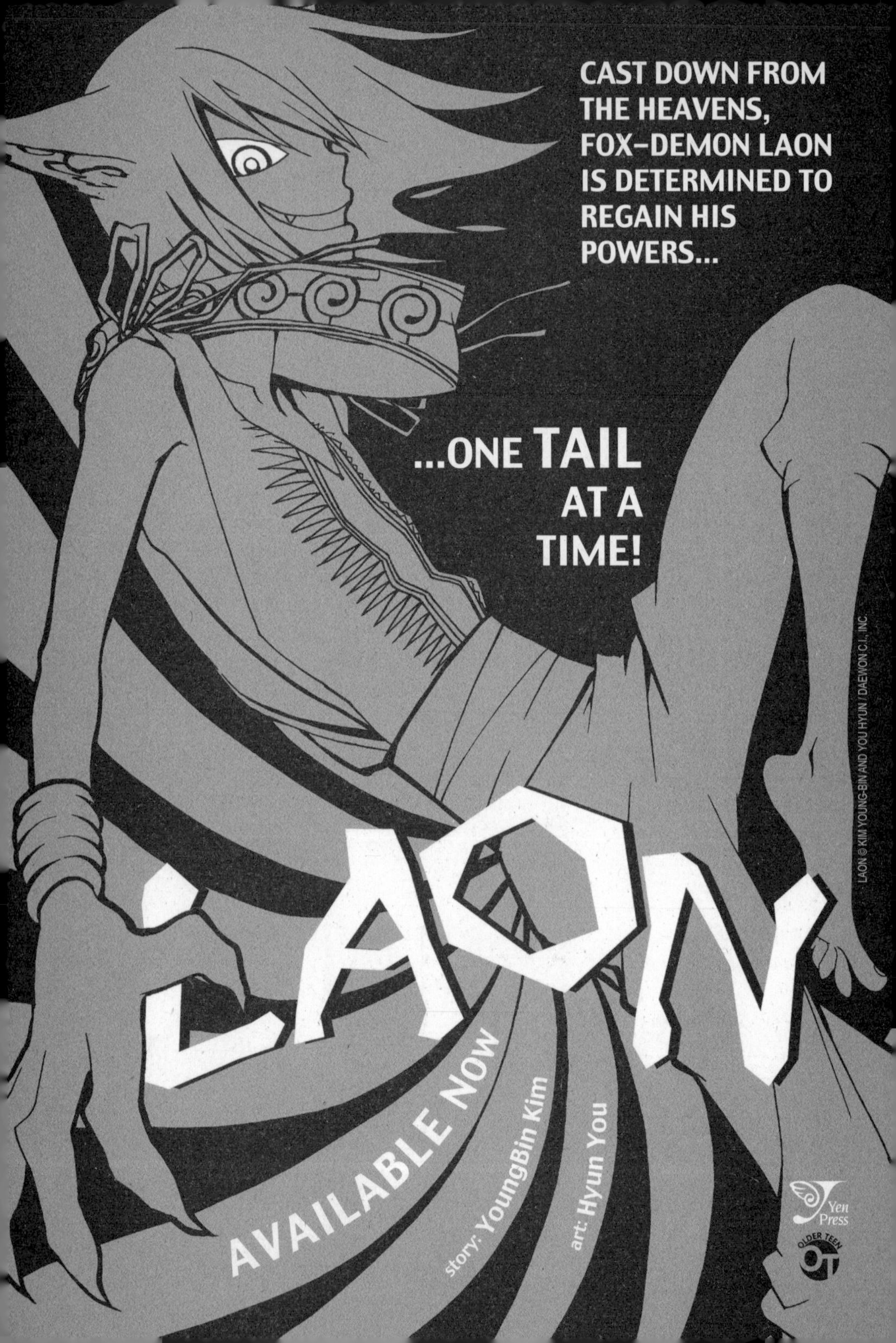
CAST DOWN FROM THE HEAVENS, FOX-DEMON LAON IS DETERMINED TO REGAIN HIS POWERS...
...ONE TAIL AT A TIME!
LAON
AVAILABLE NOW
story: YoungBin Kim
art: Hyun You
Yen Press
OLDER TEEN OT
LAON © KIM YOUNG-BIN AND YOU HYUN / DAEWON C.I., INC.

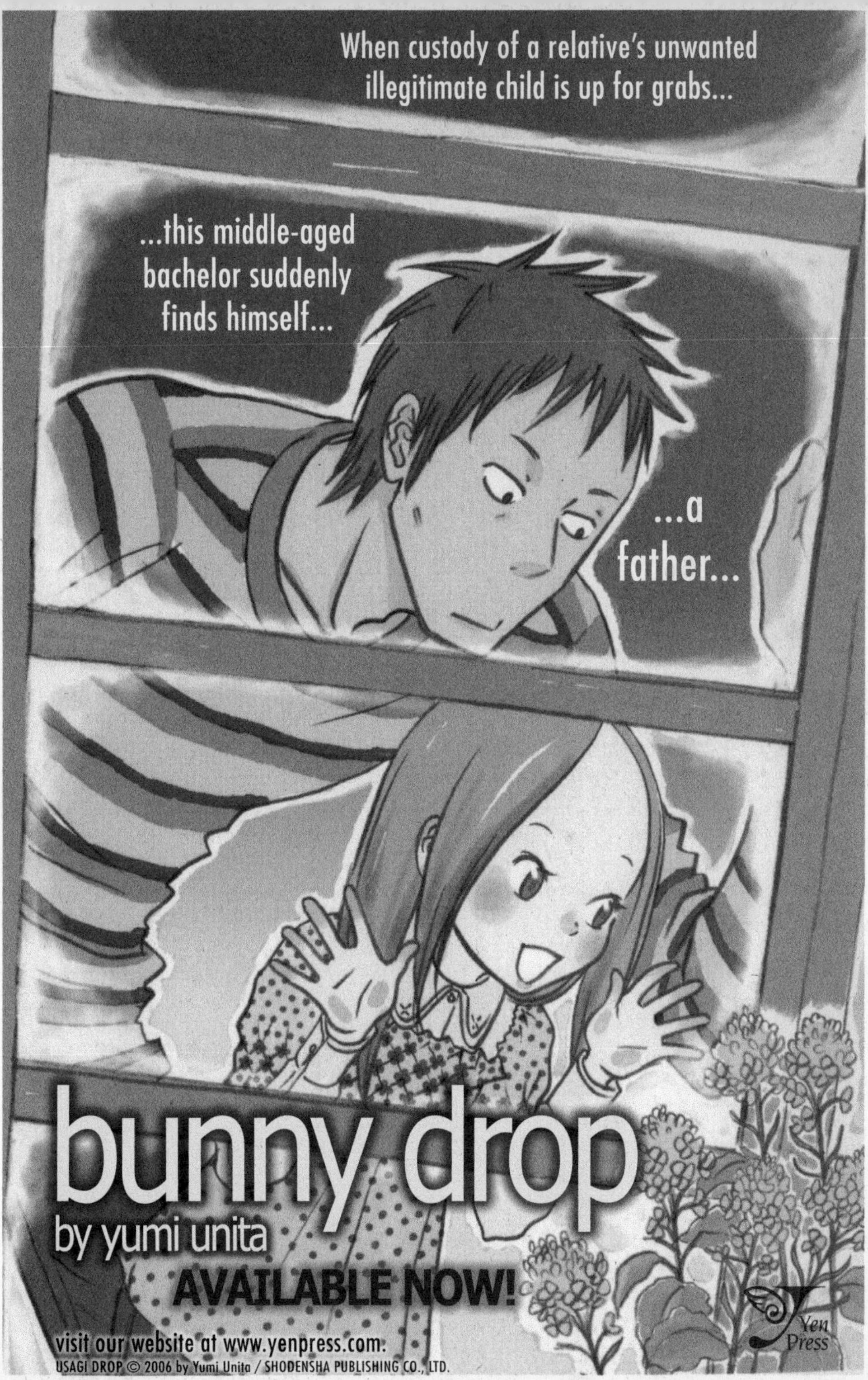

When custody of a relative's unwanted illegitimate child is up for grabs...
...this middle-aged bachelor suddenly finds himself...
...a father...
bunny drop
by yumi unita
AVAILABLE NOW!
visit our website at www.yenpress.com.
USAGI DROP © 2006 by Yumi Unita / SHODENSHA PUBLISHING CO., LTD.
Yen Press

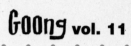

Goong vol. 11

Story and art by SoHee Park

Translation HyeYoung Im
English Adaptation Jamie S. Rich
Lettering Alexis Eckerman

Goong, Vols. 13 & 14 © 2006, 2007 SoHee Park. All rights reserved. First published in Korea in 2006, 2007 by SEOUL CULTURAL PUBLISHERS, Inc. English translation rights arranged by SEOUL CULTURAL PUBLISHERS, Inc.

English edition copyright © 2011 Hachette Book Group, Inc.

Yen Press
Hachette Book Group
237 Park Avenue, New York, NY 10017

www.HachetteBookGroup.com
www.YenPress.com

Yen Press is an imprint of Hachette Book Group, Inc.
The Yen Press name and logo are trademarks of Hachette Book Group, Inc.

First Yen Press Edition: May 2011

ISBN: 978-0-7595-3155-0

10 9 8 7 6 5 4 3 2 1

BVG

Printed in the United States of America